Shri Guru Granth Sahib, Vol. 4
of 4

Shri Guru Granth Sahib, Vol. 4 of 4

Formatted For Educational Interest

Republished 2008 by Forgotten Books

www.forgottenbooks.org

PUBLISHER'S PREFACE

About the Book

"The Granth is the central text of Sikhism, a religion that emerged in the Punjab region of India in the 15th Century. Sikhism is a unique faith which has aspects of Islam: monotheism and iconoclasm, and Hinduism: reincarnation, karma and nirvana. However Sikhism is distinct from Hinduism and Islam. The Sikh Gurus (teachers), contemporaries of Luther and Calvin, were reformers who rejected the caste system and much of the apparatus of Hindu ritual and legalism. They promoted religious tolerance and the equality of women. The founding Guru, Shri Guru Nanak Dev Ji, (1469-1538), is noted for the saying "There is no Hindu, there is no Muslim."

The Granth, compiled by Guru Gobind Singh, contains compositions of six Gurus, namely Guru Nanak, Guru Angad, Guru Amar Das, Guru Ram Das, Guru Arjan, and Guru Teg Bahadur. The hymns are arranged by the thirty one ragas (musical forms) in which they were composed. The hymns that comprise the Granth were originally written in several different languages: Persian, mediaeval Prakrit, Hindi, Marathi, old Panjabi, Multani, and several local dialects. In addition, there are Sanskrit and Arabic portions. This makes it extrordinarily difficult to translate. The translation presented here is the Khalsa Consensus Translation, which is highly regarded by scholars.
The Granth is considered the living embodiment of the Gurus, the "eleventh guru". Printed copies of the Granth are treated with the greatest respect. This is the reason for the honorific titles that make up the full name of the book. There are protocols to be observed in while reading of the Granth. A Sikh reader suggests the following: "Out of respect, it is advised that before you do read the Sri Guru Granth Sahib, that you cover your hair." This is normally with a turban or a piece of cloth provided by the gurdwara."

(Quote from sacred-texts.com)

CONTENTS

RAAG MAAROO

Section 25 - Raag Maaroo - Part 091

All the continents, islands and worlds meditate in remembrance.

The nether worlds and spheres meditate in remembrance on that True Lord.

The sources of creation and speech meditate in remembrance; all the Lord's humble servants meditate in remembrance. |2|

Brahma, Vishnu and Shiva meditate in remembrance.

The three hundred thirty million gods meditate in remembrance.

The titans and demons all meditate in remembrance; Your Praises are uncountable - they cannot be counted. |3|

All the beasts, birds and demons meditate in remembrance.

The forests, mountains and hermits meditate in remembrance.

All the vines and branches meditate in remembrance; O my Lord and Master, You are permeating and pervading all minds. |4|

All beings, both subtle and gross, meditate in remembrance.

The Siddhas and seekers meditate in remembrance on the Lord's Mantra.

Both the visible and the invisible meditate in remembrance on my God; God is the Master of all worlds. |5|

Men and women, throughout the four stages of life, meditate in remembrance on You.

All social classes and souls of all races meditate in remembrance on You.

All the virtuous, clever and wise people meditate in remembrance; night and day meditate in remembrance. |6|

Hours, minutes and seconds meditate in remembrance.

Death and life, and thoughts of purification, meditate in remembrance.

The Shaastras, with their lucky signs and joinings, meditate in remembrance; the invisible cannot be seen, even for an instant. |7|

The Lord and Master is the Doer, the Cause of causes.
He is the Inner-knower, the Searcher of all hearts.
That person, whom You bless with Your Grace, and link to Your devotional service, wins this invaluable human life. |8|

He, within whose mind God dwells,
has perfect karma, and chants the Chant of the Guru.
One who realizes God pervading deep within all, does not wander crying in reincarnation again. |9|

Pain, sorrow and doubt run away from that one, within whose mind the Word of the Guru's Shabad abides.
Intuitive peace, poise and bliss come from the sublime essence of the Naam; the unstruck sound current of the Guru's Bani intuitively vibrates and resounds. |10|

He alone is wealthy, who meditates on God.
He alone is honorable, who joins the Saadh Sangat, the Company of the Holy.
That person, within whose mind the Supreme Lord God abides, has perfect karma, and becomes famous. |11|

The Lord and Master is pervading the water, land and sky.
There is no other said to be so.
The ointment of the Guru's spiritual wisdom has eradicated all doubts; except the One Lord, I do not see any other at all. |12|

The Lord's Court is the highest of the high.
His limit and extent cannot be described.
The Lord and Master is profoundly deep, unfathomable and unweighable; how can He be measured? |13|

You are the Creator; all is created by You.
Without You, there is no other at all.
You alone, God, are in the beginning, the middle and the end. You are the root of the entire expanse. |14|

The Messenger of Death does not even approach that person
who sings the Kirtan of the Lord's Praises in the Saadh Sangat, the Company of the Holy.

All desires are fulfilled, for one who listens with his ears to the Praises of God. |15|

You belong to all, and all belong to You, O my true, deep and profound Lord and Master.

Section 25 - Raag Maaroo - Part 092

Says Nanak, those humble beings are exalted, who are pleasing to Your Mind, O my Lord and Master. |16|1|8|

Maaroo, Fifth Mehl:
God is the almighty Giver of all peace and joy.
Be merciful to me, that I may meditate in remembrance on Your Name.
The Lord is the Great Giver; all beings and creatures are beggars; His humble servants yearn to beg from Him. |1|

I beg for the dust of the feet of the humble, that I may be blessed with the supreme status,
and the filth of countless lifetimes may be erased.
The chronic diseases are cured by the medicine of the Lord's Name; I beg to be imbued with the Immaculate Lord. |2|

With my ears, I listen to the Pure Praises of my Lord and Master.
With the Support of the One Lord, I have abandoned corruption, sexuality and desire.
I humbly bow and fall at the feet of Your slaves; I do not hesitate to do good deeds. |3|

O Lord, with my tongue I sing Your Glorious Praises.
The sins which I have committed are erased.
Meditating, meditating in remembrance on my Lord and Master, my mind lives; I am rid of the five oppressive demons. |4|

Meditating on Your lotus feet, I have come aboard Your boat.
Joining the Society of the Saints, I cross over the world-ocean.
My flower-offering and worship is to realize that the Lord is dwelling alike in all; I shall not be reincarnated naked again. |5|

Please make me the slave of Your slaves, O Lord of the world.

You are the treasure of Grace, merciful to the meek.
Meet with your companion and helper, the Perfect Transcendent Lord God;
you shall never be separated from Him again. |6|

I dedicate my mind and body, and place them in offering before the Lord.
Asleep for countless lifetimes, I have awakened.
He, to whom I belong, is my cherisher and nurturer. I have killed and
discarded my murderous self-conceit. |7|

The Inner-knower, the Searcher of hearts, is pervading the water and the
land.
The undeceivable Lord and Master is permeating each and every heart.
The Perfect Guru has demolished the wall of doubt, and now I see the One
Lord pervading everywhere. |8|

Wherever I look, there I see God, the ocean of peace.
The Lord's treasure is never exhausted; He is the storehouse of jewels.
He cannot be seized; He is inaccessible, and His limits cannot be found. He
is realized when the Lord bestows His Grace. |9|

My heart is cooled, and my mind and body are calmed and soothed.
The craving for birth and death is quenched.
Grasping hold of my hand, He has lifted me up and out; He has blessed me
with His Ambrosial Glance of Grace. |10|

The One and Only Lord is permeating and pervading everywhere.
There is none other than Him at all.
God permeates the beginning, the middle and the end; He has subdued my
desires and doubts. |11|

The Guru is the Transcendent Lord, the Guru is the Lord of the Universe.
The Guru is the Creator, the Guru is forever forgiving.
Meditating, chanting the Guru's Chant, I have obtained the fruits and
rewards; in the Company of the Saints, I have been blessed with the lamp
of spiritual wisdom. |12|

Whatever I see, is my Lord and Master God.
Whatever I hear, is the Bani of God's Word.
Whatever I do, You make me do; You are the Sanctuary, the help and
support of the Saints, Your children. |13|

The beggar begs, and worships You in adoration.
You are the Purifier of the sinners, O Perfectly Holy Lord God.
Please bless me with this one gift, O treasure of all bliss and virtue; I do not ask for anything else. |14|

Section 25 - Raag Maaroo - Part 093

God is the Creator of the body-vessel.
In the Society of the Saints, the dye is produced.
Through the Word of the Lord's Bani, one's reputation becomes immaculate, and the mind is colored by the dye of the Naam, the Name of the Lord. |15|

The sixteen powers, absolute perfection and fruitful rewards are obtained, when the Lord and Master of infinite power is revealed.
The Lord's Name is Nanak's bliss, play and peace; he drinks in the Ambrosial Nectar of the Lord. |16|2|9|

Maaroo, Solhas, Fifth Mehl:
One Universal Creator God. By The Grace Of The True Guru:
You are my Lord and Master; You have made me Your servant.
My soul and body are all gifts from You.
You are the Creator, the Cause of causes; nothing belongs to me. |1|

When You sent me, I came into the world.
Whatever is pleasing to Your Will, I do.
Without You, nothing is done, so I am not anxious at all. |2|

In the world hereafter, the Hukam of Your Command is heard.
In this world, I chant Your Praises, Lord.
You Yourself write the account, and You Yourself erase it; no one can argue with You. |3|

You are our father; we are all Your children.
We play as You cause us to play.
The wilderness and the path are all made by You. No one can take the wrong path. |4|

Some remain seated within their homes.

Some wander across the country and through foreign lands.
Some are grass-cutters, and some are kings. Who among these can be called false? |5|

Who is liberated, and who will land in hell?
Who is worldly, and who is a devotee?
Who is wise, and who is shallow? Who is aware, and who is ignorant? |6|

By the Hukam of the Lord's Command, one is liberated, and by His Hukam, one falls into hell.
By His Hukam, one is worldly, and by His Hukam, one is a devotee.
By His Hukam, one is shallow, and by His Hukam, one is wise. There is no other side except His. |7|

You made the ocean vast and huge.
You made some into foolish self-willed manmukhs, and dragged them into hell.
Some are carried across, in the ship of Truth of the True Guru. |8|

You issue Your Command for this amazing thing, death.
You create all beings and creatures, and absorb them back into Yourself.
You gaze in delight upon the one arena of the world, and enjoy all the pleasures. |9|

Great is the Lord and Master, and Great is His Name.
He is the Great Giver; Great is His place.
He is inaccessible and unfathomable, infinite and unweighable. He cannot be measureed. |10|

No one else knows His value.
Only You Yourself, O Immaculate Lord, are equal to Yourself.
You Yourself are the spiritual teacher, You Yourself are the One who meditates. You Yourself are the great and immense Being of Truth. |11|

For so many days, You remained invisible.
For so many days, You were absorbed in silent absorption.
For so many days, there was only pitch darkness, and then the Creator revealed Himself. |12|

You Yourself are called the God of Supreme Power.

Section 25 - Raag Maaroo - Part 094

You Yourself are the hero, exerting Your regal power.
You Yourself spread peace within; You are cool and icy calm. |13|

One whom You bless and make Gurmukh
- the Naam abides within him, and the unstruck sound current vibrates for him.
He is peaceful, and he is the master of all; the Messenger of Death does not even approach him. |14|

His value cannot be described on paper.
Says Nanak, the Lord of the world is infinite.
In the beginning, in the middle and in the end, God exists. Judgement is in His Hands alone. |15|

No one is equal to Him.
No one can stand up against Him by any means.
Nanak's God is Himself all-in-all. He creates and stages and watches His wondrous plays. |16|1|10|

Maaroo, Fifth Mehl:
The Supreme Lord God is imperishable, the Transcendent Lord, the Inner-knower, the Searcher of hearts.
He is the Slayer of demons, our Supreme Lord and Master.
The Supreme Rishi, the Master of the sensory organs, the uplifter of mountains, the joyful Lord playing His enticing flute. |1|

The Enticer of Hearts, the Lord of wealth, Krishna, the Enemy of ego.
The Lord of the Universe, the Dear Lord, the Destroyer of demons.
The Life of the World, our eternal and ever-stable Lord and Master dwells within each and every heart, and is always with us. |2|

The Support of the Earth, the man-lion, the Supreme Lord God.
The Protector who tears apart demons with His teeth, the Upholder of the earth.
O Creator, You assumed the form of the pygmy to humble the demons; You are the Lord God of all. |3|

You are the Great Raam Chand, who has no form or feature.
Adorned with flowers, holding the chakra in Your hand, Your form is incomparably beautiful.
You have thousands of eyes, and thousands of forms. You alone are the Giver, and all are beggars of You. |4|

You are the Lover of Your devotees, the Master of the masterless.
The Lord and Master of the milk-maids, You are the companion of all.
O Lord, Immacuate Great Giver, I cannot describe even an iota of Your Glorious Virtues. |5|

Liberator, Enticing Lord, Lord of Lakshmi, Supreme Lord God.
Savior of Dropadi's honor.
Lord of Maya, miracle-worker, absorbed in delightful play, unattached. |6|

The Blessed Vision of His Darshan is fruitful and rewarding; He is not born, He is self-existent.
His form is undying; it is never destroyed.
O imperishable, eternal, unfathomable Lord, everything is attached to You. |7|

The Lover of greatness, who dwells in heaven.
By the Pleasure of His Will, He took incarnation as the great fish and the tortoise.
The Lord of beauteous hair, the Worker of miraculous deeds, whatever He wishes, comes to pass. |8|

He is beyond need of any sustenance, free of hate and all-pervading.
He has staged His play; He is called the four-armed Lord.
He assumed the beautiful form of the blue-skinned Krishna; hearing His flute, all are fascinated and enticed. |9|

He is adorned with garlands of flowers, with lotus eyes.
His ear-rings, crown and flute are so beautiful.
He carries the conch, the chakra and the war club; He is the Great Charioteer, who stays with His Saints. |10|

The Lord of yellow robes, the Master of the three worlds.
The Lord of the Universe, the Lord of the world; with my mouth, I chant His Name.

The Archer who draws the bow, the Beloved Lord God; I cannot count all His limbs. |11|

He is said to be free of anguish, and absolutely immaculate.
The Lord of prosperity, pervading the water, the land and the sky.

Section 25 - Raag Maaroo - Part 095

He is near this world and the nether regions of the underworld; His Place is permanent, ever-stable and imperishable. |12|

The Purifier of sinners, the Destroyer of pain and fear.
The Eliminator of egotism, the Eradicator of coming and going.
He is pleased with devotional worship, and merciful to the meek; He cannot be appeased by any other qualities. |13|

The Formless Lord is undeceivable and unchanging.
He is the Embodiment of Light; through Him, the whole world blossoms forth.
He alone unites with Him, whom He unites with Himself. No one can attain the Lord by himself. |14|

He Himself is the milk-maid, and He Himself is Krishna.
He Himself grazes the cows in the forest.
You Yourself create, and You Yourself destroy. Not even a particle of filth attaches to You. |15|

Which of Your Glorious Virtues can I chant with my one tongue?
Even the thousand-headed serpent does not know Your limit.
One may chant new names for You day and night, but even so, O God, no one can describe even one of Your Glorious Virtues. |16|

I have grasped the Support, and entered the Sanctuary of the Lord, the Father of the world.
The Messenger of Death is terrifying and horrendous, and sea of Maya is impassable.
Please be merciful, Lord, and save me, if it is Your Will; please lead me to join with the Saadh Sangat, the Company of the Holy. |17|

All that is seen is an illusion.

I beg for this one gift, for the dust of the feet of the Saints, O Lord of the Universe.
Applying it to my forehead, I obtain the supreme status; he alone obtains it, unto whom You give it. |18|

Those, unto whom the Lord, the Giver of peace, grants His Mercy,
grasp the feet of the Holy, and weave them into their hearts.
They obtain all the wealth of the Naam, the Name of the Lord; the unstruck sound current of the Shabad vibrates and resounds within their minds. |19|

With my tongue I chant the Names given to You.
'Sat Naam' is Your perfect, primal Name.
Says Nanak, Your devotees have entered Your Sanctuary. Please bestow the Blessed Vision of Your Darshan; their minds are filled with love for You. |20|

You alone know Your state and extent.
You Yourself speak, and You Yourself describe it.
Please make Nanak the slave of Your slaves, O Lord; as it pleases Your Will, please keep him with Your slaves. |21|2|11|

Maaroo, Fifth Mehl:
O slave of the inaccessible Lord God Allah,
forsake thoughts of worldly entanglements.
Become the dust of the feet of the humble fakeers, and consider yourself a traveller on this journey. O saintly dervish, you shall be approved in the Court of the Lord. |1|

Let Truth be your prayer, and faith your prayer-mat.
Subdue your desires, and overcome your hopes.
Let your body be the mosque, and your mind the priest. Let true purity be God's Word for you. |2|

Let your practice be to live the spiritual life.
Let your spiritual cleansing be to renounce the world and seek God.
Let control of the mind be your spiritual wisdom, O holy man; meeting with God, you shall never die again. |3|

Practice within your heart the teachings of the Koran and the Bible;

restrain the ten sensory organs from straying into evil.
Tie up the five demons of desire with faith, charity and contentment, and you shall be acceptable. |4|

Let compassion be your Mecca, and the dust of the feet of the holy your fast.
Let Paradise be your practice of the Prophet's Word.
God is the beauty, the light and the fragrance. Meditation on Allah is the secluded meditation chamber. |5|

Section 25 - Raag Maaroo - Part 096

He alone is a Qazi, who practices the Truth.
He alone is a Haji, a pilgrim to Mecca, who purifies his heart.
He alone is a Mullah, who banishes evil; he alone is a saintly dervish, who takes the Support of the Lord's Praise. |6|

Always, at every moment, remember God, the Creator within your heart.
Let your meditation beads be the subjugation of the ten senses. Let good conduct and self-restraint be your circumcision. |7|

You must know in your heart that everything is temporary.
Family, household and siblings are all entanglements.
Kings, rulers and nobles are mortal and transitory; only God's Gate is the permanent place. |8|

First, is the Lord's Praise; second, contentment;
third, humility, and fourth, giving to charities.
Fifth is to hold one's desires in restraint. These are the five most sublime daily prayers. |9|

Let your daily worship be the knowledge that God is everywhere.
Let renunciation of evil actions be the water-jug you carry.
Let realization of the One Lord God be your call to prayer; be a good child of God - let this be your trumpet. |10|

Let what is earned righteously be your blessed food.
Wash away pollution with the river of your heart.
One who realizes the Prophet attains heaven. Azraa-eel, the Messenger of Death, does not cast him into hell. |11|

Let good deeds be your body, and faith your bride.
Play and enjoy the Lord's love and delight.
Purify what is impure, and let the Lord's Presence be your religious tradition. Let your total awareness be the turban on your head. |12|

To be Muslim is to be kind-hearted,
and wash away pollution from within the heart.
He does not even approach worldly pleasures; he is pure, like flowers, silk, ghee and the deer-skin. |13|

One who is blessed with the mercy and compassion of the Merciful Lord,
is the manliest man among men.
He alone is a Shaykh, a preacher, a Haji, and he alone is God's slave, who is blessed with God's Grace. |14|

The Creator Lord has Creative Power; the Merciful Lord has Mercy.
The Praises and the Love of the Merciful Lord are unfathomable.
Realize the True Hukam, the Command of the Lord, O Nanak; you shall be released from bondage, and carried across. |15|3|12|

Maaroo, Fifth Mehl:
The Abode of the Supreme Lord God is above all.
He Himself establishes, establishes and creates.
Holding tight to the Sanctuary of God, peace is found, and one is not afflicted by the fear of Maya. |1|

He saved you from the fire of the womb,
and did not destroy you, when you were an egg in your mother's ovary.
Blessing you with meditative remembrance upon Himself, He nurtured you and cherished you; He is the Master of all hearts. |2|

I have come to the Sanctuary of His lotus feet.
In the Saadh Sangat, the Company of the Holy, I sing the Praises of the Lord.
I have erased all the pains of birth and death; meditating on the Lord, Har, Har, I have no fear of death. |3|

God is all-powerful, indescribable, unfathomable and divine.
All beings and creatures serve Him.

In so many ways, He cherishes those born from eggs, from the womb, from sweat and from the earth. |4|

He alone obtains this wealth,
who savors and enjoys, deep within his mind, the Name of the Lord.
Grasping hold of his arm, God lifts him up and pulls him out of the deep, dark pit. Such a devotee of the Lord is very rare. |5|

Section 25 - Raag Maaroo - Part 097

God exists in the beginning, in the middle and in the end.
Whatever the Creator Lord Himself does, comes to pass.
Doubt and fear are erased, in the Saadh Sangat, the Company of the Holy, and then one is not afflicted by deadly pain. |6|

I sing the most Sublime Bani, the Word of the Lord of the Universe.
I beg for the dust of the feet of the Saadh Sangat.
Eradicating desire, I have become free of desire; I have burnt away all my sins. |7|

This is the unique way of the Saints;
they behold the Supreme Lord God with them.
With each and every breath, they worship and adore the Lord, Har, Har.
How could anyone be too lazy to meditate on Him? |8|

Wherever I look, there I see the Inner-knower, the Searcher of hearts.
I never forget God, my Lord and Master, even for an instant.
Your slaves live by meditating, meditating in remembrance on the Lord;
You are permeating the woods, the water and the land. |9|

Even the hot wind does not touch one
who remains awake in meditative remembrance, night and day.
He delights and enjoys meditative remembrance on the Lord; he has no attachment to Maya. |10|

Disease, sorrow and pain do not affect him;
he sings the Kirtan of the Lord's Praises in the Saadh Sangat, the Company of the Holy.
Please bless me with Your Name, O my Beloved Lord God; please listen to my prayer, O Creator. |11|

Your Name is a jewel, O my Beloved Lord.
Your slaves are imbued with Your Infinite Love.
Those who are imbued with Your Love, become like You; it is so rare that they are found. |12|

My mind longs for the dust of the feet of those
who never forget the Lord.
Associating with them, I obtain the supreme status; the Lord, my Companion, is always with me. |13|

He alone is my beloved friend and companion,
who implants the Name of the One Lord within, and eradicates evil-mindedness.
Immaculate are the teachings of that humble servant of the Lord, who casts out sexual desire, anger and egotism. |14|

Other than You, O Lord, no one is mine.
The Guru has led me to grasp the feet of God.
I am a sacrifice to the Perfect True Guru, who has destroyed the illusion of duality. |15|

With each and every breath, I never forget God.
Twenty-four hours a day, I meditate on the Lord, Har, Har.
O Nanak, the Saints are imbued with Your Love; You are the great and all-powerful Lord. |16|4|13|

Maaroo, Fifth Mehl:
One Universal Creator God. By The Grace Of The True Guru:
I enshrine the Lord's lotus feet continually within my heart.
Each and every moment, I humbly bow to the Perfect Guru.
I dedicate my body, mind and everything, and place it in offering before the Lord. His Name is the most beautiful in this world. |1|

Why forget the Lord and Master from your mind?
He blessed you with body and soul, creating and embellishing you.
With every breath and morsel of food, the Creator takes care of His beings, who receive according to what they have done. |2|

No one returns empty-handed from Him;

twenty-four hours a day, keep the Lord in your mind.

Section 25 - Raag Maaroo - Part 098

In the Saadh Sangat, the Company of the Holy, meditate and vibrate upon your imperishable Lord and Master, and you shall be honored in the Court of the Lord. |3|

The four great blessings, and the eighteen miraculous spiritual powers,
are found in the treasure of the Naam, which brings celestial peace and poise, and the nine treasures.
If you yearn in your mind for all joys, then join the Saadh Sangat, and dwell upon your Lord and Master. |4|

The Shaastras, the Simritees and the Vedas proclaim
that the mortal must be victorious in this priceless human life.
Forsaking sexual desire, anger and slander, sing of the Lord with your tongue, O Nanak. |5|

He has no form or shape, no ancestry or social class.
The Perfect Lord is perfectly pervading day and night.
Whoever meditates on Him is very fortunate; he is not consigned to reincarnation again. |6|

One who forgets the Primal Lord, the Architect of karma,
wanders around burning, and remains tormented.
No one can save such an ungrateful person; he is thrown into the most horrible hell. |7|

He blessed you with your soul, the breath of life, your body and wealth;
He preserved and nurtured you in your mother's womb.
Forsaking His Love, you are imbued with another; you shall never achieve your goals like this. |8|

Please shower me with Your Merciful Grace, O my Lord and Master.
You dwell in each and every heart, and are near everyone.
Nothing is in my hands; he alone knows, whom You inspire to know. |9|

One who has such pre-ordained destiny inscribed upon his forehead,
that person is not afflicted by Maya.

Slave Nanak seeks Your Sanctuary forever; there is no other equal to You. |10|

In His Will, He made all pain and pleasure.
How rare are those who remember the Ambrosial Naam, the Name of the Lord.
His value cannot be described. He is prevailing everywhere. |11|

He is the devotee; He is the Great Giver.
He is the Perfect Primal Lord, the Architect of karma.
He is your help and support, since infancy; He fulfills your mind's desires. |12|

Death, pain and pleasure are ordained by the Lord.
They do not increase or decrease by anyone's efforts.
That alone happens, which is pleasing to the Creator; speaking of himself, the mortal ruins himself. |13|

He lifts us up and pulls us out of the deep dark pit;
He unites with Himself, those who were separated for so many incarnations.
Showering them with His Mercy, He protects them with His own hands.
Meeting with the Holy Saints, they meditate on the Lord of the Universe. |14|

Your worth cannot be described.
Wondrous is Your form, and Your glorious greatness.
Your humble servant begs for the gift of devotional worship. Nanak is a sacrifice, a sacrifice to You. |15|1|14|22|24|2|14|62|

Vaar Of Maaroo, Third Mehl:
One Universal Creator God. By The Grace Of The True Guru:
Shalok, First Mehl:
If virtue is sold when there is no buyer, then it is sold very cheap.
But if one meets a buyer of virtue, then virtue sells for hundreds of thousands.

Section 25 - Raag Maaroo - Part 099

Meeting with a virtuous person, virtue is obtained, and one is immersed in the True Guru.

Priceless virtues are not obtained for any price; they cannot be purchased in a store.

O Nanak, their weight is full and perfect; it never decreases at all. |1|

Fourth Mehl:

Without the Naam, the Name of the Lord, they wander around, continually coming and going in reincarnation.

Some are in bondage, and some are set free; some are happy in the Love of the Lord.

O Nanak, believe in the True Lord, and practice Truth, through the lifestyle of Truth. |2|

Pauree:

From the Guru, I have obtained the supremely powerful sword of spiritual wisdom.

I have cut down the fortress of duality and doubt, attachment, greed and egotism.

The Name of the Lord abides within my mind; I contemplate the Word of the Guru's Shabad.

Through Truth, self-discipline and sublime understanding, the Lord has become very dear to me.

Truly, truly, the True Creator Lord is all-pervading. |1|

Shalok, Third Mehl:

Among the ragas, Kaydaaraa Raga is known as good, O Siblings of Destiny, if through it, one comes to love the Word of the Shabad,

and if one remains in the Soceity of the Saints, and enshrines love for the True Lord.

Such a person washes away the pollution from within, and saves his generations as well.

He gathes in the capital of virtue, and destroys and drives out unvirtuous sins.

O Nanak, he alone is known as united, who does not forsake his Guru, and who does not love duality. |1|

Fourth Mehl:

Gazing upon the world-ocean, I am afraid of death; but if I live in the Fear of You, God, then I am not afraid.

Through the Word of the Guru's Shabad, I am content; O Nanak, I blossom forth in the Name. |2|

Fourth Mehl:

I get on board the boat and set out, but the ocean is churning with waves.

The boat of Truth encounters no obstruction, if the Guru gives encouragement.

He takes us across to the door on the other side, as the Guru keeps watch.

O Nanak, if I am blessed with His Grace, I shall go to His Court with honor. |3|

Pauree:

Enjoy your kingdom of bliss; as Gurmukh, practice Truth.

Sitting upon the throne of Truth, the Lord administers justice; He unites us in Union with the Society of the Saints.

Meditating on the Lord, through the True Teachings, we become just like the Lord.

If the Lord, the Giver of peace, abides in the mind, in this world, then in the end, He becomes our help and support.

Love for the Lord wells up, when the Guru imparts understanding. |2|

Shalok, First Mehl:

Confused and deluded, I wander around, but no one shows me the way.

I go and ask the clever people, if there is there anyone who can rid me of my pain.

If the True Guru abides within my mind, then I see the Lord, my best friend, there.

O Nanak, my mind is satisfied and fulfilled, contemplating the Praises of the True Name. |1|

Third Mehl:

He Himself is the Doer, and He is the deed; He Himself issues the Command.

He Himself forgives some, and He Himself does the deed.

O Nanak, receiving the Divine Light from the Guru, suffering and corruption are burnt away, through the Name. |2|

Pauree:

Don't be fooled by gazing at the riches of Maya, you foolish self-willed manmukh.

It shall not go along with you when you must depart; all the wealth you see is false.

The blind and ignorant do not understand, that the sword of death is hanging over their heads.

By Guru's Grace, those who drink in the sublime essence of the Lord are saved.

Section 25 - Raag Maaroo - Part 100

He Himself is the Doer, and He Himself is the Cause; the Lord Himself is our Saving Grace. |3|

Shalok, Third Mehl:
Those who do not meet with the Guru, who have no Fear of God at all, continue coming and going in reincarnation, and suffer terrible pain; their anxiety is never relieved.

They are beaten like clothes being washed on the rocks, and struck every hour like chimes.

O Nanak, without the True Name, these entanglements are not removed from hanging over one's head. |1|

Third Mehl:
I have searched throughout the three worlds, O my friend; egotism is bad for the world.

Don't worry, O my soul; speak the Truth, O Nanak, the Truth, and only the Truth. |2|

Pauree:
The Lord Himself forgives the Gurmukhs; they are absorbed and immersed in the Lord's Name.

He Himself links them to devotional worship; they bear the Insignia of the Guru's Shabad.

Those who turn towards the Guru, as sunmukh, are beautiful. They are famous in the Court of the True Lord.

In this world, and in the world hereafter, they are liberated; they realize the Lord.

Blessed, blessed are those humble beings who serve the Lord. I am a sacrifice to them. |4|

Shalok, First Mehl:
The rude, ill-mannered bride is encased in the body-tomb; she is blackened, and her mind is impure.
She can enjoy her Husband Lord, only if she is virtuous. O Nanak, the soul-bride is unworthy, and without virtue. |1|

First Mehl:
She has good conduct, true self-discipline, and a perfect family.
O Nanak, day and night, she is always good; she loves her Beloved Husband Lord. |2|

Pauree:
One who realizes his own self, is blessed with the treasure of the Naam, the Name of the Lord.
Granting His Mercy, the Guru merges him in the Word of His Shabad.
The Word of the Guru's Bani is immaculate and pure; through it, one drinks in the sublime essence of the Lord.
Those who taste the sublime essence of the Lord, forsake other flavors.
Drinking in the sublime essence of the Lord, they remain satisfied forever; their hunger and thirst are quenched. |5|

Shalok, Third Mehl:
Her Husband Lord is pleased, and He enjoys His bride; the soul-bride adorns her heart with the Naam, the Name of the Lord.
O Nanak, that bride who stands before Him, is the most noble and respected woman. |1|

First Mehl:
In her father-in-law's home hereafter, and in her parents' home in this world, she belongs to her Husband Lord. Her Husband is inaccessible and unfathomable.
O Nanak, she is the happy soul-bride, who is pleasing to her carefree, independent Lord. |2|

Pauree:
That king sits upon the throne, who is worthy of that throne.
Those who realize the True Lord, they alone are the true kings.
These mere earthly rulers are not called kings; in the love of duality, they suffer.

Why should someone praise someone else who is also created? They depart in no time at all.
The One True Lord is eternal and imperishable. One who, as Gurmukh, understands becomes eternal as well. |6|

Shalok, Third Mehl:
The One Lord is the Husband of all. No one is without the Husband Lord.
O Nanak, they are the pure soul-brides, who merge in the True Guru. |1|

Third Mehl:
The mind is churning with so many waves of desire. How can one be emancipated in the Court of the Lord?

Be absorbed in the Lord's True Love, and imbued with the deep color of the Lord's Infinite Love.
O Nanak, by Guru's Grace, one is emancipated, if the consciousness is attached to the True Lord. |2|

Pauree:
The Name of the Lord is priceless. How can its value be estimated?

Section 25 - Raag Maaroo - Part 101

He Himself created the entire universe, and He Himself is pervading it.
The Gurmukhs praise the Lord forever, and through the Truth, they assess Him.
Through the Word of the Guru's Shabad, the heart-lotus blossoms forth, and in this way, one drinks in the sublime essence of the Lord.
Coming and going in reincarnation ceases, and one sleeps in peace and poise. |7|

Shalok, First Mehl:
Neither dirty, nor dull, nor saffron, nor any color that fades.
O Nanak, crimson - deep crimson is the color of one who is imbued with the True Lord. |1|

Third Mehl:
The bumble bee intuitively and fearlessly dwells among the vegetation, flowers and fruits.
O Nanak, there is only one tree, one flower, and one bumble bee. |2|

Pauree:

Those humble beings who struggle with their minds are brave and distinguished heroes.

Those who realize their own selves, remain forever united with the Lord.

This is the glory of the spiritual teachers, that they remain absorbed in their mind.

They attain the Mansion of the Lord's Presence, and focus their meditation on the True Lord.

Those who conquer their own minds, by Guru's Grace, conquer the world. |8|

Shalok, Third Mehl:

If I were to become a Yogi, and wander around the world, begging from door to door,

then, when I am summoned to the Court of the Lord, what answer could I give?

The Naam, the Name of the Lord, is the charity I beg for; contentment is my temple. The True Lord is always with me.

Nothing is obtained by wearing religious robes; all will be seized by the Messenger of Death.

O Nanak, talk is false; contemplate the True Name. |1|

Third Mehl:

Through that door, you will be called to account; do not serve at that door.

Seek and find such a True Guru, who has no equal in His greatness.

In His Sanctuary, one is released, and no one calls him to account.

Truth is implanted within Him, and He implants Truth within others. He bestows the blessing of the True Shabad.

One who has Truth within his heart - his body and mind are also true.

O Nanak, if one submits to the Hukam, the Command of the True Lord God, he is blessed with true glory and greatness.

He is immersed and merged in the True Lord, who blesses him with His Glance of Grace. |2|

Pauree:

They are not called heroes, who die of egotism, suffering in pain.

The blind ones do not realize their own selves; in the love of duality, they rot.

They struggle with great anger; here and hereafter, they suffer in pain.

The Dear Lord is not pleased by egotism; the Vedas proclaim this clearly.
Those who die of egotism, shall not find salvation. They die, and are reborn in reincarnation. |9|

Shalok, Third Mehl:
The crow does not become white, and an iron boat does not float across.
One who puts his faith in the treasure of his Beloved Lord is blessed; he exalts and embellishes others as well.
One who realizes the Hukam of God's Command - his face is radiant and bright; he floats across, like iron upon wood.
Forsake thirst and desire, and abide in the Fear of God; O Nanak, these are the most excellent actions. |1|

Third Mehl:
The ignorant people who go to the desert to conquer their minds, are not able to conquer them.
O Nanak, if this mind is to be conquered, one must contemplate the Word of the Guru's Shabad.
This mind is not conquered by conquering it, even though everyone longs to do so.
O Nanak, the mind itself conquers the mind, if one meets with the True Guru. |2|

Section 25 - Raag Maaroo - Part 102

Pauree:
He created both sides; Shiva dwells within Shakti (the soul dwells within the material universe).
Through the material universe of Shakti, no one has ever found the Lord; they continue to be born and die in reincarnation.
Serving the Guru, peace is found, meditating on the Lord with every breath and morsel of food.
Searching and looking through the Simritees and the Shaastras, I have found that the most sublime person is the slave of the Lord.
O Nanak, without the Naam, nothing is permanent and stable; I am a sacrifice to the Naam, the Name of the Lord. |10|

Shalok, Third Mehl:
I might become a Pandit, a religious scholar, or an astrologer, and recite the four Vedas with my mouth;

I might be worshipped throughout the nine regions of the earth for my wisdom and thought;

let me not forget the Word of Truth, that no one can touch my sacred cooking square.

Such cooking squares are false, O Nanak; only the One Lord is True. |1|

Third Mehl:
He Himself creates and He Himself acts; He bestows His Glance of Grace.
He Himself grants glorious greatness; says Nanak, He is the True Lord. |2|

Pauree:
Only death is painful; I cannot conceive of anything else as painful.
It is unstoppable; it stalks and pervades the world, and fights with the sinners.
Through the Word of the Guru's Shabad, one is immersed in the Lord.
Meditating on the Lord, one comes to realize the Lord.
He alone is emancipated in the Sanctuary of the Lord, who struggles with his own mind.
One who contemplates and meditates on the Lord in his mind, succeeds in the Court of the Lord. |11|

Shalok, First Mehl:
Submit to the Will of the Lord Commander; in His Court, only Truth is accepted.
Your Lord and Master shall call you to account; do not go astray on beholding the world.
One who keeps watch over his heart, and keeps his heart pure, is a dervish, a saintly devotee.
Love and affection, O Nanak, are in the accounts placed before the Creator. |1|

First Mehl:
One who is unattached like the bumble bee, sees the Lord of the world everywhere.
The diamond of his mind is pierced through with the Diamond of the Lord's Name; O Nanak, his neck is embellished with it. |2|

Pauree:
The self-willed manmukhs are afflicted by death; they cling to Maya in emotional attachment.

In an instant, they are thrown to the ground and killed; in the love of duality, they are deluded.

This opportunity shall not come into their hands again; they are beaten by the Messenger of Death with his stick.

But Death's stick does not even strike those who remain awake and aware in the Love of the Lord.

All are Yours, and cling to You; only You can save them. |12|

Shalok, First Mehl:
See the imperishable Lord everywhere; attachment to wealth brings only great pain.

Loaded with dust, you have to cross over the world-ocean; you are not carrying the profit and capital of the Name with you. |1|

First Mehl:
My capital is Your True Name, O Lord; this wealth is inexhaustible and infinite.

O Nanak, this merchandise is immaculate; blessed is the banker who trades in it. |2|

First Mehl:
Know and enjoy the primal, eternal Love of the Great Lord and Master.

Blessed with the Naam, O Nanak, you shall strike down the Messenger of Death, and push his face to the ground. |3|

Pauree:
He Himself has embellished the body, and placed the nine treasures of the Naam within it.

He confuses some in doubt; fruitless are their actions.

Some, as Gurmukh, realize their Lord, the Supreme Soul.

Some listen to the Lord, and obey Him; sublime and exalted are their actions.

Love for the Lord wells up deep within, singing the Glorious Praises of the Lord's Name. |13|

Shalok, First Mehl:

Section 25 - Raag Maaroo - Part 103

The Fear of God abides in the mind of the innocent; this is the straight path to the One Lord.
Jealousy and envy bring terrible pain, and one is cursed throughout the three worlds. |1|

First Mehl:
The drum of the Vedas vibrates, bringing dispute and divisiveness.
O Nanak, contemplate the Naam, the Name of the Lord; there is none except Him. |2|

First Mehl:
The world-ocean of the three qualities is unfathomably deep; how can its bottom be seen?
If I meet with the great, self-sufficient True Guru, then I am carried across.
This ocean is filled up with pain and suffering.
O Nanak, without the True Name, no one's hunger is appeased. |3|

Pauree:
Those who search their inner beings, through the Word of the Guru's Shabad, are exalted and adorned.
They obtain what they wish for, meditating on the Lord's Name.
One who is blessed by God's Grace, meets with the Guru; he sings the Glorious Praises of the Lord.
The Righteous Judge of Dharma is his friend; he does not have to walk on the Path of Death.
He meditates on the Lord's Name, day and night; he is absorbed and immersed in the Lord's Name. |14|

Shalok, First Mehl:
Listen to and speak the Name of the One Lord, who permeates the heavens, this world and the nether regions of the underworld.
The Hukam of His Command cannot be erased; whatever He has written, shall go with the mortal.
Who has died, and who kills? Who comes and who goes?
Who is enraptured, O Nanak, and whose consciousness merges in the Lord? |1|

First Mehl:
In egotism, he dies; possessiveness kills him, and the breath flows out like a river.

Desire is exhausted, O Nanak, only when the mind is imbued with the Name.

His eyes are imbued with the eyes of the Lord, and his ears ring with celestial consciousness.

His tongue drinks in the sweet nectar, dyed crimson by chanting the Name of the Beloved Lord.

His inner being is drenched with the Lord's fragrance; his worth cannot be described. |2|

Pauree:

In this age, the Naam, the Name of the Lord, is the treasure. Only the Naam goes along in the end.

It is inexhaustible; it is never empty, no matter how much one may eat, consume or spend.

The Messenger of Death does not even approach the humble servant of the Lord.

They alone are the true bankers and traders, who have the wealth of the Lord in their laps.

By the Lord's Mercy, one finds the Lord, only when the Lord Himself sends for him. |15|

Shalok, Third Mehl:

The self-willed manmukh does not appreciate the excellence of trading in Truth. He deals in poison, collects poison, and is in love with poison.

Outwardly, they call themselves Pandits, religious scholars, but in their minds they are foolish and ignorant.

They do not focus their consciousness on the Lord; they love to engage in arguments.

They speak to cause arguments, and earn their living by telling lies.

In this world, only the Lord's Name is immaculate and pure. All other objects of creation are polluted.

O Nanak, those who do not remember the Naam, the Name of the Lord, are polluted; they die in ignorance. |1|

Third Mehl:

Without serving the Lord, he suffers in pain; accepting the Hukam of God's Command, pain is gone.

He Himself is the Giver of peace; He Himself awards punishment.

O Nanak, know this well; all that happens is according to His Will. |2|

Pauree:
Without the Lord's Name, the world is poor. Without the Name, no one is satisfied.
He is deluded by duality and doubt. In egotism, he suffers in pain.

Section 25 - Raag Maaroo - Part 104

Without good karma, he does not obtain anything, no matter how much he may wish for it.
Coming and going in reincarnation, and birth and death are ended, through the Word of the Guru's Shabad.
He Himself acts, so unto whom should we complain? There is no other at all. |16|

Shalok, Third Mehl:
In this world, the Saints earn the wealth; they come to meet God through the True Guru.
The True Guru implants the Truth within; the value of this wealth cannot be described.
Obtaining this wealth, hunger is relieved, and peace comes to dwell in the mind.
Only those who have such pre-ordained destiny, come to receive this.
The world of the self-willed manmukh is poor, crying out for Maya.
Night and day, it wanders continually, and its hunger is never relieved.
It never finds calm tranquility, and peace never comes to dwell in its mind.
It is always plagued by anxiety, and its cynicism never departs.
O Nanak, without the True Guru, the intellect is perverted; if one meets the True Guru, then one practices the Word of the Shabad.
Forever and ever, he dwells in peace, and merges in the True Lord. |1|

Third Mehl:
The One who created the world, takes care of it.
Meditate in remembrance on the One Lord, O Siblings of Destiny; there is none other than Him.
So eat the food of the Shabad and goodness; eating it, you shall remain satisfied forever.
Dress yourself in the Praise of the Lord. Forever and ever, it is radiant and bright; it is never polluted.
I have intuitively earned the true wealth, which never decreases.
The body is adorned with the Shabad, and is at peace forever and ever.

O Nanak, the Gurmukh realizes the Lord, who reveals Himself. |2|

Pauree:
Deep within the self are meditation and austere self-discipline, when one realizes the Word of the Guru's Shabad.
Meditating on the Name of the Lord, Har, Har, egotism and ignorance are eliminated.
One's inner being is overflowing with Ambrosial Nectar; tasting it, the flavor is known.
Those who taste it become fearless; they are satisfied with the sublime essence of the Lord.
Those who drink it in, by the Grace of the Lord, are never again afflicted by death. |17|

Shalok, Third Mehl:
People tie up bundles of demerits; no one deals in virtue.
Rare is that person, O Nanak, who purchases virtue.
By Guru's Grace, one is blessed with virtue, when the Lord bestows His Glance of Grace. |1|

Third Mehl:
Merits and demerits are the same; they are both created by the Creator.
O Nanak, one who obeys the Hukam of the Lord's Command, finds peace, contemplating the Word of the Guru's Shabad. |2|

Pauree:
The King sits on the throne within the self; He Himself administers justice.
Through the Word of the Guru's Shabad, the Lord's Court is known; within the self is the Sanctuary, the Mansion of the Lord's Presence.
The coins are assayed, and the genuine coins are placed in His treasury, while the counterfeit ones find no place.
The Truest of the True is all-pervading; His justice is forever True.
One comes to enjoy the Ambrosial essence, when the Name is enshrined in the mind. |18|

Shalok, First Mehl:
When one acts in egotism, then You are not there, Lord. Wherever You are, there is no ego.

Section 25 - Raag Maaroo - Part 105

O spiritual teachers, understand this: the Unspoken Speech is in the mind.

Without the Guru, the essence of reality is not found; the Invisible Lord dwells everywhere.

One meets the True Guru, and then the Lord is known, when the Word of the Shabad comes to dwell in the mind.

When self-conceit departs, doubt and fear also depart, and the pain of birth and death is removed.

Following the Guru's Teachings, the Unseen Lord is seen; the intellect is exalted, and one is carried across.

O Nanak, chant the chant of 'Sohang hansaa' - 'He is me, and I am Him.' The three worlds are absorbed in Him. |1|

Third Mehl:

Some assay their mind-jewel, and contemplate the Word of the Guru's Shabad.

Only a few of those humble beings are known in this world, in this Dark Age of Kali Yuga.

One's self remains blended with the Lord's Self, when egotism and duality are conquered.

O Nanak, those who are imbued with the Naam cross over the difficult, treacherous and terrifying world-ocean. |2|

Pauree:

The self-willed manmukhs do not search within their own selves; they are deluded by their egotistical pride.

Wandering in the four directions, they grow weary, tormented by burning desire within.

They do not study the Simritees and the Shaastras; the manmukhs waste away and are lost.

Without the Guru, no one finds the Naam, the Name of the True Lord.

One who contemplates the essence of spiritual wisdom and meditates on the Lord is saved. |19|

Shalok, Second Mehl:

He Himself knows, He Himself acts, and He Himself does it right.

So stand before Him, O Nanak, and offer your prayers. |1|

First Mehl:

He who created the creation, watches over it; He Himself knows.

Unto whom should I speak, O Nanak, when everything is contained within the home of the heart? |2|

Pauree:
Forget everything, and be friends with the One Lord alone.
Your mind and body shall be enraptured, and the Lord shall burn away your sins.
Your comings and goings in reincarnation shall cease; you shall not be reborn and die again.
The True Name shall be your Support, and you shall not burn in sorrow and attachment.
O Nanak, gather in the treasure of the Naam, the Name of the Lord, within your mind. |20|

Shalok, Fifth Mehl:
You do not forget Maya from your mind; you beg for it with each and every breath.
You do not even think of that God; O Nanak, it is not in your karma. |1|

Fifth Mehl:
Maya and its wealth shall not go along with you, so why do you cling to it - are you blind?
Meditate on the Guru's Feet, and the bonds of Maya shall be cut away from you. |2|

Pauree:
By the Pleasure of His Will, the Lord inspires us to obey the Hukam of His Command; by the Pleasure of His Will, we find peace.
By the Pleasure of His Will, He leads us to meet the True Guru; by the Pleasure of His Will, we meditate on the Truth.
There is no other gift as great as the Pleasure of His Will; this Truth is spoken and proclaimed.
Those who have such pre-ordained destiny, practice and live the Truth.
Nanak has entered His Sanctuary; He created the world. |21|

Shalok, Third Mehl:
Those who do not have spiritual wisdom within, do not have even an iota of the Fear of God.
O Nanak, why kill those who are already dead? The Lord of the Universe Himself has killed them. |1|

Third Mehl:
To read the horoscope of the mind, is the most sublime joyful peace.
He alone is called a good Brahmin, who understands God in contemplative meditation.
He praises the Lord, and reads of the Lord, and contemplates the Word of the Guru's Shabad.

Section 25 - Raag Maaroo - Part 106

Celebrated and approved is the coming into the world of such a person, who saves all his generations as well.
Hereafter, no one is questioned about social status; excellent and sublime is the practice of the Word of the Shabad.
Other study is false, and other actions are false; such people are in love with poison.
They do not find any peace within themselves; the self-willed manmukhs waste away their lives.
O Nanak, those who are attuned to the Naam are saved; they have infinite love for the Guru. |2|

Pauree:
He Himself creates the creation, and gazes upon it; He Himself is totally True.
One who does not understand the Hukam, the Command of his Lord and Master, is false.
By the Pleasure of His Will, the True Lord joins the Gurmukh to Himself.
He is the One Lord and Master of all; through the Word of the Guru's Shabad, we are blended with Him.
The Gurmukhs praise Him forever; all are beggars of Him.
O Nanak, as He Himself makes us dance, we dance. |22|1|

Sudh|

Vaar Of Maaroo, Fifth Mehl, Dakhanay, Fifth Mehl:
One Universal Creator God. By The Grace Of The True Guru:
If You tell me to, O my Friend, I will cut off my head and give it to You.
My eyes long for You; when will I see Your Vision? |1|

Fifth Mehl:

I am in love with You; I have seen that other love is false.

Even clothes and food are frightening to me, as long as I do not see my Beloved. |2|

Fifth Mehl:

I rise early, O my Husband Lord, to behold Your Vision.

Eye make-up, garlands of flowers, and the flavor of betel leaf, are all nothing but dust, without seeing You. |3|

Pauree:

You are True, O my True Lord and Master; You uphold all that is true.

You created the world, making a place for the Gurmukhs.

By the Will of the Lord, the Vedas came into being; they discriminate between sin and virtue.

You created Brahma, Vishnu and Shiva, and the expanse of the three qualities.

Creating the world of the nine regions, O Lord, You have embellished it with beauty.

Creating the beings of various kinds, You infused Your power into them.

No one knows Your limit, O True Creator Lord.

You Yourself know all ways and means; You Yourself save the Gurmukhs. |1|

Dakhanay, Fifth Mehl:

If You are my friend, then don't separate Yourself from me, even for an instant.

My soul is fascinated and enticed by You; when will I see You, O my Love? |1|

Fifth Mehl:

Burn in the fire, you evil person; O separation, be dead.

O my Husband Lord, please sleep upon my bed, that all my sufferings may be gone. |2|

Fifth Mehl:

The evil person is engrossed in the love of duality; through the disease of egotism, he suffers separation.

The True Lord King is my friend; meeting with Him, I am so happy. |3|

Pauree:

You are inaccessible, merciful and infinite; who can estimate Your worth?
You created the entire universe; You are the Master of all the worlds.
No one knows Your creative power, O my all-pervading Lord and Master.
No one can equal You; You are imperishable and eternal, the Savior of the world.

Section 25 - Raag Maaroo - Part 107

You established the four ages; You are the Creator of all worlds.
You created the comings and goings of reincarnation; not even a particle of filth sticks to You.
As you are merciful, You attach us to the Feet of the True Guru.
You cannot be found by any other efforts; You are the eternal, imperishable Creator of the Universe. |2|

Dakhanay, Fifth Mehl:
If You come into my courtyard, all the earth becomes beautiful.
Other than the One Lord, my Husband, no one else cares for me. |1|

Fifth Mehl:
All my adornments become beautiful, when You, O Lord, sit in my courtyard and make it Yours.
Then no traveller who comes to my home shall leave empty-handed. |2|

Fifth Mehl:
I have spread out my bed for You, O my Husband Lord, and applied all my decorations.
But even this is not pleasing to me, to wear a garland around my neck. |3|

Pauree:
O Supreme Lord God, O Transcendent Lord, You do not take birth.
By the Hukam of Your Command, You formed the Universe; forming it, You merge into it.
Your Form cannot be known; how can one meditate on You?
You are pervading and permeating all; You Yourself reveal Your creative potency.
Your treasures of devotional worship are overflowing; they never decrease.
These gems, jewels and diamonds - their value cannot be estimated.
As You Yourself become merciful, Lord, You link us to the service of the True Guru.

One who sings the Glorious Praises of the Lord, never suffers any deficiency. |3|

Dakhanay, Fifth Mehl:
When I look within my being, I find that my Beloved is with me.
All pains are relieved, O Nanak, when He bestows His Glance of Grace. |1|

Fifth Mehl:
Nanak sits, waiting for news of the Lord, and stands at the Lord's Door; serving Him for so long.
O my Beloved, only You know my objective; I stand, waiting to see the Lord's face. |2|

Fifth Mehl:
What should I say to you, you fool? Don't look at the vines of others - be a true husband.
O Nanak, the entire world is blooming, like a garden of flowers. |3|

Pauree:
You are Wise, all-knowing and beautiful; You are pervading and permeating all.
You Yourself are the Lord and Master, and the servant; You worship and adore Yourself.
You are all-wise and all-seeing; You Yourself are true and pure.
The Immaculate Lord, my Lord God, is celibate and True.
God spreads out the expanse of the entire universe, and He Himself plays in it.
He created this coming and going of reincarnation; creating the wondrous play, He gazes upon it.
One who is blessed with the Guru's Teachings, is not consigned to the womb of reincarnation, ever again.
All walk as He makes them walk; nothing is under the control of the created beings. |4|

Dakhanay, Fifth Mehl:
You are walking along the river-bank, but the land is giving way beneath you.
Watch out! Your foot might slip, and you'll fall in and die. |1|

Fifth Mehl:

You believe what is false and temporary to be true, and so you run on and on.

O Nanak, like butter in the fire, it shall melt away; it shall fade away like the water-lily. |2|

Fifth Mehl:
O my foolish and silly soul, why are you too lazy to serve?
Such a long time has passed. When will this opportunity come again? |3|

Section 25 - Raag Maaroo - Part 108

Pauree:
You have no form or shape, no social class or race.
These humans believe that You are far away; but You are quite obviously apparent.
You enjoy Yourself in every heart, and no filth sticks to You.
You are the blissful and infinite Primal Lord God; Your Light is all-pervading.
Among all divine beings, You are the most divine, O Creator-architect, Rejuvenator of all.
How can my single tongue worship and adore You? You are the eternal, imperishable, infinite Lord God.
One whom You Yourself unite with the True Guru - all his generations are saved.
All Your servants serve You; Nanak is a humble servant at Your Door. |5|

Dakhanay, Fifth Mehl:
He builds a hut of straw, and the fool lights a fire in it.
Only those who have such pre-ordained destiny on their foreheads, find Shelter with the Master. |1|

Fifth Mehl:
O Nanak, he grinds the corn, cooks it and places it before himself.
But without his True Guru, he sits and waits for his food to be blessed. |2|

Fifth Mehl:
O Nanak, the loaves of bread are baked and placed on the plate.
Those who obey their Guru, eat and are totally satisfied. |3|

Pauree:
You have staged this play in the world, and infused egotism into all beings.

In the one temple of the body are the five thieves, who continually misbehave.

The ten brides, the sensory organs were created, and the one husband, the self; the ten are engrossed in flavors and tastes.

This Maya fascinates and entices them; they wander continually in doubt.

You created both sides, spirit and matter, Shiva and Shakti.

Matter loses out to spirit; this is pleasing to the Lord.

You enshrined spirit within, which leads to merger with the Sat Sangat, the True Congregation.

Within the bubble, You formed the bubble, which shall once again merge into the water. |6|

Dakhanay, Fifth Mehl:

Look ahead; don't turn your face backwards.

O Nanak, be successful this time, and you shall not be reincarnated again. |1|

Fifth Mehl:

My joyful friend is called the friend of all.

All think of Him as their own; He never breaks anyone's heart. |2|

Fifth Mehl:

The hidden jewel has been found; it has appeared on my forehead.

Beautiful and exalted is that place, O Nanak, where You dwell, O my Dear Lord. |3|

Pauree:

When You are on my side, Lord, what do I need to worry about?

You entrusted everything to me, when I became Your slave.

My wealth is inexhaustible, no matter how much I spend and consume.

The 8.4 million species of beings all work to serve me.

All these enemies have become my friends, and no one wishes me ill.

No one calls me to account, since God is my forgiver.

I have become blissful, and I have found peace, meeting with the Guru, the Lord of the Universe.

All my affairs have been resolved, since You are pleased with me. |7|

Dakhanay, Fifth Mehl:

I am so eager to see You, O Lord; what does Your face look like?

I wandered around in such a miserable state, but when I saw You, my mind was comforted and consoled. |1|

Section 25 - Raag Maaroo - Part 109

Fifth Mehl:
The miserable endure so much suffering and pain; You alone know their pain, Lord.
I may know hundreds of thousands of remedies, but I shall live only if I see my Husband Lord. |2|

Fifth Mehl:
I have seen the river-bank washed away by the raging waters of the river.
They alone remain intact, who meet with the True Guru. |3|

Pauree:
No pain afflicts that humble being who hungers for You, Lord.
That humble Gurmukh who understands, is celebrated in the four directions.
Sins run away from that man, who seeks the Sanctuary of the Lord.
The filth of countless incarnations is washed away, bathing in the dust of the Guru's feet.
Whoever submits to the Lord's Will does not suffer in sorrow.
O Dear Lord, You are the friend of all; all believe that You are theirs.
The glory of the Lord's humble servant is as great as the Glorious Radiance of the Lord.
Among all, His humble servant is pre-eminent; through His humble servant, the Lord is known. |8|

Dakhanay, Fifth Mehl:
Those whom I followed, now follow me.
Those in whom I placed my hopes, now place their hopes in me. |1|

Fifth Mehl:
The fly flies around, and comes to the wet lump of molasses.
Whoever sits on it, is caught; they alone are saved, who have good destiny on their foreheads. |2|

Fifth Mehl:
I see Him within all. No one is without Him.

Good destiny is inscribed on the forehead of that companion, who who enjoys the Lord, my Friend. |3|

Pauree:
I am a minstrel at His Door, singing His Glorious Praises, to please to my Lord God.
My God is permanent and stable; others continue coming and going.
I beg for that gift from the Lord of the World, which will satisfy my hunger.
O Dear Lord God, please bless Your minstrel with the Blessed Vision of Your Darshan, that I might be satisfied and fulfilled.
God, the Great Giver, hears the prayer, and summons the minstrel to the Mansion of His Presence.
Gazing upon God, the minstrel is rid of pain and hunger; he does not think to ask for anything else.
All desires are fulfilled, touching the feet of God.
I am His humble, unworthy minstrel; the Primal Lord God has forgiven me. |9|

Dakhanay, Fifth Mehl:
When the soul leaves, you shall become dust, O vacant body; why do you not realize your Husband Lord?

You are in love with evil people; by what virtues will you enjoy the Lord's Love? |1|

Fifth Mehl:
O Nanak, without Him, you cannot survive, even for an instant; you cannot afford to forget Him, even for a moment.
Why are you alienated from Him, O my mind? He takes care of you. |2|

Fifth Mehl:
Those who are imbued with the Love of the Supreme Lord God, their minds and bodies are colored deep crimson.
O Nanak, without the Name, other thoughts are polluted and corrupt. |3|

Pauree:
O Dear Lord, when You are my friend, what sorrow can afflict me?
You have beaten off and destroyed the cheats that cheat the world.
The Guru has carried me across the terrifying world-ocean, and I have won the battle.

Through the Guru's Teachings, I enjoy all the pleasures in the great world-arena.

The True Lord has brought all my senses and organs under my control.

Section 25 - Raag Maaroo - Part 110

Wherever I join them, there they are joined; they do not struggle against me.

I obtain the fruits of my desires; the Guru has directed me within.

When Guru Nanak is pleased, O Siblings of Destiny, the Lord is seen to be dwelling near at hand. |10|

Dakhanay, Fifth Mehl:
When You come into my consciousness, then I obtain all peace and comfort.

Nanak: with Your Name within my mind, O my Husband Lord, I am filled with delight. |1|

Fifth Mehl:
Enjoyment of clothes and corrupt pleasures - all these are nothing more than dust.

I long for the dust of the feet of those who are imbued with the Lord's Vision. |2|

Fifth Mehl:
Why do you look in other directions? O my heart, take the Support of the Lord alone.

Become the dust of the feet of the Saints, and find the Lord, the Giver of peace. |3|

Pauree:
Without good karma, the Dear Lord is not found; without the True Guru, the mind is not joined to Him.

Only the Dharma remains stable in this Dark Age of Kali Yuga; these sinners will not last at all.

Whatever one does with this hand, he obtains with the other hand, without a moment's delay.

I have examined the four ages, and without the Sangat, the Holy Congregation, egotism does not depart.

Egotism is never eradicated without the Saadh Sangat, the Company of the Holy.

As long as one's mind is torn away from his Lord and Master, he finds no place of rest.

That humble being, who, as Gurmukh, serves the Lord, has the Support of the Imperishable Lord in the home of his heart.

By the Lord's Grace, peace is obtained, and one is attached to the feet of the Guru, the True Guru. |11|

Dakhanay, Fifth Mehl:

I have searched everywhere for the King over the heads of kings.

That Master is within my heart; I chant His Name with my mouth. |1|

Fifth Mehl:

O my mother, the Master has blessed me with the jewel.

My heart is cooled and soothed, chanting the True Name with my mouth. |2|

Fifth Mehl:

I have become the bed for my Beloved Husband Lord; my eyes have become the sheets.

If You look at me, even for an instant, then I obtain peace beyond all price. |3|

Pauree:

My mind longs to meet the Lord; how can I obtain the Blessed Vision of His Darshan?

I obtain hundreds of thousands, if my Lord and Master speaks to me, even for an instant.

I have searched in four directions; there is no other as great as You, Lord.

Show me the Path, O Saints. How can I meet God?

I dedicate my mind to Him, and renounce my ego. This is the Path which I shall take.

Joining the Sat Sangat, the True Congregation, I serve my Lord and Master continually.

All my hopes are fulfilled; the Guru has ushered me into the Mansion of the Lord's Presence.

I cannot conceive of any other as great as You, O my Friend, O Lord of the World. |12|

Dakhanay, Fifth Mehl:
I have become the throne for my Beloved Lord King.
If You place Your foot on me, I blossom forth like the lotus flower. |1|

Fifth Mehl:
If my Beloved becomes hungry, I will become food, and place myself before Him.
I may be crushed, again and again, but like sugarcane, I do not stop yielding sweet juice. |2|

Fifth Mehl:
Break off your love with the cheaters; realize that it is a mirage.
Your pleasure lasts for only two moments; this traveller wanders through countless homes. |3|

Pauree:
God is not found by intellectual devices; He is unknowable and unseen.

Section 25 - Raag Maaroo - Part 111

The followers of the six orders wander and roam around wearing religious robes, but they do not meet God.
They keep the lunar fasts, but they are of no account.
Those who read the Vedas in their entirety, still do not see the sublime essence of reality.
They apply ceremonial marks to their foreheads, and take cleansing baths, but they are blackened within.
They wear religious robes, but without the True Teachings, God is not found.
One who had strayed, finds the Path again, if such pre-ordained destiny is written on his forehead.
One who sees the Guru with his eyes, embellishes and exalts his human life. |13|

Dakhanay, Fifth Mehl:
Focus on that which will not pass away.
Abandon your false actions, and meditate on the True Master. |1|

Fifth Mehl:
God's Light is permeating all, like the moon reflected in the water.

He Himself is revealed, O Nanak, to one who has such destiny inscribed upon his forehead. |2|

Fifth Mehl:
One's face becomes beautiful, chanting the Naam, the Name of the Lord, and singing His Glorious Praises, twenty-four hours a day.
O Nanak, in the Court of the Lord, you shall be accepted; even the homeless find a home there. |3|

Pauree:
By wearing religious robes outwardly, God, the Inner-knower is not found.
Without the One Dear Lord, all wander around aimlessly.
Their minds are imbued with attachment to family, and so they continually wander around, puffed up with pride.
The arrogant wander around the world; why are they so proud of their wealth?
Their wealth shall not go with them when they depart; in an instant, it is gone.
They wander around in the world, according to the Hukam of the Lord's Command.
When one's karma is activated, one finds the Guru, and through Him, the Lord and Master is found.
That humble being, who serves the Lord, has his affairs resolved by the Lord. |14|

Dakhanay, Fifth Mehl:
All speak with their mouths, but rare are those one who realize death.
Nanak is the dust of the feet of those who have faith in the One Lord. |1|

Fifth Mehl:
Know that He dwells within all; rare are those who realize this.
There is no obscuring veil on the body of that one, O Nanak, who meets the Guru. |2|

Fifth Mehl:
I drink in the water which has washed the feet of those who share the Teachings.
My body is filled with infinite love to see my True Master. |3|

Pauree:

Forgetting the Naam, the Name of the Fearless Lord, he becomes attached to Maya.

He comes and goes, and wanders, dancing in countless incarnations.

He gives his word, but then backs out. All that he says is false.

The false person is hollow within; he is totally engrossed in falsehood.

He tries to take vengeance upon the Lord, who bears no vengeance; such a person is trapped by falsehood and greed.

The True King, the Primal Lord God, kills him when He sees what he has done.

The Messenger of Death sees him, and he rots away in pain.

Even-handed justice is administered, O Nanak, in the Court of the True Lord. |15|

Dakhanay, Fifth Mehl:
In the early hours of the morning, chant the Name of God, and meditate on the Feet of the Guru.

The filth of birth and death is erased, singing the Glorious Praises of the True Lord. |1|

Fifth Mehl:
The body is dark, blind and empty, without the Naam, the Name of the Lord.

O Nanak, fruitful is the birth of one, within whose heart the True Master dwells. |2|

Fifth Mehl:
With my eyes, I have seen the Light; my great thirst for Him is not quenched.

Section 25 - Raag Maaroo - Part 112

O Nanak, these are not the eyes which can see my Beloved Husband Lord. |3|

Pauree:
That humble being, who, as Gurmukh, serves the Lord, obtains all peace and pleasure.

He Himself is saved, along with his family, and all the world is saved as well.

He collects the wealth of the Lord's Name, and all his thirst is quenched.

He renounces worldly greed, and his inner being is lovingly attuned to the Lord.

Forever and ever, the home of his heart is filled with bliss; the Lord is his companion, help and support.

He looks alike upon enemy and friend, and wishes well to all.

He alone is fulfilled in this world, who meditates on the spiritual wisdom of the Guru.

He obtains what is pre-ordained for him, according to the Lord. |16|

Dakhanay, Fifth Mehl:
The true person is said to be beautiful; false is the reputation of the false.
O Nanak, rare are those who have Truth in their laps. |1|

Fifth Mehl:
The face of my friend, the Lord, is incomparably beautiful; I would watch Him, twenty-four hours a day.
In sleep, I saw my Husband Lord; I am a sacrifice to that dream. |2|

Fifth Mehl:
O my friend, realize the True Lord. Just to talk about Him is useless.
See Him within your mind; your Beloved is not far away. |3|

Pauree:
The earth, the Akaashic ethers of the sky, the nether regions of the underworld, the moon and the sun shall pass away.

Emperors, bankers, rulers and leaders shall depart, and their homes shall be demolished.

The poor and the rich, the humble and the intoxicated, all these people shall pass away.

The Qazis, Shaykhs and preachers shall all arise and depart.

The spiritual teachers, prophets and disciples - none of these shall remain permanently.

Fasts, calls to prayer and sacred scriptures - without understanding, all these shall vanish.

The 8.4 million species of beings of the earth shall all continue coming and going in reincarnation.

The One True Lord God is eternal and unchanging. The Lord's slave is also eternal. |17|

Dakhanay, Fifth Mehl:

I have seen and examined all; without the One Lord, there is none at all.
Come, and show me Your face, O my friend, so that my body and mind may be cooled and soothed. |1|

Fifth Mehl:
The lover is without hope, but within my mind, there is great hope.
In the midst of hope, only You, O Lord, remain free of hope; I am a sacrifice, a sacrifice, a sacrifice to You. |2|

Fifth Mehl:
Even if I just hear of separation from You, I am in pain; without seeing You, O Lord, I die.
Without her Beloved, the separated lover takes no comfort. |3|

Pauree:
River-banks, sacred shrines, idols, temples, and places of pilgrimage like Kaydarnaat'h, Mat'huraa and Benares,

the three hundred thirty million gods, along with Indra, shall all pass away.
The Simritees, Shaastras, the four Vedas and the six systems of philosophy shall vanish.
Prayer books, Pandits, religious scholars, songs, poems and poets shall also depart.
Those who are celibate, truthful and charitiable, and the Sannyaasee hermits are all subject to death.
The silent sages, the Yogis and the nudists, along with the Messengers of Death, shall pass away.
Whatever is seen shall perish; all will dissolve and disappear.
Only the Supreme Lord God, the Transcendent Lord, is permanent. His servant becomes permanent as well. |18|

Shalok Dakhanay, Fifth Mehl:
Hundreds of times naked does not make the person naked; tens of thousands of hungers do not make him hungry;

millions of pains do not cause him pain. O Nanak, the Husband Lord blesses him with his Glance of Grace. |1|

Section 25 - Raag Maaroo - Part 113

Fifth Mehl:
Even if one were to enjoy all pleasures, and be master of the entire earth,
O Nanak, all of that is just a disease. Without the Naam, he is dead. |2|

Fifth Mehl:
Yearn for the One Lord, and make Him your friend.
O Nanak, He alone fulfills your hopes; you should feel embarrassed, visiting other places. |3|

Pauree:
The One and only Lord is eternal, imperishable, inaccessible and incomprehensible.
The treasure of the Naam is eternal and imperishable. Meditating in remembrance on Him, the Lord is attained.
The Kirtan of His Praises is eternal and imperishable; the Gurmukh sings the Glorious Praises of the Lord of the Universe.
Truth, righteousness, Dharma and intense meditation are eternal and imperishable. Day and night, worship the Lord in adoration.
Compassion, righteousness, Dharma and intense meditation are eternal and imperishable; they alone obtain these, who have such pre-ordained destiny.
The inscription inscribed upon one's forehead is eternal and imperishable; it cannot be avoided by avoidance.
The Congregation, the Company of the Holy, and the word of the humble, are eternal and imperishable. The Holy Guru is eternal and imperishable.
Those who have such pre-ordained destiny worship and adore the Lord, forever and ever. |19|

Shalok, Dakhanay, Fifth Mehl:
One who himself has drowned - how can he carry anyone else across?
One who is imbued with the Love of the Husband Lord - O Nanak, he himself is saved, and he saves others as well. |1|

Fifth Mehl:
Wherever someone speaks and hears the Name of my Beloved Lord,
that is where I go, O Nanak, to see Him, and blossom forth in bliss. |2|

Fifth Mehl:
You are in love with your children and your wife; why do you keep calling them your own?

O Nanak, without the Naam, the Name of the Lord, the human body has no foundation. |3|

Pauree:
With my eyes, I gaze upon the Blessed Vision of the Guru's Darshan; I touch my forehead to the Guru's feet.
With my feet I walk on the Guru's Path; with my hands, I wave the fan over Him.
I meditate on Akaal Moorat, the undying form, within my heart; day and night, I meditate on Him.
I have renounced all possessiveness, and have placed my faith in the all-powerful Guru.
The Guru has blessed me with the treasure of the Naam; I am rid of all sufferings.
Eat and enjoy the Naam, the Name of the indescribable Lord, O Siblings of Destiny.
Confirm your faith in the Naam, charity and self-purification; chant the Guru's sermon forever.
Blessed with intuitive poise, I have found God; I am rid of the fear of the Messenger of Death. |20|

Shalok, Dakhanay, Fifth Mehl:
I am centered and focused on my Beloved, but I am not satisfied, even by seeing Him.
The Lord and Master is within all; I do not see any other. |1|

Fifth Mehl:
The sayings of the Saints are the paths of peace.
O Nanak, they alone obtain them, upon whose foreheads such destiny is written. |2|

Fifth Mehl:
He is totally permeating the mountains, oceans, deserts, lands, forests, orchards, caves,
the nether regions of the underworld, the Akaashic ethers of the skies, and all hearts.
Nanak sees that they are all strung on the same thread. |3|

Pauree:

The Dear Lord is my mother, the Dear Lord is my father; the Dear Lord cherishes and nurtures me.

The Dear Lord takes care of me; I am the child of the Lord.

Slowly and steadily, He feeds me; He never fails.

He does not remind me of my faults; He hugs me close in His embrace.

Whatever I ask for, He give me; the Lord is my peace-giving father.

Section 25 - Raag Maaroo - Part 114

He has blessed me with the capital, the wealth of spiritual wisdom; He has made me worthy of this merchandise.

He has made me a partner with the Guru; I have obtained all peace and comforts.

He is with me, and shall never separate from me; the Lord, my father, is potent to do everything. |21|

Shalok, Dakhanay, Fifth Mehl:
O Nanak, break away from the false, and seek out the Saints, your true friends.

The false shall leave you, even while you are still alive; but the Saints shall not forsake you, even when you are dead. |1|

Fifth Mehl:
O Nanak, the lightning flashes, and thunder echoes in the dark black clouds.
The downpour from the clouds is heavy; O Nanak, the soul-brides are exalted and embellished with their Beloved. |2|

Fifth Mehl:
The ponds and the lands are overflowing with water, and the cold wind is blowing.

Her bed is adorned with gold, diamonds and rubies;

she is blessed with beautiful gowns and delicacies, O Nanak, but without her Beloved, she burns in agony. |3|

Pauree:
He does the dees which the Creator causes him to do.

Even if you run in hundreds of directions, O mortal, you shall still receive what you are pre-destined to receive.

Without good karma, you shall obtain nothing, even if you wander across the whole world.

Meeting with the Guru, you shall know the Fear of God, and other fears shall be taken away.

Through the Fear of God, the attitude of detachment wells up, and one sets out in search of the Lord.

Searching and searching, intuitive wisdom wells up, and then, one is not born to die again.

Practicing meditation within my heart, I have found the Sanctuary of the Holy.

Whoever the Lord places on the boat of Guru Nanak, is carried across the terrifying world-ocean. |22|

Shalok, Dakhanay Fifth Mehl:
First, accept death, and give up any hope of life.
Become the dust of the feet of all, and then, you may come to me. |1|

Fifth Mehl:
See, that only one who has died, truly lives; one who is alive, consider him dead.
Those who are in love with the One Lord, are the supreme people. |2|

Fifth Mehl:
Pain does not even approach that person, within whose mind God abides.
Hunger and thirst do not affect him, and the Messenger of Death does not approach him. |3|

Pauree:
Your worth cannot be estimated, O True, Unmoving Lord God.
The Siddhas, seekers, spiritual teachers and meditators - who among them can measure You?
You are all-powerful, to form and break; You create and destroy all.
You are all-powerful to act, and inspire all to act; You speak through each and every heart.
You give sustanance to all; why should mankind waver?
You are deep, profound and unfathomable; Your virtuous spiritual wisdom is priceless.
They do the deeds which they are pre-ordained to do.
Without You, there is nothing at all; Nanak chants Your Glorious Praises. |23|1|2|

Raag Maaroo, The Word Of Kabeer Jee:

One Universal Creator God. By The Grace Of The True Guru:
O Pandit, O religious scholar, in what foul thoughts are you engaged?
You shall be drowned, along with your family, if you do not meditate on the Lord, you unfortunate person. |1|Pause|

What is the use of reading the Vedas and the Puraanas? It is like loading a donkey with sandalwood.

Section 25 - Raag Maaroo - Part 115

You do not know the exalted state of the Lord's Name; how will you ever cross over? |1|

You kill living beings, and call it a righteous action. Tell me, brother, what would you call an unrighteous action?

You call yourself the most excellent sage; then who would you call a butcher? |2|

You are blind in your mind, and do not understand your own self; how can you make others understand, O brother?

For the sake of Maya and money, you sell knowledge; your life is totally worthless. |3|

Naarad and Vyaasa say these things; go and ask Suk Dayv as well.
Says Kabeer, chanting the Lord's Name, you shall be saved; otherwise, you shall drown, brother. |4|1|

Living in the forest, how will you find Him? Not until you remove corruption from your mind.
Those who look alike upon home and forest, are the most perfect people in the world. |1|

You shall find real peace in the Lord,
if you lovingly dwell on the Lord within your being. |1|Pause|

What is the use of wearing matted hair, smearing the body with ashes, and living in a cave?

Conquering the mind, one conquers the world, and then remains detached from corruption. |2|

They all apply make-up to their eyes; there is little difference between their objectives.
But those eyes, to which the ointment of spiritual wisdom is applied, are approved and supreme. |3|

Says Kabeer, now I know my Lord; the Guru has blessed me with spiritual wisdom.
I have met the Lord, and I am emancipated within; now, my mind does not wander at all. |4|2|

You have riches and miraculous spiritual powers; so what business do you have with anyone else?
What should I say about the reality of your talk? I am embarrassed even to speak to you. |1|

One who has found the Lord,
does not wander from door to door. |1|Pause|

The false world wanders all around, in hopes of finding wealth to use for a few days.
That humble being, who drinks in the Lord's water, never becomes thirsty again. |2|

Whoever understands, by Guru's Grace, becomes free of hope in the midst of hope.
One comes to see the Lord everywhere, when the soul becomes detached. |3|

I have tasted the sublime essence of the Lord's Name; the Lord's Name carries everyone across.
Says Kabeer, I have become like gold; doubt is dispelled, and I have crossed over the world-ocean. |4|3|

Like drops of water in the water of the ocean, and like waves in the stream, I merge in the Lord.
Merging my being into the Absolute Being of God, I have become impartial and transparent, like the air. |1|

Why should I come into the world again?
Coming and going is by the Hukam of His Command; realizing His Hukam, I shall merge in Him. |1|Pause|

When the body, formed of the five elements, perishes, then any such doubts shall end.
Giving up the different schools of philosophy, I look upon all equally; I meditate only on the One Name. |2|

Whatever I am attached to, to that I am attached; such are the deeds I do.
When the Dear Lord grants His Grace, then I am merged in the Word of the Guru's Shabad. |3|

Die while yet alive, and by so dying, be alive; thus you shall not be reborn again.

Section 25 - Raag Maaroo - Part 116

Says Kabeer, whoever is absorbed in the Naam remains lovingly absorbed in the Primal, Absolute Lord. |4|4|

If You keep me far away from You, then tell me, what is liberation?
The One has many forms, and is contained within all; how can I be fooled now? |1|

O Lord, where will You take me, to save me?
Tell me where, and what sort of liberation shall You give me? By Your Grace, I have already obtained it. |1|Pause|

People talk of salvation and being saved, as long as they do not understand the essence of reality.
I have now become pure within my heart, says Kabeer, and my mind is pleased and appeased. |2|5|

Raawan made castles and fortresses of gold, but he had to abandon them when he left. |1|

Why do you act only to please your mind?

When Death comes and grabs you by the hair, then only the Name of the Lord will save you. |1|Pause|

Death, and deathlessness are the creations of our Lord and Master; this show, this expanse, is only an entanglement.
Says Kabeer, those who have the sublime essence of the Lord in their hearts - in the end, they are liberated. |2|6|

The body is a village, and the soul is the owner and farmer; the five farm-hands live there.
The eyes, nose, ears, tongue and sensory organs of touch do not obey any order. |1|

O father, now I shall not live in this village.
The accountants summoned Chitar and Gupat, the recording scribes of the conscious and the unconscious, to ask for an account of each and every moment. |1|Pause|

When the Righteous Judge of Dharma calls for my account, there shall be a very heavy balance against me.
The five farm-hands shall then run away, and the bailiff shall arrest the soul. |2|

Says Kabeer, listen, O Saints: settle your accounts in this farm.
O Lord, please forgive Your slave now, in this life, so that he may not have to return again to this terrifying world-ocean. |3|7|

Raag Maaroo, The Word Of Kabeer Jee:
One Universal Creator God. By The Grace Of The True Guru:
No one has seen the Fearless Lord, O renunciate.
Without the Fear of God, how can the Fearless Lord be obtained? |1|

If one sees the Presence of his Husband Lord near at hand, then he feels the Fear of God, O renunciate.
If he realizes the Hukam of the Lord's Command, then he becomes fearless. |2|

Don't practice hypocrisy with the Lord, O renunciate!
The whole world is filled with hypocrisy. |3|

Thirst and desire do not just go away, O renunciate.
The body is burning in the fire of worldly love and attachment. |4|

Anxiety is burned, and the body is burned, O renunciate,
only if one lets his mind become dead. |5|

Without the True Guru, there can be no renunciation,
even though all the people may wish for it. |6|

When God grants His Grace, one meets the True Guru, O renunciate,
and automatically, intuitively finds that Lord. |7|

Says Kabeer, I offer this one prayer, O renunciate.
Carry me across the terrifying world-ocean. |8|1|8|

Section 25 - Raag Maaroo - Part 117

O king, who will come to you?
I have seen such love from Bidur, that the poor man is pleasing to me.
|1|Pause|

Gazing upon your elephants, you have gone astray in doubt; you do not
know the Great Lord God.
I judge Bidur's water to be like ambrosial nectar, in comparison with your
milk. |1|

I find his rough vegetables to be like rice pudding; the night of my life
passes singing the Glorious Praises of the Lord.
Kabeer's Lord and Master is joyous and blissful; He does not care about
anyone's social class. |2|9|

Shalok, Kabeer:
The battle-drum beats in the sky of the mind; aim is taken, and the wound
is inflicted.
The spiritual warriors enter the field of battle; now is the time to fight! |1|

He alone is known as a spiritual hero, who fights in defense of religion.
He may be cut apart, piece by piece, but he never leaves the field of battle.
|2|2|

Shabad Of Kabeer, Raag Maaroo, The Word Of Naam Dayv Jee:
One Universal Creator God. By The Grace Of The True Guru:
I have obtained the four kinds of liberation, and the four miraculous spiritual powers, in the Sanctuary of God, my Husband Lord.
I am liberated, and famous throughout the four ages; the canopy of praise and fame waves over my head. |1|

Meditating on the Sovereign Lord God, who has not been saved?
Whoever follows the Guru's Teachings and joins the Saadh Sangat, the Company of the Holy, is called the most devoted of the devotees. |1|Pause|

He is adorned with the conch, the chakra, the mala and the ceremonial tilak mark on his forehead; gazing upon his radiant glory, the Messenger of Death is scared away.
He becomes fearless, and the power of the Lord thunders through him; the pains of birth and death are taken away. |2|

The Lord blessed Ambreek with fearless dignity, and elevated Bhabhikhan to become king.
Sudama's Lord and Master blessed him with the nine treasures; he made Dhroo permanent and unmoving; as the north star, he still hasn't moved. |3|

For the sake of His devotee Prahlaad, God assumed the form of the man-lion, and killed Harnaakhash.
Says Naam Dayv, the beautiful-haired Lord is in the power of His devotees; He is standing at Balraja's door, even now! |4|1|

Maaroo, Kabeer Jee:
You have forgotten your religion, O madman; you have forgotten your religion.
You fill your belly, and sleep like an animal; you have wasted and lost this human life. |1|Pause|

You never joined the Saadh Sangat, the Company of the Holy. You are engrossed in false pursuits.
You wander like a dog, a pig, a crow; soon, you shall have to get up and leave. |1|

You believe that you yourself are great, and that others are small.
Those who are false in thought, word and deed, I have seen them going to hell. |2|

The lustful, the angry, the clever, the deceitful and the lazy
waste their lives in slander, and never remember their Lord in meditation. |3|

Says Kabeer, the fools, the idiots and the brutes do not remember the Lord.
They do not know the Lord's Name; how can they be carried across? |4|1|

Section 25 - Raag Maaroo - Part 118

Raag Maaroo, The Word Of Jai Dayv Jee:
One Universal Creator God. By The Grace Of The True Guru:
The breath is drawn in through the left nostril; it is held in the central channel of the Sushmanaa, and exhaled through the right nostril, repeating the Lord's Name sixteen times.
I am powerless; my power has been broken. My unstable mind has been stabliized, and my unadorned soul has been adorned. I drink in the Ambrosial Nectar. |1|

Within my mind, I chant the Name of the Primal Lord God, the Source of virtue.
My vision, that You are I are separate, has melted away. |1|Pause|

I worship the One who is worthy of being worshipped. I trust the One who is worthy of being trusted. Like water merging in water, I merge in the Lord.
Says Jai Dayv, I meditate and contemplate the Luminous, Triumphant Lord.
I am lovingly absorbed in the Nirvaanaa of God. |2|1|

Kabeer, Maaroo:
Meditate in remembrance on the Lord, or else you will regret it in the end, O mind.
O sinful soul, you act in greed, but today or tomorrow, you will have to get up and leave. |1|Pause|

Clinging to greed, you have wasted your life, deluded in the doubt of Maya.
Do not take pride in your wealth and youth; you shall crumble apart like dry paper. |1|

When the Messenger of Death comes and grabs you by the hair, and knocks you down, on that day, you shall be powerless.
You do not remember the Lord, or vibrate upon Him in meditation, and you do not practice compassion; you shall be beaten on your face. |2|

When the Righteous Judge of Dharma calls for your account, what face will you show Him then?
Says Kabeer, listen, O Saints: in the Saadh Sangat, the Company of the Holy, you shall be saved. |3|1|

Raag Maaroo, The Word Of Ravi Daas Jee:
One Universal Creator God. By The Grace Of The True Guru:
O Love, who else but You could do such a thing?
O Patron of the poor, Lord of the World, You have put the canopy of Your Grace over my head. |1|Pause|

Only You can grant Mercy to that person whose touch pollutes the world.
You exalt and elevate the lowly, O my Lord of the Universe; You are not afraid of anyone. |1|

Naam Dayv, Kabeer, Trilochan, Sadhana and Sain crossed over.
Says Ravi Daas, listen, O Saints, through the Dear Lord, all is accomplished. |2|1|

MAAROO:
The Lord is the ocean of peace; the miraculous tree of life, the jewel of miracles and the wish-fulfilling cow are all under His power.
The four great blessings, the eight great miraculous spiritual powers and the nine treasures are in the palm of His hand. |1|

Why don't you chant the Lord's Name, Har, Har, Har?
Abandon all other devices of words. |1|Pause|

The many epics, the Puraanas and the Vedas are all composed out of the letters of the alphabet.
After careful thought, Vyaasa spoke the supreme truth, that there is nothing equal to the Lord's Name. |2|

In intuitive Samaadhi, their troubles are eliminated; the very fortunate ones lovingly focus on the Lord.

Says Ravi Daas, the Lord's slave remains detached from the world; the fear of birth and death runs away from his mind. |3|2|15|

RAAG TUKHAARI

Section 26 - Raag Tukhaari - Part 001

Tukhaari Chhant, First Mehl, Baarah Maahaa ~ The Twelve Months:
One Universal Creator God. By The Grace Of The True Guru:
Listen: according to the karma of their past actions, each and every person experiences happiness or sorrow; whatever You give, Lord, is good.
O Lord, the Created Universe is Yours; what is my condition? Without the Lord, I cannot survive, even for an instant.
Without my Beloved, I am miserable; I have no friend at all. As Gurmukh, I drink in the Ambrosial Nectar.
The Formless Lord is contained in His Creation. To obey God is the best course of action.
O Nanak, the soul-bride is gazing upon Your Path; please listen, O Supreme Soul. |1|

The rainbird cries out, "Pri-o! Beloved!", and the song-bird sings the Lord's Bani.
The soul-bride enjoys all the pleasures, and merges in the Being of her Beloved.
She merges into the Being of her Beloved, when she becomes pleasing to God; she is the happy, blessed soul-bride.
Establishing the nine houses, and the Royal Mansion of the Tenth Gate above them, the Lord dwells in that home deep within the self.
All are Yours, You are my Beloved; night and day, I celebrate Your Love.
O Nanak, the rainbird cries out, "Pri-o! Pri-o! Beloved! Beloved!" The song-bird is embellished with the Word of the Shabad. |2|

Please listen, O my Beloved Lord - I am drenched with Your Love.
My mind and body are absorbed in dwelling on You; I cannot forget You, even for an instant.
How could I forget You, even for an instant? I am a sacrifice to You; singing Your Glorious Praises, I live.
No one is mine; unto whom do I belong? Without the Lord, I cannot survive.

I have grasped the Support of the Lord's Feet; dwelling there, my body has become immaculate.

O Nanak, I have obtained profound insight, and found peace; my mind is comforted by the Word of the Guru's Shabad. |3|

The Ambrosial Nectar rains down on us! Its drops are so delightful!

Meeting the Guru, the Best Friend, with intuitive ease, the mortal falls in love with the Lord.

The Lord comes into the temple of the body, when it pleases God's Will; the soul-bride rises up, and sings His Glorious Praises.

In each and every home, the Husband Lord ravishes and enjoys the happy soul-brides; so why has He forgotten me?

The sky is overcast with heavy, low-hanging clouds; the rain is delightful, and my Beloved's Love is pleasing to my mind and body.

O Nanak, the Ambrosial Nectar of Gurbani rains down; the Lord, in His Grace, has come into the home of my heart. |4|

In the month of Chayt, the lovely spring has come, and the bumble bees hum with joy.

Section 26 - Raag Tukhaari - Part 002

The forest is blossoming in front of my door; if only my Beloved would return to my home!

If her Husband Lord does not return home, how can the soul-bride find peace? Her body is wasting away with the sorrow of separation.

The beautiful song-bird sings, perched on the mango tree; but how can I endure the pain in the depths of my being?

The bumble bee is buzzing around the flowering branches; but how can I survive? I am dying, O my mother!

O Nanak, in Chayt, peace is easily obtained, if the soul-bride obtains the Lord as her Husband, within the home of her own heart. |5|

Baisakhi is so pleasant; the branches blossom with new leaves.

The soul-bride yearns to see the Lord at her door. Come, O Lord, and take pity on me!

Please come home, O my Beloved; carry me across the treacherous world-ocean. Without You, I am not worth even a shell.

Who can estimate my worth, if I am pleasing to You? I see You, and inspire others to see You, O my Love.

I know that You are not far away; I believe that You are deep within me, and I realize Your Presence.

O Nanak, finding God in Baisakhi, the consciousness is filled with the Word of the Shabad, and the mind comes to believe. |6|

The month of Jayt'h is so sublime. How could I forget my Beloved?

The earth burns like a furnace, and the soul-bride offers her prayer.

The bride offers her prayer, and sings His Glorious Praises; singing His Praises, she becomes pleasing to God.

The Unattached Lord dwells in His true mansion. If He allows me, then I will come to Him.

The bride is dishonored and powerless; how will she find peace without her Lord?

O Nanak, in Jayt'h, she who knows her Lord becomes just like Him; grasping virtue, she meets with the Merciful Lord. |7|

The month of Aasaarh is good; the sun blazes in the sky.

The earth suffers in pain, parched and roasted in the fire.

The fire dries up the moisture, and she dies in agony. But even then, the sun does not grow tired.

His chariot moves on, and the soul-bride seeks shade; the crickets are chirping in the forest.

She ties up her bundle of faults and demerits, and suffers in the world hereafter. But dwelling on the True Lord, she finds peace.

O Nanak, I have given this mind to Him; death and life rest with God. |8|

In Saawan, be happy, O my mind. The rainy season has come, and the clouds have burst into showers.

My mind and body are pleased by my Lord, but my Beloved has gone away.

My Beloved has not come home, and I am dying of the sorrow of separation. The lightning flashes, and I am scared.

My bed is lonely, and I am suffering in agony. I am dying in pain, O my mother!

Tell me - without the Lord, how can I sleep, or feel hungry? My clothes give no comfort to my body.

O Nanak, she alone is a happy soul-bride, who merges in the Being of her Beloved Husband Lord. |9|

In Bhaadon, the young woman is confused by doubt; later, she regrets and repents.

The lakes and fields are overflowing with water; the rainy season has come - the time to celebrate!

In the dark of night it rains; how can the young bride find peace? The frogs and peacocks send out their noisy calls.

"Pri-o! Pri-o! Beloved! Beloved!" cries the rainbird, while the snakes slither around, biting.

The mosquitoes bite and sting, and the ponds are filled to overflowing; without the Lord, how can she find peace?

O Nanak, I will go and ask my Guru; wherever God is, there I will go. |10|

In Assu, come, my Beloved; the soul-bride is grieving to death.

She can only meet Him, when God leads her to meet Him; she is ruined by the love of duality.

If she is plundered by falsehood, then her Beloved forsakes her. Then, the white flowers of old age blossom in my hair.

Section 26 - Raag Tukhaari - Part 003

Summer is now behind us, and the winter season is ahead. Gazing upon this play, my shaky mind wavers.

In all ten directions, the branches are green and alive. That which ripens slowly, is sweet.

O Nanak, in Assu, please meet me, my Beloved. The True Guru has become my Advocate and Friend. |11|

In Katak, that alone comes to pass, which is pleasing to the Will of God.

The lamp of intuition burns, lit by the essence of reality.

Love is the oil in the lamp, which unites the soul-bride with her Lord. The bride is delighted, in ecstasy.

One who dies in faults and demerits - her death is not successful. But one who dies in glorious virtue, really truly dies.

Those who are blessed with devotional worship of the Naam, the Name of the Lord, sit in the home of their own inner being. They place their hopes in You.

Nanak: please open the shutters of Your Door, O Lord, and meet me. A single moment is like six months to me. |12|

The month of Maghar is good, for those who sing the Glorious Praises of the Lord, and merge in His Being.

The virtuous wife utters His Glorious Praises; my Beloved Husband Lord is Eternal and Unchanging.

The Primal Lord is Unmoving and Unchanging, Clever and Wise; all the world is fickle.

By virtue of spiritual wisdom and meditation, she merges in His Being; she is pleasing to God, and He is pleasing to her.

I have heard the songs and the music, and the poems of the poets; but only the Name of the Lord takes away my pain.

O Nanak, that soul-bride is pleasing to her Husband Lord, who performs loving devotional worship before her Beloved. |13|

In Poh, the snow falls, and the sap of the trees and the fields dries up.

Why have You not come? I keep You in my mind, body and mouth.

He is permeating and pervading my mind and body; He is the Life of the World. Through the Word of the Guru's Shabad, I enjoy His Love.

His Light fills all those born of eggs, born from the womb, born of sweat and born of the earth, each and every heart.

Grant me the Blessed Vision of Your Darshan, O Lord of Mercy and Compassion. O Great Giver, grant me understanding, that I might find salvation.

O Nanak, the Lord enjoys, savors and ravishes the bride who is in love with Him. |14|

In Maagh, I become pure; I know that the sacred shrine of pilgrimage is within me.

I have met my Friend with intuitive ease; I grasp His Glorious Virtues, and merge in His Being.

O my Beloved, Beauteous Lord God, please listen: I sing Your Glories, and merge in Your Being. If it is pleasing to Your Will, I bathe in the sacred pool within.

The Ganges, Jamunaa, the sacred meeting place of the three rivers, the seven seas, charity, donations, adoration and worship all rest in the Transcendent Lord God; throughout the ages, I realize the One.

O Nanak, in Maagh, the most sublime essence is meditation on the Lord; this is the cleansing bath of the sixty-eight sacred shrines of pilgrimage. |15|

In Phalgun, her mind is enraptured, pleased by the Love of her Beloved.

Night and day, she is enraptured, and her selfishness is gone.

Emotional attachment is eradicated from her mind, when it pleases Him; in His Mercy, He comes to my home.

I dress in various clothes, but without my Beloved, I shall not find a place in the Mansion of His Presence.

I have adorned myself with garlands of flowers, pearl necklaces, scented oils and silk robes.

O Nanak, the Guru has united me with Him. The soul-bride has found her Husband Lord, within the home of her own heart. |16|

The twelve months, the seasons, the weeks, the days, the hours, the minutes and the seconds are all sublime, when the True Lord comes and meets her with natural ease.

God, my Beloved, has met me, and my affairs are all resolved. The Creator Lord knows all ways and means.

I am loved by the One who has embellished and exalted me; I have met Him, and I savor His Love.

The bed of my heart becomes beautiful, when my Husband Lord ravishes me. As Gurmukh, the destiny on my forehead has been awakened and activated.

Section 26 - Raag Tukhaari - Part 004

O Nanak, day and night, my Beloved enjoys me; with the Lord as my Husband, my Marriage is Eternal. |17|1|

Tukhaari, First Mehl:
In the first watch of the dark night, O bride of splendored eyes,
protect your riches; your turn is coming soon.

When your turn comes, who will wake you? While you sleep, your juice shall be sucked out by the Messenger of Death.

The night is so dark; what will become of your honor? The thieves will break into your home and rob you.

O Saviour Lord, Inaccessible and Infinite, please hear my prayer.

O Nanak, the fool never remembers Him; what can he see in the dark of night? |1|

The second watch has begun; wake up, you unconscious being!
Protect your riches, O mortal; your farm is being eaten.

Protect your crops, and love the Lord, the Guru. Stay awake and aware, and the thieves shall not rob you.

You shall not have to go on the path of Death, and you shall not suffer in pain; your fear and terror of death shall run away.

The lamps of the sun and the moon are lit by the Guru's Teachings, through His Door, meditating on the True Lord, in the mind and with the mouth.

O Nanak, the fool still does not remember the Lord. How can he find peace in duality? |2|

The third watch has begun, and sleep has set in.

The mortal suffers in pain, from attachment to Maya, children and spouse.

Maya, his children, his wife and the world are so dear to him; he bites the bait, and is caught.

Meditating on the Naam, the Name of the Lord, he shall find peace; following the Guru's Teachings, he shall not be seized by death.

He cannot escape from birth, dying and death; without the Name, he suffers.

O Nanak, in the third watch of the three-phased Maya, the world is engrossed in attachment to Maya. |3|

The fourth watch has begun, and the day is about to dawn.

Those who remain awake and aware, night and day, preserve and protect their homes.

The night is pleasant and peaceful, for those who remain awake; following the Guru's advice, they focus on the Naam.

Those who practice the Word of the Guru's Shabad are not reincarnated again; the Lord God is their Best Friend.

The hands shake, the feet and body totter, the vision goes dark, and the body turns to dust.

O Nanak, people are miserable throughout the four ages, if the Name of the Lord does not abide in the mind. |4|

The knot has been untied; rise up - the order has come!

Pleasures and comforts are gone; like a prisoner, you are driven on.

You shall be bound and gagged, when it pleases God; you will not see or hear it coming.

Everyone will have their turn; the crop ripens, and then it is cut down.

The account is kept for every second, every instant; the soul suffers for the bad and the good.

O Nanak, the angelic beings are united with the Word of the Shabad; this is the way God made it. |5|2|

Tukhaari, First Mehl:
The meteor shoots across the sky. How can it be seen with the eyes?
The True Guru reveals the Word of the Shabad to His servant who has such perfect karma.
The Guru reveals the Shabad; dwelling on the True Lord, day and night, he beholds and reflects on God.
The five restless desires are restrained, and he knows the home of his own heart. He conquers sexual desire, anger and corruption.
His inner being is illuminated, by the Guru's Teachings; He beholds the Lord's play of karma.

Section 26 - Raag Tukhaari - Part 005

O Nanak, killing his ego, he is satisfied; the meteor has shot across the sky. |1|

The Gurmukhs remain awake and aware; their egotistical pride is eradicated.
Night and day, it is dawn for them; they merge in the True Lord.
The Gurmukhs are merged in the True Lord; they are pleasing to His Mind.
The Gurmukhs are intact, safe and sound, awake and awake.
The Guru blesses them with the Ambrosial Nectar of the True Name; they are lovingly attuned to the Lord's Feet.
The Divine Light is revealed, and in that Light, they achieve realization; the self-willed manmukhs wander in doubt and confusion.
O Nanak, when the dawn breaks, their minds are satisfied; they pass their life-night awake and aware. |2|

Forgetting faults and demerits, virtue and merit enter one's home.
The One Lord is permeating everywhere; there is no other at all.
He is All-pervading; there is no other. The mind comes to believe, from the mind.
The One who established the water, the land, the three worlds, each and every heart - that God is known by the Gurmukh.
The Infinite, All-powerful Lord is the Creator, the Cause of causes; erasing the three-phased Maya, we merge in Him.

O Nanak, then, demerits are dissolved by merits; such are the Guru's Teachings. |3|

My coming and going in reincarnation have ended; doubt and hesitation are gone.
Conquering my ego, I have met the True Lord, and now I wear the robe of Truth.
The Guru has rid me of egotism; my sorrow and suffering are dispelled.
My might merges into the Light; I realize and understand my own self.
In this world of my parents' home, I am satisfied with the Shabad; at my in-laws' home, in the world beyond, I shall be pleasing to my Husband Lord.
O Nanak, the True Guru has united me in His Union; my dependence on people has ended. |4|3|

Tukhaari, First Mehl:
Deluded by doubt, misled and confused, the soul-bride later regrets and repents.
Abandoning her Husband Lord, she sleeps, and does not appreciate His Worth.
Leaving her Husband Lord, she sleeps, and is plundered by her faults and demerits. The night is so painful for this bride.
Sexual desire, anger and egotism destroy her. She burns in egotism.
When the soul-swan flies away, by the Command of the Lord, her dust mingles with dust.
O Nanak, without the True Name, she is confused and deluded, and so she regrets and repents. |1|

Please listen, O my Beloved Husband Lord, to my one prayer.
You dwell in the home of the self deep within, while I roll around like a dust-ball.
Without my Husband Lord, no one likes me at all; what can I say or do now?
The Ambrosial Naam, the Name of the Lord, is the sweetest nectar of nectars. Through the Word of the Guru's Shabad, with my tongue, I drink in this nectar.
Without the Name, no one has any friend or companion; millions come and go in reincarnation.
Nanak: the profit is earned and the soul returns home. True, true are Your Teachings. |2|

O Friend, You have travelled so far from Your homeland; I send my message of love to You.

I cherish and remember that Friend; the eyes of this soul-bride are filled with tears.

The eyes of the soul-bride are filled with tears; I dwell upon Your Glorious Virtues. How can I meet my Beloved Lord God?

I do not know the treacherous path, the way to You. How can I find You and cross over, O my Husband Lord?

Through the Shabad, the Word of the True Guru, the separated soul-bride meets with the Lord; I place my body and mind before You.

O Nanak, the ambrosial tree bears the most delicious fruits; meeting with my Beloved, I taste the sweet essence. |3|

The Lord has called you to the Mansion of His Presence - do not delay!

Section 26 - Raag Tukhaari - Part 006

Night and day, imbued with His Love, you shall meet with Him with intuitive ease.

In celestial peace and poise, you shall meet Him; do not harbor anger - subdue your proud self!

Imbued with Truth, I am united in His Union, while the self-willed manmukhs continue coming and going.

When you dance, what veil covers you? Break the water pot, and be unattached.

O Nanak, realize your own self; as Gurmukh, contemplate the essence of reality. |4|4|

Tukhaari, First Mehl:
O my Dear Beloved, I am the slave of Your slaves.

The Guru has shown me the Invisible Lord, and now, I do not seek any other.

The Guru showed me the Invisible Lord, when it pleased Him, and when God showered His Blessings.

The Life of the World, the Great Giver, the Primal Lord, the Architect of Destiny, the Lord of the woods - I have met Him with intuitive ease.

Bestow Your Glance of Grace and carry me across, to save me. Please bless me with the Truth, O Lord, Merciful to the meek.

Prays Nanak, I am the slave of Your slaves. You are the Cherisher of all souls. |1|

My Dear Beloved is enshrined throughout the Universe.

The Shabad is pervading, through the Guru, the Embodiment of the Lord.

The Guru, the Embodiment of the Lord, is enshrined throughout the three worlds; His limits cannot be found.

He created the beings of various colors and kinds; His Blessings increase day by day.

The Infinite Lord Himself establishes and disestablishes; whatever pleases Him, happens.

O Nanak, the diamond of the mind is pierced through by the diamond of spiritual wisdom. The garland of virtue is strung. |2|

The virtuous person merges in the Virtuous Lord; his forehead bears the insignia of the Naam, the Name of the Lord.

The true person merges in the True Lord; his comings and goings are over.

The true person realizes the True Lord, and is imbued with Truth. He meets the True Lord, and is pleasing to the Lord's Mind.

No one else is seen to be above the True Lord; the true person merges in the True Lord.

The Fascinating Lord has fascinated my mind; releasing me from bondage, He has set me free.

O Nanak, my light merged into the Light, when I met my most Darling Beloved. |3|

By searching, the true home, the place of the True Guru is found.

The Gurmukh obtains spiritual wisdom, while the self-willed manmukh does not.

Whoever the Lord has blessed with the gift of Truth is accepted; the Supremely Wise Lord is forever the Great Giver.

He is known to be Immortal, Unborn and Permanent; the True Mansion of His Presence is everlasting.

The day-to-day account of deeds is not recorded for that person, who manifests the radiance of the Divine Light of the Lord.

O Nanak, the true person is absorbed in the True Lord; the Gurmukh crosses over to the other side. |4|5|

Tukhaari, First Mehl:

O my ignorant, unconscious mind, reform yourself.

O my mind, leave behind your faults and demerits, and be absorbed in virtue.

You are deluded by so many flavors and pleasures, and you act in such confusion. You are separated, and you will not meet your Lord.

How can the impassible world-ocean be crossed? The fear of the Messenger of Death is deadly. The path of Death is agonizingly painful.

The mortal does not know the Lord in the evening, or in the morning; trapped on the treacherous path, what will he do then?

Bound in bondage, he is released only by this method: as Gurmukh, serve the Lord. |1|

O my mind, abandon your household entanglements.

O my mind, serve the Lord, the Primal, Detached Lord.

Section 26 - Raag Tukhaari - Part 007

Meditate in remembrance on the One Universal Creator; the True Lord created the entire Universe.

The Guru controls the air, water and fire; He has staged the drama of the world.

Reflect on your own self, and so practice good conduct; chant the Name of the Lord as your self-discipline and meditation.

The Name of the Lord is your Companion, Friend and Dear Beloved; chant it, and meditate on it. |2|

O my mind, remain steady and stable, and you will not have to endure beatings.

O my mind, singing the Glorious Praises of the Lord, you shall merge into Him with intuitive ease.

Singing the Glorious Praises of the Lord, be happy. Apply the ointment of spiritual wisdom to your eyes.

The Word of the Shabad is the lamp which illuminates the three worlds; it slaughters the five demons.

Quieting your fears, become fearless, and you shall cross over the impassible world ocean. Meeting the Guru, your affairs shall be resolved.

You shall find the joy and the beauty of the Lord's Love and Affection; the Lord Himself shall shower you with His Grace. |3|

O my mind, why did you come into the world? What will you take with you when you go?

O my mind, you shall be emancipated, when you eliminate your doubts.

So gather the wealth and capital of the Name of the Lord, Har, Har; through the Word of the Guru's Shabad, you shall realize its value.

Filth shall be taken away, through the Immaculate Word of the Shabad; you shall know the Mansion of the Lord's Presence, your true home.

Through the Naam, you shall obtain honor, and come home. Eagerly drink in the Ambrosial Amrit.

Meditate on the Lord's Name, and you shall obtain the sublime essence of the Shabad; by great good fortune, chant the Praises of the Lord. |4|

O my mind, without a ladder, how will you climb up to the Temple of the Lord?

O my mind, without a boat, you shall not reach the other shore.

On that far shore is Your Beloved, Infinite Friend. Only your awareness of the Guru's Shabad will carry you across.

Join the Saadh Sangat, the Company of the Holy, and you shall enjoy ecstasy; you shall not regret or repent later on.

Be Merciful, O Merciful True Lord God: please give me the Blessing of the Lord's Name, and the Sangat, the Company of the Holy.

Nanak prays: please hear me, O my Beloved; instruct my mind through the Word of the Guru's Shabad. |5|6|

Tukhaari Chhant, Fourth Mehl:
One Universal Creator God. By The Grace Of The True Guru:
My inner being is filled with love for my Beloved Husband Lord. How can I live without Him?

As long as I do not have the Blessed Vision of His Darshan, how can I drink in the Ambrosial Nectar?

How can I drink in the Ambrosial Nectar without the Lord? I cannot survive without Him.

Night and day, I cry out, "Pri-o! Pri-o! Beloved! Beloved!", day and night. Without my Husband Lord, my thirst is not quenched.

Please, bless me with Your Grace, O my Beloved Lord, that I may dwell on the Name of the Lord, Har, Har, forever.

Through the Word of the Guru's Shabad, I have met my Beloved; I am a sacrifice to the True Guru. |1|

When I see my Beloved Husband Lord, I chant the Lord's Glorious Praises with love.

Section 26 - Raag Tukhaari - Part 008

My inner being blossoms forth; I continually utter, "Pri-o! Pri-o! Beloved! Beloved!"

I speak of my Dear Beloved, and through the Shabad, I am saved. Unless I can see Him, I am not satisfied.

That soul-bride who is ever adorned with the Shabad, meditates on the Name of the Lord, Har, Har.

Please bless this beggar, Your humble servant, with the Gift of Mercy; please unite me with my Beloved.

Night and day, I meditate on the Guru, the Lord of the World; I am a sacrifice to the True Guru. |2|

I am a stone in the Boat of the Guru. Please carry me across the terrifying ocean of poison.

O Guru, please, lovingly bless me with the Word of the Shabad. I am such a fool - please save me!

I am a fool and an idiot; I know nothing of Your extent. You are known as Inaccessible and Great.

You Yourself are Merciful; please, mercifully bless me. I am unworthy and dishonored - please, unite me with Yourself!

Through countless lifetimes, I wandered in sin; now, I have come seeking Your Sanctuary.

Take pity on me and save me, Dear Lord; I have grasped the Feet of the True Guru. |3|

The Guru is the Philosopher's Stone; by His touch, iron is transformed into gold.

My light merges into the Light, and my body-fortress is so beautiful.

My body-fortress is so beautiful; I am fascinated by my God. How could I forget Him, for even a breath, or a morsel of food?

I have seized the Unseen and Unfathomable Lord, through the Word of the Guru's Shabad. I am a sacrifice to the True Guru.

I place my head in offering before the True Guru, if it truly pleases the True Guru.

Take pity on me, O God, Great Giver, that Nanak may merge in Your Being. |4|1|

Tukhaari, Fourth Mehl:

The Lord, Har, Har, is Inaccessible, Unfathomable, Infinite, the Farthest of the Far.

Those who meditate on You, O Lord of the Universe - those humble beings cross over the terrifying, treacherous world-ocean.

Those who meditate on the Name of the Lord, Har, Har, easily cross over the terrifying, treacherous world-ocean.

Those who lovingly walk in harmony with the Word of the Guru, the True Guru - the Lord, Har, Har, unites them with Himself.

The mortal's light meets the Light of God, and blends with that Divine Light when the Lord, the Support of the Earth, grants His Grace.

The Lord, Har, Har, is Inaccessible, Unfathomable, Infinite, the Farthest of the Far. |1|

O my Lord and Master, You are Inaccessible and Unfathomable. You are totally pervading and permeating each and every heart.

You are Unseen, Unknowable and Unfathomable; You are found through the Word of the Guru, the True Guru.

Blessed, blessed are those humble, powerful and perfect people, who join the Guru's Sangat, the Society of the Saints, and chant His Glorious Praises.

With clear and precise understanding, the Gurmukhs contemplate the Guru's Shabad; each and every instant, they continually speak of the Lord.

When the Gurmukh sits down, he chants the Lord's Name. When the Gurmukh stands up, he chants the Lord's Name, Har, Har.

O my Lord and Master, You are Inaccessible and Unfathomable. You are totally pervading and permeating each and every heart. |2|

Those humble servants who serve are accepted. They serve the Lord, and follow the Guru's Teachings.

All their millions of sins are taken away in an instant; the Lord takes them far away.

All their sin and blame is washed away. They worship and adore the One Lord with their conscious minds.

Section 26 - Raag Tukhaari - Part 009

The Creator makes fruitful the lives of all those who, through the Guru's Word, chant the True Name.

Blessed are those humble beings, those great and perfect people, who follow the Guru's Teachings and meditate on the Lord; they cross over the terrifying and treacherous world-ocean.

Those humble servants who serve are accepted. They follow the Guru's Teachings, and serve the Lord. |3|

You Yourself, Lord, are the Inner-knower, the Searcher of hearts; as You make me walk, O my Beloved, so do I walk.
Nothing is in my hands; when You unite me, then I come to be united.
Those whom You unite with Yourself, O my Lord and Master - all their accounts are settled.
No one can go through the accounts of those, O Siblings of Destiny, who through the Word of the Guru's Teachings are united with the Lord.
O Nanak, the Lord shows Mercy to those who accept the Guru's Will as good.
You Yourself, Lord, are the Inner-knower, the Searcher of hearts; as You make me walk, O my Beloved, so do I walk. |4|2|

Tukhaari, Fourth Mehl:
You are the Life of the World, the Lord of the Universe, our Lord and Master, the Creator of all the Universe.
They alone meditate on You, O my Lord, who have such destiny recorded on their foreheads.
Those who are so pre-destined by their Lord and Master, worship and adore the Name of the Lord, Har, Har.
All sins are erased in an instant, for those who meditate on the Lord, through the Guru's Teachings.
Blessed, blessed are those humble beings who meditate on the Lord's Name. Seeing them, I am uplifted.
You are the Life of the World, the Lord of the Universe, our Lord and Master, the Creator of all the Universe. |1|

You are totally pervading the water, the land and the sky. O True Lord, You are the Master of all.
Those who meditate on the Lord in their conscious minds - all those who chant and meditate on the Lord are liberated.
Those mortal beings who meditate on the Lord are liberated; their faces are radiant in the Court of the Lord.
Those humble beings are exalted in this world and the next; the Savior Lord saves them.
Listen to the Lord's Name in the Society of the Saints, O humble Siblings of Destiny. The Gurmukh's service to the Lord is fruitful.

You are totally pervading the water, the land and the sky. O True Lord, You are the Master of all. |2|

You are the One Lord, the One and Only Lord, pervading all places and interspaces.
The forests and fields, the three worlds and the entire Universe, chant the Name of the Lord, Har, Har.
All chant the Name of the Creator Lord, Har, Har; countless, uncountable beings meditate on the Lord.
Blessed, blessed are those Saints and Holy People of the Lord, who are pleasing to the Creator Lord God.
O Creator, please bless me with the Fruitful Vision, the Darshan, of those who chant the Lord's Name in their hearts forever.
You are the One Lord, the One and Only Lord, pervading all places and interspaces. |3|

The treasures of devotional worship to You are countless; he alone is blessed with them, O my Lord and Master, whom You bless.
The Lord's Glorious Virtues abide within the heart of that person, whose forehead the Guru has touched.
The Glorious Virtues of the Lord dwell in the heart of that person, whose inner being is filled with the Fear of God, and His Love.

Section 26 - Raag Tukhaari - Part 010

Without the Fear of God, His Love is not obtained. Without the Fear of God, no one is carried across to the other side.
O Nanak, he alone is blessed with the Fear of God, and God's Love and Affection, whom You, Lord, bless with Your Mercy.
The treasures of devotional worship to You are countless; he alone is blessed with Them, O my Lord and Master, whom You bless. |4|3|

Tukhaari, Fourth Mehl:
To receive the Blessed Vision of the Darshan of the Guru, the True Guru, is to truly bathe at the Abhaijit festival.
The filth of evil-mindedness is washed off, and the darkness of ignorance is dispelled.
Blessed by the Guru's Darshan, spiritual ignorance is dispelled, and the Divine Light illuminates the inner being.

The pains of birth and death vanish in an instant, and the Eternal, Imperishable Lord God is found.

The Creator Lord God Himself created the festival, when the True Guru went to bathe at the festival in Kuruk-shaytra.

To receive the Blessed Vision of the Darshan of the Guru, the True Guru, is to truly bathe at the Abhaijit festival. |1|

The Sikhs travelled with the Guru, the True Guru, on the path, along the road.

Night and day, devotional worship services were held, each and every instant, with each step.

Devotional worship services to the Lord God were held, and all the people came to see the Guru.

Whoever was blessed with the Darshan of the Guru, the True Guru, the Lord united with Himself.

The True Guru made the pilgrimage to the sacred shrines, for the sake of saving all the people.

The Sikhs travelled with the Guru, the True Guru, on the path, along the road. |2|

When the Guru, the True Guru, first arrived at Kuruk-shaytra, it was a very auspicious time.

The news spread throughout the world, and the beings of the three worlds came.

The angelic beings and silent sages from all the three worlds came to see Him.

Those who are touched by the Guru, the True Guru - all their sins and mistakes were erased and dispelled.

The Yogis, the nudists, the Sannyaasees and those of the six schools of philosophy spoke with Him, and then bowed and departed.

When the Guru, the True Guru, first arrived at Kuruk-shaytra, it was a very auspicious time. |3|

Second, the Guru went to the river Jamunaa, where He chanted the Name of the Lord, Har, Har.

The tax collectors met the Guru and gave Him offerings; they did not impose the tax on His followers.

All the True Guru's followers were excused from the tax; they meditated on the Name of the Lord, Har, Har.

The Messenger of Death does not even approach those who have walked on the path, and followed the Guru's Teachings.

All the world said, "Guru! Guru! Guru!" Uttering the Guru's Name, they were all emancipated.

Second, the Guru went to the river Jamunaa, where He chanted the Name of the Lord, Har, Har. |4|

Third, He went to the Ganges, and a wonderful drama was played out there.

All were fascinated, gazing upon the Blessed Vision of the Saintly Guru's Darshan; no tax at all was imposed upon anyone.

No tax at all was collected, and the mouths of the tax collectors were sealed.

They said, "O brothers, what should we do? Who should we ask? Everyone is running after the True Guru."

Section 26 - Raag Tukhaari - Part 011

The tax collectors were smart; they thought about it, and saw. They broke their cash-boxes and left.

Third, He went to the Ganges, and a wonderful drama was played out there. |5|

The important men of the city met together, and sought the Protection of the Guru, the True Guru.

The Guru, the True Guru, the Guru is the Lord of the Universe. Go ahead and consult the Simritees - they will confirm this.

The Simritees and the Shaastras all confirm that Suk Dayv and Prahlaad meditated on the Guru, the Lord of the Universe, and knew Him as the Supreme Lord.

The five thieves and the highway robbers dwell in the fortress of the body-village; the Guru has destroyed their home and place.

The Puraanas continually praise the giving of charity, but devotional worship of the Lord is only obtained through the Word of Guru Nanak.

The important men of the city met together, and sought the Protection of the Guru, the True Guru. |6|4|10|

Tukhaari Chhant, Fifth Mehl:
One Universal Creator God. By The Grace Of The True Guru:

O my Beloved, I am a sacrifice to You. Through the Guru, I have dedicated my mind to You.

Hearing the Word of Your Shabad, my mind is enraptured.

This mind is enraptured, like the fish in the water; it is lovingly attached to the Lord.

Your Worth cannot be described, O my Lord and Master; Your Mansion is Incomparable and Unrivalled.

O Giver of all Virtue, O my Lord and Master, please hear the prayer of this humble person.

Please bless Nanak with the Blessed Vision of Your Darshan. I am a sacrifice, my soul is a sacrifice, a sacrifice to You. |1|

This body and mind are Yours; all virtues are Yours.

I am a sacrifice, every little bit, to Your Darshan.

Please hear me, O my Lord God; I live only by seeing Your Vision, even if only for an instant.

I have heard that Your Name is the most Ambrosial Nectar; please bless me with Your Mercy, that I may drink it in.

My hopes and desires rest in You, O my Husband Lord; like the rainbird, I long for the rain-drop.

Says Nanak, my soul is a sacrifice to You; please bless me with Your Darshan, O my Lord God. |2|

You are my True Lord and Master, O Infinite King.

You are my Dear Beloved, so dear to my life and consciousness.

You bring peace to my soul; You are known to the Gurmukh. All are blessed by Your Love.

The mortal does only those deeds which You ordain, Lord.

One who is blessed by Your Grace, O Lord of the Universe, conquers his mind in the Saadh Sangat, the Company of the Holy.

Says Nanak, my soul is a sacrifice to You; You gave me my soul and body. |3|

I am unworthy, but He has saved me, for the sake of the Saints.

The True Guru has covered by faults; I am such a sinner.

God has covered for me; He is the Giver of the soul, life and peace.

My Lord and Master is Eternal and Unchanging, Ever-present; He is the Perfect Creator, the Architect of Destiny.

Your Praise cannot be described; who can say where You are?

Slave Nanak is a sacrifice to the one who blesses him with the Lord's Name, even for an instant. |4|1|11|

RAAG KAYDAARAA

Section 27 - Raag Kaydaaraa - Part 001

Kaydaaraa, Fourth Mehl, First House:
One Universal Creator God. By The Grace Of The True Guru:
O my mind, sing continually the Name of the Lord.
The Inaccessible, Unfathomable Lord cannot be seen; meeting with the Perfect Guru, He is seen. |Pause|

That person, upon whom my Lord and Master showers His Mercy - the Lord attunes that one to Himself.
Everyone worships the Lord, but only that person who is pleasing to the Lord is accepted. |1|

The Name of the Lord, Har, Har, is priceless. It rests with the Lord. If the Lord bestows it, then we meditate on the Naam.
That person, whom my Lord and Master blesses with His Name - his entire account is forgiven. |2|

Those humble beings who worship and adore the Lord's Name, are said to be blessed. Such is the good destiny written on their foreheads.
Gazing upon them, my mind blossoms forth, like the mother who meets with her son and hugs him close. |3|

I am a child, and You, O my Lord God, are my Father; please bless me with such understanding, that I may find the Lord.
Like the cow, which is happy upon seeing her calf, O Lord, please hug Nanak close in Your Embrace. |4|1|

Kaydaaraa, Fourth Mehl, First House:
One Universal Creator God. By The Grace Of The True Guru:
O my mind, chant the Glorious Praises of the Lord, Har, Har.
Wash the Feet of the True Guru, and worship them. In this way, you shall find my Lord God. |Pause|

Sexual desire, anger, greed, attachment, egotism and corrupt pleasures - stay away from these.

Join the Sat Sangat, the True Congregation, and speak with the Holy People about the Lord. The Love of the Lord is the healing remedy; the Name of the Lord is the healing remedy. Chant the Name of the Lord, Raam, Raam. |1|

Section 27 - Raag Kaydaaraa - Part 002

So you think that the egotistical pride in power which you harbor deep within is everything. Let it go, and restrain your self-conceit.

Please be kind to servant Nanak, O Lord, my Lord and Master; please make him the dust of the Feet of the Saints. |2|1|2|

Kaydaaraa, Fifth Mehl, Second House:
One Universal Creator God. By The Grace Of The True Guru:
O mother, I have awakened in the Society of the Saints.
Seeing the Love of my Beloved, I chant His Name, the greatest treasure|Pause|

I am so thirsty for the Blessed Vision of His Darshan. my eyes are focused on Him;
I have forgotten other thirsts. |1|

Now, I have found my Peace-giving Guru with ease; seeing His Darshan, my mind clings to Him.
Seeing my Lord, joy has welled up in my mind; O Nanak, the speech of my Beloved is so sweet! |2|1|

Kaydaaraa, Fifth Mehl, Third House:
One Universal Creator God. By The Grace Of The True Guru:
Please listen to the prayers of the humble, O Merciful Lord.
The five thieves and the three dispositions torment my mind.
O Merciful Lord, Master of the masterless, please save me from them. |Pause|

I make all sorts of efforts and go on pilgrimages;
I perform the six rituals, and meditate in the right way.
I am so tired of making all these efforts, but the horrible demons still do not leave me. |1|

I seek Your Sanctuary, and bow to You, O Compassionate Lord.
You are the Destroyer of fear, O Lord, Har, Har, Har, Har.
You alone are Merciful to the meek.
Nanak takes the Support of God's Feet.
I have been rescued from the ocean of doubt,
holding tight to the feet and the robes of the Saints. |2|1|2|

Kaydaaraa, Fifth Mehl, Fourth House:
One Universal Creator God. By The Grace Of The True Guru:
I have come to Your Sanctuary, O Lord, O Supreme Treasure.
Love for the Naam, the Name of the Lord, is enshrined within my mind; I beg for the gift of Your Name. |1|Pause|

O Pefect Transcendent Lord, Giver of Peace, please grant Your Grace and save my honor.
Please bless me with such love, O my Lord and Master, that in the Saadh Sangat, the Company of the Holy, I may chant the Glorious Praises of the Lord with my tongue. |1|

O Lord of the World, Merciful Lord of the Universe, Your sermon and spiritual wisdom are immaculate and pure.
Please attune Nanak to Your Love, O Lord, and focus his meditation on Your Lotus Feet. |2|1|3|

Kaydaaraa, Fifth Mehl:
My mind yearns for the Blessed Vision of the Lord's Darshan.
Please grant Your Grace, and unite me with the Society of the Saints; please bless me with Your Name. |Pause|

I serve my True Beloved Lord. Wherever I hear His Praise, there my mind is in ecstasy.

Section 27 - Raag Kaydaaraa - Part 003

I am a sacrifice, a sacrifice, forever devoted to You. Your place is incomparably beautiful! |1|

You cherish and nurture all; You take care of all, and Your shade covers all.

You are the Primal Creator, the God of Nanak; I behold You in each and every heart. |2|2|4|

Kaydaaraa, Fifth Mehl:
I love the Love of my Beloved.
My mind is intoxicated with delight, and my consciousness is filled with hope; my eyes are drenched with Your Love. |Pause|

Blessed is that day, that hour, minute and second when the heavy, rigid shutters are opened, and desire is quenched.
Seeing the Blessed Vision of Your Darshan, I live. |1|

What is the method, what is the effort, and what is the service, which inspires me to contemplate You?
Abandon your egotistical pride and attachment; O Nanak, you shall be saved in the Society of the Saints. |2|3|5|

Kaydaaraa, Fifth Mehl:
Sing the Glorious Praises of the Lord, Har, Har, Har.
Have Mercy on me, O Life of the World, O Lord of the Universe, that I may chant Your Name. |Pause|

Please lift me up, God, out of vice and corruption, and attach my mind to the Saadh Sangat, the Company of the Holy.
Doubt, fear and attachment are eradicated from that person who follows the Guru's Teachings, and gazes on the Blessed Vision of His Darshan. |1|

Let my mind become the dust of all; may I abandon my egotistical intellect.
Please bless me with Your devotional worship, O Merciful Lord; by great good fortune, O Nanak, I have found the Lord. |2|4|6|

Kaydaaraa, Fifth Mehl:
Without the Lord, life is useless.
Those who forsake the Lord, and become engrossed in other pleasures - false and useless are the clothes they wear, and the food they eat. |Pause|

The pleasures of wealth, youth, property and comforts will not stay with you, O mother.
Seeing the mirage, the madman is entangled in it; he is imbued with pleasures that pass away, like the shade of a tree. |1|

Totally intoxicated with the wine of pride and attachment, he has fallen into the pit of sexual desire and anger.
O Dear God, please be the Help and Support of servant Nanak; please take me by the hand, and uplift me. |2|5|7|

Kaydaaraa, Fifth Mehl:
Nothing goes along with the mortal, except for the Lord.
He is the Master of the meek, the Lord of Mercy, my Lord and Master, the Master of the masterless. |Pause|

Children, possessions and the enjoyment of corrupt pleasures do not go along with the mortal on the path of Death.
Singing the Glorious Praises of the treasure of the Naam, and the Lord of the Universe, the mortal is carried across the deep ocean. |1|

In the Sanctuary of the All-powerful, Indescribable, Unfathomable Lord, meditate in remembrance on Him, and your pains shall vanish.
Nanak longs for the dust of the feet of the Lord's humble servant; he shall obtain it only if such pre-ordained destiny is written on his forehead. |2|6|8|

Kaydaaraa, Fifth Mehl, Fifth House:
One Universal Creator God. By The Grace Of The True Guru:
I do not forget the Lord in my mind.
This love has now become very strong; it has burnt away other corruption. |Pause|

How can the rainbird forsake the rain-drop? The fish cannot survive without water, even for an instant.

Section 27 - Raag Kaydaaraa - Part 004

My tongue chants the Glorious Praises of the Lord of the World; this has become part of my very nature. |1|

The deer is fascinated by the sound of the bell, and so it is shot with the sharp arrow.
God's Lotus Feet are the Source of Nectar; O Nanak, I am tied to them by a knot. |2|1|9|

Kaydaaraa, Fifth Mehl:
My Beloved dwells in the cave of my heart.
Shatter the wall of doubt, O my Lord and Master; please grab hold of me, and lift me up towards Yourself. |1|Pause|

The world-ocean is so vast and deep; please be kind, lift me up and place me on the shore.
In the Society of the Saints, the Lord's Feet are the boat to carry us across. |1|

The One who placed you in the womb of your mother's belly - no one else shall save you in the wilderness of corruption.
The power of the Lord's Sanctuary is all-powerful; Nanak does not rely on any other. |2|2|10|

Kaydaaraa, Fifth Mehl:
With your tongue, chant the Name of the Lord.
Chanting the Glorious Praises of the Lord, day and night, your sins shall be eradicated. |Pause|

You shall have to leave behind all your riches when you depart. Death is hanging over your head - know this well!

Transitory attachments and evil hopes are false. Surely you must believe this! |1|

Within your heart, focus your meditation on the True Primal Being, Akaal Moorat, the Undying Form.
Only this profitable merchandise, the treasure of the Naam, O Nanak, shall be accepted. |2|3|11|

Kaydaaraa, Fifth Mehl:
I take only the Support of the Name of the Lord.
Suffering and conflict do not afflict me; I deal only with the Society of the Saints. |Pause|

Showering His Mercy on me, the Lord Himself has saved me, and no evil thoughts arise within me.

Whoever receives this Grace, contemplates Him in meditation; he is not burned by the fire of the world. |1|

Peace, joy and bliss come from the Lord, Har, Har. God's Feet are sublime and excellent.
Slave Nanak seeks Your Sanctuary; he is the dust of the feet of Your Saints. |2|4|12|

Kaydaaraa, Fifth Mehl:
Without the Name of the Lord, one's ears are cursed.
Those who forget the Embodiment of Life - what is the point of their lives? |Pause|

One who eats and drinks countless delicacies is no more than a donkey, a beast of burden.
Twenty-four hours a day, he endures terrible suffering, like the bull, chained to the oil-press. |1|

Forsaking the Life of the World, and attached to another, they weep and wail in so many ways.
With his palms pressed together, Nanak begs for this gift; O Lord, please keep me strung around Your Neck. |2|5|13|

Kaydaaraa, Fifth Mehl:
I take the dust of the feet of the Saints and apply it to my face.
Hearing of the Imperishable, Eternally Perfect Lord, pain does not afflict me, even in this Dark Age of Kali Yuga. |Pause|

Through the Guru's Word, all affairs are resolved, and the mind is not tossed about here and there.
Whoever sees the One God to be pervading in all the many beings, does not burn in the fire of corruption. |1|

The Lord grasps His slave by the arm, and his light merges into the Light.
Nanak, the orphan, has come seeking the Sanctuary of God's Feet; O Lord, he walks with You. |2|6|14|

Kaydaaraa, Fifth Mehl:

Section 27 - Raag Kaydaaraa - Part 005

My mind is filled with yearning for the Name of the Lord.
I am totally filled with tranquility and bliss; the burning desire within has been quenched. |Pause|

Walking on the path of the Saints, millions of mortal sinners have been saved.
One who applies the dust of the feet of the humble to his forehead, is purified, as if he has bathed at countless sacred shrines. |1|

Meditating on His Lotus Feet deep within, one realizes the Lord and Master in each and every heart.
In the Sanctuary of the Divine, Infinite Lord, Nanak shall never again be tortured by the Messenger of Death. |2|7|15|

Kaydaaraa Chhant, Fifth Mehl:
One Universal Creator God. By The Grace Of The True Guru:
Please meet me, O my Dear Beloved. |Pause|

He is All-pervading amongst all, the Architect of Destiny.
The Lord God has created His Path, which is known in the Society of the Saints.
The Creator Lord, the Architect of Destiny, is known in the Society of the Saints; You are seen in each and every heart.
One who comes to His Sanctuary, finds absolute peace; not even a bit of his work goes unnoticed.
One who sings the Glorious Praises of the Lord, the Treasure of Virtue, is easily, naturally intoxicated with the supreme, sublime essence of divine love.
Slave Nanak seeks Your Sanctuary; You are the Perfect Creator Lord, the Architect of Destiny. |1|

The Lord's humble servant is pierced through with loving devotion to Him; where else can he go?
The fish cannot endure separation, and without water, it will die.
Without the Lord, how can I survive? How can I endure the pain? I am like the rainbird, thirsty for the rain-drop.
"When will the night pass?," asks the chakvi bird. "I shall find peace only when the rays of the sun shine on me."

My mind is attached to the Blessed Vision of the Lord. Blessed are the nights and days, when I sing the Glorious Praises of the Lord,

Slave Nanak utters this prayer; without the Lord, how can the breath of life continue to flow through me? |2|

Without the breath, how can the body obtain glory and fame?
Without the Blessed Vision of the Lord's Darshan, the humble, holy person does not find peace, even for an instant.
Those who are without the Lord suffer in hell; my mind is pierced through with the Lord's Feet.
The Lord is both sensual and unattached; lovingly attune yourself to the Naam, the Name of the Lord. No one can ever deny Him.
Go and meet with the Lord, and dwell in the Saadh Sangat, the Company of the Holy; no one can contain that peace within his being.
Please be kind to me, O Lord and Master of Nanak, that I may merge in You. |3|

Searching and searching, I have met with my Lord God, who has showered me with His Mercy.
I am unworthy, a lowly orphan, but He does not even consider my faults.
He does not consider my faults; He has blessed me with Perfect Peace. It is said that it is His Way to purify us.
Hearing that He is the Love of His devotees, I have grasped the hem of His robe. He is totally permeating each and every heart.
I have found the Lord, the Ocean of Peace, with intuitive ease; the pains of birth and death are gone.
Taking him by the hand, the Lord has saved Nanak, His slave; He has woven the garland of His Name into his heart. |4|1|

Section 27 - Raag Kaydaaraa - Part 006

Raag Kaydaaraa, The Word Of Kabeer Jee:
One Universal Creator God. By The Grace Of The True Guru:
Those who ignore both praise and slander, who reject egotistical pride and conceit,
who look alike upon iron and gold - they are the very image of the Lord God. |1|

Hardly anyone is a humble servant of Yours, O Lord.

Ignoring sexual desire, anger, greed and attachment, such a person becomes aware of the Lord's Feet. |1|Pause|

Raajas, the quality of energy and activity; Taamas, the quality of darkness and inertia; and Satvas, the quality of purity and light, are all called the creations of Maya, Your illusion.
That man who realizes the fourth state - he alone obtains the supreme state. |2|

Amidst pilgrimages, fasting, rituals, purification and self-discipline, he remains always without thought of reward.
Thirst and desire for Maya and doubt depart, remembering the Lord, the Supreme Soul. |3|

When the temple is illuminated by the lamp, its darkness is dispelled.
The Fearless Lord is All-pervading. Doubt has run away, says Kabeer, the Lord's humble slave. |4|1|

Some deal in bronze and copper, some in cloves and betel nuts.
The Saints deal in the Naam, the Name of the Lord of the Universe. Such is my merchandise as well. |1|

I am a trader in the Name of the Lord.
The priceless diamond has come into my hands. I have left the world behind. |1|Pause|

When the True Lord attached me, then I was attached to Truth. I am a trader of the True Lord.
I have loaded the commodity of Truth; It has reached the Lord, the Treasurer. |2|

He Himself is the pearl, the jewel, the ruby; He Himself is the jeweller.
He Himself spreads out in the ten directions. The Merchant is Eternal and Unchanging. |3|

My mind is the bull, and meditation is the road; I have filled my packs with spiritual wisdom, and loaded them on the bull.
Says Kabeer, listen, O Saints: my merchandise has reached its destination! |4|2|

You barbaric brute, with your primitive intellect - reverse your breath and turn it inward.
Let your mind be intoxicated with the stream of Ambrosial Nectar which trickles down from the furnace of the Tenth Gate. |1|

O Siblings of Destiny, call on the Lord.
O Saints, drink in this wine forever; it is so difficult to obtain, and it quenches your thirst so easily. |1|Pause|

In the Fear of God, is the Love of God. Only those few who understand His Love obtain the sublime essence of the Lord, O Siblings of Destiny.
As many hearts as there are - in all of them, is His Ambrosial Nectar; as He pleases, He causes them to drink it in. |2|

There are nine gates to the one city of the body; restrain your mind from escaping through them.
When the knot of the three qualities is untied, then the Tenth Gate opens up, and the mind is intoxicated, O Siblings of Destiny. |3|

When the mortal fully realizes the state of fearless dignity, then his sufferings vanish; so says Kabeer after careful deliberation.
Turning away from the world, I have obtained this wine, and I am intoxicated with it. |4|3|

You are engrossed with unsatisfied sexual desire and unresolved anger; you do not know the State of the One Lord.
Your eyes are blinded, and you see nothing at all. You drown and die without water. |1|

Section 27 - Raag Kaydaaraa - Part 007

Why do you walk in that crooked, zig-zag way?
You are nothing more than a bundle of bones, wrapped in skin, filled with manure; you give off such a rotten smell! |1|Pause|

You do not meditate on the Lord. What doubts have confused and deluded you? Death is not far away from you!

Making all sorts of efforts, you manage to preserve this body, but it shall only survive until its time is up. |2|

By one's own efforts, nothing is done. What can the mere mortal accomplish?
When it pleases the Lord, the mortal meets the True Guru, and chants the Name of the One Lord. |3|

You live in a house of sand, but you still puff up your body - you ignorant fool!
Says Kabeer, those who do not remember the Lord may be very clever, but they still drown. |4|4|

Your turban is crooked, and you walk crooked; and now you have started chewing betel leaves.
You have no use at all for loving devotional worship; you say you have business in court. |1|

In your egotistical pride, you have forgotten the Lord.
Gazing upon your gold, and your very beautiful wife, you believe that they are permanent. |1|Pause|

You are engrossed in greed, falsehood, corruption and great arrogance. Your life is passing away.
Says Kabeer, at the very last moment, death will come and seize you, you fool! |2|5|

The mortal beats the drum for a few days, and then he must depart.
With so much wealth and cash and buried treasure, still, he cannot take anything with him. |1|Pause|

Sitting on the threshhold, his wife weeps and wails; his mother accompanies him to the outer gate.
All the people and relatives together go to the crematorium, but the swan-soul must go home all alone. |1|

Those children, that wealth, that city and town - he shall not come to see them again.
Says Kabeer, why do you not meditate on the Lord? Your life is uselessly slipping away! |2|6|

Raag Kaydaaraa, The Word Of Ravi Daas Jee:

One Universal Creator God. By The Grace Of The True Guru:
One who performs the six religious rituals and comes from a good family, but who does not have devotion to the Lord in his heart,

one who does not appreciate talk of the Lord's Lotus Feet, is just like an outcaste, a pariah. |1|

Be conscious, be conscious, be conscious, O my unconscious mind.
Why do you not look at Baalmeek?
From such a low social status, what a high status he obtained! Devotional worship to the Lord is sublime! |1|Pause|

The killer of dogs, the lowest of all, was lovingly embraced by Krishna.
See how the poor people praise him! His praise extends throughout the three worlds. |2|

Ajaamal, Pingulaa, Lodhia and the elephant went to the Lord.
Even such evil-minded beings were emancipated. Why should you not also be saved, O Ravi Daas? |3|1|

RAAG BHAIRAO

Section 28 - Raag Bhairao - Part 001

Raag Bhairao, First Mehl, First House, Chau-Padas:
ONE Universal Creator God. Truth Is The Name. Creative Being Personified.
No Fear. No Hatred. Image Of The Undying. Beyond Birth. Self-Existent. By
Guru's Grace:
Without You, nothing happens.
You create the creatures, and gazing on them, you know them. |1|

What can I say? I cannot say anything.
Whatever exists, is by Your Will. |Pause|

Whatever is to be done, rests with You.
Unto whom should I offer my prayer? |2|

I speak and hear the Bani of Your Word.
You Yourself know all Your Wondrous Play. |3|

You Yourself act, and inspire all to act; only You Yourself know.
Says Nanak, You, Lord, see, establish and disestablish. |4|1|

One Universal Creator God. By The Grace Of The True Guru:
Raag Bhairao, First Mehl, Second House:
Through the Word of the Guru's Shabad, so many silent sages have been
saved; Indra and Brahma have also been saved.
Sanak, Sanandan and many humble men of austerity, by Guru's Grace, have
been carried across to the other side. |1|

Without the Word of the Shabad, how can anyone cross over the terrifying
world-ocean?
Without the Naam, the Name of the Lord, the world is entangled in the
disease of duality, and is drowned, drowned, and dies. |1|Pause|

The Guru is Divine; the Guru is Inscrutable and Mysterious. Serving the
Guru, the three worlds are known and understood.

The Guru, the Giver, has Himself given me the Gift; I have obtained the Inscrutable, Mysterious Lord. |2|

The mind is the king; the mind is appeased and satisfied through the mind itself, and desire is stilled in the mind.
The mind is the Yogi, the mind wastes away in separation from the Lord; singing the Glorious Praises of the Lord, the mind is instructed and reformed. |3|

How very rare are those in this world who, through the Guru, subdue their minds, and contemplate the Word of the Shabad.
O Nanak, our Lord and Master is All-pervading; through the True Word of the Shabad, we are emancipated. |4|1|2|

Bhairao, First Mehl:
The eyes lose their sight, and the body withers away; old age overtakes the mortal, and death hangs over his head.
Beauty, loving attachment and the pleasures of life are not permanent. How can anyone escape from the noose of death? |1|

O mortal, meditate on the Lord - your life is passing away!

Section 28 - Raag Bhairao - Part 002

Without the True Word of the Shabad, you shall never be released, and your life shall be totally useless. |1|Pause|

Within the body are sexual desire, anger, egotism and attachment. This pain is so great, and so difficult to endure.
As Gurmukh, chant the Lord's Name, and savor it with your tongue; in this way, you shall cross over to the other side. |2|

Your ears are deaf, and your intellect is worthless, and still, you do not intuitively understand the Word of the Shabad.
The self-willed manmukh wastes this priceless human life and loses it. Without the Guru, the blind person cannot see. |3|

Whoever remains detached and free of desire in the midst of desire - and whoever, unattached, intuitively meditates on the Celestial Lord

- prays Nanak, as Gurmukh, he is released. He is lovingly attuned to the Naam, the Name of the Lord. |4|2|3|

Bhairao, First Mehl:
His walk becomes weak and clumsy, his feet and hands shake, and the skin of his body is withered and wrinkled.
His eyes are dim, his ears are deaf, and yet, the self-willed manmukh does not know the Naam. |1|

O blind man, what have you obtained by coming into the world?
The Lord is not in your heart, and you do not serve the Guru. After wasting your capital, you shall have to depart. |1|Pause|

Your tongue is not imbued with the Love of the Lord; whatever you say is tasteless and insipid.
You indulge in slander of the Saints; becoming a beast, you shall never be noble. |2|

Only a few obtain the sublime essence of the Ambrosial Amrit, united in Union with the True Guru.
As long as the mortal does not come to understand the mystery of the Shabad, the Word of God, he shall continue to be tormented by death. |3|

Whoever finds the door of the One True Lord, does not know any other house or door.
By Guru's Grace, I have obtained the supreme status; so says poor Nanak. |4|3|4|

Bhairao, First Mehl:
He spends the entire night in sleep; the noose is tied around his neck. His day is wasted in worldly entanglements.
He does not know God, who created this world, for a moment, for even an instant. |1|

O mortal, how will you escape this terrible disaster?
What did you bring with you, and what will you take away? Meditate on the Lord, the Most Worthy and Generous Lord. |1|Pause|

The heart-lotus of the self-willed manmukh is upside-down; his intellect is shallow; his mind is blind, and his head is entangled in worldly affairs.

Death and re-birth constantly hang over your head; without the Name, your neck shall be caught in the noose. |2|

Your steps are unsteady, and your eyes are blind; you are not aware of the Word of the Shabad, O Sibling of Destiny.
The Shaastras and the Vedas keep the mortal bound to the three modes of Maya, and so he performs his deeds blindly. |3|

He loses his capital - how can he earn any profit? The evil-minded person has no spiritual wisdom at all.
Contemplating the Shabad, he drinks in the sublime essence of the Lord; O Nanak, his faith is confirmed in the Truth. |4|4|5|

Bhairao, First Mehl:
He remains with the Guru, day and night, and his tongue savors the savory taste of the Lord's Love.
He does not know any other; he realizes the Word of the Shabad. He knows and realizes the Lord deep within his own being. |1|

Such a humble person is pleasing to my mind.
He conquers his self-conceit, and is imbued with the Infinite Lord. He serves the Guru. |1|Pause|

Deep within my being, and outside as well, is the Immaculate Lord God. I bow humbly before that Primal Lord God.
Deep within each and every heart, and amidst all, the Embodiment of Truth is permeating and pervading. |2|

Section 28 - Raag Bhairao - Part 003

Those who are imbued with Truth - their tongues are tinged with Truth; they do not have even an iota of the filth of falsehood.
They taste the sweet Ambrosial Nectar of the Immaculate Naam, the Name of the Lord; imbued with the Shabad, they are blessed with honor. |3|

The virtuous meet with the virtuous, and earn the profit; as Gurmukh, they obtain the glorious greatness of the Naam.
All sorrows are erased, by serving the Guru; O Nanak, the Naam is our only Friend and Companion. |4|5|6|

Bhairao, First Mehl:
The Naam, the Name of the Lord, is the wealth and support of all; It is enshrined in the heart, by Guru's Grace.
One who gathers this imperishable wealth is fulfilled, and through intuitive meditation, is lovingly focused on the Lord. |1|

O mortal, focus your consciousness on devotional worship of the Lord.
As Gurmukh, meditate on the Name of the Lord in your heart, and you shall return to your home with intuitive ease. |1|Pause|

Doubt, separation and fear are never eradicated, and the mortal continues coming and going in reincarnation, as long as he does not know the Lord.
Without the Name of the Lord, no one is liberated; they drown and die without water. |2|

Busy with his worldly affairs, all honor is lost; the ignorant one is not rid of his doubts.
Without the Word of the Guru's Shabad, the mortal is never liberated; he remains blindly entangled in the expanse of worldly affairs. |3|

My mind is pleased and appeased with the Immaculate Lord, who has no ancestry. Through the mind itself, the mind is subdued.
Deep within my being, and outside as well, I know only the One Lord. O Nanak, there is no other at all. |4|6|7|

Bhairao, First Mehl:
You may give feasts, make burnt offerings, donate to charity, perform austere penance and worship, and endure pain and suffering in the body.
But without the Lord's Name, liberation is not obtained. As Gurmukh, obtain the Naam and liberation. |1|

Without the Lord's Name, birth into the world is useless.
Without the Name, the mortal eats poison and speaks poisonous words; he dies fruitlessly, and wanders in reincarnation. |1|Pause|

The mortal may read scriptures, study grammar and say his prayers three times a day.
Without the Word of the Guru's Shabad, where is liberation, O mortal?
Without the Lord's Name, the mortal is entangled and dies. |2|

Walking sticks, begging bowls, hair tufts, sacred threads, loin cloths, pilgrimages to sacred shrines and wandering all around

- without the Lord's Name, peace and tranquility are not obtained. One who chants the Name of the Lord, Har, Har, crosses over to the other side. |3|

The mortal's hair may be matted and tangled upon his head, and he may smear his body with ashes; he may take off his clothes and go naked.
But without the Lord's Name, he is not satisfied; he wears religious robes, but he is bound by the karma of the actions he committed in past lives. |4|

As many beings and creatures as there are in the water, on the land and in the sky - wherever they are, You are with them all, O Lord.
By Guru's Grace, please preserve Your humble servant; O Lord, Nanak stirs up this juice, and drinks it in. |5|7|8|

Raag Bhairao, Third Mehl, Chaupadas, First House:
One Universal Creator God. By The Grace Of The True Guru:
No one should be proud of his social class and status.
He alone is a Brahmin, who knows God. |1|

Do not be proud of your social class and status, you ignorant fool!

Section 28 - Raag Bhairao - Part 004

So much sin and corruption comes from this pride. |1|Pause|

Everyone says that there are four castes, four social classes.
They all emanate from the drop of God's Seed. |2|

The entire universe is made of the same clay.
The Potter has shaped it into all sorts of vessels. |3|

The five elements join together, to make up the form of the human body.
Who can say which is less, and which is more? |4|

Says Nanak, this soul is bound by its actions.
Without meeting the True Guru, it is not liberated. |5|1|

Bhairao, Third Mehl:
The Yogis, the householders, the Pandits, the religious scholars, and the beggars in religious robes
- they are all asleep in egotism. |1|

They are asleep, intoxicated with the wine of Maya.
Only those who remain awake and aware are not robbed. |1|Pause|

One who has met the True Guru, remains awake and aware.
Such a person overpowers the five thieves. |2|

One who contemplates the essence of reality remains awake and aware.
He kills his self-conceit, and does not kill anyone else. |3|

One who knows the One Lord remains awake and aware.
He abandons the service of others, and realizes the essence of reality. |4|

Of the four castes, whoever remains awake and aware
is released from birth and death. |5|

Says Nanak, that humble being remains awake and aware,
who applies the ointment of spiritual wisdom to his eyes. |6|2|

Bhairao, Third Mehl:
Whoever the Lord keeps in His Sanctuary,
is attached to the Truth, and receives the fruit of Truth. |1|

O mortal, unto whom will you complain?
The Hukam of the Lord's Command is pervasive; by the Hukam of His Command, all things happen. |1|Pause|

This Creation was established by You.
In an instant You destroy it, and You create it again without a moment's delay. |2|

By His Grace, He has staged this Play.
By the Guru's Merciful Grace, I have obtained the supreme status. |3|

Says Nanak, He alone kills and revives.
Understand this well - do not be confused by doubt. |4|3|

Bhairao, Third Mehl:
I am the bride; the Creator is my Husband Lord.
As He inspires me, I adorn myself. |1|

When it pleases Him, He enjoys me.
I am joined, body and mind, to my True Lord and Master. |1|Pause|

How can anyone praise or slander anyone else?
The One Lord Himself is pervading and permeating all. |2|

By Guru's Grace, I am attracted by His Love.
I shall meet with my Merciful Lord, and vibrate the Panch Shabad, the Five Primal Sounds. |3|

Prays Nanak, what can anyone do?
He alone meets with the Lord, whom the Lord Himself meets. |4|4|

Bhairao, Third Mehl:
He alone is a silent sage, who subdues his mind's duality.
Subduing his duality, he contemplates God. |1|

Let each person examine his own mind, O Siblings of Destiny.
Examine your mind, and you shall obtain the nine treasures of the Naam. |1|Pause|

The Creator created the world, upon the foundation of worldly love and attachment.
Attaching it to possessiveness, He has led it into confusion with doubt. |2|

From this Mind come all bodies, and the breath of life.
By mental contemplation, the mortal realizes the Hukam of the Lord's Command, and merges in Him. |3|

Section 28 - Raag Bhairao - Part 005

When the mortal has good karma, the Guru grants His Grace.
Then this mind is awakened, and the duality of this mind is subdued. |4|

It is the innate nature of the mind to remain forever detached.

The Detached, Dispassionate Lord dwells within all. |5|

Says Nanak, one who understands this mystery,
becomes the embodiment of the Primal, Immaculate, Divine Lord God.
|6|5|

Bhairao, Third Mehl:
The world is saved through Name of the Lord.
It carries the mortal across the terrifying world-ocean. |1|

By Guru's Grace, dwell upon the Lord's Name.
It shall stand by you forever. |1|Pause|

The foolish self-willed manmukhs do not remember the Naam, the Name of
the Lord.
Without the Name, how will they cross over? |2|

The Lord, the Great Giver, Himself gives His Gifts.
Celebrate and praise the Great Giver! |3|

Granting His Grace, the Lord unites the mortals with the True Guru.
O Nanak, the Naam is enshrined within the heart. |4|6|

Bhairao, Third Mehl:
All people are saved through the Naam, the Name of the Lord.
Those who become Gurmukh are blessed to receive It. |1|

When the Dear Lord showers His Mercy,
He blesses the Gurmukh with the glorious greatness of the Naam.
|1|Pause|

Those who love the Beloved Name of the Lord
save themselves, and save all their ancestors. |2|

Without the Name, the self-willed manmukhs go to the City of Death.
They suffer in pain and endure beatings. |3|

When the Creator Himself gives,
O Nanak, then the mortals receive the Naam. |4|7|

Bhairao, Third Mehl:
Love of the Lord of the Universe saved Sanak and his brother, the sons of Brahma.
They contemplated the Word of the Shabad, and the Name of the Lord. |1|

O Dear Lord, please shower me with Your Mercy,
that as Gurmukh, I may embrace love for Your Name. |1|Pause|

Whoever has true loving devotional worship deep within his being
meets the Lord, through the Perfect Guru. |2|

He naturally, intuitively dwells within the home of his own inner being.
The Naam abides within the mind of the Gurmukh. |3|

The Lord, the Seer, Himself sees.
O Nanak, enshrine the Naam within your heart. |4|8|

Bhairao, Third Mehl:
In this Dark Age of Kali Yuga, enshrine the Lord's Name within your heart.
Without the Name, ashes will be blown in your face. |1|

The Lord's Name is so difficult to obtain, O Siblings of Destiny.
By Guru's Grace, it comes to dwell in the mind. |1|Pause|

That humble being who seeks the Lord's Name,
receives it from the Perfect Guru. |2|

Those humble beings who accept the Will of the Lord, are approved and accepted.
Through the Word of the Guru's Shabad, they bear the insignia of the Naam, the Name of the Lord. |3|

So serve the One, whose power supports the Universe.
O Nanak, the Gurmukh loves the Naam. |4|9|

Bhairao, Third Mehl:
In this Dark Age of Kali Yuga, many rituals are performed.
But it is not the time for them, and so they are of no use. |1|

In Kali Yuga, the Lord's Name is the most sublime.

As Gurmukh, be lovingly attached to Truth. |1|Pause|

Searching my body and mind, I found Him within the home of my own heart.
The Gurmukh centers his consciousness on the Lord's Name. |2|

Section 28 - Raag Bhairao - Part 006

The ointment of spiritual wisdom is obtained from the True Guru.
The Lord's Name is pervading the three worlds. |3|

In Kali Yuga, it is the time for the One Dear Lord; it is not the time for anything else.
O Nanak, as Gurmukh, let the Lord's Name grow within your heart. |4|10|

Bhairao, Third Mehl, Second House:
One Universal Creator God. By The Grace Of The True Guru:
The self-willed manmukhs are afflicted with the disease of duality; they are burnt by the intense fire of desire.
They die and die again, and are reborn; they find no place of rest. They waste their lives uselessly. |1|

O my Beloved, grant Your Grace, and give me understanding.
The world was created in the disease of egotism; without the Word of the Shabad, the disease is not cured. |1|Pause|

There are so many silent sages, who read the Simritees and the Shaastras; without the Shabad, they have no clear awareness.
All those under the influence of the three qualities are afflicted with the disease; through possessiveness, they lose their awareness. |2|

O God, you save some, and you enjoin others to serve the Guru.
They obtain the treasure of the Name of the Lord; peace comes to abide within their minds. |3|

The Gurmukhs dwell in the fourth state; they obtain a dwelling in the home of their own inner being.
The Perfect True Guru shows His Mercy to them; they eradicate their self-conceit from within. |4|

Everyone must serve the One Lord, who created Brahma, Vishnu and Shiva.
O Nanak, the One True Lord is permanent and stable. He does not die, and
He is not born. |5|1|11|

Bhairao, Third Mehl:
The self-willed manmukh is afflicted with the disease of duality forever; the
entire universe is diseased.
The Gurmukh understands, and is cured of the disease, contemplating the
Word of the Guru's Shabad. |1|

O Dear Lord, please let me join the Sat Sangat, the True Congregation.
O Nanak, the Lord blesses with glorious greatness, those who focus their
consciousness on the Lord's Name. |1|Pause|

Death takes all those who are afflicted with the disease of possessiveness.
They are subject to the Messenger of Death.
The Messenger of Death does not even approach that mortal who, as
Gurmukh, enshrines the Lord within his heart. |2|

One who does not know the Lord's Name, and who does not become
Gurmukh - why did he even come into the world?
He never serves the Guru; he wastes his life uselessly. |3|

O Nanak, those whom the True Guru enjoins to His service, have perfect
good fortune.
They obtain the fruits of their desires, and find peace in the Word of the
Guru's Bani. |4|2|12|

Bhairao, Third Mehl:
In pain he is born, in pain he dies, and in pain he does his deeds.
He is never released from the womb of reincarnation; he rots away in
manure. |1|

Cursed, cursed is the self-willed manmukh, who wastes his life away.
He does not serve the Perfect Guru; he does not love the Name of the Lord.
|1|Pause|

The Word of the Guru's Shabad cures all diseases; he alone is attached to
it, whom the Dear Lord attaches.

Section 28 - Raag Bhairao - Part 007

Through the Naam, glorious greatness is obtained; he alone obtains it, whose mind is filled with the Lord. |2|

Meeting the True Guru, the fruitful rewards are obtained. This true lifestyle beings sublime peace.
Those humble beings who are attached to the Lord are immaculate; they enshrine love for the Lord's Name. |3|

If I obtain the dust of their feet, I apply it to my forehead. They meditate on the Perfect True Guru.
O Nanak, this dust is obtained only by perfect destiny. They focus their consciousness on the Lord's Name. |4|3|13|

Bhairao, Third Mehl:
That humble being who contemplates the Word of the Shabad is true; the True Lord is within his heart.
If someone performs true devotional worship day and night, then his body will not feel pain. |1|

Everyone calls him, "Devotee, devotee."
But without serving the True Guru, devotional worship is not obtained.
Only through perfect destiny does one meet God. |1|Pause|

The self-willed manmukhs lose their capital, and still, they demand profits. How can they earn any profit?
The Messenger of Death is always hovering above their heads. In the love of duality, they lose their honor. |2|

Trying on all sorts of religious robes, they wander around day and night, but the disease of their egotism is not cured.
Reading and studying, they argue and debate; attached to Maya, they lose their awareness. |3|

Those who serve the True Guru are blessed with the supreme status; through the Naam, they are blessed with glorious greatness.
O Nanak, those whose minds are filled with the Naam, are honored in the Court of the True Lord. |4|4|14|

Bhairao, Third Mehl:
The self-willed manmukh cannot escape false hope. In the love of duality, he is ruined.
His belly is like a river - it is never filled up. He is consumed by the fire of desire. |1|

Eternally blissful are those who are imbued with the sublime essence of the Lord.
The Naam, the Name of the Lord, fills their hearts, and duality runs away from their minds. Drinking in the Ambrosial Nectar of the Lord, Har, Har, they are satisfied. |1|Pause|

The Supreme Lord God Himself created the Universe; He links each and every person to their tasks.
He Himself created love and attachment to Maya; He Himself attaches the mortals to duality. |2|

If there were any other, then I would speak to him; all will be merged in You.
The Gurmukh contemplates the essence of spiritual wisdom; his light merges into the Light. |3|

God is True, Forever True, and all His Creation is True.
O Nanak, the True Guru has given me this understanding; the True Name brings emancipation. |4|5|15|

Bhairao, Third Mehl:
In this Dark Age of Kali Yuga, those who do not realize the Lord are goblins. In the Golden Age of Sat Yuga, the supreme soul-swans contemplated the Lord.
In the Silver Age of Dwaapur Yuga, and the Brass Age of Traytaa Yuga, mankind prevailed, but only a rare few subdued their egos. |1|

In this Dark Age of Kali Yuga, glorious greatness is obtained through the Lord's Name.
In each and every age, the Gurmukhs know the One Lord; without the Name, liberation is not attained. |1|Pause|

The Naam, the Name of the Lord, is revealed in the heart of the True Lord's humble servant. It dwells in the mind of the Gurmukh.

Those who are lovingly focused on the Lord's Name save themselves; they save all their ancestors as well. |2|

My Lord God is the Giver of virtue. The Word of the Shabad burns away all faults and demerits.

Section 28 - Raag Bhairao - Part 008

Those whose minds are filled with the Naam are beautiful; they enshrine the Naam within their hearts. |3|

The True Guru has revealed to me the Lord's Home and His Court, and the Mansion of His Presence. I joyfully enjoy His Love.
Whatever He says, I accept as good; Nanak chants the Naam. |4|6|16|

Bhairao, Third Mehl:
The desires of the mind are absorbed in the mind, contemplating the Word of the Guru's Shabad.
Understanding is obtained from the Perfect Guru, and then the mortal does not die over and over again. |1|

My mind takes the Support of the Lord's Name.
By Guru's Grace, I have obtained the supreme status; the Lord is the Fulfiller of all desires. |1|Pause|

The One Lord is permeating and pervading amongst all; without the Guru, this understanding is not obtained.
My Lord God has been revealed to me, and I have become Gurmukh. Night and day, I sing the Glorious Praises of the Lord. |2|

The One Lord is the Giver of peace; peace is not found anywhere else.
Those who do not serve the Giver, the True Guru, depart regretfully in the end. |3|

Serving the True Guru, lasting peace is obtained, and the mortal does not suffer in pain any longer.
Nanak has been blessed with devotional worship of the Lord; his light has merged into the Light. |4|7|17|

Bhairao, Third Mehl:

Without the Guru, the world is insane; confused and deluded, it is beaten, and it suffers.
It dies and dies again, and is reborn, always in pain, but it is unaware of the Lord's Gate. |1|

O my mind, remain always in the Protection of the True Guru's Sanctuary.
Those people, to whose hearts the Lord's Name seems sweet, are carried across the terrifying world-ocean by the Word of the Guru's Shabad. |1|Pause|

The mortal wears various religious robes, but his consciousness is unsteady; deep within, he is filled with sexual desire, anger and egotism.
Deep within is the great thirst and immense hunger; he wanders from door to door. |2|

Those who die in the Word of the Guru's Shabad are reborn; they find the door of liberation.
With constant peace and tranquility deep within, they enshrine the Lord within their hearts. |3|

As it pleases Him, He inspires us to act. Nothing else can be done.
O Nanak, the Gurmukh contemplates the Word of the Shabad, and is blessed with the glorious greatness of the Lord's Name. |4|8|18|

Bhairao, Third Mehl:
Lost in egotism, Maya and attachment, the mortal earns pain, and eats pain.
The great disease, the rabid disease of greed, is deep within him; he wanders around indiscriminately. |1|

The life of the self-willed manmukh in this world is cursed.
He does not remember the Lord's Name, even in his dreams. He is never in love with the Lord's Name. |1|Pause|

He acts like a beast, and does not understand anything. Practicing falsehood, he becomes false.
But when the mortal meets the True Guru, his way of looking at the world changes. How rare are those humble beings who seek and find the Lord. |2|

That person, whose heart is forever filled with the Name of the Lord, Har, Har, obtains the Lord, the Treasure of Virtue.

By Guru's Grace, he finds the Perfect Lord; the egotistical pride of his mind is eradicated. |3|

The Creator Himself acts, and causes all to act. He Himself places us on the path.

Section 28 - Raag Bhairao - Part 009

He Himself blesses the Gurmukh with glorious greatness; O Nanak, he merges in the Naam. |4|9|19|

Bhairao, Third Mehl:
Upon my writing tablet, I write the Name of the Lord, the Lord of the Universe, the Lord of the World.
In the love of duality, the mortals are caught in the noose of the Messenger of Death.
The True Guru nurtures and sustains me.
The Lord, the Giver of peace, is always with me. |1|

Following his Guru's instructions, Prahlaad chanted the Lord's Name;
he was a child, but he was not afraid when his teacher yelled at him.
|1|Pause|

Prahlaad's mother gave her beloved son some advice:
"My son, you must abandon the Lord's Name, and save your life!"
Prahlaad said: "Listen, O my mother;
I shall never give up the Lord's Name. My Guru has taught me this."|2|

Sandaa and Markaa, his teachers, went to his father the king, and complained:
"Prahlaad himself has gone astray, and he leads all the other pupils astray."
In the court of the wicked king, a plan was hatched.
God is the Savior of Prahlaad. |3|

With sword in hand, and with great egotistical pride, Prahlaad's father ran up to him.
"Where is your Lord, who will save you?"

In an instant, the Lord appeared in a dreadful form, and shattered the pillar.
Harnaakhash was torn apart by His claws, and Prahlaad was saved. |4|

The Dear Lord completes the tasks of the Saints.
He saved twenty-one generations of Prahlaad's descendents.
Through the Word of the Guru's Shabad, the poison of egotism is neutralized.
O Nanak, through the Name of the Lord, the Saints are emancipated. |5|10|20|

Bhairao, Third Mehl:
The Lord Himself makes demons pursue the Saints, and He Himself saves them.
Those who remain forever in Your Sanctuary, O Lord - their minds are never touched by sorrow. |1|

In each and every age, the Lord saves the honor of His devotees.
Prahlaad, the demon's son, knew nothing of the Hindu morning prayer, the Gayatri, and nothing about ceremonial water-offerings to his ancestors; but through the Word of the Shabad, he was united in the Lord's Union. |1|Pause|

Night and day, he performed devotional worship service, day and night, and through the Shabad, his duality was eradicated.
Those who are imbued with Truth are immaculate and pure; the True Lord abides within their minds. |2|

The fools in duality read, but they do not understand anything; they waste their lives uselessly.
The wicked demon slandered the Saint, and stirred up trouble. |3|

Prahlaad did not read in duality, and he did not abandon the Lord's Name; he was not afraid of any fear.
The Dear Lord became the Savior of the Saint, and the demonic Death could not even approach him. |4|

The Lord Himself saved his honor, and blessed his devotee with glorious greatness.

O Nanak, Harnaakhash was torn apart by the Lord with His claws; the blind demon knew nothing of the Lord's Court. |5|11|21|

Raag Bhairao, Fourth Mehl, Chaupadas, First House:
One Universal Creator God. By The Grace Of The True Guru:
The Lord, in His Mercy, attaches mortals to the feet of the Saints.

Section 28 - Raag Bhairao - Part 010

Through the Word of the Guru's Shabad, vibrate and meditate on the Lord; let your awareness be absorbed in Him. |1|

O my mind, vibrate and meditate on the Lord and the Name of the Lord.
The Lord, Har, Har, the Giver of Peace, grants His Grace; the Gurmukh crosses over the terrifying world-ocean through the Name of the Lord. |1|Pause|

Joining the Saadh Sangat, the Company of the Holy, sing of the Lord.
Follow the Guru's Teachings, and you shall obtain the Lord, the Source of Nectar. |2|

Bathe in the pool of ambrosial nectar, the spiritual wisdom of the Holy Guru.
All sins will be eliminated and eradicated. |3|

You Yourself are the Creator, the Support of the Universe.
Please unite servant Nanak with Yourself; he is the slave of Your slaves. |4|1|

Bhairao, Fourth Mehl:
Fruitful is that moment when the Lord's Name is spoken.
Following the Guru's Teachings, all pains are taken away. |1|

O my mind, vibrate the Name of the Lord.
O Lord, be merciful, and unite me with the Perfect Guru. Joining with the Sat Sangat, the True Congregation, I shall cross over the terrifying world-ocean. |1|Pause|

Meditate on the Life of the World; remember the Lord in your mind.
Millions upon millions of your sins shall be taken away. |2|

In the Sat Sangat, apply the dust of the feet of the holy to your face;
this is how to bathe in the sixty-eight sacred shrines, and the Ganges. |3|

I am a fool; the Lord has shown mercy to me.
The Savior Lord has saved servant Nanak. |4|2|

Bhairao, Fourth Mehl:
To do good deeds is the best rosary.
Chant on the beads within your heart, and it shall go along with you. |1|

Chant the Name of the Lord, Har, Har, the Lord of the forest.
Have mercy on me, Lord, and unite me with the Sat Sangat, the True
Congregation, so that I may be released from Maya's noose of death.
|1|Pause|

Whoever, as Gurmukh, serves and works hard,
is molded and shaped in the true mint of the Shabad, the Word of God. |2|

The Guru has revealed to me the Inaccessible and Unfathomable Lord.
Searching within the body-village, I have found the Lord. |3|

I am just a child; the Lord is my Father, who nurtures and cherishes me.
Please save servant Nanak, Lord; bless him with Your Glance of Grace.
|4|3|

Bhairao, Fourth Mehl:
All hearts are Yours, Lord; You are in all.
There is nothing at all except You. |1|

O my mind, meditate on the Lord, the Giver of peace.
I praise You, O Lord God, You are my Father. |1|Pause|

Wherever I look, I see only the Lord God.
All are under Your control; there is no other at all. |2|

O Lord, when it is Your Will to save someone,
then nothing can threaten him. |3|

You are totally pervading and permeating the waters, the lands, the skies and all places.
Servant Nanak meditates on the Ever-present Lord. |4|4|

Bhairao, Fourth Mehl, Second House:
One Universal Creator God. By The Grace Of The True Guru:
The Lord's Saint is the embodiment of the Lord; within his heart is the Name of the Lord.
One who has such destiny inscribed on his forehead, follows the Guru's Teachings, and contemplates the Name of the Lord within his heart. |1|

Section 28 - Raag Bhairao - Part 011

Enshrine Him in your heart, and meditate on the Lord.
The five plundering thieves are in the body-village; through the Word of the Guru's Shabad, the Lord has beaten them and driven them out. |1|Pause|

Those whose minds are satisfied with the Lord - the Lord Himself resolves their affairs.
Their subservience and their dependence on other people is ended; the Creator Lord is on their side. |2|

If something were beyond the realm of the Lord's Power, only then would we have recourse to consult someone else.
Whatever the Lord does is good. Meditate on the Name of the Lord, night and day. |3|

Whatever the Lord does, He does by Himself. He does not ask or consult anyone else.
O Nanak, meditate forever on God; granting His Grace, He unites us with the True Guru. |4|1|5|

Bhairao, Fourth Mehl:
O my Lord and Master, please unite me with the Holy people; meditating on You, I am saved.
Gazing upon the Blessed Vision of their Darshan, my mind blossoms forth. Each and every moment, I am a sacrifice to them. |1|

Meditate within your heart on the Name of the Lord.

Show Mercy, Mercy to me, O Father of the World, O my Lord and Master; make me the water-carrier of the slave of Your slaves. |1|Pause|

Their intellect is sublime and exalted, and so is their honor; the Lord, the Lord of the forest, abides within their hearts.
O my Lord and Master, please link me to the service of those who meditate in remembrance on You, and are saved. |2|

Those who do not find such a Holy True Guru are beaten, and driven out of the Court of the Lord.
These slanderous people have no honor or reputation; their noses are cut by the Creator Lord. |3|

The Lord Himself speaks, and the Lord Himself inspires all to speak; He is Immaculate and Formless, and needs no sustenance.
O Lord, he alone meets You, whom You cause to meet. Says servant Nanak, I am a wretched creature. What can I do? |4|2|6|

Bhairao, Fourth Mehl:
That is Your True Congregation, Lord, where the Kirtan of the Lord's Praises are heard.
The minds of those who listen to the Lord's Name are drenched with bliss; I worship their feet continually. |1|

Meditating on the Lord, the Life of the World, the mortals cross over.
Your Names are so many, they are countless, O Lord. This tongue of mine cannot even count them. |1|Pause|

O Gursikhs, chant the Lord's Name, and sing the Praises of the Lord. Take the Guru's Teachings, and meditate on the Lord.
Whoever listens to the Guru's Teachings - that humble being receives countless comforts and pleasures from the Lord. |2|

Blessed is the ancestry, blessed is the father, and blessed is that mother who gave birth to this humble servant.
Those who meditate on my Lord, Har, Har, with every breath and morsel of food - those humble servants of the Lord look beautiful in the True Court of the Lord. |3|

O Lord, Har, Har, Your Names are profound and infinite; Your devotees cherish them deep within.
Servant Nanak has obained the wisdom of the Guru's Teachings; meditating on the Lord, Har, Har, he crosses over to the other side. |4|3|7|

Section 28 - Raag Bhairao - Part 012

Bhairao, Fifth Mehl, First House:
One Universal Creator God. By The Grace Of The True Guru:
Setting aside all other days, it is said that the Lord was born on the eighth lunar day. |1|

Deluded and confused by doubt, the mortal practices falsehood.
The Lord is beyond birth and death. |1|Pause|

You prepare sweet treats and feed them to your stone god.
God is not born, and He does not die, you foolish, faithless cynic! |2|

You sing lullabyes to your stone god - this is the source of all your mistakes.
Let that mouth be burnt, which says that our Lord and Master is subject to birth. |3|

He is not born, and He does not die; He does not come and go in reincarnation.
The God of Nanak is pervading and permeating everywhere. |4|1|

Bhairao, Fifth Mehl:
Standing up, I am at peace; sitting down, I am at peace.
I feel no fear, because this is what I understand. |1|

The One Lord, my Lord and Master, is my Protector.
He is the Inner-knower, the Searcher of Hearts. |1|Pause|

I sleep without worry, and I awake without worry.
You, O God, are pervading everywhere. |2|

I dwell in peace in my home, and I am at peace outside.
Says Nanak, the Guru has implanted His Mantra within me. |3|2|

Bhairao, Fifth Mehl:

I do not keep fasts, nor do I observe the month of Ramadaan.
I serve only the One, who will protect me in the end. |1|

The One Lord, the Lord of the World, is my God Allah.
He adminsters justice to both Hindus and Muslims. |1|Pause|

I do not make pilgrimages to Mecca, nor do I worship at Hindu sacred shrines.
I serve the One Lord, and not any other. |2|

I do not perform Hindu worship services, nor do I offer the Muslim prayers.
I have taken the One Formless Lord into my heart; I humbly worship Him there. |3|

I am not a Hindu, nor am I a Muslim.
My body and breath of life belong to Allah - to Raam - the God of both. |4|

Says Kabeer, this is what I say:
meeting with the Guru, my Spiritual Teacher, I realize God, my Lord and Master. |5|3|

Bhairao, Fifth Mehl:
I easily tied up the deer - the ten sensory organs.
I shot five of the desires with the Word of the Lord's Bani. |1|

I go out hunting with the Saints,
and we capture the deer without horses or weapons. |1|Pause|

My mind used to run around outside hunting.
But now, I have found the game within the home of my body-village. |2|

I caught the deer and brought them home.
Dividing them up, I shared them, bit by bit. |3|

God has given this gift.
Nanak's home is filled with the Naam, the Name of the Lord. |4|4|

Bhairao, Fifth Mehl:
Even though he may be fed with hundreds of longings and yearnings,
still the faithless cynic does not remember the Lord, Har, Har. |1|

Take in the teachings of the humble Saints.
In the Saadh Sangat, the Company of the Holy, you shall obtain the supreme status. |1|Pause|

Stones may be kept under water for a long time.
Even so, they do not absorb the water; they remain hard and dry. |2|

Section 28 - Raag Bhairao - Part 013

The six Shaastras may be read to a fool,
but it is like the wind blowing in the ten directions. |3|

It is like threshing a crop without any corn - nothing is gained.
In the same way, no benefit comes from the faithless cynic. |4|

As the Lord attaches them, so are all attached.
Says Nanak, God has formed such a form. |5|5|

Bhairao, Fifth Mehl:
He created the soul, the breath of life and the body.
He created all beings, and knows their pains. |1|

The Guru, the Lord of the Universe, is the Helper of the soul.
Here and herafter, He always provides shade. |1|Pause|

Worship and adoration of God is the pure way of life.
In the Saadh Sangat, the Company of the Holy, the love of duality vanishes.
|2|

Friends, well-wishers and wealth will not support you.
Blessed, blessed is my Lord. |3|

Nanak utters the Ambrosial Bani of the Lord.
Except the One Lord, he does not know any other at all. |4|6|

Bhairao, Fifth Mehl:
The Lord is in front of me, and the Lord is behind me.
My Beloved Lord, the Source of Nectar, is in the middle as well. |1|

God is my Shaastra and my favorable omen.
In His Home and Mansion, I find peace, poise and bliss. |1|Pause|

Chanting the Naam, the Name of the Lord, with my tongue, and hearing it with my ears, I live.
Meditating, meditating in remembrance on God, I have become eternal, permanent and stable. |2|

The pains of countless lifetimes have been erased.
The Unstruck Sound-current of the Shabad, the Word of God, vibrates in the Court of the Lord. |3|

Granting His Grace, God has blended me with Himself.
Nanak has entered the Sanctuary of God. |4|7|

Bhairao, Fifth Mehl:
It brings millions of desires to fulfillment.
On the Path of Death, It will go with you and help you. |1|

The Naam, the Name of the Lord of the Universe, is the holy water of the Ganges.
Whoever meditates on it, is saved; drinking it in, the mortal does not wander in reincarnation again. |1|Pause|

It is my worship, meditation, austerity and cleansing bath.
Meditating in remembrance on the Naam, I have become free of desire. |2|

It is my domain and empire, wealth, mansion and court.
Meditating in remembrance on the Naam brings perfect conduct. |3|

Slave Nanak has deliberated, and has come to this conclusion:
Without the Lord's Name, everything is false and worthless, like ashes. |4|8|

Bhairao, Fifth Mehl:
The poison had absolutely no harmful effect.
But the wicked Brahmin died in pain. |1|

The Supreme Lord God Himself has saved His humble servant.

The sinner died through the Power of the Guru. |1|Pause|

The humble servant of the Lord and Master meditates on Him.
He Himself has destroyed the ignorant sinner. |2|

God is the Mother, the Father and the Protector of His slave.
The face of the slanderer, here and hereafter, is blackened. |3|

The Transcendent Lord has heard the prayer of servant Nanak.
The filthy sinner lost hope and died. |4|9|

Bhairao, Fifth Mehl:
Excellent, excellent, excellent, excellent, excellent is Your Name.
False, false, false, false is pride in the world. |1|Pause|

The glorious vision of Your slaves, O Infinite Lord, is wonderful and beauteous.

Section 28 - Raag Bhairao - Part 014

Without the Naam, the Name of the Lord, the whole world is just ashes. |1|

Your Creative Power is marvellous, and Your Lotus Feet are admirable.
Your Praise is priceless, O True King. |2|

God is the Support of the unsupported.
Meditate day and night on the Cherisher of the meek and humble. |3|

God has been merciful to Nanak.
May I never forget God; He is my heart, my soul, my breath of life. |4|10|

Bhairao, Fifth Mehl:
As Gurmukh, obtain the true wealth.
Accept the Will of God as True. |1|

Live, live, live forever.
Rise early each day, and drink in the Nectar of the Lord.
With your tongue, chant the Name of the Lord, Har, Har, Har, Har. |1|Pause|

In this Dark Age of Kali Yuga, the One Name alone shall save you.
Nanak speaks the wisdom of God. |2|11|

Bhairao, Fifth Mehl:
Serving the True Guru, all fruits and rewards are obtained.
The filth of so many lifetimes is washed away. |1|

Your Name, God, is the Purifier of sinners.
Because of the karma of my past deeds, I sing the Glorious Praises of the
Lord. |1|Pause|

In the Saadh Sangat, the Company of the Holy, I am saved.
I am blessed with honor in God's Court. |2|

Serving at God's Feet, all comforts are obtained.
All the angels and demi-gods long for the dust of the feet of such beings.
|3|

Nanak has obtained the treasure of the Naam.
Chanting and meditating on the Lord, the whole world is saved. |4|12|

Bhairao, Fifth Mehl:
God hugs His slave close in His Embrace.
He throws the slanderer into the fire. |1|

The Lord saves His servants from the sinners.
No one can save the sinner. The sinner is destroyed by his own actions.
|1|Pause|

The Lord's slave is in love with the Dear Lord.
The slanderer loves something else. |2|

The Supreme Lord God has revealed His Innate Nature.
The evil-doer obtains the fruits of his own actions. |3|

God does not come or go; He is All-pervading and permeating.
Slave Nanak seeks the Sanctuary of the Lord. |4|13|

Raag Bhairao, Fifth Mehl, Chaupadas, Second House:

One Universal Creator God. By The Grace Of The True Guru:
The Fascinating Lord, the Creator of all, the Formless Lord, is the Giver of Peace.
You have abandoned this Lord, and you serve another. Why are you intoxicated with the pleasures of corruption? |1|

O my mind, meditate on the Lord of the Universe.
I have seen all other sorts of efforts; whatever you can think of, will only bring failure. |1|Pause|

The blind, ignorant, self-willed manmukhs forsake their Lord and Master, and dwell on His slave Maya.
They slander those who worship their Lord; they are like beasts, without a Guru. |2|

Soul, life, body and wealth all belong to God, but the faithless cynics claim that they own them.

Section 28 - Raag Bhairao - Part 015

They are proud and arrogant, evil-minded and filthy; without the Guru, they are reincarnated into the terrifying world-ocean. |3|

Through burnt offerings, charitable feasts, ritualistic chants, penance, all sorts of austere self-discipline and pilgrimages to sacred shrines and rivers, they do not find God.
Self-conceit is only erased when one seeks the Lord's Sanctuary and becomes Gurmukh; O Nanak, he crosses over the world-ocean. |4|1|14|

Bhairao, Fifth Mehl:
I have seen Him in the woods, and I have seen Him in the fields. I have seen Him in the household, and in renunciation.
I have seen Him as a Yogi carrying His staff, as a Yogi with matted hair, fasting, making vows, and visiting sacred shrines of pilgrimage. |1|

I have seen Him in the Society of the Saints, and within my own mind.
In the sky, in the nether regions of the underworld, and in everything, He is pervading and permeating. With love and joy, I sing His Glorious Praises. |1|Pause|

I have seen Him among the Yogis, the Sannyaasees, the celibates, the wandering hermits and the wearers of patched coats.

I have seen Him among the men of severe self-discipline, the silent sages, the actors, dramas and dances. |2|

I have seen Him in the four Vedas, I have seen Him in the six Shaastras, in the eighteen Puraanas and the Simritees as well.

All together, they declare that there is only the One Lord. So tell me, from whom is He hidden? |3|

Unfathomable and Inaccessible, He is our Infinite Lord and Master; His Value is beyond valuation.

Servant Nanak is a sacrifice, a sacrifice to those, within whose heart He is revealed. |4|2|15|

Bhairao, Fifth Mehl:
How can anyone do evil, if he realizes that the Lord is near?
One who gathers corruption, constantly feels fear.
He is near, but this mystery is not understood.
Without the True Guru, all are enticed by Maya. |1|

Everyone says that He is near, near at hand.
But rare is that person, who, as Gurmukh, understands this mystery. |1|Pause|

The mortal does not see the Lord near at hand; instead, he goes to the homes of others.
He steals their wealth and lives in falsehood.
Under the influence of the drug of illusion, he does not know that the Lord is with him.
Without the Guru, he is confused and deluded by doubt. |2|

Not understanding that the Lord is near, he tells lies.
In love and attachment to Maya, the fool is plundered.
That which he seeks is within his own self, but he looks for it outside.
Without the Guru, he is confused and deluded by doubt. |3|

One whose good karma is recorded on his forehead
serves the True Guru; thus the hard and heavy shutters of his mind are opened wide.

Within his own being and beyond, he sees the Lord near at hand.
O servant Nanak, he does not come and go in reincarnation. |4|3|16|

Bhairao, Fifth Mehl:
Who can kill that person whom You protect, O Lord?
All beings, and the entire universe, is within You.
The mortal thinks up millions of plans,
but that alone happens, which the Lord of wondrous plays does. |1|

Save me, save me, O Lord; shower me with Your Mercy.
I seek Your Sanctuary, and Your Court. |1|Pause|

Whoever serves the Fearless Lord, the Giver of Peace,
is rid of all his fears; he knows the One Lord.
Whatever You do, that alone comes to pass in the end.
There is no other who can kill or protect us. |2|

What do you think, with your human understanding?
The All-knowing Lord is the Searcher of Hearts.
The One and only Lord is my Support and Protection.
The Creator Lord knows everything. |3|

That person who is blessed by the Creator's Glance of Grace

Section 28 - Raag Bhairao - Part 016

- all his affairs are resolved.
The One Lord is his Protector.
O servant Nanak, no one can equal him. |4|4|17|

Bhairao, Fifth Mehl:
We should feel sad, if God were beyond us.
We should feel sad, if we forget the Lord.
We should feel sad, if we are in love with duality.
But why should we feel sad? The Lord is pervading everywhere. |1|

In love and attachment to Maya, the mortals are sad, and are consumed by sadness.
Without the Name, they wander and wander and wander, and waste away. |1|Pause|

We should feel sad, if there were another Creator Lord.
We should feel sad, if someone dies by injustice.
We should feel sad, if something were not known to the Lord.
But why should we feel sad? The Lord is totally permeating everywhere.
|2|

We should feel sad, if God were a tyrant.
We should feel sad, if He made us suffer by mistake.
The Guru says that whatever happens is all by God's Will.
So I have abandoned sadness, and I now sleep without anxiety. |3|

O God, You alone are my Lord and Master; all belong to You.
According to Your Will, You pass judgement.
There is no other at all; the One Lord is permeating and pervading everywhere.
Please save Nanak's honor; I have come to Your Sanctuary. |4|5|18|

Bhairao, Fifth Mehl:
Without music, how is one to dance?
Without a voice, how is one to sing?
Without strings, how is a guitar to be played?
Without the Naam, all affairs are useless. |1|

Without the Naam - tell me: who has ever been saved?
Without the True Guru, how can anyone cross over to the other side?
|1|Pause|

Without a tongue, how can anyone speak?
Without ears, how can anyone hear?
Without eyes, how can anyone see?
Without the Naam, the mortal is of no account at all. |2|

Without learning, how can one be a Pandit - a religious scholar?
Without power, what is the glory of an empire?
Without understanding, how can the mind become steady?
Without the Naam, the whole world is insane. |3|

Without detachment, how can one be a detached hermit?
Without renouncing egotism, how can anyone be a renunciate?

Without overcoming the five thieves, how can the mind be subdued?
Without the Naam, the mortal regrets and repents forever and ever. |4|

Without the Guru's Teachings, how can anyone obtain spiritual wisdom?
Without seeing - tell me: how can anyone visualize in meditation?
Without the Fear of God, all speech in useless.
Says Nanak, this is the wisdom of the Lord's Court. |5|6|19|

Bhairao, Fifth Mehl:
Mankind is afflicted with the disease of egotism.
The disease of sexual desire overwhelms the elephant.
Because of the disease of vision, the moth is burnt to death.
Because of the disease of the sound of the bell, the deer is lured to its death. |1|

Whoever I see is diseased.
Only my True Guru, the True Yogi, is free of disease. |1|Pause|

Because of the disease of taste, the fish is caught.
Because of the disease of smell, the bumble bee is destroyed.
The whole world is caught in the disease of attachment.
In the disease of the three qualities, corruption is multiplied. |2|

In disease the mortals die, and in disease they are born.
In disease they wander in reincarnation again and again.

Section 28 - Raag Bhairao - Part 017

Entangled in disease, they cannot stay still, even for an instant.
Without the True Guru, the disease is never cured. |3|

When the Supreme Lord God grants His Mercy,
He grabs hold of the mortal's arm, and pulls him up and out of the disease.
Reaching the Saadh Sangat, the Company of the Holy, the mortal's bonds are broken.
Says Nanak, the Guru cures him of the disease. |4|7|20|

Bhairao, Fifth Mehl:
When He comes to mind, then I am in supreme bliss.
When He comes to mind, then all my pains are shattered.

When He comes to mind, my hopes are fulfilled.
When He comes to mind, I never feel sadness. |1|

Deep within my being, my Sovereign Lord King has revealed Himself to me.
The Perfect Guru has inspired me to love Him. |1|Pause|

When He comes to mind, I am the king of all.
When He comes to mind, all my affairs are completed.
When He comes to mind, I am dyed in the deep crimson of His Love.
When He comes to mind, I am ecstatic forever. |2|

When He comes to mind, I am wealthy forever.
When He comes to mind, I am free of doubt forever.
When He comes to mind, then I enjoy all pleasures.
When He comes to mind, I am rid of fear. |3|

When He comes to mind, I find the home of peace and poise.
When He comes to mind, I am absorbed in the Primal Void of God.
When He comes to mind, I continually sing the Kirtan of His Praises.
Nanak's mind is pleased and satisfied with the Lord God. |4|8|21|

Bhairao, Fifth Mehl:
My Father is Eternal, forever alive.
My brothers live forever as well.
My friends are permanent and imperishable.
My family abides in the home of the self within. |1|

I have found peace, and so all are at peace.
The Perfect Guru has united me with my Father. |1|Pause|

My mansions are the highest of all.
My countries are infinite and uncountable.
My kingdom is eternally stable.
My wealth is inexhaustible and permanent. |2|

My glorious reputation resounds throughout the ages.
My fame has spread in all places and interspaces.
My praises echo in each and every house.
My devotional worship is known to all people. |3|

My Father has revealed Himself within me.
The Father and son have joined together in partnership.
Says Nanak, when my Father is pleased,
then the Father and son are joined together in love, and become one. |4|9|22|

Bhairao, Fifth Mehl:
The True Guru, the Primal Being, is free of revenge and hate; He is God, the Great Giver.
I am a sinner; You are my Forgiver.
That sinner, who finds no protection anywhere
- if he comes seeking Your Sanctuary, then he becomes immaculate and pure. |1|

Pleasing the True Guru, I have found peace.
Meditating on the Guru, I have obtained all fruits and rewards. |1|Pause|

I humbly bow to the Supreme Lord God, the True Guru.
My mind and body are Yours; all the world is Yours.
When the veil of illusion is removed, then I come to see You.
You are my Lord and Master; You are the King of all. |2|

When it pleases Him, even dry wood becomes green.
When it pleases Him, rivers flow across the desert sands.
When it pleases Him, all fruits and rewards are obtained.
Grasping hold of the Guru's feet, my anxiety is dispelled. |3|

Section 28 - Raag Bhairao - Part 018

I am unworthy and ungrateful, but He has been merciful to me.
My mind and body have been cooled and soothed; the Ambrosial Nectar rains down in my mind.
The Supreme Lord God, the Guru, has become kind and compassionate to me.
Slave Nanak beholds the Lord, enraptured. |4|10|23|

Bhairao, Fifth Mehl:
My True Guru is totally independent.
My True Guru is adorned with Truth.
My True Guru is the Giver of all.

My True Guru is the Primal Creator Lord, the Architect of Destiny. |1|

There is no deity equal to the Guru.
Whoever has good destiny inscribed on his forehead, applies himself to seva - selfless service. |1|Pause|

My True Guru is the Sustainer and Cherisher of all.
My True Guru kills and revives.
The glorious greatness of my True Guru has become manifest everywhere. |2|

My True Guru is the power of the powerless.
My True Guru is my home and court.
I am forever a sacrifice to the True Guru.
He has shown me the path. |3|

One who serves the Guru is not afflicted with fear.
One who serves the Guru does not suffer in pain.
Nanak has studied the Simritees and the Vedas.
There is no difference between the Supreme Lord God and the Guru. |4|11|24|

Bhairao, Fifth Mehl:
Repeating the Naam, the Name of the Lord, the mortal is exalted and glorified.
Repeating the Naam, sin is banished from the body.
Repeating the Naam, all festivals are celebrated.
Repeating the Naam, one is cleansed at the sixty-eight sacred shrines. |1|

My sacred shrine of pilgrimage is the Name of the Lord.
The Guru has instructed me in the true essence of spiritual wisdom. |1|Pause|

Repeating the Naam, the mortal's pains are taken away.
Repeating the Naam, the most ignorant people become spiritual teachers.
Repeating the Naam, the Divine Light blazes forth.
Repeating the Naam, one's bonds are broken. |2|

Repeating the Naam, the Messenger of Death does not draw near.
Repeating the Naam, one finds peace in the Court of the Lord.

Repeating the Naam, God gives His Approval.
The Naam is my true wealth. |3|

The Guru has instructed me in these sublime teachings.
The Kirtan of the Lord's Praises and the Naam are the Support of the mind.
Nanak is saved through the atonement of the Naam.
Other actions are just to please and appease the people. |4|12|25|

Bhairao, Fifth Mehl:
I bow in humble worship, tens of thousands of times.
I offer this mind as a sacrifice.
Meditating in remembrance on Him, sufferings are erased.
Bliss wells up, and no disease is contracted. |1|

Such is the diamond, the Immaculate Naam, the Name of the Lord.
Chanting it, all works are perfectly completed. |1|Pause|

Beholding Him, the house of pain is demolished.
The mind seizes the cooling, soothing, Ambrosial Nectar of the Naam.
Millions of devotees worship His Feet.
He is the Fulfiller of all the mind's desires. |2|

In an instant, He fills the empty to over-flowing.
In an instant, He transforms the dry into green.
In an instant, He gives the homeless a home.
In an instant, He bestows honor on the dishonored. |3|

Section 28 - Raag Bhairao - Part 019

The One Lord is totally pervading and permeating all.
He alone meditates on the Lord, whose True Guru is Perfect.
Such a person has the Kirtan of the Lord's Praises for his Support.
Says Nanak, the Lord Himself is merciful to him. |4|13|26|

Bhairao, Fifth Mehl:
I was discarded and abandoned, but He has embellished me.
He has blessed me with beauty and His Love; through His Name, I am exalted.
All my pains and sorrows have been eradicated.
The Guru has become my Mother and Father. |1|

O my friends and companions, my household is in bliss.
Granting His Grace, my Husband Lord has met me. |1|Pause|

The fire of desire has been extinguished, and all my desires have been fulfilled.
The darkness has been dispelled, and the Divine Light blazes forth.
The Unstruck Sound-current of the Shabad, the Word of God, is wondrous and amazing!
Perfect is the Grace of the Perfect Guru. |2|

That person, unto whom the Lord reveals Himself
- by the Blessed Vision of his Darshan, I am forever enraptured.
He obtains all virtues and so many treasures.
The True Guru blesses him with the Naam, the Name of the Lord. |3|

That person who meets with his Lord and Master
- his mind and body are cooled and soothed, chanting the Name of the Lord, Har, Har.
Says Nanak, such a humble being is pleasing to God;
only a rare few are blessed with the dust of his feet. |4|14|27|

Bhairao, Fifth Mehl:
The mortal does not hesitate to think about sin.
He is not ashamed to spend time with prostitutes.
He works all day long,
but when it is time to remember the Lord, then a heavy stone falls on his head. |1|

Attached to Maya, the world is deluded and confused.
The Deluder Himself has deluded the mortal, and now he is engrossed in worthless worldly affairs. |1|Pause|

Gazing on Maya's illusion, its pleasures pass away.
He loves the shell, and ruins his life.
Bound to blind worldly affairs, his mind wavers and wanders.
The Creator Lord does not come into his mind. |2|

Working and working like this, he only obtains pain,
and his affairs of Maya are never completed.

His mind is saturated with sexual desire, anger and greed.
Wiggling like a fish out of water, he dies. |3|

One who has the Lord Himself as his Protector,
chants and meditates forever on the Name of the Lord, Har, Har.
In the Saadh Sangat, the Company of the Holy, he chants the Glorious
Praises of the Lord.
O Nanak, he has found the Perfect True Guru. |4|15|28|

Bhairao, Fifth Mehl:
He alone obtains it, unto whom the Lord shows Mercy.
He enshrines the Name of the Lord in his mind.
With the True Word of the Shabad in his heart and mind,
the sins of countless incarnations vanish. |1|

The Lord's Name is the Support of the soul.
By Guru's Grace, chant the Name continually, O Siblings of Destiny; It shall
carry you across the world-ocean. |1|Pause|

Those who have this treasure of the Lord's Name written in their destiny,
those humble beings are honored in the Court of the Lord.
Singing His Glorious Praises with peace, poise and bliss,
even the homeless obtain a home hereafter. |2|

Throughout the ages, this has been the essence of reality.
Meditate in remembrance on the Lord, and contemplate the Truth.

Section 28 - Raag Bhairao - Part 020

He alone is attached to the hem of the Lord's robe, whom the Lord Himself
attaches.
Asleep for countless incarnations, he now awakens. |3|

Your devotees belong to You, and You belong to Your devotees.
You Yourself inspire them to chant Your Praises.
All beings and creatures are in Your Hands.
Nanak's God is always with him. |4|16|29|

Bhairao, Fifth Mehl:
The Naam, the Name of the Lord, is the Inner-knower of my heart.

The Naam is so useful to me.
The Lord's Name permeates each and every hair of mine.
The Perfect True Guru has given me this gift. |1|

The Jewel of the Naam is my treasure.
It is inaccessible, priceless, infinite and incomparable. |1|Pause|

The Naam is my unmoving, unchanging Lord and Master.
The glory of the Naam spreads over the whole world.
The Naam is my perfect master of wealth.
The Naam is my independence. |2|

The Naam is my food and love.
The Naam is the objective of my mind.
By the Grace of the Saints, I never forget the Naam.
Repeating the Naam, the Unstruck Sound-current of the Naad resounds.
|3|

By God's Grace, I have obtained the nine treasures of the Naam.
By Guru's Grace, I am tuned in to the Naam.
They alone are wealthy and supreme,
O Nanak, who have the treasure of the Naam. |4|17|30|

Bhairao, Fifth Mehl:
You are my Father, and You are my Mother.
You are my Soul, my Breath of Life, the Giver of Peace.
You are my Lord and Master; I am Your slave.
Without You, I have no one at all. |1|

Please bless me with Your Mercy, God, and give me this gift,
that I may sing Your Praises, day and night. |1|Pause|

I am Your musical instrument, and You are the Musician.
I am Your beggar; please bless me with Your charity, O Great Giver.
By Your Grace, I enjoy love and pleasures.
You are deep within each and every heart. |2|

By Your Grace, I chant the Name.
In the Saadh Sangat, the Company of the Holy, I sing Your Glorious Praises.
In Your Mercy, You take away our pains.

By Your Mercy, the heart-lotus blossoms forth. |3|

I am a sacrifice to the Divine Guru.
The Blessed Vision of His Darshan is fruitful and rewarding; His service is immaculate and pure.
Be Merciful to me, O my Lord God and Master,
that Nanak may continually sing Your Glorious Praises. |4|18|31|

Bhairao, Fifth Mehl:
His Regal Court is the highest of all.
I humbly bow to Him, forever and ever.
His place is the highest of the high.
Millions of sins are erased by the Name of the Lord. |1|

In His Sanctuary, we find eternal peace.
He Mercifully unites us with Himself. |1|Pause|

His wondrous actions cannot even be described.
All hearts rest their faith and hope in Him.
He is manifest in the Saadh Sangat, the Company of the Holy.
The devotees lovingly worship and adore Him night and day. |2|

He gives, but His treasures are never exhausted.
In an instant, He establishes and disestablishes.
No one can erase the Hukam of His Command.
The True Lord is above the heads of kings. |3|

He is my Anchor and Support; I place my hopes in Him.

Section 28 - Raag Bhairao - Part 021

I place my pain and pleasure before Him.
He covers the faults of His humble servant.
Nanak sings His Praises. |4|19|32|

Bhairao, Fifth Mehl:
The whiner whines every day.
His attachment to his household and entanglements cloud his mind.
If someone becomes detached through understanding,
he will not have to suffer in birth and death again. |1|

All of his conflicts are extensions of his corruption.
How rare is that person who takes the Naam as his Support. |1|Pause|

The three-phased Maya infects all.
Whoever clings to it suffers pain and sorrow.
There is no peace without meditating on the Naam, the Name of the Lord.
By great good fortune, the treasure of the Naam is received. |2|

One who loves the actor in his mind,
later regrets it when the actor takes off his costume.
The shade from a cloud is transitory,
like the worldly paraphernalia of attachment and corruption. |3|

If someone is blessed with the singular substance,
then all of his tasks are accomplished to perfection.
One who obtains the Naam, by Guru's Grace
- O Nanak, his coming into the world is certified and approved. |4|20|33|

Bhairao, Fifth Mehl:
Slandering the Saints, the mortal wanders in reincarnation.
Slandering the Saints, he is diseased.
Slandering the Saints, he suffers in pain.
The slanderer is punished by the Messenger of Death. |1|

Those who argue and fight with the Saints
- those slanderers find no happiness at all. |1|Pause|

Slandering the devotees, the wall of the mortal's body is shattered.
Slandering the devotees, he suffers in hell.
Slandering the devotees, he rots in the womb.
Slandering the devotees, he loses his realm and power. |2|

The slanderer finds no salvation at all.
He eats only that which he himself has planted.
He is worse than a thief, a lecher, or a gambler.
The slanderer places an unbearable burden upon his head. |3|

The devotees of the Supreme Lord God are beyond hate and vengeance.
Whoever worships their feet is emancipated.

The Primal Lord God has deluded and confused the slanderer.
O Nanak, the record of one's past actions cannot be erased. |4|21|34|

Bhairao, Fifth Mehl:
The Naam, the Name of the Lord, is for me the Vedas and the Sound-current of the Naad.
Through the Naam, my tasks are perfectly accomplished.
The Naam is my worship of deities.
The Naam is my service to the Guru. |1|

The Perfect Guru has implanted the Naam within me.
The highest task of all is the Name of the Lord, Har, Har. |1|Pause|

The Naam is my cleansing bath and purification.
The Naam is my perfect donation of charity.
Those who repeat the Naam are totally purified.
Those who chant the Naam are my friends and Siblings of Destiny. |2|

The Naam is my auspicious omen and good fortune.
The Naam is the sublime food which satisfies me.
The Naam is my good conduct.
The Naam is my immaculate occupation. |3|

All those humble beings whose minds are filled with the One God
have the Support of the Lord, Har, Har.
O Nanak, sing the Glorious Praises of the Lord with your mind and body.
In the Saadh Sangat, the Company of the Holy, the Lord bestows His Name.
|4|22|35|

Section 28 - Raag Bhairao - Part 022

Bhairao, Fifth Mehl:
You bless the poor with wealth, O Lord.
Countless sins are taken away, and the mind becomes immaculate and pure.
All the mind's desires are fulfilled, and one's tasks are perfectly accomplished.
You bestow Your Name upon Your devotee. |1|

Service to the Lord, our Sovereign King, is fruitful and rewarding.

Our Lord and Master is the Creator, the Cause of causes; no one is turned away from His Door empty-handed. |1|Pause|

God eradicates the disease from the diseased person.
God takes away the sorrows of the suffering.
And those who have no place at all - You seat them upon the place.
You link Your slave to devotional worship. |2|

God bestows honor on the dishonored.
He makes the foolish and ignorant become clever and wise.
The fear of all fear disappears.
The Lord dwells within the mind of His humble servant. |3|

The Supreme Lord God is the Treasure of Peace.
The Ambrosial Name of the Lord is the essence of reality.
Granting His Grace, He enjoins the mortals to serve the Saints.
O Nanak, such a person merges in the Saadh Sangat, the Company of the Holy. |4|23|36|

Bhairao, Fifth Mehl:
In the Realm of the Saints, the Lord dwells in the mind.
In the Realm of the Saints, all sins run away.
In the Realm of the Saints, one's lifestyle is immaculate.
In the Society of the Saints, one comes to love the One Lord. |1|

That alone is called the Realm of the Saints,
where only the Glorious Praises of the Supreme Lord God are sung. |1|Pause|

In the Realm of the Saints, birth and death are ended.
In the Realm of the Saints, the Messenger of Death cannot touch the mortal.
In the Society of the Saints, one's speech becomes immaculate
In the realm of the saints, the Lord's Name is chanted. |2|

The Realm of the Saints is the eternal, ever-stable place.
In the Realm of the Saints, sins are destroyed.
In the Realm of the Saints, the immaculate sermon is spoken.
In the Society of the Saints, the pain of egotism runs away. |3|

The Realm of the Saints cannot be destroyed.
In the Realm of the Saints, is the Lord, the Treasure of Virtue.
The Realm of the Saints is the resting place of our Lord and Master.
O Nanak, He is woven into the fabric of His devotees, through and through.
|4|24|37|

Bhairao, Fifth Mehl:
Why worry about disease, when the Lord Himself protects us?
That person whom the Lord protects, does not suffer pain and sorrow.
That person, upon whom God showers His Mercy
- Death hovering above him is turned away. |1|

The Name of the Lord, Har, Har, is forever our Help and Support.
When He comes to mind, the mortal finds lasting peace, and the Messenger of Death cannot even approach him. |1|Pause|

When this being did not exist, who created him then?
What has been produced from the source?
He Himself kills, and He Himself rejuvenates.
He cherishes His devotees forever. |2|

Know that everything is in His Hands.
My God is the Master of the masterless.
His Name is the Destroyer of pain.
Singing His Glorious Praises, you shall find peace. |3|

O my Lord and Master, please listen to the prayer of Your Saint.
I place my soul, my breath of life and wealth before You.
All this world is Yours; it meditates on You.

Section 28 - Raag Bhairao - Part 023

Please shower Nanak with Your Mercy and bless him with peace.
|4|25|38|

Bhairao, Fifth Mehl:
With Your Support, I survive in the Dark Age of Kali Yuga.
With Your Support, I sing Your Glorious Praises.
With Your Support, death cannot even touch me.
With Your Support, my entanglements vanish. |1|

In this world and the next, I have Your Support.
The One Lord, our Lord and Master, is all-pervading. |1|Pause|

With Your Support, I celebrate blissfully.
With Your Support, I chant the Guru's Mantra.
With Your Support, I cross over the terrifying world-ocean.
The Perfect Lord, our Protector and Savior, is the Ocean of Peace. |2|

With Your Support, I have no fear.
The True Lord is the Inner-knower, the Searcher of hearts.
With Your Support, my mind is filled with Your Power.
Here and there, You are my Court of Appeal. |3|

I take Your Support, and place my faith in You.
All meditate on God, the Treasure of Virtue.
Chanting and meditating on You, Your slaves celebrate in bliss.
Nanak meditates in remembrance on the True Lord, the Treasure of Virtue.
|4|26|39|

Bhairao, Fifth Mehl:
First, I gave up slandering others.
All the anxiety of my mind was dispelled.
Greed and attachment were totally banished.
I see God ever-present, close at hand; I have become a great devotee. |1|

Such a renunciate is very rare.
Such a humble servant chants the Name of the Lord, Har, Har. |1|Pause|

I have forsaken my egotistical intellect.
The love of sexual desire and anger has vanished.
I meditate on the Naam, the Name of the Lord, Har, Har.
In the Company of the Holy, I am emancipated. |2|

Enemy and friend are all the same to me.
The Perfect Lord God is permeating all.
Accepting the Will of God, I have found peace.
The Perfect Guru has implanted the Name of the Lord within me. |3|

That person, whom the Lord, in His Mercy, saves

- that devotee chants and meditates on the Naam.
That person, whose mind is illumined, and who obtains understanding through the Guru
- says Nanak, he is totally fulfilled. |4|27|40|

Bhairao, Fifth Mehl:
There is no peace in earning lots of money.
There is no peace in watching dances and plays.
There is no peace in conquering lots of countries.
All peace comes from singing the Glorious Praises of the Lord, Har, Har. |1|

You shall obtain peace, poise and bliss,
when you find the Saadh Sangat, the Company of the Holy, by great good fortune. As Gurmukh, utter the Name of the Lord, Har, Har. |1|Pause|

Mother, father, children and spouse - all place the mortal in bondage.
Religious rituals and actions done in ego place the mortal in bondage.
If the Lord, the Shatterer of bonds, abides in the mind,
then peace is obtained, dwelling in the home of the self deep within. |2|

Everyone is a beggar; God is the Great Giver.
The Treasure of Virtue is the Infinite, Endless Lord.
That person, unto whom God grants His Mercy
- that humble being chants the Name of the Lord, Har, Har. |3|

I offer my prayer to my Guru.
O Primal Lord God, Treasure of Virtue, please bless me with Your Grace.
Says Nanak, I have come to Your Sanctuary.
If it pleases You, please protect me, O Lord of the World. |4|28|41|

Bhairao, Fifth Mehl:
Meeting with the Guru, I have forsaken the love of duality.

Section 28 - Raag Bhairao - Part 024

As Gurmukh, I chant the Name of the Lord.
My anxiety is gone, and I am in love with the Naam, the Name of the Lord.
I was asleep for countless lifetimes, but I have now awakened. |1|

Granting His Grace, He has linked me to His service.

In the Saadh Sangat, the Company of the Holy, all pleasures are found.
|1|Pause|

The Word of the Guru's Shabad has eradicated disease and evil.
My mind has absorbed the medicine of the Naam.
Meeting with the Guru, my mind is in bliss.
All treasures are in the Name of the Lord God. |2|

My fear of birth and death and the Messenger of Death has been dispelled.
In the Saadh Sangat, the inverted lotus of my heart has blossomed forth.
Singing the Glorious Praises of the Lord, I have found eternal, abiding peace.
All my tasks are perfectly accomplished. |3|

This human body, so difficult to obtain, is approved by the Lord.
Chanting the Name of the Lord, Har, Har, it has become fruitful.
Says Nanak, God has blessed me with His Mercy.
With every breath and morsel of food, I meditate on the Lord, Har, Har.
|4|29|42|

Bhairao, Fifth Mehl:
His Name is the Highest of all.
Sing His Glorious Praises, forever and ever.
Meditating in remembrance on Him, all pain is dispelled.
All pleasures come to dwell in the mind. |1|

O my mind, meditate in remembrance on the True Lord.
In this world and the next, you shall be saved. |1|Pause|

The Immaculate Lord God is the Creator of all.
He gives sustenance to all beings and creatures.
He forgives millions of sins and mistakes in an instant.
Through loving devotional worship, one is emancipated forever. |2|

True wealth and true glorious greatness,
and eternal, unchanging wisdom, are obtained from the Perfect Guru.
When the Protector, the Savior Lord, bestows His Mercy,
all spiritual darkness is dispelled. |3|

I focus my meditation on the Supreme Lord God.

The Lord of Nirvaanaa is totally pervading and permeating all.
Eradicating doubt and fear, I have met the Lord of the World.
The Guru has become merciful to Nanak. |4|30|43|

Bhairao, Fifth Mehl:
Meditating in remembrance on Him, the mind is illumined.
Suffering is eradicated, and one comes to dwell in peace and poise.
They alone receive it, unto whom God gives it.
They are blessed to serve the Perfect Guru. |1|

All peace and comfort are in Your Name, God.
Twenty-four hours a day, O my mind, sing His Glorious Praises. |1|Pause|

You shall receive the fruits of your desires,
when the Name of the Lord comes to dwell in the mind.
Meditating on the Lord, your comings and goings cease.
Through loving devotional worship, lovingly focus your attention on God.
|2|

Sexual desire, anger and egotism are dispelled.
Love and attachment to Maya are broken.
Lean on God's Support, day and night.
The Supreme Lord God has given this gift. |3|

Our Lord and Master is the Creator, the Cause of causes.
He is the Inner-knower, the Searcher of all hearts.
Bless me with Your Grace, Lord, and link me to Your service.
Slave Nanak has come to Your Sanctuary. |4|31|44|

Bhairao, Fifth Mehl:
One who does not repeat the Naam, the Name of the Lord, shall die of shame.
Without the Name, how can he ever sleep in peace?
The mortal abandons meditative remembrance of the Lord, and then wishes for the state of supreme salvation;

Section 28 - Raag Bhairao - Part 025

but without roots, how can there be any branches? |1|

O my mind, meditate on the Guru, the Lord of the Universe.
The filth of countless incarnations shall be washed away. Breaking your
bonds, you shall be united with the Lord. |1|Pause|

How can a stone be purified by bathing at a sacred shrine of pilgrimage?
The filth of egotism clings to the mind.
Millions of rituals and actions taken are the root of entanglements.
Without meditating and vibrating on the Lord, the mortal gathers only
worthless bundles of straw. |2|

Without eating, hunger is not satisfied.
When the disease is cured, then the pain goes away.
The mortal is engrossed in sexual desire, anger, greed and attachment.
He does not meditate on God, that God who created him. |3|

Blessed, blessed is the Holy Saint, and blessed is the Name of the Lord.
Twenty-four hours a day, sing the Kirtan, the Glorious Praises of the Lord.
Blessed is the devotee of the Lord, and blessed is the Creator Lord.
Nanak seeks the Sanctuary of God, the Primal, the Infinite. |4|32|45|

Bhairao, Fifth Mehl:
When the Guru was totally pleased, my fear was taken away.
I enshrine the Name of the Immaculate Lord within my mind.
He is Merciful to the meek, forever Compassionate.
All my entanglements are finished. |1|

I have found peace, poise, and myriads of pleasures.
In the Saadh Sangat, the Company of the Holy, fear and doubt are
dispelled. My tongue chants the Ambrosial Name of the Lord, Har, Har.
|1|Pause|

I have fallen in love with the Lord's Lotus Feet.
In an instant, the terrible demons are destroyed.
Twenty-four hours a day, I meditate and chant the Name of the Lord, Har,
Har.
The Guru is Himself the Savior Lord, the Lord of the Universe. |2|

He Himself cherishes His servant forever.
He watches over every breath of His humble devotee.
Tell me, what is the nature of human beings?

The Lord extends His Hand, and saves them from the Messenger of Death. |3|

Immaculate is the Glory, and Immaculate is the way of life,
of those who remember the Supreme Lord God in their minds.
The Guru, in His Mercy, has granted this Gift.
Nanak has obtained the treasure of the Naam, the Name of the Lord. |4|33|46|

Bhairao, Fifth Mehl:
My Guru is the All-powerful Lord, the Creator, the Cause of causes.
He is the Soul, the Breath of Life, the Giver of Peace, always near.
He is the Destroyer of fear, the Eternal, Unchanging, Sovereign Lord King.
Gazing upon the Blessed Vision of His Darshan, all fear is dispelled. |1|

Wherever I look, is the Protection of Your Sanctuary.
I am a sacrifice, a sacrifice to the Feet of the True Guru. |1|Pause|

My tasks are perfectly accomplished, meeting the Divine Guru.
He is the Giver of all rewards. Serving Him, I am immaculate.
He reaches out with His Hand to His slaves.
The Name of the Lord abides in their hearts. |2|

They are forever in bliss, and do not suffer at all.
No pain, sorrow or disease afflicts them.
Everything is Yours, O Creator Lord.
The Guru is the Supreme Lord God, the Inaccessible and Infinite. |3|

His Glorious Grandeur is immaculate, and the Bani of His Word is wonder-ful!
The Perfect Supreme Lord God is pleasing to my mind.
He is permeating the waters, the lands and the skies.
O Nanak, everything comes from God. |4|34|47|

Bhairao, Fifth Mehl:
My mind and body are imbued with the Love of the Lord's Feet.

Section 28 - Raag Bhairao - Part 026

All the desires of my mind have been perfectly fulfilled.

Twenty-four hours a day, I sing of the Lord God.
The True Guru has imparted this perfect wisdom. |1|

Very fortunate are those who love the Naam, the Name of the Lord.
Associating with them, we cross over the world-ocean. |1|Pause|

They are spiritual teachers, who meditate in remembrance on the One
Lord.
Wealthy are those who have a discriminating intellect.
Noble are those who remember their Lord and Master in meditation.
Honorable are those who understand their own selves. |2|

By Guru's Grace, I have obtained the supreme status.
Day and night I meditate on the Glories of God.
My bonds are broken, and my hopes are fulfilled.
The Feet of the Lord now abide in my heart. |3|

Says Nanak, one whose karma is perfect
- that humble being enters the Sanctuary of God.
He himself is pure, and he sanctifies all.
His tongue chants the Name of the Lord, the Source of Nectar. |4|35|48|

Bhairao, Fifth Mehl:
Repeating the Naam, the Name of the Lord, no obstacles block the way.
Listening to the Naam, the Messenger of Death runs far away.
Repeating the Naam, all pains vanish.
Chanting the Naam, the Lord's Lotus Feet dwell within. |1|

Meditating, vibrating the Name of the Lord, Har, Har, is unobstructed
devotional worship.
Sing the Glorious Praises of the Lord with loving affection and energy.
|1|Pause|

Meditating in remembrance on the Lord, the Eye of Death cannot see you.
Meditating in remembrance on the Lord, demons and ghosts shall not
touch you.
Meditating in remembrance on the Lord, attachment and pride shall not
bind you.
Meditating in remembrance on the Lord, you shall not be consigned to the
womb of reincarnation. |2|

Any time is a good time to meditate in remembrance on the Lord.
Among the masses, only a few meditate in remembrance on the Lord.
Social class or no social class, anyone may meditate on the Lord.
Whoever meditates on Him is emancipated. |3|

Chant the Name of the Lord in the Saadh Sangat, the Company of the Holy.
Perfect is the Love of the Lord's Name.
O God, shower Your Mercy on Nanak,
that he may think of you with each and every breath. |4|36|49|

Bhairao, Fifth Mehl:
He Himself is the Shaastras, and He Himself is the Vedas.
He knows the secrets of each and every heart.
He is the Embodiment of Light; all beings belong to Him.
The Creator, the Cause of causes, the Perfect All-powerful Lord. |1|

Grab hold of the Support of God, O my mind.
As Gurmukh, worship and adore His Lotus Feet; enemies and pains shall
not even approach you. |1|Pause|

He Himself is the Essence of the forests and fields, and all the three worlds.
The universe is strung on His Thread.
He is the Uniter of Shiva and Shakti - mind and matter.
He Himself is in the detachment of Nirvaanaa, and He Himself is the
Enjoyer. |2|

Wherever I look, there He is.
Without Him, there is no one at all.
In the Love of the Naam, the world-ocean is crossed.
Nanak sings His Glorious Praises in the Saadh Sangat, the Company of the
Holy. |3|

Liberation, the ways and means of enjoyment and union are under His
Control.
His humble servant lacks nothing.
That person, with whom the Lord, in His Mercy, is pleased
- O slave Nanak, that humble servant is blessed. |4|37|50|

Bhairao, Fifth Mehl:

The minds of the Lord's devotee are filled with bliss.
They become stable and permanent, and all their anxiety is gone.

Section 28 - Raag Bhairao - Part 027

Their fears and doubts are dispelled in an instant.
The Supreme Lord God comes to dwell in their minds. |1|

The Lord is forever the Help and Support of the Saints.
Inside the home of the heart, and outside as well, the Transcendent Lord is always with us, permeating and pervading all places. |1|Pause|

The Lord of the World is my wealth, property, youth and ways and means.
He continually cherishes and brings peace to my soul and breath of life.
He reaches out with His Hand and saves His slave.
He does not abandon us, even for an instant; He is always with us. |2|

There is no other Beloved like the Lord.
The True Lord takes care of all.
The Lord is our Mother, Father, Son and Relation.
Since the beginning of time, and throughout the ages, His devotees sing His Glorious Praises. |3|

My mind is filled with the Support and the Power of the Lord.
Without the Lord, there is no other at all.
Nanak's mind is encouraged by this hope,
that God will accomplish my objectives in life. |4|38|51|

Bhairao, Fifth Mehl:
Fear itself becomes afraid, when the mortal remembers the Lord's Name in meditation.
All the diseases of the three gunas - the three qualities - are cured, and tasks of the Lord's slaves are perfectly accomplished. |1|Pause|

The people of the Lord always sing His Glorious Praises; they attain His Perfect Mansion.
Even the Righteous Judge of Dharma and the Messenger of Death yearn, day and night, to be sanctified by the Blessed Vision of the Lord's humble servant. |1|

Sexual desire, anger, intoxication, egotism, slander and egotistical pride are eradicted in the Saadh Sangat, the Company of the Holy.
By great good fortune, such Saints are met. Nanak is forever a sacrifice to them. |2|39|52|

Bhairao, Fifth Mehl:
One who harbors the five thieves, becomes the embodiment of these five.
He gets up each day and tells lies.
He applies ceremonial religious marks to his body, but practices hypocrisy.
He wastes away in sadness and pain, like a lonely widow. |1|

Without the Name of the Lord, everything is false.
Without the Perfect Guru, liberation is not obtained. In the Court of the True Lord, the faithless cynic is plundered. |1|Pause|

One who does not know the Lord's Creative Power is polluted.
Ritualistically plastering one's kitchen square does not make it pure in the Eyes of the Lord.
If a person is polluted within, he may wash himself everyday on the outside,
but in the Court of the True Lord, he forfeits his honor. |2|

He works for the sake of Maya,
but he never places his feet on the right path.
He never even remembers the One who created him.
He speaks falsehood, only falsehood, with his mouth. |3|

That person, unto whom the Creator Lord shows Mercy,
deals with the Saadh Sangat, the Company of the Holy.
One who lovingly worships the Lord's Name,
says Nanak - no obstacles ever block his way. |4|40|53|

Bhairao, Fifth Mehl:
The entire universe curses the slanderer.
False are the dealings of the slanderer.
The slanderer's lifestyle is filthy and polluted.
The Lord is the Saving Grace and the Protector of His slave. |1|

The slanderer dies with the rest of the slanderers.

The Supreme Lord God, the Transcendent Lord, protects and saves His humble servant. Death roars and thunders over the head of the slanderer. |1|Pause|

Section 28 - Raag Bhairao - Part 028

No one belives what the slanderer says.
The slanderer tells lies, and later regrets and repents.
He wrings his hands, and hits his head against the ground.
The Lord does not forgive the slanderer. |2|

The Lord's slave does not wish anyone ill.
The slanderer suffers, as if stabbed by a spear.
Like a crane, he spreads his feathers, to look like a swan.
When he speaks with his mouth, then he is exposed and driven out. |3|

The Creator is the Inner-knower, the Searcher of hearts.
That person, whom the Lord makes His Own, becomes stable and steady.
The Lord's slave is true in the Court of the Lord.
Servant Nanak speaks, after contemplating the essence of reality. |4|41|54|

Bhairao, Fifth Mehl:
With my palms pressed together, I offer this prayer.
My soul, body and wealth are His property.
He is the Creator, my Lord and Master.
Millions of times, I am a sacrifice to Him. |1|

The dust of the feet of the Holy brings purity.
Remembering God in meditation, the mind's corruption is eradicated, and the filth of countless incarnations is washed away. |1|Pause|

All treasures are in His household.
Serving Him, the mortal attains honor.
He is the Fulfiller of the mind's desires.
He is the Support of the soul and the breath of life of His devotees. |2|

His Light shines in each and every heart.
Chanting and meditating on God, the Treasure of Virtue, His devotees live.
Service to Him does not go in vain.

Deep within your mind and body, meditate on the One Lord. |3|

Following the Guru's Teachings, compassion and contentment are found.
This Treasure of the Naam, the Name of the Lord, is the immaculate object.
Please grant Your Grace, O Lord, and attach me to the hem of Your robe.
Nanak meditates continually on the Lord's Lotus Feet. |4|42|55|

Bhairao, Fifth Mehl:
The True Guru has listened to my prayer.
All my affairs have been resolved.
Deep within my mind and body, I meditate on God.
The Perfect Guru has dispelled all my fears. |1|

The All-powerful Divine Guru is the Greatest of all.
Serving Him, I obtain all comforts. |Pause|

Everything is done by Him.
No one can erase His Eternal Decree.
The Supreme Lord God, the Transcendent Lord, is incomparably beautiful.
The Guru is the Image of Fulfillment, the Embodiment of the Lord. |2|

The Name of the Lord abides deep within him.
Wherever he looks, he sees the Wisdom of God.
His mind is totally enlightened and illuminated.
Within that person, the Supreme Lord God abides. |3|

I humbly bow to that Guru forever.
I am forever a sacrifice to that Guru.
I wash the feet of the Guru, and drink in this water.
Chanting and meditating forever on Guru Nanak, I live. |4|43|56|

Section 28 - Raag Bhairao - Part 029

Raag Bhairao, Fifth Mehl, Partaal, Third House:
One Universal Creator God. By The Grace Of The True Guru:
God is the Compassionate Cherisher. Who can count His Glorious Virtues?
Countless colors, and countless waves of joy; He is the Master of all.
|1|Pause|

Endless spiritual wisdom, endless meditations, endless chants, intense meditations and austere self-disciplines.
Countless virtues, musical notes and playful sports; countless silent sages enshrine Him in their hearts. |1|

Countless melodies, countless instruments, countless tastes, each and every instant. Countless mistakes and countless diseases are removed by hearing His Praise.
O Nanak, serving the Infinite, Divine Lord, one earns all the rewards and merits of performing the six rituals, fasts, worship services, pilgrimages to sacred rivers, and journeys to sacred shrines. |2|1|57|8|21|7|57|93|

Bhairao, Ashtapadees, First Mehl, Second House:
One Universal Creator God. By The Grace Of The True Guru:
The Lord is in the soul, and the soul is in the Lord. This is realized through the Guru's Teachings.
The Ambrosial Word of the Guru's Bani is realized through the Word of the Shabad. Sorrow is dispelled, and egotism is eliminated. |1|

O Nanak, the disease of egotism is so very deadly.
Wherever I look, I see the pain of the same disease. The Primal Lord Himself bestows the Shabad of His Word. |1|Pause|

When the Appraiser Himself appraises the mortal, then he is not tested again.
Those who are blessed with His Grace meet with the Guru. They alone are true, who are pleasing to God. |2|

Air, water and fire are diseased; the world with its enjoyments is diseased.
Mother, father, Maya and the body are diseased; those united with their relatives are diseased. |3|

Brahma, Vishnu and Shiva are diseased; the whole world is diseased.
Those who remember the Lord's Feet and contemplate the Word of the Guru's Shabad are liberated. |4|

The seven seas are diseased, along with the rivers; the continents and the nether regions of the underworlds are full of disease.
The people of the Lord dwell in Truth and peace; He blesses them with His Grace everywhere. |5|

The six Shaastras are diseased, as are the many who follow the different religious orders.
What can the poor Vedas and Bibles do? People do not understand the One and Only Lord. |6|

Eating sweet treats, the mortal is filled with disease; he finds no peace at all.
Forgetting the Naam, the Name of the Lord, they walk on other paths, and at the very last moment, they regret and repent. |7|

Wandering around at sacred shrines of pilgrimage, the mortal is not cured of his disease. Reading scripture, he gets involved in useless arguments.
The disease of duality is so very deadly; it causes dependence on Maya. |8|

One who becomes Gurmukh and praises the True Shabad with the True Lord in his mind is cured of his disease.
O Nanak, the humble servant of the Lord is immaculate, night and day; he bears the insignia of the Lord's Grace. |9|1|

Section 28 - Raag Bhairao - Part 030

Bhairao, Third Mehl, Second House:
One Universal Creator God. By The Grace Of The True Guru:
The Creator has staged His Wondrous Play.
I listen to the Unstruck Sound-current of the Shabad, and the Bani of His Word.
The self-willed manmukhs are deluded and confused, while the Gurmukhs understand.
The Creator creates the Cause that causes. |1|

Deep within my being, I meditate on the Word of the Guru's Shabad.
I shall never forsake the Name of the Lord. |1|Pause|

Prahlaad's father sent him to school, to learn to read.
He took his writing tablet and went to the teacher.
He said, "I shall not read anything except the Naam, the Name of the Lord.
Write the Lord's Name on my tablet."|2|

Prahlaad's mother said to her son,

"I advise you not to read anything except what you are taught."
He answered, "The Great Giver, my Fearless Lord God is always with me.
If I were to forsake the Lord, then my family would be disgraced." |3|

"Prahlaad has corrupted all the other students.
He does not listen to what I say, and he does his own thing.
He instigated devotional worship in the townspeople."
The gathering of the wicked people could not do anything against him. |4|

Sanda and Marka, his teachers, made the complaint.
All the demons kept trying in vain.
The Lord protected His humble devotee, and preserved his honor.
What can be done by mere created beings? |5|

Because of his past karma, the demon ruled over his kingdom.
He did not realize the Lord; the Lord Himself confused him.
He started an argument with his son Prahlaad.
The blind one did not understand that his death was approaching. |6|

Prahlaad was placed in a cell, and the door was locked.
The fearless child was not afraid at all. He said, "Within my being, is the Guru, the Lord of the World."
The created being tried to compete with his Creator, but he assumed this name in vain.
That which was predestined for him has come to pass; he started an argument with the Lord's humble servant. |7|

The father raised the club to strike down Prahlaad, saying,
"Where is your God, the Lord of the Universe, now?"
He replied, "The Life of the World, the Great Giver, is my Help and Support in the end.
Wherever I look, I see Him permeating and prevailing." |8|

Tearing down the pillars, the Lord Himself appeared.
The egotistical demon was killed and destroyed.
The minds of the devotees were filled with bliss, and congratulations poured in.
He blessed His servant with glorious greatness. |9|

He created birth, death and attachment.

The Creator has ordained coming and going in reincarnation.
For the sake of Prahlaad, the Lord Himself appeared.
The word of the devotee came true. |10|

The gods proclaimed the victory of Lakshmi, and said,
"O mother, make this form of the Man-lion disappear!"
Lakshmi was afraid, and did not approach.

Section 28 - Raag Bhairao - Part 031

The humble servant Prahlaad came and fell at the Lord's Feet. |11|

The True Guru implanted the treasure of the Naam within.
Power, property and all Maya is false.
But still, the greedy people continue clinging to them.
Without the Name of the Lord, the mortals are punished in His Court. |12|

Says Nanak, everyone acts as the Lord makes them act.
They alone are approved and accepted, who focus their consciousness on the Lord.
He has made His devotees His Own.
The Creator has appeared in His Own Form. |13|1|2|

Bhairao, Third Mehl:
Serving the Guru, I obtain the Ambrosial Fruit; my egotism and desire have been quenched.
The Name of the Lord dwells within my heart and mind, and the desires of my mind are quieted. |1|

O Dear Lord, my Beloved, please bless me with Your Mercy.
Night and day, Your humble servant begs for Your Glorious Praises; through the Word of the Guru's Shabad, he is saved. |1|Pause|

The Messenger of Death cannot even touch the humble Saints; it does not cause them even an iota of suffering or pain.
Those who enter Your Sanctuary, Lord, save themselves, and save all their ancestors as well. |2|

You Yourself save the honor of Your devotees; this is Your Glory, O Lord.

You cleanse them of the sins and the pains of countless incarnations; You love them without even an iota of duality. |3|

I am foolish and ignorant, and understand nothing. You Yourself bless me with understanding.
You do whatever You please; nothing else can be done at all. |4|

Creating the world, You have linked all to their tasks - even the evil deeds which men do.
They lose this precious human life in the gamble, and do not understand the Word of the Shabad. |5|

The self-willed manmukhs die, understanding nothing; they are enveloped by the darkness of evil-mindedness and ignorance.
They do not cross over the terrible world-ocean; without the Guru, they drown and die. |6|

True are those humble beings who are imbued with the True Shabad; the Lord God unites them with Himself.
Through the Word of the Guru's Bani, they come to understand the Shabad. They remain lovingly focused on the True Lord. |7|

You Yourself are Immaculate and Pure, and pure are Your humble servants who contemplate the Word of the Guru's Shabad.
Nanak is forever a sacrifice to those, who enshrine the Lord's Name within their hearts. |8|2|3|

Bhairao, Fifth Mehl, Ashtapadees, Second House:
One Universal Creator God. By The Grace Of The True Guru:
He alone is a great king, who keeps the Naam, the Name of the Lord, within his heart.
One who keeps the Naam in his heart - his tasks are perfectly accomplished.
One who keeps the Naam in his heart, obtains millions of treasures.
Without the Naam, life is useless. |1|

I praise that person, who has the capital of the Lord's Wealth.
He is very fortunate, on whose forehead the Guru has placed His Hand. |1|Pause|

One who keeps the Naam in his heart, has many millions of armies on his side.

One who keeps the Naam in his heart, enjoys peace and poise.

Section 28 - Raag Bhairao - Part 032

One who keeps the Naam in his heart becomes cool and calm.
Without the Naam, both life and death are cursed. |2|

One who keeps the Naam in his heart is Jivan-mukta, liberated while yet alive.
One who keeps the Naam in his heart knows all ways and means.
One who keeps the Naam in his heart obtains the nine treasures.
Without the Naam, the mortal wanders, coming and going in reincarnation. |3|

One who keeps the Naam in his heart is carefree and independent.
One who keeps the Naam in his heart always earns a profit.
One who keeps the Naam in his heart has a large family.
Without the Naam, the mortal is just an ignorant, self-willed manmukh. |4|

One who keeps the Naam in his heart has a permanent position.
One who keeps the Naam in his heart is seated on the throne.
One who keeps the Naam in his heart is the true king.
Without the Naam, no one has any honor or respect. |5|

One who keeps the Naam in his heart is famous everywhere.
One who keeps the Naam in his heart is the Embodiment of the Creator Lord.
One who keeps the Naam in his heart is the highest of all.
Without the Naam, the mortal wanders in reincarnation. |6|

One who keeps the Naam in his heart sees the Lord manifested in His Creation.
One who keeps the Naam in his heart - his darkness is dispelled.
One who keeps the Naam in his heart is approved and accepted.
Without the Naam, the mortal continues coming and going in reincarnation. |7|

He alone receives the Naam, who is blessed by the Lord's Mercy.

In the Saadh Sangat, the Company of the Holy, the Lord of the World is understood.
Coming and going in reincarnation ends, and peace is found.
Says Nanak, my essence has merged in the Essence of the Lord. |8|1|4|

Bhairao, Fifth Mehl:
He created millions of incarnations of Vishnu.
He created millions of universes as places to practice righteousness.
He created and destroyed millions of Shivas.
He employed millions of Brahmas to create the worlds. |1|

Such is my Lord and Master, the Lord of the Universe.
I cannot even describe His Many Virtues. |1|Pause|

Millions of Mayas are His maid-servants.
Millions of souls are His beds.
Millions of universes are the limbs of His Being.
Millions of devotees abide with the Lord. |2|

Millions of kings with their crowns and canopies bow before Him.
Millions of Indras stand at His Door.
Millions of heavenly paradises are within the scope of His Vision.
Millions of His Names cannot even be appraised. |3|

Millions of celestial sounds resound for Him.
His Wondrous Plays are enacted on millions of stages.
Millions of Shaktis and Shivas are obedient to Him.
He gives sustenance and support to millions of beings. |4|

In His Feet are millions of sacred shrines of pilgrimage.
Millions chant His Sacred and Beautiful Name.
Millions of worshippers worship Him.
Millions of expanses are His; there is no other at all. |5|

Millions of swan-souls sing His Immaculate Praises.
Millions of Brahma's sons sing His Praises.
He creates and destroys millions, in an instant.
Millions are Your Virtues, Lord - they cannot even be counted. |6|

Millions of spiritual teachers teach His spiritual wisdom.

Millions of meditators focus on His meditation.
Millions of austere penitents practice austerities.

Section 28 - Raag Bhairao - Part 033

Millions of silent sages dwell in silence. |7|

Our Eternal, Imperishable, Incomprehensible Lord and Master, the Inner-knower, the Searcher of hearts, is permeating all hearts.
Wherever I look, I see Your Dwelling, O Lord.
The Guru has blessed Nanak with enlightenment. |8|2|5|

Bhairao, Fifth Mehl:
The True Guru has blessed me with this gift.
He has given me the Priceless Jewel of the Lord's Name.
Now, I intuitively enjoy endless pleasures and wondrous play.
God has spontaneously met with Nanak. |1|

Says Nanak, True is the Kirtan of the Lord's Praise.
Again and again, my mind remains immersed in it. |1|Pause|

Spontaneously, I feed on the Love of God.
Spontaneously, I take God's Name.
Spontaneously, I am saved by the Word of the Shabad.
Spontaneously, my treasures are filled to overflowing. |2|

Spontaneously, my works are perfectly accomplished.
Spontaneously, I am rid of sorrow.
Spontaneously, my enemies have become friends.
Spontaneously, I have brought my mind under control. |3|

Spontaneously, God has comforted me.
Spontaneously, my hopes have been fulfilled.
Spontaneously, I have totally realized the essence of reality.
Spontaneously, I have been blessed with the Guru's Mantra. |4|

Spontaneously, I am rid of hatred.
Spontaneously, my darkness has been dispelled.
Spontaneously, the Kirtan of the Lord's Praise seems so sweet to my mind.
Spontaneously, I behold God in each and every heart. |5|

Spontaneously, all my doubts have been dispelled.
Spontaneously, peace and celestial harmony fill my mind.
Spontaneously, the Unstruck Melody of the Sound-current resounds within me.
Spontaneously, the Lord of the Universe has revealed Himself to me. |6|

Spontaneously, my mind has been pleased and appeased.
I have spontaneously realized the Eternal, Unchanging Lord.
Spontaneously, all wisdom and knowledge has welled up within me.
Spontaneously, the Support of the Lord, Har, Har, has come into my hands. |7|

Spontaneously, God has recorded my pre-ordained destiny.
Spontaneously, the One Lord and Master God has met me.
Spontaneously, all my cares and worries have been taken away.
Nanak, Nanak, Nanak, has merged into the Image of God. |8|3|6|

Bhairao, The Word Of The Devotees, Kabeer Jee, First House:
One Universal Creator God. By The Grace Of The True Guru:
The Name of the Lord - this alone is my wealth.
I do not tie it up to hide it, nor do I sell it to make my living. |1|Pause|

The Name is my crop, and the Name is my field.
As Your humble servant, I perform devotional worship to You; I seek Your Sanctuary. |1|

The Name is Maya and wealth for me; the Name is my capital.
I do not forsake You; I do not know any other at all. |2|

The Name is my family, the Name is my brother.
The Name is my companion, who will help me in the end. |3|

One whom the Lord keeps detached from Maya
- says Kabeer, I am his slave. |4|1|

Naked we come, and naked we go.
No one, not even the kings and queens, shall remain. |1|

Section 28 - Raag Bhairao - Part 034

The Sovereign Lord is the nine treasures for me.
The possessions and the spouse to which the mortal is lovingly attached, are Your wealth, O Lord. |1|Pause|

They do not come with the mortal, and they do not go with him.
What good does it do him, if he has elephants tied up at his doorway? |2|

The fortress of Sri Lanka was made out of gold,
but what could the foolish Raawan take with him when he left? |3|

Says Kabeer, think of doing some good deeds.
In the end, the gambler shall depart empty-handed. |4|2|

Brahma is polluted, and Indra is polluted.
The sun is polluted, and the moon is polluted. |1|

This world is polluted with pollution.
Only the One Lord is Immaculate; He has no end or limitation. |1|Pause|

The rulers of kingdoms are polluted.
Nights and days, and the days of the month are polluted. |2|

The pearl is polluted, the diamond is polluted.
Wind, fire and water are polluted. |3|

Shiva, Shankara and Mahaysh are polluted.
The Siddhas, seekers and strivers, and those who wear religious robes, are polluted. |4|

The Yogis and wandering hermits with their matted hair are polluted.
The body, along with the swan-soul, is polluted. |5|

Says Kabeer, those humble beings are approved and pure, who know the Lord. |6|3|

Let your mind be Mecca, and your body the temple of worship.
Let the Supreme Guru be the One who speaks. |1|

O Mullah, utter the call to prayer.

The one mosque has ten doors. |1|Pause|

So slaughter your evil nature, doubt and cruelty;
consume the five demons and you shall be blessed with contentment. |2|

Hindus and Muslims have the same One Lord and Master.
What can the Mullah do, and what can the Shaykh do? |3|

Says Kabeer, I have gone insane.
Slaughtering, slaughtering my mind, I have merged into the Celestial Lord.
|4|4|

When the stream flows into the Ganges, then it becomes the Ganges. |1|

Just so, Kabeer has changed.
He has become the Embodiment of Truth, and he does not go anywhere
else. |1|Pause|

Associating with the sandalwood tree, the tree nearby is changed;
that tree begins to smell just like the sandalwood tree. |2|

Coming into contact with the philosophers' stone, copper is transformed;
that copper is transformed into gold. |3|

In the Society of the Saints, Kabeer is transformed;
that Kabeer is transformed into the Lord. |4|5|

Some apply ceremonial marks to their foreheads, hold malas in their hands,
and wear religious robes.
Some people think that the Lord is a play-thing. |1|

If I am insane, then I am Yours, O Lord.
How can people know my secret? |1|Pause|

I do not pick leaves as offerings, and I do not worship idols.
Without devotional worship of the Lord, service is useless. |2|

I worship the True Guru; forever and ever, I surrender to Him.
By such service, I find peace in the Court of the Lord. |3|

People say that Kabeer has gone insane.
Only the Lord realizes the secret of Kabeer. |4|6|

Turning away from the world, I have forgotten both my social class and ancestry.
My weaving now is in the most profound celestial stillness. |1|

I have no quarrel with anyone.

Section 28 - Raag Bhairao - Part 035

I have abandoned both the Pandits, the Hindu religious scholars, and the Mullahs, the Muslim priests. |1|Pause|

I weave and weave, and wear what I weave.
Where egotism does not exist, there I sing God's Praises. |2|

Whatever the Pandits and Mullahs have written,
I reject; I do not accept any of it. |3|

My heart is pure, and so I have seen the Lord within.
Searching, searching within the self, Kabeer has met the Lord. |4|7|

No one respects the poor man.
He may make thousands of efforts, but no one pays any attention to him.
|1|Pause|

When the poor man goes to the rich man,
and sits right in front of him, the rich man turns his back on him. |1|

But when the rich man goes to the poor man,
the poor man welcomes him with respect. |2|

The poor man and the rich man are both brothers.
God's pre-ordained plan cannot be erased. |3|

Says Kabeer, he alone is poor,
who does not have the Naam, the Name of the Lord, in his heart. |4|8|

Serving the Guru, devotional worship is practiced.

Then, this human body is obtained.
Even the gods long for this human body.
So vibrate that human body, and think of serving the Lord. |1|

Vibrate, and meditate on the Lord of the Universe, and never forget Him.
This is the blessed opportunity of this human incarnation. |1|Pause|

As long as the disease of old age has not come to the body,
and as long as death has not come and seized the body,
and as long as your voice has not lost its power,
O mortal being, vibrate and meditate on the Lord of the World. |2|

If you do not vibrate and meditate on Him now, when will you, O Sibing of Destiny?
When the end comes, you will not be able to vibrate and meditate on Him.
Whatever you have to do - now is the best time to do it.
Otherwise, you shall regret and repent afterwards, and you shall not be carried across to the other side. |3|

He alone is a servant, whom the Lord enjoins to His service.
He alone attains the Immaculate Divine Lord.
Meeting with the Guru, his doors are opened wide,
and he does not have to journey again on the path of reincarnation. |4|

This is your chance, and this is your time.
Look deep into your own heart, and reflect on this.
Says Kabeer, you can win or lose.
In so many ways, I have proclaimed this out loud. |5|1|9|

In the City of God, sublime understanding prevails.
There, you shall meet with the Lord, and reflect on Him.
Thus, you shall understand this world and the next.
What is the use of claiming that you own everything, if you only die in the end? |1|

I focus my meditation on my inner self, deep within.
The Name of the Sovereign Lord is my spiritual wisdom. |1|Pause|

In the first chakra, the root chakra, I have grasped the reins and tied them.
I have firmly placed the moon above the sun.

The sun blazes forth at the western gate.
Through the central channel of the Shushmanaa, it rises up above my head.
|2|

There is a stone at that western gate,
and above that stone, is another window.
Above that window is the Tenth Gate.
Says Kabeer, it has no end or limitation. |3|2|10|

He alone is a Mullah, who struggles with his mind,
and through the Guru's Teachings, fights with death.
He crushes the pride of the Messenger of Death.
Unto that Mullah, I ever offer greetings of respect. |1|

Section 28 - Raag Bhairao - Part 036

God is present, right here at hand; why do you say that He is far away?
Tie up your disturbing passions, and find the Beauteous Lord. |1|Pause|

He alone is a Qazi, who contemplates the human body,
and through the fire of the body, is illumined by God.
He does not lose his semen, even in his dreams;
for such a Qazi, there is no old age or death. |2|

He alone is a sultan and a king, who shoots the two arrows,
gathers in his outgoing mind,
and assembles his army in the realm of the mind's sky, the Tenth Gate.
The canopy of royalty waves over such a sultan. |3|

The Yogi cries out, "Gorakh, Gorakh".
The Hindu utters the Name of Raam.
The Muslim has only One God.
The Lord and Master of Kabeer is all-pervading. |4|3|11|

Fifth Mehl:
Those who call a stone their god
- their service is useless.
Those who fall at the feet of a stone god
- their work is wasted in vain. |1|

My Lord and Master speaks forever.
God gives His gifts to all living beings. |1|Pause|

The Divine Lord is within the self, but the spiritually blind one does not know this.
Deluded by doubt, he is caught in the noose.
The stone does not speak; it does not give anything to anyone.
Such religious rituals are useless; such service is fruitless. |2|

If a corpse is anointed with sandalwood oil,
what good does it do?
If a corpse is rolled in manure,
what does it lose from this? |3|

Says Kabeer, I proclaim this out loud
- behold, and understand, you ignorant, faithless cynic.
The love of duality has ruined countless homes.
The Lord's devotees are forever in bliss. |4|4|12|

The fish in the water is attached to Maya.
The moth fluttering around the lamp is pierced through by Maya.
The sexual desire of Maya afflicts the elephant.
The snakes and bumble bees are destroyed through Maya. |1|

Such are the enticements of Maya, O Siblings of Destiny.
As many living beings are there are, have been deceived. |1|Pause|

The birds and the deer are imbued with Maya.
Sugar is a deadly trap for the flies.
Horses and camels are absorbed in Maya.
The eighty-four Siddhas, the beings of miraculous spiritual powers, play in Maya. |2|

The six celibates are slaves of Maya.
So are the nine masters of Yoga, and the sun and the moon.
The austere disciplinarians and the Rishis are asleep in Maya.
Death and the five demons are in Maya. |3|

Dogs and jackals are imbued with Maya.
Monkeys, leopards and lions,

cats, sheep, foxes,
trees and roots are planted in Maya. |4|

Even the gods are drenched with Maya,
as are the oceans, the sky and the earth.
Says Kabeer, whoever has a belly to fill, is under the spell of Maya.
The mortal is emancipated only when he meets the Holy Saint. |5|5|13|

As long as he cries out, "Mine! Mine!",
none of his tasks is accomplished.
When such possessiveness is erased and removed,

Section 28 - Raag Bhairao - Part 037

then God comes and resolves his affairs. |1|

Contemplate such spiritual wisdom, O mortal man.
Why not meditate in remembrance on the Lord, the Destroyer of pain?
|1|Pause|

As long as the tiger lives in the forest,
the forest does not flower.
But when the jackal eats the tiger,
then the entire forest flowers. |2|

The victorious are drowned, while the defeated swim across.
By Guru's Grace, one crosses over and is saved.
Slave Kabeer speaks and teaches:
remain lovingly absorbed, attuned to the Lord alone. |3|6|14|

He has 7,000 commanders,
and hundreds of thousands of prophets;
He is said to have 88,000,000 shaykhs,
and 56,000,000 attendants. |1|

I am meek and poor - what chance do I have of being heard there?
His Court is so far away; only a rare few attain the Mansion of His Presence.
|1|Pause|

He has 33,000,000 play-houses.

His beings wander insanely through 8.4 million incarnations.
He bestowed His Grace on Adam, the father of mankind,
who then lived in paradise for a long time. |2|

Pale are the faces of those whose hearts are disturbed.
They have forsaken their Bible, and practice Satanic evil.
One who blames the world, and is angry with people,
shall receive the fruits of his own actions. |3|

You are the Great Giver, O Lord; I am forever a beggar at Your Door.
If I were to deny You, then I would be a wretched sinner.
Slave Kabeer has entered Your Shelter.
Keep me near You, O Merciful Lord God - that is heaven for me. |4|7|15|

Everyone speaks of going there,
but I do not even know where heaven is. |1|Pause|

One who does not even know the mystery of his own self,
speaks of heaven, but it is only talk. |1|

As long as the mortal hopes for heaven,
he will not dwell at the Lord's Feet. |2|

Heaven is not a fort with moats and ramparts, and walls plastered with
mud;
I do not know what heaven's gate is like. |3|

Says Kabeer, now what more can I say?
The Saadh Sangat, the Company of the Holy, is heaven itself. |4|8|16|

How can the beautiful fortress be conquered, O Siblings of Destiny?
It has double walls and triple moats. |1|Pause|

It is defended by the five elements, the twenty-five categories, attachment,
pride, jealousy and the awesomely powerful Maya.
The poor mortal being does not have the strength to conquer it; what
should I do now, O Lord? |1|

Sexual desire is the window, pain and pleasure are the gate-keepers, virtue
and sin are the gates.

Anger is the great supreme commander, full of argument and strife, and the mind is the rebel king there. |2|

Their armor is the pleasure of tastes and flavors, their helmets are worldly attachments; they take aim with their bows of corrupt intellect.
The greed that fills their hearts is the arrow; with these things, their fortress is impregnable. |3|

But I have made divine love the fuse, and deep meditation the bomb; I have launched the rocket of spiritual wisdom.
The fire of God is lit by intuition, and with one shot, the fortress is taken. |4|

Taking truth and contentment with me, I begin the battle and storm both the gates.
In the Saadh Sangat, the Company of the Holy, and by Guru's Grace, I have captured the king of the fortress. |5|

Section 28 - Raag Bhairao - Part 038

With the army of God's devotees, and Shakti, the power of meditation, I have snapped the noose of the fear of death.
Slave Kabeer has climbed to the top of the fortress; I have obtained the eternal, imperishable domain. |6|9|17|

The mother Ganges is deep and profound.
Tied up in chains, they took Kabeer there. |1|

My mind was not shaken; why should my body be afraid?
My consciousness remained immersed in the Lotus Feet of the Lord. |1|Pause|

The waves of the Ganges broke the chains,
and Kabeer was seated on a deer skin. |2|

Says Kabeer, I have no friend or companion.
On the water, and on the land, the Lord is my Protector. |3|10|18|

Bhairao, Kabeer Jee, Ashtapadees, Second House:
One Universal Creator God. By The Grace Of The True Guru:

God constructed a fortress, inaccessible and unreachable, in which He dwells.
There, His Divine Light radiates forth.
Lightning blazes, and bliss prevails there,
where the Eternally Young Lord God abides. |1|

This soul is lovingly attuned to the Lord's Name.
It is saved from old age and death, and its doubt runs away. |1|Pause|

Those who believe in high and low social classes,
only sing songs and chants of egotism.
The Unstruck Sound-current of the Shabad, the Word of God, resounds in that place,
where the Supreme Lord God abides. |2|

He creates planets, solar systems and galaxies;
He destroys the three worlds, the three gods and the three qualities.
The Inaccessible and Unfathomable Lord God dwells in the heart.
No one can find the limits or the secrets of the Lord of the World. |3|

The Lord shines forth in the plantain flower and the sunshine.
He dwells in the pollen of the lotus flower.
The Lord's secret is within the twelve petals of the heart-lotus.
The Supreme Lord, the Lord of Lakshmi dwells there. |4|

He is like the sky, stretching across the lower, upper and middle realms.
In the profoundly silent celestial realm, He radiates forth.
Neither the sun nor the moon are there,
but the Primal Immaculate Lord celebrates there. |5|

Know that He is in the universe, and in the body as well.
Take your cleansing bath in the Mansarovar Lake.
Chant "Sohang" - "He is me."
He is not affected by either virtue or vice. |6|

He is not affected by either high or low social class, sunshine or shade.
He is in the Guru's Sanctuary, and nowhere else.
He is not diverted by diversions, comings or goings.
Remain intuitively absorbed in the celestial void. |7|

One who knows the Lord in the mind
- whatever he says, comes to pass.
One who firmly implants the Lord's Divine Light, and His Mantra within the mind
- says Kabeer, such a mortal crosses over to the other side. |8|1|

Millions of suns shine for Him,
millions of Shivas and Kailash mountains.
Millions of Durga goddesses massage His Feet.
Millions of Brahmas chant the Vedas for Him. |1|

When I beg, I beg only from the Lord.
I have nothing to do with any other deities. |1|Pause|

Millions of moons twinkle in the sky.

Section 28 - Raag Bhairao - Part 039

Three hundred thirty million gods eat the Lord's offerings.
The nine stars, a million times over, stand at His Door.
Millions of Righteous Judges of Dharma are His gate-keepers. |2|

Millions of winds blow around Him in the four directions.
Millions of serpents prepare His bed.
Millions of oceans are His water-carriers.
The eighteen million loads of vegetation are His Hair. |3|

Millions of treasurers fill His Treasury.
Millions of Lakshmis adorn themselves for Him.
Many millions of vices and virtues look up to Him.
Millions of Indras serve Him. |4|

Fifty-six million clouds are His.
In each and every village, His infinite fame has spread.
Wild demons with dishevelled hair move about.
The Lord plays in countless ways. |5|

Millions of charitable feasts are held in His Court,
and millions of celestial singers celebrate His victory.
Millions of sciences all sing His Praises.

Even so, the limits of the Supreme Lord God cannot be found. |6|

Rama, with millions of monkeys, conquered Raawan's army.
Billions of Puraanas greatly praise Him;
He humbled the pride of Duyodhan. |7|

Millions of gods of love cannot compete with Him.
He steals the hearts of mortal beings.
Says Kabeer, please hear me, O Lord of the World.
I beg for the blessing of fearless dignity. |8|2|18|20|

Bhairao, The Word Of Naam Dayv Jee, First House:
One Universal Creator God. By The Grace Of The True Guru:
O my tongue, I will cut you into a hundred pieces,
if you do not chant the Name of the Lord. |1|

O my tongue, be imbued with the Lord's Name.
Meditate on the Name of the Lord, Har, Har, and imbue yourself with this
most excellent color. |1|Pause|

O my tongue, other occupations are false.
The state of Nirvaanaa comes only through the Lord's Name. |2|

The performance of countless millions of other devotions
is not equal to even one devotion to the Name of the Lord. |3|

Prays Naam Dayv, this is my occupation.
O Lord, Your Forms are endless. |4|1|

One who stays away from others' wealth and others' spouses
- the Lord abides near that person. |1|

Those who do not meditate and vibrate on the Lord
- I do not even want to see them. |1|Pause|

Those whose inner beings are not in harmony with the Lord,
are nothing more than beasts. |2|

Prays Naam Dayv, a man without a nose
does not look handsome, even if he has the thirty-two beauty marks. |3|2|

Naam Dayv milked the brown cow, and brought a cup of milk and a jug of water to his family god. |1|

"Please drink this milk, O my Sovereign Lord God.
Drink this milk and my mind will be happy.
Otherwise, my father will be angry with me."|1|Pause|

Taking the golden cup, Naam Dayv filled it with the ambrosial milk,
and placed it before the Lord. |2|

The Lord looked upon Naam Dayv and smiled. "This one devotee abides within my heart."|3|

The Lord drank the milk, and the devotee returned home.

Section 28 - Raag Bhairao - Part 040

Thus did Naam Dayv come to receive the Blessed Vision of the Lord's Darshan. |4|3|

I am crazy - the Lord is my Husband.
I decorate and adorn myself for Him. |1|

Slander me well, slander me well, slander me well, O people.
My body and mind are united with my Beloved Lord. |1|Pause|

Do not engage in any arguments or debates with anyone.
With your tongue, savor the Lord's sublime essence. |2|

Now, I know within my soul, that such an arrangement has been made;
I will meet with my Lord by the beat of the drum. |3|

Anyone can praise or slander me.
Naam Dayv has met the Lord. |4|4|

Sometimes, people do not appreciate milk, sugar and ghee.
Sometimes, they have to beg for bread from door to door.
Sometimes, they have to pick out the grain from the chaff. |1|

As the Lord keeps us, so do we live, O Siblings of Destiny.
The Lord's Glory cannot even be described. |1|Pause|

Sometimes, people prance around on horses.
Sometimes, they do not even have shoes for their feet. |2|

Sometimes, people sleep on cozy beds with white sheets.
Sometimes, they do not even have straw to put down on the ground. |3|

Naam Dayv prays, only the Naam, the Name of the Lord, can save us.
One who meets the Guru, is carried across to the other side. |4|5|

Laughing and playing, I came to Your Temple, O Lord.
While Naam Dayv was worshipping, he was grabbed and driven out. |1|

I am of a low social class, O Lord;
why was I born into a family of fabric dyers? |1|Pause|

I picked up my blanket and went back,
to sit behind the temple. |2|

As Naam Dayv uttered the Glorious Praises of the Lord,
the temple turned around to face the Lord's humble devotee. |3|6|

Bhairao, Naam Dayv Jee, Second House:
One Universal Creator God. By The Grace Of The True Guru:
As the hungry person loves food,
and the thirsty person is obsessed with water,
and as the fool is attached to his family
- just so, the Lord is very dear to Naam Dayv. |1|

Naam Dayv is in love with the Lord.
He has naturally and intuitively become detached from the world.
|1|Pause|

Like the woman who falls in love with another man,
and the greedy man who loves only wealth,
and the sexually promiscuous man who loves women and sex,
just so, Naam Dayv is in love with the Lord. |2|

But that alone is real love, which the Lord Himself inspires;
by Guru's Grace, duality is eradicated.
Such love never breaks; through it, the mortal remains merged in the Lord.
Naam Dayv has focused his consciousness on the True Name. |3|

Like the love between the child and its mother,
so is my mind imbued with the Lord.
Prays Naam Dayv, I am in love with the Lord.
The Lord of the Universe abides within my consciousness. |4|1|7|

The blind fool abandons the wife of his own home,

Section 28 - Raag Bhairao - Part 041

and has an affair with another woman.
He is like the parrot, who is pleased to see the simbal tree;
but in the end, he dies, stuck to it. |1|

The home of the sinner is on fire.
It keeps burning, and the fire cannot be extinguished. |1|Pause|

He does not go to see where the Lord is being worshipped.
He abandons the Lord's Path, and takes the wrong path.
He forgets the Primal Lord God, and is caught in the cycle of reincarnation.
He throws away the Ambrosial Nectar, and gathers poison to eat. |2|

He is like the prostitute, who comes to dance,
wearing beautiful clothes, decorated and adorned.
She dances to the beat, exciting the breath of those who watch her.
But the noose of the Messenger of Death is around her neck. |3|

One who has good karma recorded on his forehead,
hurries to enter the Guru's Sanctuary.
Says Naam Dayv, consider this:
O Saints, this is the way to cross over to the other side. |4|2|8|

Sanda and Marka went and complained to Harnaakhash,
"Your son does not read his lessons. We are tired of trying to teach him.
He chants the Lord's Name, clapping his hands to keep the beat; he has
spoiled all the other students. |1|

He chants the Lord's Name,
and he has enshrined meditative remembrance of the Lord within his heart."|1|Pause|

"Your father the king has conquered the whole world", said his mother the queen.
"O Prahlad my son, you do not obey him, so he has decided to deal with you in another way."|2|

The council of villians met and resolved to send Prahlaad into the life hereafter.
Prahlaad was thrown off a mountain, into the water, and into a fire, but the Sovereign Lord God saved him, by changing the laws of nature. |3|

Harnaakhash thundered with rage and threatened to kill Prahlaad. "Tell me, who can save you?"
Prahlaad answered, "The Lord, the Master of the three worlds, is contained even in this pillar to which I am tied."|4|

The Lord who tore Harnaakhash apart with His nails proclaimed Himself the Lord of gods and men.
Says Naam Dayv, I meditate on the Lord, the Man-lion, the Giver of fearless dignity. |5|3|9|

The Sultan said, "Listen, Naam Dayv:
let me see the actions of your Lord."|1|

The Sultan arrested Naam Dayv,
and said, "Let me see your Beloved Lord."|1|Pause|

"Bring this dead cow back to life.
Otherwise, I shall cut off your head here and now."|2|

Naam Dayv answered, "O king, how can this happen?
No one can bring the dead back to life. |3|

I cannot do anything by my own actions.
Whatever the Lord does, that alone happens."|4|

The arrogant king was enraged at this reply.
He incited an elephant to attack. |5|

Naam Dayv's mother began to cry,
and she said, "Why don't you abandon your Lord Raam, and worship his Lord Allah?" |6|

Naam Dayv answered, "I am not your son, and you are not my mother.
Even if my body dies, I will still sing the Glorious Praises of the Lord." |7|

The elephant attacked him with his trunk,
but Naam Dayv was saved, protected by the Lord. |8|

The king said, "The Qazis and the Mullahs bow down to me,
but this Hindu has trampled my honor." |9|

The people pleaded with the king, "Hear our prayer, O king.

Section 28 - Raag Bhairao - Part 042

Here, take Naam Dayv's weight in gold, and release him." |10|

The king replied, "If I take the gold, then I will be consigned to hell,
by forsaking my faith and gathering worldly wealth." |11|

With his feet in chains, Naam Dayv kept the beat with his hands,
singing the Praises of the Lord. |12|

"Even if the Ganges and the Jamunaa rivers flow backwards,
I will still continue singing the Praises of the Lord." |13|

Three hours passed,
and even then, the Lord of the three worlds had not come. |14|

Playing on the instrument of the feathered wings,
the Lord of the Universe came, mounted on the eagle garura. |15|

He cherished His devotee,
and the Lord came, mounted on the eagle garura. |16|

The Lord said to him, "If you wish, I shall turn the earth sideways.
If you wish, I shall turn it upside down. |17|

If you wish, I shall bring the dead cow back to life.
Everyone will see and be convinced."|18|

Naam Dayv prayed, and milked the cow.
He brought the calf to the cow, and milked her. |19|

When the pitcher was filled with milk,
Naam Dayv took it and placed it before the king. |20|

The king went into his palace,
and his heart was troubled. |21|

Through the Qazis and the Mullahs, the king offered his prayer,
"Forgive me, please, O Hindu; I am just a cow before you."|22|

Naam Dayv said, "Listen, O king:
have I done this miracle? |23|

The purpose of this miracle is
that you, O king, should walk on the path of truth and humility."|24|

Naam Dayv became famous everywhere for this.
The Hindus all went together to Naam Dayv. |25|

If the cow had not been revived,
people would have lost faith in Naam Dayv. |26|

The fame of Naam Dayv spread throughout the world.
The humble devotees were saved and carried across with him. |27|

All sorts of troubles and pains afflicted the slanderer.
There is no difference between Naam Dayv and the Lord. |28|1|10|

SECOND HOUSE:
By the Grace of the Divine Guru, one meets the Lord.
By the Grace of the Divine Guru, one is carried across to the other side.
By the Grace of the Divine Guru, one swims across to heaven.

By the Grace of the Divine Guru, one remains dead while yet alive. |1|

True, True, True True, True is the Divine Guru.
False, false, false, false is all other service. |1|Pause|

When the Divine Guru grants His Grace, the Naam, the Name of the Lord, is implanted within.
When the Divine Guru grants His Grace, one does not wander in the ten directions.
When the Divine Guru grants His Grace, the five demons are kept far away.
When the Divine Guru grants His Grace, one does not die regretting. |2|

When the Divine Guru grants His Grace, one is blessed with the Ambrosial Bani of the Word.
When the Divine Guru grants His Grace, one speaks the Unspoken Speech.
When the Divine Guru grants His Grace, one's body becomes like ambrosial nectar.
When the Divine Guru grants His Grace, one utters and chants the Naam, the Name of the Lord. |3|

When the Divine Guru grants His Grace, one sees the three worlds.
When the Divine Guru grants His Grace, one understands the state of supreme dignity.
When the Divine Guru grants His Grace, one's head is in the Akaashic ethers.
When the Divine Guru grants His Grace, one is always congratulated everywhere. |4|

When the Divine Guru grants His Grace, one remains detached forever.
When the Divine Guru grants His Grace, one forsakes the slander of others.

Section 28 - Raag Bhairao - Part 043

When the Divine Guru grants His Grace, one looks upon good and bad as the same.
When the Divine Guru grants His Grace, one has good destiny written on his forehead. |5|

When the Divine Guru grants His Grace, the wall of the body is not eroded.

When the Divine Guru grants His Grace, the temple turns itself towards the mortal.
When the Divine Guru grants His Grace, one's home is constructed.
When the Divine Guru grants His Grace, one's bed is lifted up out of the water. |6|

When the Divine Guru grants His Grace, one has bathed at the sixty-eight sacred shrines of pilgrimage.
When the Divine Guru grants His Grace, one's body is stamped with the sacred mark of Vishnu.
When the Divine Guru grants His Grace, one has performed the twelve devotional services.
When the Divine Guru grants His Grace, all poison is transformed into fruit. |7|

When the Divine Guru grants His Grace, skepticism is shattered.
When the Divine Guru grants His Grace, one escapes from the Messenger of Death.
When the Divine Guru grants His Grace, one crosses over the terrifying world-ocean.
When the Divine Guru grants His Grace, one is not subject to the cycle of reincarnation. |8|

When the Divine Guru grants His Grace, one understands the rituals of the eighteen Puraanas.
When the Divine Guru grants His Grace, it is as if one has made an offering of the eighten loads of vegetation.
When the Divine Guru grants His Grace, one needs no other place of rest.
Naam Dayv has entered the Sanctuary of the Guru. |9|1|2|11|

Bhairao, The Word Of Ravi Daas Jee, Second House:
One Universal Creator God. By The Grace Of The True Guru:
Without seeing something, the yearning for it does not arise.
Whatever is seen, shall pass away.
Whoever chants and praises the Naam, the Name of the Lord,
is the true Yogi, free of desire. |1|

When someone utters the Name of the Lord with love,
it is as if he has touched the philosopher's stone; his sense of duality is eradicated. |1|Pause|

He alone is a silent sage, who destroys the duality of his mind.
Keeping the doors of his body closed, he merges in the Lord of the three worlds.
Everyone acts according to the inclinations of the mind.
Attuned to the Creator Lord, one remains free of fear. |2|

Plants blossom forth to produce fruit.
When the fruit is produced, the flowers wither away.
For the sake of spiritual wisdom, people act and practice rituals.
When spiritual wisdom wells up, then actions are left behind. |3|

For the sake of ghee, wise people churn milk.
Those who are Jivan-mukta, liberated while yet alive - are forever in the state of Nirvaanaa.
Says Ravi Daas, O you unfortunate people,
why not meditate on the Lord with love in your heart? |4|1|

NAAM DAYV:
Come, O Lord of beautiful hair,
wearing the robes of a Sufi Saint. |Pause|

Your cap is the realm of the Akaashic ethers; the seven nether worlds are Your sandals.
The body covered with skin is Your temple; You are so beautiful, O Lord of the World. |1|

The fifty-six million clouds are Your gowns, the 16,000 milkmaids are your skirts.
The eighteen loads of vegetation is Your stick, and all the world is Your plate. |2|

The human body is the mosque, and the mind is the priest, who peacefully leads the prayer.
You are married to Maya, O Formless Lord, and so You have taken form. |3|

Performing devotional worship services to You, my cymbals were taken away; unto whom should I complain?

Naam Dayv's Lord and Master, the Inner-knower, the Searcher of hearts, wanders everywhere; He has no specific home. |4|1|

RAAG BASANT

Section 29 - Raag Basant - Part 001

Raag Basant, First Mehl, First House, Chau-Padas, Du-Tukas:
ONE Universal Creator God. Truth Is The Name. Creative Being Personified. No Fear. No Hatred. Image Of The Undying. Beyond Birth. Self-Existent. By Guru's Grace:
Among the months, blessed is this month, when spring always comes.
Blossom forth, O my consciousness, contemplating the Lord of the Universe, forever and ever. |1|

O ignorant one, forget your egotistical intellect.
Subdue your ego, and contemplate Him in your mind; gather in the virtues of the Sublime, Virtuous Lord. |1|Pause|

Karma is the tree, the Lord's Name the branches, Dharmic faith the flowers, and spiritual wisdom the fruit.
Realization of the Lord are the leaves, and eradication of the pride of the mind is the shade. |2|

Whoever sees the Lord's Creative Power with his eyes, and hears the Guru's Bani with his ears, and utters the True Name with his mouth,

attains the perfect wealth of honor, and intuitively focuses his meditation on the Lord. |3|

The months and the seasons come; see, and do your deeds.
O Nanak, those Gurmukhs who remain merged in the Lord do not wither away; they remain green forever. |4|1|

First Mehl, Basant:
The season of spring, so delightful, has come.
Those who are imbued with love for You, O Lord, chant Your Name with joy.
Whom else should I worship? At whose feet should I bow? |1|

I am the slave of Your slaves, O my Sovereign Lord King.
O Life of the Universe, there is no other way to meet You. |1|Pause|

You have only One Form, and yet You have countless forms.
Which one should I worship? Before which one should I burn incense?
Your limits cannot be found. How can anyone find them?
I am the slave of Your slaves, O my Sovereign Lord King. |2|

The cycles of years and the places of pilgrimage are Yours, O Lord.
Your Name is True, O Transcendent Lord God.
Your State cannot be known, O Eternal, Unchanging Lord God.
Although You are unknown, still we chant Your Name. |3|

What can poor Nanak say?
All people praise the One Lord.
Nanak places his head on the feet of such people.
I am a sacrifice to Your Names, as many as there are, O Lord. |4|2|

Basant, First Mehl:
The kitchen is golden, and the cooking pots are golden.
The lines marking the cooking square are silver.
The water is from the Ganges, and the firewood is sanctified.
The food is soft rice, cooked in milk. |1|

O my mind, these things are worthless,

Section 29 - Raag Basant - Part 002

if you are not drenched with the True Name. |1|Pause|

One may have the eighteen Puraanas written in his own hand;
he may recite the four Vedas by heart,
and take ritual baths at holy festivals and give charitable donations;
he may observe the ritual fasts, and perform religious ceremonies day and night. |2|

He may be a Qazi, a Mullah or a Shaykh,
a Yogi or a wandering hermit wearing saffron-colored robes;
he may be a householder, working at his job;

but without understanding the essence of devotional worship, all people are eventually bound and gagged, and driven along by the Messenger of Death. |3|

Each person's karma is written on his forehead.
According to their deeds, they shall be judged.
Only the foolish and the ignorant issue commands.
O Nanak, the treasure of praise belongs to the True Lord alone. |4|3|

Basant, Third Mehl:
A person may take off his clothes and be naked.
What Yoga does he practice by having matted and tangled hair?
If the mind is not pure, what use is it to hold the breath at the Tenth Gate?
The fool wanders and wanders, entering the cycle of reincarnation again and again. |1|

Meditate on the One Lord, O my foolish mind,
and you shall cross over to the other side in an instant. |1|Pause|

Some recite and expound on the Simritees and the Shaastras;
some sing the Vedas and read the Puraanas;
but they practice hypocrisy and deception with their eyes and minds.
The Lord does not even come near them. |2|

Even if someone practices such self-discipline,
compassion and devotional worship
- if he is filled with greed, and his mind is engrossed in corruption,
how can he find the Immaculate Lord? |3|

What can the created being do?
The Lord Himself moves him.
If the Lord casts His Glance of Grace, then his doubts are dispelled.
If the mortal realizes the Hukam of the Lord's Command, he obtains the True Lord. |4|

If someone's soul is polluted within,
what is the use of his traveling to sacred shrines of pilgrimage all over the world?
O Nanak, when one joins the Society of the True Guru,
then the bonds of the terrifying world-ocean are broken. |5|4|

Basant, First Mehl:
All the worlds have been fascinated and enchanted by Your Maya, O Lord.
I do not see any other at all - You are everywhere.
You are the Master of Yogis, the Divinity of the divine.
Serving at the Guru's Feet, the Name of the Lord is received. |1|

O my Beauteous, Deep and Profound Beloved Lord.
As Gurmukh, I sing the Glorious Praises of the Lord's Name. You are Infinite, the Cherisher of all. |1|Pause|

Without the Holy Saint, association with the Lord is not obtained.
Without the Guru, one's very fiber is stained with filth.
Without the Lord's Name, one cannot become pure.
Through the Word of the Guru's Shabad, sing the Praises of the True Lord. |2|

O Savior Lord, that person whom You have saved
- You lead him to meet the True Guru, and so take care of him.
You take away his poisonous egotism and attachment.
You dispel all his sufferings, O Sovereign Lord God. |3|

His state and condition are sublime; the Lord's Glorious Virtues permeate his body.
Through the Word of the Guru's Teachings, the diamond of the Lord's Name is revealed.
He is lovingly attuned to the Naam; he is rid of the love of duality.
O Lord, let servant Nanak meet the Guru. |4|5|

Basant, First Mehl:
O my friends and companions, listen with love in your heart.
My Husband Lord is Incomparably Beautiful; He is always with me.
He is Unseen - He cannot be seen. How can I describe Him?

Section 29 - Raag Basant - Part 003

The Guru has shown me that my Sovereign Lord God is with me. |1|

Joining together with my friends and companions, I am adorned with the Lord's Glorious Virtues.

The sublime soul-brides play with their Lord God. The Gurmukhs look within themselves; their minds are filled with faith. |1|Pause|

The self-willed manmukhs, suffering in separation, do not understand this mystery.
The Beloved Lord of all celebrates in each and every heart.
The Gurmukh is stable, knowing that God is always with him.
The Guru has implanted the Naam within me; I chant it, and meditate on it. |2|

Without the Guru, devotional love does not well up within.
Without the Guru, one is not blessed with the Society of the Saints.
Without the Guru, the blind cry out, entangled in worldly affairs.
That mortal who becomes Gurmukh becomes immaculate; the Word of the Shabad washes away his filth. |3|

Uniting with the Guru, the mortal conquers and subdues his mind.
Day and night, he savors the Yoga of devotional worship.
Associating with the Saint Guru, suffering and sickness are ended.
Servant Nanak merges with his Husband Lord, in the Yoga of intuitive ease. |4|6|

Basant, First Mehl:
By His Creative Power, God fashioned the creation.
The King of kings Himself adminsters true justice.
The most sublime Word of the Guru's Teachings is always with us.
The wealth of the Lord's Name, the source of nectar, is easily acquired. |1|

So chant the Name of the Lord; do not forget it, O my mind.
The Lord is Infinite, Inaccessible and Incomprehensible; His weight cannot be weighed, but He Himself allows the Gurmukh to weigh Him. |1|Pause|

Your GurSikhs serve at the Guru's Feet.
Serving the Guru, they are carried across; they have abandoned any distinction between 'mine' and 'yours'.
The slanderous and greedy people are hard-hearted.
Those who do not love to serve the Guru are the most thieving of thieves. |2|

When the Guru is pleased, He blesses the mortals with loving devotional worship of the Lord.

When the Guru is pleased, the mortal obtains a place in the Mansion of the Lord's Presence.

So renounce slander, and awaken in devotional worship of the Lord.

Devotion to the Lord is wonderful; it comes through good karma and destiny. |3|

The Guru unites in union with the Lord, and grants the gift of the Name.

The Guru loves His Sikhs, day and night.

They obtain the fruit of the Naam, when the Guru's favor is bestowed.

Says Nanak, those who receive it are very rare indeed. |4|7|

Basant, Third Mehl, Ik-Tukas:

When it pleases our Lord and Master, His servant serves Him.

He remains dead while yet alive, and redeems all his ancestors. |1|

I shall not renounce Your devotional worship, O Lord; what does it matter if people laugh at me?

The True Name abides within my heart. |1|Pause|

Just as the mortal remains engrossed in attachment to Maya,

so does the Lord's humble Saint remain absorbed in the Lord's Name. |2|

I am foolish and ignorant, O Lord; please be merciful to me.

May I remain in Your Sanctuary. |3|

Says Nanak, worldly affairs are fruitless.

Only by Guru's Grace does one receive the Nectar of the Naam, the Name of the Lord. |4|8|

First Mehl, Basant Hindol, Second House:

One Universal Creator God. By The Grace Of The True Guru:

O Brahmin, you worship and believe in your stone-god, and wear your ceremonial rosary beads.

Chant the Name of the Lord. Build your boat, and pray, "O Merciful Lord, please be merciful to me."|1|

Section 29 - Raag Basant - Part 004

Why do you irrigate the barren, alkaline soil? You are wasting your life away!

This wall of mud is crumbling. Why bother to patch it with plaster? |1|Pause|

Let your hands be the buckets, strung on the chain, and yoke the mind as the ox to pull it; draw the water up from the well.

Irrigate your fields with the Ambrosial Nectar, and you shall be owned by God the Gardener. |2|

Let sexual desire and anger be your two shovels, to dig up the dirt of your farm, O Siblings of Destiny.

The more you dig, the more peace you shall find. Your past actions cannot be erased. |3|

The crane is again transformed into a swan, if You so will, O Merciful Lord.

Prays Nanak, the slave of Your slaves: O Merciful Lord, have mercy on me. |4|1|9|

Basant, First Mehl, Hindol:

In the House of the Husband Lord - in the world hereafter, everything is jointly owned; but in this world - in the house of the soul-bride's parents, the soul-bride owns them separately.

She herself is ill-mannered; how can she blame anyone else? She does not know how to take care of these things. |1|

O my Lord and Master, I am deluded by doubt.

I sing the Word which You have written; I do not know any other Word. |1|Pause|

She alone is known as the Lord's bride, who embroiders her gown in the Name.

She who preserves and protects the home of her own heart and does not taste of evil, shall be the Beloved of her Husband Lord. |2|

If you are a learned and wise religious scholar, then make a boat of the letters of the Lord's Name.

Prays Nanak, the One Lord shall carry you across, if you merge in the True Lord. |3|2|10|

Basant Hindol, First Mehl:
The king is just a boy, and his city is vulnerable. He is in love with his wicked enemies.
He reads of his two mothers and his two fathers; O Pandit, reflect on this. |1|

O Master Pandit, teach me about this.
How can I obtain the Lord of life? |1|Pause|

There is fire within the plants which bloom; the ocean is tied into a bundle.
The sun and the moon dwell in the same home in the sky. You have not obtained this knowledge. |2|

One who knows the All-pervading Lord, eats up the one mother - Maya.
Know that the sign of such a person is that he gathers the wealth of compassion. |3|

The mind lives with those who do not listen, and do not admit what they eat.
Prays Nanak, the slave of the Lord's slave: one instant the mind is huge, and the next instant, it is tiny. |4|3|11|

Basant Hindol, First Mehl:
The Guru is the True Banker, the Giver of peace; He unites the mortal with the Lord, and satisfies his hunger.
Granting His Grace, He implants devotional worship of the Lord within; and then night and day, we sing the Glorious Praises of the Lord. |1|

O my mind, do not forget the Lord; keep Him in your consciousness.
Without the Guru, no one is liberated anywhere in the three worlds. The Gurmukh obtains the Lord's Name. |1|Pause|

Without devotional worship, the True Guru is not obtained. Without good destiny, devotional worship of the Lord is not obtained.
Without good destiny, the Sat Sangat, the True Congregation, is not obtained. By the grace of one's good karma, the Lord's Name is received. |2|

In each and every heart, the Lord is hidden; He creates and watches over all. He reveals Himself in the humble, Saintly Gurmukhs.

Those who chant the Name of the Lord, Har, Har, are drenched with the Lord's Love. Their minds are drenched with the Ambrosial Water of the Naam, the Name of the Lord. |3|

Section 29 - Raag Basant - Part 005

Those who are blessed with the glory of the Lord's Throne - those Gurmukhs are renowned as supreme.
Touching the philosopher's stone, they themselves becomes the philosopher's stone; they become the companions of the Lord, the Guru. |4|4|12|

Basant, Third Mehl, First House, Du-Tukas:
One Universal Creator God. By The Grace Of The True Guru:
Throughout the months and the seasons, the Lord is always in bloom.
He rejuvenates all beings and creatures.
What can I say? I am just a worm.
No one has found Your beginning or Your end, O Lord. |1|

Those who serve You, Lord,
obtain the greatest peace; their souls are so divine. |1|Pause|

If the Lord is merciful, then the mortal is allowed to serve Him.
By Guru's Grace, he remains dead while yet alive.
Night and day, he chants the True Name;
in this way, he crosses over the treacherous world-ocean. |2|

The Creator created both poison and nectar.
He attached these two fruits to the world-plant.
The Creator Himself is the Doer, the Cause of all.
He feeds all as He pleases. |3|

O Nanak, when He casts His Glance of Grace,
He Himself bestows His Ambrosial Naam.
Thus, the desire for sin and corruption is ended.
The Lord Himself carries out His Own Will. |4|1|

Basant, Third Mehl:
Those who are attuned to the True Lord's Name are happy and exalted.
Take pity on me, O God, Merciful to the meek.
Without Him, I have no other at all.

As it pleases His Will, He keeps me. |1|

The Guru, the Lord, is pleasing to my mind.
I cannot even survive, without the Blessed Vision of His Darshan. But I shall easily unite with the Guru, if He unites me in His Union. |1|Pause|

The greedy mind is enticed by greed.
Forgetting the Lord, it regrets and repents in the end.
The separated ones are reunited, when they are inspired to serve the Guru.
They are blessed with the Lord's Name - such is the destiny written on their foreheads. |2|

This body is built of air and water.
The body is afflicted with the terribly painful illness of egotism.
The Gurmukh has the Medicine: singing the Glorious Praises of the Lord's Name.
Granting His Grace, the Guru has cured the illness. |3|

The four evils are the four rivers of fire flowing through the body.
It is burning in desire, and burning in egotism.
Those whom the Guru protects and saves are very fortunate.
Servant Nanak enshrines the Ambrosial Name of the Lord in his heart. |4|2|

Basant, Third Mehl:
One who serves the Lord is the Lord's person.
He dwells in intuitive peace, and never suffers in sorrow.
The self-willed manmukhs are dead; the Lord is not within their minds.
They die and die again and again, and are reincarnated, only to die once more. |1|

They alone are alive, whose minds are filled with the Lord.
They contemplate the True Lord, and are absorbed in the True Lord. |1|Pause|

Those who do not serve the Lord are far away from the Lord.
They wander in foreign lands, with dust thrown on their heads.
The Lord Himself enjoins His humble servants to serve Him.
They live in peace forever, and have no greed at all. |2|

Section 29 - Raag Basant - Part 006

When the Lord bestows His Glance of Grace, egotism is eradicated.
Then, the mortal is honored in the Court of the True Lord.
He sees the Dear Lord always close at hand, ever-present.
Through the Word of the Guru's Shabad, he sees the Lord pervading and permeating all. |3|

The Lord cherishes all beings and creatures.
By Guru's Grace, contemplate Him forever.
You shall go to your true home in the Lord's Court with honor.
O Nanak, through the Naam, the Name of the Lord, you shall be blessed with glorious greatness. |4|3|

Basant, Third Mehl:
One who worships the Lord within his mind,
sees the One and Only Lord, and no other.
People in duality suffer terrible pain.
The True Guru has shown me the One Lord. |1|

My God is in bloom, forever in spring.
This mind blossoms forth, singing the Glorious Praises of the Lord of the Universe. |1|Pause|

So consult the Guru, and reflect upon His wisdom;
then, you shall be in love with the True Lord God.
Abandon your self-conceit, and be His loving servant.
Then, the Life of the World shall come to dwell in your mind. |2|

Worship Him with devotion, and see Him always ever-present, close at hand.
My God is forever permeating and pervading all.
Only a rare few know the mystery of this devotional worship.
My God is the Enlightener of all souls. |3|

The True Guru Himself unites us in His Union.
He Himself links our consciousness to the Lord, the Life of the World.
Thus, our minds and bodies are rejuvenated with intuitive ease.
O Nanak, through the Naam, the Name of the Lord, we remain attuned to the String of His Love. |4|4|

Basant, Third Mehl:
The Lord is the Lover of His devotees; He dwells within their minds,
by Guru's Grace, with intuitive ease.
Through devotional worship, self-conceit is eradicated from within,
and then, one meets the True Lord. |1|

His devotees are forever beauteous at the Door of the Lord God.
Loving the Guru, they have love and affection for the True Lord. |1|Pause|

That humble being who worships the Lord with devotion becomes
immaculate and pure.
Through the Word of the Guru's Shabad, egotism is eradicated from within.
The Dear Lord Himself comes to dwell within the mind,
and the mortal remains immersed in peace, tranquility and intuitive ease.
|2|

Those who are imbued with Truth, are forever in the bloom of spring.
Their minds and bodies are rejuvenated, uttering the Glorious Praises of
the Lord of the Universe.
Without the Lord's Name, the world is dry and parched.
It burns in the fire of desire, over and over again. |3|

One who does only that which is pleasing to the Dear Lord
- his body is forever at peace, and his consciousness is attached to the
Lord's Will.
He serves His God with intuitive ease.
O Nanak, the Naam, the Name of the Lord, comes to abide in his mind.
|4|5|

Basant, Third Mehl:
Attachment to Maya is burnt away by the Word of the Shabad.
The mind and body are rejuvenated by the Love of the True Guru.
The tree bears fruit at the Lord's Door,
in love with the True Bani of the Guru's Word, and the Naam, the Name of
the Lord. |1|

This mind is rejuvenated, with intuitive ease;
loving the True Guru, it bears the fruit of truth. |1|Pause|

He Himself is near, and He Himself is far away.
Through the Word of the Guru's Shabad, He is seen to be ever-present, close at hand.
The plants have blossomed forth, giving a dense shade.
The Gurmukh blossoms forth, with intuitive ease. |2|

Night and day, he sings the Kirtan of the Lord's Praises, day and night.
The True Guru drives out sin and doubt from within.

Section 29 - Raag Basant - Part 007

Gazing upon the wonder of God's Creation, I am wonder-struck and amazed.
The Gurmukh obtains the Naam, the Name of the Lord, by His Grace. |3|

The Creator Himself enjoys all delights.
Whatever He does, surely comes to pass.
He is the Great Giver; He has no greed at all.
O Nanak, living the Word of the Shabad, the mortal meets with God. |4|6|

Basant, Third Mehl:
By perfect destiny, one acts in truth.
Remembering the One Lord, one does not have to enter the cycle of reincarnation.
Fruitful is the coming into the world, and the life of one
who remains intuitively absorbed in the True Name. |1|

The Gurmukh acts, lovingly attuned to the Lord.
Be dedicated to the Lord's Name, and eradicate self-conceit from within. |1|Pause|

True is the speech of that humble being;
through the Word of the Guru's Shabad, it is spread throughout the world.
Throughout the four ages, his fame and glory spread.
Imbued with the Naam, the Name of the Lord, the Lord's humble servant is recognized and renowned. |2|

Some remain lovingly attuned to the True Word of the Shabad.
True are those humble beings who love the True Lord.

They meditate on the True Lord, and behold Him near at hand, ever-present.
They are the dust of the lotus feet of the humble Saints. |3|

There is only One Creator Lord; there is no other at all.
Through the Word of the Guru's Shabad, comes Union with the Lord.
Whoever serves the True Lord finds joy.
O Nanak, he is intuitively absorbed in the Naam, the Name of the Lord. |4|7|

Basant, Third Mehl:
The Lord's humble servant worships Him, and beholds Him ever-present, near at hand.
He is the dust of the lotus feet of the humble Saints.
Those who remain lovingly attuned to the Lord forever
are blessed with understanding by the Perfect True Guru. |1|

How rare are those who become the slave of the Lord's slaves.
They attain the supreme status. |1|Pause|

So serve the One Lord, and no other.
Serving Him, eternal peace is obtained.
He does not die; He does not come and go in reincarnation.
Why should I serve any other than Him, O my mother? |2|

True are those humble beings who realize the True Lord.
Conquering their self-conceit, they merge intuitively into the Naam, the Name of the Lord.
The Gurmukhs gather in the Naam.
Their minds are immaculate, and their reputations are immaculate. |3|

Know the Lord, who gave you spiritual wisdom,
and realize the One God, through the True Word of the Shabad.
When the mortal tastes the sublime essence of the Lord, he becomes pure and holy.
O Nanak, those who are imbued with the Naam - their reputations are true. |4|8|

Basant, Third Mehl:

Those who are imbued with the Naam, the Name of the Lord - their generations are redeemed and saved.
True is their speech; they love the Naam.
Why have the wandering self-willed manmukhs even come into the world?
Forgetting the Naam, the mortals waste their lives away. |1|

One who dies while yet alive, truly dies, and embellishes his death.
Through the Word of the Guru's Shabad, he enshrines the True Lord within his heart. |1|Pause|

Truth is the food of the Gurmukh; his body is sanctified and pure.
His mind is immaculate; he is forever the ocean of virtue.
He is not forced to come and go in the cycle of birth and death.
By Guru's Grace, he merges in the True Lord. |2|

Serving the True Lord, one realizes Truth.
Through the Word of the Guru's Shabad, he goes to the Lord's Court with his banners flying proudly.

Section 29 - Raag Basant - Part 008

In the Court of the True Lord, he obtains true glory.
He comes to dwell in the home of his own inner being. |3|

He cannot be fooled; He is the Truest of the True.
All others are deluded; in duality, they lose their honor.
So serve the True Lord, through the True Bani of His Word.
O Nanak, through the Naam, merge in the True Lord. |4|9|

Basant, Third Mehl:
Without the grace of good karma, all are deluded by doubt.
In attachment to Maya, they suffer in terrible pain.
The blind, self-willed manmukhs find no place of rest.
They are like maggots in manure, rotting away in manure. |1|

That humble being who obeys the Hukam of the Lord's Command is accepted.
Through the Word of the Guru's Shabad, he is blessed with the insignia and the banner of the Naam, the Name of the Lord. |1|Pause|

Those who have such pre-ordained destiny are imbued with the Naam.
The Name of the Lord is forever pleasing to their minds.
Through the Bani, the Word of the True Guru, eternal peace is found.
Through it, one's light merges into the Light. |2|

Only the Naam, the Name of the Lord, can save the world.
By Guru's Grace, one comes to love the Naam.
Without the Naam, no one obtains liberation.
Through the Perfect Guru, the Naam is obtained. |3|

He alone understands, whom the Lord Himself causes to understand.
Serving the True Guru, the Naam is implanted within.
Those humble beings who know the One Lord are approved and accepted.
O Nanak, imbued with the Naam, they go to the Lord's Court with His banner and insignia. |4|10|

Basant, Third Mehl:
Granting His Grace, the Lord leads the mortal to meet the True Guru.
The Lord Himself comes to abide in his mind.
His intellect becomes steady and stable, and his mind is strengthened forever.
He sings the Glorious Praises of the Lord, the Ocean of Virtue. |1|

Those who forget the Naam, the Name of the Lord - those mortals die eating poison.
Their lives are wasted uselessly, and they continue coming and going in reincarnation. |1|Pause|

They wear all sorts of religious robes, but their minds are not at peace.
In great egotism, they lose their honor.
But those who realize the Word of the Shabad, are blessed by great good fortune.
They bring their distractible minds back home. |2|

Within the home of the inner self is the inaccessible and infinite substance.
Those who find it, by following the Guru's Teachings, contemplate the Shabad.
Those who obtain the nine treasures of the Naam within the home of their own inner being,

are forever dyed in the color of the Lord's Love; they are absorbed in the Truth. |3|

God Himself does everything; no one can do anything at all by himself.
When God so wills, He merges the mortal into Himself.
All are near Him; no one is far away from Him.
O Nanak, the Naam is permeating and pervading everywhere. |4|11|

Basant, Third Mehl:
Through the Word of the Guru's Shabad, remember the Lord with love,
and you shall remain satisfied by the sublime essence of the Lord's Name.
The sins of millions upon millions of lifetimes shall be burnt away.
Remaining dead while yet alive, you shall be absorbed in the Lord's Name.
|1|

The Dear Lord Himself knows His own bountiful blessings.
This mind blossoms forth in the Guru's Shabad, chanting the Name of the Lord, the Giver of virtue. |1|Pause|

No one is liberated by wandering around in saffron-colored robes.
Tranquility is not found by strict self-discipline.
But by following the Guru's Teachings, one is blessed to receive the Naam, the Name of the Lord.
By great good fortune, one finds the Lord. |2|

In this Dark Age of Kali Yuga, glorious greatness comes through the Lord's Name.

Section 29 - Raag Basant - Part 009

Through the Perfect Guru, it is obtained.
Those who are imbued with the Naam find everlasting peace.
But without the Naam, mortals burn in egotism. |3|

By great good furtune, some contemplate the Lord's Name.
Through the Lord's Name, all sorrows are eradicated.
He dwells within the heart, and pervades the external universe as well.
O Nanak, the Creator Lord knows all. |4|12|

Basant, Third Mehl, Ik-Tukas:

I am just a worm, created by You, O Lord.
If you bless me, then I chant Your Primal Mantra. |1|

I chant and reflect on His Glorious Virtues, O my mother.
Meditating on the Lord, I fall at the Lord's Feet. |1|Pause|

By Guru's Grace, I am addicted to the favor of the Naam, the Name of the
Lord.
Why waste your life in hatred, vengeance and conflict? |2|

When the Guru granted His Grace, my egotism was eradicated,
and then, I obtained the Lord's Name with intuitive ease. |3|

The most lofty and exalted occupation is to contemplate the Word of the
Shabad.
Nanak chants the True Name. |4|1|13|

Basant, Third Mehl:
The season of spring has come, and all the plants have blossomed forth.
This mind blossoms forth, in association with the True Guru. |1|

So meditate on the True Lord, O my foolish mind.
Only then shall you find peace, O my mind. |1|Pause|

This mind blossoms forth, and I am in ecstasy.
I am blessed with the Ambrosial Fruit of the Naam, the Name of the Lord of
the Universe. |2|

Everyone speaks and says that the Lord is the One and Only.
By understanding the Hukam of His Command, we come to know the One
Lord. |3|

Says Nanak, no one can describe the Lord by speaking through ego.
All speech and insight comes from our Lord and Master. |4|2|14|

Basant, Third Mehl:
All the ages were created by You, O Lord.
Meeting with the True Guru, one's intellect is awakened. |1|

O Dear Lord, please blend me with Yourself;

let me merge in the True Name, through the Word of the Guru's Shabad. |1|Pause|

When the mind is in spring, all people are rejuvenated.
Blossoming forth and flowering through the Lord's Name, peace is obtained. |2|

Contemplating the Word of the Guru's Shabad, one is in spring forever, with the Lord's Name enshrined in the heart. |3|

When the mind is in spring, the body and mind are rejuvenated.
O Nanak, this body is the tree which bears the fruit of the Lord's Name. |4|3|15|

Basant, Third Mehl:
They alone are in the spring season, who sing the Glorious Praises of the Lord.
They come to worship the Lord with devotion, through their perfect destiny. |1|

This mind is not even touched by spring.
This mind is burnt by duality and double-mindedness. |1|Pause|

This mind is entangled in worldly affairs, creating more and more karma.
Enchanted by Maya, it cries out in suffering forever. |2|

This mind is released, only when it meets with the True Guru.
Then, it does not suffer beatings by the Messenger of Death. |3|

This mind is released, when the Guru emancipates it.
O Nanak, attachment to Maya is burnt away through the Word of the Shabad. |4|4|16|

Basant, Third Mehl:
Spring has come, and all the plants are flowering.
These beings and creatures blossom forth when they focus their consciousness on the Lord. |1|

Section 29 - Raag Basant - Part 010

In this way, this mind is rejuvenated.
Chanting the Name of the Lord, Har, Har, day and night, egotism is removed and washed away from the Gurmukhs. |1|Pause|

The True Guru speaks the Bani of the Word, and the Shabad, the Word of God.
This world blossoms forth in its greenery, through the love of the True Guru. |2|

The mortal blossoms forth in flower and fruit, when the Lord Himself so wills.
He is attached to the Lord, the Primal Root of all, when he finds the True Guru. |3|

The Lord Himself is the season of spring; the whole world is His Garden.
O Nanak, this most unique devotional worship comes only by perfect destiny. |4|5|17|

Basant Hindol, Third Mehl, Second House:
One Universal Creator God. By The Grace Of The True Guru:
I am a sacrifice to the Word of the Guru's Bani, O Siblings of Destiny. I am devoted and dedicated to the Word of the Guru's Shabad.
I praise my Guru forever, O Siblings of Destiny. I focus my consciousness on the Guru's Feet. |1|

O my mind, focus your consciousness on the Lord's Name.
Your mind and body shall blossom forth in lush greenery, and you shall obtain the fruit of the Name of the One Lord. |1|Pause|

Those who are protected by the Guru are saved, O Siblings of Destiny. They drink in the Ambrosial Nectar of the Lord's sublime essence.
The pain of egotism within is eradicated and banished, O Siblings of Destiny, and peace comes to dwell in their minds. |2|

Those whom the Primal Lord Himself forgives, O Siblings of Destiny, are united with the Word of the Shabad.
The dust of their feet brings emancipation; in the company of Sadh Sangat, the True Congregation, we are united with the Lord. |3|

He Himself does, and causes all to be done, O Siblings of Destiny; He makes everything blossom forth in green abundance.
O Nanak, peace fills their minds and bodies forever, O Siblings of Destiny; they are united with the Shabad. |4|1|18|12|18|30|

Raag Basant, Fourth Mehl, First House, Ik-Tukay:
One Universal Creator God. By The Grace Of The True Guru:
Just as the light of the sun's rays spread out,
the Lord permeates each and every heart, through and through. |1|

The One Lord is permeating and pervading all places.
Through the Word of the Guru's Shabad, we merge with Him, O my mother. |1|Pause|

The One Lord is deep within each and every heart.
Meeting with the Guru, the One Lord becomes manifest, radiating forth. |2|

The One and Only Lord is present and prevailing everywhere.
The greedy, faithless cynic thinks that God is far away. |3|

The One and Only Lord permeates and pervades the world.
O Nanak, whatever the One Lord does comes to pass. |4|1|

Basant, Fourth Mehl:
Day and night, the two calls are sent out.
O mortal, meditate in remembrance on the Lord, who protects you forever, and saves you in the end. |1|

Concentrate forever on the Lord, Har, Har, O my mind.
God the Destroyer of all depression and suffering is found, through the Guru's Teachings, singing the Glorious Praises of God. |1|Pause|

The self-willed manmukhs die of their egotism, over and over again.

Section 29 - Raag Basant - Part 011

They are destroyed by Death's demons, and they must go to the City of Death. |2|

The Gurmukhs are lovingly attached to the Lord, Har, Har, Har.
Their pains of both birth and death are taken away. |3|

The Lord showers His Mercy on His humble devotees.
Guru Nanak has shown mercy to me; I have met the Lord, the Lord of the forest. |4|2|

Basant Hindol, Fourth Mehl, Second House:
One Universal Creator God. By The Grace Of The True Guru:
The Lord's Name is a jewel, hidden in a chamber of the palace of the body-fortress.
When one meets the True Guru, then he searches and finds it, and his light merges with the Divine Light. |1|

O Lord, lead me to meet with the Holy Person, the Guru.
Gazing upon the Blessed Vision of His Darshan, all my sins are erased, and I obtain the supreme, sublime, sanctified status. |1|Pause|

The five thieves join together and plunder the body-village, stealing the wealth of the Lord's Name.
But through the Guru's Teachings, they are traced and caught, and this wealth is recovered intact. |2|

Practicing hypocrisy and superstition, people have grown weary of the effort, but still, deep within their hearts, they yearn for Maya, Maya.
By the Grace of the Holy Person, I have met with the Lord, the Primal Being, and the darkness of ignorance is dispelled. |3|

The Lord, the Lord of the Earth, the Lord of the Universe, in His Mercy, leads me to meet the Holy Person, the Guru.
O Nanak, peace then comes to abide deep within my mind, and I constantly sing the Glorious Praises of the Lord within my heart. |4|1|3|

Basant, Fourth Mehl, Hindol:
You are the Great Supreme Being, the Vast and Inaccessible Lord of the World; I am a mere insect, a worm created by You.
O Lord, Merciful to the meek, please grant Your Grace; O God, I long for the feet of the Guru, the True Guru. |1|

O Dear Lord of the Universe, please be merciful and unite me with the Sat Sangat, the True Congregation.

I was overflowing with the filthy sins of countless past lives. But joining the Sangat, God made me pure again. |1|Pause|

Your humble servant, whether of high class or low class, O Lord - by meditating on You, the sinner becomes pure.

The Lord exalts and elevates him above the whole world, and the Lord God blesses him with the Lord's Glory. |2|

Anyone who meditates on God, whether of high class or low class, will have all of his hopes and desires fulfilled.

Those humble servants of the Lord who enshrine the Lord within their hearts, are blessed, and are made great and totally perfect. |3|

I am so low, I am an utterly heavy lump of clay. Please shower Your Mercy on me, Lord, and unite me with Yourself.

The Lord, in His Mercy, has led servant Nanak to find the Guru; I was a sinner, and now I have become immaculate and pure. |4|2|4|

Basant Hindol, Fourth Mehl:

My mind cannot survive, even for an instant, without the Lord. I drink in continually the sublime essence of the Name of the Lord, Har, Har.

It is like a baby, who joyfully sucks at his mother's breast; when the breast is withdrawn, he weeps and cries. |1|

O Dear Lord of the Universe, my mind and body are pierced through by the Name of the Lord.

By great good fortune, I have found the Guru, the True Guru, and in the body-village, the Lord has revealed Himself. |1|Pause|

Section 29 - Raag Basant - Part 012

Each and every breath of the Lord's humble servant is pierced through with love of the Lord God.

As the lotus is totally in love with the water and withers away without seeing the water, so am I in love with the Lord. |2|

The Lord's humble servant chants the Immaculate Naam, the Name of the Lord; through the Guru's Teachings, the Lord reveals Himself.

The filth of egotism which stained me for countless lifetimes has been washed away, by the Ambrosial Water of the Ocean of the Lord. |3|

Please, do not take my karma into account, O my Lord and Master; please save the honor of Your slave.
O Lord, if it pleases You, hear my prayer; servant Nanak seeks Your Sanctuary. |4|3|5|

Basant Hindol, Fourth Mehl:
Each and every moment, my mind roams and rambles, and runs all over the place. It does not stay in its own home, even for an instant.
But when the bridle of the Shabad, the Word of God, is placed over its head, it returns to dwell in its own home. |1|

O Dear Lord of the Universe, lead me to join the Sat Sangat, the True Congregation, so that I may meditate on You, Lord.
I am cured of the disease of egotism, and I have found peace; I have intuitively entered into the state of Samaadhi. |1|Pause|

This house is loaded with countless gems, jewels, rubies and emeralds, but the wandering mind cannot find them.
As the water-diviner finds the hidden water, and the well is then dug in an instant, so do we find the object of the Name through the True Guru. |2|

Those who do not find such a Holy True Guru - cursed, cursed are the lives of those people.
The treasure of this human life is obtained when one's virtues bear fruit, but it is lost in exchange for a mere shell. |3|

O Lord God, please be merciful to me; be merciful, and lead me to meet the Guru.
Servant Nanak has attained the state of Nirvaanaa; meeting with the Holy people, he sings the Glorious Praises of the Lord. |4|4|6|

Basant Hindol, Fourth Mehl:
Coming and going, he suffers the pains of vice and corruption; the body of the self-willed manmukh is desolate and vacant.
He does not dwell on the Lord's Name, even for an instant, and so the Messenger of Death seizes him by his hair. |1|

O Dear Lord of the Universe, please rid me of the poison of egotism and attachment.

The Sat Sangat, Guru's True Congregation is so dear to the Lord. So join the Sangat, and taste the sublime essence of the Lord. |1|Pause|

Please be kind to me, and unite me with the Sat Sangat, the True Congregation of the Holy; I seek the Sanctuary of the Holy.

I am a heavy stone, sinking down - please lift me up and pull me out! O God, Merciful to the meek, You are the Destroyer of sorrow. |2|

I enshrine the Praises of my Lord and Master within my heart; joining the Sat Sangat, my intellect is enlightened.

I have fallen in love with the Lord's Name; I am a sacrifice to the Lord. |3|

O Lord God, please fulfill the desires of Your humble servant; please bless me with Your Name, O Lord.

Servant Nanak's mind and body are filled with ecstasy; the Guru has blessed him with the Mantra of the Lord's Name. |4|5|7|12|18|7|37|

Section 29 - Raag Basant - Part 013

Basant, Fifth Mehl, First House, Du-Tukay:
One Universal Creator God. By The Grace Of The True Guru:
I serve the Guru, and humbly bow to Him.
Today is a day of celebration for me.
Today I am in supreme bliss.
My anxiety is dispelled, and I have met the Lord of the Universe. |1|

Today, it is springtime in my household.
I sing Your Glorious Praises, O Infinite Lord God. |1|Pause|

Today, I am celebrating the festival of Phalgun.
Joining with God's companions, I have begun to play.
I celebrate the festival of Holi by serving the Saints.
I am imbued with the deep crimson color of the Lord's Divine Love. |2|

My mind and body have blossomed forth, in utter, incomparable beauty.
They do not dry out in either sunshine or shade;
they flourish in all seasons.
It is always springtime, when I meet with the Divine Guru. |3|

The wish-fulfilling Elysian Tree has sprouted and grown.
It bears flowers and fruits, jewels of all sorts.
I am satisfied and fulfilled, singing the Glorious Praises of the Lord.
Servant Nanak meditates on the Lord, Har, Har, Har. |4|1|

Basant, Fifth Mehl:
The shopkeeper deals in merchandise for profit.
The gambler's consciousness is focused on gambling.
The opium addict lives by consuming opium.
In the same way, the humble servant of the Lord lives by meditating on the Lord. |1|

Everyone is absorbed in his own pleasures.
He is attached to whatever God attaches him to. |1|Pause|

When the clouds and the rain come, the peacocks dance.
Seeing the moon, the lotus blossoms.
When the mother sees her infant, she is happy.
In the same way, the humble servant of the Lord lives by meditating on the Lord of the Universe. |2|

The tiger always wants to eat meat.
Gazing upon the battlefield, the warrior's mind is exalted.
The miser is totally in love with his wealth.
The humble servant of the Lord leans on the Support of the Lord, Har, Har. |3|

All love is contained in the Love of the One Lord.
All comforts are contained in the Comfort of the Lord's Name.
He alone receives this treasure,
O Nanak, unto whom the Guru gives His gift. |4|2|

Basant, Fifth Mehl:
He alone experiences this springtime of the soul, unto whom God grants His Grace.
He alone experiences this springtime of the soul, unto whom the Guru is merciful.
He alone is joyful, who works for the One Lord.

He alone experiences this eternal springtime of the soul, within whose heart the Naam, the Name of the Lord, abides. |1|

This spring comes only to those homes,
in which the melody of the Kirtan of the Lord's Praises resounds. |1|Pause|

O mortal, let your love for the Supreme Lord God blossom forth.
Practice spiritual wisdom, and consult the humble servants of the Lord.
He alone is an ascetic, who joins the Saadh Sangat, the Company of the Holy.
He alone dwells in deep, continual meditation, who loves his Guru. |2|

He alone is fearless, who has the Fear of God.
He alone is peaceful, whose doubts are dispelled.
He alone is a hermit, who heart is steady and stable.
He alone is steady and unmoving, who has found the true place. |3|

He seeks the One Lord, and loves the One Lord.
He loves to gaze upon the Blessed Vision of the Lord's Darshan.
He intuitively enjoys the Love of the Lord.
Slave Nanak is a sacrifice to that humble being. |4|3|

Section 29 - Raag Basant - Part 014

Basant, Fifth Mehl:
You gave us our soul, breath of life and body.
I am a fool, but You have made me beautiful, enshrining Your Light within me.
We are all beggars, O God; You are merciful to us.
Chanting the Naam, the Name of the Lord, we are uplifted and exalted. |1|

O my Beloved, only You have the potency to act,
and cause all to be done. |1|Pause|

Chanting the Naam, the mortal is saved.
Chanting the Naam, sublime peace and poise are found.
Chanting the Naam, honor and glory are received.
Chanting the Naam, no obstacles shall block your way. |2|

For this reason, you have been blessed with this body, so difficult to obtain.

O my Dear God, please bless me to speak the Naam.
This tranquil peace is found in the Saadh Sangat, the Company of the Holy.
May I always chant and meditate within my heart on Your Name, O God.
|3|

Other than You, there is no one at all.
Everything is Your play; it all merges again into You.
As it pleases Your Will, save me, Lord.
O Nanak, peace is obtained by meeting with the Perfect Guru. |4|4|

Basant, Fifth Mehl:
My Beloved God, my King is with me.
Gazing upon Him, I live, O my mother.
Remembering Him in meditation, there is no pain or suffering.
Please, take pity on me, and lead me on to meet Him. |1|

My Beloved is the Support of my breath of life and mind.
This soul, breath of life, and wealth are all Yours, O Lord. |1|Pause|

He is sought by the angels, mortals and divine beings.
The silent sages, the humble, and the religious teachers do not understand
His mystery.
His state and extent cannot be described.
In each and every home of each and every heart, He is permeating and
pervading. |2|

His devotees are totally in bliss.
His devotees cannot be destroyed.
His devotees are not afraid.
His devotees are victorious forever. |3|

What Praises of Yours can I utter?
God, the Giver of peace, is all-pervading, permeating everywhere.
Nanak begs for this one gift.
Be merciful, and bless me with Your Name. |4|5|

Basant, Fifth Mehl:
As the plant turns green upon receiving water,
just so, in the Saadh Sangat, the Company of the Holy, egotism is eradicated.

Just as the servant is encouraged by his ruler,
we are saved by the Guru. |1|

You are the Great Giver, O Generous Lord God.
Each and every instant, I humbly bow to You. |1|Pause|

Whoever enters the Saadh Sangat
- that humble being is imbued with the Love of the Supreme Lord God.
He is liberated from bondage.
His devotees worship Him in adoration; they are united in His Union. |2|

My eyes are content, gazing upon the Blessed Vision of His Darshan.
My tongue sings the Infinite Praises of God.
My thirst is quenched, by Guru's Grace.
My mind is satisfied, with the sublime taste of the Lord's subtle essence.
|3|

Your servant is committed to the service of Your Feet,
O Primal Infinite Divine Being.
Your Name is the Saving Grace of all.
Nanak has received this teasure. |4|6|

Basant, Fifth Mehl:
You are the Great Giver; You continue to give.
You permeate and pervade my soul, and my breath of life.
You have given me all sorts of foods and dishes.
I am unworthy; I know none of Your Virtues at all. |1|

I do not understand anything of Your Worth.

Section 29 - Raag Basant - Part 015

Save me, O my Merciful Lord God. |1|Pause|

I have not practiced meditation, austerities or good actions.
I do not know the way to meet You.
Within my mind, I have placed my hopes in the One Lord alone.
The Support of Your Name shall carry me across. |2|

You are the Expert, O God, in all powers.

The fish cannot find the limits of the water.
You are Inaccessible and Unfathomable, the Highest of the High.
I am small, and You are so very Great. |3|

Those who meditate on You are wealthy.
Those who attain You are rich.
Those who serve You are peaceful.
Nanak seeks the Sanctuary of the Saints. |4|7|

Basant, Fifth Mehl:
Serve the One who created You.
Worship the One who gave you life.
Become His servant, and you shall never again be punished.
Become His trustee, and you shall never again suffer sorrow. |1|

That mortal who is blessed with such great good fortune,
attains this state of Nirvaanaa. |1|Pause|

Life is wasted uselessly in the service of duality.
No efforts shall be rewarded, and no works brought to fruition.
It is so painful to serve only mortal beings.
Service to the Holy brings lasting peace and bliss. |2|

If you long for eternal peace, O Siblings of Destiny,
then join the Saadh Sangat, the Company of the Holy; this is the Guru's
advice.
There, the Naam, the Name of the Lord, is meditated on.
In the Saadh Sangat, you shall be emancipated. |3|

Among all essences, this is the essence of spiritual wisdom.
Among all meditations, meditation on the One Lord is the most sublime.
The Kirtan of the Lord's Praises is the ultimate melody.
Meeting with the Guru, Nanak sings the Glorious Praises of the Lord. |4|8|

Basant, Fifth Mehl:
Chanting His Name, one's mouth becomes pure.
Meditating in remembrance on Him, one's reputation becomes stainless.
Worshipping Him in adoration, one is not tortured by the Messenger of
Death.
Serving Him, everything is obtained. |1|

The Lord's Name - chant the Lord's Name.
Abandon all the desires of your mind. |1|Pause|

He is the Support of the earth and the sky.
His Light illuminates each and every heart.
Meditating in remembrance on Him, even fallen sinners are sanctified;
in the end, they will not weep and wail over and over again. |2|

Among all religions, this is the ultimate religion.
Among all rituals and codes of conduct, this is above all.
The angels, mortals and divine beings long for Him.
To find Him, commit yourself to the service of the Society of the Saints. |3|

One whom the Primal Lord God blesses with His bounties,
obtains the treasure of the Lord.
His state and extent cannot be described.
Servant Nanak meditates on the Lord, Har, Har. |4|9|

Basant, Fifth Mehl:
My mind and body are gripped by thirst and desire.
The Merciful Guru has fulfilled my hopes.
In the Saadh Sangat, the Company of the Holy, all my sins have been taken away.
I chant the Naam, the Name of the Lord; I am in love with the Name of the Lord. |1|

By Guru's Grace, this spring of the soul has come.
I enshrine the Lord's Lotus Feet within my heart; I listen to the Lord's Praise, forever and ever. |1|Pause|

Section 29 - Raag Basant - Part 016

Our All-powerful Lord and Master is the Doer of all, the Cause of all causes.
I am an orphan - I seek Your Sanctuary, God.
All beings and creatures take Your Support.
Be merciful, God, and save me. |2|

God is the Destroyer of fear, the Remover of pain and suffering.
The angelic beings and silent sages serve Him.

The earth and the sky are in His Power.
All beings eat what You give them. |3|

O Merciful God, O Searcher of hearts,
please bless Your slave with Your Glance of Grace.
Please be kind and bless me with this gift,
that Nanak may live in Your Name. |4|10|

Basant, Fifth Mehl:
Loving the Lord, one's sins are taken away.
Meditating on the Lord, one does not suffer at all.
Meditating on the Lord of the Universe, all darkness is dispelled.
Meditating in remembrance on the Lord, the cycle of reincarnation comes
to an end. |1|

The love of the Lord is springtime for me.
I am always with the humble Saints. |1|Pause|

The Saints have shared the Teachings with me.
Blessed is that country where the devotees of the Lord of the Universe
dwell.
But that place where the Lord's devotees are not, is wilderness.
By Guru's Grace, realize the Lord in each and every heart. |2|

Sing the Kirtan of the Lord's Praises, and enjoy the nectar of His Love.
O mortal, you must always restrain yourself from committing sins.
Behold the Creator Lord God near at hand.
Here and hereafter, God shall resolve your affairs. |3|

I focus my meditation on the Lord's Lotus Feet.
Granting His Grace, God has blessed me with this Gift.
I yearn for the dust of the feet of Your Saints.
Nanak meditates on his Lord and Master, who is ever-present, near at
hand. |4|11|

Basant, Fifth Mehl:
The True Transcendent Lord is always new, forever fresh.
By Guru's Grace, I continually chant His Name.
God is my Protector, my Mother and Father.
Meditating in remembrance on Him, I do not suffer in sorrow. |1|

I meditate on my Lord and Master, single-mindedly, with love.
I seek the Sanctuary of the Perfect Guru forever. My True Lord and Master hugs me close in His Embrace. |1|Pause|

God Himself protects His humble servants.
The demons and wicked enemies have grown weary of struggling against Him.
Without the True Guru, there is no place to go.
Wandering through the lands and foreign countries, people only grow tired and suffer in pain. |2|

The record of their past actions cannot be erased.
They harvest and eat what they have planted.
The Lord Himself is the Protector of His humble servants.
No one can rival the humble servant of the Lord. |3|

By His own efforts, God protects His slave.
God's Glory is perfect and unbroken.
So sing the Glorious Praises of the Lord of the Universe with your tongue forever.
Nanak lives by meditating on the Feet of the Lord. |4|12|

Basant, Fifth Mehl:
Dwelling at the Guru's Feet, pain and suffering go away.
The Supreme Lord God has shown mercy to me.
All my desires and tasks are fulfilled.
Chanting the Lord's Name, Nanak lives. |1|

How beautiful is that season, when the Lord fills the mind.
Without the True Guru, the world weeps. The faithless cynic comes and goes in reincarnation, over and over again. |1|Pause|

Section 29 - Raag Basant - Part 017

They alone are rich, who have the Wealth of the Lord God.
Through the Word of the Guru's Shabad, sexual desire and anger are eradicated.
Their fear is dispelled, and they attain the state of fearlessness.
Meeting with the Guru, Nanak meditates on his Lord and Master. |2|

God dwells in the Saadh Sangat, the Company of the Holy.
Chanting and meditating on the Lord, one's hopes are fulfilled.
God permeates and pervades the water, the land and the sky.
Meeting with the Guru, Nanak chants the Name of the Lord, Har, Har. |3|

The eight miraculous spiritual powers and the nine treasures are contained in the Naam, the Name of the Lord. This is bestowed when God grants His Grace.
Your slaves, O God, live by chanting and meditating on Your Name.
O Nanak, the heart-lotus of the Gurmukh blossoms forth. |4|13|

Basant, Fifth Mehl, First House, Ik-Tukay:
One Universal Creator God. By The Grace Of The True Guru:
Meditating on the Lord, all desires are fulfilled,
and the mortal is re-united with God, after having been separated for so long. |1|

Meditate on the Lord of the Universe, who is worthy of meditation.
Meditating on Him, enjoy celestial peace and poise. |1|Pause|

Bestowing His Mercy, He blesses us with His Glance of Grace.
God Himself takes care of His slave. |2|

My bed has been beautified by His Love.
God, the Giver of Peace, has come to meet me. |3|

He does not consider my merits and demerits.
Nanak worships at the Feet of God. |4|1|14|

Basant, Fifth Mehl:
The sins are erased, singing the Glories of God;
night and day, celestial joy wells up. |1|

My mind has blossomed forth, by the touch of the Lord's Feet.
By His Grace, He has led me to meet the Holy men, the humble servants of the Lord. I remain continually imbued with the love of the Lord's Name. |1|Pause|

In His Mercy, the Lord of the World has revealed Himself to me.

The Lord, Merciful to the meek, has attached me to the hem of His robe and saved me. |2|

This mind has become the dust of the Holy;
I behold my Lord and Master, continually, ever-present. |3|

Sexual desire, anger and desire have vanished.
O Nanak, God has become kind to me. |4|2|15|

Basant, Fifth Mehl:
God Himself has cured the disease.
He laid on His Hands, and protected His child. |1|

Celestial peace and tranquility fill my home forever, in this springtime of the soul.
I have sought the Sanctuary of the Perfect Guru; I chant the Mantra of the Name of the Lord, Har, Har, the Embodiment of emancipation. |1|Pause|

God Himself has dispelled my sorrow and suffering.
I meditate continually, continuously, on my Guru. |2|

That humble being who chants Your Name,
obtains all fruits and rewards; singing the Glories of God, he becomes steady and stable. |3|

O Nanak, the way of the devotees is good.
They meditate continually, continuously, on the Lord, the Giver of peace. |4|3|16|

Basant, Fifth Mehl:
By His Will, He makes us happy.
He shows Mercy to His servant. |1|

The Perfect Guru makes everything perfect.
He implants the Amrosial Naam, the Name of the Lord, in the heart. |1|Pause|

He does not consider the karma of my actions, or my Dharma, my spiritual practice.

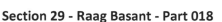

Section 29 - Raag Basant - Part 018

Taking me by the arm, He saves me and carries me across the terrifying world-ocean. |2|

God has rid me of my filth, and made me stainless and pure.
I have sought the Sanctuary of the Perfect Guru. |3|

He Himself does, and causes everything to be done.
By His Grace, O Nanak, He saves us. |4|4|17|

Basant, Fifth Mehl:
One Universal Creator God. By The Grace Of The True Guru:
Behold the flowers flowering, and the blossoms blossoming forth!
Renounce and abandon your egotism.
Grasp hold of His Lotus Feet.
Meet with God, O blessed one.
O my mind, remain conscious of the Lord. |Pause|

The tender young plants smell so good,
while others remain like dry wood.
The season of spring has come;
it blossoms forth luxuriantly. |1|

Now, the Dark Age of Kali Yuga has come.
Plant the Naam, the Name of the One Lord.
It is not the season to plant other seeds.
Do not wander lost in doubt and delusion.
One who has such destiny written on his forehead, shall meet with the Guru and find the Lord.
O mortal, this is the season of the Naam.
Nanak utters the Glorious Praises of the Lord, Har, Har, Har, Har. |2|18|

Basant, Fifth Mehl, Second House, Hindol:
One Universal Creator God. By The Grace Of The True Guru:
Come and join together, O my Siblings of Destiny; dispel your sense of duality and let yourselves be lovingly absorbed in the Lord.
Let yourselves be joined to the Name of the Lord; become Gurmukh, spread out your mat, and sit down. |1|

In this way, throw the dice, O brothers.
As Gurmukh, chant the Naam, the Name of the Lord, day and night. At the very last moment, you shall not have to suffer in pain. |1|Pause|

Let righteous actions be your gameboard, and let the truth be your dice.
Conquer sexual desire, anger, greed and worldly attachment; only such a game as this is dear to the Lord. |2|

Rise in the early hours of the morning, and take your cleansing bath. Before you go to bed at night, remember to worship the Lord.
My True Guru will assist you, even on your most difficult moves; you shall reach your true home in celestial peace and poise. |3|

The Lord Himself plays, and He Himself watches; the Lord Himself created the creation.
O servant Nanak, that person who plays this game as Gurmukh, wins the game of life, and returns to his true home. |4|1|19|

Basant, Fifth Mehl, Hindol:
You alone know Your Creative Power, O Lord; no one else knows it.
He alone realizes You, O my Beloved, unto whom You show Your Mercy. |1|

I am a sacrifice to Your devotees.
Your place is eternally beautiful, God; Your wonders are infinite. |1|Pause|

Only You Yourself can perform Your service. No one else can do it.
He alone is Your devotee, who is pleasing to You. You bless them with Your Love. |2|

Section 29 - Raag Basant - Part 019

You are the Great Giver; You are so very Wise. There is no other like You.
You are my All-powerful Lord and Master; I do not know how to worship You. |3|

Your Mansion is imperceptible, O my Beloved; it is so difficult to accept Your Will.
Says Nanak, I have collapsed at Your Door, Lord. I am foolish and ignorant - please save me! |4|2|20|

Basant Hindol, Fifth Mehl:
The mortal does not know the Primal Lord God; he does not understand hmself. He is engrossed in doubt and egotism. |1|

My Father is the Supreme Lord God, my Master.
I am unworthy, but please save me anyway. |1|Pause|

Creation and destruction come only from God; this is what the Lord's humble servants believe. |2|

Only those who are imbued with God's Name are judged to be peaceful in this Dark Age of Kali Yuga. |3|

It is the Guru's Word that carries us across; Nanak cannot think of any other way. |4|3|21|

One Universal Creator God. By The Grace Of The True Guru:
Raag Basant Hindol, Ninth Mehl:
O Holy Saints, know that this body is false.
The Lord who dwells within it - recognize that He alone is real. |1|Pause|

The wealth of this world is only a dream; why are you so proud of it?
None of it shall go along with you in the end; why do you cling to it? |1|

Leave behind both praise and slander; enshrine the Kirtan of the Lord's Praises within your heart.
O servant Nanak, the One Primal Being, the Lord God, is totally permeating everywhere. |2|1|

Basant, Ninth Mehl:
The heart of the sinner is filled with unfulfilled sexual desire.
He cannot control his fickle mind. |1|Pause|

The Yogis, wandering ascetics and renunciates
- this net is cast over them all. |1|

Those who contemplate the Name of the Lord
cross over the terrifying world-ocean. |2|

Servant Nanak seeks the Sanctuary of the Lord.
Please bestow the blessing of Your Name, that he may continue to sing
Your Glorious Praises. |3|2|

Basant, Ninth Mehl:
O mother, I have gathered the wealth of the Lord's Name.
My mind has stopped its wanderings, and now, it has come to rest.
|1|Pause|

Attachment to Maya has run away from my body, and immaculate spiritual
wisdom has welled up within me.
Greed and attachment cannot even touch me; I have grasped hold of
devotional worship of the Lord. |1|

The cynicism of countless lifetimes has been eradicated, since I obtained
the jewel of the Naam, the Name of the Lord.
My mind was rid of all its desires, and I was absorbed in the peace of my
own inner being. |2|

That person, unto whom the Merciful Lord shows compassion, sings the
Glorious Praises of the Lord of the Universe.
Says Nanak, this wealth is gathered only by the Gurmukh. |3|3|

Basant, Ninth Mehl:
O my mind, how can you forget the Lord's Name?
When the body perishes, you shall have to deal with the Messenger of
Death. |1|Pause|

This world is just a hill of smoke.

Section 29 - Raag Basant - Part 020

What makes you think that it is real? |1|

Wealth, spouse, property and household
- none of them shall go along with you; you must know that this is true! |2|

Only devotion to the Lord shall go with you.
Says Nanak, vibrate and meditate on the Lord with single-minded love.
|3|4|

Basant, Ninth Mehl:
Why do you wander lost, O mortal, attached to falsehood and greed?
Nothing has been lost yet - there is still time to wake up! |1|Pause|

You must realize that this world is nothing more than a dream.
In an instant, it shall perish; know this as true. |1|

The Lord constantly abides with you.
Night and day, vibrate and meditate on Him, O my friend. |2|

At the very last instant, He shall be your Help and Support.
Says Nanak, sing His Praises. |3|5|

Basant, First Mehl, Ashtapadees, First House, Du-Tukees:
One Universal Creator God. By The Grace Of The True Guru:
The world is a crow; it does not remember the Naam, the Name of the
Lord.
Forgetting the Naam, it sees the bait, and pecks at it.
The mind wavers unsteadily, in guilt and deceit.
I have shattered my attachment to the false world. |1|

The burden of sexual desire, anger and corruption is unbearable.
Without the Naam, how can the mortal maintain a virtuous lifestyle?
|1|Pause|

The world is like a house of sand, built on a whirlpool;
it is like a bubble formed by drops of rain.
It is formed from a mere drop, when the Lord's wheel turns round.
The lights of all souls are the servants of the Lord's Name. |2|

My Supreme Guru has created everything.
I perform devotional worship service to You, and fall at Your Feet, O Lord.
Imbued with Your Name, I long to be Yours.
Those who do not let the Naam become manifest within themselves,
depart like thieves in the end. |3|

The mortal loses his honor, gathering sin and corruption.
But imbued with the Lord's Name, you shall go to your true home with
honor.

God does whatever He wills.
One who abides in the Fear of God, becomes fearless, O my mother. |4|

The woman desires beauty and pleasure.
But betel leaves, garlands of flowers and sweet tastes lead only to disease.
The more she plays and enjoys, the more she suffers in sorrow.
But when she enters into the Sanctuary of God, whatever she wishes comes to pass. |5|

She wears beautiful clothes with all sorts of decorations.
But the flowers turn to dust, and her beauty leads her into evil.
Hope and desire have blocked the doorway.
Without the Naam, one's hearth and home are deserted. |6|

O princess, my daughter, run away from this place!
Chant the True Name, and embellish your days.
Serve your Beloved Lord God, and lean on the Support of His Love.
Through the Word of the Guru's Shabad, abandon your thirst for corruption and poison. |7|

My Fascinating Lord has fascinated my mind.
Through the Word of the Guru's Shabad, I have realized You, Lord.
Nanak stands longingly at God's Door.
I am content and satisfied with Your Name; please shower me with Your Mercy. |8|1|

Basant, First Mehl:
The mind is deluded by doubt; it comes and goes in reincarnation.
It is lured by the poisonous lure of Maya.
It does not remain stable in the Love of the One Lord.
Like the fish, its neck is pierced by the hook. |1|

The deluded mind is instructed by the True Name.
It contemplates the Word of the Guru's Shabad, with intuitive ease. |1|Pause|

Section 29 - Raag Basant - Part 021

The mind, deluded by doubt, buzzes around like a bumble bee.

The holes of the body are worthless, if the mind is filled with such great desire for corrupt passions.

It is like the elephant, trapped by its own sexual desire.

It is caught and held tight by the chains, and beaten on its head. |2|

The mind is like a foolish frog, without devotional worship.

It is cursed and condemned in the Court of the Lord, without the Naam, the Name of the Lord.

He has no class or honor, and no one even mentions his name.

That person who lacks virtue - all of his pains and sorrows are his only companions. |3|

His mind wanders out, and cannot be brought back or restrained.

Without being imbued with the sublime essence of the Lord, it has no honor or credit.

You Yourself are the Listener, Lord, and You Yourself are our Protector.

You are the Support of the earth; You Yourself behold and understand it. |4|

When You Yourself make me wander, unto whom can I complain?

Meeting the Guru, I will tell Him of my pain, O my mother.

Abandoning my worthless demerits, now I practice virtue.

Imbued with the Word of the Guru's Shabad, I am absorbed in the True Lord. |5|

Meeting with the True Guru, the intellect is elevated and exalted.

The mind becomes immaculate, and egotism is washed away.

He is liberated forever, and no one can put him in bondage.

He chants the Naam forever, and nothing else. |6|

The mind comes and goes according to the Will of the Lord.

The One Lord is contained amongst all; nothing else can be said.

The Hukam of His Command pervades everywhere, and all merge in His Command.

Pain and pleasure all come by His Will. |7|

You are infallible; You never make mistakes.

Those who listen to the Word of the Guru's Shabad - their intellects become deep and profound.

You, O my Great Lord and Master, are contained in the Shabad.

O Nanak, my mind is pleased, praising the True Lord. |8|2|

Basant, First Mehl:
That person, who thirsts for the Blessed Vision of the Lord's Darshan,
is absorbed in the One Lord, leaving duality behind.
His pains are taken away, as he churns and drinks in the Ambrosial Nectar.
The Gurmukh understands, and merges in the One Lord. |1|

So many cry out for Your Darshan, Lord.
How rare are those who realize the Word of the Guru's Shabad and merge
with Him. |1|Pause|

The Vedas say that we should chant the Name of the One Lord.
He is endless; who can find His limits?
There is only One Creator, who created the world.
Without any pillars, He supports the earth and the sky. |2|

Spiritual wisdom and meditation are contained in the melody of the Bani,
the Word of the One Lord.
The One Lord is Untouched and Unstained; His story is unspoken.
The Shabad, the Word, is the Insignia of the One True Lord.
Through the Perfect Guru, the Knowing Lord is known. |3|

There is only one religion of Dharma; let everyone grasp this truth.
Through the Guru's Teachings, one becomes perfect, all the ages through.
Imbued with the Unmanifest Celestial Lord, and lovingly absorbed in the
One,
the Gurmukh attains the invisible and infinite. |4|

There is one celestial throne, and One Supreme King.
The Independent Lord God is pervading all places.
The three worlds are the creation of that Sublime Lord.
The One Creator of the Creation is Unfathomable and Incomprehensible.
|5|

His Form is One, and True is His Name.
True justice is administered there.
Those who practice Truth are honored and accepted.
They are honored in the Court of the True Lord. |6|

Devotional worship of the One Lord is the expression of love for the One Lord.

Without the Fear of God and devotional worship of Him, the mortal comes and goes in reincarnation.

One who obtains this understanding from the Guru dwells like an honored guest in this world.

Section 29 - Raag Basant - Part 022

That humble being who is imbued with the sublime essence of the Lord is certified and approved. |7|

I see Him here and there; I dwell on Him intuitively.
I do not love any other than You, O Lord and Master.
O Nanak, my ego has been burnt away by the Word of the Shabad.
The True Guru has shown me the Blessed Vision of the True Lord. |8|3|

Basant, First Mehl:
The fickle consciousness cannot find the Lord's limits.
It is caught in non-stop coming and going.
I am suffering and dying, O my Creator.
No one cares for me, except my Beloved. |1|

All are high and exalted; how can I call anyone low?
Devotional worship of the Lord and the True Name has satisfied me. |1|Pause|

I have taken all sorts of medicines; I am so tired of them.
How can this disease be cured, without my Guru?
Without devotional worship of the Lord, the pain is so great.
My Lord and Master is the Giver of pain and pleasure. |2|

The disease is so deadly; how can I find the courage?
He knows my disease, and only He can take away the pain.
My mind and body are filled with faults and demerits.
I searched and searched, and found the Guru, O my brother! |3|

The Word of the Guru's Shabad, and the Lord's Name are the cures.
As You keep me, so do I remain.
The world is sick; where should I look?

The Lord is Pure and Immaculate; Immaculate is His Name. |4|

The Guru sees and reveals the Lord's home, deep within the home of the self;
He ushers the soul-bride into the Mansion of the Lord's Presence.
When the mind remains in the mind, and the consciousness in the consciousness,
such people of the Lord remain unattached. |5|

They remain free of any desire for happiness or sorrow;
tasting the Amrit, the Ambrosial Nectar, they abide in the Lord's Name.
They recognize their own selves, and remain lovingly attuned to the Lord.
They are victorious on the battlefield of life, following the Guru's Teachings, and their pains run away. |6|

The Guru has given me the True Ambrosial Nectar; I drink it in.
Of course, I have died, and now I am alive to live.
Please, protect me as Your Own, if it pleases You.
One who is Yours, merges into You. |7|

Painful diseases afflict those who are sexually promiscuous.
God appears permeating and pervading in each and every heart.
One who remains unattached, through the Word of the Guru's Shabad
- O Nanak, his heart and consciousness dwell upon and savor the Lord. |8|4|

Basant, First Mehl, Ik-Tukee:
Do not make such a show of rubbing ashes on your body.
O naked Yogi, this is not the way of Yoga! |1|

You fool! How can you have forgotten the Lord's Name?
At the very last moment, it and it alone shall be of any use to you. |1|Pause|

Consult the Guru, reflect and think it over.
Wherever I look, I see the Lord of the World. |2|

What can I say? I am nothing.
All my status and honor are in Your Name. |3|

Why do you take such pride in gazing upon your property and wealth?
When you must leave, nothing shall go along with you. |4|

So subdue the five thieves, and hold your consciousness in its place.
This is the basis of the way of Yoga. |5|

Your mind is tied with the rope of egotism.
You do not even think of the Lord - you fool! He alone shall liberate you.
|6|

If you forget the Lord, you will fall into the clutches of the Messenger of
Death.
At that very last moment, you fool, you shall be beaten. |7|

Section 29 - Raag Basant - Part 023

Contemplate the Word of the Guru's Shabad, and be rid of your ego.
True Yoga shall come to dwell in your mind. |8|

He blessed you with body and soul, but you do not even think of Him.
You fool! Visiting graves and cremation grounds is not Yoga. |9|

Nanak chants the sublime, glorious Bani of the Word.
Understand it, and appreciate it. |10|5|

Basant, First Mehl:
In duality and evil-mindedness, the mortal acts blindly.
The self-willed manmukh wanders, lost in the darkness. |1|

The blind man follows blind advice.
Unless one takes the Guru's Way, his doubt is not dispelled. |1|Pause|

The manmukh is blind; he does not like the Guru's Teachings.
He has become a beast; he cannot get rid of his egotistical pride. |2|

God created 8.4 million species of beings.
My Lord and Master, by the Pleasure of His Will, creates and destroys
them. |3|

All are deluded and confused, without the Word of the Shabad and good conduct.
He alone is instructed in this, who is blessed by the Guru, the Creator. |4|

The Guru's servants are pleasing to our Lord and Master.
The Lord forgives them, and they no longer fear the Messenger of Death. |5|

Those who love the One Lord with all their heart
- He dispels their doubts and unites them with Himself. |6|

God is Independent, Endless and Infinite.
The Creator Lord is pleased with Truth. |7|

O Nanak, the Guru instructs the mistaken soul.
He implants the Truth within him, and shows him the One Lord. |8|6|

Basant, First Mehl:
He Himself is the bumble bee, the fruit and the vine.
He Himself unites us with the Sangat - the Congregation, and the Guru, our Best Friend. |1|

O bumble bee, suck in that fragrance,
which causes the trees to flower, and the woods to grow lush foliage. |1|Pause|

He Himself is Lakshmi, and He Himself is her husband.
He established the world by Word of His Shabad, and He Himself ravishes it. |2|

He Himself is the calf, the cow and the milk.
He Himself is the Support of the body-mansion. |3|

He Himself is the Deed, and He Himself is the Doer.
As Gurmukh, He contemplates Himself. |4|

You create the creation, and gaze upon it, O Creator Lord.
You give Your Support to the uncounted beings and creatures. |5|

You are the Profound, Unfathomable Ocean of Virtue.

You are the Unknowable, the Immaculate, the most Sublime Jewel. |6|

You Yourself are the Creator, with the Potency to create.
You are the Independent Ruler, whose people are at peace. |7|

Nanak is satisfied with the subtle taste of the Lord's Name.
Without the Beloved Lord and Master, life is meaningless. |8|7|

Basant Hindol, First Mehl, Second House:
One Universal Creator God. By The Grace Of The True Guru:
The nine regions, the seven continents, the fourteen worlds, the three qualities and the four ages - You established them all through the four sources of creation, and You seated them in Your mansions.
He placed the four lamps, one by one, into the hands of the four ages. |1|

O Merciful Lord, Destroyer of demons, Lord of Lakshmi, such is Your Power - Your Shakti. |1|Pause|

Your army is the fire in the home of each and every heart. And Dharma - righteous living is the ruling chieftain.
The earth is Your great cooking pot; Your beings receive their portions only once. Destiny is Your gate-keeper. |2|

But the mortal becomes unsatisfied, and begs for more; his fickle mind brings him disgrace.

Section 29 - Raag Basant - Part 024

Greed is the dark dungeon, and demerits are the shackles on his feet. |3|

His wealth constantly batters him, and sin acts as the police officer.
Whether the mortal is good or bad, he is as You look upon him, O Lord. |4|

The Primal Lord God is called Allah. The Shaykh's turn has now come.
The temples of the gods are subject to taxes; this is what it has come to. |5|

The Muslim devotional pots, calls to prayer, prayers and prayer mats are everywhere; the Lord appears in blue robes.

In each and every home, everyone uses Muslim greetings; your speech has changed, O people. |6|

You, O my Lord and Master, are the King of the earth; what power do I have to challenge You?
In the four directions, people bow in humble adoration to You; Your Praises are sung in each and every heart. |7|

Making pilgrimages to sacred shrines, reading the Simritees and giving donations in charity - these do bring any profit.
O Nanak, glorious greatness is obtained in an instant, remembering the Naam, the Name of the Lord. |8|1|8|

Basant Hindol, Second House, Fourth Mehl:
One Universal Creator God. By The Grace Of The True Guru:
Within the body-village there lives a child who cannot hold still, even for an instant.
It makes so many efforts, and grows weary, but still, it wanders restlessly again and again. |1|

O my Lord and Master, Your child has come home, to be one with You.
Meeting the True Guru, he finds the Perfect Lord. Meditating and vibrating on the Name of the Lord, he receives the Insignia of the Lord. |1|Pause|

These are dead corpses, these bodies of all the people of the world; the Name of the Lord does not dwell in them.
The Guru leads us to taste the water of the Lord's Name, and then we savor and enjoy it, and our bodies are rejuvenated. |2|

I have examined and studied and searched my entire body, and as Gurmukh, I behold a miraculous wonder.
All the faithless cynics searched outside and died, but following the Guru's Teachings, I have found the Lord within the home of my own heart. |3|

God is Merciful to the meekest of the meek; Krishna came to the house of Bidar, a devotee of low social status.
Sudama loved God, who came to meet him; God sent everything to his home, and ended his poverty. |4|

Great is the glory of the Name of the Lord. My Lord and Master Himself has enshrined it within me.
Even if all the faithless cynics continue slandering me, it is not diminished by even one iota. |5|

The Lord's Name is the praise of His humble servant. It brings him honor in the ten directions.
The slanderers and the faithless cynics cannot endure it at all; they have set fire to their own houses. |6|

The humble person meeting with another humble person obtains honor. In the glory of the Lord, their glory shines forth.
The servants of my Lord and Master are loved by the Beloved. They are the slaves of His slaves. |7|

The Creator Himself is the Water; He Himself unites us in His Union.
O Nanak, the Gurmukh is absorbed in celestial peace and poise, like water blending with water. |8|1|9|

Section 29 - Raag Basant - Part 025

Basant, Fifth Mehl, First House, Du-Tukee:
One Universal Creator God. By The Grace Of The True Guru:
Listen to the stories of the devotees, O my mind, and meditate with love.
Ajaamal uttered the Lord's Name once, and was saved.
Baalmeek found the Saadh Sangat, the Company of the Holy.
The Lord definitely met Dhroo. |1|

I beg for the dust of the feet of Your Saints.
Please bless me with Your Mercy, Lord, that I may apply it to my forehead.
|1|Pause|

Ganika the prostitute was saved, when her parrot uttered the Lord's Name.
The elephant meditated on the Lord, and was saved.
He delivered the poor Brahmin Sudama out of poverty.
O my mind, you too must meditate and vibrate on the Lord of the Universe.
|2|

Even the hunter who shot an arrow at Krishna was saved.
Kubija the hunchback was saved, when God placed His Feet on her thumb.

Bidar was saved by his attitude of humility.
O my mind, you too must meditate on the Lord. |3|

The Lord Himself saved the honor of Prahlaad.
Even when she was being disrobed in court, Dropatee's honor was preserved.
Those who have served the Lord, even at the very last instant of their lives, are saved.
O my mind, serve Him, and you shall be carried across to the other side. |4|

Dhanna served the Lord, with the innocence of a child.
Meeting with the Guru, Trilochan attained the perfection of the Siddhas.
The Guru blessed Baynee with His Divine Illumination.
O my mind, you too must be the Lord's slave. |5|

Jai Dayv gave up his egotism.
Sain the barber was saved through his selfless service.
Do not let your mind waver or wander; do not let it go anywhere.
O my mind, you too shall cross over; seek the Sanctuary of God. |6|

O my Lord and Master, You have shown Your Mercy to them.
You saved those devotees.
You do not take their merits and demerits into account.
Seeing these ways of Yours, I have dedicated my mind to Your service. |7|

Kabeer meditated on the One Lord with love.
Naam Dayv lived with the Dear Lord.
Ravi Daas meditated on God, the Incomparably Beautiful.
Guru Nanak Dayv is the Embodiment of the Lord of the Universe. |8|1|

Basant, Fifth Mehl:
The mortal wanders in reincarnation through countless lifetimes.
Without meditating in remembrance on the Lord, he falls into hell.
Without devotional worship, he is cut apart into pieces.
Without understanding, he is punished by the Messenger of Death. |1|

Meditate and vibrate forever on the Lord of the Universe, O my friend.
Love forever the True Word of the Shabad. |1|Pause|

Contentment does not come by any endeavors.
All the show of Maya is just a cloud of smoke.
The mortal does not hesitate to commit sins.
Intoxicated with poison, he comes and goes in reincarnation. |2|

Acting in egotism and self-conceit, his corruption only increases.
The world is drowning in attachment and greed.
Sexual desire and anger hold the mind in its power.
Even in his dreams, he does not chant the Lord's Name. |3|

Sometimes he is a king, and sometimes he is a beggar.
The world is bound by pleasure and pain.
The mortal makes no arrangements to save himself.
The bondage of sin continues to hold him. |4|

He has no beloved friends or companions.
He himself eats what he himself plants.

Section 29 - Raag Basant - Part 026

He gathers up that which brings corruption;
leaving them, the fool must depart in an instant. |5|

He wanders in attachment to Maya.
He acts in accordance with the karma of his past actions.
Only the Creator Himself remains detached.
God is not affected by virtue or vice. |6|

Please save me, O Merciful Lord of the Universe!
I seek Your Sanctuary, O Perfect Compassionate Lord.
Without You, I have no other place of rest.
Please take pity on me, God, and bless me with Your Name. |7|

You are the Creator, and You are the Doer.
You are High and Exalted, and You are totally Infinite.
Please be merciful, and attach me to the hem of Your robe.
Slave Nanak has entered the Sanctuary of God. |8|2|

Basant Kee Vaar, Fifth Mehl:
One Universal Creator God. By The Grace Of The True Guru:

Meditate on the Lord's Name, and blossom forth in green abundance.

By your high destiny, you have been blessed with this wondrous spring of the soul.

See all the three worlds in bloom, and obtain the Fruit of Ambrosial Nectar.

Meeting with the Holy Saints, peace wells up, and all sins are erased.

O Nanak, remember in meditation the One Name, and you shall never again be consigned to the womb of reincarnation.. |1|

The five powerful desires are bound down, when you lean on the True Lord.

The Lord Himself leads us to dwell at His Feet. He stands right in our midst.

All sorrows and sicknesses are eradicated, and you become ever-fresh and rejuvenated.

Night and day, meditate on the Naam, the Name of the Lord. You shall never again die.

And the One, from whom we came, O Nanak, into Him we merge once again. |2|

Where do we come from? Where do we live? Where do we go in the end?

All creatures belong to God, our Lord and Master. Who can place a value on Him?

Those who meditate, listen and chant, those devotees are blessed and beautified.

The Lord God is Inaccessible and Unfathomable; there is no other equal to Him.

The Perfect Guru has taught this Truth. Nanak proclaims it to the world. |3|1|

Basant, The Word Of The Devotees,
Kabeer Jee, First House:
One Universal Creator God. By The Grace Of The True Guru:
The earth is in bloom, and the sky is in bloom.
Each and every heart has blossomed forth, and the soul is illumined. |1|

My Sovereign Lord King blossoms forth in countless ways.
Wherever I look, I see Him there pervading. |1|Pause|

The four Vedas blossom forth in duality.
The Simritees blossom forth, along with the Koran and the Bible. |2|

Shiva blossoms forth in Yoga and meditation.
Kabeer's Lord and Master pervades in all alike. |3|1|

The Pandits, the Hindu religious scholars, are intoxicated, reading the Puraanas.
The Yogis are intoxicated in Yoga and meditation.
The Sannyaasees are intoxicated in egotism.
The penitents are intoxicated with the mystery of penance. |1|

All are intoxicated with the wine of Maya; no one is awake and aware.
The thieves are with them, plundering their homes. |1|Pause|

Suk Dayv and Akrur are awake and aware.

Section 29 - Raag Basant - Part 027

Hanuman with his tail is awake and aware.
Shiva is awake, serving at the Lord's Feet.
Naam Dayv and Jai Dayv are awake in this Dark Age of Kali Yuga. |2|

There are many ways of being awake, and sleeping.
To be awake as Gurmukh is the most excellent way.
The most sublime of all the actions of this body,
says Kabeer, is to meditate and vibrate on the Lord's Name. |3|2|

The wife gives birth to her husband.
The son leads his father in play.
Without breasts, the mother nurses her baby. |1|

Behold, people! This is how it is in the Dark Age of Kali Yuga.
The son marries his mother. |1|Pause|

Without feet, the mortal jumps.
Without a mouth, he bursts into laughter.
Without feeling sleepy, he lays down and sleeps.
Without a churn, the milk is churned. |2|

Without udders, the cow gives milk.
Without travelling, a long journey is made.
Without the True Guru, the path is not found.

Says Kabeer, see this, and understand. |3|3|

Prahlaad was sent to school.
He took many of his friends along with him.
He asked his teacher, "Why do you teach me about worldly affairs?
Write the Name of the Dear Lord on my tablet." |1|

O Baba, I will not forsake the Name of the Lord.
I will not bother with any other lessons. |1|Pause|

Sanda and Marka went to the king to complain.
He sent for Prahlaad to come at once.
He said to him, "Stop uttering the Lord's Name.
I shall release you at once, if you obey my words." |2|

Prahlaad answered, "Why do you annoy me, over and over again?
God created the water, land, hills and mountains.
I shall not forsake the One Lord; if I did, I would be going against my Guru.
You might as well throw me into the fire and kill me." |3|

The king became angry and drew his sword.
"Show me your protector now!"
So God emerged out of the pillar, and assumed a mighty form.
He killed Harnaakhash, tearing him apart with his nails. |4|

The Supreme Lord God, the Divinity of the divine,
for the sake of His devotee, assumed the form of the man-lion.
Says Kabeer, no one can know the Lord's limits.
He saves His devotees like Prahlaad over and over again. |5|4|

Within the body and mind are thieves like sexual desire,
which has stolen my jewel of spiritual wisdom.
I am a poor orphan, O God; unto whom should I complain?
Who has not been ruined by sexual desire? What am I? |1|

O Lord, I cannot endure this agonizing pain.
What power does my fickle mind have against it? |1|Pause|

Sanak, Sanandan, Shiva and Suk Dayv
were born out of Brahma's naval chakra.

The poets and the Yogis with their matted hair
all lived their lives with good behavior. |2|

You are Unfathomable; I cannot know Your depth.
O God, Master of the meek, unto whom should I tell my pains?
Please rid me of the pains of birth and death, and bless me with peace.
Kabeer utters the Glorious Praises of God, the Ocean of peace. |3|5|

There is one merchant and five traders.
The twenty-five oxen carry false merchandise.
There are nine poles which hold the ten bags.
The body is tied by the seventy-two ropes. |1|

I don't care at all about such commerce.

Section 29 - Raag Basant - Part 028

It depletes my capital, and the interest charges only increase. |Pause|

Weaving the seven threads together, they carry on their trade.
They are led on by the karma of their past actions.
The three tax-collectors argue with them.
The traders depart empty-handed. |2|

Their capital is exhausted, and their trade is ruined.
The caravan is scattered in the ten directions.
Says Kabeer, O mortal, your tasks will be accomplished,
when you merge in the Celestial Lord; let your doubts run away. |3|6|

Basant Hindol, Second House:
One Universal Creator God. By The Grace Of The True Guru:
The mother is impure, and the father is impure. The fruit they produce is
impure.
Impure they come, and impure they go. The unfortunate ones die in
impurity. |1|

Tell me, O Pandit, O religious scholar, which place is uncontaminated?
Where should I sit to eat my meal? |1|Pause|

The tongue is impure, and its speech is impure. The eyes and ears are totally impure.
The impurity of the sexual organs does not depart; the Brahmin is burnt by the fire. |2|

The fire is impure, and the water is impure. The place where you sit and cook is impure.
Impure is the ladle which serves the food. Impure is the one who sits down to eat it. |3|

Impure is the cow dung, and impure is the kitchen square. Impure are the lines that mark it off.
Says Kabeer, they alone are pure, who have obtained pure understanding. |4|1|7|

Raamaanand Jee, First House:
One Universal Creator God. By The Grace Of The True Guru:
Where should I go? My home is filled with bliss.
My consciousness does not go out wandering. My mind has become crippled. |1|Pause|

One day, a desire welled up in my mind.
I ground up sandalwood, along with several fragrant oils.
I went to God's place, and worshipped Him there.
That God showed me the Guru, within my own mind. |1|

Wherever I go, I find water and stones.
You are totally pervading and permeating in all.
I have searched through all the Vedas and the Puraanas.
I would go there, only if the Lord were not here. |2|

I am a sacrifice to You, O my True Guru.
You have cut through all my confusion and doubt.
Raamaanand's Lord and Master is the All-pervading Lord God.
The Word of the Guru's Shabad eradicates the karma of millions of past actions. |3|1|

Basant, The Word Of Naam Dayv Jee:
One Universal Creator God. By The Grace Of The True Guru:
If the servant runs away when his master is in trouble,

he will not have a long life, and he brings shame to all his family. |1|

I shall not abandon devotional worship of You, O Lord, even if the people laugh at me.
The Lord's Lotus Feet abide within my heart. |1|Pause|

The mortal will even die for the sake of his wealth;
in the same way, the Saints do not forsake the Lord's Name. |2|

Pilgrimages to the Ganges, the Gaya and the Godawari are merely worldly affairs.

Section 29 - Raag Basant - Part 029

If the Lord were totally pleased, then He would let Naam Dayv be His servant. |3|1|

The tidal waves of greed constantly assault me.
My body is drowning, O Lord. |1|

Please carry me across the world-ocean, O Lord of the Universe.
Carry me across, O Beloved Father. |1|Pause|

I cannot steer my ship in this storm.
I cannot find the other shore, O Beloved Lord. |2|

Please be merciful, and unite me with the True Guru;
carry me across, O Lord. |3|

Says Naam Dayv, I do not know how to swim.
Give me Your Arm, give me Your Arm, O Beloved Lord. |4|2|

Slowly at first, the body-cart loaded with dust starts to move.
Later, it is driven on by the stick. |1|

The body moves along like the ball of dung, driven on by the dung-beetle.
The beloved soul goes down to the pool to wash itself clean. |1|Pause|

The washerman washes, imbued with the Lord's Love.
My mind is imbued with the Lord's Lotus Feet. |2|

Prays Naam Dayv, O Lord, You are All-pervading.
Please be kind to Your devotee. |3|3|

Basant, The Word Of Ravi Daas Jee:
One Universal Creator God. By The Grace Of The True Guru:
You know nothing.
Seeing your clothes, you are so proud of yourself.
The proud bride shall not find a place with the Lord.
Above your head, the crow of death is cawing. |1|

Why are you so proud? You are insane.
Even the mushrooms of summer live longer than you. |1|Pause|

The deer does not know the secret;
the musk is within its own body, but it searches for it outside.
Whoever reflects on his own body
- the Messenger of Death does not abuse him. |2|

The man is so proud of his sons and his wife;
his Lord and Master shall call for his account.
The soul suffers in pain for the actions it has committed.
Afterwards, whom shall you call, "Dear, Dear."|3|

If you seek the Support of the Holy,
millions upon millions of your sins shall be totally erased.
Says Ravi Daas, one who chants the Naam, the Name of the Lord,
is not concerned with social class, birth and rebirth. |4|1|

Basant, Kabeer Jee:
One Universal Creator God. By The Grace Of The True Guru:
You walk like a cow.
The hair on your tail is shiny and lustrous. |1|

Look around, and eat anything in this house.
But do not go out to any other. |1|Pause|

You lick the grinding bowl, and eat the flour.
Where have you taken the kitchen rags? |2|

Your gaze is fixed on the basket in the cupboard.
Watch out - a stick may strike you from behind. |3|

Says Kabeer, you have over-indulged in your pleasures.
Watch out - someone may throw a brick at you. |4|1|

RAAG SAARANG

Section 30 - Raag Saarang - Part 001

Raag Saarang, Chau-Padas, First Mehl, First House:
ONE Universal Creator God. Truth Is The Name. Creative Being Personified.
No Fear. No Hatred. Image Of The Undying. Beyond Birth. Self-Existent. By
Guru's Grace:
I am the hand-maiden of my Lord and Master.
I have grasped the Feet of God, the Life of the world. He has killed and
eradicated my egotism. |1|Pause|

He is the Perfect, Supreme Light, the Supreme Lord God, my Beloved, my
Breath of Life.
The Fascinating Lord has fascinated my mind; contemplating the Word of
the Shabad, I have come to understand. |1|

The worthless self-willed manmukh, with false and shallow understanding -
his mind and body are held in pain's grip.
Since I came to be imbued with the Love of my Beautiful Lord, I meditate
on the Lord, and my mind is encouraged. |2|

Abandoning egotism, I have become detached. And now, I absorb true
intuitive understanding.
The mind is pleased and appeased by the Pure, Immaculate Lord; the
opinions of other people are irrelevant. |3|

There is no other like You, in the past or in the future, O my Beloved, my
Breath of Life, my Support.
The soul-bride is imbued with the Name of the Lord; O Nanak, the Lord is
her Husband. |4|1|

Saarang, First Mehl:
How can I survive without the Lord? I am suffering in pain.
My tongue does not taste - all is bland without the Lord's sublime essence.
Without God, I suffer and die. |1|Pause|

As long as I do not attain the Blessed Vision of my Beloved, I remain hungry and thirsty.

Gazing upon the Blessed Vision of His Darshan, my mind is pleased and appeased. The lotus blossoms forth in the water. |1|

The low-hanging clouds crack with thunder and burst. The cuckoos and the peacocks are filled with passion,

along with the birds in the trees, the bulls and the snakes. The soul-bride is happy when her Husband Lord returns home. |2|

She is filthy and ugly, unfeminine and ill-mannered - she has no intuitive understanding of her Husband Lord.

She is not satisfied by the sublime essence of her Lord's Love; she is evil-minded, immersed in her pain. |3|

The soul-bride does not come and go in reincarnation or suffer in pain; her body is not touched by the pain of disease.

O Nanak, she is intuitively embellished by God; seeing God, her mind is encouraged. |4|2|

Saarang, First Mehl:

My Beloved Lord God is not far away.

My mind is pleased and appeased by the Word of the True Guru's Teachings. I have found the Lord, the Support of my breath of life. |1|Pause|

Section 30 - Raag Saarang - Part 002

This is the way to meet your Husband Lord. Blessed is the soul-bride who is loved by her Husband Lord.

Social class and status, race, ancestry and skepticism are eliminated, following the Guru's Teachings and contemplating the Word of the Shabad. |1|

One whose mind is pleased and appeased, has no egotistical pride. Violence and greed are forgotten.

The soul-bride intuitively ravishes and enjoys her Husband Lord; as Gurmukh, she is embellished by His Love. |2|

Burn away any love of family and relatives, which increases your attachment to Maya.

One who does not savor the Lord's Love deep within, lives in duality and corruption. |3|

His Love is a priceless jewel deep within my being; the Lover of my Beloved is not hidden.

O Nanak, as Gurmukh, enshrine the Priceless Naam deep within your being, all the ages through. |4|3|

Saarang, Fourth Mehl, First House:
One Universal Creator God. By The Grace Of The True Guru:
I am the dust of the feet of the humble Saints of the Lord.

Joining the Sat Sangat, the True Congregation, I have obtained the supreme status. The Lord, the Supreme Soul, is all-pervading everywhere. |1|Pause|

Meeting the Saintly True Guru, I have found peace and tranquility. Sins and painful mistakes are totally erased and taken away.

The Divine Light of the soul radiates forth, gazing upon the Presence of the Immaculate Lord God. |1|

By great good fortune, I have found the Sat Sangat; the Name of the Lord, Har, Har, is all-prevading everywhere.

I have taken my cleansing bath at the sixty-eight sacred shrines of pilgrimage, bathing in the dust of the feet of the True Congregation. |2|

Evil-minded and corrupt, filthy-minded and shallow, with impure heart, attached to enticement and falsehood.

Without good karma, how can I find the Sangat? Engrossed in egotism, the mortal remains stuck in regret. |3|

Be kind and show Your Mercy, O Dear Lord; I beg for the dust of the feet of the Sat Sangat.

O Nanak, meeting with the Saints, the Lord is attained. The Lord's humble servant obtains the Presence of the Lord. |4|1|

Saarang, Fourth Mehl:
I am a sacrifice to the Feet of the Lord of the Universe.

I cannot swim across the terrifying world ocean. But chanting the Name of the Lord, Har, Har, I am carried across across. |1|Pause|

Faith in God came to fill my heart; I serve Him intuitively, and contemplate Him.

Night and day, I chant the Lord's Name within my heart; it is all-powerful and virtuous. |1|

God is Inaccessible and Unfathomable, All-pervading everywhere, in all minds and bodies; He is Infinite and Invisible.

When the Guru bebomes merciful, then the Unseen Lord is seen within the heart. |2|

Deep within the inner being is the Name of the Lord, the Support of the entire earth, but to the egotistical shaakta, the faithless cynic, He seems far away.

His burning desire is never quenched, and he loses the game of life in the gamble. |3|

Standing up and sitting down, the mortal sings the Glorious Praises of the Lord, when the Guru bestows even a tiny bit of His Grace.

O Nanak, those who are blessed by His Glance of Grace - He saves and protects their honor. |4|2|

Section 30 - Raag Saarang - Part 003

Saarang, Fourth Mehl:

O my Beloved Lord, Har, Har, please bless me with Your Ambrosial Name.

Those whose minds are pleased to be Gurmukh - the Lord completes their projects. |1|Pause|

Those humble beings who become meek before the Guru-their pains are taken away.

Night and day, they perform devotional worship services to the Guru; they are embellished with the Word of the Guru's Shabad. |1|

Within their hearts is the ambrosial essence of the Naam, the Name of the Lord; they savor this essence, sing the praises of this essence, and contemplate this essence.

By Guru's Grace, they are aware of this ambrosial essence; they find the Gate of Salvation. |2|

The True is the Primal Being, Unmoving and Unchanging. One who takes the Support of the Naam, the Name of the Lord - his intellect becomes focused and steady.
I offer my soul to Him; I am a sacrifice to my True Guru. |3|

The self-willed manmukhs are stuck in doubt and attached to duality; the darkness of spiritual ignorance is within them.
They do not see the True Guru, the Giver; they are not on this shore, or the other. |4|

Our Lord and Master is permeating and pervading each and every heart; He is supremely Potent to exercise His Might.
Nanak, the slave of His slaves, says, please, be merciful and save me! |5|3|

Saarang, Fourth Mehl:
This is the way to work for the Lord.
Whatever He does, accept that as true. As Gurmukh, remain lovingly absorbed in His Name. |1|Pause|

The Love of the Lord of the Universe seems supremely sweet. Everything else is forgotten.
Night and day, he is in ecstasy; his mind is pleased and appeased, and his light merges into the Light. |1|

Singing the Glorious Praises of the Lord, his mind is satisfied. Peace and tranquility come to abide within his mind.
When the Guru becomes merciful, the mortal finds the Lord; he focuses his consciousness on the Lord's Lotus Feet. |2|

The intellect is enlightened, meditating on the Lord. He remains lovingly attuned to the essence of spiritual wisdom.
The Divine Light radiates forth deep within his being; his mind is pleased and appeased. He merges intuitively into Celestial Samaadhi. |3|

One whose heart is filled with falsehood, continues to practice falsehood, even while he teaches and preaches about the Lord.
Within him is the utter darkness of greed. He is thrashed like wheat, and suffers in pain. |4|

When my God is totally pleased, the mortal tunes in and becomes Gurmukh.

Nanak has obtained the Immaculate Naam, the Name of the Lord. Chanting the Naam, he has found peace. |5|4|

Saarang, Fourth Mehl:
My mind is pleased and appeased by the Name of the Lord.

The True Guru has implanted divine love within my heart. The Sermon of the Lord, Har, Har, is pleasing to my mind. |1|Pause|

Please be merciful to Your meek and humble servant; please bless Your humble servant with Your Unspoken Speech.

Meeting with the humble Saints, I have found the sublime essence of the Lord. The Lord seems so sweet to my mind and body. |1|

They alone are unattached, who are imbued with the Lord's Love; through the Guru's Teachings, they realize the Naam, the Name of the Lord.

Meeting with the Primal Being, one finds peace, and one's comings and goings in reincarnation are ended. |2|

With my eyes, I gaze lovingly upon God, my Lord and Master. I chant His Name with my tongue.

Section 30 - Raag Saarang - Part 004

With my ears, I listen to the Kirtan of His Praises, day and night. I love the Lord, Har, Har, with all my heart. |3|

When the Guru helped me to overcome the five thieves, then I found ultimate bliss, attached to the Naam.

The Lord has showered His Mercy on servant Nanak; he merges in the Lord, in the Name of the Lord. |4|5|

Saarang, Fourth Mehl:
O my mind, chant the Name of the Lord, and study His Excellence.

Without the Lord's Name, nothing is steady or stable. All the rest of the show is useless. |1|Pause|

What is there to accept, and what is there to reject, O madman? Whatever is seen shall turn to dust.

That poison which you believe to be your own - you must abandon it and leave it behind. What a load you have to carry on your head! |1|

Moment by moment, instant by instant, your life is running out. The fool cannot understand this.
He does things which will not go along with him in the end. This is the lifestyle of the faithless cynic. |2|

So join together with the humble Saints, O madman, and you shall find the Gate of Salvation.
Without the Sat Sangat, the True Congregation, no one finds any peace. Go and ask the scholars of the Vedas. |3|

All the kings and queens shall depart; they must leave this false expanse.
O Nanak, the Saints are eternally steady and stable; they take the Support of the Name of the Lord. |4|6|

Saarang, Fourth Mehl, Third House, Du-Padas:
One Universal Creator God. By The Grace Of The True Guru:
O son, why do you argue with your father?
It is a sin to argue with the one who fathered you and raised you. |1|Pause|

That wealth, which you are so proud of - that wealth does not belong to anyone.
In an instant, you shall have to leave behind all your corrupt pleasures; you shall be left to regret and repent. |1|

He is God, your Lord and Master - chant the Chant of that Lord.
Servant Nanak spreads the Teachings; if you listen to it, you shall be rid of your pain. |2|1|7|

Saarang, Fourth Mehl, Fifth House, Du-Padas, Partaal:
One Universal Creator God. By The Grace Of The True Guru:
O my mind, meditate on the Lord of the World, the Master of the Universe, the Life of the World, the Enticer of the mind; fall in love with Him. I take the Support of the Lord, Har, Har, Har, all day and all night. |1|Pause|

Endless, endless, endless are the Praises of the Lord. Suk Dayv, Naarad and the gods like Brahma sing His Glorious Praises. Your Glorious Virtues, O my Lord and Master, cannot even be counted.

O Lord, You are Infinite, O Lord, You are Infinite, O Lord, You are my Lord and Master; only You Yourself know Your Own Ways. |1|

Those who are near, near to the Lord - those who dwell near the Lord - those humble servants of the Lord are the Holy, the devotees of the Lord. Those humble servants of the Lord merge with their Lord, O Nanak, like water merging with water. |2|1|8|

Section 30 - Raag Saarang - Part 005

Saarang, Fourth Mehl:
O my mind, meditate on the Lord, the Lord, your Lord and Master. The Lord is the Most Divine of all the divine beings. Chant the Name of the Lord, Raam, Raam, the Lord, my most Dear Beloved. |1|Pause|

That household, in which the Glorious Praises of the Lord are sung, in which the Glorious Praises of the Lord are sung, in which His Glorious Praises are sung, where the Panch Shabad, the Five Primal Sounds, resound - great is the destiny w

All the sins of that humble being are taken away, all the pains are taken away, all diseases are taken away; sexual desire, anger, greed, attachment and egotistical pride are taken away. The Lord drives the five thieves out of such a person

Chant the Name of the Lord, O Holy Saints of the Lord; meditate on the Lord of the Universe, O Holy people of the Lord. Meditate in thought, word and deed on the Lord, Har, Har. Worship and adore the Lord, O Holy people of the Lord.

Chant the Name of the Lord, chant the Name of the Lord. It shall rid you of all your sins.

Continually and continuously remain awake and aware. You shall be in ecstasy forever and ever, meditating on the Lord of the Universe.

Servant Nanak: O Lord, Your devotees obtain the fruits of their minds' desires; they obtain all the fruits and rewards, and the four great blessings - Dharmic faith, wealth and riches, sexual success and liberation. |2|2|9|

Saarang, Fourth Mehl:
O my mind, meditate on the Lord, the Lord of Wealth, the Source of Nectar, the Supreme Lord God, the True Transcendent Being, God, the Inner-knower, the Searcher of hearts.
He is the Destroyer of all suffering, the Giver of all peace; sing the Praises of my Beloved Lord God. |1|Pause|

The Lord dwells in the home of each and every heart. The Lord dwells in the water, and the Lord dwells on the land. The Lord dwells in the spaces and interspaces. I have such a great longing to see the Lord.
If only some Saint, some humble Saint of the Lord, my Holy Beloved, would come, to show me the way.
I would wash and massage the feet of that humble being. |1|

The Lord's humble servant meets the Lord, through his faith in the Lord; meeting the Lord, he becomes Gurmukh.
My mind and body are in ecstasy; I have seen my Sovereign Lord King.
Servant Nanak has been blessed with Grace, blessed with the Lord's Grace, blessed with the Grace of the Lord of the Universe.
I meditate on the Lord, the Name of the Lord, night and day, forever, forever and ever. |2|3|10|

Saarang, Fourth Mehl:
O my mind, meditate on the Fearless Lord,
who is True, True, Forever True.
He is free of vengeance, the Image of the Undying,
beyond birth, Self-existent.
O my mind, meditate night and day on the Formless, Self-sustaining Lord.
|1|Pause|

For the Blessed Vision of the Lord's Darshan, for the Blessed Vision of the Lord's Darshan, the three hundred thirty million gods, and millions of Siddhas, celibates and Yogis make their pilgrimages to sacred shrines and rivers, and go on f

The service of the humble person is approved, unto whom the Lord of the World shows His Mercy. |1|

They alone are the good Saints of the Lord, the best and most exalted devotees, who are pleasing to their Lord.

Those who have my Lord and Master on their side - O Nanak, the Lord saves their honor. |2|4|11|

Section 30 - Raag Saarang - Part 006

Saarang, Fourth Mehl, Partaal:
O my mind, meditate on the Lord of the Universe, the Lord, the Lord of the Universe, the Treasure of Virtue, the God of all creation. O my mind, chant the Name of the Lord, the Lord, the Eternal, Imperishable, Primal Lord God. |1|Pause|

The Name of the Lord is the Ambrosial Nectar, Har, Har, Har. He alone drinks it in, whom the Lord inspires to drink it.
The Merciful Lord Himself bestows His Mercy, and He leads the mortal to meet with the True Guru. That humble being tastes the Ambrosial Name of the Lord, Har, Har. |1|

Those who serve my Lord, forever and ever - all their pain, doubt and fear are taken away.
Servant Nanak chants the Naam, the Name of the Lord, and so he lives, like the song-bird, which is satisfied only by drinking in the water. |2|5|12|

Saarang, Fourth Mehl:
O my mind, meditate on the Supreme Lord.
The Lord, the Lord is All-pervading.
True, True is the Lord.
O Siblings of Destiny, chant the Name of the Lord, Raam, Raam, Raam, forever. He is All-pervading everywhere. |1|Pause|

The Lord Himself is Himself the Creator of all. The Lord Himself is Himself pervading the whole world.
That person, upon whom my Sovereign Lord King, Raam, Raam, Raam, bestows His Mercy - that person is lovingly attuned to the Lord's Name. |1|

O Saints of the Lord, behold the Glory of the Name of the Lord; His Name saves the honor of His humble devotees in this Dark Age of Kali Yuga.
My Sovereign Lord King has taken servant Nanak's side; his enemies and attackers have all run away. |2|6|13|

Saarang, Fifth Mehl, Chau-Padas, First House:

One Universal Creator God. By The Grace Of The True Guru:
I am a sacrifice to the Image of the True Guru.
My inner being is filled with a great thirst, like that of the song-bird for water. When shall I find the Fruitful Vision of His Darshan? |1|Pause|

He is the Master of the masterless, the Cherisher of all. He is the Lover of the devotees of His Name.
That mortal, whom no one can protect - You bless him with Your Support, O Lord. |1|

Support of the unsupported, Saving Grace of the unsaved, Home of the homeless.
Wherever I go in the ten directions, You are there with me. The only thing I do is sing the Kirtan of Your Praises. |2|

From Your Oneness, You become tens of thousands, and from tens of thousands, You become One. I cannot describe Your state and extent.
You are Infinite - Your value cannot be appraised. Everything I see is Your play. |3|

I speak with the Company of the Holy; I am in love with the Holy people of the Lord.
Servant Nanak has found the Lord through the Guru's Teachings; please bless me with Your Blessed Vision; O Lord, my mind yearns for it. |4|1|

Saarang, Fifth Mehl:
The Dear Lord is the Inner-knower, the Searcher of hearts.
The mortal does evil deeds, and hides from others, but like the air, the Lord is present everywhere. |1|Pause|

You call yourself a devotee of Vishnu and you practice the six rituals, but your inner being is polluted with greed.
Those who slander the Society of the Saints, shall all be drowned in their ignorance. |1|

Section 30 - Raag Saarang - Part 007

The mortal eats the food which he has carefully prepared, and then steals the wealth of others. His inner being is filled with falsehood and pride.

He knows nothing of the Vedas or the Shaastras; his mind is gripped by pride. |2|

He says his evening prayers, and observes all the fasts, but this is all just a show.
God made him stray from the path, and sent him into the wilderness. All his actions are useless. |3|

He alone is a spiritual teacher, and he alone is a devotee of Vishnu and a scholar, whom the Lord God blesses with His Grace.
Serving the True Guru, he obtains the supreme status and saves the whole world. |4|

What can I say? I don't know what to say. As God wills, so do I speak.
I ask only for the dust of the feet of the Saadh Sangat, the Company of the Holy. Servant Nanak seeks their Sanctuary. |5|2|

Saarang, Fifth Mehl:
Now, my dancing is over.
I have intuitively obtained my Darling Beloved. Through the Word of the True Guru's Teachings, I found Him. |1|Pause|

The virgin speaks with her friends about her husband and they laugh together;
but when he comes home, she becomes shy, and modestly covers her face. |1|

When gold is melted in the crucible, it flows freely everywhere.
But when it is made into pure solid bars of gold, then it remains stationary. |2|

As long as the days and the nights of one's life last, the clock strikes the hours, minutes and seconds.
But when the gong player gets up and leaves, the gong is not sounded again. |3|

When the pitcher is filled with water, the water contained within it seems distinct.
Says Nanak, when the pitcher is emptied out, the water mingles again with water. |4|3|

Saarang, Fifth Mehl:
Now if he is asked, what can he say?
He was supposed to have gathered the sublime essence of the Ambrosial Naam, the Name of the Lord, but instead, the mad-man was busy with poison. |1|Pause|

This human life, so difficult to obtain, was finally obtained after such a long time. He is losing it in exchange for a shell.
He came to buy musk, but instead, he has loaded dust and thistle grass. |1|

He comes in search of profits, but he is entangled in the enticing illusion of Maya.
He loses the jewel, in exchange for mere glass. When will he have this blessed opportunity again? |2|

He is full of sins, and he has not even one redeeming virtue. Forsaking his Lord and Master, he is involved with Maya, God's slave.
And when the final silence comes, like inanimate matter, he is caught like a thief at the door. |3|

I cannot see any other way out. I seek the Sanctuary of the Lord's slaves.
Says Nanak, the mortal is emancipated, only when all his demerits and faults are erased and eradicated. |4|4|

Saarang, Fifth Mehl:
O mother, my patience is gone. I am in love with my Husband Lord.
There are so many kinds of incomparable pleasures, but I am not interested in any of them. |1|Pause|

Night and day, I utter, "Pri-a, Pri-a - Beloved, Beloved" with my mouth. I cannot sleep, even for an instant; I remain awake and aware.
Necklaces, eye make-up, fancy clothes and decorations - without my Husband Lord, these are all poison to me. |1|

Section 30 - Raag Saarang - Part 008

I ask and ask, with humility, "Who can tell me which country my Husband Lord lives in?"

I would dedicate my heart to him, I offer my mind and body and every-thing; I place my head at his feet. |2|

I bow at the feet of the voluntary slave of the Lord; I beg him to bless me with the Saadh Sangat, the Company of the Holy.
Show Mercy to me, that I may meet God, and gaze upon the Blessed Vision of His Darshan every moment. |3|

When He is Kind to me, He comes to dwell within my being. Night and day, my mind is calm and peaceful.
Says Nanak, I sing the Songs of Joy; the Unstruck Word of the Shabad resounds within me. |4|5|

Saarang, Fifth Mehl:
O mother, True, True True is the Lord, and True, True, True is His Holy Saint.
The Word which the Perfect Guru has spoken, I have tied to my robe. |1|Pause|

Night and day, and the stars in the sky shall vanish. The sun and the moon shall vanish.
The mountains, the earth, the water and the air shall pass away. Only the Word of the Holy Saint shall endure. |1|

Those born of eggs shall pass away, and those born of the womb shall pass away. Those born of the earth and sweat shall pass away as well.
The four Vedas shall pass away, and the six Shaastras shall pass away. Only the Word of the Holy Saint is eternal. |2|

Raajas, the quality of energetic activity shall pass away. Taamas, the quality of lethargic darkness shall pass away. Saatvas, the quality of peaceful light shall pass away as well.
All that is seen shall pass away. Only the Word of the Holy Saint is beyond destruction. |3|

He Himself is Himself by Himself. All that is seen is His play.
He cannot be found by any means. O Nanak, meeting with the Guru, God is found. |4|6|

Saarang, Fifth Mehl:

The Guru, the Lord of the Universe, dwells within my mind.
Wherever my Lord and Master is remembered in meditation - that village is filled with peace and bliss. |1|Pause|

Wherever my Beloved Lord and Master is forgotten - all misery and misfortune is there.
Where the Praises of my Lord, the Embodiment of Bliss and Joy are sung - eternal peace and wealth are there. |1|

Wherever they do not listen to the Stories of the Lord with their ears - the utterly desolate wilderness is there.
Where the Kirtan of the Lord's Praises are sung with love in the Saadh Sangat - there is fragrance and fruit and joy in abundance. |2|

Without meditative remembrance on the Lord, one may live for millions of years, but his life would be totally useless.
But if he vibrates and meditates on the Lord of the Universe, for even a moment, then he shall live forever and ever. |3|

O God, I seek Your Sanctuary, Your Sanctuary, Your Sanctuary; please mercifully bless me with the Saadh Sangat, the Company of the Holy.
O Nanak, the Lord is All-pervading everywhere, amongst all. He knows the qualities and the condition of all. |4|7|

Saarang, Fifth Mehl:
Now, I have obtained the Support of the Lord.
Those who seek the Sanctuary of the Ocean of Mercy are carried across the world-ocean. |1|Pause|

They sleep in peace, and intuitively merge into the Lord. The Guru takes away their cynicism and doubt.
Whatever they wish for, the Lord does; they obtain the fruits of their minds' desires. |1|

In my heart, I meditate on Him; with my eyes, I focus my meditation on Him. With my ears, I listen to His Sermon.

Section 30 - Raag Saarang - Part 009

With my feet, I walk on my Lord and Mater's Path. With my tongue, I sing the Glorious Praises of the Lord. |2|

With my eyes, I see the Lord, the Embodiment of Absolute Bliss; the Saint has turned away from the world.
I have found the Priceless Name of the Beloved Lord; it never leaves me or goes anywhere else. |3|

What praise, what glory and what virtues should I utter, in order to please the Lord?
That humble being, unto whom the Merciful Lord is kind - O servant Nanak, he is the slave of God's slaves. |4|8|

Saarang, Fifth Mehl:
Who can I tell, and with whom can I speak, about this state of peace and bliss?
I am in ecstasy and delight, gazing upon the Blessed Vision of God's Darshan. My mind sings His Songs of Joy and His Glories. |1|Pause|

I am wonderstruck, gazing upon the Wondrous Lord. The Merciful Lord is All-pervading everywhere.
I drink in the Invaluable Nectar of the Naam, the Name of the Lord. Like the mute, I can only smile - I cannot speak of its flavor. |1|

As the breath is held in bondage, no one can understand its coming in and going out.
So is that person, whose heart is enlightened by the Lord - his story cannot be told. |2|

As many other efforts as you can think of - I have seen them and studied them all.
My Beloved, Carefree Lord has revealed Himself within the home of my own heart; thus I have realized the Inaccessible Lord. |3|

The Absolute, Formless, Eternally Unchanging, Immeasurable Lord cannot be masured.
Says Nanak, whoever endures the unendurable - this state belongs to him alone. |4|9|

Saarang, Fifth Mehl:

The corrupt person passes his days and nights uselessly.
He does not vibrate and meditate on the Lord of the Universe; he is intoxicated with egotistical intellect. He loses his life in the gamble. |1|Pause|

The Naam, the Name of the Lord, is priceless, but he is not in love with it. He loves only to slander others.
Weaving the grass, he builds his house of straw. At the door, he builds a fire. |1|

He carries a load of sulfur on his head, and drives the Ambrosial Nectar out of his mind.
Wearing his good clothes, the mortal falls into the coal-pit; again and again, he tries to shake it off. |2|

Standing on the branch, eating and eating and smiling, he cuts down the tree.
He falls down head-first and is shattered into bits and pieces. |3|

He bears vengeance against the Lord who is free of vengeance. The fool is not up to the task.
Says Nanak, the Saving Grace of the Saints is the Formless, Supreme Lord God. |4|10|

Saarang, Fifth Mehl:
All the others are deluded by doubt; they do not understand.
That person, within whose heart the One Pure Word abides, realizes the essence of the Vedas. |1|Pause|

He walks in the ways of the world, trying to please people.
But as long as his heart is not enlightened, he is stuck in pitch black darkness. |1|

The land may be prepared in every way, but nothing sprouts without being planted.
Just so, without the Lord's Name, no one is liberated, nor is egotistical pride eradicated. |2|

The mortal may churn water until he is sore, but how can butter be produced?

Without meeting the Guru, no one is liberated, and the Lord of the Universe is not met. |3|

Section 30 - Raag Saarang - Part 010

Searching and searching, I have come to this realization: all peace and bliss are in the Name of the Lord.
Says Nanak, he alone receives it, upon whose forehead such destiny is inscribed. |4|11|

Saarang, Fifth Mehl:
Night and day, utter the Glorious Praises of the Lord.
You shall obtain all wealth, all pleasures and successes, and the fruits of your mind's desires. |1|Pause|

Come, O Saints, let us meditate in remembrance on God; He is the Eternal, Imperishable Giver of Peace and Praanaa, the Breath of Life.
Master of the masterless, Destroyer of the pains of the meek and the poor; He is All-pervading and permeating, abiding in all hearts. |1|

The very fortunate ones drink in the Sublime Essence of the Lord, singing, reciting and listening to the Lord's Praises.
All their sufferings and struggles are wiped away from their bodies; they remain lovingly awake and aware in the Name of the Lord. |2|

So abandon your sexual desire, greed, falsehood and slander; meditating in remembrance on the Lord, you shall be released from bondage.
The intoxication of loving attachments, egotism and blind possessiveness are eradicated by Guru's Grace. |3|

You are All-Powerful, O Supreme Lord God and Master; please be Merciful to Your humble servant.
My Lord and Master is All-pervading and prevailing everywhere; O Nanak, God is Near. |4|12|

Saarang, Fifth Mehl:
I am a sacrifice to the Feet of the Divine Guru.
I meditate with Him on the Supreme Lord God; His Teachings have emancipated me. |1|Pause|

All pains, diseases and fears are erased, for one who comes to the Sanctuary of the Lord's Saints.
He Himself chants, and inspires others to chant the Naam, the Name of the Lord. He is Utterly All-Powerful; He carries us across to the other side. |1|

His Mantra drives out cynicism, and totally fills the empty one.
Those who obey the Order of the Lord's slaves, do not enter into the womb of reincarnation ever again. |2|

Whoever works for the Lord's devotees and sings His Praises - his pains of birth and death are taken away.
Those unto whom my Beloved becomes Merciful, endure the Unendurable Ecstasy of the Lord, Har, Har. |3|

Those who are satisfied by the Sublime Essence of the Lord, merge intuitively into the Lord; no mouth can describe their state.
By Guru's Grace, O Nanak, they are content; chanting and meditating on God's Name, they are saved. |4|13|

Saarang, Fifth Mehl:
I sing, O I sing the Songs of Joy of my Lord, the Treasure of Virtue.
Fortunate is the time, fortunate is the day and the moment, when I become pleasing to the Lord of the World. |1|Pause|

I touch my forehead to the Feet of the Saints.
The Saints have placed their hands on my forehead. |1|

My mind is filled with the Mantra of the Holy Saints,
and I have risen above the three qualities|2|

Gazing upon the Blessed Vision, the Darshan of God's devotees, my eyes are filled with love.
Greed and attachment are gone, along with doubt. |3|

Says Nanak, I have found intuitive peace, poise and bliss.
Tearing down the wall, I have met the Lord, the Embodiment of Supreme Bliss. |4|14|

Saarang, Fifth Mehl, Second House:
One Universal Creator God. By The Grace Of The True Guru:

How can I express the pain of my soul?
I am so thirsty for the Blessed Vision, the Darshan of my Enticing and Lovely Beloved. My mind cannot survive - it yearns for Him in so many ways. |1|Pause|

Section 30 - Raag Saarang - Part 011

I think thoughts of Him; I miss the Love of my Beloved. When will I obtain the Blessed Vision of the Lord's Darshan?
I try, but this mind is not encouraged. Is there any Saint who can lead me to God? |1|

Chanting, penance, self-control, good deeds and charity - I sacrifice all these in fire; I dedicate all peace and places to Him.
One who helps me to behold the Blessed Vision of my Beloved, for even an instant - I am a sacrifice to that Saint. |2|

I offer all my prayers and entreaties to him; I serve him, day and night.
I have renounced all pride and egotism; he tells me the stories of my Beloved. |3|

I am wonder-struck, gazing upon the wondrous play of God. The Guru, the True Guru, has led me to meet the Primal Lord.
I have found God, my Merciful Loving Lord, within the home of my own heart. O Nanak, the fire within me has been quenched. |4|1|15|

Saarang, Fifth Mehl:
You fool, why are you not meditating on the Lord now?
In the awful hell of the fire of the womb, you did penance, upside-down; each and every instant, you sang His Glorious Praises. |1|Pause|

You wandered through countless incarnations, until finally you attained this priceless human birth.
Leaving the womb, you were born, and when you came out, you became attached to other places. |1|

You practiced evil and fraud day and night, and did useless deeds.
You thrash the straw, but it has no wheat; running around and hurrying, you obtain only pain. |2|

The false person is attached to falsehood; he is entangled with transitory things.

And when the Righteous Judge of Dharma seizes you, O madman, you shall arise and depart with your face blackened. |3|

He alone meets with God, whom God Himself meets, by such pre-ordained destiny written on his forehead.

Says Nanak, I am a sacrifice to that humble being, who remains unattached within his mind. |4|2|16|

Saarang, Fifth Mehl:

How can I live without my Beloved, O my mother?

Separated from Him, the mortal becomes a corpse, and is not allowed to remain within the house. |1|Pause|

He is the Giver of the soul, the heart, the breath of life. Being with Him, we are embellished with joy.

Please bless me with Your Gace, O Saint, that I may sing the songs of joyful praise to my God. |1|

I touch my forehead to the feet of the Saints. My eyes long for their dust.

By His Grace, we meet God; O Nanak, I am a sacrifice, a sacrifice to Him. |2|3|17|

Saarang, Fifth Mehl:

I am a sacrifice to that occasion.

Twenty-four hours a day, I meditate in remembrance on my God; by great good fortune, I have found the Lord. |1|Pause|

Kabeer is good, the slave of the Lord's slaves; the humble barber Sain is sublime.

Highest of the high is Naam Dayv, who looked upon all alike; Ravi Daas was in tune with the Lord. |1|

My soul, body and wealth belong to the Saints; my mind longs for the dust of the Saints.

And by the radiant Grace of the Saints, all my doubts have been erased. O Nanak, I have met the Lord. |2|4|18|

Saarang, Fifth Mehl:

The True Guru fulfills the mind's desires.

Section 30 - Raag Saarang - Part 012

All wealth and treasures are obtained by remembering Him in meditation; twenty-four hours a day, O my mind, meditate on Him. |1|Pause|

Your Name is Ambrosial Nectar, O my Lord and Master. Whoever drinks it in is satisfied.
The sins of countless incarnations are erased, and hereafter, he shall be saved and redeemed in the Court of the Lord. |1|

I have come to Your Sanctuary, O Creator, O Perfect Supreme Eternal Lord God.
Please be kind to me, that I may meditate on Your Lotus Feet. O Nanak, my mind and body thirst for the Blessed Vision of Your Darshan. |2|5|19|

Saarang, Fifth Mehl, Third House:
One Universal Creator God. By The Grace Of The True Guru:
O my mind, why are you lured away by otherness?
Here and hereafter, God is forever your Help and Support. He is your soul-mate; He will help you succeed. |1|Pause|

The Name of your Beloved Lover, the Fascinating Lord, is Ambrosial Nectar. Drinking it in, you shall find satisfaction.
The Being of Immortal Manifestation is found in the Saadh Sangat, the Company of the Holy. Meditate on Him in that most sublime place. |1|

The Bani, the Word of the Supreme Lord God, is the greatest Mantra of all. It eradicates pride from the mind.
Searching, Nanak found the home of peace and bliss in the Name of the Lord. |2|1|20|

Saarang, Fifth Mehl:
O my mind, sing forever the Songs of Joy of the Lord of the Universe.
All your disease, sorrow and sin will be erased, if you meditate on the Lord's Name, even for an instant. |1|Pause|

Abandon all your clever tricks; go and enter the Sanctuary of the Holy.

When the Lord, the Destroyer of the pains of the poor becomes merciful, the Messenger of Death is changed into the Righteous Judge of Dharma. |1|

Without the One Lord, there is no other at all. No one else can equal Him. The Lord is Nanak's Mother, Father and Sibling, the Giver of Peace, his Breath of Life. |2|2|21|

Saarang, Fifth Mehl:
The Lord's humble servant saves those who accompany him.
Their minds are sanctified and rendered pure, and they are rid of the pains of countless incarnations. |1|Pause|

Those who walk on the path find peace; they are saved, along with those who speak with them.
Even those who are drowning in the horrible, deep dark pit are carried across in the Saadh Sangat, the Company of the Holy. |1|

Those who have such high destiny turn their faces toward the Saadh Sangat.
Nanak longs for the dust of their feet; O God, please shower Your Mercy on me! |2|3|22|

Saarang, Fifth Mehl:
The humble servant of the Lord meditates on the Lord, Raam, Raam, Raam.
One who enjoys peace in the Company of the Holy, even for an instant, obtains millions of heavenly paradises. |1|Pause|

This human body, so difficult to obtain, is sanctified by meditating on the Lord. It takes away the fear of death.
Even the sins of terrible sinners are washed away, by cherishing the Lord's Name within the heart. |1|

Whoever listens to the Immaculate Praises of the Lord - his pains of birth and death are dispelled.
Says Nanak, the Lord is found by great good fortune, and then the mind and body blossom forth. |2|4|23|

Section 30 - Raag Saarang - Part 013

Saarang, Fifth Mehl, Du-Padas, Fourth House:
One Universal Creator God. By The Grace Of The True Guru:
O my Fascinating Lord, I pray to You: come into my house.
I act in pride, and speak in pride. I am mistaken and wrong, but I am still Your hand-maiden, O my Beloved. |1|Pause|

I hear that You are near, but I cannot see You. I wander in suffering, deluded by doubt.
The Guru has become merciful to me; He has removed the veils. Meeting with my Beloved, my mind blossoms forth in abundance. |1|

If I were to forget my Lord and Master, even for an instant, it would be like millions of days, tens of thousands of years.
When I joined the Saadh Sangat, the Company of the Holy, O Nanak, I met my Lord. |2|1|24|

Saarang, Fifth Mehl:
Now what should I think? I have given up thinking.
You do whatever You wish to do. Please bless me with Your Name - I am a sacrifice to You. |1|Pause|

The poison of corruption is flowering forth in the four directions; I have taken the GurMantra as my antidote.
Giving me His Hand, He has saved me as His Own; like the lotus in the water, I remain unattached. |1|

I am nothing. What am I? You hold all in Your Power.
Nanak has run to Your Sanctuary, Lord; please save him, for the sake of Your Saints. |2|2|25|

Saarang, Fifth Mehl:
Now I have abandoned all efforts and devices.
My Lord and Master is the All-powerful Creator, the Cause of causes, my only Saving Grace. |1|Pause|

I have seen numerous forms of incomparable beauty, but nothing is like You.
You give Your Support to all, O my Lord and Master; You are the Giver of peace, of the soul and the breath of life. |1|

Wandering, wandering, I grew so tired; meeting the Guru, I fell at His Feet.
Says Nanak, I have found total peace; this life-night of mine passes in peace. |2|3|26|

Saarang, Fifth Mehl:
Now I have found the Support of my Lord.
The Guru, the Giver of peace, has become merciful to me. I was blind - I see the jewel of the Lord. |1|Pause|

I have cut away the darkness of ignorance and become immaculate; my discriminationg intellect has blossomed forth.
As the waves of water and the foam become water again, the Lord and His servant become One. |1|

He is taken in again, into what from which he came; all is one in the One Lord.
O Nanak, I have come to see the Master of the breath of life, all-pervading everywhere. |2|4|27|

Saarang, Fifth Mehl:
My mind longs for the One Beloved Lord.
I have looked everywhere in every country, but nothing equals even a hair of my Beloved. |1|Pause|

All sorts of delicacies and dainties are placed before me, but I do not even want to look at them.
I long for the sublime essence of the Lord, calling, "Pri-o! Pri-o! - Beloved! Beloved!", like the Bumble bee longing for the lotus flower. |1|

Section 30 - Raag Saarang - Part 014

The Treasure of Virtue, the Enticer of the mind, my Beloved is the Giver of peace to all.
Guru Nanak has led me to You, O God. Join with me, O my Best Friend, and hold me close in Your Embrace. |2|5|28|

Saarang, Fifth Mehl:
Now my mind is pleased and appeased by my Lord and Master.
The Holy Saint has become kind and compassionate to me, and has destroyed this demon of duality. |1|Pause|

You are so beautiful, and You are so wise; You are elegant and all-knowing.
All the Yogis, spiritual teachers and meditators do not know even a bit of Your value. |1|

You are the Master, You are the Lord under the royal canopy; You are the perfectly pervading Lord God.
Please bless me with the gift of service to the Saints; O Nanak, I am a sacrifice to the Lord. |2|6|29|

Saarang, Fifth Mehl:
The Love of my Beloved comes into my conscious mind.
I have forgotten the entangling affairs of Maya, and I spend my life-night fighting with evil. |1|Pause|

I serve the Lord; the Lord abides within my heart. I have found my Lord in the Sat Sangat, the True Congregation.
So I have met with my enticingly beautiful Beloved; I have obtained the peace which I asked for. |1|

The Guru has brought my Beloved under my control, and I enjoy Him with unrestrained pleasure.
I have become fearless; O Nanak, my fears have been eradicated. Chanting the Word, I have found the Lord. |2|7|30|

Saarang, Fifth Mehl:
I am a sacrifice to the Blessed Vision, the Darshan of my Dear Lord.
The Naad, the Sound-current of His Word fills my ears; my body has settled gently into the Lap of my Beloved. |1|Pause|

I was a discarded bride, and the Guru has made me a happy soul-bride. I have found the Elegant and All-knowing Lord.
That home, in which I was not even allowed to sit - I have found that place in which I can dwell. |1|

God, the Love of His devotees, has come under the control of those who protect the honor of His Saints.
Says Nanak, my mid is pleased and appeased with the Lord, and my subservience to other people has come to an end. |2|8|31|

Saarang, Fifth Mehl:
Now my association with the five thieves has come to an end.
Gazing upon the Blessed Vision of the Lord's Darshan, my mind is in ecstasy; by Guru's Grace, I am released. |1|Pause|

The impregnable place is guarded by countless ramparts and warriors.
This impregnable fortress cannot be touched, but with the assistance of the Saints, I have entered and robbed it. |1|

I have found such a great treasure, a priceless, inexhaustible supply of jewels.
O servant Nanak, when God showered His Mercy on me, my mind drank in the sublime essence of the Lord. |2|9|32|

Saarang, Fifth Mehl:
Now my mind is absorbed in my Lord and Master.
The Perfect Guru has blessed me with the gift of the breath of life. I am involved with the Lord, like the fish with the water. |1|Pause|

I have cast out sexual desire, anger, greed, egotism and envy; I have offered all this as a gift.
The Guru has implanted the medicine of the Lord's Mantra within me, and I have met with the All-knowing Lord God. |1|

My household belongs to You, O my Lord and Master; the Guru has blessed me with God, and rid me of egotism.

Section 30 - Raag Saarang - Part 015

Says Nanak, I have found the Lord with intuitive ease, within the home of my own heart. Devotional worship of the Lord is a treasure over-flowing. |2|10|33|

Saarang, Fifth Mehl:
O my Enticing Lord, all beings are Yours - You save them.
Even a tiny bit of Your Mercy ends all cruelty and tyranny. You save and redeem millions of universes. |1|Pause|

I offer countless prayers; I remember You each and every instant.

Please be merciful to me, O Destroyer of the pains of the poor; please give me Your hand and save me. |1|

And what about these poor kings? Tell me, who can they kill?
Save me, save me, save me, O Giver of peace; O Nanak, all the world is Yours. |2|11|34|

Saarang, Fifth Mehl:
Now I have obtained the wealth of the Lord's Name.
I have become carefree, and all my thirsty desires are satisfied. Such is the destiny written on my forehead. |1|Pause|

Searching and searching, I became depressed; I wandered all around, and finally came back to my body-village.
The Merciful Guru made this deal, and I have obtained the priceless jewel. |1|

The other deals and trades which I did, brought only sorrow and suffering.
Fearless are those traders who deal in meditation on the Lord of the Universe. O Nanak, the Lord's Name is their capital. |2|12|35|

Saarang, Fifth Mehl:
The Speech of my Beloved seems so sweet to my mind.
The Guru has taken hold of my arm, and linked me to God's service. My Beloved Lord is forever merciful to me. |1|Pause|

O God, You are my Lord and Master; You are the Cherisher of all. My wife and I are totally Your slaves.
You are all my honor and power - You are. Your Name is my only Support. |1|

If You seat me on the throne, then I am Your slave. If You make me a grass-cutter, then what can I say?
Servant Nanak's God is the Primal Lord, the Architect of Destiny, Unfathomable and Immeasurable. |2|13|36|

Saarang, Fifth Mehl:
The tongue becomes beautiful, uttering the Glorious Praises of the Lord.
In an instant, He creates and destroys. Gazing upon His Wondrous Plays, my mind is fascinated. |1|Pause|

Listening to His Praises, my mind is in utter ecstasy, and my heart is rid of pride and pain.

I have found peace, and my pains have been taken away, since I became one with God. |1|

Sinful resides have been wiped away, and my mind is immaculate. The Guru has lifted me up and pulled me out of the deception of Maya.

Says Nanak, I have found God, the All-powerful Creator, the Cause of causes. |2|14|37|

Saarang, Fifth Mehl:
With my eyes, I have seen the marvellous wonders of the Lord.

He is far from all, and yet near to all. He is Inaccessible and Unfathomable, and yet He dwells in the heart. |1|Pause|

The Infallible Lord never makes a mistake. He does not have to write His Orders, and He does not have to consult with anyone.

In an instant, He creates, embellishes and destroys. He is the Lover of His devotees, the Treasure of Excellence. |1|

Lighting the lamp in the deep dark pit, the Guru illumines and enlightens the heart.

Section 30 - Raag Saarang - Part 016

Says Nanak, gazing upon the Blessed Vision of His Darshan, I have found peace, and all my hopes have been fulfilled. |2|15|38|

Saarang, Fifth Mehl:
The most beautiful path for the feet is to follow the Lord of the Universe.

The more you walk on any other path, the more you suffer in pain. |1|Pause|

The eyes are sanctified, gazing upon the Blessed Vision of the Lord's Darshan. Serving Him, the hands are sanctified.

The heart is sanctified, when the Lord abides within the heart; that forehead which touches the dust of the feet of the Saints is sanctified. |1|

All treasures are in the Name of the Lord, Har, Har; he alone obtains it, who has it written in his karma.

Servant Nanak has met with the Perfect Guru; he passes his life-night in peace, poise and pleasure. |2|16|39|

Saarang, Fifth Mehl:

Meditate on the Naam, the Name of the Lord; at the very last instant, it shall be your Help and Support.

In that place where your mother, father, children and siblings shall be of no use to you at all, there, the Name alone shall save you. |1|Pause|

He alone meditates on the Lord in the deep dark pit of his own household, upon whose forehead such destiny is written.

His bonds are loosened, and the Guru liberates him. He sees You, O Lord, everywhere. |1|

Drinking in the Ambrosial Nectar of the Naam, his mind is satisfied. Tasting it, his tongue is satiated.

Says Nanak, I have obtained celestial peace and poise; the Guru has quenched all my thirst. |2|17|40|

Saarang, Fifth Mehl:

Meeting the Guru, I meditate on God in such a way,

that He has become kind and compassionate to me. He is the Destroyer of pain; He does not allow the hot wind to even touch me. |1|Pause|

With each and every breath I take, I sing the Glorious Praises of the Lord.

He is not separated from me, even for an instant, and I never forget Him. He is always with me, wherever I go. |1|

I am a sacrifice, a sacrifice, a sacrifice, a sacrifice to His Lotus Feet. I am a sacrifice, a sacrifice to the Blessed Vision of the Guru's Darshan.

Says Nanak, I do not care about anything else; I have found the Lord, the Ocean of peace. |2|18|41|

Saarang, Fifth Mehl:

The Word of the Guru's Shabad seems so sweet to my mind.

My karma has been activated, and the Divine Radiance of the Lord, Har, Har, is manifest in each and every heart. |1|Pause|

The Supreme Lord God, beyond birth, Self-existent, is seated within every heart everywhere.

I have come to obtain the Ambrosial Nectar of the Naam, the Name of the Lord. I am a sacrifice, a sacrifice to the Lotus Feet of God. |1|

I anoint my forehead with the dust of the Society of the Saints; it is as if I have bathed at all the sacred shrines of pilgrimage.

Says Nanak, I am dyed in the deep crimson color of His Love; the Love of my Lord shall never fade away. |2|19|42|

Saarang, Fifth Mehl:

The Guru has given me the Name of the Lord, Har, Har, as my Companion.

If the Word of God dwells within my heart for even an instant, all my hunger is relieved. |1|Pause|

O Treasure of Mercy, Master of Excellence, my Lord and Master, Ocean of peace, Lord of all.

My hopes rest in You alone, O my Lord and Master; hope in anything else is useless. |1|

My eyes were satisfied and fulfilled, gazing upon the Blessed Vision of His Darshan, when the Guru placed His Hand on my forehead.

Section 30 - Raag Saarang - Part 017

Says Nanak, I have found immeasurable peace; my fear of birth and death is gone. |2|20|43|

Saarang, Fifth Mehl:

You fool: why are you going somewhere else?

The Enticing Ambrosial Amrit is with you, but you are deluded, totally deluded, and you eat poison. |1|Pause|

God is Beautiful, Wise and Incomparable; He is the Creator, the Architect of Destiny, but you have no love for Him.

The mad-man's mind is enticed by Maya, the enticer; he has taken the intoxicating drug of falsehood. |1|

The Destroyer of pain has become kind and compassionate to me, and I am in tune with the Saints.

I have obtained all treasures within the home of my own heart; says Nanak, my light has merged into the Light. |2|21|44|

Saarang, Fifth Mehl:
My consciousness has loved my Beloved God, since the very beginning of time.
When You blessed me with the Teachings, O my True Guru, I was embellished with beauty. |1|Pause|

I am mistaken; You are never mistaken. I am a sinner; You are the Saving Grace of sinners.
I am a lowly thorn-tree, and You are the sandalwood tree. Please preserve my honor by staying with me; please stay with me. |1|

You are deep and profound, calm and benevolent. What am I? Just a poor helpless being.
The Merciful Guru Nanak has united me with the Lord. I lay on His Bed of Peace. |2|22|45|

Saarang, Fifth Mehl:
O my mind, blessed and approved is that day,
and fruitful is that hour, and lucky is that moment, when the True Guru blesses me with spirtual wisdom. |1|Pause|

Blessed is my good destiny, and blessed is my Husband Lord. Blessed are those upon whom honor is bestowed.
This body is Yours, all my home and wealth are Yours; I offer my heart as a sacrifice to You. |1|

I obtain tens of thousands and millions of regal pleasures, if I gaze upon Your Blessed Vision, even for an instant.
When You, O God, say, "My servant, stay here with me", Nanak knows unlimited peace. |2|23|46|

Saarang, Fifth Mehl:
Now I am rid of my skepticism and sorrow.
I have abandoned and forsaken all other efforts, and come to the Sanctuary of the True Guru. |1|Pause|

I have attained total perfection, and all my works are perfectly completed; the illness of egotism has been totally eradicated.

Millions of sins are destroyed in an instant; meeting with the Guru, I chant the Name of the Lord, Har, Har. |1|

Subduing the five thieves, he Guru has made them my slaves; my mind has become stable and steady and fearless.

It does not come or go in reincarnation; it does not waver or wander anywhere. O Nanak, my empire is eternal. |2|24|47|

Saarang, Fifth Mehl:
Here and hereafter, God is forever my Help and Support.
He is the Enticer of my mind, the Beloved of my soul. What Glorious Praises of His can I sing and chant? |1|Pause|

He plays with me, He fondles and caresses me. Forever and ever, He blesses me with bliss.
He cherishes me, like the father and the mother love their child. |1|

I cannot survive without Him, even for an instant; I shall never forget Him.

Section 30 - Raag Saarang - Part 018

Says Nanak, joining the Society of the Saints, I am enraptured, lovingly attuned to my Lord. |2|25|48|

Saarang, Fifth Mehl:
Sing of your Lord and Master, your Best Friend.
Do not place your hopes in anyone else; meditate on God, the Giver of peace. |1|Pause|

Peace, joy and salvation are in His Home. Seek the Protection of His Sanctuary.
But if you forsake Him, and serve mortal beings, your honor will dissolve like salt in water. |1|

I have grasped the Anchor and Support of my Lord and Master; meeting with the Guru, I have found wisdom and understanding.
Nanak has met God, the Treasure of Excellence; all dependence on others is gone. |2|26|49|

Saarang, Fifth Mehl:
I have the Almighty Support of my Dear Lord God.
I do not look up to anyone else. My honor and glory are Yours, O God.
|1|Pause|

God has taken my side; He has lifted me up and pulled me out of the whirlpool of corruption.
He has poured the medicine of the Naam, the Ambrosial Name of the Lord, into my mouth; I have fallen at the Guru's Feet. |1|

How can I praise You with only one mouth? You are generous, even to the unworthy.
You cut away the noose, and now You own me; Nanak is blessed with myriad joys. |2|27|50|

Saarang, Fifth Mehl:
Remembering God in meditation, pains are dispelled.
When the Giver of peace to the soul becomes merciful, the mortal is totally redeemed. |1|Pause|

I know of none other than God; tell me, who else should I approach?
As You know me, so do You keep me, O my Lord and Master.I have surrendered everything to You. |1|

God gave me His Hand and saved me; He has blessed me with eternal life.
Says Nanak, my mind is in ecstasy; the noose of death has been cut away from my neck. |2|28|51|

Saarang, Fifth Mehl:
My mind contemplates You, O Lord, all the time.
I am Your meek and helpless child; You are God my Father. As You know me, You save me. |1|Pause|

When I am hungry, I ask for food; when I am full, I am totally at peace.
When I dwell with You, I am free of disease; if I become separated from You, I turn to dust. |1|

What power does the slave of Your slave have, O Establisher and Disestablisher?

If I do not forget the Naam, the Name of the Lord, then I die. Nanak offers this prayer. |2|29|52|

Saarang, Fifth Mehl:
I have shaken off fear and dread from my mind.
With intuitive ease, peace and poise, I sing the Glorious Praises of my Kind, Sweet, Darling Beloved. |1|Pause|

Practicing the Guru's Word, by His Grace, I do not wander anywhere anymore.
The illusion has been dispelled; I am in Samaadhi, Sukh-aasan, the position of peace. I have found the Lord, the Lover of His devotees, within the home of my own heart. |1|

| The Sound-current of the Naad, playful joys and pleasures - I am intuitively, easily absorbed into the Celestial Lord.
He Himself is the Creator, the Cause of causes. Says Nanak, He Himself is All-in-all. |2|30|53|

Section 30 - Raag Saarang - Part 019

Saarang, Fifth Mehl:
The Ambrosial Nectar of the Naam, the Name of the Lord, is the Support of the mind.
I am a sacrifice to the One who gave it to me; I humbly bow to the Perfect Guru. |1|Pause|

My thirst is quenched, and I have been intuitively embellished. The poisons of sexual desire and anger have been burnt away.
This mind does not come and go; it abides in that place, where the Formless Lord sits. |1|

The One Lord is manifest and radiant; the One Lord is hidden and myste-rious. The One Lord is abysmal darkness.
From the beginning, throughout the middle and until the end, is God. Says Nanak, reflect on the Truth. |2|31|54|

Saarang, Fifth Mehl:
Without God, I cannot survive, even for an instant.
One who finds joy in the Lord finds total peace and perfection. |1|Pause|

God is the Embodiment of bliss, the Breath of Life and Wealth; remembering Him in meditation, I am blessed with absolute bliss.
He is utterly All-powerful, with me forever and ever; what tongue can utter His Glorious Praises? |1|

His Place is sacred, and His Glory is sacred; sacred are those who listen and speak of Him.
Says Nanak, that dwelling is sacred, in which Your Saints live. |2|32|55|

Saarang, Fifth Mehl:
My tongue chants Your Name, Your Name.
In the mother's womb, You sustained me, and in this mortal world, You alone help me. |1|Pause|

You are my Father, and You are my Mother; You are my Loving Friend and Sibling.
You are my Family, and You are my Support. You are the Giver of the Breath of Life. |1|

You are my Treasure, and You are my Wealth. You are my Gems and Jewels.
You are the wish-fulfilling Elysian Tree. Nanak has found You through the Guru, and now he is enraptured. |2|33|56|

Saarang, Fifth Mehl:
Wherever he goes, his consciousness turns to his own.
Whoever is a chaylaa (a servant) goes only to his Lord and Master. |1|Pause|

He shares his sorrows, his joys and his condition only with his own.
He obtains honor from his own, and strength from his own; he gets an advantage from his own. |1|

Some have regal power, youth, wealth and property; some have a father and a mother.
I have obtained all things, O Nanak, from the Guru. My hopes have been fulfilled. |2|34|57|

Saarang, Fifth Mehl:

False is intoxication and pride in Maya.
Get rid of your fraud and attachment, O wretched mortal, and remember that the Lord of the World is with you. |1|Pause|

False are royal powers, youth, nobility, kings, rulers and aristocrats.
False are the fine clothes, perfumes and clever tricks; false are the foods and drinks. |1|

O Patron of the meek and the poor, I am the slave of Your slaves; I seek the Sanctuary of Your Saints.
I humbly ask, I beg of You, please relieve my anxiety; O Lord of Life, please unite Nanak with Yourself. |2|35|58|

Saarang, Fifth Mehl:
By himself, the mortal cannot accomplish anything.
He runs around chasing all sorts of projects, engrossed in other entangle-ments. |1|Pause|

His companions of these few days will not be there when he is in trouble.

Section 30 - Raag Saarang - Part 020

He is hand and glove with those who are of no use to him; the poor wretch is affectionately involved with them. |1|

I am nothing; nothing belongs to me. I have no power or control.
O Creator, Cause of causes, Lord God of Nanak, I am saved and redeemed in the Society of the Saints. |2|36|59|

Saarang, Fifth Mehl:
The Great Enticer Maya keeps enticing, and cannot be stopped.
She is the Beloved of all the Siddhas and seekers; no one can fend her off. |1|Pause|

Reciting the six Shaastras and visiting sacred shrines of pilgrimage do not decrease her power.
Devotional worship, ceremonial religious marks, fasting, vows and penance - none of these will make her release her hold. |1|

The world has fallen into the deep dark pit. O Saints, please bless me with the supreme status of salvation.
In the Saadh Sangat, the Company of the Holy, Nanak has been liberated, gazing upon the Blessed Vision of their Darshan, even for an instant. |2|37|60|

Saarang, Fifth Mehl:
Why are you working so hard to earn profits?
You are puffed up like a bag of air, and your skin is very brittle. Your body has grown old and dusty. |1|Pause|

You move things from here to there, like the hawk swooping down on the flesh of its prey.
You are blind - you have forgotten the Great Giver. You fill your belly like a traveller at an inn. |1|

You are entangled in the taste of false pleasures and corrupt sins; the path which you have to take is very narrow.
Says Nanak: figure it out, you ignorant fool! Today or tomorrow, the knot will be untied! |2|38|61|

Saarang, Fifth Mehl:
O Dear Guru, by associating with You, I have come to know the Lord.
There are millions of heroes, and no one pays any attention to them, but in the Court of the Lord, I am honored and respected. |1|Pause|

What is the origin of the human beings? How beautiful they are!
When God infuses His Light into clay, the human body is judged to be precious. |1|

From You, I have learned to serve; from You, I have learned to chant and meditate; from You, I have realized the essence of reality.
Placing His Hand on my forehead, He has cut away the bonds which held me; O Nanak, I am the slave of His slaves. |2|39|62|

Saarang, Fifth Mehl:
The Lord has blessed His servant with His Name.
What can any poor mortal do to someone who has the Lord as his Savior and Protector? |1|Pause|

He Himself is the Great Being; He Himself is the Leader. He Himself accomplishes the tasks of His servant.
Our Lord and Master destroys all demons; He is the Inner-knower, the Searcher of hearts. |1|

He Himself saves the honor of His servants; He Himself blesses them with stability.
From the very beginning of time, and throughout the ages, He saves His servants. O Nanak, how rare is the person who knows God. |2|40|63|

Saarang, Fifth Mehl:
O Lord, You are my Best Friend, my Companion, my Breath of Life.
My mind, wealth, body and soul are all Yours; this body is sewn together by Your Blessing. |1|Pause|

You have blessed me with all sorts of gifts; you have blessed me with honor and respect.
Forever and ever, You preserve my honor, O Inner-knower, O Searcher of hearts. |1|

Section 30 - Raag Saarang - Part 021

Those Saints who know You, O Lord and Master - blessed and approved is their coming into the world.
The Congregation of those humble beings is obtained by great good fortune; Nanak is a sacrifice to the Saints. |2|41|64|

Saarang, Fifth Mehl:
Save me, O Merciful Saint!
You are the All-powerful Cause of causes. You have ended my separation, and joined me with God. |1|Pause|

You save us from the corruption and sins of countless incarnations; associating with You, we obtain sublime understanding.
Forgetting God, we wandered through countless incarnations; with each and every breath, we sing the Lord's Praises. |1|

Whoever meets with the Holy Saints - those sinners are sanctified.
Says Nanak, those who have such high destiny, win this invaluable human life. |2|42|65|

Saarang, Fifth Mehl:
O my Lord and Master, Your humble servant has come to offer this prayer.
Hearing Your Name, I am blessed with total peace, bliss, poise and pleasure. |1|Pause|

The Treasure of Mercy, the Ocean of Peace - His Praises are diffused everywhere.
O Lord, You celebrate in the Society of the Saints; You reveal Yourself to them. |1|

With my eyes I see the Saints, and dedicate myself to serving them; I wash their feet with my hair.
Twenty-four hours a day, I gaze upon the Blessed Vision, the Darshan of the Saints; this is the peace and comfort which Nanak has received. |2|43|66|

Saarang, Fifth Mehl:
One who is lovingly absorbed in the Lord's Name
is a good-hearted friend, intuitively embellished with happiness. He is said to be blessed and fortunate. |1|Pause|

He is rid of sin and corruption, and detached from Maya; he has renounced the poison of egotistical intellect.
He thirsts for the Blessed Vision of the Lord's Darshan, and he places his hopes in the One Lord alone. The Feet of his Beloved are the Support of his heart. |1|

He sleeps, wakes, rises up and sits down without anxiety; he laughs and cries without anxiety.
Says Nanak, she who has cheated the world - that Maya is cheated by the humble servant of the Lord. |2|44|67|

Saarang, Fifth Mehl:
Now, no one complains about the Lord's humble servant.
Whoever tries to complain is destroyed by the Guru, the Transcendent Lord God. |1|Pause|

Whoever harbors vengeance against the One who is beyond all vengenace, shall lose in the Court of the Lord.

From the very beginning of time, and throughout the ages, it is the glorious greatness of God, that He preserves the honor of His humble servants. |1|

The mortal becomes fearless, and all his fears are taken away, when he leans on the Support of the Lord's Lotus Feet.
Chanting the Name, through the Guru's Word, Nanak has become famous throughout the world. |2|45|68|

Saarang, Fifth Mehl:
The Lord's humble servant has discarded all self-conceit.
As You see fit, You save us, O Lord of the World. Beholding Your Glorious Grandeur, I live. |1|Pause|

Through the Guru's Instruction, and the Saadh Sangat, the Company of the Holy, all sorrow and suffering is taken away.
I look upon friend and enemy alike; all that I speak is the Lord's meditation. |1|

The fire within me is quenched; I am cool, calm and tranquil. Hearing the unstruck celestial melody, I am wonder-struck and amazed.
I am in ecstasy, O Nanak, and my mind is filled with Truth, through the perfect perfection of the Sound-current of the Naad. |2|46|69|

Section 30 - Raag Saarang - Part 022

Saarang, Fifth Mehl:
My Guru has rid me of my cynicism.
I am a sacrifice to that Guru; I am devoted to Him, forever and ever. |1|Pause|

I chant the Guru's Name day and night; I enshrine the Guru's Feet within my mind.
I bathe continually in the dust of the Guru's Feet, washing off my dirty sins. |1|

I continually serve the Perfect Guru; I humbly bow to my Guru.
The Perfect Guru has blessed me with all fruitful rewards; O Nanak, the Guru has emancipated me. |2|47|70|

Saarang, Fifth Mehl:

Meditating in remembrance on the Naam, the Name of the Lord, the mortal attains salvation.
His sorrows are dispelled, and his fears are all erased; he is in love with the Saadh Sangat, the Company of the Holy. |1|Pause|

His mind worships and adores the Lord, Har, Har, Har, Har; his tongue sings the Praises of the Lord.
Abandoning egotistical pride, sexual desire, anger and slander, he embraces love for the Lord. |1|

Worship and adore the Merciful Lord God; chanting the Name of the Lord of the Universe, you shall be embellished and exalted.
Says Nanak, whoever becomes the dust of all, merges in the Blesed Vision of the Lord, Har, Har. |2|48|71|

Saarang, Fifth Mehl:
I am a sacrifice to my Perfect Guru.
My Savior Lord has saved me; He has revealed the Glory of His Name. |1|Pause|

He makes His servants and slaves fearless, and takes away all their pain.
So renounce all other efforts, and enshrine the Lord's Lotus Feet within your mind. |1|

God is the Support of the breath of life, my Best Friend and Companion, the One and Only Creator of the Universe.
Nanak's Lord and Master is the Highest of all; again and again, I humbly bow to Him. |2|49|72|

Saarang, Fifth Mehl:
Tell me: other than the Lord, who exists?
The Creator, the Embodiment of Mercy, bestows all comforts; meditate forever on that God. |1|Pause|

All creatures are strung on His Thread; sing the Praises of that God.
Meditate in remembrance on that Lord and Master who gives you everything. Why would you go to anyone else? |1|

Service to my Lord and Master is fruitful and rewarding; from Him, you shall obtain the fruits of your mind's desires.

Says Nanak, take your profits and leave; you shall go to your true home in peace. |2|50|73|

Saarang, Fifth Mehl:
O my Lord and Master, I have come to Your Sanctuary.
The anxiety of my mind departed, when I gazed upon the Blessed Vision of Your Darshan. |1|Pause|

You know my condition, without my speaking. You inspire me to chant Your Name.
My pains are gone, and I am absorbed in peace, poise and bliss, singing Your Glorious Praises. |1|

Taking me by the arm, You lifted me up, out of the deep dark pit of household and Maya.
Says Nanak, the Guru has broken my bonds, and ended my separaation; He has united me with God. |2|51|74|

Section 30 - Raag Saarang - Part 023

Saarang, Fifth Mehl:
The Name of the Lord is cooling and soothing.
Searching, searching the Vedas, the Puraanas and the Simritees, the Holy Saints have realized this. |1|Pause|

In the worlds of Shiva, Brahma and Indra, I wandered around, burning up with envy.
Meditating, meditating in remembrance on my Lord and Master, I became cool and calm; my pains, sorrows and doubts are gone. |1|

Whoever has been saved in the past or the present, was saved through loving devotional worship of the Divine Lord.
This is Nanak's prayer: O Dear God, please let me serve the humble Saints. |2|52|75|

Saarang, Fifth Mehl;
O my tongue, sing the Ambrosial Praises of the Lord.
Chant the Name of the Lord, Har, Har, listen to the Lord's Sermon, and chant God's Name. |1|Pause|

So gather in the jewel, the wealth of the Lord's Name; love God with your mind and body.
You must realize that all other wealth is false; this alone is the true purpose of life. |1|

He is the Giver of the soul, the breath of life and liberation; lovingly tune in to the One and Only Lord.
Says Nanak, I have entered His Sanctuary; He gives sustenance to all. |2|53|76|

Saarang, Fifth Mehl:
I cannot do anything else.
I have taken this Support, meeting the Saints; I have entered the Sanctuary of the One Lord of the World. |1|Pause|

The five wicked enemies are within this body; they lead the mortal to practice evil and corruption.
He has infinite hope, but his days are numbered, and old age is sapping his strength. |1|

He is the Help of the helpless, the Merciful Lord, the Ocean of Peace, the Destroyer of all pains and fears.
Slave Nanak longs for this blessing, that he may live, gazing upon the Feet of God. |2|54|77|

Saarang, Fifth Mehl:
Without the Lord's Name, flavors are tasteless and insipid.
Sing the Sweet Ambrosial Praises of the Lord's Kirtan; day and night, the Sound-current of the Naad will resonate and resound. |1|Pause|

Meditating in remembrance on the Lord, total peace and bliss are obtained, and all sorrows are taken away.
The profit of the Lord, Har, Har, is found in the Saadh Sangat, the Company of the Holy; so load it and bring it on home. |1|

He is the Highest of all, the Highest of the high; His celestial ecomomy has no limit.
Nanak cannot even express His Glorious Grandeur; gazing upon Him, he is wonder-struck. |2|55|78|

Saarang, Fifth Mehl:
The mortal came to hear and chant the Word of the Guru's Bani.
But he has forgotten the Naam, the Name of the Lord, and he has become attached to other temptations. His life is totally worthless! |1|Pause|

O my unconscious mind, become conscious and figure it out; the Saints speak the Unspoken Speech of the Lord.
So gather in your profits - worship and adore the Lord within your heart; your coming and going in reincarnation shall end. |1|

Efforts, powers and clever tricks are Yours; if You bless me with them, I repeat Your Name.
They alone are devotees, and they alone are attached to devotional worship, O Nanak, who are pleasing to God. |2|56|79|

Saarang, Fifth Mehl:
Those who deal in the Naam, the Name of the Lord, are wealthy.
So become a partner with them, and earn the wealth of the Naam. Contemplate the Word of the Guru's Shabad. |1|Pause|

Section 30 - Raag Saarang - Part 024

Abandon your deception, and go beyond vengeance; see God who is always with you.
Deal only in this true wealth and gather in this true wealth, and you shall never suffer loss. |1|

Eating and consuming it, it is never exhausted; God's treasures are overflowing.
Says Nanak, you shall go home to the Court of the Supreme Lord God with honor and respect. |2|57|80|

Saarang, Fifth Mehl:
O Dear God, I am wretched and helpless!
From what source did you create humans? This is Your Glorious Grandeur. |1|Pause|

You are the Giver of the soul and the breath of life to all; Your Infinite Glories cannot be spoken.

You are the Beloved Lord of all, the Cherisher of all, the Support of all hearts. |1|

No one knows Your state and extent. You alone created the expanse of the Universe.
Please, give me a seat in the boat of the Holy; O Nanak, thus I shall cross over this terrifying world-ocean, and reach the other shore. |2|58|81|

Saarang, Fifth Mehl:
One who comes to the Lord's Sanctuary is very fortunate.
He knows of no other than the One Lord. He has renounced all other efforts. |1|Pause|

He worships and adores the Lord, Har, Har, in thought, word and deed; in the Saadh Sangat, the Company of the Holy, he finds peace.
He enjoys bliss and pleasure, and savors the Unspoken Speech of the Lord; he merges intuitively into the True Lord. |1|

Sublime and exalted is the speech of one whom the Lord, in His Mercy makes His Own.
Those who are imbued with God in the state of Nirvaanaa, O Nanak, are emancipated in the Saadh Sangat. |2|59|82|

Saarang, Fifth Mehl:
Since I grasped hold of the Sanctuary of the Holy,
my mind is illuminated with tranquility, peace and poise, and I am rid of all my pain. |1|Pause|

Please be merciful to me, O Lord, and bless me with Your Name; this is the prayer I offer to You.
I have forgotten my other occupations; remembering God in meditation, I have obtained the true profit. |1|

We shall merge again into the One from whom we came; He is the Essence of Being.
Says Nanak, the Guru has eradicated my doubt; my light has merged into the Light. |2|60|83|

Saarang, Fifth Mehl:
O my tongue, sing the Praises of the Lord.

Abandon all other tastes and flavors; the taste of the Naam, the Name of the Lord, is so sublime. |1|Pause|

Enshrine the Lord's Lotus Feet within your heart; let yourself be lovingly attuned to the One Lord.
In the Saadh Sangat, the Company of the Holy, you shall become immaculate and pure; you shall not come to be reincarnated again. |1|

You are the Support of the soul and the breath of life; You are the Home of the homeless.
With each and every breath, I dwell on the Lord, Har, Har; O Nanak, I am forever a sacrifice to Him. |2|61|84|

Saarang, Fifth Mehl:
To meditate on the Lotus Feet of the Lord of the Universe is heaven for me.
In the Saadh Sangat, the Company of the Holy, is the treasure of liberation and the Lord's Ambrosial Name. |1|Pause|

O Lord God, please be kind to me, that I may hear with my ears Your Sublime and Exalted Sermon.
My cycle of coming and going is finally completed, and I have attained peace and tranquility. |1|

Section 30 - Raag Saarang - Part 025

Searching and searching, I have realized the essence of reality: devotional worship is the most sublime fulfillment.
Says Nanak, without the Name of the One Lord, all other ways are imperfect. |2|62|85|

Saarang, Fifth Mehl:
The True Guru is the True Giver.
Gazing upon the Blessed Vision of His Darshan, all my pains are dispelled. I am a sacrifice to His Lotus Feet. |1|Pause|

The Supreme Lord God is True, and True are the Holy Saints; the Name of the Lord is steady and stable.
So worship the Imperishable, Supreme Lord God with love, and sing His Glorious Praises. |1|

The limits of the Inaccessible, Unfathomable Lord cannot be found; He is the Support of all hearts.

O Nanak, chant, "Waaho! Waaho!" to Him, who has no end or limitation. |2|63|86|

Saarang, Fifth Mehl:
The Feet of the Guru abide within my mind.

My Lord and Master is permeating and pervading all places; He dwells nearby, close to all. |1|Pause|

Breaking my bonds, I have lovingly tuned in to the Lord, and now the Saints are pleased with me.

This precious human life has been sanctified, and all my desires have been fulfilled. |1|

O my God, whoever You bless with Your Mercy - he alone sings Your Glorious Praises.

Servant Nanak is a sacrifice to that person who sings the Glorious Praises of the Lord of the Universe, twenty-four hours a day. |2|64|87|

Saarang, Fifth Mehl:
A person is judged to be alive, only if he sees the Lord.

Please be merciful to me, O my Enticing Beloved Lord, and erase the record of my doubts. |1|Pause|

By speaking and listening, tranquility and peace are not found at all. What can anyone learn without faith?

One who renounces God and longs for another - his face is blackened with filth. |1|

One who is blessed with the wealth of our Lord and Master, the Embodiment of Peace, does not believe in any other religious doctrine.

O Nanak, one whose mind is fascinated and intoxicated with the Blessed Vision of the Lord's Darshan - his tasks are perfectly accomplished. |2|65|88|

Saarang, Fifth Mehl:
Meditate in remembrance on the Naam, the Name of the One Lord.

In this way, the sins of your past mistakes shall be burnt off in an instant. It is like giving millions in charity, and bathing at sacred shrines of pilgrimage. |1|Pause|

Entangled in other affairs, the mortal suffers uselessly in sorrow. Without the Lord, wisdom is useless.
The mortal is freed of the anguish of death and birth, meditating and vibrating on the Blissful Lord of the Universe. |1|

I seek Your Sancutary, O Perfect Lord, Ocean of Peace. Please be merciful, and bless me with this gift.
Meditating, meditating in remembrance on God, Nanak lives; his egotistical pride has been eradicated. |2|66|89|

Saarang, Fifth Mehl:
He alone is a Dhoorat, who is attached to the Primal Lord God.
He alone is a Dhurandhar, and he alone is a Basundhar, who is absorbed in the sublime essence of Love of the One Lord. |1|Pause|

One who practices deception and does not know where true profit lies is not a Dhoorat - he is a fool.
He abandons profitable enterprises and is involved in unprofitable ones. He does not meditate on the Beauteous Lord God. |1|

He alone is clever and wise and a religious scholar, he alone is a brave warrior, and he alone is intelligent,

who chants the Name of the Lord, Har, Har, in the Saadh Sangat, the Company of the Holy. O Nanak, he alone is approved. |2|67|90|

Section 30 - Raag Saarang - Part 026

Saarang, Fifth Mehl:
The Lord, Har, Har, is the life of the humble Saints.
Instead of enjoying corrupt pleasures, they drink in the Ambrosial Essence of the Name of the Lord, the Ocean of Peace. |1|Pause|

They gather up the priceless wealth of the Lord's Name, and weave it into the fabric of their mind and body.

Imbued with the Lord's Love, their minds are dyed in the deep crimson color of devotional love; they are intoxicated with the sublime essence of the Lord's Name. |1|

As the fish is immersed in water, they are absorbed in the Lord's Name. O Nanak, the Saints are like the rainbirds; they are comforted, drinking in the drops of the Lord's Name. |2|68|91|

Saarang, Fifth Mehl:
Without the Name of the Lord, the mortal is a ghost.
All the actions he commits are just shackles and bonds. |1|Pause|

Without serving God, one who serves another wastes his time uselessly.
When the Messenger of Death comes to kill you, O mortal, what will your condition be then? |1|

Please protect Your slave, O Eternally Merciful Lord.
O Nanak, my God is the Treasure of Peace; He is the wealth and property of the Saadh Sangat, the Company of the Holy. |2|69|92|

Saarang, Fifth Mehl:
My mind and body deal only in the Lord.
Imbued with loving devotional worship, I sing His Glorious Praises; I am not affected by worldly affairs. |1|Pause|

This is the way of life of the Holy Saint: he listens to the Kirtan, the Praises of his Lord and Master, and meditates in remembrance on Him.
He implants the Lord's Lotus Feet deep within his heart; worship of the Lord is the support of his breath of life. |1|

O God, Merciful to the meek, please hear my prayer, and shower Your Blessings upon me.
I continually chant the treasure of the Naam with my tongue; Nanak is forever a sacrifice. |2|70|93|

Saarang, Fifth Mehl:
Without the Name of the Lord, his intellect is shallow.
He does not meditate in remembrance on the Lord, his Lord and Master; the blind fool suffers in terrible agony. |1|Pause|

He does not embrace love for the Name of the Lord; he is totally attached to various religious robes.

His attachments are shattered in an instant; when the pitcher is broken, the water runs out. |1|

Please bless me, that I may worship You in loving devotion. My mind is absorbed and intoxicated with Your Delicious Love.

Nanak, Your slave, has entered Your Sanctuary; without God, there is no other at all. |2|71|94|

Saarang, Fifth Mehl:
In my mind, I think about that moment,
when I join the Gathering of the Friendly Saints, constantly singing the Glorious Praises of the Lord of the Universe. |1|Pause|

Without vibrating and meditating on the Lord, whatever deeds you do will be useless.

The Perfect Embodiment of Supreme Bliss is so sweet to my mind. Without Him, there is no other at all. |1|

Chanting, deep meditation, austere self-discipline, good deeds and other techniques to being peace - they are not equal to even a tiny bit of the Lord's Name.

Nanak's mind is pierced through by the Lotus Feet of the Lord; it is absorbed in His Lotus Feet. |2|72|95|

Saarang, Fifth Mehl:
My God is always with me; He is the Inner-knower, the Searcher of hearts.
I find happiness in the world hereafter, and peace and pleasure in this world, meditating in remembrance on the Name of my Lord and Master. |1|Pause|

Section 30 - Raag Saarang - Part 027

The Lord is my Best Friend, my Buddy, my Companion. I sing the Glorious Praises of my Sovereign Lord King.

I shall not forget Him in my heart, even for an instant; I have met with the Perfect Guru. |1|

In His Mercy, He protects His slave; all beings and creatures are in His Power.
One who is lovingly attuned to the One, the Perfect Transcendent Lord God, O Nanak, is rid of all fear. |2|73|96|

Saarang, Fifth Mehl:
One who has the Lord's Power on his side
- all his desires are fulfilled, and no pain afflicts him. |1|Pause|

That humble devotee is a slave of his God, who listens to Him, and so lives.
I have made the effort to gaze upon the Blessed Vision of His Darshan; it is obtained only by good karma. |1|

It is only by Guru's Grace that I see His Vision with my eyes which none can equal.
Please bless Nanak with this Gift, that he may wash the Feet of the Saints, and so live. |2|74|97|

Saarang, Fifth Mehl:
I live by singing the Glorious Praises of the Lord.
Please be Merciful to me, O my Loving Lord of the Universe, that I may never forget You. |1|Pause|

My mind, body, wealth and all are Yours, O my Lord and Master; there is nowhere else for me at all.
As You keep me, so do I survive; I eat and I wear whatever You give me. |1|

I am a sacrifice, a sacrifice to the Saadh Sangat, the Company of the Holy; I shall never again fall into reincarnation.
Slave Nanak seeks Your Sancuary, Lord; as it pleases Your Will, so do You guide him. |2|75|98|

Saarang, Fifth Mehl:
O my mind, the Naam is the most sublime peace.
Other affairs of Maya are corrupt. They are nothing more than dust. |1|Pause|

The mortal has fallen into the deep dark pit of household attachment; it is a horrible, dark hell.

He wanders in various incarnations, growing weary; he wanders through them again and again. |1|

O Purifier of sinners, O Lover of Your devotees, please shower Your Mercy on Your meek servant.
With palms pressed together, Nanak begs for this blessing: O Lord, please save me in the Saadh Sangat, the Company of the Holy. |2|76|99|

Saarang, Fifth Mehl:
The Glorious Radiance of the Lord has spread out everywhere.
The doubts of my mind and body are all erased, and I am rid of the three diseases. |1|Pause|

My thirst is quenched, and my hopes have all been fulfilled; my sorrows and sufferings are over.
Singing the Glorious Praises of the Unmoving, Eternal, Unchanging Lord God, my mind, body and soul are comforted and encouraged. |1|

Sexual desire, anger, greed, pride and envy are destroyed in the Saadh Sangat, the Company of the Holy.
He is the Lover of His devotees, the Destroyer of fear; O Nanak, He is our Mother and Father. |2|77|100|

Saarang, Fifth Mehl:
Without the Naam, the Name of the Lord, the world is miserable.
Like a dog, its desires are never satisfied; it clings to the ashes of corruption. |1|Pause|

Administering the intoxicating drug, God Himself leads the mortals astray; they are reincarnated again and again.
He does not meditate in remembrance on the Lord, even for an instant, and so the Messenger of Death makes him suffer. |1|

Please be merciful to me, O Destroyer of the pains of the meek and the poor; let me be the dust of the feet of the Saints.

Section 30 - Raag Saarang - Part 028

Slave Nanak asks for the Blessed Vision of God. It is the Support of his mind and body. |2|78|101|

Saarang, Fifth Mehl:
Without the Name of the Lord, the soul is polluted.
The True Lord God has Himself administered the intoxicating drug of corruption, and led the mortal astray. |1|Pause|

Wandering through millions of incarnations in countless ways, he does not find stability anywhere.
The faithless cynic does not intuitively meet with the Perfect True Guru; he continues coming and going in reincarnation. |1|

Please save me, O All-powerful Lord God, O Great Giver; O God, You are Inaccessible and Infinite.
Slave Nanak seeks Your Sanctuary, to cross over the terrible world-ocean, and reach the other shore. |2|79|102|

Saarang, Fifth Mehl:
To chant the Glorious Praises of the Lord is Sublime.
In the Saadh Sangat, the Company of the Holy, meditate on the Transcendent Lord God; The taste of His essence is Ambrosial Nectar. |1|Pause|

Meditating in remembrance on the One Unmoving, Eternal, Unchanging Lord God, the intoxication of Maya wears off.
One who is blessed with intuitive peace and poise, and the vibrations of the Unstruck Celestial Bani, never suffers again. |1|

Even Brahma and his sons sing God's Praises; Sukdayv and Prahlaad sing His Praises as well.
Drinking in the fascinating Ambrosial Nectar of the Lord's sublime essence, Nanak meditates on the Amazing Lord. |2|80|103|

Saarang, Fifth Mehl:
He commits many millions of sins.
Day and night, he does not get tired of them, and he never finds release. |1|Pause|

He carries on his head a terrible, heavy load of sin and corruption.
In an instant, he is exposed. The Messenger of Death seizes him by his hair. |1|

He is consigned to countless forms of reincarnation, into beasts, ghosts, camels and donkeys.

Vibrating and meditating on the Lord of the Universe in the Saadh Sangat, the Company of the Holy, O Nanak, you shall never be struck or harmed at all. |2|81|104|

Saarang, Fifth Mehl:
He is so blind! He is eating loads of poison.
His eyes, ears and body are totally exhausted; he shall lose his breath in an instant. |1|Pause|

Making the poor suffer, he fills his belly, but the wealth of Maya shall not go with him.
Committing sinful mistakes again and again, he regrets and repents, but he can never give them up. |1|

The Messenger of Death comes to slaughter the slanderer; he beats him on his head.
O Nanak, he cuts himself with his own dagger, and damages his own mind. |2|82|105|

Saarang, Fifth Mehl:
The slanderer is destroyed in mid-stream.
Our Lord and Master is the Saving Grace, the Protector of His humble servants; those who have turned their backs on the Guru are overtaken by death. |1|Pause|

No one listens to what he says; he is not allowed to sit anywhere.
He suffers in pain here, and falls into hell hereafter. He wanders in endless reincarnations. |1|

He has become infamous across worlds and galaxies; he receives according to what he has done.
Nanak seeks the Sanctuary of the Fearless Creator Lord; he sings His Glorious Praises in ecstasy and bliss. |2|83|106|

Saarang, Fifth Mehl:
Desire plays itself out in so many ways.

Section 30 - Raag Saarang - Part 029

But it is not fulfilled at all, and in the end, it dies, exhausted. |1|Pause|

It does not produce tranquility, peace and poise; this is the way it works.
He does not know what belongs to him, and to others. He burns in sexual desire and anger. |1|

The world is enveloped by an ocean of pain; O Lord, please save Your slave!
Nanak seeks the Sanctuary of Your Lotus Feet; Nanak is forever and ever a sacrifice. |2|84|107|

Saarang, Fifth Mehl:
O sinner, who taught you to sin?
You do not contemplate your Lord and Master, even for an instant; it was He who gave you your body and soul. |1|Pause|

Eating, drinking and sleeping, you are happy, but contemplating the Naam, the Name of the Lord, you are miserable.
In the womb of your mother, you cried and whined like a wretch. |1|

And now, bound by great pride and corruption, you shall wander in endless incarnations.
You have forgotten the Lord of the Universe; what misery will be your lot now? O Nanak, peace is found by realizing the sublime state of the Lord. |2|85|108|

Saarang, Fifth Mehl:
O mother, I have grasped the Protection, the Sanctuary of the Lord's Feet.
Gazing upon the Blessed Vision of His Darshan, my mind is fascinated, and evil-mindedness is taken away. |1|Pause|

He is Unfathomable, Incomprehensible, Exalted and High, Eternal and Imperishable; His worth cannot be appraised.
Gazing upon Him, gazing upon Him in the water and on the land, my mind has blossomed forth in ecstasy. He is totally pervading and permeating all. |1|

Merciful to the meek, my Beloved, Enticer of my mind; meeting with the Holy, He is known.

Meditating, meditating in remembrance on the Lord, Nanak lives; the Messenger of Death cannot catch or torment him. |2|86|109|

Saarang, Fifth Mehl:
O mother, my mind is intoxicated.
Gazing upon the Merciful Lord, I am filled with bliss and peace; imbued with the sublime essence of the Lord, I am intoxicated. |1|Pause|

I have become spotless and pure, singing the Sacred Praises of the Lord; I shall never again be dirtied.
My awareness is focused on the Lotus Feet of God; I have met the Infinite, Supreme Being. |1|

Taking me by the hand, He has given me everything; He has lit up my lamp.
O Nanak, savoring the Naam, the Name of the Lord, I have become detached; my generations have been carried across as well. |2|87|110|

Saarang, Fifth Mehl:
O mother, by meditating in remembrance on some other, the mortal dies.
Forsaking the Lord of the Universe, the Giver of souls, the mortal is engrossed and entangled in Maya. |1|Pause|

Forgetting the Naam, the Name of the Lord, he walks on some other path, and falls into the most horrible hell.
He suffers uncounted punishments, and wanders from womb to womb in reincarnation. |1|

They alone are wealthy, and they alone are honorable, who are absorbed in the Sanctuary of the Lord.
By Guru's Grace, O Nanak, they conquer the world; they do not come and go in reincarnation ever again. |2|88|111|

Saarang, Fifth Mehl:
The Lord has cut down the crooked tree of my deceit.
The forest of doubt is burnt away in an instant, by the fire of the Lord's Name. |1|Pause|

Sexual desire, anger and slander are gone; in the Saadh Sangat, the Company of the Holy, I have beaten them and driven them out.

Section 30 - Raag Saarang - Part 030

The Gurmukh is successful in this priceless human life; he shall not lose it in the gamble ever again. |1|

Twenty-four hours a day, I sing the Glorious Praises of the Lord, and contemplate the Perfect Word of the Shabad.
Servant Nanak is the slave of Your slaves; over and over again, he bows in humble reverence to You. |2|89|112|

Saarang, Fifth Mehl:
This Holy Book is the home of the Transcendent Lord God.
Whoever sings the Glorious Praises of the Lord of the Universe in the Saadh Sangat, the Company of the Holy, has the perfect knowledge of God. |1|Pause|

The Siddhas and seekers and all the silent sages long for the Lord, but those who meditate on Him are rare.
That person, unto whom my Lord and Master is merciful - all his tasks are perfectly accomplished. |1|

One whose heart is filled with the Lord, the Destroyer of fear, knows the whole world.
May I never forget You, even for an instant, O my Creator Lord; Nanak begs for this blessing. |2|90|113|

Saarang, Fifth Mehl:
The rain has fallen everywhere.
Singing the Lord's Praises with ecstasy and bliss, the Perfect Lord is revealed. |1|Pause|

On all four sides and in the ten directions, the Lord is an ocean. There is no place where He does not exist.
O Perfect Lord God, Ocean of Mercy, You bless all with the gift of the soul. |1|

True, True, True is my Lord and Master; True is the Saadh Sangat, the Company of the Holy.
True are those humble beings, within whom faith wells up; O Nanak, they are not deluded by doubt. |2|91|114|

Saarang, Fifth Mehl:
O Dear Lord of the Universe, You are the Support of my breath of life.
You are my Best Friend and Companion, my Help and Support; You are my family. |1|Pause|

You placed Your Hand on my forehead; in the Saadh Sangat, the Company of the Holy, I sing Your Glorious Praises.
By Your Grace, I have obtained all fruits and rewards; I meditate on the Lord's Name with delight. |1|

The True Guru has laid the eternal foundation; it shall never be shaken.
Guru Nanak has become merciful to me, and I have been blessed with the treasure of absolute peace. |2|92|115|

Saarang, Fifth Mehl:
Only the true merchandise of the Naam, the Name of the Lord, stays with you.
Sing the Glorious Praises of the Lord, the treasure of wealth, and earn your profit; in the midst of corruption, remain untouched. |1|Pause|

All beings and creatures find contentment, meditating on their God.
The priceless jewel of infinite worth, this human life, is won, and they are not consigned to reincarnation ever again. |1|

When the Lord of the Universe shows His kindness and compassion, the mortal finds the Saadh Sangat, the Company of the Holy,

Nanak has found the wealth of the Lotus Feet of the Lord; he is imbued with the Love of God. |2|93|116|

Saarang, Fifth Mehl:
O mother, I am wonder-struck, gazing upon the Lord.
My mind is enticed by the unstruck celestial melody; its flavor is amazing! |1|Pause|

He is my Mother, Father and Relative. My mind delights in the Lord.
Singing the Glorious Praises of the Lord of the Universe in the Saadh Sangat, the Company of the Holy, all my illusions are dispelled. |1|

I am lovingly attached to His Lotus Feet; my doubt and fear are totally consumed.
Servant Nanak has taken the Support of the One Lord. He shall not wander in reincarnation ever again. |2|94|117|

Section 30 - Raag Saarang - Part 031

Saarang, Fifth Mehl:
O mother, I am totally intoxicated with the Lord's Feet.
I know of none other than the Lord. I have totally burnt off my sense of duality. |1|Pause|

To abandon the Lord of the World, and become involved with anything else, is to fall into the pit of corruption.
My mind is enticed, thirsty for the Blessed Vision of His Darshan. He has lifted me up and out of hell. |1|

By the Grace of the Saints, I have met the Lord, the Giver of peace; the noise of egotism has been stilled.
Slave Nanak is imbued with the Love of the Lord; the forests of his mind and body have blossomed forth. |2|95|118|

Saarang, Fifth Mehl:
The false dealings are finished.
Join the Saadh Sangat, the Company of the Holy, and meditate, vibrate on the Lord. This is the most excellent thing in the world. |1|Pause|

Here and hereafter, you shall never waver; enshrine the Naam, the Name of the Lord, within your heart.
The boat of the Guru's Feet is found by great good fortune; it shall carry you across the world-ocean. |1|

The Infinite Lord is totally permeating and pervading the water, the land and the sky.
Drink in the Ambrosial Nectar of the Lord's Name; O Nanak, all other tastes are bitter. |2|96|119|

Saarang, Fifth Mehl:
You whine and cry

- you are intoxicated with the great corruption of attachment and pride, but you do not remember the Lord in meditation. |1|Pause|

Those who meditate on the Lord in the Saadh Sangat, the Company of the Holy - the guilt of their minstakes is burnt away.
Fruitful is the body, and blessed is the birth of those who merge with God. |1|

The four great blessings, and the eighteen supernatural spiritual powers - above all these are the Holy Saints.
Slave Nanak longs for the dust of the feet of the humble; attached to the hem of His robe, he is saved. |2|97|120|

Saarang, Fifth Mehl:
The Lord's humble servants yearn for the Lord's Name.
In thought, word and deed, they long for this peace, to gaze with their eyes upon the Blessed Vision of God's Darshan. |1|Pause|

You are Endless, O God, my Supreme Lord and Master; Your state cannot be known.
My mind is pierced through by the Love of Your Lotus Feet; this is every-thing to me - I enshrine it deep within my being. |1|

In the Vedas, the Puraanas and the Simritees, the humble and the Holy chant this Bani with their tongues.
Chanting the Lord's Name, O Nanak, I am emancipated; other teachings of duality are useless. |2|98|121|

Saarang, Fifth Mehl:
A fly! You are just a fly, created by the Lord.
Wherever it stinks, you land there; you suck in the most toxic stench. |1|Pause|

You don't stay put anywhere; I have seen this with my eyes.
You have not spared anyone, except the Saints - the Saints are on the side of the Lord of the Universe. |1|

You have enticed all beings and creatures; no one knows You, except the Saints.

Slave Nanak is imbued with the Kirtan of the Lord's Praises. Focusing his consciousness on the Word of the Shabad, he realizes the Presence of the True Lord. |2|99|122|

Saarang, Fifth Mehl:
O mother, the noose of Death has been cut away.
Chanting the Name of the Lord, Har, Har, I have found total peace. I remain unattached in the midst of my household. |1|Pause|

Section 30 - Raag Saarang - Part 032

Granting His Grace, He has made me His Own. The thirst for the Blessed Vision of His Darshan wells up within me.
Joining the Society of the Saints, I sing the Glorious Praises of the Lord; I have given up other hopes. |1|

The Saint has pulled me out of the utterly desolate wilderness, and shown me the path.
Gazing upon His Darshan, all sins are taken away; Nanak is blessed with the jewel of the Lord. |2|100|123|

Saarang, Fifth Mehl:
O mother, I am involved with the Love of the Lord;
I am intoxicated with it. My mind has such a longing and thirst for the Blessed Vision, the Darshan of my Beauteous Lord. No one can break this. |1|Pause|

The Lord is my breath of life, honor, spouse, parent, child, relative, wealth - everything.
Cursed is this body of bones, this pile of maggots and manure, if it knows any other than the Lord. |1|

The Destroyer of the pains of the poor has become merciful to me, by the power of the karma of my past actions.
Nanak seeks the Sanctuary of God, the Treasure, the Ocean of Mercy; my subservience to others is past. |2|101|124|

Saarang, Fifth Mehl:
The Lord's melody is noble and sublime.

The Lotus Feet of my Lord and Master are incomparably beautiful. Meditating on them, one becomes Holy. |1|Pause|

Just by thinking of the Darshan, the Blessed Vision of the Lord of the World, the dirty sins are washed away.
The Lord cuts down and weeds out the corruption of the cycle of birth and death. |1|

How rare is that person who has such pre-ordained destiny, to find the Lord.
Chanting the Glorious Praises of the Creator, the Lord of the Universe - O Nanak, this is Truth. |2|102|125|

Saarang, Fifth Mehl:
The intellect of one who dwells on the Name of the Lord is excellent.
One who forgets the Lord and becomes involved with some other - all his showy pretensions are false. |1|Pause|

Meditate, vibrate on our Lord and Master in the Company of the Holy, and your sins shall be eradicated.
When the Lord's Lotus Feet abide within the heart, the mortal is never again caught in the cycle of death and birth. |1|

He showers us with His kindness and compassion; He saves and protects those who take the Support of the Naam, the Name of the One Lord.
Meditating in remembrance on Him, day and night, O Nanak, your face shall be radiant in the Court of the Lord. |2|103|126|

Saarang, Fifth Mehl:
Honored - you shall be honored in the Court of the Lord.
Join the Saadh Sangat, the Company of the Holy, and sing the Glorious Praises of the Lord; your egotistical pride will be totally dispelled. |1|Pause|

Showering His kindness and compassion, He shall make you His Own. As Gurmukh, your spiritual wisdom shall be perfect.
All peace and all sorts of ecstasy are obtained, by meditating on the Darshan, the Blessed Vision of my Lord and Master. |1|

She who dwells close to her Lord is always the pure, happy soul-bride; she is famous in the ten directions.
She is imbued with the Love of her Loving Beloved Lord; Nanak is a sacrifice to her. |2|104|127|

Saarang, Fifth Mehl:
O Lord, I take the Support of Your Lotus Feet.
You are my Best Friend and Companion; I am with You. You are our Protector, O Lord of the Universe. |1|Pause|

You are mine, and I am Yours; here and hereafter, You are my Saving Grace.
You are Endess and Infinite, O my Lord and Master; by Guru's Grace, a few understand. |1|

Without being spoken, without being told, You know all, O Searcher of hearts.
One whom God unites with Himself, O Nanak, that humble being is honored in the Court of the Lord. |2|105|128|

Section 30 - Raag Saarang - Part 033

Saarang, Fifth Mehl, Chau-Padas, Fifth House:
One Universal Creator God. By The Grace Of The True Guru:
Meditate, vibrate on the Lord; other actions are corrupt.
Pride, attachment and desire are not quenched; the world is in the grip of death. |1|Pause|

Eating, drinking, laughing and sleeping, life passes uselessly.
The mortal wanders in reincarnation, burning in the hellish environment of the womb; in the end, he is destroyed by death. |1|

He practices fraud, cruelty and slander against others; he sins, and washes his hands.
Without the True Guru, he has no understanding; he is lost in the utter darkness of anger and attachment. |2|

He takes the intoxicating drugs of cruelty and corruption, and is plundered.
He is not conscious of the Creator Lord God.

The Lord of the Universe is hidden and unattached. The mortal is like a wild elephant, intoxicated with the wine of egotism. |3|

In His Mercy, God saves His Saints; they have the Support of His Lotus Feet. With his palms pressed together, Nanak has come to the Sanctuary of the Primal Being, the Infinite Lord God. |4|1|129|

Saarang, Fifth Mehl, Sixth House, Partaal:
One Universal Creator God. By The Grace Of The True Guru:
Chant His Sublime Word and His Priceless Glories.
Why are you indulding in corrupt actions?
Look at this, see and understand!
Meditate on the Word of the Guru's Shabad, and attain the Mansion of the Lord's Presence.
Imbued with the Love of the Lord, you shall totally play with Him. |1|Pause|

The world is a dream.
Its expanse is false.
O my companion, why are you so enticed by the Enticer? Enshrine the Love of Your Beloved within your heart. |1|

He is total love and affection.
God is always merciful.
Others - why are you involved with others?
Remain involved with the Lord.
When you join the Saadh Sangat, the Company of the Holy,
says Nanak, meditate on the Lord.
Now, your association with death is ended. |2|1|130|

Saarang, Fifth Mehl:
You may make donations of gold,
and give away land in charity
and purify your mind in various ways,
but none of this is equal to the Lord's Name. Remain attached to the Lord's Lotus Feet. |1|Pause|

You may recite the four Vedas with your tongue,
and listen to the eighteen Puraanas and the six Shaastras with your ears,

but these are not equal to the celestial melody of the Naam, the Name of the Lord of the Universe.
Remain attached to the Lord's Lotus Feet. |1|

You may observe fasts, and say your prayers, purify yourself
and do good deeds; you may go on pilgrimages everywhere and eat nothing at all.
You may cook your food without touching anyone;
you may make a great show of cleansing techniques,
and burn incense and devotional lamps, but none of these are equal to the Lord's Name.
O Merciful Lord, please hear the prayer of the meek and the poor.
Please grant me the Blessed Vision of Your Darshan, that I may see You with my eyes. The Naam is so sweet to servant Nanak. |2|2|131|

Saarang, Fifth Mehl:
Meditate on the Lord, Raam, Raam, Raam. The Lord is your Help and Support. |1|Pause|

Section 30 - Raag Saarang - Part 034

Grasping hold of the Feet of the Saints, I have abandoned sexual desire, anger and greed. The Guru, the Lord of the World, has been kind to me, and I have realized my destiny. |1|

My doubts and attachments have been dispelled, and the blinding bonds of Maya have been broken. My Lord and Master is pervading and permeating everywhere; no one is an enemy.
My Lord and Master is totally satisfied with me; He has rid me of the pains of death and birth. Grasping hold of the Feet of the Saints, Nanak sings the Glorious Praises of the Lord. |2|3|132|

Saarang, Fifth Mehl:
Chant the Name of the Lord, Har, Har, Har; enshrine the Lord, Har, Har, within your mind. |1|Pause|

Hear Him with your ears, and practice devotional worship - these are good deeds, which make up for past evils.
So seek the Sanctuary of the Holy, and forget all your other habits. |1|.

Love the Lord's Feet, continually and continuously - the most sacred and sanctified.

Fear is taken away from the servant of the Lord, and the dirty sins and mistakes of the past are burnt away.

Those who speak are liberated, and those who listen are liberated; those who keep the Rehit, the Code of Conduct, are not reincarnated again.

The Lord's Name is the most sublime essence; Nanak contemplates the nature of reality. |2|4|133|

Saarang, Fifth Mehl:

I beg for devotion to the Naam, the Name of the Lord; I have forsaken all other activities. |1|Pause|

Meditate lovingly on the Lord, and sing forever the Glorious Praises of the Lord of the Universe.

I long for the dust of the feet of the Lord's humble servant, O Great Giver, my Lord and Master. |1|

The Naam, the Name of the Lord, is the ultimate ecstasy, bliss, happiness, peace and tranquility. The fear is death is dispelled by meditating in remembrance on the Inner-knower, the Searcher of hearts.

Only the Sanctuary of the Feet of the Lord of the Universe can destroy all the suffering of the world.

The Saadh Sangat, the Company of the Holy, is the boat, O Nanak, to carry us across to the other side. |2|5|134|

Saarang, Fifth Mehl:

Gazing upon my Guru, I sing the Praises of my Beloved Lord.

I escape from the five thieves, and I find the One, when I join the Saadh Sangat, the Company of the Holy. |1|Pause|

Nothing of the visible world shall go along with you; abandon your pride and attachment.

Love the One Lord, and join the Saadh Sangat, and you shall be embellished and exalted. |1|

I have found the Lord, the Treasure of Excellence; all my hopes have been fulfilled.

Nanak's mind is in ecstasy; the Guru has shattered the impregnable fortress. |2|6|135|

Saarang, Fifth Mehl:
My mind is neutral and detached; I seek only the Blessed Vision of His Darshan. |1|Pause|

Serving the Holy Saints, I meditate on my Beloved within my heart.
Gazing upon the Embodiment of Ecstasy, I rise to the Mansion of His Presence. |1|

I work for Him; I have forsaken everything else. I seek only His Sanctuary.
O Nanak, my Lord and Master hugs me close in His Embrace; the Guru is pleased and satisfied with me. |2|7|136|

Saarang, Fifth Mehl:
This is my condition.
Only my Merciful Lord knows it. |1|Pause|

I have abandoned my mother and father, and sold my mind to the Saints.
I have lost my social status, birth-right and ancestry; I sing the Glorious Praises of the Lord, Har, Har. |1|

I have broken away from other people and family; I work only for God.
The Guru has taught me, O Nanak, to serve only the One Lord. |2|8|137|

Section 30 - Raag Saarang - Part 035

Saarang, Fifth Mehl:
You are my Loving Beloved Enticing Lord of the World.
You are in worms, elephants, stones and all beings and creatures; You nourish and cherish them all. |1|Pause|

You are not far away; You are totally present with all.
You are Beautiful, the Source of Nectar. |1|

You have no caste or social class, no ancestry or family.
Nanak: God, You are Merciful. |2|9|138|

Saarang, Fifth Mehl:
Acting and play-acting, the mortal sinks into corruption. Even the moon and the sun are enticed and bewitched.

The disturbing noise of corruption wells up, in the tinkling ankle bells of Maya the beautiful. With her beguiling gestures of love, she seduces everyone except the Lord. |Pause|

Maya clings to the three worlds; those who are stuck in wrong actions cannot escape her. Drunk and engrossed in blind worldly affairs, they are tossed about on the mighty ocean. |1|

The Saint, the slave of the Lord is saved; the noose of the Messenger of Death is snapped.
The Naam, the Name of the Lord, is the Purifier of sinners; O Nanak, remember Him in meditation. |2|10|139|3|13|155|

One Universal Creator God. By The Grace Of The True Guru:
Raag Saarang, Ninth Mehl:
No one will be your help and support, except the Lord.
Who has any mother, father, child or spouse? Who is anyone's brother or sister? |1|Pause|

All the wealth, land and property which you consider your own
- when you leave your body, none of it shall go along with you. Why do you cling to them? |1|

God is Merciful to the meek, forever the Destroyer of fear, and yet you do not develop any loving relationship with Him.
Says Nanak, the whole world is totally false; it is like a dream in the night. |2|1|

Saarang, Ninth Mehl:
O mortal, why are you engrossed in corruption?
No one is allowed to remain in this world; one comes, and another departs. |1|Pause|

Who has a body? Who has wealth and property? With whom should we fall in love?
Whatever is seen, shall all disappear, like the shade of a passing cloud. |1|

Abandon egotism, and grasp the Sanctuary of the Saints; you shall be liberated in an instant.

O servant Nanak, without meditating and vibrating on the Lord God, there is no peace, even in dreams. |2|2|

Saarang, Ninth Mehl:
O mortal, why have you wasted your life?
Intoxicated with Maya and its riches, involved in corrupt pleasures, you have not sought the Sanctuary of the Lord. |1|Pause|

This whole world is just a dream; why does seeing it fill you with greed?
Everything that has been created will be destroyed; nothing will remain. |1|

You see this false body as true; in this way, you have placed yourself in bondage.
O servant Nanak, he is a liberated being, whose consciousness lovingly vibrates, and meditates on the Lord. |2|3|

Saarang, Fifth Mehl:
In my mind, I never sang the Glorious Praises of the Lord.

Section 30 - Raag Saarang - Part 036

I remained under the influence of corruption, night and day; I did whatever I pleased. |1|Pause|

I never listened to the Guru's Teachings; I was entangled with others' spouses.
I ran all around slandering others; I was taught, but I never learned. |1|

How can I even describe my actions? This is how I wasted my life.
Says Nanak, I am totally filled with faults. I have come to Your Sanctuary - please save me, O Lord! |2|4|3|13|139|4|159|

Raag Saarang, Ashtapadees, First Mehl, First House:
One Universal Creator God. By The Grace Of The True Guru:
How can I live, O my mother?
Hail to the Lord of the Universe. I ask to sing Your Praises; without You, O Lord, I cannot even survive. |1|Pause|

I am thirsty, thirsty for the Lord; the soul-bride gazes upon Him all through the night.
My mind is absorbed into the Lord, my Lord and Master. Only God knows the pain of another. |1|

My body suffers in pain, without the Lord; through the Word of the Guru's Shabad, I find the Lord.
O Dear Lord, please be kind and compassionate to me, that I might remain merged in You, O Lord. |2|

Follow such a path, O my conscious mind, that you may remain focused on the Feet of the Lord.
I am wonder-struck, singing the Glorious Praises of my Fascinating Lord; I am intuitively absorbed in the Fearless Lord. |3|

That heart, in which the Eternal, Unchanging Naam vibrates and resounds, does not diminish, and cannot be evaluated.
Without the Name, everyone is poor; the True Guru has imparted this understanding. |4|

My Beloved is my breath of life - listen, O my companion. The demons have taken poison and died.
As love for Him welled up, so it remains. My mind is imbued with His Love. |5|

I am absorbed in celestial samaadhi, lovingly attached to the Lord forever. I live by singing the Glorious Praises of the Lord.
Imbued with the Word of the Guru's Shabad, I have become detached from the world. In the profound primal trance, I dwell within the home of my own inner being. |6|

The Naam, the Name of the Lord, is sublimely sweet and supremely delicious; within the home of my own self, I understand the essence of the Lord.
Wherever You keep my mind, there it is. This is what the Guru has taught me. |7|

Sanak and Sanandan, Brahma and Indra, were imbued with devotional worship, and came to be in harmony with Him.

O Nanak, without the Lord, I cannot live, even for an instant. The Name of the Lord is glorious and great. |8|1|

Saarang, First Mehl:
Without the Lord, how can my mind be comforted?
The guilt and sin of millions of ages is erased, and one is released from the cycle of reincarnation, when the Truth is implanted within. |1|Pause|

Anger is gone, egotism and attachment have been burnt away; I am imbued with His ever-fresh Love.
Other fears are forgotten, begging at God's Door. The Immaculate Lord is my Companion. |1|

Forsaking my fickle intellect, I have found God, the Destroyer of fear; I am lovingly attuned to the One Word, the Shabad.
Tasting the sublime essence of the Lord, my thirst is quenched; by great good fortune, the Lord has united me with Himself. |2|

The empty tank has been filled to overflowing. Following the Guru's Teachings, I am enraptured with the True Lord.

Section 30 - Raag Saarang - Part 037

My mind is imbued with love for the Naam. The Immaculate Lord is merciful, from the beginning of time, and througout the ages. |3|

My mind is fascinated with the Fascinating Lord. By great good fortune, I am lovingly attuned to Him.
Contemplating the True Lord, all the resides of sins and mistakes are wiped away. My mind is pure and immaculate in His Love. |4|

God is the Deep and Unfathomable Ocean, the Source of all jewels; no other is worthy of worship.
I contemplate the Shabad, the Destroyer of doubt and fear; I do not know any other at all. |5|

Subduing my mind, I have realized the pure status; I am totally imbued with the sublime essence of the Lord.
I do not know any other except the Lord. The True Guru has imparted this understanding. |6|

God is Inaccessible and Unfathomable, Unmastered and Unborn; through the Guru's Teachings, I know the One Lord.
Filled to overflowing, my consciousness does not waver; through the Mind, my mind is pleased and appeased. |7|

By Guru's Grace, I speak the Unspoken; I speak what He makes me speak.
O Nanak, my Lord is Merciful to the meek; I do not know any other at all. |8|2|

Saarang, Third Mehl, Ashtapadees, First House:
One Universal Creator God. By The Grace Of The True Guru:
O my mind, the Name of the Lord is glorious and great.
I know of none, other than the Lord; through the Lord's Name, I have attained liberation and emancipation. |1|Pause|

Through the Word of the Shabad, I am lovingly attuned to the Lord, the Destroyer of fear, the Destroyer of the Messenger of Death.
As Gurmukh, I have realized the Lord, the Giver of peace; I remain intuitively absorbed in Him. |1|

The Immaculate Name of the Lord is the food of His devotees; they wear the glory of devotional worship.
They abide in the home of their inner beings, and they serve the Lord forever; they are honored in the Court of the Lord. |2|

The intellect of the self-willed manmukh is false; his mind wavers and wobbles, and he cannot speak the Unspoken Speech.
Following the Guru's Teachings, the Eternal Unchanging Lord abides within the mind; the True Word of His Bani is Ambrosial Nectar. |3|

The Shabad calms the turbulent waves of the mind; the tongue is intuively imbued with peace.
So remain united forever with your True Guru, who is lovingly attuned to the Lord. |4|

If the mortal dies in the Shabad, then he is liberated; he focuses his consciousness on the Lord's Feet.
The Lord is an Ocean; His Water is Forever Pure. Whoever bathes in it is intuitively imbued with peace. |5|

Those who contemplate the Shabad are forever imbued with His Love; their egotism and desires are subdued.
The Pure, Unattached Lord permeates their inner beings; the Lord, the Supreme Soul, is pervading all. |6|

Your humble servants serve You, O Lord; those who are imbued with the Truth are pleasing to Your Mind.
Those who are involved in duality do not find the Mansion of the Lord's Presence; caught in the false nature of the world, they do not discriminate between merits and demerits. |7|

When the Lord merges us into Himself, we speak the Unspoken Speech; True is the Shabad, and True is the Word of His Bani.
O Nanak, the true people are absorbed in the Truth; they chant the Name of the Lord. |8|1|

Saarang, Third Mehl:
O my mind, the Name of the Lord is supremely sweet.

Section 30 - Raag Saarang - Part 038

It is the Destroyer of the sins, the guilt and fears of countless incarnations; the Gurmukh sees the One Lord. |1|Pause|

Millions upon millions of sins are erased, when the mind comes to love the True Lord.
I do not know any other, except the Lord; the True Guru has revealed the One Lord to me. |1|

Those whose hearts are filled with the wealth of the Lord's Love, remain intuitively absorbed in Him.
Imbued with the Shabad, they are dyed in the deep crimson color of His Love. They are imbued with the Lord's celestial peace and poise. |2|

Contemplating the Shabad, the tongue is imbued with joy; embracing His Love, it is dyed a deep crimson.
I have come to know the Name of the Pure Detached Lord; my mind is satisfied and comforted. |3|

The Pandits, the religious scholars, read and study, and all the silent sages have grown weary; they have grown weary of wearing their religious robes and wandering all around.

By Guru's Grace, I have found the Immaculate Lord; I contemplate the True Word of the Shabad. |4|

My coming and going in reincarnation is ended, and I am imbued with Truth; the True Word of the Shabad is pleasing to my mind.

Serving the True Guru, eternal peace is found, and self-conceit is eliminated from within. |5|

Through the True Word of the Shabad, the celestial melody wells up, and the mind is lovingly focused on the True Lord.

The Immaculate Naam, the Name of the Inaccessible and Unfathomable Lord, abides in the mind of the Gurmukh. |6|

The whole world is contained in the One Lord. How rare are those who understand the One Lord.

One who dies in the Shabad comes to know everything; night and day, he realizes the One Lord. |7|

That humble being, upon whom the Lord casts His Glance of Grace, understands. Nothing else can be said.

O Nanak, those who are imbued with the Naam are forever detached from the world; they are lovingly attuned to the One Word of the Shabad. |8|2|

Saarang, Third Mehl:

O my mind, the Speech of the Lord is unspoken.

That humble being who is blessed by the Lord's Glance of Grace, obtains it. How rare is that Gurmukh who understands. |1|Pause|

The Lord is Deep, Profound and Unfathomable, the Ocean of Excellence; He is realized through the Word of the Guru's Shabad.

Mortals do their deeds in all sorts of ways, in the love of duality; but without the Shabad, they are insane. |1|

That humble being who bathes in the Lord's Name becomes immaculate; he never becomes polluted again.

Without the Name, the whole world is polluted; wandering in duality, it loses its honor. |2|

What should I grasp? What should I gather up or leave behind? I do not know.
O Dear Lord, Your Name is the Help and Support of those whom You bless with Your kindness and compassion. |3|

The True Lord is the True Giver, the Architect of Destiny; as He pleases, He links mortals to the Name.
He alone comes to understand, who enters the Guru's Gate, whom the Lord Himself instructs. |4|

Even gazing upon the wonders of the Lord, this mind does not think of Him. The world comes and goes in reincarnation.
Serving the True Guru, the mortal comes to understand, and finds the Door of Salvation. |5|

Those who understand the Lord's Court, never suffer separation from him. The True Guru has imparted this understanding.
They practice truth, self-restraint and good deeds; their comings and goings are ended. |6|

In the Court of the True Lord, they practice Truth. The Gurmukhs take the Support of the True Lord.

Section 30 - Raag Saarang - Part 039

The self-willed manmukhs wander, lost in doubt and duality. They do not know how to contemplate the Lord. |7|

He Himself is the Gurmukh, and He Himself gives; He Himself creates and beholds.
O Nanak, those humble beings are approved, whose honor the Lord Himself accepts. |8|3|

Saarang, Fifth Mehl, Ashtapadees, First House:
One Universal Creator God. By The Grace Of The True Guru:
O Lord of the World, I gaze upon Your wondrous glory.
You are the Doer, the Cause of causes, the Creator and Destroyer. You are the Sovereign Lord of all. |1|Pause|

The rulers and nobles and kings shall become beggars. Their ostentatious shows are false
. My Sovereign Lord King is eternally stable. His Praises are sung in every heart. |1|

Listen to the Praises of my Lord King, O Saints. I chant them as best I can.
My Lord King, the Great Giver, is Immeasurable. He is the Highest of the high. |2|

He has strung His Breath throughout the creation; He locked the fire in the wood.
He placed the water and the land together, but neither blends with the other. |3|

In each and every heart, the Story of our Sovereign Lord is told; in each and every home, they yearn for Him.
Afterwards, He created all beings and creatures; but first, He provided them with sustenance. |4|

Whatever He does, He does by Himself. Who has ever given Him advice?
The mortals make all sorts of efforts and showy displays, but He is realized only through the Teachings of Truth. |5|

The Lord protects and saves His devotees; He blesses them with the glory of His Name.
Whoever is disrespectful to the humble servant of the Lord, shall be swept away and destroyed. |6|

Those who join the Saadh Sangat, the Company of the Holy, are liberated; all their demerits are taken away.
Seeing them, God becomes merciful; they are carried across the terrifying world-ocean. |7|

I am lowly, I am nothing at all; You are my Great Lord and Master - how can I even contemplate Your creative potency?
My mind and body are cooled and soothed, gazing upon the Blessed Vision of the Guru's Darshan. Nanak takes the Support of the Naam, the Name of the Lord. |8|1|

Saarang, Fifth Mehl, Ashtapadees, Sixth House:

One Universal Creator God. By The Grace Of The True Guru:
Listen to the Story of the Inaccessible and Unfathomable.
The glory of the Supreme Lord God is wondrous and amazing! |1|Pause|

Forever and ever, humbly bow to the True Guru.
By Guru's Grace, sing the Glorious Praises of the Infinite Lord.
His Light shall radiate deep within your mind.
With the healing ointment of spiritual wisdom, ignorance is dispelled. |1|

There is no limit to His Expanse.
His Glory is Infinite and Endless.
His many plays cannot be counted.
He is not subject to pleasure or pain. |2|

Many Brahmas vibrate Him in the Vedas.
Many Shivas sit in deep meditation.

Section 30 - Raag Saarang - Part 040

Many beings take incarnation.
Many Indras stand at the Lord's Door. |3|

Many winds, fires and waters.
Many jewels, and oceans of butter and milk.
Many suns, moons and stars.
Many gods and goddesses of so many kinds. |4|

Many earths, many wish-fulfilling cows.
Many miraculous Elysian trees, many Krishnas playing the flute.
Many Akaashic ethers, many nether regions of the underworld.
Many mouths chant and meditate on the Lord. |5|

Many Shaastras, Simritees and Puraanas.
Many ways in which we speak.
Many listeners listen to the Lord of Treasure.
The Lord God totally permeates all beings. |6|

Many righteous judges of Dharma, many gods of wealth.
Many gods of water, many mountains of gold.
Many thousand-headed snakes, chanting ever-new Names of God.

They do not know the limits of the Supreme Lord God. |7|

Many solar systems, many galaxies.
Many forms, colors and celestial realms.
Many gardens, many fruits and roots.
He Himself is mind, and He Himself is matter. |8|

Many ages, days and nights.
Many apocalypses, many creations.
Many beings are in His home.
The Lord is perfectly pervading all places. |9|

Many Mayas, which cannot be known.
Many are the ways in which our Sovereign Lord plays.
Many exquisite melodies sing of the Lord.
Many recording scribes of the conscious and subconscious are revealed there. |10|

He is above all, and yet He dwells with His devotees.
Twenty-four hours a day, they sing His Praises with love.
Many unstruck melodies resound and resonate with bliss.
There is no end or limit of that sublime essence. |11|

True is the Primal Being, and True is His dwelling.
He is the Highest of the high, Immaculate and Detached, in Nirvaanaa.
He alone knows His handiwork.
He Himself pervades each and every heart.
The Merciful Lord is the Treasure of Compassion, O Nanak.
Those who chant and meditate on Him, O Nanak, are exalted and enraptured. |12|1|2|2|3|7|

Saarang, Chhant, Fifth Mehl:
One Universal Creator God. By The Grace Of The True Guru:
See the Giver of fearlessness in all.
The Detached Lord is totally permeating each and every heart.
Like waves in the water, He created the creation.
He enjoys all tastes, and takes pleasure in all hearts. There is no other like Him at all.
The color of the Lord's Love is the one color of our Lord and Master; in the Saadh Sangat, the Company of the Holy, God is realized.

O Nanak, I am drenched with the Blessed Vision of the Lord, like the fish in the water. I see the Giver of fearlessness in all. |1|

What praises should I give, and what approval should I offer to Him?
The Perfect Lord is totally pervading and permeating all places.
The Perfect Enticing Lord adorns each and every heart. When He withdraws, the mortal turns to dust.

Section 30 - Raag Saarang - Part 041

Why do you not worship and adore Him? Join together with the Holy Saints; any instant, your time shall come.
All your property and wealth, and all that you see - none of it will go along with you.
Says Nanak, worship and adore the Lord, Har, Har. What praise, and what approval, can I offer to Him? |2|

I ask the Saints, what is my Lord and Master like?
I offer my heart, to one who brings me news of Him.
Give me news of my Dear God; where does the Enticer live?
He is the Giver of peace to life and limb; God is totally permeating all places, interspaces and countries.
He is liberated from bondage, joined to each and every heart. I cannot say what the Lord is like.
Gazing upon His wondrous play, O Nanak, my mind is fascinated. I humbly ask, what is my Lord and Master like? |3|

In His Kindness, He has come to His humble servant.
Blessed is that heart, in which the Lord's Feet are enshrined.
His Feet are enshrined within, in the Society of the Saints; the darkness of ignorance is dispelled.
The heart is enlightened and illumined and enraptured; God has been found.
Pain is gone, and peace has come to my house. The ultimate intuitive peace prevails.
Says Nanak, I have found the Perfect Lord; in His Kindness, He has come to His humble servant. |4|1|

Vaar Of Saarang, Fourth Mehl, To Be Sung To The Tune Of Mehma-Hasna:
One Universal Creator God. By The Grace Of The True Guru:

Shalok, Second Mehl:
The key of the Guru opens the lock of attachment, in the house of the mind, under the roof of the body.
O Nanak, without the Guru, the door of the mind cannot be opened. No one else holds the key in hand. |1|

First Mehl:
He is not won over by music, songs or the Vedas.
He is not won over by intuitive wisdom, meditation or Yoga.
He is not won over by feeling sad and depressed forever.
He is not won over by beauty, wealth and pleasures.
He is not won over by wandering naked at sacred shrines.
He is not won over by giving donations in charity.
He is not won over by living alone in the wilderness.
He is not won over by fighting and dying as a warrior in battle.
He is not won over by becoming the dust of the masses.
The account is written of the loves of the mind.
O Nanak, the Lord is won over only by His Name. |2|

First Mehl:
You may study the nine grammars, the six Shaastras and the six divions of the Vedas.
You may recite the Mahaabhaarata.
Even these cannot find the limits of the Lord.
Without the Naam, the Name of the Lord, how can anyone be liberated?
Brahma, in the lotus of the navel, does not know the limits of God.
The Gurmukh, O Nanak, realizes the Naam. |3|

Pauree:
The Immaculate Lord Himself, by Himself, created Himself.
He Himself created the whole drama of all the world's play.
He Himself formed the three gunas, the three qualities; He increased the attachment to Maya.
By Guru's Grace, they are saved - those who love the Will of God.
O Nanak, the True Lord is pervading everywhere; all are contained within the True Lord. |1|

Section 30 - Raag Saarang - Part 042

Shalok, Second Mehl:

He Himself creates, O Nanak; He establishes the various creatures.

How can anyone be called bad? We have only One Lord and Master.

There is One Lord and Master of all; He watches over all, and assigns all to their tasks.

Some have less, and some have more; no one is allowed to leave empty.

Naked we come, and naked we go; in between, we put on a show.

O Nanak, one who does not understand the Hukam of God's Command - what will he have to do in the world hereafter? |1|

First Mehl:

He sends out the various created beings, and he calls back the various created beings again.

He himself establishes, and He Himself disestablishes. He fashions them in various forms.

And all the human beings who wander around as beggars, He Himself gives in charity to them.

As it is recorded, the mortals speak, and as it is recorded, they walk. So why put on all this show?

This is the basis of intelligence; this is certified and approved. Nanak speaks and proclaims it.

By past actions, each being is judged; what else can anyone say? |2|

Pauree:

The Guru's Word makes the drama play itself out. Through virtue, this becomes evident.

Whoever utters the Word of the Guru's Bani - the Lord is enshrined in his mind.

Maya's power is gone, and doubt is eradicated; awaken to the Light of the Lord.

Those who hold onto goodness as their treasure meet the Guru, the Primal Being.

O Nanak, they are intuitively absorbed and blended into the Name of the Lord. |2|

Shalok, Second Mehl:

The merchants come from the Banker; He sends the account of their destiny with them.

On the basis of their accounts, He issues the Hukam of His Command, and they are left to take care of their merchandise.

The merchants have purchased their merchandise and packed up their cargo.

Some depart after having earned a good profit, while others leave, having lost their investment altogether.

No one asks to have less; who should be celebrated?

The Lord casts His Glance of Grace, O Nanak, upon those who have preserved their capital investment. |1|

First Mehl:
United, the united separate, and separated, they unite again.

Living, the living die, and dying, they live again.

They become the fathers of many, and the sons of many; they become the gurus of many, and the disciples.

No account can be made of the future or the past; who knows what shall be, or what was?

All the actions and events of the past are recorded; the Doer did, He does, and He will do.

The self-willed manmukh dies, while the Gurmukh is saved; O Nanak, the Gracious Lord bestows His Glance of Grace. |2|

Pauree:
The self-willed manmukh wanders in duality, lured and enticed by duality.

He practices falsehood and deception, telling lies.

Love and attachment to children and spouse is total misery and pain.

He is gagged and bound at the door of the Messenger of Death; he dies, and wanders lost in reincarnation.

The self-willed manmukh wastes his life; Nanak loves the Lord. |3|

Shalok, Second Mehl:
Those who are blessed with the glorious greatness of Your Name - their minds are imbued with Your Love.

O Nanak, there is only One Ambrosial Nectar; there is no other nectar at all.

O Nanak, the Ambrosial Nectar is obtained within the mind, by Guru's Grace.

They alone drink it in with love, who have such pre-ordained destiny. |1|

Section 30 - Raag Saarang - Part 043

Second Mehl:
Why praise the created being? Praise the One who created all.

O Nanak, there is no other Giver, except the One Lord.

Praise the Creator Lord, who created the creation.

Praise the Great Giver, who gives sustenence to all.

O Nanak, the treasure of the Eternal Lord is over-flowing.

Praise and honor the One, who has no end or limitation. |2|

Pauree:

The Name of the Lord is a treasure. Serving it, peace is obtained.

I chant the Name of the Immaculate Lord, so that I may go home with honor.

The Word of the Gurmukh is the Naam; I enshrine the Naam within my heart.

The bird of the intellect comes under one's control, by meditating on the True Guru.

O Nanak, if the Lord becomes merciful, the mortal lovingly tunes in to the Naam. |4|

Shalok, Second Mehl:

How can we speak of Him? Only He knows Himself.

His decree cannot be challenged; He is our Supreme Lord and Master.

By His Decree, even kings, nobles and commanders must step down.

Whatever is pleasing to His Will, O Nanak, is a good deed.

By His Decree, we walk; nothing rests in our hands.

When the Order comes from our Lord and Master, all must rise up and take to the road.

As His Decree is issued, so is His Command obeyed.

Those who are sent, come, O Nanak; when they are called back, they depart and go. |1|

Second Mehl:

Those whom the Lord blesses with His Praises, are the true keepers of the treasure.

Those who are blessed with the key - they alone receive the treasure.

That treasure, from which virtue wells up - that treasure is approved.

Those who are blessed by His Glance of Grace, O Nanak, bear the Insignia of the Naam. |2|

Pauree:

The Naam, the Name of the Lord, is immaculate and pure; hearing it, peace is obtained.

Listening and hearing, It is enshrined in the mind; how rare is that humble being who realizes it.

Sitting down and standing up, I shall never forget Him, the Truest of the true.

His devotees have the Support of His Name; in His Name, they find peace.

O Nanak, He permeates and pervades mind and body; He is the Lord, the Guru's Word. |5|

Shalok, First Mehl:
O Nanak, the weight is weighed out, when the soul is placed on the scale.

Nothing is equal to speaking of the One, who perfectly unites us with the Perfect Lord.

To call Him glorious and great carries such a heavy weight.

Other intellectualisms are lightweight; other words are lightweight as well.

The weight of the earth, water and mountains
- how can the goldsmith weigh it on the scale?

What weights can balance the scale?

O Nanak, when questioned, the answer is given.

The blind fool is running around, leading the blind.

The more they say, the more they expose themselves. |1|

First Mehl:
It is difficult to chant it; it is difficult to listen to it. It cannot be chanted with the mouth.

Some speak with their mouths and chant the Word of the Shabad - the low and the high, day and night.

If He were something, then He would be visible. His form and state cannot be seen.

The Creator Lord does all deeds; He is established in the hearts of the high and the low.

Section 30 - Raag Saarang - Part 044

It is so difficult to chant it, O Nanak; it cannot be chanted with the mouth. |2|

Pauree:
Hearing the Name, the mind is delighted. The Name brings peace and tranquility.

Hearing the Name, the mind is satisfied, and all pains are taken away.

Hearing the Name, one becomes famous; the Name brings glorious greatness.

The Name brings all honor and status; through the Name, salvation is obtained.

The Gurmukh meditates on the Name; Nanak is lovingly attuned to the Name. |6|

Shalok, First Mehl:

Impurity does not come from music; impurity does not come from the Vedas.

Impurity does not come from the phases of the sun and the moon.

Impurity does not come from food; impurity does not come from ritual cleansing baths.

Impurity does not come from the rain, which falls everywhere.

Impurity does not come from the earth; impurity does not come from the water.

Impurity does not come from the air which is diffused everywhere.

O Nanak, the one who has no Guru, has no redeeming virtues at all.

Impurity comes from turning one's face away from God. |1|

First Mehl:

O Nanak, the mouth is truly cleansed by ritual cleansing, if you really know how to do it.

For the intuitively aware, cleansing is spiritual wisdom. For the Yogi, it is self-control.

For the Brahmin, cleansing is contentment; for the householder, it is truth and charity.

For the king, cleansing is justice; for the scholar, it is true meditation.

The consciousness is not washed with water; you drink it to quench your thirst.

Water is the father of the world; in the end, water destroys it all. |2|

Pauree:

Hearing the Name, all supernatural spiritual powers are obtained, and wealth follows along.

Hearing the Name, the nine treasures are received, and the mind's desires are obtained.

Hearing the Name, contentment comes, and Maya meditates at one's feet.

Hearing the Name, intuitive peace and poise wells up.

Through the Guru's Teachings, the Name is obtained; O Nanak, sing His Glorious Praises. |7|

Shalok, First Mehl:
In pain, we are born; in pain, we die. In pain, we deal with the world.
Hereafter, there is said to be pain, only pain; the more the mortals read, the more they cry out.
The packages of pain are untied, but peace does not emerge.
In pain, the soul burns; in pain, it departs weeping and wailing.
O Nanak, imbued with the Lord's Praise, the mind and body blossom forth, rejuvenated.
In the fire of pain, the mortals die; but pain is also the cure. |1|

First Mehl:
O Nanak, worldly pleasures are nothing more than dust. They are the dust of the dust of ashes.
The mortal earns only the dust of the dust; his body is covered with dust.
When the soul is taken out of the body, it too is covered with dust.
And when one's account is called for in the world hereafter, he receives only ten times more dust. |2|

Pauree:
Hearing the Name, one is blessed with purity and self-control, and the Messenger of Death will not draw near.
Hearing the Name, the heart is illumined, and darkness is dispelled.
Hearing the Name, one comes to understand his own self, and the profit of the Name is obtained.
Hearing the Name, sins are eradicated, and one meets the Immaculate True Lord.
O Nanak, hearing the Name, one's face becomes radiant. As Gurmukh, meditate on the Name. |8|

Shalok, First Mehl:
In your home, is the Lord God, along with all your other gods.

Section 30 - Raag Saarang - Part 045

You wash your stone gods and worship them.
You offer saffron, sandalwood and flowers.
Falling at their feet, you try so hard to appease them.

Begging, begging from other people, you get things to wear and eat.
For your blind deeds, you will be blindly punished.
Your idol does not feed the hungry, or save the dying.
The blind assembly argues in blindness. |1|

First Mehl:
All intuitive understanding, all Yoga, all the Vedas and Puraanas.
All actions, all penances, all songs and spiritual wisdom.
All intellect, all enlightenment, all sacred shrines of pilgrimage.
All kingdoms, all royal commands, all joys and all delicacies.
All mankind, all divinites, all Yoga and meditation.
All worlds, all celestial realms; all the beings of the universe.
According to His Hukam, He commands them. His Pen writes out the account of their actions.
O Nanak, True is the Lord, and True is His Name. True is His Congregation and His Court. |2|

Pauree:
With faith in the Name, peace wells up; the Name brings emancipation.
With faith in the Name, honor is obtained. The Lord is enshrined in the heart.
With faith in the Name, one crosses over the terrifying world-ocean, and no obstructions are ever again encountered.
With faith in the Name, the Path is revealed; through the Name, one is totally enlightened.
O Nanak, meeting with the True Guru, one comes to have faith in the Name; he alone has faith, who is blessed with it. |9|

Shalok, First Mehl:
The mortal walks on his head through the worlds and realms; he meditates, balaced on one foot.
Controlling the wind of the breath, he meditates within his mind, tucking his chin down into his chest.
What does he lean on? Where does he get his power?
What can be said, O Nanak? Who is blessed by the Creator?
God keeps all under His Command, but the fool shows off himself. |1|

First Mehl:
He is, He is - I say it millions upon millions, millions upon millions of times.
With my mouth I say it, forever and ever; there is no end to this speech.

I do not get tired, and I will not be stopped; this is how great my determination is.

O Nanak, this is tiny and insignificant. To say that it is more, is wrong. |2|

Pauree:
With faith in the Name, all one's ancestors and family are saved.
With faith in the Name, one's associates are saved; enshrine it within your heart.
With faith in the Name, those who hear it are saved; let your tongue delight in it.
With faith in the Name, pain and hunger are dispelled; let your consciousness be attached to the Name.
O Nanak, they alone Praise the Name, who meet with the Guru. |10|

Shalok, First Mehl:
All nights, all days, all dates, all days of the week;
All seasons, all months, all the earth and everything on it.
All waters, all winds, all fires and underworlds.
All solar systems and galaxies, all worlds, people and forms.
No one knows how great the Hukam of His Command is; no one can describe His actions.
Mortals may utter, chant, recite and contemplate His Praises until they grow weary.
The poor fools, O Nanak, cannot find even a tiny bit of the Lord. |1|

First Mehl:
If I were to walk around with my eyes wide open, gazing at all the created forms;
I could ask the spiritual teachers and religious scholars, and those who contemplate the Vedas;

Section 30 - Raag Saarang - Part 046

I could ask the gods, mortal men, warriors and divine incarnations;
I could consult all the Siddhas in Samaadhi, and go to see the Lord's Court.
Hereafter, Truth is the Name of all; the Fearless Lord has no fear at all.
False are other intellectualisms, false and shallow; blind are the contemplations of the blind.
O Nanak, by the karma of good actions, the mortal comes to meditate on the Lord; by His Grace, we are carried across. |2|

Pauree:
With faith in the Name, evil-mindedness is eradicated, and the intellect is enlightened.
With faith in the Name, egotism is eradicated, and all sickness is cured.
Believing in the Name, The Name wells up, and intuitive peace and poise are obtained.
Believing in the Name, tranquility and peace well up, and the Lord is enshrined in the mind.
O Nanak, the Name is a jewel; the Gurmukh meditates on the Lord. |11|

Shalok, First Mehl:
If there were any other equal to You, O Lord, I would speak to them of You.
You, I praise You; I am blind, but through the Name, I am all-seeing.
Whatever is spoken, is the Word of the Shabad. Chanting it with love, we are embellished.
Nanak, this is the greatest thing to say: all glorious greatness is Yours. |1|

First Mehl:
When there was nothing, what happened? What happens when one is born?
The Creator, the Doer, does all; He watches over all, again and again
. Whether we keep silent or beg out loud, the Great Giver blesses us with His gifts.
The One Lord is the Giver; we are all beggars. I have seen this throughout the Universe.
Nanak knows this: the Great Giver lives forever. |2|

Pauree:
With faith in the Name, intuitive awareness wells up; through the Name, intelligence comes.
With faith in the Name, chant the Glories of God; through the Name, peace is obtained.
With faith in the Name, doubt is eradicated, and the mortal never suffers again.
With faith in the Name, sing His Praises, and your sinful intellect shall be washed clean.
O Nanak, through the Perfect Guru, one comes to have faith in the Name; they alone receive it, unto whom He gives it. |12|

Shalok, First Mehl:
Some read the Shaastras, the Vedas and the Puraanas.
They recite them, out of ignorance.
If they really understood them, they would realize the Lord.
Nanak says, there is no need to shout so loud. |1|

First Mehl:
When I am Yours, then everything is mine. When I am not, You are.
You Yourself are All-powerful, and You Yourself are the Intuitive Knower.
The whole world is strung on the Power of Your Shakti.
You Yourself send out the mortal beings, and You Yourself call them back home. Having created the creation, You behold it.
O Nanak, True is the Name of the True Lord; through Truth, one is accepted by the Primal Lord God. |2|

Pauree:
The Name of the Immaculate Lord is unknowable. How can it be known?
The Name of the Immaculate Lord is with the mortal being. How can it be obtained, O Siblings of Destiny?
The Name of the Immaculate Lord is all-pervading and permeating everywhere.
Through the Perfect Guru, it is obtained. It is revealed within the heart.
O Nanak, when the Merciful Lord grants His Grace, the mortal meets with the Guru, O Siblings of Desitny. |13|

Shalok, First Mehl:
In this Dark Age of Kali Yuga, people have faces like dogs; they eat rotting carcasses for food.
They bark and speak, telling only lies; all thought of righteousness has left them.
Those who have no honor while alive, will have an evil reputation after they die.

Section 30 - Raag Saarang - Part 047

Whatever is predestined, happens, O Nanak; whatever the Creator does, comes to pass. |1|

First Mehl:
Women have become advisors, and men have become hunters.

Humility, self-control and purity have run away; people eat the uneatable, forbidden food.

Modesty has left her home, and honor has gone away with her.

O Nanak, there is only One True Lord; do not bother to search for any other as true. |2|

Pauree:

You smear your outer body with ashes, but within, you are filled with darkness.

You wear the patched coat and all the right clothes and robes, but you are still egotistical and proud.

You do not chant the Shabad, the Word of Your Lord and Master; you are attached to the expanse of Maya.

Within, you are filled with greed and doubt; you wander around like a fool.

Says Nanak, you never even think of the Naam; you have lost the game of life in the gamble. |14|

Shalok, First Mehl:

You may be in love with tens of thousands, and live for thousands of years; but what good are these pleasures and occupations?

And when you must separate from them, that separation is like poison, but they will be gone in an instant.

You may eat sweets for a hundred years, but eventually, you will have to eat the bitter as well.

Then, you will not remember eating the sweets; bitterness will permeate you.

The sweet and the bitter are both diseases.

O Nanak, eating them, you will come to ruin in the end.

It is useless to worry and struggle to death.

Entangled in worries and struggles, people exhaust themselves. |1|

First Mehl:

They have fine clothes and furniture of various colors.

Their houses are painted beautifully white.

In pleasure and poise, they play their mind games.

When they approach You, O Lord, they shall be spoken to.

They think it is sweet, so they eat the bitter.

The bitter disease grows in the body.

If, later on, they receive the sweet,

then their bitterness shall be gone, O mother.

O Nanak, the Gurmukh is blessed to receive
what he is predestined to receive. |2|

Pauree:
Those whose hearts are filled with the filth of deception, may wash
themselves on the outside.
They practice falsehood and deception, and their falsehood is revealed.
That which is within them, comes out; it cannot be concealed by conceal-
ment.
Attached to falsehood and greed, the mortal is consigned to reincarnation
over and over again.
O Nanak, whatever the mortal plants, he must eat. The Creator Lord has
written our destiny. |15|

Shalok, Second Mehl:
The Vedas bring forth stories and legends, and thoughts of vice and virtue.
What is given, they receive, and what is received, they give. They are
reincarnated in heaven and hell.
High and low, social class and status - the world wanders lost in supersti-
tion.
The Ambrosial Word of Gurbani proclaims the essence of reality. Spiritual
wisdom and meditation are contained within it.
The Gurmukhs chant it, and the Gurmukhs realize it. Intuitively aware, they
meditate on it.
By the Hukam of His Command, He formed the Universe, and in His Hukam,
He keeps it. By His Hukam, He keeps it under His Gaze.
O Nanak, if the mortal shatters his ego before he departs, as it is pre-
ordained, then he is approved. |1|

First Mehl:
The Vedas proclaim that vice and virtue are the seeds of heaven and hell.
Whatever is planted, shall grow. The soul eats the fruits of its actions, and
understands.
Whoever praises spiritual wisdom as great, becomes truthful in the True
Name.
When Truth is planted, Truth grows. In the Court of the Lord, you shall find
your place of honor.

Section 30 - Raag Saarang - Part 048

The Vedas are only merchants; spiritual wisdom is the capital; by His Grace, it is received.
O Nanak, without capital, no one has ever departed with profit. |2|

Pauree:
You can water a bitter neem tree with ambrosial nectar.
You can feed a venomous snake lots of milk.
The self-willed manmukh is resistant; he cannot be softened. You might as well water a stone.
Irrigating a poisonous plant with ambrosial nectar, only poisonous fruit is obtained.
O Lord, please unite Nanak with the Sangat, the Holy Congregation, so that he may be rid of all poison. |16|

Shalok, First Mehl:
Death does not ask the time; it does not ask the date or the day of the week.
Some have packed up, and some who have packed up have gone.
Some are severely punished, and some are taken care of.
They must leave their armies and drums, and their beautiful mansions.
O Nanak, the pile of dust is once again reduced to dust. |1|

First Mehl:
O Nanak, the pile shall fall apart; the fortress of the body is made of dust.
The thief has settled within you; O soul, your life is false. |2|

Pauree:
Those who are filled with vicious slander, shall have their noses cut, and be shamed.
They are totally ugly, and always in pain. Their faces are blackened by Maya.
They rise early in the morning, to cheat and steal from others; they hide from the Lord's Name.
O Dear Lord, let me not even associate with them; save me from them, O my Sovereign Lord King.
O Nanak, the self-willed manmukhs act according to their past deeds, producing nothing but pain. |17|

Shalok, Fourth Mehl:
Everyone belongs to our Lord and Master. Everyone came from Him.

Only by realizing the Hukam of His Command, is Truth obtained.
The Gurmukh realizes his own self; no one appears evil to him.
O Nanak, the Gurmukh meditates on the Naam, the Name of the Lord.
Fruitful is his coming into the world. |1|

Fourth Mehl:
He Himself is the Giver of all; He unites all with Himself.
O Nanak, they are united with the Word of the Shabad; serving the Lord,
the Great Giver, they shall never be separated from Him again. |2|

Pauree:
Peace and tranquility fill the heart of the Gurmukh; the Name wells up
within them.
Chanting and meditation, penance and self-discipline, and bathing at
sacred shrines of pilgrimage - the merits of these come by pleasing my God.
So serve the Lord with a pure heart; singing His Glorious Praises, you shall
be embellished and exalted.
My Dear Lord is pleased by this; he carries the Gurmukh across.
O Nanak, the Gurmukh is merged with the Lord; he is embellished in His
Court. |18|

Shalok, First Mehl:
Thus speaks the wealthy man: I should go and get more wealth.
Nanak becomes poor on that day when he forgets the Lord's Name. |1|

First Mehl:
The sun rises and sets, and the lives of all run out.
The mind and body experience pleasures; one loses, and another wins.
Everyone is puffed up with pride; even after they are spoken to, they do
not stop.
O Nanak, the Lord Himself sees all; when He takes the air out of the
balloon, the body falls. |2|

Pauree:
The treasure of the Name is in the Sat Sangat, the True Congregation.
There, the Lord is found.

Section 30 - Raag Saarang - Part 049

By Guru's Grace, the heart is illumined, and darkness is dispelled.

Iron is transformed into gold, when it touches the Philosopher's Stone.

O Nanak, meeting with the True Guru, the Name is obtained. Meeting Him, the mortal meditates on the Name.

Those who have virtue as their treasure, obtain the Blessed Vision of His Darshan. |19|

Shalok, First Mehl:

Cursed are the lives of those who read and write the Lord's Name to sell it.

Their crop is devastated - what harvest will they have?

Lacking truth and humility, they shall not be appreciated in the world hereafter.

Wisdom which leads to arguments is not called wisdom.

Wisdom leads us to serve our Lord and Master; through wisdom, honor is obtained.

Wisdom does not come by reading textbooks; wisdom inspires us to give in charity.

Says Nanak, this is the Path; other things lead to Satan. |1|

Second Mehl:

Mortals are known by their actions; this is the way it has to be.

They should show goodness, and not be deformed by their actions; this is how they are called beautiful.

Whatever they desire, they shall receive; O Nanak, they become the very image of God. |2|

Pauree:

The True Guru is the tree of ambrosia. it bears the fruit of sweet nectar.

He alone receives it, who is so pre-destined, through the Word of the Guru's Shabad.

One who walks in harmony with the Will of the True Guru, is blended with the Lord.

The Messenger of Death cannot even see him; his heart is illumined with God's Light.

O Nanak, God forgives him, and blends him with Himself; he does not rot away in the womb of reincarnation ever again. |20|

Shalok, First Mehl:

Those who have truth as their fast, contentment as their sacred shrine of pilgrimage, spiritual wisdom and meditation as their cleansing bath, kindness as their deity, and forgiveness as their chanting beads - they are the most excellent people.

Those who take the Way as their loincloth, and intuitive awareness their ritualistically purified enclosure, with good deeds their ceremonial forehead mark,

and love their food - O Nanak, they are very rare. |1|

Third Mehl:

On the ninth day of the month, make a vow to speak the Truth,

and your sexual desire, anger and desire shall be eaten up.

On the tenth day, regulate your ten doors; on the eleventh day, know that the Lord is One.

On the twelfth day, the five thieves are subdued, and then, O Nanak, the mind is pleased and appeased.

Observe such a fast as this, O Pandit, O religious scholar; of what use are all the other teachings? |2|

Pauree:

Kings, rulers and monarchs enjoy pleasures and gather the poison of Maya.

In love with it, they collect more and more, stealing the wealth of others.

They do not trust their own children or spouses; they are totally attached to the love of Maya.

But even as they look on, Maya cheats them, and they come to regret and repent.

Bound and gagged at Death's door, they are beaten and punished; O Nanak, it pleases the Will of the Lord. |21|

Shalok, First Mehl:

The one who lacks spiritual wisdom sings religious songs.

The hungry Mullah turns his home into a mosque.

The lazy unemployed has his ears pierced to look like a Yogi.

Someone else becomes a pan-handler, and loses his social status.

One who calls himself a guru or a spiritual teacher, while he goes around begging

- don't ever touch his feet.

One who works for what he eats, and gives some of what he has

- O Nanak, he knows the Path. |1|

Section 30 - Raag Saarang - Part 050

First Mehl:
Those mortals whose minds are like deep dark pits do not understand the purpose of life, even when it is explained to them.
Their minds are blind, and their heart-lotuses are upside-down; they look totally ugly.
Some know how to speak, and understand what they are told. They are wise and beautiful.
Some do not understand about the Sound-current of the Naad or the Vedas, music, virtue or vice.
Some are not blessed with understanding, intelligence, or sublime intellect; they do not grasp the mystery of God's Word.
O Nanak, they are donkeys; they are very proud of themselves, but they have no virtues at all. |2|

Pauree:
To the Gurmukh, everything is sacred: wealth, property, Maya.
Those who spend the wealth of the Lord find peace through giving.
Those who meditate on the Lord's Name shall never be deprived.
The Gurmukhs come to see the Lord, and leave behind the things of Maya.
O Nanak, the devotees do not think of anything else; they are absorbed in the Name of the Lord. |22|

Shalok, Fourth Mehl:
Those who serve the True Guru are very fortunate.
They are lovingly attuned to the True Shabad, the Word of the One God.
In their own household and family, they are in natural Samaadhi.
O Nanak, those who are attuned to the Naam are truly detached from the world. |1|

Fourth Mehl:
Calculated service is not service at all, and what is done is not approved.
The flavor of the Shabad, the Word of God, is not tasted if the mortal is not in love with the True Lord God.
The stubborn-minded person does not even like the True Guru; he comes and goes in reincarnation.
He takes one step forward, and ten steps back.
The mortal works to serve the True Guru, if he walks in harmony with the True Guru's Will.

He loses his self-conceit, and meets the True Guru; he remains intuitively absorbed in the Lord.

O Nanak, they never forget the Naam, the Name of the Lord; they are united in Union with the True Lord. |2|

Pauree:
They call themselves emperors and rulers, but none of them will be allowed to stay.

Their sturdy forts and mansions - none of them will go along with them.

Their gold and horses, fast as the wind, are cursed, and cursed are their clever tricks.

Eating the thirty-six delicacies, they become bloated with pollution.

O Nanak, the self-willed manmukh does not know the One who gives, and so he suffers in pain. |23|

Shalok, Third Mehl:
The Pandits, the religious scholars and the silent sages read and recite until they get tired. They wander through foreign lands in their religious robes, until they are exhausted.

In love with duality, they never receive the Name. Held in the grasp of pain, they suffer terribly.

The blind fools serve the three gunas, the three dispositions; they deal only with Maya.

With deception in their hearts, the fools read sacred texts to fill their bellies.

One who serves the True Guru finds peace; he eradicates egotism from within.

O Nanak, there is One Name to chant and dwell on; how rare are those who reflect on this and understand. |1|

Third Mehl:
Naked we come, and naked we go. This is by the Lord's Command; what else can we do?

The object belongs to Him; He shall take it away; with whom should one be angry.

One who becomes Gurmukh accepts God's Will; he intuitively drinks in the Lord's sublime essence.

O Nanak, praise the Giver of peace forever; with your tongue, savor the Lord. |2|

Section 30 - Raag Saarang - Part 051

Pauree:
The fortress of the body has been decorated and adorned in so many ways.
The wealthy wear beautiful silk robes of various colors.
They hold elegant and beautiful courts, on red and white carpets.
But they eat in pain, and in pain they seek pleasure; they are very proud of their pride.
O Nanak, the mortal does not even think of the Name, which shall deliver him in the end. |24|

Shalok, Third Mehl:
She sleeps in intuitive peace and poise, absorbed in the Word of the Shabad.
God hugs her close in His Embrace, and merges her into Himself.
Duality is eradicated with intuitive ease.
The Naam comes to abide in her mind.
He hugs close in His Embrace those who shatter and reform their beings.
O Nanak, those who are predestined to meet Him, come and meet Him now. |1|

Third Mehl:
Those who forget the Naam, the Name of the Lord - so what if they chant other chants?
They are maggots in manure, plundered by the thief of worldly entanglements.
O Nanak, never forget the Naam; greed for anything else is false. |2|

Pauree:
Those who praise the Naam, and believe in the Naam, are eternally stable in this world.
Within their hearts, they dwell on the Lord, and nothing else at all.
With each and every hair, they chant the Lord's Name, each and every instant, the Lord.
The birth of the Gurmukh is fruitful and certified; pure and unstained, his filth is washed away.
O Nanak, meditating on the Lord of eternal life, the status of immortality is obtained. |25|

Shalok, Third Mehl:

Those who forget the Naam and do other things,
O Nanak, will be bound and gagged and beaten in the City of Death, like the thief caught red-handed. |1|

Fifth Mehl:
The earth is beauteous, and the sky is lovely, chanting the Name of the Lord.
O Nanak, those who lack the Naam - their carcasses are eaten by the crows. |2|

Pauree:
Those who lovingly praise the Naam, and dwell in the mansion of the self deep within,
do not enter into reincarnation ever again; they shall never be destroyed.
They remain immersed and absorbed in the love of the Lord, with every breath and morsel of food.
The color of the Lord's Love never fades away; the Gurmukhs are enlightened.
Granting His Grace, He unites them with Himself; O Nanak, the Lord keeps them by His side. |26|

Shalok, Third Mehl:
As long as his mind is disturbed by waves, he is caught in ego and egotistical pride.
He does not find the taste of the Shabad, and he does not embrace love for the Name.
His service is not accepted; worrying and worrying, he wastes away in misery.
O Nanak, he alone is called a selfless servant, who cuts off his head, and offers it to the Lord.
He accepts the Will of the True Guru, and enshrines the Shabad within his heart. |1|

Third Mehl:
That is chanting and meditation, work and selfless service, which is pleasing to our Lord and Master.
The Lord Himself forgives, and takes away self-conceit, and unites the mortals with Himself.
United with the Lord, the mortal is never separated again; his light merges into the Light.

O Nanak, by Guru's Grace, the mortal understands, when the Lord allows him to understand. |2|

Pauree:
All are held accountable, even the egotistical self-willed manmukhs.
They never even think of the Name of the Lord; the Messenger of Death shall hit them on their heads.

Section 30 - Raag Saarang - Part 052

Their sin and corruption are like rusty slag; they carry such a heavy load.
The path is treacherous and terrifying; how can they cross over to the other side?
O Nanak, those whom the Guru protects are saved. They are saved in the Name of the Lord. |27|

Shalok, Third Mehl:
Without serving the True Guru, no one finds peace; mortals die and are reborn, over and over again.
They have been given the drug of emotional attachment; in love with duality, they are totally corrupt.
Some are saved, by Guru's Grace. Everyone humbly bows before such humble beings.
O Nanak, meditate on the Naam, deep within yourself, day and night. You shall find the Door of Salvation. |1|

Third Mehl:
Emotionally attached to Maya, the mortal forgets truth, death and the Name of the Lord.
Engaged in worldly affairs, his life wastes away; deep within himself, he suffers in pain.
O Nanak, those who have the karma of such pre-ordained destiny, serve the True Guru and find peace. |2|

Pauree:
Read the account of the Name of the Lord, and you shall never again be called to account.
No one will question you, and you will always be safe in the Court of the Lord.
The Messenger of Death will meet you, and be your constant servant.

Through the Perfect Guru, you shall find the Mansion of the Lord's Presence. You shall be famous throughout the world.

O Nanak, the unstruck celestial melody vibrates at your door; come and merge with the Lord. |28|

Shalok, Third Mehl:

Whoever follows the Guru's Teachings, attains the most sublime peace of all peace.

Acting in accordance with the Guru, his fear is cut away; O Nanak, he is carried across. |1|

Third Mehl:

The True Lord does not grow old; His Naam is never dirtied.

Whoever walks in harmony with the Guru's Will, shall not be reborn again.

O Nanak, those who forget the Naam, come and go in reincarnation. |2|

Pauree:

I am a beggar; I ask this blessing of You: O Lord, please embellish me with Your Love.

I am so thirsty for the Blessed Vision of the Lord's Darshan; His Darshan brings me satisfaction.

I cannot live for a moment, for even an instant, without seeing Him, O my mother.

The Guru has shown me that the Lord is always with me; He is permeating and pervading all places.

He Himself wakes the sleepers, O Nanak, and lovingly attunes them to Himself. |29|

Shalok, Third Mehl:

The self-willed manmukhs do not even know how to speak. They are filled with sexual desire, anger and egotism.

They do not know the difference between good and bad; they constantly think of corruption.

In the Lord's Court, they are called to account, and they are judged to be false.

He Himself creates the Universe. He Himself contemplates it.

O Nanak, whom should we tell? The True Lord is permeating and pervading all. |1|

Third Mehl:

The Gurmukhs worship and adore the Lord; they receive the good karma of their actions.

O Nanak, I am a sacrifice to those whose minds are filled with the Lord. |2|

Pauree:
All people cherish hope, that they will live long lives.
They wish to live forever; they adorn and embellish their forts and mansions.
By various frauds and deceptions, they steal the wealth of others.
But the Messenger of Death keeps his gaze on their breath, and the life of those goblins decreases day by day.

Section 30 - Raag Saarang - Part 053

Nanak has come to the Sanctuary of the Guru, and is saved. The Guru, the Lord, is his Protector. |30|

Shalok, Third Mehl:
Reading and writing, the Pandits engage in debates and disputes; they are attached to the flavors of Maya.
In the love of duality, they forget the Naam. Those foolish mortals shall receive their punishment.
They do not serve the One who created them, who gives sustenance to all.
The noose of Death around their necks is not cut off; they come and go in reincarnation, over and over again.
The True Guru comes and meets those who have such pre-ordained destiny.
Night and day, they meditate on the Naam, the Name of the Lord; O Nanak, they merge into the True Lord. |1|

Third Mehl:
Those Gurmukhs who fall at His Feet deal with the True Lord and serve the True Lord.
O Nanak, those who walk in harmony with the Guru's Will are intuitively absorbed in the True Lord. |2|

Pauree:
In hope, there is very great pain; the self-willed manmukh focuses his consciousness on it.
The Gurmukhs become desireless, and attain supreme peace.

In the midst of their household, they remain detached; they are lovingly attuned to the Detached Lord.

Sorrow and separation do not cling to them at all. They are pleased with the Lord's Will.

O Nanak, they remain forever immersed in the Primal Lord, who blends them with Himself. |31|

Shalok, Third Mehl:

Why keep what is held in trust for another? Giving it back, peace is found.

The Word of the Guru's Shabad rests in the Guru; it does not appear through anyone else.

The blind man finds a jewel, and goes from house to house selling it.

But they cannot appraise it, and they do not offer him even half a shell for it.

If he cannot appraise it himself, then he should have it appraised by an appraiser.

If he focuses his consciousness, then he obtains the true object, and he is blessed with the nine treasures.

The wealth is within the house, while the world is dying of hunger. Without the True Guru, no one has a clue.

When the cooling and soothing Shabad comes to dwell in the mind and body, there is no sorrow or separation there.

The object belongs to someone else, but the fool is proud of it, and shows his shallow nature.

O Nanak, without understanding, no one obtains it; they come and go in reincarnation, over and over again. |1|

Third Mehl:

My mind is in ecstasy; I have met my Beloved Lord. My beloved friends, the Saints, are delighted.

Those who are united with the Primal Lord shall never be separated again. The Creator has united them with Himself.

The Shabad permeates my inner being, and I have found the Guru; all my sorrows are dispelled.

I praise forever the Lord, the Giver of peace; I keep Him enshrined deep within my heart.

How can the self-willed manmukh gossip about those who are embellished and exalted in the True Word of the Shabad?

My Beloved Himself preserves the honor of those who have come to the Guru's Door seeking Sanctuary.

O Nanak, the Gurmukhs are filled with joy; their faces are radiant in the Court of the Lord. |2|

Pauree:
The husband and wife are very much in love; joining together, their love increases.
Gazing on his children and his wife, the man is pleased and attached to Maya.
Stealing the wealth of his own country and other lands, he brings it home and feeds them.

Section 30 - Raag Saarang - Part 054

In the end, hatred and conflict well up, and no one can save him.
O Nanak, without the Name, those loving attachments are cursed; engrossed in them, he suffers in pain. |32|

Shalok, Third Mehl:
The Guru's Word is the Ambrosial Nectar of the Naam. Eating it, all hunger departs.
There is no thirst or desire at all, when the Naam comes to dwell in the mind.
Eating anything other than the Name, disease runs to afflict the body.
O Nanak, whoever takes the Praise of the Shabad as his spices and flavors - the Lord unites him in His Union. |1|

Third Mehl:
The life within all living beings is the Word of the Shabad. Through it, we meet our Husband Lord.
Without the Shabad, the world is in darkness. Through the Shabad, it is enlightened.
The Pandits, the religious scholars, and the silent sages read and write until they are weary. The religious fanatics are tired of washing their bodies.
Without the Shabad, no one attains the Lord; the miserable depart weeping and wailing.
O Nanak, by His Glance of Grace, the Merciful Lord is attained. |2|

Pauree:
The husband and wife are very much in love; sitting together, they make evil plans.

All that is seen shall pass away. This is the Will of my God.
How can anyone remain in this world forever? Some may try to devise a plan.
Working for the Perfect Guru, the wall becomes permanent and stable.
O Nanak, the Lord forgives them, and merges them into Himself; they are absorbed in the Lord's Name. |33|

Shalok, Third Mehl:
Attached to Maya, the mortal forgets the Fear of God and Guru, and love for the Infinite Lord.
The waves of greed take away his wisdom and understanding, and he does not embrace love for the True Lord.
The Word of the Shabad abides in the mind of the Gurmukhs, who find the Gate of Salvation.
O Nanak, the Lord Himself forgives them, and unites them in Union with Himself. |1|

Fourth Mehl:
O Nanak, without Him, we could not live for a moment. Forgetting Him, we could not succeed for an instant.
O mortal, how can you be angry with the One who cares for you? |2|

Fourth Mehl:
The rainy season of Saawan has come. The Gurmukh meditates on the Lord's Name.
All pain, hunger and misfortune end, when the rain falls in torrents.
The entire earth is rejuvenated, and the grain grows in abundance.
The Carefree Lord, by His Grace, summons that mortal whom the Lord Himself approves.
So meditate on the Lord, O Saints; He shall save you in the end.
The Kirtan of the Lord's Praises and devotion to Him is bliss; peace shall come to dwell in the mind.
Those Gurmukhs who worship the Naam, the Name of the Lord - their pain and hunger departs.
Servant Nanak is satisfied, singing the Glorious Praises of the Lord. Please embellish him with the Blessed Vision of Your Darshan. |3|

Pauree:
The Perfect Guru bestows His gifts, which increase day by day.

The Merciful Lord Himself bestows them; they cannot be concealed by concealment.

The heart-lotus blossoms forth, and the mortal is lovingly absorbed in the state of supreme bliss.

If anyone tries to challenge him, the Lord throws dust on his head.

O Nanak, no one can equal the glory of the Perfect True Guru. |34|

Section 30 - Raag Saarang - Part 055

Shalok, Third Mehl:

The Order of the Lord is beyond challenge. Clever tricks and arguments will not work against it.

So abandon your self-conceit, and take to His Sanctuary; accept the Order of His Will.

The Gurmukh eliminates self-conceit from within himself; he shall not be punished by the Messenger of Death.

O Nanak, he alone is called a selfless servant, who remains lovingly attuned to the True Lord. |1|

Third Mehl:

All gifts, light and beauty are Yours.

Excessive cleverness and egotism are mine.

The mortal performs all sorts of rituals in greed and attachment; engrossed in egotsim, he shall never escape the cycle of reincarnation.

O Nanak, the Creator Himself inspires all to act. Whatever pleases Him is good. |2|

Pauree, Fifth Mehl:

Let Truth be your food, and Truth your clothes, and take the Support of the True Name.

The True Guru shall lead you to meet God, the Great Giver.

When perfect destiny is activated, the mortal meditates on the Formless Lord.

Joining the Saadh Sangat, the Company of the Holy, you shall cross over the world-ocean.

O Nanak, chant God's Praises, and celebrate His Victory. |35|

Shalok, Fifth Mehl:

In Your Mercy, You care for all beings and creatures.

You produce corn and water in abundance; You eliminate pain and poverty, and carry all beings across.

The Great Giver listened to my prayer, and the world has been cooled and comforted.

Take me into Your Embrace, and take away all my pain.

Nanak meditates on the Naam, the Name of the Lord; the House of God is fruitful and prosperous. |1|

Fifth Mehl:

Rain is falling from the clouds - it is so beautiful! The Creator Lord issued His Order.

Grain has been produced in abundance; the world is cooled and comforted.

The mind and body are rejuvenated, meditating in remembrance on the Inaccessible and Infinite Lord.

O my True Creator Lord God, please shower Your Mercy on me.

He does whatever He pleases; Nanak is forever a sacrifice to Him. |2|

Pauree:

The Great Lord is Inaccessible; His glorious greatness is glorious!

Gazing upon Him through the Word of the Guru's Shabad, I blossom forth in ecstasy; tranquility comes to my inner being.

All by Himself, He Himself is pervading everywhere, O Siblings of Destiny.

He Himself is the Lord and Master of all. He has subdued all, and all are under the Hukam of His Command.

O Nanak, the Lord does whatever He pleases. Everyone walks in harmony with His Will. |36|1|

SUDH|

Raag Saarang, The Word Of The Devotees.

Kabeer Jee:

One Universal Creator God. By The Grace Of The True Guru:

O mortal, why are you so proud of small things?

With a few pounds of grain and a few coins in your pocket, you are totally puffed up with pride. |1|Pause|

With great pomp and ceremony, you control a hundred villages, with an income of hundreds of thousands of dollars.

The power you exert will last for only a few days, like the green leaves of the forest. |1|

No one has brought this wealth with him, and no one will take it with him when he goes.

Emperors, even greater than Raawan, passed away in an instant. |2|

Section 30 - Raag Saarang - Part 056

The Lord's Saints are steady and stable forever; they worship and adore Him, and chant the Lord's Name.

Those who are mercifully blessed by the Lord of the Universe, join the Sat Sangat, the True Congregation. |3|

Mother, father, spouse, children and wealth will not go along with you in the end.

Says Kabeer, meditate and vibrate on the Lord, O madman. Your life is uselessly wasting away. |4|1|

I do not know the limits of Your Royal Ashram.

I am the humble slave of Your Saints. |1|Pause|

The one who goes laughing returns crying, and the one who goes crying returns laughing.

What is inhabited becomes deserted, and what is deserted becomes inhabited. |1|

The water turns into a desert, the desert turns into a well, and the well turns into a mountain.

From the earth, the mortal is exalted to the Akaashic ethers; and from the ethers on high, he is thrown down again. |2|

The beggar is transformed into a king, and the king into a beggar.

The idiotic fool is transformed into a Pandit, a religious scholar, and the Pandit into a fool. |3|

The woman is transformed into a man, and the men into women.

Says Kabeer, God is the Beloved of the Holy Saints. I am a sacrifice to His image. |4|2|

Saarang, The Word Of Naam Dayv Jee:

One Universal Creator God. By The Grace Of The True Guru:

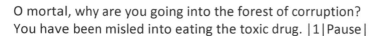

O mortal, why are you going into the forest of corruption?
You have been misled into eating the toxic drug. |1|Pause|

You are like a fish living in the water;
you do not see the net of death.
Trying to taste the flavor, you swallow the hook.
You are bound by attachment to wealth and woman. |1|

The bee stores up loads of honey;
then someone comes and takes the honey, and throws dust in its mouth.
The cow stores up loads of milk;
then the milkman comes and ties it by its neck and milks it. |2|

For the sake of Maya, the mortal works very hard.
He takes the wealth of Maya, and buries it in the ground.
He acquires so much, but the fool does not appreciate it.
His wealth remains buried in the ground, while his body turns to dust. |3|

He burns in tremendous sexual desire, unresolved anger and desire.
He never joins the Saadh Sangat, the Company of the Holy.
Says Naam Dayv, seek God's Shelter;
be fearless, and vibrate on the Lord God. |4|1|

Why not make a bet with me, O Lord of Wealth?
From the master comes the servant, and from the servant, comes the master. This is the game I play with You. |1|Pause|

You Yourself are the deity, and You are the temple of worship. You are the devoted worshipper.
From the water, the waves rise up, and from the waves, the water. They are only different by figures of speech. |1|

You Yourself sing, and You Yourself dance. You Yourself blow the bugle.
Says Naam Dayv, You are my Lord and Master. Your humble servant is imperfect; You are perfect. |2|2|

Says God: my slave is devoted only to me; he is in my very image.
The sight of him, even for an instant, cures the three fevers; his touch brings liberation from the deep dark pit of household affairs. |1|Pause|

The devotee can release anyone from my bondage, but I cannot release anyone from his.

Section 30 - Raag Saarang - Part 057

If, at any time, he grabs and binds me, even then, I cannot protest. |1|

I am bound by virtue; I am the Life of all. My slaves are my very life.
Says Naam Dayv, as is the quality of his soul, so is my love which illuminates him. |2|3|

Saarang:
One Universal Creator God. By The Grace Of The True Guru:
So what have you accomplished by listening to the Puraanas?
Faithful devotion has not welled up within you, and you have not been inspired to give to the hungry. |1|Pause|

You have not forgotten sexual desire, and you have not forgotten anger; greed has not left you either.
Your mouth has not stopped slandering and gossiping about others. Your service is useless and fruitless. |1|

By breaking into the houses of others and robbing them, you fill your belly, you sinner.
But when you go to the world beyond, your guilt will be well known, by the acts of ignorance which you committed. |2|

Cruelty has not left your mind; you have not cherished kindness for other living beings.
Parmaanand has joined the Saadh Sangat, the Company of the Holy. Why have you not followed the sacred teachings? |3|1|6|

O mind, do not even associate with those who have turned their backs on the Lord.
Saarang, Fifth Mehl, Sur Daas:
One Universal Creator God. By The Grace Of The True Guru:
The people of the Lord dwell with the Lord.
They dedicate their minds and bodies to Him; they dedicate everything to Him. They are intoxicated with the celestial melody of intuitive ecstasy. |1|Pause|

Gazing upon the Blessed Vision of the Lord's Darshan, they are cleansed of corruption. They obtain absolutely everything.
They have nothing to do with anything else; they gaze on the beauteous Face of God. |1|

But one who forsakes the elegantly beautiful Lord, and harbors desire for anything else, is like a leech on the body of a leper.
Says Sur Daas, God has taken my mind in His Hands. He has blessed me with the world beyond. |2|1|8|

Saarang, Kabeer Jee:
One Universal Creator God. By The Grace Of The True Guru:
Other than the Lord, who is the Help and Support of the mind?
Love and attachment to mother, father, sibling, child and spouse, is all just an illusion. |1|Pause|

So build a raft to the world hereafter; what faith do you place in wealth?
What confidence do you place in this fragile vessel; it breaks with the slightest stroke. |1|

You shall obtain the rewards of all righteousness and goodness, if you desire to be the dust of all.
Says Kabeer, listen, O Saints: this mind is like the bird, flying above the forest. |2|1|9|

RAAG MALAAR

Section 31 - Raag Malaar - Part 001

Raag Malaar, Chau-Padas, First Mehl, First House:
ONE Universal Creator God. Truth Is The Name. Creative Being Personified.
No Fear. No Hatred. Image Of The Undying. Beyond Birth. Self-Existent. By
Guru's Grace:
Eating, drinking, laughing and sleeping, the mortal forgets about dying.
Forgetting his Lord and Master, the mortal is ruined, and his life is cursed.
He cannot remain forever. |1|

O mortal, meditate on the One Lord.
You shall go to your true home with honor. |1 Pause|

Those who serve You - what can they give You? They beg for and receive
what cannot remain.
You are the Great Giver of all souls; You are the Life within all living beings.
|2|

The Gurmukhs meditate, and receive the Ambrosial Nectar; thus they
become pure.
Day and night, chant the Naam, the Name of the Lord, O mortal. It makes
the filthy immacuate. |3|

As is the season, so is the comfort of the body, and so is the body itself.
O Nanak, that season is beautiful; without the Name, what season is it?
|4|1|

Malaar, First Mehl:
I offer prayers to my Beloved Guru, that He may unite me with my Husband
Lord.
I hear the thunder in the clouds, and my mind is cooled and soothed;
imbued with the Love of my Dear Beloved, I sing His Glorious Praises. |1|

The rain pours down, and my mind is drenched with His Love.

The drop of Ambrosial Nectar pleases my heart; the Guru has fascinated my mind, which is drenched in the sublime essence of the Lord. |1|Pause|

With intuitive peace and poise, the soul-bride is loved by her Husband Lord; her mind is pleased and appeased by the Guru's Teachings.
She is the happy soul-bride of her Husband Lord; her mind and body are filled with joy by His Love. |2|

Discarding her demerits, she becomes detached; with the Lord as her Husband, her marriage is eternal.
She never suffers separation or sorrow; her Lord God showers her with His Grace. |3|

Her mind is steady and stable; she does not come and go in reincarnation.
She takes the Shelter of the Perfect Guru. O Nanak, as Gurmukh, chant the Naam; you shall be accepted as the true soul-bride of the Lord. |4|2|

Malaar, First Mehl:
They pretend to understand the Truth, but they are not satisfied by the Naam; they waste their lives in egotism.

Section 31 - Raag Malaar - Part 002

Caught in slander and attachment to the wealth and women of others, they eat poison and suffer in pain.
They think about the Shabad, but they are not released from their fear and fraud; the minds and mouths are filled with Maya, Maya.
Loading the heavy and crushing load, they die, only to be reborn, and waste their lives again. |1|

The Word of the Shabad is so very beautiful; it is pleasing to my mind.
The mortal wanders lost in reincarnation, wearing various robes and clothes; when he is saved and protected by the Guru, then he finds the Truth. |1|Pause|

He does not try to wash away his angry passions by bathing at sacred shrines. He does not love the Name of the Lord.
He abandons and discards the priceless jewel, and he goes back from where he came.
And so he becomes a maggot in manure, and in that, he is absorbed.

The more he tastes, the more he is diseased; without the Guru, there is no peace and poise. |2|

Focusing my awareness on selfless service, I joyfully sing His Praises. As Gurmukh, I contemplate spiritual wisdom.
The seeker comes forth, and the debater dies down; I am a sacrifice, a sacrifice to the Guru, the Creator Lord.
I am low and wretched, with shallow and false understanding; You embellish and exalt me through the Word of Your Shabad.
And wherever there is self-realization, You are there; O True Lord Savior, You save us and carry us across. |3|

Where should I sit to chant Your Praises; which of Your Infinite Praises should I chant?
The Unknown cannot be known; O Inaccessible, Unborn Lord God, You are the Lord and Master of masters.
How can I compare You to anyone else I see? All are beggars - You are the Great Giver.
Lacking devotion, Nanak looks to Your Door; please bless him with Your One Name, that he may enshrine it in his heart. |4|3|

Malaar, First Mehl:
The soul-bride who has not known delight with her Husband Lord, shall weep and wail with a wretched face.
She becomes hopeless, caught in the noose of her own karma; without the Guru, she wanders deluded by doubt. |1|

So rain down, O clouds. My Husband Lord has come home.
I am a sacrifice to my Guru, who has led me to meet my Lord God. |1|Pause|

My love, my Lord and Master is forever fresh; I am embellished with devotional worship night and day.
I am liberated, gazing on the Blessed Vision of the Guru's Darshan. Devotional worship has made me glorious and exalted throughout the ages. |2|

I am Yours; the three worlds are Yours as well. You are mine, and I am Yours.

Meeting with the True Guru, I have found the Immaculate Lord; I shall not be consigned to this terrifying world-ocean ever again. |3|

If the soul-bride is filled with delight on seeing her Husband Lord, then her decorations are true.
With the Immaculate Celestial Lord, she becomes the truest of the true.
Following the Guru's Teachings, she leans on the Support of the Naam. |4|

She is liberated; the Guru has untied her bonds. Focusing her awareness on the Shabad, she attains honor.
O Nanak, the Lord's Name is deep within her heart; as Gurmukh, she is united in His Union. |5|4|

First Mehl, Malaar:
Others' wives, others' wealth, greed, egotism, corruption and poison;
evil passions, slander of others, sexual desire and anger - give up all these. |1|

The Inaccessible, Infinite Lord is sitting in His Mansion.
That humble being, whose conduct is in harmony with the jewel of the Guru's Shabad, obtains the Ambrosial Nectar. |1|Pause|

Section 31 - Raag Malaar - Part 003

He sees pleasure and pain as both the same, along with good and bad in the world.
Wisdom, understanding and awareness are found in the Name of the Lord.
In the Sat Sangat, the True Congregation, embrace love for the Guru. |2|

Day and night, profit is obtained through the Lord's Name. The Guru, the Giver, has given this gift.
That Sikh who becomes Gurmukh obtains it. The Creator blesses him with His Glance of Grace. |3|

The body is a mansion, a temple, the home of the Lord; He has infused His Infinite Light into it.
O Nanak, the Gurmukh is invited to the Mansion of the Lord's Presence; the Lord unites him in His Union. |4|5|

Malaar, First Mehl, Second House:

One Universal Creator God. By The Grace Of The True Guru:
Know that the creation was formed through air and water;
have no doubt that the body was made through fire.
And if you know where the soul comes from,
you shall be known as a wise religious scholar. |1|

Who can know the Glorious Praises of the Lord of the Universe, O mother?
Without seeing Him, we cannot say anything about Him.
How can anyone speak and describe Him, O mother? |1|Pause|

He is high above the sky, and beneath the nether worlds.
How can I speak of Him? Let me understand.
Who knows what sort of Name is chanted, in the heart, without the tongue? |2|

Undoubtedly, words fail me.
He alone understands, who is blessed.
Day and night, deep within, he remains lovingly attuned to the Lord.
He is the true person, who is merged in the True Lord. |3|

If someone of high social standing becomes a selfless servant,
then his praises cannot even be expressed.
And if someone from a low social class becomes a selfless servant,
O Nanak, he shall wear shoes of honor. |4|1|6|

Malaar, First Mehl:
The pain of separation - this is the hungry pain I feel.
Another pain is the attack of the Messenger of Death.
Another pain is the disease consuming my body.
O foolish doctor, don't give me medicine. |1|

O foolish doctor, don't give me medicine.
The pain persists, and the body continues to suffer.
Your medicine has no effect on me. |1|Pause|

Forgetting his Lord and Master, the mortal enjoys sensual pleasures;
then, disease rises up in his body.
The blind mortal receives his punishment.
O foolish doctor, don't give me medicine. |2|

The value of sandalwood lies in its fragrance.
The value of the human lasts only as long as the breath in the body.
When the breath is taken away, the body crumbles into dust.
After that, no one takes any food. |3|

The mortal's body is golden, and the soul-swan is immaculate and pure,
if even a tiny particle of the Immaculate Naam is within.
All pain and disease are eradicated.
O Nanak, the mortal is saved through the True Name. |4|2|7|

Malaar, First Mehl:
Pain is the poison. The Lord's Name is the antidote.
Grind it up in the mortar of contentment, with the pestle of charitable giving.

Section 31 - Raag Malaar - Part 004

Take it each and every day, and your body shall not waste away.
At the very last instant, you shall strike down the Messenger of Death. |1|

So take such medicine, O fool,
by which your corruption shall be taken away. |1|Pause|

Power, wealth and youth are all just shadows,
as are the vehicles you see moving around.
Neither your body, nor your fame, nor your social status shall go along with you.
In the next world it is day, while here, it is all night. |2|

Let your taste for pleasures be the firewood, let your greed be the ghee,
and your sexual desire and anger the cooking oil; burn them in the fire.
Some make burnt offerings, hold sacred feasts, and read the Puraanas.
Whatever pleases God is acceptable. |3|

Intense meditation is the paper, and Your Name is the insignia.
Those for whom this treasure is ordered,
look wealthy when they reach their true home.
O Nanak, blessed is that mother who gave birth to them. |4|3|8|

Malaar, First Mehl:

You wear white clothes, and speak sweet words.
Your nose is sharp, and your eyes are black.
Have you ever seen your Lord and Master, O sister? |1|

O my All-powerful Lord and Master, by Your power, I fly and soar, and ascend to the heavens.
I see Him in the water, on the land, in the mountains, on the river-banks, in all places and interspaces, O brother. |2|

He fashioned the body, and gave it wings;
He gave it great thirst and desire to fly.
When He bestows His Glance of Grace, I am comforted and consoled.
As He makes me see, so do I see, O brother. |3|

Neither this body, nor its wings, shall go to the world hereafter.
It is a fusion of air, water and fire.
O Nanak, if it is in the mortal's karma, then he meditates on the Lord, with the Guru as his Spiritual Teacher.
This body is absorbed in the Truth. |4|4|9|

Malaar, Third Mehl, Chau-Padas, First House:
One Universal Creator God. By The Grace Of The True Guru:
The Formless Lord is formed by Himself. He Himself deludes in doubt.
Creating the Creation, the Creator Himself beholds it; He enjoins us as He pleases.
This is the true greatness of His servant, that he obeys the Hukam of the Lord's Command. |1|

Only He Himself knows His Will. By Guru's Grace, it is grasped.
When this play of Shiva and Shakti comes to his home, he remains dead while yet alive. |1|Pause|

They read the Vedas, and read them again, and engage in arguments about Brahma, Vishnu and Shiva.
This three-phased Maya has deluded the whole world into cynicism about death and birth.
By Guru's Grace, know the One Lord, and the anxiety of your mind will be allayed. |2|

I am meek, foolish and thoughtless, but still, You take care of me.

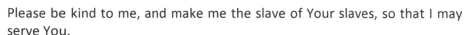

Please be kind to me, and make me the slave of Your slaves, so that I may serve You.
Please bless me with the treasure of the One Name, that I may chant it, day and night. |3|

Says Nanak, by Guru's Grace, understand. Hardly anyone considers this.
Like foam bubbling up on the surface of the water, so is this world.

Section 31 - Raag Malaar - Part 005

It shall eventually merge back into that from which it came, and all its expanse shall be gone. |4|1|

Malaar, Third Mehl:
Those who realize the Hukam of the Lord's Command are united with Him; through the Word of His Shabad, their egotism is burnt away.
They perform true devotional worship day and night; they remain lovingly attuned to the True Lord.
They gaze on their True Lord forever, through the Word of the Guru's Shabad, with loving ease. |1|

O mortal, accept His Will and find peace.
God is pleased by the Pleasure of His Own Will. Whomever He forgives, meets no obstacles on the way. |1|Pause|

Under the influence of the three gunas, the three dispositions, the mind wanders everywhere, without love or devotion to the Lord.
No one is ever saved or liberated, by doing deeds in ego.
Whatever our Lord and Master wills, comes to pass. People wander according to their past actions. |2|

Meeting with the True Guru, the mind is overpowered; the Lord's Name comes to abide in the mind.
The value of such a person cannot be estimated; nothing at all can be said about him.
He comes to dwell in the fourth state; he remains merged in the True Lord. |3|

My Lord God is Inaccessible and Unfathomable. His value cannot be expressed.

By Guru's Grace, he comes to understand, and live the Shabad.
O Nanak, praise the Naam, the Name of the Lord, Har, Har; you shall be honored in the Court of the Lord. |4|2|

Malaar, Third Mehl:
Rare is that person who, as Gurmukh, understands; the Lord has bestowed His Glance of Grace.
There is no Giver except the Guru. He grants His Grace and forgives.
Meeting the Guru, peace and tranquility well up; chant the Naam, the Name of the Lord, day and night. |1|

O my mind, meditate on the Ambrosial Name of the Lord.
Meeting with the True Guru and the Primal Being, the Name is obtained, and one remains forever absorbed in the Lord's Name. |1|Pause|

The self-willed manmukhs are forever separated from the Lord; no one is with them.
They are stricken with the great disease of egotism; they are hit on the head by the Messenger of Death.
Those who follow the Guru's Teachings are never separated from the Sat Sangat, the True Congregation. They dwell on the Naam, night and day. |2|

You are the One and Only Creator of all. You continually create, watch over and contemplate.
Some are Gurmukh - You unite them with Yourself. You bless then with the treasure of devotion.
You Yourself know everything. Unto whom should I complain? |3|

The Name of the Lord, Har, Har, is Ambrosial Nectar. By the Lord's Grace, it is obtained.
Chanting the Name of the Lord, Har, Har, night and day, the intuitive peace and poise of the Guru is obtained.
O Nanak, the Naam is the greatest treasure. Focus your consciousness on the Naam. |4|3|

Malaar, Third Mehl:
I praise the Guru, the Giver of peace, forever. He truly is the Lord God.
By Guru's Grace, I have obtained the supreme status. His glorious greatness is glorious!

One who sings the Glorious Praises of the True Lord, merges in the True Lord. |1|

O mortal, contemplate the Guru's Word in your heart.
Abandon your false family, poisonous egotism and desire; remember in your heart, that you will have to leave. |1|Pause|

The True Guru is the Giver of the Lord's Name. There is no other giver at all.

Section 31 - Raag Malaar - Part 006

Bestowing the gift of the soul, He satisfies the mortal beings, and merges them in the True Name.
Night and day, they ravish and enjoy the Lord within the heart; they are intuitively absorbed in Samaadhi. |2|

The Shabad, the Word of the True Guru, has pierced my mind. The True Word of His Bani permeates my heart.
My God is Unseen; He cannot be seen. The Gurmukh speaks the Unspoken.
When the Giver of peace grants His Grace, the mortal being meditates on the Lord, the Life of the Universe. |3|

He does not come and go in renicarnation any longer; the Gurmukh meditates intuitively.
From the mind, the mind merges into our Lord and Master; the mind is absorbed into the Mind.
In truth, the True Lord is pleased with truth; eradicate egotism from within yourself. |4|

Our One and Only Lord and Master dwells within the mind; there is no other at all.
The One Name is Sweet Ambrosial Nectar; it is Immaculate Truth in the world.
O Nanak, the Name of God is obtained, by those who are so predestined. |5|4|

Malaar, Third Mehl:
All the heavenly heralds and celestial singers are saved through the Naam, the Name of the Lord.

They contemplate the Word of the Guru's Shabad. Subduing their ego, the Name abides in their minds; they keep the Lord enshrined in their hearts.

He alone understands, whom the Lord causes to understand; the Lord unites him with Himself.

Night and day, he sings the Word of the Shabad and the Guru's Bani; he remains lovingly attuned to the True Lord. |1|

O my mind, each and every moment, dwell on the Naam.

The Shabad is the Guru's Gift. It shall bring you lasting peace deep within; it shall always stand by you. |1|Pause|

The self-willed manmukhs never give up their hypocrisy; in the love of duality, they suffer in pain.

Forgetting the Naam, their minds are imbued with corruption. They waste away their lives uselessly.

This opportunity shall not come into their hands again; night and day, they shall always regret and repent.

They die and die again and again, only to be reborn, but they never understand. They rot away in manure. |2|

The Gurmukhs are imbued with the Naam, and are saved; they contemplate the Word of the Guru's Shabad.

Meditating on the Name of the Lord, they are Jivan-mukta, liberated while yet alive. They enshrine the Lord within their hearts.

Their minds and bodies are immaculate, their intellect is immaculate and sublime. Their speech is sublime as well.

They realize the One Primal Being, the One Lord God. There is no other at all. |3|

God Himself is the Doer, and He Himself is the Cause of causes. He Himself bestows His Glance of Grace.

My mind and body are imbued with the Word of the Guru's Bani. My consciousness is immersed in His service.

The Unseen and Inscrutable Lord dwells deep within. He is seen only by the Gurmukh.

O Nanak, He gives to whomever He pleases. According to the Pleasure of His Will, He leads the mortals on. |4|5|

Malaar, Third Mehl, Du-Tukas:

Through the True Guru, the mortal obtains the special place, the Mansion of the Lord's Presence in his own home.
Through the Word of the Guru's Shabad, his egotistical pride is dispelled. |1|

Those who have the Naam inscribed on their foreheads,
meditate on the Naam night and day, forever and ever. They are honored in the True Court of the Lord. |1|Pause|

From the True Guru, they learn the ways and means of the mind. Night and day, they focus their meditation on the Lord forever.

Section 31 - Raag Malaar - Part 007

Imbued with the Word of the Guru's Shabad, they remain forever detached. They are honored in the True Court of the Lord. |2|

This mind plays, subject to the Lord's Will; in an instant, it wanders out in the ten directions and returns home again.
When the True Lord God Himself bestows His Glance of Grace, then this mind is instantly brought under control by the Gurmukh. |3|

The mortal comes to know the ways and means of the mind, realizing and contemplating the Shabad.
O Nanak, meditate forever on the Naam, and cross over the terrifying world-ocean. |4|6|

Malaar, Third Mehl:
Soul, body and breath of life are all His; He is permeating and pervading each and every heart.
Except the One Lord, I do not know any other at all. The True Guru has revealed this to me. |1|

O my mind, remain lovingly attuned to the Naam, the Name of the Lord.
Through the Word of the Guru's Shabad, I meditate on the Lord, the Unseen, Unfathomable and Infinite Creator. |1|Pause|

Mind and body are pleased, lovingly attuned to the One Lord, intuitively absorbed in peace and poise.

By Guru's Grace, doubt and fear are dispelled, being lovingly attuned to the One Name. |2|

When the mortal follows the Guru's Teachings, and lives the Truth, then he attains the state of emancipation.
Among millions, how rare is that one who understands, and is lovingly attuned to the Name of the Lord. |3|

Wherever I look, there I see the One. This understanding has come through the Guru's Teachings.
I place my mind, body and breath of life in offering before Him; O Nanak, self-conceit is gone. |4|7|

Malaar, Third Mehl:
My True Lord God, the Eradicator of suffering, is found through the Word of the Shabad.
Imbued with devotional worship, the mortal remains forever detached. He is honored in the True Court of the Lord. |1|

O mind, remain absorbed in the Mind.
The mind of the Gurmukh is pleased with the Lord's Name, lovingly attuned to the Lord. |1|Pause|

My God is totally Inaccessible and Unfathomable; through the Guru's Teachings, He is understood.
True self-discipline rests in singing the Kirtan of the Lord's Praises, lovingly attuned to the Lord. |2|

He Himself is the Shabad, and He Himself is the True Teachings; He merges our light into the Light.
The breath vibrates through this frail body; the Gurmukh obtains the ambrosial nectar. |3|

He Himself fashions, and He Himself links us to our tasks; the True Lord is pervading everywhere.
O Nanak, without the Naam, the Name of the Lord, no one is anything. Through the Naam, we are blessed with glory. |4|8|

Malaar, Third Mehl:

The mortal is enticed by the poison of corruption, burdened with such a heavy load.
The Lord has placed the magic spell of the Shabad into his mouth, and destroyed the poison of ego. |1|

O mortal, egotism and attachment are such heavy loads of pain.
This terrifying world-ocean cannot be crossed; through the Lord's Name, the Gurmukh crosses over to the other side. |1|Pause|

Attachment to the three-phased show of Maya pervades all the created forms.
In the Sat Sangat, the Society of the Saints, the state of supreme awareness is attained. The Merciful Lord carries us across. |2|

The smell of sandalwood is so sublime; its fragrance spreads out far and wide.

Section 31 - Raag Malaar - Part 008

The lifestyle of the Lord's humble servant is exalted and sublime. He spreads the Kirtan of the Lord's Praises throughout the world. |3|

O my Lord and Master, please be merciful, merciful to me, that I may enshrine the Lord, Har, Har, Har, within my heart.
Nanak has found the Perfect True Guru; in his mind, he chants the Name of the Lord. |4|9|

Malaar, Third Mehl, Second House:
One Universal Creator God. By The Grace Of The True Guru:
Is this mind a householder, or is this mind a detached renunciate?
Is this mind beyond social class, eternal and unchanging?
Is this mind fickle, or is this mind detached?
How has this mind been gripped by possessiveness? |1|

O Pandit, O religious scholar, reflect on this in your mind.
Why do you read so many other things, and carry such a heavy load? |1|Pause|

The Creator has attached it to Maya and possessiveness.
Enforcing His Order, He created the world.

By Guru's Grace, understand this, O Siblings of Destiny.
Remain forever in the Sanctuary of the Lord. |2|

He alone is a Pandit, who sheds the load of the three qualities.
Night and day, he chants the Name of the One Lord.
He accepts the Teachings of the True Guru.
He offers his head to the True Guru.
He remains forever unattached in the state of Nirvaanaa.
Such a Pandit is accepted in the Court of the Lord. |3|

He preaches that the One Lord is within all beings.
As he sees the One Lord, he knows the One Lord.
That person, whom the Lord forgives, is united with Him.
He finds eternal peace, here and hereafter. |4|

Says Nanak, what can anyone do?
He alone is liberated, whom the Lord blesses with His Grace.
Night and day, he sings the Glorious Praises of the Lord.
Then, he no longer bothers with the proclamations of the Shaastras or the Vedas. |5|1|10|

Malaar, Third Mehl:
The self-willed manmukhs wander lost in reincarnation, confused and deluded by doubt.
The Messenger of Death constantly beats them and disgraces them.
Serving the True Guru, the mortal's subservience to Death is ended.
He meets the Lord God, and enters the Mansion of His Presence. |1|

O mortal, as Gurmukh, meditate on the Naam, the Name of the Lord.
In duality, you are ruining and wasting this priceless human life. You trade it away in exchange for a shell. |1|Pause|

The Gurmukh falls in love with the Lord, by His Grace.
He enshrines loving devotion to the Lord, Har, Har, deep within his heart.
The Word of the Shabad carries him across the terrifying world-ocean.
He appears true in the True Court of the Lord. |2|

Performing all sorts of rituals, they do not find the True Guru.
Without the Guru, so many wander lost and confused in Maya.
Egotism, possessiveness and attachment rise up and increase within them.

In the love of duality, the self-willed manmukhs suffer in pain. |3|

The Creator Himself is Inaccessible and Infinite.
Chant the Word of the Guru's Shabad, and earn the true profit.
The Lord is Independent, Ever-present, here and now.

Section 31 - Raag Malaar - Part 009

O Nanak, the Gurmukh merges in the Naam. |4|2|11|

Malaar, Third Mehl:
Those who are attached to the Guru's Teachings, are Jivan-mukta, liberated while yet alive.
They remain forever awake and aware night and day, in devotional worship of the Lord.
They serve the True Guru, and eradicate their self-conceit.
I fall at the feet of such humble beings. |1|

Constantly singing the Glorious Praises of the Lord, I live.
The Word of the Guru's Shabad is such totally sweet elixir. Through the Name of the Lord, I have attained the state of liberation. |1|Pause|

Attachment to Maya leads to the darkness of ignorance.
The self-willed manukhs are attached, foolish and ignorant.
Night and day, their lives pass away in worldly entanglements.
They die and die again and again, only to be reborn and receive their punishment. |2|

The Gurmukh is lovingly attuned to the Name of the Lord.
He does not cling to false greed.
Whatever he does, he does with intuitive poise.
He drinks in the sublime essence of the Lord; his tongue delights in its flavor. |3|

Among millions, hardly any understand.
The Lord Himself forgives, and bestows His glorious greatness.
Whoever meets with the Primal Lord God, shall never be separated again.
Nanak is absorbed in the Name of the Lord, Har, Har. |4|3|12|

Malaar, Third Mehl:

Everyone speaks the Name of the Lord with the tongue.

But only by serving the True Guru does the mortal receive the Name.

His bonds are shattered, and he stays in the house of liberation.

Through the Word of the Guru's Shabad, he sits in the eternal, unchanging house. |1|

O my mind, why are you angry?

In this Dark Age of Kali Yuga, the Lord's Name is the source of profit.

Contemplate and appreciate the Guru's Teachings within your heart, night and day. |1|Pause|

Each and every instant, the rainbird cries and calls.

Without seeing her Beloved, she does not sleep at all.

She cannot endure this separation.

When she meets the True Guru, then she intuitively meets her Beloved. |2|

Lacking the Naam, the Name of the Lord, the mortal suffers and dies.

He is burnt in the fire of desire, and his hunger does not depart.

Without good destiny, he cannot find the Naam.

He performs all sorts of rituals until he is exhausted. |3|

The mortal thinks about the Vedic teachings of the three gunas, the three dispositions.

He deals in corruption, filth and vice.

He dies, only to be reborn; he is ruined over and over again.

The Gurmukh enshrines the glory of the supreme state of celestial peace. |4|

One who has faith in the Guru - everyone has faith in him.

Through the Guru's Word, the mind is cooled and soothed.

Throughout the four ages, that humble being is known to be pure.

O Nanak, that Gurmukh is so rare. |5|4|13|9|13|22|

Raag Malaar, Fourth Mehl, First House, Chau-Padas:

One Universal Creator God. By The Grace Of The True Guru:

Night and day, I meditate on the Lord, Har, Har, within my heart; through the Guru's Teachings, my pain is forgotten.

The chains of all my hopes and desires have been snapped; my Lord God has showered me with His Mercy. |1|

My eyes gaze eternally on the Lord, Har, Har.
Gazing on the True Guru, my mind blossoms forth. I have met with the Lord, the Lord of the World. |1|Pause|

Section 31 - Raag Malaar - Part 010

One who forgets such a Name of the Lord, Har, Har - his family is disho-nored.
His family is sterile and barren, and his mother is made a widow. |2|

O Lord, let me meet the Holy Guru, who night and day keep the Lord enshrined in his heart.
Seeing the Guru, the GurSikh blossoms forth, like the child seeing his mother. |3|

The soul-bride and the Husband Lord live together as one, but the hard wall of egotism has come between them.
The Perfect Guru demolishes the wall of egotism; servant Nanak has met the Lord, the Lord of the World. |4|1|

Malaar, Fourth Mehl:
The Ganges, the Jamunaa, the Godaavari and the Saraswati - these rivers strive for the dust of the feet of the Holy.
Overflowing with their filthy sins, the mortals take cleansing baths in them; the rivers' pollution is washed away by the dust of the feet of the Holy. |1|

Instead of bathing at the sixty-eight sacred shrines of pilgrimage, take your cleansing bath in the Name.
When the dust of the feet of the Sat Sangat rises up into the eyes, all filthy evil-mindedness is removed. |1|Pause|

Bhaageerat'h the penitent brought the Ganges down, and Shiva established Kaydaar.
Krishna grazed cows in Kaashi; through the humble servant of the Lord, these places became famous. |2|

And all the sacred shrines of pilgrimage established by the gods, long for the dust of the feet of the Holy.

Meeting with the Lord's Saint, the Holy Guru, I apply the dust of His feet to my face. |3|

And all the creatures of Your Universe, O my Lord and Master, long for the dust of the feet of the Holy.
O Nanak, one who has such destiny inscribed on his forehead, is blessed with the dust of the feet of the Holy; the Lord carries him across. |4|2|

Malaar, Fourth Mehl:
The Lord seems sweet to that humble being who is blessed by the Grace of the Lord.
His hunger and pain are totally taken away; he chants the Glorious Praises of the Lord, Har, Har. |1|

Meditating on the Lord, Har, Har, Har, the mortal is emancipated.
One who listens to the Guru's Teachings and meditates on them, is carried across the terrifying world-ocean. |1|Pause|

I am the slave of that humble being, who is blessed by the Grace of the Lord, Har, Har.
Meeting with the Lord's humble servant, peace is obtained; all the pollution and filth of evil-mindedness is washed away. |2|

The humble servant of the Lord feels hunger only for the Lord. He is satisfied only when he chants the Lord's Glories.
The humble servant of the Lord is a fish in the Water of the Lord. Forgetting the Lord, he would dry up and die. |3|

He alone knows this love, who enshrines it within his mind.
Servant Nanak gazes upon the Lord and is at peace; The hunger of his body is totally satisfied. |4|3|

Malaar, Fourth Mehl:
All the beings and creatures which God has created - on their foreheds, He has written their destiny.
The Lord blesses His humble servant with glorious greatness. The Lord enjoins him to his tasks. |1|

The True Guru implants the Naam, the Name of the Lord, Har, Har, within.

Section 31 - Raag Malaar - Part 011

Chant the Name of the Lord, O Sikhs of the Guru, O my Siblings of Destiny. Only the Lord will carry you across the terrifying world-ocean. |1|Pause|

That humble being who worships, adores and serves the Guru is pleasing to my Lord God.
To worship and adore the True Guru is to serve the Lord. In His Mercy, He saves us and carries us across. |2|

The ignorant and the blind wander deluded by doubt; deluded and confused, they pick flowers to offer to their idols.
They worship lifeless stones and serve the tombs of the dead; all their efforts are useless. |3|

He alone is said to be the True Guru, who realizes God, and proclaims the Sermon of the Lord, Har, Har.
Offer the Guru sacred foods, clothes, silk and satin robes of all sorts; know that He is True. The merits of this shall never leave you lacking. |4|

The Divine True Guru is the Embodiment, the Image of the Lord; He utters the Ambrosial Word.
O Nanak, blessed and good is the destiny of that humble being, who focuses his consciousness on the Feet of the Lord. |5|4|

Malaar, Fourth Mehl:
Those whose hearts are filled with my True Guru - those Saints are good and noble in every way.
Seeing them, my mind blossoms forth in bliss; I am forever a sacrifice to them. |1|

O spiritual teacher, chant the Name of the Lord, day and night.
All hunger and thirst are satisfied, for those who partake of the sublime essence of the Lord, through the Guru's Teachings. |1|Pause|

The slaves of the Lord are our Holy companions. Meeting with them, doubt is taken away.
As the swan separates the milk from the water, the Holy Saint removes the fire of egotism from the body. |2|

Those who do not love the Lord in their hearts are deceitful; they continually practice deception.

What can anyone give them to eat? Whatever they themselves plant, they must eat. |3|

This is the Quality of the Lord, and of the Lord's humble servants as well; the Lord places His Own Essence within them.

Blessed, blessed, is Guru Nanak, who looks impartially on all; He crosses over and transcends both slander and praise. |4|5|

Malaar, Fourth Mehl:

The Name of the Lord is inaccessible, unfathomable, exalted and sublime. It is chanted by the Lord's Grace.

By great good fortune, I have found the True Congregation, and in the Company of the Holy, I am carried across. |1|

My mind is in ecstasy, night and day.

By Guru's Grace, I chant the Name of the Lord. Doubt and fear are gone from my mind. |1|Pause|

Those who chant and meditate on the Lord - O Lord, in Your Mercy, please unite me with them.

Gazing upon them, I am at peace; the pain and disease of egotism are gone. |2|

Those who meditate on the Naam, the Name of the Lord in their hearts - their lives become totally fruitful.

They themselves swim across, and carry the world across with them. Their ancestors and family cross over as well. |3|

You Yourself created the whole world, and You Yourself keep it under Your control.

Section 31 - Raag Malaar - Part 012

God has showered His Mercy on servant Nanak; He has lifted him up, and rescued him from the ocean of poison. |4|6|

Malaar, Fourth Mehl:

Those who do not drink in the Ambrosial Nectar by Guru's Grace - their thirst and hunger are not relieved.

The foolish self-willed manmukh burns in the fire of egotistical pride; he suffers painfully in egotism.

Coming and going, he wastes his life uselessly; afflicted with pain, he regrets and repents.

He does not even think of the One, from whom he originated. Cursed is his life, and cursed is his food. |1|

O mortal, as Gurmukh, meditate on the Naam, the Name of the Lord.

The Lord, Har, Har, in His Mercy leads the mortal to meet the Guru; he is absorbed in the Name of the Lord, Har, Har. |1|Pause|

The life of the self-willed manmukh is useless; he comes and goes in shame. In sexual desire and anger, the proud ones are drowned. They are burnt in their egotism.

They do not attain perfection or understanding; their intellect is dimmed. Tossed by the waves of greed, they suffer in pain.

Without the Guru, they suffer in terrible pain. Seized by Death, they weep and wail. |2|

As Gurmukh, I have attained the Unfathomable Name of the Lord, with intuitive peace and poise.

The treasure of the Naam abides deep within my heart. My tongue sings the Glorious Praises of the Lord.

I am forever in bliss, day and night, lovingly attuned to the One Word of the Shabad.

I have obtained the treasure of the Naam with intuitive ease; this is the glorious greatness of the True Guru. |3|

Through the True Guru, the Lord, Har, Har, comes to dwell within my mind. I am forever a sacrifice to the True Guru.

I have dedicated my mind and body to Him, and placed everything before Him in offering. I focus my consciousness on His Feet.

Please be merciful to me, O my Perfect Guru, and unite me with Yourself.

I am just iron; the Guru is the boat, to carry me across. |4|7|

Malaar, Fourth Mehl, Partaal, Third House:
One Universal Creator God. By The Grace Of The True Guru:

The humble servant of the Lord chants the Name of the Supreme Lord; he joins the Saadh Sangat, the Company of the Lord's Holy. |1|Pause|

Deal only in the wealth of the Lord, and gather only the wealth of the Lord. No thief can ever steal it. |1|

The rainbirds and the peacocks sing day and night, hearing the thunder in the clouds. |2|

Whatever the deer, the fish and the birds sing, they chant to the Lord, and no other. |3|

Servant Nanak sings the Kirtan of the Lord's Praises; the sound and fury of Death has totally gone away. |4|1|8|

Malaar, Fourth Mehl:
They speak and chant the Name of the Lord, Raam, Raam; the very fortunate ones seek Him.
Whoever shows me the Way of the Lord - I fall at his feet. |1|Pause|

The Lord is my Friend and Compansion; I am in love with the Lord.

Section 31 - Raag Malaar - Part 013

I sing of the Lord, and I speak of the Lord; I have discarded all other loves. |1|

My Beloved is the Enticer of the mind; The Detached Lord God is the Embodiment of Supreme bliss.
Nanak lives by gazing upon the Lord; may I see Him for a moment, for even just an instant. |2|2|9|9|13|9|31|

Raag Malaar, Fifth Mehl, Chau-Padas, First House:
One Universal Creator God. By The Grace Of The True Guru:
What are you so worried about? What are you thinking? What have you tried?
Tell me - the Lord of the Universe - who controls Him? |1|

The rain showers down from the clouds, O companion. The Guest has come into my home.

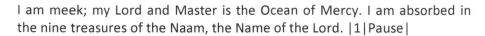

I am meek; my Lord and Master is the Ocean of Mercy. I am absorbed in the nine treasures of the Naam, the Name of the Lord. |1|Pause|

I have prepared all sorts of foods in various ways, and all sorts of sweet deserts.
I have made my kitchen pure and sacred. Now, O my Sovereign Lord King, please sample my food. |2|

The villains have been destroyed, and my friends are delighted. This is Your Own Mansion and Temple, O Lord.
When my Playful Beloved came into my household, then I found total peace. |3|

In the Society of the Saints, I have the Support and Protection of the Perfect Guru; this is the pre-ordained destiny inscribed upon my forehead.
Servant Nanak has found his Playful Husband Lord. He shall never suffer in sorrow again. |4|1|

Malaar, Fifth Mehl:
When the baby's only food is milk, it cannot survive without its milk.
The mother takes care of it, and pours milk into its mouth; then, it is satisfied and fulfilled. |1|

I am just a baby; God, the Great Giver, is my Father.
The child is so foolish; it makes so many mistakes. But it has nowhere else to go. |1|Pause|

The mind of the poor child is fickle; he touches even snakes and fire.
His mother and father hug him close in their embrace, and so he plays in joy and bliss. |2|

What hunger can the child ever have, O my Lord and Master, when You are his Father?
The treasure of the Naam and the nine treasures are in Your celestial household. You fulfill the desires of the mind. |3|

My Merciful Father has issued this Command: whatever the child asks for, is put into his mouth.
Nanak, the child, longs for the Blessed Vision of God's Darshan. May His Feet always dwell within my heart. |4|2|

Malaar, Fifth Mehl:
I tried everything, and gathered all devices together; I have discarded all my anxieties.
I have begun to set all my household affairs right; I have placed my faith in my Lord and Master. |1|

I listen to the celestial vibrations resonating and resounding.
Sunrise has come, and I gaze upon the Face of my Beloved. My household is filled with peace and pleasure. |1|Pause|

I focus my mind, and embellish and adorn the place within; then I go out to speak with the Saints.
Seeking and searching, I have found my Husband Lord; I bow at His Feet and worship Him with devotion. |2|

Section 31 - Raag Malaar - Part 014

When my Beloved came to live in my house, I began to sing the songs of bliss.
My friends and companions are happy; God leads me to meet the Perfect Guru. |3|

My friends and companions are in ecstasy; the Guru has completed all my projects.
Says Nanak, I have met my Husband, the Giver of peace; He shall never leave me and go away. |4|3|

Malaar, Fifth Mehl:
From a king to a worm, and from a worm to the lord of gods, they engage in evil to fill their bellies.
They renounce the Lord, the Ocean of Mercy, and worship some other; they are thieves and killers of the soul. |1|

Forgetting the Lord, they suffer in sorrow and die.
They wander lost in reincarnation through all sorts of species; they do not find shelter anywhere. |1|Pause|

Those who abandon their Lord and Master and think of some other, are foolish, stupid, idiotic donkeys.

How can they cross over the ocean in a paper boat? Their eogtistical boasts that they will cross over are meaningless. |2|

Shiva, Brahma, angels and demons, all burn in the fire of death.
Nanak seeks the Sanctuary of the Lord's Lotus Feet; O God, Creator, please do not send me into exile. |3|4|

Raag Malaar, Fifth Mehl, Du-Padas, First House:
One Universal Creator God. By The Grace Of The True Guru:
My God is detached and free of desire.
I cannot survive without Him, even for an instant. I am so in love with Him. |1|Pause|

Associating with the Saints, God has come into my consciousness. By their Grace, I have been awakened.
Hearing the Teachings, my mind has become immaculate. Imbued with the Lord's Love, I sing His Glorious Praises. |1|

Dedicating this mind, I have made friends with the Saints. They have become merciful to me; I am very fortunate.
I have found absolute peace - I cannot describe it. Nanak has obtained the dust of the feet of the humble. |2|1|5|

Malaar, Fifth Mehl:
O mother, please lead me to union with my Beloved.
All my friends and companions sleep totally in peace; their Beloved Lord has come into the homes of their hearts. |1|Pause|

I am worthless; God is forever Merciful. I am unworthy; what clever tricks could I try?
I claim to be on a par with those who are imbued with the Love of their Beloved. This is my stubborn egotism. |1|

I am dishonored - I seek the Sanctuary of the One, the Guru, the True Guru, the Primal Being, the Giver of peace.
In an instant, all my pains have been taken away; Nanak passes the night of his life in peace. |2|2|6|

Malaar, Fifth Mehl:
Rain down, O cloud; do not delay.

O beloved cloud, O support of the mind, you bring lasting bliss and joy to the mind. |1|Pause|

I take to Your Support, O my Lord and Master; how could You forget me?

Section 31 - Raag Malaar - Part 015

I am Your beautiful bride, Your servant and slave. I have no nobility without my Husband Lord. |1|

When my Lord and Master listened to my prayer, He hurried to shower me with His Mercy.
Says Nanak, I have become just like my Husband Lord; I am blessed with honor, nobility and the lifestyle of goodness. |2|3|7|

Malaar, Fifth Mehl:
Meditate on the True Name of your Beloved.
The pains and sorrows of the terrifying world-ocean are dispelled, by enshrining the Image of the Guru within your heart. |1|Pause|

Your enemies shall be destroyed, and all the evil-doers shall perish, when you come to the Sanctuary of the Lord.
The Savior Lord has given me His Hand and saved me; I have obtained the wealth of the Naam. |1|

Granting His Grace, He has eradicated all my sins; He has placed the Immaculate Naam within my mind.
O Nanak, the Treasure of Virtue fills my mind; I shall never again suffer in pain. |2|4|8|

Malaar, Fifth Mehl:
My Beloved God is the Lover of my breath of life.
Please bless me with the loving devotional worship of the Naam, O Kind and Compassionate Lord. |1|Pause|

I meditate in remembrance on Your Feet, O my Beloved; my heart is filled with hope.
I offer my prayer to the humble Saints; my mind thirsts for the Blssed Vision of the Lord's Darshan. |1|

Separation is death, and Union with the Lord is life. Please bless Your humble servant with Your Darshan.

O my God, please be Merciful, and bless Nanak with the support, the life and wealth of the Naam. |2|5|9|

Malaar, Fifth Mehl:
Now, I have become just like my Beloved.
Dwelling on my Sovereign Lord King, I have found peace. Rain down, O peace-giving cloud. |1|Pause|

I cannot forget Him, even for an instant; He is the Ocean of peace. Through the Naam, the Name of the Lord, I have obtained the nine treasures.
My perfect destiny has been activated, meeting with the Saints, my help and support. |1|

Peace has welled up, and all pain has been dispelled, lovingly attuned to the Supreme Lord God.
The arduous and terrifying world-ocean is crossed over, O Nanak, by meditating on the Feet of the Lord. |2|6|10|

Malaar, Fifth Mehl:
The clouds have rained down all over the world.
My Beloved Lord God has become merciful to me; I am blessed with ecstasy, bliss and peace. |1|Pause|

My sorrows are erased, and all my thirsts are quenched, meditating on the Supreme Lord God.
In the Saadh Sangat, the Company of the Holy, death and birth come to an end, and the mortal does not wander anywhere, ever again. |1|

My mind and body are imbued with the Immaculate Naam, the Name of the Lord; I am lovingly attuned to His Lotus Feet.
God has made Nanak His Own; slave Nanak seeks His Sanctuary. |2|7|11|

Malaar, Fifth Mehl:
Separated from the Lord, how can any living being live?
My consciousness is filled with yearning and hope to meet my Lord, and drink in the sublime essence of His Lotus Feet. |1|Pause|

Those who are thirsty for You, O my Beloved, are not separated from You.

Those who forget my Beloved Lord are dead and dying. |1|

Section 31 - Raag Malaar - Part 016

The Lord of the Universe is permeating and pervading my mind and body; I see Him Ever-present, here and now

. O Nanak, He is permeating the inner being of all; He is all-pervading everywhere. |2|8|12|

Malaar, Fifth Mehl:
Vibrating and meditating on the Lord, who has not been carried across?
Those reborn into the body of a bird, the body of a fish, the body of a deer, and the body of a bull - in the Saadh Sangat, the Company of the Holy, they are saved. |1|Pause|

The families of gods, the families of demons, titans, celestial singers and human beings are carried across the ocean.
Whoever meditates and vibrates on the Lord in the Saadh Sangat - his pains are taken away. |1|

Sexual desire, anger and the pleasures of terrible corruption - he keeps away from these.
He meditates on the Lord, Merciful to the meek, the Embodiment of Compassion; Nanak is forever a sacrifice to Him. |2|9|13|

Malaar, Fifth Mehl:
Today, I am seated in the Lord's store.
With the wealth of the Lord, I have entered into partnership with the humble; I shall not have take the Highway of Death. |1|Pause|

Showering me with His Kindness, the Supreme Lord God has saved me; the doors of doubt have been opened wide.
I have found God, the Banker of Infinity; I have earned the profit of the wealth of His Feet. |1|

I have grasped the protection of the Sanctuary of the Unchanging, Unmoving, Imperishable Lord; He has picked up my sins and thrown them out.

Slave Nanak's sorrow and suffering has ended. He shall never again be squeezed into the mold of reincarnation. |2|10|14|

Malaar, Fifth Mehl:
In so many ways, attachment to Maya leads to ruin.
Among millions, it is very rare to find a selfless servant who remains a perfect devotee for very long. |1|Pause|

Roaming and wandering here and there, the mortal finds only trouble; his body and wealth become strangers to himself.
Hiding from people, he practices deception; he does not know the One who is always with him. |1|

He wanders through troubled incarnations of low and wretched species as a deer, a bird and a fish.
Says Nanak, O God, I am a stone - please carry me across, that I may enjoy peace in the Saadh Sangat, the Company of the Holy. |2|11|15|

Malaar, Fifth Mehl:
The cruel and evil ones died after taking poison, O mother.
And the One, to whom all creatures belong, has saved us. God has granted His Grace. |1|Pause|

The Inner-knower, the Searcher of hearts, is contained within all; why should I be afraid, O Siblings of Destiny?
God, my Help and Support, is always with me. He shall never leave; I see Him everywhere. |1|

He is the Master of the masterless, the Destroyer of the pains of the poor; He has attached me to the hem of His robe.
O Lord, Your slaves live by Your Support; Nanak has come to the Sanctuary of God. |2|12|16|

Malaar, Fifth Mehl:
O my mind, dwell on the Feet of the Lord.
My mind is enticed by thirst for the Blessed Vision of the Lord; I would take wings and fly out to meet Him. |1|Pause|

Searching and seeking, I have found the Path, and now I serve the Holy.

O my Lord and Master, please be kind to me, that I may drink in Your most sublime essence. |1|

Begging and pleading, I have come to Your Sanctuary; I am on fire - please shower me with Your Mercy!
Please give me Your Hand - I am Your slave, O Lord. Please make Nanak Your Own. |2|13|17|

Section 31 - Raag Malaar - Part 017

Malaar, Fifth Mehl:
It is God's Nature to love His devotees.
He destroys the slanderers, crushing them beneath His Feet. His Glory is manifest everywhere. |1|Pause|

His Victory is celebrated all throughout the world. He blesses all creatures with compassion.
Hugging him close in His Embrace, the Lord saves and protects His slave. The hot winds cannot even touch him. |1|

My Lord and Master has made me His Own; dispelling my doubts and fears, He has made me happy.
The Lord's slaves enjoy ultimate ecstasy; O Nanak, faith has welled up in my mind. |2|14|18|

Raag Malaar, Fifth Mehl, Chau-Padas, Second House:
One Universal Creator God. By The Grace Of The True Guru:
The Gurmukh sees God pervading everywhere.
The Gurmukh knows that the universe is the extension of the three gunas, the three dispositions.
The Gurmukh reflects on the Sound-current of the Naad, and the wisdom of the Vedas.
Without the Perfect Guru, there is only pitch-black darkness. |1|

O my mind, calling on the Guru, eternal peace is found.
Following the Guru's Teachings, the Lord comes to dwell within the heart; I meditate on my Lord and Master with every breath and morsel of food. |1|Pause|

I am a sacrifice to the Guru's Feet.

Night and day, I continually sing the Glorious Praises of the Guru.
I take my cleansing bath in the dust of the Guru's Feet.
I am honored in the True Court of the Lord. |2|

The Guru is the boat, to carry me across the terrifying world-ocean.
Meeting with the Guru, I shall not be reincarnated ever again.
That humble being serves the Guru,
who has such karma inscribed on his forehead by the Primal Lord. |3|

The Guru is my life; the Guru is my support.
The Guru is my way of life; the Guru is my family.
The Guru is my Lord and Master; I seek the Sanctuary of the True Guru.
O Nanak, the Guru is the Supreme Lord God; His value cannot be estimated. |4|1|19|

Malaar, Fifth Mehl:
I enshrine the Lord's Feet within my heart;
in His Mercy, God has united me with Himself.
God enjoins His servant to his tasks.
His worth cannot be expressed. |1|

Please be merciful to me, O Perfect Giver of peace.
By Your Grace, You come to mind; I am imbued with Your Love, twenty-four hours a day. |1|Pause|

Singing and listening, it is all by Your Will.
One who understands the Hukam of Your Command is absorbed in Truth.
Chanting and meditating on Your Name, I live.
Without You, there is no place at all. |2|

Pain and pleasure come by Your Command, O Creator Lord.
By the Pleasure of Your Will You forgive, and by the Pleasure of Your Will You award punishment.
You are the Creator of both realms.
I am a sacrifice to Your Glorious Grandeur. |3|

You alone know Your value.
You alone understand, You Yourself speak and listen.
They alone are devotees, who are pleasing to Your Will.

Section 31 - Raag Malaar - Part 018

Nanak is forever a sacrifice to them. |4|2|20|

Malaar, Fifth Mehl:
The Transcendent Lord God has become merciful;
Ambrosial Nectar is raining down from the clouds.
All beings and creatures are satisfied;
their affairs are perfectly resolved. |1|

O my mind, dwell on the Lord, forever and ever.
Serving the Perfect Guru, I have obtained it. It shall stay with me both here and hereafter. |1|Pause|

He is the Destroyer of pain, the Eradicator of fear.
He takes care of His beings.
The Savior Lord is kind and compassionate forever.
I am a sacrifice to Him, forever and ever. |2|

The Creator Himself has eliminated death.
Meditate on Him forever and ever, O my mind.
He watches all with His Glance of Grace and protects them.
Continually and continuously, sing the Glorious Praises of the Lord God. |3|

The One and Only Creator Lord is Himself by Himself.
The Lord's devotees know His Glorious Grandeur.
He preserves the Honor of His Name.
Nanak speaks as the Lord inspires him to speak. |4|3|21|

Malaar, Fifth Mehl:
All treasures are found in the Sanctuary of the Guru.
Honor is obtained in the True Court of the Lord.
Doubt, fear, pain and suffering are taken away,
forever singing the Glorious Praises of the Lord in the Saadh Sangat, the Company of the Holy. |1|

O my mind, praise the Perfect Guru.
Chant the treasure of the Naam, the Name of the Lord, day and night. You shall obtain the fruits of your mind's desires. |1|Pause|

No one else is as great as the True Guru.
The Guru is the Supreme Lord, the Transcendent Lord God.
He saves us from the pains of death and birth,
and we will not have to taste the poison of Maya ever again. |2|

The Guru's glorious grandeur cannot be described.
The Guru is the Transcendent Lord, in the True Name.
True is His self-discipline, and True are all His actions.
Immaculate and pure is that mind, which is imbued with love for the Guru.
|3|

The Perfect Guru is obtained by great good fortune.
Drive out sexual desire, anger and greed from your mind.
By His Grace, the Guru's Feet are enshrined within.
Nanak offers his prayer to the True Lord God. |4|4|22|

Raag Malaar, Fifth Mehl, Partaal, Third House:
One Universal Creator God. By The Grace Of The True Guru:
Pleasing the Guru, I have fallen in love with my Merciful Beloved Lord.
I have made all my decorations,
and renounced all corruption;
my wandering mind has become steady and stable. |1|Pause|

O my mind, lose your self-conceit by associating with the Holy, and you
shall find Him.
The unstruck celestial melody vibrates and resounds; like a song-bird, chant
the Lord's Name, with words of sweetness and utter beauty. |1|

Such is the glory of Your Darshan, so utterly inifinte and fruitful, O my Love;
so do we become by associating with the Saints.
Vibrating, chanting Your Name, we cross over the terrifying world-ocean.
They dwell on the Lord, Raam, Raam, chanting on their malas;

Section 31 - Raag Malaar - Part 019

their minds are turned towards the Lord in the Saadh Sangat, the Company
of the Holy.
O servant Nanak, their Beloved Lord seems so sweet to them. |2|1|23|

Malaar, Fifth Mehl:

My mind wanders through the dense forest.
It walks with eagerness and love,
hoping to meet God. |1|Pause|

Maya with her three gunas - the three dispositions - has come to entice
me; whom can I tell of my pain? |1|

I tried everything else, but nothing could rid me of my sorrow.
So hurry to the Sanctuary of the Holy, O Nanak; joining them, sing the
Glorious Praises of the Lord of the Universe. |2|2|24|

Malaar, Fifth Mehl:
The glory of my Beloved is noble and sublime.
The celestial singers and angels sing His Sublime Praises in ecstasy,
happiness and joy. |1|Pause|

The most worthy beings sing God's Praises in beautiful harmonies, in all
sorts of ways, in myriads of sublime forms. |1|

Throughout the mountains, trees, deserts, oceans and galaxies, permeating
each and every heart, the sublime grandeur of my Love is totally pervading.
In the Saadh Sangat, the Company of the Holy, the Love of the Lord is
found; O Nanak, sublime is that faith. |2|3|25|

Malaar, Fifth Mehl:
With love for the Guru, I enshrine the Lotus Feet of my Lord deep within
my heart. |1|Pause|

I gaze on the Blessed Vision of His Fruitful Darshan; my sins are erased and
taken away.
My mind is immaculate and enlightened. |1|

I am wonderstruck, stunned and amazed.
Chanting the Naam, the Name of the Lord, millions of sins are destroyed.
I fall at His Feet, and touch my forehead to them.
You alone are, You alone are, O God.
Your devotees take Your Support.
Servant Nanak has come to the Door of Your Sanctuary. |2|4|26|

Malaar, Fifth Mehl:

Rain down with happiness in God's Will.
Bless me with total bliss and good fortune. |1|Pause|

My mind blossoms forth in the Society of the Saints; soaking up the rain, the earth is blessed and beautified. |1|

The peacock loves the thunder of the rain clouds.
The rainbird's mind is drawn to the rain-drop
- so is my mind enticed by the Lord.
I have renounced Maya, the deceiver.
Joining with the Saints, Nanak is awakened. |2|5|27|

Malaar, Fifth Mehl:
Sing forever the Glorious Praises of the Lord of the World.
Enshrine the Lord's Name in your consciousness. |1|Pause|

Forsake your pride, and abandon your ego; join the Saadh Sangat, the Company of the Holy.
Meditate in loving remembrance on the One Lord; your sorrows shall be ended, O friend. |1|

The Supreme Lord God has become merciful;
corrupt entanglements have come to an end.
Grasping the feet of the Holy,
Nanak sings forever the Glorious Praises of the Lord of the World. |2|6|28|

Malaar, Fifth Mehl:
The Embodiment of the Lord of the Universe roars like the thunder-cloud.
Singing His Glorious Praises brings peace and bliss. |1|Pause|

The Sanctuary of the Lord's Feet carries us across the world-ocean. His Sublime Word is the unstruck celestial melody. |1|

The thirsty traveller's consciousness obtains the water of the soul from the pool of nectar.
Servant Nanak loves the Blessed Vision of the Lord; in His Mercy, God has blessed him with it. |2|7|29|

Section 31 - Raag Malaar - Part 020

Malaar, Fifth Mehl:
O Lord of the Universe, O Lord of the World, O Dear Merciful Beloved. |1|Pause|

You are the Master of the breath of life, the Companion of the lost and forsaken, the Destroyer of the pains of the poor. |1|

O All-powerful, Inaccessible, Perfect Lord, please shower me with Your Mercy. |2|

Please, carry Nanak across the terrible, deep dark pit of the world to the other side. |3|8|30|

Malaar, First Mehl, Ashtapadees, First House:
One Universal Creator God. By The Grace Of The True Guru:
The chakvi bird does not long for sleepy eyes; without her beloved, she does not sleep.
When the sun rises, she sees her beloved with her eyes; she bows and touches his feet. |1|

The Love of my Beloved is pleasing; it is my Companion and Support.
Without Him, I cannot live in this world even for an instant; such is my hunger and thirst. |1|Pause|

The lotus in the pool blossoms forth intuitively and naturally, with the rays of the sun in the sky.
Such is the love for my Beloved which imbues me; my light has merged into the Light. |2|

Without water, the rainbird cries out, "Pri-o! Pri-o! - Beloved! Beloved!" It cries and wails and laments.
The thundering clouds rain down in the ten directions; its thirst is not quenched until it catches the rain-drop in its mouth. |3|

The fish lives in water, from which it was born. It finds peace and pleasure according to its past actions.
It cannot survive without water for a moment, even for an instant. Life and death depend on it. |4|

The soul-bride is separated from her Husband Lord, who lives in His Own Country. He sends the Shabad, His Word, through the True Guru.
She gathers virtues, and enshrines God within her heart. Imbued with devotion, she is happy. |5|

Everyone cries out, "Beloved! Beloved!" But she alone finds her Beloved, who is pleasing to the Guru.
Our Beloved is always with us; through the Truth, He blesses us with His Grace, and unites us in His Union. |6|

He is the life of the soul in each and every soul; He permeates and pervades each and every heart.
By Guru's Grace, He is revealed within the home of my heart; I am intuitively, naturally, absorbed into Him. |7|

He Himself shall resolve all your affairs, when you meet with the Giver of peace, the Lord of the World.
By Guru's Grace, you shall find your Husband Lord within your own home; then, O Nanak, the fire within you shall be quenched. |8|1|

Malaar, First Mehl:
Remain awake and aware, serving the Guru; except for the Lord, no one is mine.
Even by making all sorts of efforts, you shall not remain here; it shall melt like glass in the fire. |1|

Tell me - why are you so proud of your body and wealth?
They shall vanish in an instant; O madman, this is how the world is wasting away, in egotism and pride. |1|Pause|

Hail to the Lord of the Universe, God, our Saving Grace; He judges and saves the mortal beings.
All that is, belongs to You. No one else is equal to You. |2|

Creating all beings and creatures, their ways and means are under Your control; You bless the Gurmukhs with the ointment of spiritual wisdom.
My Eternal, Unmastered Lord is over the heads of all. He is the Destroyer of death and rebirth, doubt and fear. |3|

Section 31 - Raag Malaar - Part 021

This wretched world is a fortress of paper, of color and form and clever tricks.
A tiny drop of water or a little puff of wind destroys its glory; in an instant, its life is ended. |4|

It is like a tree-house near the bank of a river, with a serpent's den in that house.
When the river overflows, what happens to the tree house? The snake bites, like duality in the mind. |5|

Through the magic spell of the Guru's spiritual wisdom, and meditation on the Word of the Guru's Teachings, vice and corruption are burnt away.
The mind and body are cooled and soothed and Truth is obtained, through the wondrous and unique devotional worship of the Lord. |6|

All that exists begs of You; You are merciful to all beings.
I seek Your Sanctuary; please save my honor, O Lord of the World, and bless me with Truth. |7|

Bound in worldly affairs and entanglements, the blind one does not understand; he acts like a murderous butcher.
But if he meets with the True Guru, then he comprehends and understands, and his mind is imbued with true spiritual wisdom. |8|

Without the Truth, this worthless body is false; I have consulted my Guru on this.
O Nanak, that God has revealed God to me; without the Truth, all the world is just a dream. |9|2|

Malaar, First Mehl:
The rainbird and the fish find peace in water; the deer is pleased by the sound of the bell. |1|

The rainbird chirps in the night, O my mother. |1|Pause|

O my Beloved, my love for You shall never end, if it is Your Will. |2|

Sleep is gone, and egotism is exhausted from my body; my heart is permeated with the Teachings of Truth. |3|

Flying among the trees and plants, I remain hungry; lovingly drinking in the Naam, the Name of the Lord, I am satisfied. |4|

I stare at You, and my tongue cries out to You; I am so thirsty for the Blessed Vision of Your Darshan. |5|

Without my Beloved, the more I decorate myself, the more my body burns; these clothes do not look good on my body. |6|

Without my Beloved, I cannot survive even for an instant; without meeting Him, I cannot sleep. |7|

Her Husband Lord is nearby, but the wretched bride does not know it. The True Guru reveals Him to her. |8|

When she meets Him with intuitive ease, she finds peace; the Word of the Shabad quenches the fire of desire. |9|

Says Nanak, through You, O Lord, my mind is pleased and appeased; I cannot express Your worth. |10|3|

Malaar, First Mehl, Ashtapadees, Second House:
One Universal Creator God. By The Grace Of The True Guru:
The earth bends under the weight of the water,
the lofty mountains and the caverns of the underworld.
Contemplating the Word of the Guru's Shabad, the oceans become calm.
The path of liberation is found by subduing the ego. |1|

I am blind; I seek the Light of the Name.
I take the Support of the Naam, the Name of the Lord. I walk on the path of mystery of the Guru's Fear. |1|Pause|

Section 31 - Raag Malaar - Part 022

Through the Shabad, the Word of the True Guru, the Path is known.
With the Guru's Support, one is blessed with the strength of the True Lord.
Dwell on the Naam, and realize the Beauteous Word of His Bani.
If it is Your Will, Lord, You lead me to find Your Door. |2|

Flying high or sitting down, I am lovingly focused on the One Lord.
Through the Word of the Guru's Shabad, I take the Naam as my Suppport.
There is no ocean of water, no mountain ranges rising up.
I dwell within the home of my own inner being, where there is no path and no one travelling on it. |3|

You alone know the way to that House in which You dwell. No one else knows the Mansion of Your Presence.
Without the True Guru, there is no understanding. The whole world is buried under its nightmare.
The mortal tries all sorts of things, and weeps and wails, but without the Guru, he does not know the Naam, the Name of the Lord.
In the twinkling of an eye, the Naam saves him, if he realizes the Word of the Guru's Shabad. |4|

Some are foolish, blind, stupid and ignorant.
Some, through fear of the True Guru, take the Support of the Naam.
The True Word of His Bani is sweet, the source of ambrosial nectar.
Whoever drinks it in, finds the Door of Salvation. |5|

One who, through the love and fear of God, enshrines the Naam within his heart, acts according to the Guru's Instructions and knows the True Bani.
When the clouds release their rain, the earth becomes beautiful; God's Light permeates each and every heart.
The evil-minded ones plant their seed in the barren soil; such is the sign of those who have no Guru.
Without the True Guru, there is utter darkness; they drown there, even without water. |6|

Whatever God does, is by His Own Will.
That which is pre-ordained cannot be erased.
Bound to the Hukam of the Lord's Command, the mortal does his deeds.
Permeated by the One Word of the Shabad, the mortal is immersed in Truth. |7|

Your Command, O God, rules in the four directions; Your Name pervades the four corners of the nether regions as well.
The True Word of the Shabad is pervading amongst all. By His Grace, the Eternal One unites us with Himself.

Birth and death hang over the heads of all beings, along with hunger, sleep and dying.
The Naam is pleasing to Nanak's mind; O True Lord, Source of bliss, please bless me with Your Grace. |8|1|4|

Malaar, First Mehl:
You do not understand the nature of death and liberation.
You are sitting on the river-bank; realize the Word of the Guru's Shabad. |1|

You stork! - how were you caught in the net?
You do not remember in your heart the Unseen Lord God. |1|Pause|

For your one life, you consume many lives.
You were supposed to swim in the water, but you are drowning in it instead. |2|

You have tormented all beings.
When Death seizes you, then you shall regret and repent. |3|

When the heavy noose is placed around your neck,
you may spread your wings, but you shall not be able to fly. |4|

You enjoy the tastes and flavors, you foolish self-willed manmukh.
You are trapped. You can only be saved by virtuous conduct, spiritual wisdom and contemplation. |5|

Serving the True Guru, you will shatter the Messenger of Death.
In your heart, dwell on the True Word of the Shabad. |6|

The Guru's Teachings, the True Word of the Shabad, is excellent and sublime.
Keep the Name of the Lord enshrined in your heart. |7|

One who is obsessed with enjoying pleasures here, shall suffer in pain hereafter.
O Nanak, there is no liberation without the True Name. |8|2|5|

Section 31 - Raag Malaar - Part 023

Malaar, Third Mehl, Ashtapadees, First House:
One Universal Creator God. By The Grace Of The True Guru:
If it is in his karma, then he finds the True Guru; without such karma, He cannot be found.
He meets the True Guru, and he is transformed into gold, if it is the Lord's Will. |1|

O my mind, focus your consciousness on the Name of the Lord, Har, Har.
The Lord is found through the True Guru, and then he remains merged with the True Lord. |1|Pause|

Spiritual wisdom wells up through the True Guru, and then this cynicism is dispelled.
Through the True Guru, the Lord is realized, and then, he is not consigned to the womb of reincarnation ever again. |2|

By Guru's Grace, the mortal dies in life, and by so dying, lives to practice the Word of the Shabad.
He alone finds the Door of Salvation, who eradicates self-conceit from within himself. |3|

By Guru's Grace, the mortal is reincarnated into the Home of the Lord, having eradicated Maya from within.
He eats the uneatable, and is blessed with a discriminating intellect; he meets the Supreme Person, the Primal Lord God. |4|

The world is unconscious, like a passing show; the mortal departs, having lost his capital.
The profit of the Lord is obtained in the Sat Sangat, the True Congregation; by good karma, it is found. |5|

Without the True Guru, no one finds it; see this in your mind, and consider this in your heart.
By great good fortune, the mortal finds the Guru, and crosses over the terrifying world-ocean. |6|

The Name of the Lord is my Anchor and Support. I take only the Support of the Name of the Lord, Har, Har.
O Dear Lord, please be kind and lead me to meet the Guru, that I may find the Door of Salvation. |7|

The pre-ordained destiny inscribed on the mortal's forehead by our Lord and Master cannot be erased.

O Nanak, those humble beings are perfect, who are pleased by the Lord's Will. |8|1|

Malaar, Third Mehl:
The world is involved with the words of the Vedas, thinking about the three gunas - the three dispositions.
Without the Name, it suffers punishment by the Messenger of Death; it comes and goes in reincarnation, over and over again.
Meeting with the True Guru, the world is liberated, and finds the Door of Salvation. |1|

O mortal, immerse yourself in service to the True Guru.
By great good fortune, the mortal finds the Perfect Guru, and meditates on the Name of the Lord, Har, Har. |1|Pause|

The Lord, by the Pleasure of His Own Will, created the Universe, and the Lord Himself gives it sustenance and support.
The Lord, by His Own Will, makes the mortal's mind immaculate, and lovingly attunes him to the Lord.
The Lord, by His Own Will, leads the mortal to meet the True Guru, the Embellisher of all his lives. |2|

Waaho! Waaho! Blessed and Great is the True Word of His Bani. Only a few, as Gurmukh, understand.
Waaho! Waaho! Praise God as Great! No one else is as Great as He.
When God's Grace is received, He Himself forgives the mortal, and unites him with Himself. |3|

The True Guru has revealed our True, Supreme Lord and Master.
The Ambrosial Nectar rains down and the mind is satisfied, remaining lovingly attuned to the True Lord.
In the Lord's Name, it is forever rejuvenated; it shall never wither and dry up again. |4|

Section 31 - Raag Malaar - Part 024

Without the True Guru, no one finds the Lord; anyone can try and see.

By the Lord's Grace, the True Guru is found, and then the Lord is met with intuitive ease.
The self-willed manmukh is deluded by doubt; without good destiny, the Lord's wealth is not obtained. |5|

The three dispositions are completely distracting; people read and study and contemplate them.
Those people are never liberated; they do not find the Door of Salvation.
Without the True Guru, they are never released from bondage; they do not embrace love for the Naam, the Name of the Lord. |6|

The Pandits, the religious scholars, and the silent sages, reading and studying the Vedas, have grown weary.
They do not even think of the Lord's Name; they do not dwell in the home of their own inner being.
The Messenger of Death hovers over their heads; they are ruined by the deceit within themselves. |7|

Everyone longs for the Name of the Lord; without good destiny, it is not obtained.
When the Lord bestows His Glance of Grace, the mortal meets the True Guru, and the Lord's Name comes to dwell within the mind.
O Nanak, through the Name, honor wells up, and the mortal remains immersed in the Lord. |8|2|

Malaar, Third Mehl, Ashtapadees, Second House:
One Universal Creator God. By The Grace Of The True Guru:
When the Lord shows His Mercy, He enjoins the mortal to work for the Guru.
His pains are taken away, and the Lord's Name comes to dwell within.
True deliverance comes by focusing one's consciousness on the True Lord.
Listen to the Shabad, and the Word of the Guru's Bani. |1|

O my mind, serve the Lord, Har, Har, the true treasure.
By Guru's Grace, the wealth of the Lord is obtained. Night and day, focus your meditation on the Lord. |1|Pause|

The soul-bride who adorns herself without her Husband Lord,
is ill-mannered and vile, wasted away into ruin.
This is the useless way of life of the self-willed manmukh.

Forgetting the Naam, the Name of the Lord, he performs all sorts of empty rituals. |2|

The bride who is Gurmukh is beautifully embellished.
Through the Word of the Shabad, she enshrines her Husband Lord within her heart.
She realizes the One Lord, and subdues her ego.
That soul-bride is virtuous and noble. |3|

Without the Guru, the Giver, no one finds the Lord.
The greedy self-willed manmukh is attracted and engrossed in duality.
Only a few spiritual teachers realize this,
that without meeting the Guru, liberation is not obtained. |4|

Everyone tells the stories told by others.
Without subduing the mind, devotional worship does not come.
When the intellect achieves spiritual wisdom, the heart-lotus blossoms forth.
The Naam, the Name of the Lord, comes to abide in that heart. |5|

In egotism, everyone can pretend to worship God with devotion.
But this does not soften the mind, and it does not bring peace.
By speaking and preaching, the mortal only shows off his self-conceit.
His devotional worship is useless, and his life is a total waste. |6|

They alone are devotees, who are pleasing to the Mind of the True Guru.
Night and day, they remain lovingly attuned to the Name.
They behold the Naam, the Name of the Lord, ever-present, near at hand.

Section 31 - Raag Malaar - Part 025

Through the Word of the Guru's Shabad, He is pervading and permeating everywhere. |7|

God Himself forgives, and bestows His Love.
The world is suffering from the terrible disease of egotism.
By Guru's Grace, this disease is cured.
O Nanak, through the Truth, the mortal remains immersed in the True Lord. |8|1|3|5|8|

Raag Malaar, Chhant, Fifth Mehl:
One Universal Creator God. By The Grace Of The True Guru:
My Beloved Lord is the Giver of loving devotional worship.
His humble servants are imbued with His Love.
He is imbued with His servants, day and night; He does not forget them from His Mind, even for an instant.
He is the Lord of the World, the Treasure of virtue; He is always with me. All glorious virtues belong to the Lord of the Universe.
With His Feet, He has fascinated my mind; as His humble servant, I am intoxicated with love for His Name.
O Nanak, my Beloved is forever Merciful; out of millions, hardly anyone realizes Him. |1|

O Beloved, Your state is inaccessible and infinite.
You save even the worst sinners.
He is the Purifier of sinners, the Lover of His devotees, the Ocean of mercy, our Lord and Master.
In the Society of the Saints, vibrate and meditate on Him with commitment forever; He is the Inner-knower, the Searcher of hearts.
Those who wander in reincarnation through millions of births, are saved and carried across, by meditating in remembrance on the Naam.
Nanak is thirsty for the Blessed Vision of Your Darshan, O Dear Lord; please take care of him. |2|

My mind is absorbed in the Lotus Feet of the Lord.
O God, You are the water; Your humble servants are fish.
O Dear God, You alone are the water and the fish. I know that there is no difference between the two.
Please take hold of my arm and bless me with Your Name. I am honored only by Your Grace.
In the Saadh Sangat, the Company of the Holy, vibrate and meditate with love on the One Lord of the Universe, who is Merciful to the meek.
Nanak, the lowly and helpless, seeks the Sanctuary of the Lord, who in His Kindness has made him His Own. |3|

He unites us with Himself.
Our Sovereign Lord King is the Destroyer of fear.
My Wondrous Lord and Master is the Inner-knower, the Searcher of hearts.
My Beloved, the Treasure of virtue, has met me.

Supreme happiness and peace well up, as I cherish the Glorious Virtues of the Lord of the Universe.

Meeting with Him, I am embellished and exalted; gazing on Him, I am fascinated, and I realize my pre-ordained destiny.

Prays Nanak, I seek the Sanctuary of those who meditate on the Lord, Har, Har. |4|1|

Vaar Of Malaar, First Mehl, Sung To The Tune Of Rana Kailaash And Malda:
One Universal Creator God. By The Grace Of The True Guru:
Shalok, Third Mehl:
Meeting with the Guru, the mind is delighted, like the earth embellished by the rain.

Everything becomes green and lush; the pools and ponds are filled to overflowing.

The inner self is imbued with the deep crimson color of love for the True Lord.

The heart-lotus blossoms forth and the mind becomes true; through the Word of the Guru's Shabad, it is ecstatic and exalted.

Section 31 - Raag Malaar - Part 026

The self-willed manmukh is on the wrong side. You can see this with your own eyes.

He is caught in the trap like the deer; the Messenger of Death hovers over his head.

Hunger, thirst and slander are evil; sexual desire and anger are horrible.

These cannot be seen with your eyes, until you contemplate the Word of the Shabad.

Whoever is pleasing to You is content; all his entanglements are gone.

Serving the Guru, his capital is preserved. The Guru is the ladder and the boat.

O Nanak, whoever is attached to the Lord receives the essence; O True Lord, You are found when the mind is true. |1|

First Mehl:
There is one path and one door. The Guru is the ladder to reach one's own place.

Our Lord and Master is so beautiful, O Nanak; all comfort and peace are in the Name of the True Lord. |2|

Pauree:
He Himself created Himself; He Himself understands Himself.
Separating the sky and the earth, He has spread out His canopy.
Without any pillars, He supports the sky, through the insignia of His Shabad.
Creating the sun and the moon, He infused His Light into them.
He created the night and the day; Wondrous are His miraculous plays.
He created the sacred shrines of pilgrimage, where people contemplate righteousness and Dharma, and take cleansing baths on special occasions.
There is no other equal to You; how can we speak and describe You?
You are seated on the throne of Truth; all others come and go in reincarnation. |1|

Shalok, First Mehl:
O Nanak, when it rains in the month of Saawan, four are delighted:
the snake, the deer, the fish and the wealthy people who seek pleasure. |1|

First Mehl:
O Nanak, when it rains in the month of Saawan, four suffer the pains of separation:
the cow's calves, the poor, the travellers and the servants. |2|

Pauree:
You are True, O True Lord; You dispense True Justice.
Like a lotus, You sit in the primal celestial trance; You are hidden from view.
Brahma is called great, but even he does not know Your limits.
You have no father or mother; who gave birth to You?
You have no form or feature; You transcend all social classes.
You have no hunger or thirst; You are satisfied and satiated.
You have merged Yourself into the Guru; You are pervading through the Word of Your Shabad.
When he is pleasing to the True Lord, the mortal merges in Truth. |2|

Shalok, First Mehl:
The physician was called in; he touched my arm and felt my pulse.
The foolish physician did not know that the pain was in the mind. |1|

Second Mehl:

O physician, you are a competent physician, if you first diagnose the disease.

Prescribe such a remedy, by which all sorts of illnesses may be cured.

Administer that medicine, which will cure the disease, and allow peace to come and dwell in the body.

Only when you are rid of your own disease, O Nanak, will you be known as a physician. |2|

Pauree:

Brahma, Vishnu, Shiva and the deities were created.

Brahma was given the Vedas, and enjoined to worship God.

The ten incarnations, and Rama the king, came into being.

According to His Will, they quickly killed all the demons.

Shiva serves Him, but cannot find His limits.

He established His throne on the principles of Truth.

He enjoined all the world to its tasks, while He keeps Himself hidden from view.

Section 31 - Raag Malaar - Part 027

The Primal Lord has ordained that mortals must practice righteousness. |3|

Shalok, Second Mehl:

The month of Saawan has come, O my companions; think of your Husband Lord.

O Nanak, the discarded bride is in love with another; now she weeps and wails, and dies. |1|

Second Mehl:

The month of Saawan has come, O my companions; the clouds have burst forth with rain.

O Nanak, the blessed soul-brides sleep in peace; they are in love with their Husband Lord. |2|

Pauree:

He Himself has staged the tournament, and arranged the arena for the wrestlers.

They have entered the arena with pomp and ceremony; the Gurmukhs are joyful.

The false and foolish self-willed manmukhs are defeated and overcome.

The Lord Himself wrestles, and He Himself defeats them. He Himself staged this play.

The One God is the Lord and Master of all; this is known by the Gurmukhs.

He writes the inscription of His Hukam on the foreheads of all, without pen or ink.

In the Sat Sangat, the True Congregation, Union with Him is obtained; there, the Glorious Praises of the Lord are chanted forever.

O Nanak, praising the True Word of His Shabad, one comes to realize the Truth. |4|

Shalok, Third Mehl:

Hanging low, low and thick in the sky, the clouds are changing color.

How do I know whether my love for my Husband Lord shall endure?

The love of those soul-brides endures, if their minds are filled with the Love and the Fear of God.

O Nanak, she who has no Love and Fear of God - her body shall never find peace. |1|

Third Mehl:

Hanging low, low and thick in the sky, the clouds come, and pure water rains down.

O Nanak, that soul-bride suffers in pain, whose mind is torn away from her Husband Lord. |2|

Pauree:

The One Lord created both sides and pervades the expanse.

The words of the Vedas became pervasive, with arguments and divisions.

Attachment and detachment are the two sides of it; Dharma, true religion, is the guide between the two.

The self-willed manmukhs are worthless and false. Without a doubt, they lose in the Court of the Lord.

Those who follow the Guru's Teachings are the true spiritual warriors; they have conquered sexual desire and anger.

They enter into the True Mansion of the Lord's Presence, embellished and exalted by the Word of the Shabad.

Those devotees are pleasing to Your Will, O Lord; they dearly love the True Name.

I am a sacrifice to those who serve their True Guru. |5|

Shalok, Third Mehl:

Hanging low, low and thick in the sky, the clouds come, and water rains down in torrents.

O Nanak, she walks in harmony with the Will of her Husband Lord; she enjoys peace and pleasure forever. |1|

Third Mehl:
Why are you standing up, standing up to look? You poor wretch, this cloud has nothing in its hands.

The One who sent this cloud - cherish Him in your mind.

He alone enshrines the Lord in his mind, upon whom the Lord bestows His Glance of Grace.

O Nanak, all those who lack this Grace, cry and weep and wail. |2|

Pauree:
Serve the Lord forever; He acts in no time at all.

He stretched the sky across the heavens; in an instant, He creates and destroys.

He Himself created the world; He contemplates His Creative Omnipotence.

The self-willed manmukh will be called to account hereafter; he will be severely punished.

Section 31 - Raag Malaar - Part 028

The Gurmukh's account is settled with honor; the Lord blesses him with the treasure of His Praise.

No one's hands can reach there; no one will hear anyone's cries.

The True Guru will be your best friend there; at the very last instant, He will save you.

These beings should serve no other than the True Guru or the Creator Lord above the heads of all. |6|

Shalok, Third Mehl:
O rainbird, the One unto whom you call - everyone longs for that Lord.

When He grants His Grace, it rains, and the forests and fields blossom forth in their greenery.

By Guru's Grace, He is found; only a rare few understand this.

Sitting down and standing up, meditate continually on Him, and be at peace forever and ever.

O Nanak, the Ambrosial Nectar rains down forever; the Lord gives it to the Gurmukh. |1|

Third Mehl:
When the people of the world are suffering in pain, they call upon the Lord in loving prayer.
The True Lord naturally listens and hears and gives comfort.
He commands the god of rain, and the rain pours down in torrents.
Corn and wealth are produced in great abundance and prosperity; their value cannot be estimated.
O Nanak, praise the Naam, the Name of the Lord; He reaches out and gives sustenance to all beings.
Eating this, peace is produced, and the mortal never again suffers in pain. |2|

Pauree:
O Dear Lord, You are the Truest of the True. You blend those who are truthful into Your Own Being.
Those caught in duality are on the side of duality; entrenched in falsehood, they cannot merge into the Lord.
You Yourself unite, and You Yourself separate; You display Your Creative Omnipotence.
Attachment brings the sorrow of separation; the mortal acts in accordance with pre-ordained destiny.
I am a sacrifice to those who remain lovingly attached to the Lord's Feet.
They are like the lotus which remains detached, floating upon the water.
They are peaceful and beautiful forever; they eradicate self-conceit from within.
They never suffer sorrow or separation; they are merged in the Being of the Lord. |7|

Shalok, Third Mehl:
O Nanak, praise the Lord; everything is in His power.
Serve Him, O mortal beings; there is none other than Him.
The Lord God abides within the mind of the Gurmukh, and then he is at peace, forever and ever.
He is never cynical; all anxiety has been taken out from within him.
Whatever happens, happens naturally; no one has any say about it.
When the True Lord abides in the mind, then the mind's desires are fulfilled.
O Nanak, He Himself hears the words of those, whose accounts are in His Hands. |1|

Third Mehl:
The Ambrosial Nectar rains down continually; realize this through realization.
Those who, as Gurmukh, realize this, keep the Lord's Ambrosial Nectar enshrined within their hearts.
They drink in the Lord's Ambrosial Nectar, and remain forever imbued with the Lord; they conquer egotism and thirsty desires.
The Name of the Lord is Ambrosial Nectar; the Lord showers His Grace, and it rains down.
O Nanak, the Gurmukh comes to behold the Lord, the Supreme Soul. |2|

Section 31 - Raag Malaar - Part 029

Pauree:
How can the unweighable be weighed? Without weighing Him, He cannot be obtained.
Reflect on the Word of the Guru's Shabad, and immerse yourself in His Glorious Virtues.
He Himself weighs Himself; He unites in Union with Himself.
His value cannot be estimated; nothing can be said about this.
I am a sacrifice to my Guru; He has made me realize this true realization.
The world has been deceived, and the Ambrosial Nectar is being plundered. The self-willed manmukh does not realize this.
Without the Name, nothing will go along with him; he wastes his life, and departs.
Those who follow the Guru's Teachings and remain awake and aware, preserve and protect the home of their heart; demons have no power against them. |8|

Shalok, Third Mehl:
O rainbird, do not cry out. Do not let this mind of yours be so thirsty for a drop of water. Obey the Hukam, the Command of your Lord and Master,

and your thirst shall be quenched. Your love for Him shall increase four-fold. |1|

Third Mehl:
O rainbird, your place is in the water; you move around in the water.
But you do not appreciate the water, and so you cry out.

In the water and on the land, it rains down in the ten directions. No place is left dry.

With so much rain, those who are die of thirst are very unfortunate.

O Nanak, the Gurmukhs understand; the Lord abides within their minds. |2|

Pauree:

The Yogic Masters, celibates, Siddhas and spiritual teachers - none of them has found the limits of the Lord.

The Gurmukhs meditate on the Naam, and merge in You, O Lord.

For thirty-six ages, God remained in utter darkness, as He pleased.

The vast expanse of water swirled around.

The Creator of all is Infinite, Endless and Inaccessible.

He formed fire and conflict, hunger and thirst.

Death hangs over the heads of the people of the world, in the love of duality.

The Savior Lord saves those who realize the Word of the Shabad. |9|

Shalok, Third Mehl:

This rain pours down on all; it rains down in accordance with God's Loving Will.

Those trees become green and lush, which remain immersed in the Guru's Word.

O Nanak, by His Grace, there is peace; the pain of these creatures is gone. |1|

Third Mehl:

The night is wet with dew; lightning flashes, and the rain pours down in torrents.

Food and wealth are produced in abundance when it rains, if it is the Will of God.

Consuming it, the minds of His creatures are satisfied, and they adopt the lifestyle of the way.

This wealth is the play of the Creator Lord. Sometimes it comes, and sometimes it goes.

The Naam is the wealth of the spiritually wise. It is permeating and pervading forever.

O Nanak, those who are blessed with His Glance of Grace receive this wealth. |2|

Pauree:
He Himself does, and causes all to be done. Unto whom can I complain?
He Himself calls the mortal beings to account; He Himself causes them to act.
Whatever pleases Him happens. Only a fool issues commands.
He Himself saves and redeems; He Himself is the Forgiver.
He Himself sees, and He Himself hears; He gives His Support to all.
He alone is pervading and permeating all; He considers each and every one.

Section 31 - Raag Malaar - Part 030

The Gurmukh reflects on the self, lovingly attached to the True Lord.
O Nanak, whom can we ask? He Himself is the Great Giver. |10|

Shalok, Third Mehl:
This world is a rainbird; let no one be deluded by doubt.
This rainbird is an animal; it has no understanding at all.
The Name of the Lord is Ambrosial Nectar; drinking it in, thirst is quenched.
O Nanak, those Gurmukhs who drink it in shall never again be afflicted by thirst. |1|

Third Mehl:
Malaar is a calming and soothing raga; meditating on the Lord brings peace and tranquility.
When the Dear Lord grants His Grace, then the rain falls on all the people of the world.
From this rain, all creatures find the ways and means to live, and the earth is embellished.
O Nanak, this world is all water; everything came from water.
By Guru's Grace, a rare few realize the Lord; such humble beings are liberated forever. |2|

Pauree:
O True and Independent Lord God, You alone are my Lord and Master.
You Yourself are everything; who else is of any account?
False is the pride of man. True is Your glorious greatness.
Coming and going in reincarnation, the beings and species of the world came into being.
But if the mortal serves his True Guru, his coming into the world is judged to be worthwhile.

And if he eradicates eogtism from within himself, then how can he be judged?

The self-willed manmukh is lost in the darkness of emotional attachment, like the man lost in the wilderness.

Countless sins are erased, by even a tiny particle of the Lord's Name. |11|

Shalok, Third Mehl:

O rainbird, you do not know the Mansion of your Lord and Master's Presence. Offer your prayers to see this Mansion.

You speak as you please, but your speech is not accepted.

Your Lord and Master is the Great Giver; whatever you desire, you shall receive from Him.

Not only the thirst of the poor rainbird, but the thirst of the whole world is quenched. |1|

Third Mehl:

The night is wet with dew; the rainbird sings the True Name with intuitive ease.

This water is my very soul; without water, I cannot survive.

Through the Word of the Guru's Shabad, this water is obtained, and egotism is eradicated from within.

O Nanak, I cannot live without Him, even for a moment; the True Guru has led me to meet Him. |2|

Pauree:

There are countless worlds and nether regions; I cannot calculate their number.

You are the Creator, the Lord of the Universe; You create it, and You destroy it.

The 8.4 million species of beings issued forth from You.

Some are called kings, emperors and nobles.

Some claim to be bankers and accumulate wealth, but in duality they lose their honor.

Some are givers, and some are beggars; God is above the heads of all.

Without the Name, they are vulgar, dreadful and wretched.

Falsehood shall not last, O Nanak; whatever the True Lord does, comes to pass. |12|

Shalok, Third Mehl:

O rainbird, the virtuous soul-bride attains the Mansion of her Lord's Presence; the unworthy, unvirtuous one is far away.

Deep within your inner being, the Lord abides. The Gurmukh beholds Him ever-present.

When the Lord bestows His Glance of Grace, the mortal no longer weeps and wails.

O Nanak, those who are imbued with the Naam intuitively merge with the Lord; they practice the Word of the Guru's Shabad. |1|

Section 31 - Raag Malaar - Part 031

Third Mehl:
The rainbird prays: O Lord, grant Your Grace, and bless me with the gift of the life of the soul.

Without the water, my thirst is not quenched, and my breath of life is ended and gone.

You are the Giver of peace, O Infinite Lord God; You are the Giver of the treasure of virtue.

O Nanak, the Gurmukh is forgiven; in the end, the Lord God shall be your only friend. |2|

Pauree:
He created the world; He considers the merits and demerits of the mortals.

Those who are entangled in the three gunas - the three dispositions - do not love the Naam, the Name of the Lord.

Forsaking virtue, they practice evil; they shall be miserable in the Court of the Lord.

They lose their life in the gamble; why did they even come into the world?

But those who conquer and subdue their minds, through the True Word of the Shabad - night and day, they love the Naam.

Those people enshrine the True, Invisible and Infinite Lord in their hearts.

You, O Lord, are the Giver, the Treasure of virtue; I am unvirtuous and unworthy.

He alone finds You, whom You bless and forgive, and inspire to contemplate the Word of the Guru's Shabad. |13|

Shalok, Fifth Mehl:
The faithless cynics forget the Name of the Lord; the night of their lives does not pass in peace.

Their days and nights become comfortable, O Nanak, singing the Glorious Praises of the Lord. |1|

Fifth Mehl:
All sorts of jewels and gems, diamonds and rubies, shine forth from their foreheads.
O Nanak, those who are pleasing to God, look beautiful in the Court of the Lord. |2|

Pauree:
Serving the True Guru, I dwell on the True Lord.
The work you have done for the True Guru shall be very useful in the end.
The Messenger of Death cannot even touch that person who is protected by the True Lord.
Lighting the lamp of the Guru's Teachings, my awareness has been awakened.
The self-willed manmukhs are false; without the Name, they wander around like demons.
They are nothing more than beasts, wrapped up in human skin; they are black-hearted within.
The True Lord is pervading all; through the True Word of the Shabad, He is seen.
O Nanak, the Naam is the greatest treasure. The Perfect Guru has revealed it to me. |14|

Shalok, Third Mehl:
The rainbird realizes the Hukam of the Lord's Command with intuitive ease through the Guru.
The clouds mercifully burst forth, and the rain pours down in torrents.
The cries and wailings of the rainbird have ceased, and peace has come to abide in its mind.
O Nanak, praise that Lord, who reaches out and gives sustenance to all beings and creatures. |1|

Third Mehl:
O rainbird, you do not know what thirst is within you, or what you can drink to quench it.
You wander in the love of duality, and you do not obtain the Ambrosial Water.

When God casts His Glance of Grace, then the mortal automatically meets the True Guru.

O Nanak, the Ambrosial Water is obtained from the True Guru, and then the mortal remains merged in the Lord with intuitive ease. |2|

Pauree:
Some go and sit in the forest realms, and do not answer any calls.

Some, in the dead of winter, break the ice and immerse themselves in freezing water.

Some rub ashes on their bodies, and never wash off their dirt.

Some look hideous, with their uncut hair matted and dishevelled. They bring dishonor to their family and ancestry.

Section 31 - Raag Malaar - Part 032

Some wander naked day and night and never sleep.

Some burn their limbs in fire, damaging and ruining themselves.

Without the Name, the body is reduced to ashes; what good is it to speak and cry then?

Those who serve the True Guru, are embellished and exalted in the Court of their Lord and Master. |15|

Shalok, Third Mehl:
The rainbird chirps in the ambrosial hours of the morning before the dawn; its prayers are heard in the Court of the Lord.

The order is issued to the clouds, to let the rains of mercy shower down.

I am a sacrifice to those who enshrine the True Lord within their hearts.

O Nanak, through the Name, all are rejuvenated, contemplating the Word of the Guru's Shabad. |1|

Third Mehl:
O rainbird, this is not the way to quench your thirst, even though you may cry out a hundred times.

By God's Grace, the True Guru is found; by His Grace, love wells up.

O Nanak, when the Lord and Master abides in the mind, corruption and evil leave from within. |2|

Pauree:
Some are Jains, wasting their time in the wilderness; by their pre-ordained destiny, they are ruined.

The Naam, the Name of the Lord, is not on their lips; they do not bathe at sacred shrines of pilgrimage.

They pull out their hair with their hands, instead of shaving.

They remain unclean day and night; they do not love the Word of the Shabad.

They have no status, no honor, and no good karma. They waste away their lives in vain.

Their minds are false and impure; that which they eat is impure and defiled.

Without the Shabad, no one achieves a lifestyle of good conduct.

The Gurmukh is absorbed in the True Lord God, the Universal Creator. |16|

Shalok, Third Mehl:

In the month of Saawan, the bride is happy, contemplating the Word of the Guru's Shabad.

O Nanak, she is a happy soul-bride forever; her love for the Guru is unlimited. |1|

Third Mehl:

In Saawan, she who has no virtue is burned, in attachment and love of duality.

O Nanak, she does not appreciate the value of her Husband Lord; all her decorations are worthless. |2|

Pauree:

The True, Unseen, Mysterious Lord is not won over by stubbornness.

Some sing according to traditional ragas, but the Lord is not pleased by these ragas.

Some dance and dance and keep the beat, but they do not worship Him with devotion.

Some refuse to eat; what can be done with these fools?

Thirst and desire have greatly increased; nothing brings satisfaction.

Some are tied down by rituals; they hassle themselves to death.

In this world, profit comes by drinking in the Ambrosial Nectar of the Naam.

The Gurmukhs gather in loving devotional worship of the Lord. |17|

Shalok, Third Mehl:

Those Gurmukhs who sing in the Raga of Malaar - their minds and bodies become cool and calm.

Through the Word of the Guru's Shabad, they realize the One, the One True Lord.

Their minds and bodies are true; they obey the True Lord, and they are known as true.

True devotional worship is deep within them; they are automatically blessed with honor.

In this Dark Age of Kali Yuga, there is utter darkness; the self-willed manmukh cannot find the way.

O Nanak, very blessed are those Gurmukhs, unto whom the Lord is revealed. |1|

Third Mehl:

The clouds rain down mercifully, and joy wells up in the minds of the people.

I am forever a sacrifice to the One, by whose Command the clouds burst forth with rain.

Section 31 - Raag Malaar - Part 033

The Gurmukhs dwell on the Word of the Shabad. They sing the Glorious Praises of the True Lord.

O Nanak, those humble beings who are imbued with the Naam are pure and immaculate. They are intuitively merged in the True Lord. |2|

Pauree:

Serving the Perfect True Guru, I have found the Perfect Lord.

Meditating on the Perfect Lord, by perfect karma, I have enshrined the Shabad within my mind.

Through perfect spiritual wisdom and meditation, my filth has been washed away.

The Lord is my sacred shrine of pilgrimage and pool of purification; I wash my mind in Him.

One who dies in the Shabad and conquers his mind - blessed is the mother who gave birth to him.

He is true in the Court of the Lord, and his coming into this world is judged to be true.

No one can challenge that person, with whom our Lord and Master is pleased.

O Nanak, praising the True Lord, his pre-ordained destiny is activated. |18|

Shalok, Third Mehl:

Those who give out ceremonial hats of recognition are fools; those who receive them have no shame.

The mouse cannot enter its hole with a basket tied around its waist.

Those who give out blessings shall die, and those that they bless shall also depart.

O Nanak, no one knows the Lord's Command, by which all must depart.

The spring harvest is the Name of the One Lord; the harvest of autumn is the True Name.

I receive a letter of pardon from my Lord and Master, when I reach His Court.

There are so many courts of the world, and so many who come and go there.

There are so many beggars begging; so many beg and beg until death. |1|

First Mehl:

The elephant eats a hundred pounds of ghee and molasses, and five hundred pounds of corn.

He belches and grunts and scatters dust, and when the breath leaves his body, he regrets it.

The blind and arrogant die insane.

Submitting to the Lord, one become pleasing to Him.

The sparrow eats only half a grain, then it flies through the sky and chirps.

The good sparrow is pleasing to her Lord and Master, if she chirps the Name of the Lord.

The powerful tiger kills hundreds of deer, and all sorts of other animals eat what it leaves.

It becomes very strong, and cannot be contained in its den, but when it must go, it regrets.

So who is impressed by the roar of the blind beast?

He is not pleasing at all to his Lord and Master.

The insect loves the milkweed plant; perched on its branch, it eats it.

It becomes good and pleasing to its Lord and Master, if it chirps the Name of the Lord.

O Nanak, the world lasts for only a few days; indulging in pleasures, pain is produced.

There are many who boast and brag, but none of them can remain detached from the world.

The fly dies for the sake of sweets.

O Lord, death does not even approach those whom You protect. You carry them across the terrifying world-ocean. |2|

Pauree:
You are Inaccessible and Unfathomable, O Invisible and Infinite True Lord Master.
You are the Giver, all are beggars of You. You alone are the Great Giver.
Those who serve You find peace, reflecting on the Guru's Teachings.
Some, according to Your Will, are in love with Maya.
Through the Word of the Guru's Shabad, praise the Lord with love and affection within.
Without love, there is no devotion. Without the True Guru, love is not enshrined.
You are the Lord God; everyone serves You. This is the prayer of Your humble minstrel.
Please bless me with the gift of contentment, that I may receive the True Name as my Support. |19|

Section 31 - Raag Malaar - Part 034

Shalok, First Mehl:
Through the night the time ticks away; through the day the time ticks away.
The body wears away and turns to straw.
All are involved and entangled in worldly entanglements.
The mortal has mistakenly renounced the way of service.
The blind fool is caught in conflict, bothered and bewildered.
Those who weep after someone has died - can they bring him back to life?
Without realization, nothing can be understood.
The weepers who weep for the dead shall themselves die as well.
O Nanak, this is the Will of our Lord and Master.
Those who do not remember the Lord, are dead. |1|

First Mehl:
Love dies, and affection dies; hatred and strife die.
The color fades, and beauty vanishes; the body suffers and collapses.
Where did he come from? Where is he going? Did he exist or not?
The self-willed manmukh made empty boasts, indulging in parties and pleasures.
O Nanak, without the True Name, his honor is torn away, from head to foot. |2|

Pauree:

The Ambrosial Naam, the Name of the Lord, is forever the Giver of peace. It shall be your Help and Support in the end.

Without the Guru, the world is insane. It does not appreciate the worth of the Name.

Those who serve the True Guru are accepted and approved. Their light merges into the Light.

That servant who enshrines the Lord's Will within his mind, becomes just like his Lord and Master.

Tell me, who has ever found peace by following his own will? The blind act in blindness.

No one is ever satisfied and fulfilled by evil and corruption. The hunger of the fool is not satisfied.

Attached to duality, all are ruined; without the True Guru, there is no understanding.

Those who serve the True Guru find peace; they are blessed with Grace by the Will of the Lord. |20|

Shalok, First Mehl:

Modesty and righteousness both, O Nanak, are qualities of those who are blessed with true wealth.

Do not refer to that wealth as your friend, which leads you to get your head beaten.

Those who possess only this worldly wealth are known as paupers.

But those, within whose hearts You dwell, O Lord - those people are oceans of virtue. |1|

First Mehl:

Worldly possessions are obtained by pain and suffering; when they are gone, they leave pain and suffering.

O Nanak, without the True Name, hunger is never satisfied.

Beauty does not satisfy hunger; when the man sees beauty, he hungers even more.

As many as are the pleasures of the body, so many are the pains which afflict it. |2|

First Mehl:

Acting blindly, the mind becomes blind. The blind mind makes the body blind.

Why make a dam with mud and plaster? Even a dam made of stones gives way.

The dam has burst. There is no boat. There is no raft. The water's depth is unfathomable.

O Nanak, without the True Name, many multitudes have drowned. |3|

First Mehl:

Thousands of pounds of gold, and thousands of pounds of silver; the king over the heads of thousands of kings.

Thousands of armies, thousands of marching bands and spearmen; the emperor of thousands of horsemen.

The unfathomable ocean of fire and water must be crossed.

The other shore cannot be seen; only the roar of pitiful cries can be heard.

O Nanak, there, it shall be known, whether anyone is a king or an emperor. |4|

Pauree:

Some have chains around their necks, in bondage to the Lord.

They are released from bondage, realizing the True Lord as True.

Section 31 - Raag Malaar - Part 035

One whose pre-ordained destiny is activated, comes to know the True Lord.

By God's Command, it is ordained. When the mortal goes, he knows.

Realize the Word of the Shabad, and cross over the terrifying world-ocean.

Thieves, adulterers and gamblers are pressed like seeds in the mill.

Slanderers and gossipers are hand-cuffed.

The Gurmukh is absorbed in the True Lord, and is famous in the Court of the Lord. |21|

Shalok, Second Mehl:

The beggar is known as an emperor, and the fool is known as a religious scholar.

The blind man is known as a seer; this is how people talk.

The trouble-maker is called a leader, and the liar is seated with honor.

O Nanak, the Gurmukhs know that this is justice in the Dark Age of Kali Yuga. |1|

First Mehl:

Deer, falcons and government officials are known to be trained and clever.

When the trap is set, they trap their own kind; hereafter they will find no place of rest.

He alone is learned and wise, and he alone is a scholar, who practices the Name.

First, the tree puts down its roots, and then it spreads out its shade above.

The kings are tigers, and their officials are dogs;

they go out and awaken the sleeping people to harass them.

The public servants inflict wounds with their nails.

The dogs lick up the blood that is spilled.

But there, in the Court of the Lord, all beings will be judged.

Those who have violated the people's trust will be disgraced; their noses will be cut off. |2|

Pauree:

He Himself creates the world, and He himself takes care of it.

Without the Fear of God, doubt is not dispelled, and love for the Name is not embraced.

Through the True Guru, the Fear of God wells up, and the Door of Salvation is found.

Through the Fear of God, intuitive ease is obtained, and one's light merges into the Light of the Infinite.

Through the Fear of God, the terrifying world-ocean is crossed over, reflecting on the Guru's Teachings.

Through the Fear of God, the Fearless Lord is found; He has no end or limitation.

The self-willed manmukhs do not appreciate the value of the Fear of God. Burning in desire, they weep and wail.

O Nanak, through the Name, peace is obtained, by enshrining the Guru's Teachings within the heart. |22|

Shalok, First Mehl:

Beauty and sexual desire are friends; hunger and tasty food are tied together.

Greed is bound up in its search for wealth, and sleep will use even a tiny space as a bed.

Anger barks and brings ruin on itself, blindly pursuing useless conflicts.

It is good to be silent, O Nanak; without the Name, one's mouth spews forth only filth. |1|

First Mehl:

Royal power, wealth, beauty, social status and youth are the five thieves.

These thieves have plundered the world; no one's honor has been spared.

But these thieves themselves are robbed, by those who fall at the Guru's Feet.

O Nanak, the multitudes who do not have good karma are plundered. |2|

Pauree:

The learned and educated are called to account for their actions.

Without the Name, they are judged false; they become miserable and suffer hardship.

Their path becomes treacherous and difficult, and their way is blocked.

Through the Shabad, the Word of the True and Independent Lord God, one becomes content.

The Lord is deep and profound and unfathomable; His depth cannot be measured.

Without the Guru, the mortals are beaten and punched in the face and the mouth, and no one is released.

Chanting the Naam, the Name of the Lord, one returns to his true home with honor.

Know that the Lord, by the Hukam of His Command, gives sustenance and the breath of life. |23|

Section 31 - Raag Malaar - Part 036

Shalok, First Mehl:

Living beings are formed of air, water and fire. They are subject to pleasure and pain.

In this world, in the nether regions of the underworld, and in the Akaashic ethers of the heavens, some remain ministers in the Court of the Lord.

Some live long lives, while others suffer and die.

Some give and consume, and still their wealth is not exhausted, while others remain poor forever.

In His Will He creates, and in His Will He destroys thousands in an instant.

He has harnessed everyone with His harness; when He forgives, he breaks the harness.

He has no color or features; He is invisible and beyond calculation.

How can He be described? He is known as the Truest of the True.

All the actions which are done and described, O Nanak, are done by the Indescribable Lord Himself.

Whoever hears the description of the indescribable,

is blessed with wealth, intelligence, perfection, spiritual wisdom and eternal peace. |1|

First Mehl:
One who bears the unbearable, controls the nine holes of the body.
One who worships and adores the Lord with his breath of life, gains stability in his body-wall.
Where has he come from, and where will he go?
Remaining dead while yet alive, he is accepted and approved.
Whoever understands the Hukam of the Lord's Command, realizes the essence of reality.
This is known by Guru's Grace.
O Nanak, know this: egotism leads to bondage.
Only those who have no ego and no self-conceit, are not consigned to reincarnation. |2|

Pauree:
Read the Praise of the Lord's Name; other intellectual pursuits are false.
Without dealing in Truth, life is worthless.
No one has ever found the Lord's end or limitation.
All the world is enveloped by the darkness of egotistical pride. It does not like the Truth.
Those who depart from this world, forgetting the Naam, shall be roasted in the frying pan.
They pour the oil of duality within, and burn.
They come into the world and wander around aimlessly; they depart when the play is finished.
O Nanak, imbued with Truth, the mortals merge in Truth. |24|

Shalok, First Mehl:
First, the mortal is conceived in the flesh, and then he dwells in the flesh.
When he comes alive, his mouth takes flesh; his bones, skin and body are flesh.
He comes out of the womb of flesh, and takes a mouthful of flesh at the breast.
His mouth is flesh, his tongue is flesh; his breath is in the flesh.
He grows up and is married, and brings his wife of flesh into his home.
Flesh is produced from flesh; all relatives are made of flesh.
When the mortal meets the True Guru, and realizes the Hukam of the Lord's Command, then he comes to be reformed.

Releasing himself, the mortal does not find release; O Nanak, through empty words, one is ruined. |1|

First Mehl:
The fools argue about flesh and meat, but they know nothing about meditation and spiritual wisdom.
What is called meat, and what is called green vegetables? What leads to sin?
It was the habit of the gods to kill the rhinoceros, and make a feast of the burnt offering.
Those who renounce meat, and hold their noses when sitting near it, devour men at night.
They practice hypocrisy, and make a show before other people, but they do not understand anything about meditation or spiritual wisdom.
O Nanak, what can be said to the blind people? They cannot answer, or even understand what is said.
They alone are blind, who act blindly. They have no eyes in their hearts.
They are produced from the blood of their mothers and fathers, but they do not eat fish or meat.

Section 31 - Raag Malaar - Part 037

But when men and women meet in the night, they come together in the flesh.
In the flesh we are conceived, and in the flesh we are born; we are vessels of flesh.
You know nothing of spiritual wisdom and meditation, even though you call yourself clever, O religious scholar.
O master, you believe that flesh on the outside is bad, but the flesh of those in your own home is good.
All beings and creatures are flesh; the soul has taken up its home in the flesh.
They eat the uneatable; they reject and abandon what they could eat. They have a teacher who is blind.
In the flesh we are conceived, and in the flesh we are born; we are vessels of flesh.
You know nothing of spiritual wisdom and meditation, even though you call yourself clever, O religious scholar.
Meat is allowed in the Puraanas, meat is allowed in the Bible and the Koran. Throughout the four ages, meat has been used.

It is featured in sacred feasts and marriage festivities; meat is used in them. Women, men, kings and emperors originate from meat.

If you see them going to hell, then do not accept charitable gifts from them.

The giver goes to hell, while the receiver goes to heaven - look at this injustice.

You do not understand your own self, but you preach to other people. O Pandit, you are very wise indeed.

O Pandit, you do not know where meat originated.

Corn, sugar cane and cotton are produced from water. The three worlds came from water.

Water says, "I am good in many ways." But water takes many forms.

Forsaking these delicacies, one becomes a true Sannyaasee, a detached hermit. Nanak reflects and speaks. |2|

Pauree:
What can I say with only one tongue? I cannot find your limits.

Those who contemplate the True Word of the Shabad are absorbed into You, O Lord.

Some wander around in saffron robes, but without the True Guru, no one finds the Lord.

They wander in foreign lands and countries until they grow weary, but You hide Yourself within them.

The Word of the Guru's Shabad is a jewel, through which the Lord shines forth and reveals Himself.

Realizing one's own self, following the Guru's Teachings, the mortal is absorbed into Truth.

Coming and going, the tricksters and magicians put on their magic show.

But those whose minds are pleased by the True Lord, praise the True One, the Ever-stable Lord. |25|

Shalok, First Mehl:
O Nanak, the tree of actions done in Maya yields ambrosial fruit and poisonous fruit.

The Creator does all deeds; we eat the fruits as He ordains. |1|

Second Mehl:
O Nanak, burn worldly greatness and glory in the fire.

These burnt offerings have caused mortals to forget the Naam, the Name of the Lord. Not even one of them will go along with you in the end. |2|

Pauree:

He judges each and every being; by the Hukam of His Command, He leads us on.

Justice is in Your Hands, O Lord; You are pleasing to my mind.

The mortal is bound and gagged by Death and lead away; no one can rescue him.

Old age, the tyrant, dances on the mortal's shoulders.

So climb aboard the boat of the True Guru, and the True Lord will rescue you.

The fire of desire burns like an oven, consuming mortals night and day.

Like trapped birds, the mortals peck at the corn; only through the Lord's Command will they find release.

Whatever the Creator does, comes to pass; falsehood shall fail in the end. |26|

Section 31 - Raag Malaar - Part 038

Shalok, First Mehl:

The True Guru is the All-knowing Primal Being; He shows us our true home within the home of the self.

The Panch Shabad, the Five Primal Sounds, resonate and resound within; the insignia of the Shabad is revealed there, vibrating gloriously.

Worlds and realms, nether regions, solar systems and galaxies are wondrously revealed.

The strings and the harps vibrate and resound; the true throne of the Lord is there.

Listen to the music of the home of the heart - Sukhmani, peace of mind. Lovingly tune in to His state of celestial ecstasy.

Contemplate the Unspoken Speech, and the desires of the mind are dissolved.

The heart-lotus is turned upside-down, and is filled with Ambrosial Nectar. This mind does not go out; it does not get distracted.

It does not forget the Chant which is chanted without chanting; it is immersed in the Primal Lord God of the ages.

All the sister-companions are blessed with the five virtues. The Gurmukhs dwell in the home of the self deep within.

Nanak is the slave of that one who seeks the Shabad and finds this home within. |1|

First Mehl:

The extravagant glamor of the world is a passing show.

My twisted mind does not believe that it will end up in a grave.

I am meek and lowly; You are the great river.

Please, bless me with the one thing; everything else is poison, and does not tempt me.

You filled this fragile body with the water of life, O Lord, by Your Creative Power.

By Your Omnipotence, I have become powerful.

Nanak is a dog in the Court of the Lord, intoxicated more and more, all the time.

The world is on fire; the Name of the Lord is cooling and soothing. |2|

New Pauree, Fifth Mehl:

His wonderful play is all-pervading; it is wonderful and amazing!

As Gurmukh, I know the the Transcendent Lord, the Supreme Lord God.

All my sins and corruption are washed away, through the insignia of the Shabad, the Word of God.

In the Saadh Sangat, the Company of the Holy, one is saved, and becomes free.

Meditating, meditating in remembrance on the Great Giver, I enjoy all comforts and pleasures.

I have become famous throughout the world, under the canopy of His kindness and grace.

He Himself has forgiven me, and united me with Himself; I am forever a sacrifice to Him.

O Nanak, by the Pleasure of His Will, my Lord and Master has blended me with Himself. |27|

Shalok, First Mehl:

Blessed is the paper, blessed is the pen, blessed is the inkwell, and blessed is the ink.

Blessed is the writer, O Nanak, who writes the True Name. |1|

First Mehl:

You Yourself are the writing tablet, and You Yourself are the pen. You are also what is written on it.

Speak of the One Lord, O Nanak; how could there be any other? |2|

Pauree:

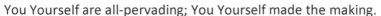

You Yourself are all-pervading; You Yourself made the making.

Without You, there is no other at all; You are permeating and pervading everywhere.

You alone know Your state and extent. Only You can estimate Your worth.

You are invisible, imperceptible and inaccessible. You are revealed through the Guru's Teachings.

Deep within, there is ignorance, suffering and doubt; through the spiritual wisdom of the Guru, they are eradicated.

He alone meditates on the Naam, whom You unite with Yourself, in Your Mercy.

You are the Creator, the Inaccessible Primal Lord God; You are all-pervading everywhere.

To whatever You link the mortal, O True Lord, to that he is linked. Nanak sings Your Glorious Praises. |28|1|

SUDH|

Section 31 - Raag Malaar - Part 039

Raag Malaar, The Word Of The Devotee Naam Dayv Jee:
One Universal Creator God. By The Grace Of The True Guru:
Serve the King, the Sovereign Lord of the World. He has no ancestry; He is immaculate and pure.
Please bless me with the gift of devotion, which the humble Saints beg for. |1|Pause|

His Home is the pavilion seen in all directions; His ornamental heavenly realms fill the seven worlds alike.
In His Home, the virgin Lakshmi dwells. The moon and the sun are His two lamps; the wretched Messenger of Death stages his dramas, and levies taxes on all.
Such is my Sovereign Lord King, the Supreme Lord of all. |1|

In His House, the four-faced Brahma, the cosmic potter lives. He created the entire universe.
In His House, the insane Shiva, the Guru of the World, lives; he imparts spiritual wisdom to expain the essence of reality.
Sin and virtue are the standard-bearers at His Door; Chitr and Gupt are the recording angels of the conscious and subconscious.
The Righteous Judge of Dharma, the Lord of Destruction, is the door-man.

Such is the Supreme Sovereign Lord of the World. |2|

In His Home are the heavenly heralds, celestial singers, Rishis and poor minstrels, who sing so sweetly.
All the Shaastras take various forms in His theater, singing beautiful songs.
The wind waves the fly-brush over Him;
His hand-maiden is Maya, who has conquered the world.
The shell of the earth is His fireplace.
Such is the Sovereign Lord of the three worlds. |3|

In His Home, the celestial turtle is the bed-frame, woven with the strings of the thousand-headed snake.
His flower-girls are the eighteen loads of vegetation; His water-carriers are the nine hundred sixty million clouds.
His sweat is the Ganges River.
The seven seas are His water-pitchers.
The creatures of the world are His household utensils.
Such is the Sovereign Lord King of the three worlds. |4|

In His home are Arjuna, Dhroo, Prahlaad, Ambreek, Naarad, Nayjaa, the Siddhas and Buddhas, the ninety-two heavenly heralds and celestial singers in their wondrous play.
All the creatures of the world are in His House.
The Lord is diffused in the inner beings of all.
Prays Naam Dayv, seek His Protection.
All the devotees are His banner and insignia. |5|1|

MALAAR:
Please do not forget me; please do not forget me,
please do not forget me, O Lord. |1|Pause|

The temple priests have doubts about this, and everyone is furious with me.
Calling me low-caste and untouchable, they beat me and drove me out; what should I do now, O Beloved Father Lord? |1|

If You liberate me after I am dead, no one will know that I am liberated.
These Pandits, these religious scholars, call me low-born; when they say this, they tarnish Your honor as well. |2|

You are called kind and compassionate; the power of Your Arm is absolutely unrivalled.

The Lord turned the temple around to face Naam Dayv; He turned His back on the Brahmins. |3|2|

Section 31 - Raag Malaar - Part 040

Malaar, The Word Of The Devotee Ravi Daas Jee:
One Universal Creator God. By The Grace Of The True Guru:
O humble townspeople, I am obviously just a shoemaker.
In my heart I cherish the Glories of the Lord, the Lord of the Universe. |1|Pause|

Even if wine is made from the water of the Ganges, O Saints, do not drink it.
This wine, and any other polluted water which mixes with the Ganges, is not separate from it. |1|

The palmyra palm tree is considered impure, and so its leaves are considered impure as well.
But if devotional prayers are written on paper made from its leaves, then people bow in reverence and worship before it. |2|

It is my occupation to prepare and cut leather; each day, I carry the carcasses out of the city.
Now, the important Brahmins of the city bow down before me; Ravi Daas, Your slave, seeks the Sanctuary of Your Name. |3|1|

MALAAR:
Those humble beings who meditate on the Lord's Lotus Feet - none are equal to them.
The Lord is One, but He is diffused in many forms. Bring in, bring in, that All-pervading Lord. |Pause|

He who writes the Praises of the Lord God, and sees nothing else at all, is a low-class, untouchable fabric-dyer by trade.
The Glory of the Name is seen in the writings of Vyaas and Sanak, throughout the seven continents. |1|

And he whose family used to kill cows at the festivals of Eed and Bakareed, who worshipped Shayks, martyrs and spiritual teachers,

whose father used to do such things - his son Kabeer became so successful that he is now famous throughout the three worlds. |2|

And all the leather-workers in those families still go around Benares removing the dead cattle
- the ritualistic Brahmins bow in reverence before their son Ravi Daas, the slave of the Lord's slaves. |3|2|

Malaar:
One Universal Creator God. By The Grace Of The True Guru:
What sort of devotional worship will lead me to meet my Beloved, the Lord of my breath of life?
In the Saadh Sangat, the Company of the Holy, I have obtained the supreme status. |Pause|

How long shall I wash these dirty clothes?
How long shall I remain asleep? |1|

Whatever I was attached to, has perished.
The shop of false merchandise has closed down. |2|

Says Ravi Daas, when the account is called for and given,
whatever the mortal has done, he shall see. |3|1|3|

RAAG KAANRAA

Section 32 - Raag Kaanraa - Part 001

Raag Kaanraa, Chau-Padas, Fourth Mehl, First House:
ONE Universal Creator God. Truth Is The Name. Creative Being Personified.
No Fear. No Hatred. Image Of The Undying. Beyond Birth. Self-Existent. By
Guru's Grace:
Meeting with the Holy people, my mind blossoms forth.
I am a sacrifice, a sacrifice, a sacrifice, a sacrifice to those Holy beings;
joining the Sangat, the Congregation, I am carried across to the other side.
|1|Pause|

O Lord, Har, Har, please bless me with Your Mercy, God, that I may fall at
the feet of the Holy.
Blessed, blessed are the Holy, who know the Lord God. Meeting with the
Holy, even sinners are saved. |1|

The mind roams and rambles all around in all directions. Meeting with the
Holy, it is overpowered and brought under control,

just as when the fisherman spreads his net over the water, he catches and
overpowers the fish. |2|

The Saints, the Saints of the Lord, are noble and good. Meeting with the
humble Saints, filth is washed away.
All the sins and egotism are washed away, like soap washing dirty clothes.
|3|

According to that pre-ordained destiny inscribed on my forehead by my
Lord and Master, I have enshrined the Feet of the Guru, the True Guru,
within my heart.
I have found God, the Destroyer of all poverty and pain; servant Nanak is
saved through the Naam. |4|1|

Kaanraa, Fourth Mehl:
My mind is the dust of the feet of the Saints.

Joining the Sangat, the Congregation, I listen to the sermon of the Lord, Har, Har. My crude and uncultured mind is drenched with the Love of the Lord. |1|Pause|

I am thoughtless and unconscious; I do not know God's state and extent. The Guru has made me thoughtful and conscious.
God is Merciful to the meek; He has made me His Own. My mind chants and meditates on the Name of the Lord, Har, Har. |1|

Meeting with the Lord's Saints, the Beloveds of the mind, I would cut out my heart, and offer it to them.
Meeting with the Lord's Saints, I meet with the Lord; this sinner has been sanctified. |2|

The humble servants of the Lord are said to be exalted in this world; meeting with them, even stones are softened.

Section 32 - Raag Kaanraa - Part 002

I cannot even describe the noble grandeur of such humble beings; the Lord, Har, Har, has made them sublime and exalted. |3|

You, Lord are the Great Merchant-Banker; O God, my Lord and Master, I am just a poor peddler; please bless me with the wealth.
Please bestow Your Kindness and Mercy upon servant Nanak, God, so that he may load up the merchandise of the Lord, Har, Har. |4|2|

Kaanraa, Fourth Mehl:
O mind, chant the Name of the Lord, and be enlightened.
Meet with the Saints of the Lord, and focus your love; remain balanced and detached within your own household. |1|Pause|

I chant the Name of the Lord, Nar-Har, within my heart; God the Merciful has shown His Mercy.
Night and day, I am in ecstasy; my mind has blossomed forth, rejuvenated. I am trying - I hope to meet my Lord. |1|

I am in love with the Lord, my Lord and Master; I love Him with every breath and morsel of food I take.

My sins were burnt away in an instant; the noose of the bondage of Maya was loosened. |2|

I am such a worm! What karma am I creating? What can I do? I am a fool, a total idiot, but God has saved me.
I am unworthy, heavy as stone, but joining the Sat Sangat, the True Congregation, I am carried across to the other side. |3|

The Universe which God created is all above me; I am the lowest, en-grossed in corruption.
With the Guru, my faults and demerits have been erased. Servant Nanak has been united with God Himself. |4|3|

Kaanraa, Fourth Mehl:
O my mind, chant the Name of the Lord, through the Guru's Word.
The Lord, Har, Har, has shown me His Mercy, and my evil-mindedness, love of duality and sense of alienation are totally gone, thanks to the Lord of the Universe. |1|Pause|

There are so many forms and colors of the Lord. The Lord is pervading each and every heart, and yet He is hidden from view.
Meeting with the Lord's Saints, the Lord is revealed, and the doors of corruption are shattered. |1|

The glory of the Saintly beings is absolutely great; they lovingly enshrine the Lord of Bliss and Delight within their hearts.
Meeting with the Lord's Saints, I meet with the Lord, just as when the calf is seen - the cow is there as well. |2|

The Lord, Har, Har, is within the humble Saints of the Lord; they are exalted - they know, and they inspire others to know as well.
The fragrance of the Lord permeates their hearts; they have abandoned the foul stench. |3|

You make those humble beings Your Own, God; You protect Your Own, O Lord.
The Lord is servant Nanak's companion; the Lord is his sibling, mother, father, relative and relation. |4|4|

Kaanraa, Fourth Mehl:

O my mind, consciously chant the Name of the Lord, Har, Har.
The commodity of the Lord, Har, Har, is locked in the fortress of Maya; through the Word of the Guru's Shabad, I have conquered the fortress. |1|Pause|

In false doubt and superstition, people wander all around, lured by love and emotional attachment to their children and families.
But just like the passing shade of the tree, your body-wall shall crumble in an instant. |1|

The humble beings are exalted; they are my breath of life and my beloveds; meeting them, my mind is filled with faith.
Deep within the heart, I am happy with the Pervading Lord; with love and joy, I dwell upon the Steady and Stable Lord. |2|

Section 32 - Raag Kaanraa - Part 003

The humble Saints, the Saints of the Lord, are noble and sublime; meeting them, the mind is tinged with love and joy.
The Lord's Love never fades away, and it never wears off. Through the Lord's Love, one goes and meets the Lord, Har, Har. |3|

I am a sinner; I have committed so many sins. The Guru has cut them, cut them, and hacked them off.
The Guru has placed the healing remedy of the Name of the Lord, Har, Har, into my mouth. Servant Nanak, the sinner, has been purified and sanctified. |4|5|

Kaanraa, Fourth Mehl:
Chant, O my mind, the Name of the Lord, the Lord of the Universe.
I was caught in the whirlpool of poisonous sin and corruption. The True Guru gave me His Hand; He lifted me up and pulled me out. |1|Pause|

O my Fearless, Immaculate Lord and Master, please save me - I am a sinner, a sinking stone.
I am lured and enticed by sexual desire, anger, greed and corruption, but associating with You, I am carried across, like iron in the wooden boat. |1|

You are the Great Primal Being, the most Inaccessible and Unfathomable Lord God; I search for You, but cannot find Your depth

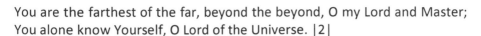

You are the farthest of the far, beyond the beyond, O my Lord and Master; You alone know Yourself, O Lord of the Universe. |2|

I meditate on the Name of the Unseen and Unfathomable Lord; joining the Sat Sangat, the True Congregation, I have found the Path of the Holy.
Joining the congregation, I listen to the Gospel of the Lord, Har, Har; I meditate on the Lord, Har, Har, and speak the Unspoken Speech. |3|

My God is the Lord of the World, the Lord of the Universe; please save me, O Lord of all Creation.
Servant Nanak is the slave of the slave of Your slaves. O God, please bless me with Your Grace; please protect me and keep me with Your humble servants. |4|6|

Kaanraa, Fourth Mehl, Partaal, Fifth House:
One Universal Creator God. By The Grace Of The True Guru:
O mind, meditate on the Lord, the Lord of the World.
The Lord is the Jewel, the Diamond, the Ruby.
The Lord fashions the Gurmukhs in His Mint.
O Lord, please, please, be Merciful to me. |1|Pause|

Your Glorious Virtues are inaccessible and unfathomable; how can my one poor tongue describe them? O my Beloved Lord, Raam, Raam, Raam, Raam.
O Dear Lord, You, You, You alone know Your Unspoken Speech. I have become enraptured, enraptured, enraptured, meditating on the Lord. |1|

The Lord, my Lord and Master, is my Companion and my Breath of Life; the Lord is my Best Friend. My mind, body and tongue are attuned to the Lord, Har, Haray, Haray. The Lord is my Wealth and Property.
She alone obtains her Husband Lord, who is so pre-destined. Through the Guru's Teachings, she sings the Glorious Praises of the Lord, Har, Har, Haray, Haray. I am a sacrifice, a sacrifice, I am a sacrifice, a sacrifice to the Lord, O servan

Kaanraa, Fourth Mehl:
Sing the Glorious Praises of the Lord, the Lord of the Universe.
Let my one tongue become two hundred thousand
- with them all, I will meditate on the Lord, Har, Har, and chant the Word of the Shabad.

O Lord, please, please, be Merciful to me. |1|Pause|

O Lord, my Lord and Master, please be Merciful to me; please enjoin me to serve You. I chant and meditate on the Lord, I chant and meditate on the Lord, I chant and meditate on the Lord of the Universe.
Your humble servants chant and meditate on You, O Lord; they are sublime and exalted. I am a sacrifice, a sacrifice, a sacrifice, a sacrifice to them. |1|

Section 32 - Raag Kaanraa - Part 004

O Lord, You are the Greatest of the Great, the Greatest of the Great, the most Lofty and High. You do whatever You please.
Servant Nanak drinks in the Ambrosial Nectar through the Guru's Teachings. Blessed, blessed, blessed, blessed, blessed and praised is the Guru. |2|2|8|

Kaanraa, Fourth Mehl:
O mind, meditate and vibrate on the Lord, Raam, Raam.
He has no form or feature - He is Great!
Joining the Sat Sangat, the True Congregation, vibrate and meditate on the Lord.
This is the high destiny written on your forehead. |1|Pause|

That household, that mansion, in which the Lord's Praises are sung - that home is filled with ecstasy and joy; so vibrate and meditate on the Lord, Raam, Raam, Raam.
Sing the Glorious Praises of the Name of the Lord, the Beloved Lord. Through the Teachings of the Guru, the Guru, the True Guru, you shall find peace. So vibrate and meditate on the Lord, Har, Haray, Har, Haray, Haray, the Lord, Raam, Raam,

You are the Support of the whole universe, Lord; O Merciful Lord, You, You, You are the Creator of all, Raam, Raam, Raam.
Servant Nanak seeks Your Sanctuary; please bless him with the Guru's Teachings, that he may vibrate and meditate on the Lord, Raam, Raam, Raam. |2|3|9|

Kaanraa, Fourth Mehl:
I eagerly kiss the Feet of the True Guru.
Meeting Him, the Path to the Lord becomes smooth and easy.

I lovingly vibrate and meditate on the Lord, and gulp down His Sublime Essence.

The Lord has written this destiny on my forehead. |1|Pause|

Some perform the six rituals and rites; the Siddhas, seekers and Yogis put on all sorts of pompous shows, with their hair all tangled and matted.

Yoga - Union with the Lord God - is not obtained by wearing religious robes; the Lord is found in the Sat Sangat, the True Congregation, and the Guru's Teachings. The humble Saints throw the doors wide open. |1|

O my Lord and Master, You are the farthest of the far, utterly unfathomable. You are totally pervading the water and the land. You alone are the One and Only Unique Lord of all creation.

You alone know all Your ways and means. You alone understand Yourself. Servant Nanak's Lord God is in each heart, in every heart, in the home of each and every heart. |2|4|10|

Kaanraa, Fourth Mehl:

O mind, chant and meditate on the Lord, the Lord of the Universe.

The Lord, Har, Har, is inaccessible and unfathomable.

Through the Guru's Teachings, my intellect attains the Lord God.

This is the pre-ordained destiny written on my forehead. |1|Pause|

Collecting the poison of Maya, people think of all sorts of evil. But peace is found only by vibrating and meditating on the Lord; with the Saints, in the Sangat, the Society of the Saints, meet the True Guru, the Holy Guru.

Just as when the iron slag is transmuted into gold by touching the Philosopher's Stone - when the sinner joins the Sangat, he becomes pure, through the Guru's Teachings. |1|

Just like the heavy iron which is carried across on the wooden raft, sinners are carried across in the Saadh Sangat, the Company of the Holy, and the Guru, the True Guru, the Holy Guru.

There are four castes, four social classes, and four stages of life. Whoever meets the Guru, Guru Nanak, is himself carried across, and he carries all his ancestors and generations across as well. |2|5|11|

Kaanraa, Fourth Mehl:

Sing the Praises of the Lord God.

Singing His Praises, sins are washed away.

Through the Word of the Guru's Teachings, listen to His Praises with your ears.
The Lord shall be Merciful to you. |1|Pause|

Section 32 - Raag Kaanraa - Part 005

Your humble servants focus their consciousness and meditate on You with one-pointed mind; those Holy beings find peace, chanting the Name of the Lord, Har, Har, the Treasure of Bliss.
They sing Your Praises, God, meeting with the Holy, the Holy people, and the Guru, the True Guru, O Lord God. |1|

They alone obtain the fruit of peace, within whose hearts You, O my Lord and Master, abide. They cross over the terrifying world-ocean - they are known as the Lord's devotees.
Please enjoin me to their service, Lord, please enjoin me to their service. O Lord God, You, You, You, You, You are the Lord of servant Nanak. |2|6|12|

Kaanraa, Fifth Mehl, Second House:
One Universal Creator God. By The Grace Of The True Guru:
Sing the Glorious Praises of the Lord of the World, the Treasure of Mercy.
The True Guru is the Destroyer of pain, the Giver of peace; meeting Him, one is totally fulfilled. |1|Pause|

Meditate in remembrance on the Naam, the Support of the mind.
Millions of sinners are carried across in an instant. |1|

Whoever remembers his Guru,
shall not suffer sorrow, even in dreams. |2|

Whoever keeps his Guru enshrined within
- that humble being tastes the sublime essence of the Lord with his tongue. |3|

Says Nanak, the Guru has been Kind to me;
here and herafter, my face is radiant. |4|1|

Kaanraa, Fifth Mehl:
I worship and adore You, my Lord and Master.

Standing up and sitting down, while sleeping and awake, with each and every breath, I meditate on the Lord. |1|Pause|

The Naam, the Name of the Lord, abides within the hearts of those, whose Lord and Master blesses them with this gift. |1|

Peace and tranquility come into the hearts of those who meet their Lord and Master, through the Word of the Guru. |2|

Those whom the Guru blesses with the Mantra of the Naam are wise, and blessed with all powers,. |3|

Says Nanak, I am a sacrifice to those who are blessed with the Name in this Dark Age of Kali Yuga. |4|2|

Kaanraa, Fifth Mehl:
Sing the Praises of God, O my tongue.
Humbly bow to the Saints, over and over again; through them, the Feet of the Lord of the Universe shall come to abide within you. |1|Pause|

The Door to the Lord cannot be found by any other means.
When He becomes Merciful, we come to meditate on the Lord, Har, Har. |1|

The body is not purified by millions of rituals.
The mind is awakened and enlightened only in the Saadh Sangat, the Company of the Holy. |2|

Thirst and desire are not quenched by enjoying the many pleasures of Maya.
Chanting the Naam, the Name of the Lord, total peace is found. |3|

When the Supreme Lord God becomes Merciful,
says Nanak, then one is rid of worldly entanglements. |4|3|

Kaanraa, Fifth Mehl:
Beg for such blessings from the Lord of the Universe:
to work for the Saints, and the Saadh Sangat, the Company of the Holy.
Chanting the Name of the Lord, the supreme status is obtained. |1|Pause|

Worship the Feet of Your Lord and Master, and seek His Sanctuary.
Take joy in whatever God does. |1|

This precious human body becomes fruitful,

Section 32 - Raag Kaanraa - Part 006

when the True Guru shows His Kindness. |2|

The house of ignorance, doubt and pain is destroyed,
for those within whose hearts the Guru's Feet abide. |3|

In the Saadh Sangat, lovingly meditate on God.
Says Nanak, you shall obtain the Perfect Lord. |4|4|

Kaanraa, Fifth Mehl:
Devotion is the natural quality of God's devotees.
Their bodies and minds are blended with their Lord and Master; He unites them with Himself. |1|Pause|

The singer sings the songs,
but she alone is saved, within whose consciousness the Lord abides. |1|

The one who sets the table sees the food,
but only one who eats the food is satisfied. |2|

People disguise themselves with all sorts of costumes,
but in the end, they are seen as they truly are. |3|

Speaking and talking are all just entanglements.
O slave Nanak, the true way of life is excellent. |4|5|

Kaanraa, Fifth Mehl:
Your humble servant listens to Your Praises with delight. |1|Pause|

My mind is enlightened, gazing upon the Glory of God. Wherever I look, there He is. |1|

You are the farthest of all, the highest of the far, profound, unfathomable and unreachable. |2|

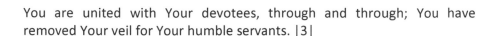

You are united with Your devotees, through and through; You have removed Your veil for Your humble servants. |3|

By Guru's Grace, Nanak sings Your Glorious Praises; he is intuitively absorbed in Samaadhi. |4|6|

Kaanraa, Fifth Mehl:
I have come to the Saints to save myself. |1|Pause|

Gazing upon the Blessed Vision of their Darshan, I am sanctified; they have implanted the Mantra of the Lord, Har, Har, within me. |1|

The disease has been eradicated, and my mind has become immaculate. I have taken the healing medicine of the Lord, Har, Har. |2|

I have become steady and stable, and I dwell in the home of peace. I shall never again wander anywhere. |3|

By the Grace of the Saints, the people and all their generations are saved; O Nanak, they are not engrossed in Maya. |4|7|

Kaanraa, Fifth Mehl:
I have totally forgotten my jealousy of others,
since I found the Saadh Sangat, the Company of the Holy. |1|Pause|

No one is my enemy, and no one is a stranger. I get along with everyone. |1|

Whatever God does, I accept that as good. This is the sublime wisdom I have obtained from the Holy. |2|

The One God is pervading in all. Gazing upon Him, beholding Him, Nanak blossoms forth in happiness. |3|8|

Kaanraa, Fifth Mehl:
O my Dear Lord and Master, You alone are my Support.
You are my Honor and Glory; I seek Your Support, and Your Sanctuary. |1|Pause|

You are my Hope, and You are my Faith. I take Your Name and enshrine it within my heart.
You are my Power; associating with You, I am embellished and exalted. I do whatever You say. |1|

Through Your Kindness and Compassion, I find peace; when You are Merciful, I cross over the terrifying world-ocean.
Through the Name of the Lord, I obtain the gift of fearlessness; Nanak places his head on the feet of the Saints. |2|9|

Section 32 - Raag Kaanraa - Part 007

Kaanraa, Fifth Mehl:
In the Sanctuary of the Holy, I focus my consciousness on the Lord's Feet.
When I was dreaming, I heard and saw only dream-objects. The True Guru has implanted the Mantra of the Naam, the Name of the Lord, within me. |1|Pause|

Power, youth and wealth do not bring satisfaction; people chase after them again and again.
I have found peace and tranquility, and all my thirsty desires have been quenched, singing His Glorious Praises. |1|

Without understanding, they are like beasts, engrossed in doubt, emotional attachment and Maya.
But in the Saadh Sangat, the Company of the Holy, the noose of Death is cut, O Nanak, and one intuitively merges in celestial peace. |2|10|

Kaanraa, Fifth Mehl:
Sing of the Lord's Feet within your heart.
Meditate, meditate in constant remembrance on God, the Embodiment of soothing peace and cooling tranquility. |1|Pause|

All your hopes shall be fulfilled, and the pain of millions of deaths and births shall be gone. |1|

Immerse yourself in the Saadh Sangat, the Company of the Holy, and you shall obtain the benefits of giving charitable gifts, and all sorts of good deeds.

Sorrow and suffering shall be erased, O Nanak, and you shall never again be devoured by death. |2|11|

Kaanraa, Fifth Mehl, Third House:
One Universal Creator God. By The Grace Of The True Guru:
Speak of God's Wisdom in the Sat Sangat, the True Congregation.
Meditating in remembrance on the Perfect Supreme Divine Light, the Transcendent Lord God, honor and glory are obtained. |1|Pause|

One's comings and goings in reincarnation cease, and suffering is dispelled, meditating in remembrance in the Saadh Sangat, the Company of the Holy.
Sinners are sanctified in an instant, in the love of the Supreme Lord God. |1|

Whoever speaks and listens to the Kirtan of the Lord's Praises is rid of evil-mindedness.
All hopes and desires, O Nanak, are fulfilled. |2|1|12|

Kaanraa, Fifth Mehl:
The Treasure of the Naam, the Name of the Lord, is found in the Saadh Sangat, the Company of the Holy.
It is the Companion of the soul, its Helper and Support. |1|Pause|

Continually bathing in the dust of the feet of the Saints,
the sins of countless incarnations are washed away. |1|

The words of the humble Saints are lofty and exalted.
Meditating, meditating in remembrance, O Nanak, mortal beings are carried across and saved. |2|2|13|

Kaanraa, Fifth Mehl:
O Holy people, sing the Glorious Praises of the Lord, Har, Haray.
Mind, body, wealth and the breath of life - all come from God; remembering Him in meditation, pain is taken away. |1|Pause|

Why are you entangled in this and that? Let your mind be attuned to the One. |1|

The place of the Saints is utterly sacred; meet with them, and meditate on the Lord of the Universe. |2|

O Nanak, I have abandoned everything and come to Your Sanctuary. Please let me merge with You. |3|3|14|

Kaanraa, Fifth Mehl:
Gazing upon and beholding my Best Friend, I blossom forth in bliss; my God is the One and Only. |1|Pause|

He is the Image of Ecstasy, Intuitive Peace and Poise. There is no other like Him. |1|

Meditating in remembrance on the Lord, Har, Har, even once, millions of sins are erased. |2|

Section 32 - Raag Kaanraa - Part 008

Uttering His Glorious Praises, suffering is eradicated, and the heart becomes tranquil and calm. |3|

Drink in the Sweet, Sublime Ambrosial Nectar, O Nanak, and be imbued with the Love of the Lord. |4|4|15|

Kaanraa, Fifth Mehl:
O friends, O Saints, come to me. |1|Pause|

Singing the Glorious Praises of the Lord with pleasure and joy, the sins will be erased and thrown away. |1|

Touch your forehead to the feet of the Saints, and your dark household shall be illumined. |2|

By the Grace of the Saints, the heart-lotus blossoms forth. Vibrate and meditate on the Lord of the Universe, and see Him near at hand. |3|

By the Grace of God, I have found the Saints. Over and over again, Nanak is a sacrifice to that moment. |4|5|16|

Kaanraa, Fifth Mehl:
I seek the Sanctuary of Your Lotus Feet, O Lord of the World.

Save me from emotional attachment, pride, deception and doubt; please cut away these ropes which bind me. |1|Pause|

I am drowning in the world-ocean.
Meditating in remembrance on the Lord, the Source of Jewels, I am saved. |1|

Your Name, Lord, is cooling and soothing.
God, my Lord and Master, is Perfect. |2|

You are the Deliverer, the Destroyer of the sufferings of the meek and the poor.
The Lord is the Treasure of Mercy, the Saving Grace of sinners. |3|

I have suffered the pains of millions of incarnations.
Nanak is at peace; the Guru has implanted the Naam, the Name of the Lord, within me. |4|6|17|

Kaanraa, Fifth Mehl:
Blessed is that love, which is attuned to the Lord's Feet.
The peace which comes from millions of chants and deep meditations is obtained by perfect good fortune and destiny. |1|Pause|

I am Your helpless servant and slave; I have given up all other support.
Every trace of doubt has been eradicated, remembering God in meditation.
I have applied the ointment of spiritual wisdom, and awakened from my sleep. |1|

You are Unfathomably Great and Utterly Vast, O my Lord and Master, Ocean of Mercy, Source of Jewels.
Nanak, the beggar, begs for the Name of the Lord, Har, Har; he rests his forehead upon God's Feet. |2|7|18|

Kaanraa, Fifth Mehl:
I am filthy, hard-hearted, deceitful and obsessed with sexual desire.
Please carry me across, as You wish, O my Lord and Master. |1|Pause|

You are All-powerful and Potent to grant Sanctuary. Exerting Your Power, You protect us. |1|

Chanting and deep meditation, penance and austere self-discipline, fasting and purification - salvation does not come by any of these means.
Please lift me up and out of this deep, dark ditch; O God, please bless Nanak with Your Glance of Grace. |2|8|19|

Kaanraa, Fifth Mehl, Fourth House:
One Universal Creator God. By The Grace Of The True Guru:
The one who bows in humble reverence to the Primal Lord, the Lord of all beings
- I am a sacrifice, a sacrifice to such a Guru; He Himself is liberated, and He carries me across as well. |1|Pause|

Which, which, which of Your Glorious Virtues should I chant? There is no end or limitation to them.
There are thousands, tens of thousands, hundreds of thousands, many millions of them, but those who contemplate them are very rare. |1|

Section 32 - Raag Kaanraa - Part 009

I am wonder-struck, wonder-struck, wonder-struck and amazed, dyed in the deep crimson color of my Beloved.
Says Nanak, the Saints savor this sublime essence, like the mute, who tastes the sweet candy, but only smiles. |2|1|20|

Kaanraa, Fifth Mehl:
The Saints do not know any other except God.
They look upon all equally, the high and the low; they speak of Him with their mouths, and honor Him in their minds. |1|Pause|

He is pervading and permeating each and every heart; He is the Ocean of Peace, the Destroyer of fear. He is my praanaa - the Breath of Life.
My mind was enlightened, and my doubt was dispelled, when the Guru whispered His Mantra into my ears. |1|

He is All-powerful, the Ocean of Mercy, the All-knowing Searcher of Hearts.
Twenty-four hours a day Nanak sings His Praises, and begs for the Gift of the Lord. |2|2|21|

Kaanraa, Fifth Mehl:
Many speak and talk about God.

But one who understands the essence of Yoga - such a humble servant is very rare |1|Pause|

He has no pain - he is totally at peace. With his eyes, he sees only the One Lord.
No one seems evil to him - all are good. There is no defeat - he is totally victorious. |1|

He is never in sorrow - he is always happy; but he gives this up, and does not take anything.
Says Nanak, the humble servant of the Lord is himself the Lord, Har, Har; he does not come and go in reincarnation. |2|3|22|

Kaanraa, Fifth Mehl:
I pray that my heart may never forget my Beloved.
My body and mind are blended with Him, but the Enticer, Maya, is enticing me, O my mother. |1|Pause|

Those unto whom I tell my pain and frustration - they themselves are caught and stuck.
In all sorts of ways, Maya has cast the net; the knots cannot be loosened. |1|

Wandering and roaming, slave Nanak has come to the Sanctuary of the Saints.
The bonds of ignorance, doubt, emotional attachment and the love of Maya have been cut; God hugs me close in His Embrace. |2|4|23|

Kaanraa, Fifth Mehl:
My home is filled with ecstasy, pleasure and joy.
I sing the Naam, and I meditate on the Naam. The Naam is the Support of my breath of life. |1|Pause|

The Naam is spiritual wisdom, the Naam is my purifying bath. The Naam resolves all my affairs.
The Naam, the Name of the Lord, is glorious grandeur; the Naam is glorious greatness. The Name of the Lord carries me across the terrifying world-ocean. |1|

The Unfathomable Treasure, the Priceless Gem - I have received it, through the Guru's Feet.
Says Nanak, God has become Merciful; my heart is intoxicated by the Blessed Vision of His Darshan. |2|5|24|

Kaanraa, Fifth Mehl:
My Friend, my Best Friend, my Lord and Master, is near.
He sees and hears everything; He is with everyone. You are here for such short time - why do you do evil? |1|Pause|

Except for the Naam, whatever you are involved with is nothing - nothing is yours.
Hereafter, everything is revealed to your gaze; but in this world, all are enticed by the darkness of doubt. |1|

People are caught in Maya, attached to their children and spouses. They have forgotten the Great and Generous Giver.

Section 32 - Raag Kaanraa - Part 010

Says Nanak, I have one article of faith; my Guru is the One who releases me from bondage. |2|6|25|

Kaanraa, Fifth Mehl:
Your Saints have overwhelmed the wicked army of corruption.
They take Your Support and place their faith in You, O my Lord and Master; they seek Your Sanctuary. |1|Pause|

Gazing upon the Blessed Vision of Your Darshan, the terrible sins of countless lifetimes are erased.
I am illumined, enlightened and filled with ecstasy. I am intuitively absorbed in Samaadhi. |1|

Who says that You cannot do everything? You are Infinitely All-powerful.
O Treasure of Mercy, Nanak savors Your Love and Your Blissful Form, earning the Profit of the Naam, the Name of the Lord. |2|7|26|

Kaanraa, Fifth Mehl:
The drowning mortal is comforted and consoled, meditating on the Lord.
He is rid of emotional attachment, doubt, pain and suffering. |1|Pause|

I meditate in remembrance, day and night, on the Guru's Feet.
Wherever I look, I see Your Sanctuary. |1|

By the Grace of the Saints, I sing the Glorious Praises of the Lord.
Meeting with the Guru, Nanak has found peace. |2|8|27|

Kaanraa, Fifth Mehl:
Meditating in remembrance on the Naam, peace of mind is found.
Meeting the Holy Saint, sing the Praises of the Lord. |1|Pause|

Granting His Grace, God has come to dwell within my heart.
I touch my forehead to the feet of the Saints. |1|

Meditate, O my mind, on the Supreme Lord God.
As Gurmukh, Nanak listens to the Praises of the Lord. |2|9|28|

Kaanraa, Fifth Mehl:
My mind loves to touch the Feet of God.
My tongue is satisfied with the Food of the Lord, Har, Har. My eyes are contented with the Blessed Vision of God. |1|Pause|

My ears are filled with the Praise of my Beloved; all my foul sins and faults are erased.
My feet follow the Path of Peace to my Lord and Master; my body and limbs joyfully blossom forth in the Society of the Saints. |1|

I have taken Sanctuary in my Perfect, Eternal, Imperishable Lord. I do not bother trying anything else.
Taking them by the hand, O Nanak, God saves His humble servants; they shall not perish in the deep, dark world-ocean. |2|10|29|

Kaanraa, Fifth Mehl:
Those fools who bellow with rage and destructive deceit, are crushed and killed innumerable times. |1|Pause|

Intoxicated with egotism and imbued with other tastes, I am in love with my evil enemies. My Beloved watches over me as I wander through thousands of incarnations. |1|

My dealings are false, and my lifestyle is chaotic. Intoxicated with the wine of emotion, I am burning in the fire of anger.
O Merciful Lord of the World, Embodiment of Compassion, Relative of the meek and the poor, please save Nanak; I seek Your Sanctuary. |2|11|30|

Kaanraa, Fifth Mehl:
The Giver of the soul, the breath of life and honor
- forgetting the Lord, all is lost. |1|Pause|

You have forsaken the Lord of the Universe, and become attached to another - you are throwing away the Ambrosial Nectar, to take dust.
What do you expect from corrupt pleasures? You fool! What makes you think that they will bring peace? |1|

Section 32 - Raag Kaanraa - Part 011

Engrossed in unfulfilled sexual desire, unresolved anger and greed, you shall be consigned to reincarnation.
But I have entered the Sanctuary of the Purifier of sinners. O Nanak, I know that I shall be saved. |2|12|31|

Kaanraa, Fifth Mehl:
I gaze on the Lotus-like Face of the Lord.
Searching and seeking, I have found the Jewel. I am totally rid of all anxiety. |1|Pause|

Enshrining His Lotus Feet within my heart,
pain and wickedness have been dispelled. |1|

The Lord of all the Universe is my kingdom, wealth and family.
In the Saadh Sangat, the Company of the Holy, Nanak has earned the Profit; he shall never die again. |2|13|32|

Kaanraa, Fifth Mehl, Fifth House:
One Universal Creator God. By The Grace Of The True Guru:
Worship God, and adore His Name.
Grasp the Feet of the Guru, the True Guru.
The Unfathomable Lord shall come into your mind,
and by Guru's Grace, you shall be victorious in this world. |1|Pause|

I have studied countless ways of worship in all sorts of ways, but that alone is worship, which is pleasing to the Lord's Will.
This body-puppet is made of clay - what can it do by itself?
O God, those humble beings meet You, whom You grasp by the arm, and place on the Path. |1|

I do not know of any other support; O Lord, You are my only Hope and Support.
I am meek and poor - what prayer can I offer?
God abides in every heart.
My mind is thirsty for the Feet of God.
Servant Nanak, Your slave, speaks: I am a sacrifice, a sacrifice, forever a sacrifice to You. |2|1|33|

Kaanraa, Fifth Mehl, Sixth House:
One Universal Creator God. By The Grace Of The True Guru:
Your Name, O my Beloved, is the Saving Grace of the world.
The Lord's Name is the wealth of the nine treasures.
One who is imbued with the Love of the Incomparably Beautiful Lord is joyful.
O mind, why do you cling to emotional attachments?
With your eyes, gaze upon the Blessed Vision, the Darshan of the Holy.
They alone find it, who have such destiny inscribed upon their foreheads. |1|Pause|

I serve at the feet of the Holy Saints.
I long for the dust of their feet, which purifies and sanctifies.
Just like the sixty-eight sacred shrines of pilgrimage, it washes away filth and pollution.
With each and every breath I meditate on Him, and never turn my face away.
Of your thousands and millions, nothing shall go along with you.
Only the Name of God will call to you in the end. |1|

Let it be your wish to honor and obey the One Formless Lord.
Abandon the love of everything else.
What Glorious Praises of Yours can I utter, O my Beloved?
I cannot describe even one of Your Virtues.
My mind is so thirsty for the Blessed Vision of His Darshan.
Please come and meet Nanak, O Divine Guru of the World. |2|1|34|

Section 32 - Raag Kaanraa - Part 012

Kaanraa, Fifth Mehl:
How may I obtain the Blessed Vision of Your Darshan? |1|Pause|

I hope and thirst for Your wish-fulfilling image; my heart yearns and longs for You. |1|

The meek and humble Saints are like thirsty fish; the Saints of the Lord are absorbed in Him.
I am the dust of the feet of the Lord's Saints.
I dedicate my heart to them.
God has become Merciful to me.
Renouncing pride and leaving behind emotional attachment, O Nanak, one meets with the Dear Lord. |2|2|35|

Kaanraa, Fifth Mehl:
The Playful Lord imbues all with the Color of His Love.
From the ant to the elephant, He is permeating and pervading all. |1|Pause|

Some go on fasts, make vows, and take pilgrimages to sacred shrines on the Ganges.
They stand naked in the water, enduring hunger and poverty.
They sit cross-legged, perform worship services and do good deeds.
They apply religious symbols to their bodies, and ceremonial marks to their limbs.
They read through the Shaastras, but they do not join the Sat Sangat, the True Congregation. |1|

They stubbornly practice ritualistic postures, standing on their heads.
They are afflicted with the disease of egotism, and their faults are not covered up.
They burn in the fire of sexual frustration, unresolved anger and compulsive desire.
He alone is liberated, O Nanak, whose True Guru is Good. |2|3|36|

Kaanraa, Fifth Mehl, Seventh House:
One Universal Creator God. By The Grace Of The True Guru.

My thirst has been quenched, meeting with the Holy.
The five thieves have run away, and I am in peace and poise; singing, singing, singing the Glorious Praises of the Lord, I obtain the Blessed Vision of my Beloved. |1|Pause|

That which God has done for me - how can I do that for Him in return?
I make my heart a sacrifice, a sacrifice, a sacrifice, a sacrifice, a sacrifice to You. |1|

First, I fall at the feet of the Saints; I meditate, meditate, lovingly attuned to You.
O God, where is that Place, where You contemplate all Your beings?
Countless slaves sing Your Praises.
He alone meets You, who is pleasing to Your Will. Servant Nanak remains absorbed in his Lord and Master.
You, You, You alone, Lord. |2|1|37|

Kaanraa, Fifth Mehl, Eighth House:
One Universal Creator God. By The Grace Of The True Guru:
Give up your pride and your self-conceit; the Loving, Merciful Lord is watching over all. O mind, become the dust of His Feet. |1|Pause|

Through the Mantra of the Lord's Saints, experience the spiritual wisdom and meditation of the Lord of the World. |1|

Within your heart, sing the Praises of the Lord of the Universe, and be lovingly attuned to His Lotus Feet. He is the Fascinating Lord, Merciful to the meek and the humble.
O Merciful Lord, please bless me with Your Kindness and Compassion.
Nanak begs for the Gift of the Naam, the Name of the Lord.
I have abandoned emotional attachment, doubt and all egotistical pride. |2|1|38|

Kaanraa, Fifth Mehl:
Speaking of God, filth and pollution are burnt away; This comes by meeting with the Guru, and not by any other efforts. |1|Pause|

Section 32 - Raag Kaanraa - Part 013

Making pilgrimages to sacred rivers, observing the six rituals, wearing matted and tangled hair, performing fire sacrifices and carrying ceremonial walking sticks - none of these are of any use. |1|

All sorts of efforts, austerities, wanderings and various speeches - none of these will lead you to find the Lord's Place.
I have considered all considerations, O Nanak, but peace comes only by vibrating and meditating on the Name. |2|2|39|

Kaanraa, Fifth Mehl, Ninth House:
One Universal Creator God. By The Grace Of The True Guru:
The Purifier of sinners, the Lover of His devotees, the Destroyer of fear - He carries us across to the other side. |1|Pause|

My eyes are satisfied, gazing upon the Blessed Vision of His Darshan; my ears are satisfied, hearing His Praise. |1|

He is the Master of the praanaa, the breath of life; He is the Giver of Support to the unsupported. I am meek and poor - I seek the Sanctuary of the Lord of the Universe.
He is the Fulfiller of hope, the Destroyer of pain. Nanak grasps the Support of the Feet of the Lord. |2|1|40|

Kaanraa, Fifth Mehl:
I seek the Sanctuary of the Feet of my Merciful Lord and Master; I do not go anywhere else.
It is the Inherent Nature of our Lord and Master to purify sinners. Those who meditate on the Lord are saved. |1|Pause|

The world is a swamp of wickedness and corruption. The blind sinner has fallen into the ocean of emotional attachment and pride,

bewildered by the entanglements of Maya.
God Himself has taken me by the hand and lifted me up and out of it; save me, O Sovereign Lord of the Universe. |1|

He is the Master of the masterless, the Supporting Lord of the Saints, the Neutralizer of millions of sins.
My mind thirsts for the Blessed Vision of His Darshan.
God is the Perfect Treasure of Virtue

O Nanak, sing and savor the Glorious Praises of the Lord, the Kind and Compassionate Lord of the World. |2|2|41|

Kaanraa, Fifth Mehl:
Countless times, I am a sacrifice, a sacrifice
to that moment of peace, on that night when I was joined with my Beloved. |1|Pause|

Mansions of gold, and beds of silk sheets - O sisters, I have no love for these. |1|

Pearls, jewels and countless pleasures, O Nanak, are useless and destructive without the Naam, the Name of the Lord.
Even with only dry crusts of bread, and a hard floor on which to sleep, my life passes in peace and pleasure with my Beloved, O sisters. |2|3|42|

Kaanraa, Fifth Mehl:
Give up your ego, and turn your face to God.
Let your yearning mind call out, "Guru, Guru".
My Beloved is the Lover of Love. |1|Pause|

The bed of your household shall be cozy, and your courtyard shall be comfortable; shatter and break the bonds which tie you to the five thieves. |1|

You shall not come and go in reincarnation; you shall dwell in your own home deep within, and your inverted heart-lotus shall blossom forth.
The turmoil of egotism shall be silenced.
Nanak sings - he sings the Praises of God, the Ocean of Virtue. |2|4|43|

Kaanraa, Fifth Mehl, Ninth House:
This is why you should chant and meditate on the Lord, O mind.
The Vedas and the Saints say that the path is treacherous and difficult. You are intoxicated with emotional attachment and the fever of egotism. |Pause|

Those who are imbued and intoxicated with the wretched Maya, suffer the pains of emotional attachment. |1|

That humble being is saved, who chants the Naam; You Yourself save him.

Emotional attachment, fear and doubt are dispelled, O Nanak, by the Grace of the Saints. |2|5|44|

Section 32 - Raag Kaanraa - Part 014

Kaanraa, Fifth Mehl, Tenth House:
One Universal Creator God. By The Grace Of The True Guru:
Give me that blessing, O Dear Saints, for which my soul would be a sacrifice.
Enticed by pride, entrapped and plundered by the five thieves, still, you live near them. I have come to the Sanctuary of the Holy, and I have been rescued from my association with those demons. |1|Pause|

I wandered through millions of lifetimes and incarnations. I am so very tired - I have fallen at God's Door. |1|

The Lord of the Universe has become Kind to me; He has blessed me with the Support of the Naam.
This precious human life has become fruitful and prosperous; O Nanak, I am carried across the terrifying world-ocean. |2|1|45|

Kaanraa, Fifth Mehl, Eleventh House:
One Universal Creator God. By The Grace Of The True Guru:
He Himself has come to me, in His Natural Way.
I know nothing, and I show nothing.
I have met God through innocent faith, and He has blessed me with peace. |1|Pause|

By the good fortune of my destiny, I have joined the Saadh Sangat, the Company of the Holy.
I do not go out anywhere; I dwell in my own home.
God, the Treasure of Virtue, has been revealed in this body-robe. |1|

I have fallen in love with His Feet; I have abandoned everything else.
In the places and interspaces, He is All-pervading.
With loving joy and excitement, Nanak speaks His Praises. |2|1|46|

Kaanraa, Fifth Mehl:
It is so hard to meet the Lord of the Universe, my Lord and Master.

His Form is Immeasurable, Inaccessible and Unfathomable; He is All-pervading everywhere. |1|Pause|

By speaking and wandering, nothing is gained; nothing is obtained by clever tricks and devices. |1|

People try all sorts of things, but the Lord is only met when He shows His Mercy.
God is Kind and Compassionate, the Treasure of Mercy; servant Nanak is the dust of the feet of the Saints. |2|2|47|

Kaanraa, Fifth Mehl:
O mother, I meditate on the Lord, Raam, Raam, Raam.
Without God, there is no other at all.
I remember His Lotus Feet with every breath, night and day. |1|Pause|

He loves me and makes me His Own; my union with Him shall never be broken.
He is my breath of life, mind, wealth and everything. The Lord is the Treasure of Virtue and Peace. |1|

Here and hereafter, the Lord is perfectly pervading; He is seen deep within the heart.
In the Sanctuary of the Saints, I am carried across; O Nanak, the terrible pain has been taken away. |2|3|48|

Kaanraa, Fifth Mehl:
God's humble servant is in love with Him.
You are my Friend, my very best Friend; everything is in Your Home. |1|Pause|

I beg for honor, I beg for strength; please bless me with wealth, property and children. |1|

You are the Technology of liberation, the Way to worldly success, the Perfect Lord of Supreme Bliss, the Transcendent Treasure.

Section 32 - Raag Kaanraa - Part 015

In the Fear of God and loving devotion, Nanak is exalted and enraptured, forever and ever a sacrifice to Him. |2|4|49|

Kaanraa, Fifth Mehl:
The debaters debate and argue their arguments.
The Yogis and meditators, religious and spiritual teachers roam and ramble, wandering endlessly all over the earth. |1|Pause|

They are egotistical, self-centered and conceited, foolish, stupid, idiotic and insane.
Wherever they go and wander, death is always with them, forever and ever and ever and ever. |1|

Give up your pride and stubborn self-conceit; death, yes, death, is always close and near at hand.
Vibrate and meditate on the Lord, Har, Haray, Haray. Says Nanak, listen you fool: without vibrating, and meditating, and dwelling on Him, your life is uselessly wasting away. |2|5|50|12|62|

Kaanraa, Ashtapadees, Fourth Mehl, First House:
One Universal Creator God. By The Grace Of The True Guru:
Chant the Name of the Lord, O mind, and find peace.
The more you chant and meditate, the more you will be at peace; serve the True Guru, and merge in the Lord. |1|Pause|

Each and every instant, the humble devotees long for Him; chanting the Naam, they find peace.
The taste of other pleasures is totally eradicated; nothing pleases them, except the Name. |1|

Following the Guru's Teachings, the Lord seems sweet to them; the Guru inspires them to speak sweet words.
Through the Word of the True Guru's Bani, the Primal Lord God is revealed; so focus your consciousness on His Bani. |2|

Hearing the Word of the Guru's Bani, my mind has been softened and saturated with it; my mind has returned to its own home deep within.
The Unstruck Melody resonates and resounds there continuously; the stream of nectar trickles down constantly. |3|

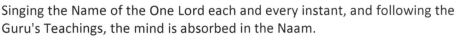

Singing the Name of the One Lord each and every instant, and following the Guru's Teachings, the mind is absorbed in the Naam.
Listening to the Naam, the mind is pleased with the Naam, and satisfied with the Naam. |4|

People wear lots of bracelets, glittering with gold; they wear all sorts of fine clothes.
But without the Naam, they are all bland and insipid. They are born, only to die again, in the cycle of reincarnation. |5|

The veil of Maya is a thick and heavy veil, a whirlpool which destroys one's home.
Sins and corrupt vices are totally heavy, like rusted slag. They will not let you cross over the poisonous and treacherous world-ocean. |6|

Let the Fear of God and neutral detachment be the boat; the Guru is the Boatman, who carries us across in the Word of the Shabad.
Meeting with the Lord, the Name of the Lord, merge in the Lord, the Name of the Lord. |7|

Attached to ignorance, people are falling asleep; attached to the Guru's spiritual wisdom, they awaken.
O Nanak, by His Will, He makes us walk as He pleases. |8|1|

Kaanraa, Fourth Mehl:
O mind, chant the Name of the Lord, Har, Har, and be carried across.
Whoever chants and meditates on it is emancipated. Like Dhroo and Prahlaad, they merge in the Lord. |1|Pause|

Section 32 - Raag Kaanraa - Part 016

Mercy, mercy, mercy - O Dear Lord, please shower Your Mercy on me, and attach me to Your Name.
Please be Merciful, and lead me to meet the True Guru; meeting the True Guru, I meditate on the Naam, the Name of the Lord. |1|

The filth of egotism from countless incarnations sticks to me; joining the Sangat, the Holy Congregation, this filth is washed away.
As iron is carried across if it is attached to wood, one who is attached to the Word of the Guru's Shabad finds the Lord. |2|

Joining the Society of the Saints, joining the Sat Sangat, the True Congregation, you shall come to receive the Sublime Essence of the Lord.
But not joining the Sangat, and committing actions in egotistical pride, is like drawing out clean water, and throwing it in the mud. |3|

The Lord is the Protector and Saving Grace of His humble devotees. The Lord's Sublime Essence seems so sweet to these humble beings.
Each and every instant, they are blessed with the Glorious Greatness of the Naam; through the Teachings of the True Guru, they are absorbed in Him. |4|

Bow forever in deep respect to the humble devotees; if you bow to those humble beings, you shall obtain the fruit of virtue.
Those wicked enemies who slander the devotees are destroyed, like Harnaakhash. |5|

Brahma, the son of the lotus, and Vyaas, the son of the fish, practiced austere penance and were worshipped.
Whoever is a devotee - worship and adore that person. Get rid of your doubts and superstitions. |6|

Do not be fooled by appearances of high and low social class. Suk Dayv bowed at the feet of Janak, and meditated.
Even though Janak threw his left-overs and garbage on Suk Dayv's head, his mind did not waver, even for an instant. |7|

Janak sat upon his regal throne, and applied the dust of the nine sages to his forehead.
Please shower Nanak with your Mercy, O my Lord and Master; make him the slave of Your slaves. |8|2|

Kaanraa, Fourth Mehl:
O mind, follow the Guru's Teachings, and joyfully sing God's Praises.
If my one tongue became hundreds of thousands and millions, I would meditate on Him millions and millions of times. |1|Pause|

The serpent king chants and meditates on the Lord with his thousands of heads, but even by these chants, he cannot find the Lord's limits.

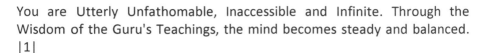

You are Utterly Unfathomable, Inaccessible and Infinite. Through the Wisdom of the Guru's Teachings, the mind becomes steady and balanced. |1|

Those humble beings who meditate on You are noble and exalted. Meditating on the Lord, they are at peace.
Bidur, the son of a slave-girl, was an untouchable, but Krishna hugged him close in His Embrace. |2|

Wood is produced from water, but by holding onto wood, one is saved from drowning.
The Lord Himself embellishes and exalts His humble servants; He confirms His Innate Nature. |3|

I am like a stone, or a piece of iron, heavy stone and iron; in the Boat of the Guru's Congregation, I am carried across,

like Kabeer the weaver, who was saved in the Sat Sangat, the True Congregation. He became pleasing to the minds of the humble Saints. |4|

Standing up, sitting down, rising up and walking on the path, I meditate.
The True Guru is the Word, and the Word is the True Guru, who teaches the Path of Liberation. |5|

By His Training, I find strength with each and every breath; now that I am trained and tamed, I meditate on the Naam, the Name of the Lord.
By Guru's Grace, egotism is extinguished, and then, through the Guru's Teachings, I merge in the Naam. |6|

Section 32 - Raag Kaanraa - Part 017

The True Guru is the Giver of the life of the soul, but the unfortunate ones do not love Him.
This opportunity shall not come into their hands again; in the end, they will suffer in torment and regret. |7|

If a good person seeks goodness for himself, he should bow low in humble surrender to the Guru.
Nanak prays: please show kindness and compassion to me, O my Lord and Master, that I may apply the dust of the True Guru to my forehead. |8|3|

Kaanraa, Fourth Mehl:
O mind, be attuned to His Love, and sing.
The Fear of God makes me fearless and immaculate; I am dyed in the color of the Guru's Teachings. |1|Pause|

Those who are attuned to the Lord's Love remain balanced and detached forever; they live near the Lord, who comes into their house.
If I am blessed with the dust of their feet, then I live. Granting His Grace, He Himself bestows it. |1|

Mortal beings are attached to greed and duality. Their minds are unripe and unfit, and will not accept the Dye of His Love.
But their lives are transformed through the Word of the Guru's Teachings. Meeting with the Guru, the Primal Being, they are dyed in the color of His Love. |2|

There are ten organs of sense and action; the ten wander unrestrained. Under the influence of the three dispositions, they are not stable, even for an instant.
Coming in contact with the True Guru, they are brought under control; then, salvation and liberation are attained. |3|

The One and Only Creator of the Universe is All-pervading everywhere. All shall once again merge into the One.
His One Form has one, and many colors; He leads all according to His One Word. |4|

The Gurmukh realizes the One and Only Lord; He is revealed to the Gurmukh.
The Gurmukh goes and meets the Lord in His Mansion deep within; the Unstruck Word of the Shabad vibrates there. |5|

God created all the beings and creatures of the universe; He blesses the Gurmukh with glory.
Without meeting the Guru, no one obtains the Mansion of His Presence. They suffer the agony of coming and going in reincarnation. |6|

For countless lifetimes, I have been separated from my Beloved; in His Mercy, the Guru has united me with Him.

Meeting the True Guru, I have found absolute peace, and my polluted intellect blossoms forth. |7|

O Lord, Har, Har, please grant Your Grace; O Life of the World, instill faith in the Naam within me.
Nanak is the Guru, the Guru, the True Guru; I am immersed in the Sanctuary of the True Guru. |8|4|

Kaanraa, Fourth Mehl:
O mind, walk on the Path of the Guru's Teachings.
Just as the wild elephant is subdued by the prod, the mind is disciplined by the Word of the Guru's Shabad. |1|Pause|

The wandering mind wanders, roams and rambles in the ten directions; but the Guru holds it, and lovingly attunes it to the Lord.
The True Guru implants the Word of the Shabad deep within the heart; the Ambrosial Naam, the Name of the Lord, trickles into the mouth. |1|

The snakes are filled with poisonous venom; the Word of the Guru's Shabad is the antidote - place it in your mouth.
Maya, the serpent, does not even approach one who is rid of the poison, and lovingly attuned to the Lord. |2|

The dog of greed is very powerful in the village of the body; the Guru strikes it and drives it out in an instant.
Truth, contentment, righteousness and Dharma have settled there; in the village of the Lord, sing the Glorious Praises of the Lord. |3|

Section 32 - Raag Kaanraa - Part 018

The mortal beings are sinking in the swamp of emotional attachment; the Guru lifts them up, and saves them from sinking.
Crying, "Save me! Save me!", the humble come to His Sanctuary; the Guru reaches out His Hand, and lifts them up. |4|

The whole world is like a game in a dream, all a game. God plays and causes the game to be played.
So earn the Profit of the Naam by following the Guru's Teachings; you shall go to the Court of the Lord in robes of honor. |5|

They act in egotism, and make others act in egotism; they collect and gather up the blackness of sin.
And when death comes, they suffer in agony; they must eat what they have planted. |6|

O Saints, gather the Wealth of the Lord's Name; if you depart after packing these provisions, you shall be honored.
So eat, spend, consume and give abundantly; the Lord will give - there will be no deficiency. |7|

The wealth of the Lord's Name is deep within the heart. In the Sanctuary of the Guru, this wealth is found.
O Nanak, God has been kind and compassionate; He has blessed me. Removing pain and poverty, He has blended me with Himself. |8|5|

Kaanraa, Fourth Mehl:
O mind, seek the Sanctuary of the True Guru, and meditate.
Iron is transformed into gold by touching the philosopher's stone; it takes on its qualities. |1|Pause|

The True Guru, the Great Primal Being, is the philosopher's stone. Whoever is attached to Him receives fruitful rewards.
Just as Prahlaad was saved by the Guru's Teachings, the Guru protects the honor of His servant. |1|

The Word of the True Guru is the most Sublime and Noble Word. Through the Guru's Word, the Ambrosial Nectar is obtained.
Ambreek the king was blessed with the status of immortality, meditating on the Word of the True Guru. |2|

The Sanctuary, the Protection and Sanctuary of the True Guru is pleasing to the mind. It is sacred and pure - meditate on it.
The True Guru has become Merciful to the meek and the poor; He has shown me the Path, the Way to the Lord. |3|

Those who enter the Sanctuary of the True Guru are firmly established; God comes to protect them.
If someone aims an arrow at the Lord's humble servant, it will turn around and hit him instead. |4|

Those who bathe in the Sacred Pool of the Lord, Har, Har, Har, Har, Har, are blessed with honor in His Court.
Those who meditate on the Guru's Teachings, the Guru's Instructions, the Guru's Wisdom, are united in the Lord's Union; He hugs them close in His Embrace. |5|

The Guru's Word is the Sound-current of the Naad, The Guru's Word is the wisdom of the Vedas; coming in contact with the Guru, meditate on the Naam.
In the Image of the Lord, Har, Har, one becomes the Embodiment of the Lord. The Lord makes His humble servant worthy of worship. |6|

The faithless cynic does not submit to the True Guru; the Lord makes the non-believer wander in confusion.
The waves of greed are like packs of dogs. The poison of Maya sticks to the body-skeleton. |7|

The Lord's Name is the Saving Grace of the whole world; join the Sangat, and meditate on the Naam.
O my God, please protect and preserve Nanak in the Sat Sangat, the True Congregation; save him, and let him merge in You. |8|6|

FIRST SET OF SIX|

Section 32 - Raag Kaanraa - Part 019

Kaanraa, Chhant, Fifth Mehl:
One Universal Creator God. By The Grace Of The True Guru:
They alone are saved, who meditate on the Lord.
Working for Maya is useless.
Meditating on the Lord, all fruits and rewards are obtained. They are blessed, blessed and very fortunate.
They are awake and aware in the True Congregation; attached to the Naam, they are lovingly attuned to the One.
I have renounced pride, emotional attachment, wickedness and corruption; attached to the Holy, I am carried across at their feet.
Prays Nanak, I have come to the Sanctuary of my Lord and Master; by great good fortune, I obtain the Blessed Vision of His Darshan. |1|

The Holy meet together, and continually vibrate and meditate on the Lord.

With love and excitement, they sing the Glorious Praises of their Lord and Master.

Singing His Praises they live, drinking in the Lord's Nectar; the cycle of birth and death is over for them.

Finding the True Congregation and meditating on the Lord, one is never again afflicted with pain.

By the Grace of the Great Giver, the Architect of Destiny, we work to serve the Saints.

Prays Nanak, I long for the dust of the feet of the humble; I am intuitively absorbed in the Blessed Vision of the Lord. |2|

All beings vibrate and meditate on the Lord of the World.

This brings the merits of chanting and meditation, austere self-discipline and perfect service.

Vibrating and meditating continuously on our Lord and Master, the Inner-knower, the Searcher of hearts, one's life becomes totally fruitful.

Those who sing and meditate continually on the Lord of the Universe - their coming into the world is blessed and approved.

The Immaculate Lord, Har, Har, is meditation and chanting, and austere self-discipline; only the Wealth of the Lord of the Universe shall go along with you in the end.

Prays Nanak, please grant Your Grace, O Lord, and bless me with the Jewel, that I may carry it in my pocket. |3|

His Wondrous and Amazing Plays are blissful
- granting His Grace, He bestows supreme ecstasy.

God, my Lord and Master, the Bringer of peace, has met me, and the desires of my mind are fulfilled.

Congratulations pour in; I am intuitively absorbed in the Lord. I shall never again cry out in pain.

He hugs me close in His Embrace, and blesses me with peace; the evil of sin and corruption is gone.

Prays Nanak, I have met my Lord and Master, the Primal Lord, the Embodiment of Bliss. |4|1|

Vaar Of Kaanraa, Fourth Mehl, Sung To The Tune Of The Ballad Of Musa:
One Universal Creator God. By The Grace Of The True Guru:
Shalok, Fourth Mehl:
Follow the Guru's Teachings, and enshrine the Treasure of the Lord's Name within your heart.

Become the slave of the Lord's slaves, and conquer egotism and corruption.
You shall win this treasure of life; you shall never lose.
Blessed, blessed and very fortunate are those, O Nanak, who savor the
Sublime Essence of the Lord through the Guru's Teachings. |1|

Fourth Mehl:
Govind, Govind, Govind - the Lord God, the Lord of the Universe is the
Treasure of Virtue.
Meditating on Govind, Govind, the Lord of the Universe, through the Guru's
Teachings, you shall be honored in the Court of the Lord.

Section 32 - Raag Kaanraa - Part 020

Meditating on God, chanting Govind, Govind, Govind, your face shall be
radiant; you shall be famous and exalted.
O Nanak, the Guru is the Lord God, the Lord of the Universe; meeting Him,
you shall obtain the Name of the Lord. |2|

Pauree:
You Yourself are the Siddha and the seeker; You Yourself are the Yoga and
the Yogi.
You Yourself are the Taster of tastes; You Yourself are the Enjoyer of
pleasures.
You Yourself are All-pervading; whatever You do comes to pass.
Blessed, blessed, blessed, blessed, blessed is the Sat Sangat, the True
Congregation of the True Guru. Join them - speak and chant the Lord's
Name.
Let everyone chant together the Name of the Lord, Har, Har, Haray, Har,
Har, Haray; chanting Har, all sins are washed away. |1|

Shalok, Fourth Mehl:
Har, Har, Har, Har is the Name of the Lord; rare are those who, as Gur-
mukh, obtain it.
Egotism and possessiveness are eradicated, and evil-mindedness is washed
away.
O Nanak, one who is blessed with such pre-ordained destiny chants the
Lord's Praises, night and day. |1|

Fourth Mehl:

The Lord Himself is Merciful; whatever the Lord Himself does, comes to pass.

The Lord Himself is All-pervading. There is no other as Great as the Lord.

Whatever pleases the Lord God's Will comes to pass; whatever the Lord God does is done.

No one can appraise His Value; the Lord God is Endless.

O Nanak, as Gurmukh, praise the Lord; your body and mind shall be cooled and soothed. |2|

Pauree:

You are the Light of all, the Life of the World; You imbue each and every heart with Your Love.

All meditate on You, O my Beloved; You are the True, True Primal Being, the Immaculate Lord.

The One is the Giver; the whole world is the beggar. All the beggars beg for His Gifts.

You are the servant, and You are the Lord and Master of all. Through the Guru's Teachings, we are ennobled and uplifted.

Let everyone say that the Lord is the Master of the senses, the Master of all faculties; through Him, we obtain all fruits and rewards. |2|

Shalok, Fourth Mehl:

O mind, meditate on the Name of the Lord, Har, Har; you shall be honored in the Court of the Lord.

You shall obtain the fruits that you desire, focusing your meditation on the Word of the Guru's Shabad.

All your sins and mistakes shall be wiped away, and you shall be rid of egotism and pride.

The heart-lotus of the Gurmukh blossoms forth, recognizing God within every soul.

O Lord God, please shower Your Mercy upon servant Nanak, that he may chant the Lord's Name. |1|

Fourth Mehl:

The Name of the Lord, Har, Har, is Sacred and Immaculate. Chanting the Naam, pain is dispelled.

God comes to abide in the minds of those who have such pre-ordained destiny.

Those who walk in harmony with the Will of the True Guru are rid of pain and poverty.

No one finds the Lord by his own will; see this, and satisfy your mind.
Servant Nanak is the slave of the slave of those who fall at the Feet of the
True Guru. |2|

Pauree:

Section 32 - Raag Kaanraa - Part 021

You are pervading and permeating all places and interspaces, O Creator.
You made all that has been made.
You created the entire universe, with all its colors and shades; in so many
ways and means and forms You formed it.
O Lord of Light, Your Light is infused within all; You link us to the Guru's
Teachings.
They alone meet the True Guru, unto whom You are Merciful; O Lord, You
instruct them in the Guru's Word.
Let everyone chant the Name of the Lord, chant the Name of the Great
Lord; all poverty, pain and hunger shall be taken away. |3|

Shalok, Fourth Mehl:
The Ambrosial Nectar of the Name of the Lord, Har, Har, is sweet; enshrine
this Ambrosial Nectar of the Lord within your heart.
The Lord God prevails in the Sangat, the Holy Congregation; reflect upon
the Shabad and understand.
Meditating on the Name of the Lord, Har, Har, within the mind, the poison
of egotism is eradicated.
One who does not remember the Name of the Lord, Har, Har, shall totally
lose this life in the gamble.
By Guru's Grace, one remembers the Lord, and enshrines the Lord's Name
within the heart.
O servant Nanak, his face shall be radiant in the Court of the True Lord. |1|

Fourth Mehl:
To chant the Lord's Praise and His Name is sublime and exalted. This is the
most excellent deed in this Dark Age of Kali Yuga.
His Praises come through the Guru's Teachings and Instructions; wear the
Necklace of the Lord's Name.
Those who meditate on the Lord are very fortunate. They are entrusted
with the Treasure of the Lord.

Without the Name, no matter what people may do, they continue to waste away in egotism.

Elephants can be washed and bathed in water, but they only throw dust on their heads again.

O Kind and Compassionate True Guru, please unite me with the Lord, that the One Creator of the Universe may abide within my mind.

Those Gurmukhs who listen to the Lord and believe in Him - servant Nanak salutes them. |2|

Pauree:

The Lord's Name is the most sublime and precious merchandise. The Primal Lord God is my Lord and Master.

The Lord has staged His Play, and He Himself permeates it. The whole world deals in this merchandise.

Your Light is the light in all beings, O Creator. All Your Expanse is True.

All those who meditate on You become prosperous; through the Guru's Teachings, they sing Your Praises, O Formless Lord.

Let everyone chant the Lord, the Lord of the World, the Lord of the Universe, and cross over the terrifying world-ocean. |4|

Shalok, Fourth Mehl:

I have only one tongue, and the Glorious Virtues of the Lord God are Unapproachable and Unfathomable.

I am ignorant - how can I meditate on You, Lord? You are Great, Unapproachable and Immeasurable.

O Lord God, please bless me with that sublime wisdom, that I may fall at the Feet of the Guru, the True Guru.

O Lord God, please lead me to the Sat Sangat, the True Congregation, where even a sinner like myself may be saved.

O Lord, please bless and forgive servant Nanak; please unite him in Your Union.

O Lord, please be merciful and hear my prayer; I am a sinner and a worm - please save me! |1|

Fourth Mehl:

O Lord, Life of the World, please bless me with Your Grace, and lead me to meet the Guru, the Merciful True Guru.

I am happy to serve the Guru; the Lord has become merciful to me.

Section 32 - Raag Kaanraa - Part 022

All my hopes and desires have been forgotten; my mind is rid of its worldly entanglements.

The Guru, in His Mercy, implanted the Naam within me; I am enraptured with the Word of the Shabad.

Servant Nanak has obtained the inexhaustible wealth; the Lord's Name is his wealth and property. |2|

Pauree:

O Lord, You are the Greatest of the Great, the Greatest of the Great, the Most Lofty and Exalted of all, the Greatest of the Great.

Those who meditate on the Infinite Lord, who meditate on the Lord, Har, Har, Har, are rejuvenated.

Those who sing and listen to Your Praises, O my Lord and Master, have millions of sins destroyed.

I know that those divine beings who follow the Guru's Teachings are just like You, Lord. They are the greatest of the great, so very fortunate.

Let everyone meditate on the Lord, who was True in the primal beginning, and True throughout the ages; He is revealed as True here and now, and He shall be True forever and ever. Servant Nanak is the slave of His slaves. |5|

Shalok, Fourth Mehl:

I meditate on my Lord, the Life of the World, the Lord, chanting the Guru's Mantra.

The Lord is Unapproachable, Inaccessible and Unfathomable; the Lord, Har, Har, has spontaneously come to meet me.

The Lord Himself is pervading each and every heart; the Lord Himself is Endless.

The Lord Himself enjoys all pleasures; the Lord Himself is the Husband of Maya.

The Lord Himself gives in charity to the whole world, and all the beings and creatures which He created.

O Merciful Lord God, please bless me with Your Bountiful Gifts; the humble Saints of the Lord beg for them.

O God of servant Nanak, please come and meet me; I sing the Songs of the Glorious Praises of the Lord. |1|

Fourth Mehl:

The Name of the Lord God is my Best Friend. My mind and body are drenched with the Naam.

All the hopes of the Gurmukh are fulfilled; servant Nanak is comforted, hearing the Naam, the Name of the Lord. |2|

Pauree:
The Lord's Sublime Name is energizing and rejuvenating. The Immaculate Lord, the Primal Being, blossoms forth.
Maya serves at the feet of those who chant and meditate on the Lord, Har, Har, day and night.
The Lord always looks after and cares for all His beings and creatures; He is with all, near and far.
Those whom the Lord inspires to understand, understand; the True Guru, God, the Primal Being, is pleased with them.
Let everyone sing the Praise of the Lord of the Universe, the Lord, the Lord of the Universe, the Lord, the Lord of the Universe; singing the Praise of the Lord, one is absorbed in His Glorious Virtues. |6|

Shalok, Fourth Mehl:
O mind, even in sleep, remember the Lord God; let yourself be intuitively absorbed into the Celestial State of Samaadhi.
Servant Nanak's mind longs for the Lord, Har, Har. As the Guru pleases, he is absorbed into the Lord, O mother. |1|

Fourth Mehl:
I am in love with the One and Only Lord; the One Lord fills my consciousness.
Servant Nanak takes the Support of the One Lord God; through the One, he obtains honor and salvation. |2|

Pauree:
The Panch Shabad, the Five Primal Sounds, vibrate with the Wisdom of the Guru's Teachings; by great good fortune, the Unstruck Melody resonates and resounds.
I see the Lord, the Source of Bliss, everywhere; through the Word of the Guru's Shabad, the Lord of the Universe is revealed.
From the primal beginning, and throughout the ages, the Lord has One Form. Through the Wisdom of the Guru's Teachings, I vibrate and meditate on the Lord God.
O Merciful Lord God, please bless me with Your Bounty; O Lord God, please preserve and protect the honor of Your humble servant.

Section 32 - Raag Kaanraa - Part 023

Let everyone proclaim: Blessed is the Guru, the True Guru, the Guru, the True Guru; meeting Him, the Lord covers their faults and deficiencies. |7|

Shalok, Fourth Mehl:
The sacred pool of devotional worship is filled to the brim and overflowing in torrents.
Those who obey the True Guru, O servant Nanak, are very fortunate - they find it. |1|

Fourth Mehl:
The Names of the Lord, Har, Har, are countless. The Glorious Virtues of the Lord, Har, Har, cannot be described.
The Lord, Har, Har, is Inaccessible and Unfathomable; how can the humble servants of the Lord be united in His Union?
Those humble beings meditate and chant the Praises of the Lord, Har, Har, but they do not attain even a tiny bit of His Worth.
O servant Nanak, the Lord God is Inaccessible; the Lord has attached me to His Robe, and united me in His Union. |2|

Pauree:
The Lord is Inaccessible and Unfathomable. How will I see the Blessed Vision of the Lord's Darshan?
If He were a material object, then I could describe Him, but He has no form or feature.
Understanding comes only when the Lord Himself gives understanding; only such a humble being sees it.
The Sat Sangat, the True Congregation of the True Guru, is the school of the soul, where the Glorious Virtues of the Lord are studied.
Blessed, blessed is the tongue, blessed is the hand, and blessed is the Teacher, the True Guru; meeting Him, the Account of the Lord is written. |8|

Shalok, Fourth Mehl:
The Name of the Lord, Har, Har, is Ambrosial Nectar. Meditate on the Lord, with love for the True Guru.
The Name of the Lord, Har, Har is Sacred and Pure. Chanting it and listening to it, pain is taken away.

They alone worship and adore the Lord's Name, upon whose foreheads such pre-ordained destiny is written.

Those humble beings are honored in the Court of the Lord; the Lord comes to abide in their minds.

O servant Nanak, their faces are radiant. They listen to the Lord; their minds are filled with love. |1|

Fourth Mehl:

The Name of the Lord, Har, Har, is the greatest treasure. The Gurmukhs obtain it.

The True Guru comes to meet those who have such pre-ordained destiny written upon their foreheads.

Their bodies and minds are cooled and soothed; peace and tranquility come to dwell in their minds.

O Nanak, chanting the Name of the Lord, Har, Har, all poverty and pain is dispelled. |2|

Pauree:

I am a sacrifice, forever and ever, to those who have seen my Beloved True Guru.

They alone meet my True Guru, who have such pre-ordaind destiny written upon their foreheads.

I meditate on the Inaccessible Lord, according to the Guru's Teachings; God has no form or feature.

Those who follow the Guru's Teachings and meditate on the Inaccessible Lord, merge with their Lord and Master and become one with Him.

Let everyone proclaim out loud, the Name of the Lord, the Lord, the Lord; the profit of devotional worship of the Lord is blessed and sublime. |9|

Shalok, Fourth Mehl:

The Lord's Name is permeating and pervading all. Repeat the Name of the Lord, Raam, Raam.

The Lord is in the home of each and every soul. God created this play with its various colors and forms.

The Lord, the Life of the World, dwells near at hand. The Guru, my Friend, has made this clear.

Section 32 - Raag Kaanraa - Part 024

They alone meet the Lord, the Lord God, their Lord and Master, whose love for the Lord is pre-ordained.

Servant Nanak meditates on the Naam, the Name of the Lord; through the Word of the Guru's Teachings, chant it consciously with your mind. |1|

Fourth Mehl:

Seek the Lord God, your Best Friend; by great good fortune, He comes to dwell with the very fortunate ones.

Through the Perfect Guru, He is revealed, O Nanak, and one is lovingly attuned to the Lord. |2|

Pauree:

Blessed, blessed, beauteous and fruitful is that moment, when service to the Lord becomes pleasing to the mind.

So proclaim the story of the Lord, O my GurSikhs; speak the Unspoken Speech of my Lord God.

How can I attain Him? How can I see Him? My Lord God is All-knowing and All-seeing.

Through the Word of the Guru's Teachings, the Lord reveals Himself; we merge in absorption in the Naam, the Name of the Lord.

Nanak is a sacrifice unto those who meditate on the Lord of Nirvaanaa. |10|

Shalok, Fourth Mehl:

One's eyes are anointed by the Lord God, when the Guru bestows the ointment of spiritual wisdom.

I have found God, my Best Friend; servant Nanak is intuitively absorbed into the Lord. |1|

Fourth Mehl:

The Gurmukh is filled with peace and tranquility deep within. His mind and body are absorbed in the Naam, the Name of the Lord.

He thinks of the Naam, and reads the Naam; he remains lovingly attuned to the Naam.

He obtains the Treasure of the Naam, and is rid of anxiety.

Meeting with the True Guru, the Naam wells up, and all hunger and thirst depart.

O Nanak, one who is imbued with the Naam, gathers the Naam in his lap. |2|

Pauree:

You Yourself created the world, and You Yourself control it.

Some are self-willed manmukhs - they lose. Others are united with the Guru - they win.

The Name of the Lord, the Lord God is Sublime. The fortunate ones chant it, through the Word of the Guru's Teachings.

All pain and poverty are taken away, when the Guru bestows the Lord's Name.

Let everyone serve the Enticing Enticer of the Mind, the Enticer of the World, who created the world, and controls it all. |11|

Shalok, Fourth Mehl:

The disease of egotism is deep within the mind; the self-willed manmukhs and the evil beings are deluded by doubt.

O Nanak, the disease is cured only by meeting with the True Guru, the Holy Friend. |1|

Fourth Mehl:

My mind and body are embellished and exalted, when I behold the Lord with my eyes.

O Nanak, meeting with that God, I live, hearing His Voice. |2|

Pauree:

The Creator is the Lord of the World, the Master of the Universe, the Infinite Primal Immeasurable Being.

Meditate on the Lord's Name, O my GurSikhs; the Lord is Sublime, the Lord's Name is Invaluable.

Those who meditate on Him in their hearts, day and night, merge with the Lord - there is no doubt about it.

By great good fortune, they join the Sangat, the Holy Congregation, and speak the Word of the Guru, the Perfect True Guru.

Let everyone meditate on the Lord, the Lord, the All-pervading Lord, by which all disputes and conflicts with Death are ended. |12|

Shalok, Fourth Mehl:

The humble servant of the Lord chants the Name, Har, Har. The foolish idiot shoots arrows at him.

O Nanak, the humble servant of the Lord is saved by the Love of the Lord. The arrow is turned around, and kills the one who shot it. |1|

Section 32 - Raag Kaanraa - Part 025

Fourth Mehl:
The eyes which are attracted by the Lord's Love behold the Lord through the Name of the Lord.
If they gaze upon something else, O servant Nanak, they ought to be gouged out. |2|

Pauree:
The Infinite Lord totally permeates the water, the land and the sky.
He cherishes and sustains all beings and creatures; whatever He does comes to pass.
Without Him, we have no mother, father, children, sibling or friend.
He is permeating and pervading deep within each and every heart; let everyone meditate on Him.
Let all chant the Glorious Praises of the Lord of the World, who is manifest all over the world. |13|

Shalok, Fourth Mehl:
Those Gurmukhs who meet as friends are blessed with the Lord God's Love.
O servant Nanak, praise the Naam, the Name of the Lord; you shall go to His court in joyous high spirits. |1|

Fourth Mehl:
Lord, You are the Great Giver of all; all beings are Yours.
They all worship You in adoration; You bless them with Your Bounty, O Beloved.
The Generous Lord, the Great Giver reaches out with His Hands, and the rain pours down on the world.
The corn germinates in the fields; contemplate the Lord's Name with love.
Servant Nanak begs for the Gift of the Support of the Name of his Lord God. |2|

Pauree:
The desires of the mind are satisfied, meditating on the Ocean of Peace.
Worship and adore the Feet of the Lord, through the Word of the Guru's Shabad, the jewel mine.
Joining the Saadh Sangat, the Company of the Holy, one is saved, and the Decree of Death is torn up.

The treasure of this human life is won, meditating on the Lord of Detachment.
Let everyone seek the Sanctuary of the True Guru; let the black spot of pain, the scar of suffering, be erased. |14|

Shalok, Fourth Mehl:
I was seeking, searching for my Friend, but my Friend is right here with me.
O servant Nanak, the Unseen is not seen, but the Gurmukh is given to see Him. |1|

Fourth Mehl:
O Nanak, I am in love with the True Lord; I cannot survive without Him.
Meeting the True Guru, the Perfect Lord is found, and the tongue savors His Sublime Essence. |2|

Pauree:
Some sing, some listen, and some speek and preach.
The filth and pollution of countless lifetimes is washed away, and the wishes of the mind are fulfilled.
Coming and going in reincarnation ceases, singing the Glorious Praises of the Lord.
They save themselves, and save their companions; they save all their generations as well.
Servant Nanak is a sacrifice to those who are pleasing to my Lord God. |15|1|

Sudh|

Raag Kaanraa, The Word Of Naam Dayv Jee:
One Universal Creator God. By The Grace Of The True Guru:
Such is the Sovereign Lord, the Inner-knower, the Searcher of Hearts;
He sees everything as clearly as one's face reflected in a mirror. |1|Pause|

He dwells in each and every heart; no stain or stigma sticks to Him.
He is liberated from bondage; He does not belong to any social class. |1|

As one's face is reflected in the water,
so does Naam Dayv's Beloved Lord and Master appear. |2|1|

RAAG KALYAAN

Section 33 - Raag Kalyaan - Part 001

Raag Kalyaan, Fourth Mehl:
ONE Universal Creator God. Truth Is The Name. Creative Being Personified.
No Fear. No Hatred. Image Of The Undying. Beyond Birth. Self-Existent. By
Guru's Grace:
The Lord, the Beauteous Lord - no one has found His limits.
I am a child - You cherish and sustain me. You are the Great Primal Being,
my Mother and Father. |1|Pause|

The Names of the Lord are Countless and Unfathomable. My Sovereign
Lord is Unfathomable and Incomprehensible.
The virtuous and the spiritual teachers have given it great thought, but they
have not found even an iota of His Value. |1|

They sing the Glorious Praises of the Lord, the Lord of the Universe forever.
They sing the Glorious Praises of the Lord of the Universe, but they do not
find His limits.
You are Immeasurable, Unweighable, and Infinite, O Lord and Master; no
matter how much one may meditate on You, Your Depth cannot be
fathomed. |2|

Lord, Your humble servants praise You, singing Your Glorious Praises, O
Sovereign Lord.
You are the ocean of water, and I am Your fish. No one has ever found Your
limits. |3|

Please be Kind to Your humble servant, Lord; please bless me with the
meditation of Your Name.
I am a blind fool; Your Name is my only Support. Servant Nanak, as
Gurmukh, has found it. |4|1|

Kalyaan, Fourth Mehl:
The humble servant of the Lord sings the Lord's Praise, and blossoms forth.

My intellect is embellished with devotion to the Lord, Har, Har, through the Guru's Teachings. This is the destiny which God has recorded on my forehead. |1|Pause|

I meditate in remembrance on the Guru's Feet, day and night. The Lord, Har, Har, Har, comes to dwell in my mind.
The Praise of the Lord, Har, Har, Har, is Excellent and Sublime in this world. His Praise is the sandalwood paste which I rub. |1|

The humble servant of the Lord is lovingly attuned to the Lord, Har, Har, Har; all the faithless cynics pursue him.
The slanderous person acts in accordance with the record of his past deeds; his foot trips over the snake, and he is stung by its bite. |2|

O my Lord and Master, You are the Saving Grace, the Protector of Your humble servants. You protect them, age after age.
What does it matter, if a demon speaks evil? By doing so, he only gets frustrated. |3|

All the beings and creatures created by God are caught in the mouth of Death.
The humble servants of the Lord are protected by the Lord God, Har, Har, Har; servant Nanak seeks His Sanctuary. |4|2|

Kalyaan, Fourth Mehl:

Section 33 - Raag Kalyaan - Part 002

O my mind, chant and meditate on the Master of the Universe.
Through the Guru's Teachings, meditate on the Lord's Name, and be rid of all the painful past sins. |1|Pause|

I have only one tongue - I cannot sing His Praises. Please bless me with many, many tongues.
Again and again, each and every instant, with all of them, I would sing His Glorious Praises; but even then, I would not be able to sing all of Your Praises, God. |1|

I am so deeply in love with God, my Lord and Master; I long to see God's Vision.

You are the Great Giver of all beings and creatures; only You know our inner pain. |2|

If only someone would show me the Way, the Path of God. Tell me - what could I give him?
I would surrender, offer and dedicate all my body and mind to him; if only someone would unite me in God's Union! |3|

The Glorious Praises of the Lord are so many and numerous; I can describe only a tiny bit of them.
My intellect is under Your control, God; You are the All-powerful Lord God of servant Nanak. |4|3|

Kalyaan, Fourth Mehl:
O my mind, chant the Glorious Praises of the Lord, which are said to be inexpressible.
Rightousness and Dharmic faith, success and prosperity, pleasure, the fulfillment of desires and liberation - all follow the humble servant of the Lord like a shadow. |1|Pause|

That humble servant of the Lord who has such good fortune written on his forehead meditates on the Name of the Lord, Har, Har.
In that Court, where God calls for the accounts, there, you shall be saved only by meditating on the Naam, the Name of the Lord. |1|

I am stained with the filth of the mistakes of countless lifetimes, the pain and pollution of egotism.
Showering His Mercy, the Guru bathed me in the Water of the Lord, and all my sins and mistakes were taken away. |2|

God, our Lord and Master, is deep within the hearts of His humble servants. They vibrate the Naam, the Name of the Lord, Har, Har.
And when that very last moment comes, then the Naam is our Best Friend and Protector. |3|

Your humble servants sing Your Praises, O Lord, Har, Har; they chant and meditate on the Lord God, the Master of the Universe.
O God, my Saving Grace, Lord and Master of servant Nanak, please save me, the sinking stone. |4|4|

Kalyaan, Fourth Mehl:
Only the Lord God knows my innermost thoughts.
If someone slanders the humble servant of the Lord, God does not believe even a tiny bit of what he says. |1|Pause|

So give up everything else, and serve the Imperishable; The Lord God, our Lord and Master, is the Highest of all.
When you serve the Lord, Death cannot even see you. It comes and falls at the feet of those who know the Lord. |1|

Those whom my Lord and Master protects - a balanced wisdom comes to their ears.
No one can equal them; their devotional worship is accepted by my God. |2|

So behold the Wondrous and Amazing Play of the Lord. In an instant, He distinguishes the genuine from the counterfeit.
And that is why His humble servant is in bliss. Those of pure heart meet together, while the evil ones regret and repent. |3|

Lord, You are the Great Giver, our All-powerful Lord and Master; O Lord, I beg for only one gift from You.
Lord, please bless servant Nanak with Your Grace, that Your Feet may abide forever within my heart. |4|5|

Section 33 - Raag Kalyaan - Part 003

Kalyaan, Fourth Mehl:
O God, Treasure of Mercy, please bless me, that I may sing the Glorious Praises of the Lord.
I always place my hopes in You; O God, when will you take me in Your Embrace? |1|Pause|

I am a foolish and ignorant child; Father, please teach me!
Your child makes mistakes again and again, but still, You are pleased with him, O Father of the Universe. |1|

Whatever You give me, O my Lord and Master - that is what I receive.
There is no other place where I can go. |2|

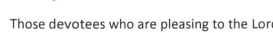

Those devotees who are pleasing to the Lord - the Lord is pleasing to them. Their light merges into the Light; the lights are merged and blended together. |3|

The Lord Himself has shown mercy; He lovingly attunes me to Himself. Servant Nanak seeks the Sanctuary of the Door of the Lord, who protects his honor. |4|6|

First Set Of Six|

Kalyaan Bhopaalee, Fourth Mehl:
One Universal Creator God. By The Grace Of The True Guru:
O Supreme Lord God, Transcendent Lord and Master, Destroyer of pain, Transcendental Lord God.
All Your devotees beg of You. Ocean of peace, carry us across the terrifying world-ocean; You are the Wish-fulfilling Jewel. |1|Pause|

Merciful to the meek and poor, Lord of the world, Support of the earth, Inner-knower, Searcher of hearts, Lord of the Universe.
Those who meditate on the Supreme Lord become fearless. Through the Wisdom of the Guru's Teachings, they meditate on the Lord, the Liberator Lord. |1|

Those who come to Sanctuary at the Feet of the Lord of the Universe - those humble beings cross over the terrifying world-ocean.
The Lord preserves the honor of His humble devotees; O servant Nanak, the Lord Himself showers them with His Grace. |2|1|7|

Raag Kalyaan, Fifth Mehl, First House:
One Universal Creator God. By The Grace Of The True Guru:
Please grant me this blessing:
May the bumble-bee of my mind be immersed again and again in the Honey of Your Lotus Feet. |1|Pause|

I am not concerned with any other water; please bless this songbird with a Drop of Your Water, Lord. |1|

Unless I meet my Lord, I am not satisfied. Nanak lives, gazing upon the Blessed Vision of His Darshan. |2|1|

Kalyaan, Fifth Mehl:
This beggar begs and begs for Your Name, Lord.
You are the Support of all, the Master of all, the Giver of absolute peace. |1|Pause|

So many, so very many, beg for charity at Your Door; they receive only what You are pleased to give. |1|

Fruitful, fruitful, fruitful is the Blessed Vision of His Darshan; touching His Touch, I sing His Glorious Praises.
O Nanak, one's essence is blended into the Essence; the diamond of the mind is pierced through by the Diamond of the Lord. |2|2|

Section 33 - Raag Kalyaan - Part 004

Kalyaan, Fifth Mehl:
O, the Wondrous Glory of my Beloved!
My mind is rejuvenated forever by His Wondrous Love. |1|Pause|

Brahma, Shiva, the Siddhas, the silent sages and Indra beg for the charity of His Praise and devotion to Him. |1|

Yogis, spiritual teachers, meditators and the thousand-headed serpent all meditate on the Waves of God.
Says Nanak, I am a sacrifice to the Saints, who are the Eternal Companions of God. |2|3|

Kalyaan, Fifth Mehl, Second House:
One Universal Creator God. By The Grace Of The True Guru:
Belief in You, Lord, brings honor.
To see with my eyes, and hear with my ears - every limb and fiber of my being, and my breath of life are in bliss. |1|Pause|

Here and there, and in the ten directions You are pervading, in the mountain and the blade of grass. |1|

Wherever I look, I see the Lord, the Supreme Lord, the Primal Being.
In the Saadh Sangat, the Company of the Holy, doubt and fear are dispelled. Nanak speaks the Wisdom of God. |2|1|4|

Kalyaan, Fifth Mehl:
The Glory of God is the Sound-current of the Naad, the Celestial Music of Bliss, and the Wisdom of the Vedas.
Speaking and listening, the silent sages and humble beings join together, in the Realm of the Saints. |1|Pause|

Spiritual wisdom, meditation, faith and charity are there; their minds savor the Taste of the Naam, the Name of the Lord. Chanting it, sins are destroyed. |1|

This is the technology of Yoga, spiritual wisdom, devotion, intuitive knowledge of the Shabad, certain knowledge of the Essence of Reality, chanting and unbroken intensive meditation.
Through and through, O Nanak, merging into the Light, you shall never again suffer pain and punishment. |2|2|5|

Kalyaan, Fifth Mehl:
What should I do, and how should I do it?
Should I center myself in meditation, or study the spiritual wisdom of the Shaastras? How can I endure this unendurable state? |1|Pause|

Vishnu, Shiva, the Siddhas, the silent sages and Indra - at whose door should I seek sanctuary? |1|

Some have power and influence, and some are blessed with heavenly paradise, but out of millions, will anyone find liberation?
Says Nanak, I have attained the Sublime Essence of the Naam, the Name of the Lord. I touch the feet of the Holy. |2|3|6|

Kalyaan, Fifth Mehl:
The Lord of the Breath of Life, the Merciful Primal Lord God, is my Friend.
The Lord saves us from the womb of reincarnation and the noose of death in this Dark Age of Kali Yuga; He takes away our pain. |1|Pause|

I enshrine the Naam, the Name of the Lord, within; I seek Your Sanctuary, Lord.
O Merciful Lord God, You are my only Support. |1|

You are the only Hope of the helpless, the meek and the poor.
Your Name, O my Lord and Master, is the Mantra of the mind. |2|

I know of nothing except You, God.
Throughout all the ages, I realize You. |3|

O Lord, You dwell in my mind night and day.
The Lord of the Universe is Nanak's only Support. |4|4|7|

Kalyaan, Fifth Mehl:
Within my mind and body I meditate on the Lord God.
The Perfect Guru is pleased and satisfied; I am blessed with eternal peace
and happiness. |1|Pause|

All affairs are successfuly resolved, singing the Glorious Praises of the Lord
of the World.
Joining the Saadh Sangat, the Company of the Holy, I dwell upon God, and
the pain of death is taken away. |1|

Please take pity on me, O my God, that I may serve You day and night.

Section 33 - Raag Kalyaan - Part 005

Slave Nanak seeks the Sanctuary of the Lord, the Perfect, Divine Primal
Being. |2|5|8|

Kalyaan, Fifth Mehl:
My God is the Inner-knower, the Searcher of Hearts.
Take pity on me, O Perfect Transcendent Lord; bless me with the True
Eternal Insignia of the Shabad, the Word of God. |1|Pause|

O Lord, other than You, no one is all-powerful. You are the Hope and the
Strength of my mind.
You are the Giver to the hearts of all beings, O Lord and Master. I eat and
wear whatever You give me. |1|

Intuitive understanding, wisdom and cleverness, glory and beauty,
pleasure, wealth and honor,
all comforts, bliss, happiness and salvation, O Nanak, come by chanting the
Lord's Name. |2|6|9|

Kalyaan, Fifth Mehl:

The Sanctuary of the Lord's Feet bring salvation.
God's Name is the Purifier of sinners. |1|Pause|

Whoever chants and meditates in the Saadh Sangat, the Company of the Holy, shall undoubtedly escape being consumed by the Messenger of Death. |1|

Liberation, the key to success, and all sorts of comforts do not equal loving devotional worship of the Lord.
Slave Nanak longs for the Blessed Vision of God's Darshan; he shall never again wander in reincarnation. |2|7|10|

Kalyaan, Fourth Mehl, Ashtapadees:
One Universal Creator God. By The Grace Of The True Guru:
Hearing the Name of the Lord, the All-pervading Lord, my mind is drenched with joy.
The Name of the Lord, Har, Har, is Ambrosial Nectar, the most Sweet and Sublime Essence; through the Guru's Teachings, drink it in with intuitive ease. |1|Pause|

The potential energy of fire is within the wood; it is released if you know how to rub it and generate friction.
In just the same way, the Lord's Name is the Light within all; the Essence is extracted by following the Guru's Teachings. |1|

There are nine doors, but the taste of these nine doors is bland and insipid.
The Essence of Ambrosial Nectar trickles down through the Tenth Door.
Please take pity on me - be kind and compassionate, O my Beloved, that I may drink in the Sublime Essence of the Lord, through the Word of the Guru's Shabad. |2|

The body-village is the most sublime and exalted village, in which the merchandise of the Lord's Sublime Essence is traded.
The most precious and priceless gems and jewels are obtained by serving the True Guru. |3|

The True Guru is Inaccessible; Inaccessible is our Lord and Master. He is the overflowing Ocean of bliss - worship Him with loving devotion.
Please take pity on me, and be Merciful to this meek song-bird; please pour a drop of Your Name into my mouth. |4|

O Beloved Lord, please color my mind with the Deep Crimson Color of Your Love; I have surrendered my mind to the Guru.

Those who are imbued with the Love of the Lord, Raam, Raam, Raam, continually drink in this essence in big gulps, savoring its sweet taste. |5|

If all the gold of the seven continents and the oceans was taken out and placed before them,

the humble servants of my Lord and Master would not even want it. They beg for the Lord to bless them with the Lord's Sublime Essence. |6|

The faithless cynics and mortal beings remain hungry forever; they continually cry out in hunger.

They hurry and run, and wander all around, caught in the love of Maya; they cover hundreds of thousands of miles in their wanderings. |7|

The humble servants of the Lord, Har, Har, Har, Har, Har, are sublime and exalted. What praise can we bestow upon them?

Section 33 - Raag Kalyaan - Part 006

Nothing else can equal the Glory of the Lord's Name; please bless servant Nanak with Your Grace. |8|1|

Kalyaan, Fourth Mehl:
O Lord, please bless me with the Touch of the Guru, the Philosopher's Stone.

I was unworthy, utterly useless, rusty slag; meeting with the True Guru, I was transformed by the Philosopher's Stone. |1|Pause|

Everyone longs for paradise, liberation and heaven; all place their hopes in them.

The humble long for the Blessed Vision of His Darshan; they do not ask for liberation. Their minds are satisfied and comforted by His Darshan. |1|

Emotional attachment to Maya is very powerful; this attachment is a black stain which sticks.

The humble servants of my Lord and Master are unattached and liberated. They are like ducks, whose feathers do not get wet. |2|

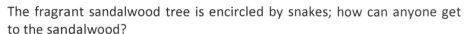

The fragrant sandalwood tree is encircled by snakes; how can anyone get to the sandalwood?
Drawing out the Mighty Sword of the Guru's Spiritual Wisdom, I slaughter and kill the poisonous snakes, and drink in the Sweet Nectar. |3|

You may gather wood and stack it in a pile, but in an instant, fire reduces it to ashes.
The faithless cynic gathers the most horrendous sins, but meeting with the Holy Saint, they are placed in the fire. |4|

The Holy, Saintly devotees are sublime and exalted. They enshrine the Naam, the Name of the Lord, deep within.
By the touch of the Holy and the humble servants of the Lord, the Lord God is seen. |5|

The thread of the faithless cynic is totally knotted and tangled; how can anything be woven with it?
This thread cannot be woven into yarn; do not associate with those faithless cynics. |6|

The True Guru and the Saadh Sangat, the Company of the Holy, are exalted and sublime. Joining the Congregation, meditate on the Lord.
The gems, jewels and precious stones are deep within; by Guru's Grace, they are found. |7|

My Lord and Master is Glorious and Great. How can I be united in His Union?
O Nanak, the Perfect Guru unites His humble servant in His Union, and blesses him with perfection. |8|2|

Kalyaan, Fourth Mehl:
Chant the Name of the Lord, the Lord, the All-pervading Lord.
The Holy, the humble and Holy, are noble and sublime. Meeting with the Holy, I joyfully love the Lord. |1|Pause|

The minds of all the beings and creatures of the world waver unsteadily.
Please take pity on them, be merciful to them, and unite them with the Holy; establish this support to support the world. |1|

The earth is beneath us, and yet its dust falls down on all; let yourself be covered by the dust of the feet of the Holy.
You shall be utterly exalted, the most noble and sublime of all; the whole world will place itself at your feet. |2|

The Gurmukhs are blessed with the Divine Light of the Lord; Maya comes to serve them.
Through the Word of the Guru's Teachings, they bite with teeth of wax and chew iron, drinking in the Sublime Essence of the Lord. |3|

The Lord has shown great mercy, and bestowed His Name; I have met with the Holy Guru, the Primal Being.
The Glorious Praises of the Lord's Name have spread out everywhere; the Lord bestows fame all over the world. |4|

The Beloved Lord is within the minds of the Holy, the Holy Saadhus; without seeing Him, they cannot survive.
The fish in the water loves only the water. Without water, it bursts and dies in an instant. |5|

Section 33 - Raag Kalyaan - Part 007

Those who have terrible luck and bad fortune do not drink in the water which washes the dust of the feet of the Holy.
The burning fire of their desires is not extinguished; they are beaten and punished by the Righteous Judge of Dharma. |6|

You may visit all the sacred shrines, observe fasts and sacred feasts, give generously in charity and waste away the body, melting it in the snow.
The weight of the Lord's Name is unweighable, according to the Guru's Teachings; nothing can equal its weight. |7|

O God, You alone know Your Glorious Virtues. Servant Nanak seeks Your Sanctuary.
You are the Ocean of water, and I am Your fish. Please be kind, and keep me always with You. |8|3|

Kalyaan, Fourth Mehl:
I worship and adore the Lord, the All-pervading Lord.

I surrender my mind and body, and place everything before Him; following the Guru's Teachings, spiritual wisdom is implanted within me. |1|Pause|

God's Name is the tree, and His Glorious Virtues are the branches. Picking and gathering up the fruit, I worship Him.
The soul is divine; divine is the soul. Worship Him with love. |1|

One of keen intellect and precise understanding is immaculate in all this world. In thoughtful consideration, he drinks in the sublime essence.
By Guru's Grace, the treasure is found; dedicate this mind to the True Guru. |2|

Priceless and utterly sublime is the Diamond of the Lord. This Diamond pierces the diamond of the mind.
The mind becomes the jeweller, through the Word of the Guru's Shabad; it appraises the Diamond of the Lord. |3|

Attaching oneself to the Society of the Saints, one is exalted and uplifted, as the palaas tree is absorbed by the peepal tree.
That mortal being is supreme among all people, who is perfumed by the fragrance of the Lord's Name. |4|

One who continually acts in goodness and immaculate purity, sprouts green branches in great abundance.
The Guru has taught me that Dharmic faith is the flower, and spiritual wisdom is the fruit; this fragrance permeates the world. |5|

The One, the Light of the One, abides within my mind; God, the One, is seen in all.
The One Lord, the Supreme Soul, is spread out everywhere; all place their heads beneath His Feet. |6|

Without the Naam, the Name of the Lord, people look like criminals with their noses cut off; bit by bit, their noses are cut off.
The faithless cynics are called egotistical; without the Name, their lives are cursed. |7|

As long as the breath breathes through the mind deep within, hurry and seek God's Sanctuary.

Please shower Your Kind Mercy and take pity upon Nanak, that he may wash the feet of the Holy. |8|4|

Kalyaan, Fourth Mehl:
O Lord, I wash the feet of the Holy.
May my sins be burnt away in an instant; O my Lord and Master, please bless me with Your Mercy. |1|Pause|

The meek and humble beggars stand begging at Your Door. Please be generous and give to those who are yearning.
Save me, save me, O God - I have come to Your Sanctuary. Please implant the Guru's Teachings, and the Naam within me. |1|

Sexual desire and anger are very powerful in the body-village; I rise up to fight the battle against them.
Please make me Your Own and save me; through the Perfect Guru, I drive them out. |2|

The powerful fire of corruption is raging violently within; the Word of the Guru's Shabad is the ice water which cools and soothes.

Section 33 - Raag Kalyaan - Part 008

My mind and body are calm and tranquil; the disease has been cured, and now I sleep in peace. |3|

As the rays of the sun spread out everywhere, the Lord pervades each and every heart.
Meeting the Holy Saint, one drinks in the Sublime Essence of the Lord; sitting in the home of your own inner being, drink in the essence. |4|

The humble being is in love with the Guru, like the chakvi bird which loves to see the sun.
She watches, and keeps on watching all through the night; and when the sun shows its face, she drinks in the Amrit. |5|

The faithless cynic is said to be very greedy - he is a dog. He is overflowing with the filth and pollution of evil-mindedness.
He talks excessively about his own interests. How can he be trusted? |6|

I have sought the Sanctuary of the Saadh Sangat, the Company of the Holy; I have found the Sublime Essence of the Lord.

They do good deeds for others, and speak of the Lord's many Glorious Virtues; please bless me to meet these Saints, these devotees of the Lord. |7|

You are the Inaccessible Lord, Kind and Compassionate, the Great Giver; please shower us with Your Mercy, and save us.

You are the Life of all the beings of the world; please cherish and sustain Nanak. |8|5|

Kalyaan, Fourth Mehl:
O Lord, please make me the slave of Your slaves.

As long as there is breath deep within my mind, let me drink in the dust of the Holy. |1|Pause|

Shiva, Naarad, the thousand-headed cobra king and the silent sages long for the dust of the Holy.

All the worlds and realms where the Holy place their feet are sanctified. |1|

So let go of your shame and renounce all your egotism; join with the Saadh Sangat, the Company of the Holy, and remain there.

Give up your fear of the Righteous Judge of Dharma, and you shall be lifted up and saved from drowning in the sea of poison. |2|

Some are standing, parched and shrivelled up by their doubts; joining the Saadh Sangat, they are rejuvenated.

So do not delay, even for an instant - go and fall at the feet of the Holy. |3|

The Kirtan of the Praise of the Lord's Name is a priceless jewel. The Lord has given it for the Holy to keep.

Whoever accepts and follows the Word of the Guru's Teachings as True - this Jewel is taken out and given to him. |4|

Listen, O Saints; listen, humble Siblings of Destiny: the Guru raises His Arms and sends out the call.

If you long for everlasting peace and comfort for your soul, then enter the Sanctuary of the True Guru. |5|

If you have great good fortune and are very noble, then implant the Guru's Teachings and the Naam, the Name of the Lord, within.

Emotional attachment to Maya is totally treacherous; drinking in the Sublime Essence of the Lord, you shall easily, intuitively cross over the world-ocean. |6|

Those who are totally in love with Maya, Maya, shall rot away in Maya.

The path of ignorance and darkness is utterly treacherous; they are loaded down with the crushing load of egotism. |7|

O Nanak, chanting the Name of the Lord, the All-pervading Lord, one is emancipated.

Meeting the True Guru, the Naam is implanted within; we are united and blended with the Lord's Name. |8|6|

First Set Of Six|

RAAG PRABHAATEE

Section 34 - Raag Prabhaatee - Part 001

ONE Universal Creator God. Truth Is The Name. Creative Being Personified. No Fear. No Hatred. Image Of The Undying. Beyond Birth. Self-Existent. By Guru's Grace:

Raag Parbhaatee Bibhaas, First Mehl, Chau-Padas, First House:
Your Name carries us across; Your Name brings respect and worship.
Your Name embellishes us; it is the object of the awakened mind.
Your Name brings honor to everyone's name.
Without Your Name, no one is ever respected. |1|

All other clever tricks are just for show.
Whoever the Lord blesses with forgiveness - his affairs are perfectly resolved. |1|Pause|

Your Name is my strength; Your Name is my support.
Your Name is my army; Your Name is my king.
Your Name brings honor, glory and approval.
By Your Grace, one is blessed with the banner and the insignia of Your Mercy. |2|

Your Name brings intuitive peace and poise; Your Name brings praise.
Your Name is the Ambrosial Nectar which cleans out the poison.
Through Your Name, all peace and comfort comes to abide in the mind.
Without the Name, they are bound and gagged, and dragged off to the City of Death. |3|

Man is involved with his wife, hearth and home, land and country,
the pleasures of the mind and fine clothes;
but when the call comes, he cannot delay.
O Nanak, in the end, the false turn out to be false. |4|1|

Prabhaatee, First Mehl:

Your Name is the Jewel, and Your Grace is the Light. In awareness, there is Your Light.
Darkness fills the dark, and then everything is lost. |1|

This whole world is corrupt.
Your Name is the only cure; nothing else works, O Infinite Creator Lord. |1|Pause|

One side of the scale holds tens of thousands, millions of nether regions and realms.
O my Beloved, Your Worth could only be estimated if something else could be placed on the other side of the scale. |2|

Section 34 - Raag Prabhaatee - Part 002

Out of pain, pleasure is produced, and out of pleasure comes pain.
That mouth which praises You - what hunger could that mouth ever suffer? |3|

O Nanak, you alone are foolish; all the rest of the world is good.
That body in which the Naam does not well up - that body becomes miserable. |4|2|

Prabhaatee, First Mehl:
For His sake, Brahma uttered the Vedas, and Shiva renounced Maya.
For His sake, the Siddhas became hermits and renunciates; even the gods have not realized His Mystery. |1|

O Baba, keep the True Lord in your mind, and utter the Name of the True Lord with your mouth; the True Lord will carry you across.
Enemies and pain shall not even approach you; only a rare few realize the Wisdom of the Lord. |1|Pause|

Fire, water and air make up the world; these three are the slaves of the Naam, the Name of the Lord.
One who does not chant the Naam is a thief, dwelling in the fortress of the five thieves. |2|

If someone does a good deed for someone else, he totally puffs himself up in his conscious mind.

The Lord bestows so many virtues and so much goodness; He does not ever regret it. |3|

Those who praise You gather the wealth in their laps; this is Nanak's wealth.
Whoever shows respect to them is not summoned by the Messenger of Death. |4|3|

Prabhaatee, First Mehl:
One who has no beauty, no social status, no mouth, no flesh
- meeting with the True Guru, he finds the Immaculate Lord, and dwells in Your Name. |1|

O detached Yogi, contemplate the essence of reality,
and you shall never again come to be born into the world. |1|Pause|

One who does not have good karma or Dharmic faith, sacred rosary or mala
- through the Light of God, wisdom is bestowed; the True Guru is our Protector. |2|

One who does not observe any fasts, make religious vows or chant
- he does not have to worry about good luck or bad, if he obeys the Command of the True Guru. |3|

One who is not hopeful, nor hopeless, who has trained his intuitive consciousness
- his being blends with the Supreme Being. O Nanak, his awareness is awakened. |4|4|

Prabhaatee, First Mehl:
What he says is approved in the Court of the Lord.
He looks upon poison and nectar as one and the same. |1|

What can I say? You are permeating and pervading all.
Whatever happens, is all by Your Will. |1|Pause|

The Divine Light shines radiantly, and egotistical pride is dispelled.
The True Guru bestows the Ambrosial Naam, the Name of the Lord. |2|

In this Dark Age of Kali Yuga, one's birth is approved,
if one is honored in the True Court. |3|

Speaking and listening, one goes to the Celestial Home of the Indescribable
Lord.
Mere words of mouth, O Nanak, are burnt away. |4|5|

Prabhaatee, First Mehl:
One who bathes in the Ambrosial Water of spiritual wisdom takes with him
the virtues of the sixty-eight sacred shrines of pilgrimage.
The Guru's Teachings are the gems and jewels; the Sikh who serves Him
searches and finds them. |1|

There is no sacred shrine equal to the Guru.
The Guru encompasses the ocean of contentment. |1|Pause|

Section 34 - Raag Prabhaatee - Part 003

The Guru is the River, from which the Pure Water is obtained forever; it
washes away the filth and pollution of evil-mindedness.
Finding the True Guru, the perfect cleansing bath is obtained, which
transforms even beasts and ghosts into gods. |2|

He is said to be the Guru, with the scent of sandalwood, who is imbued
with the True Name to the bottom of His Heart.
By His Fragrance, the world of vegetation is perfumed. Lovingly focus
yourself on His Feet. |3|

The life of the soul wells up for the Gurmukh; the Gurmukh goes to the
House of God.
The Gurmukh, O Nanak, merges in the True One; the Gurmukh attains the
exalted state of the self. |4|6|

Prabhaatee, First Mehl:
By Guru's Grace, contemplate spiritual knowledge; read it and study it, and
you shall be honored.
Within the self, the self is revealed, when one is blessed with the Ambrosial
Naam, the Name of the Lord. |1|

O Creator Lord, You alone are my Benefactor.

I beg for only one blessing from You: please bless me with Your Name. |1|Pause|

The five wandering thieves are captured and held, and the egotistical pride of the mind is subdued.
Visions of corruption, vice and evil-mindedness run away. Such is the spiritual wisdom of God. |2|

Please bless me with the rice of truth and self-restraint, the wheat of compassion, and the leaf-plate of meditation.
Bless me with the milk of good karma, and the clarified butter, the ghee, of compassion. Such are the gifts I beg of You, Lord. |3|

Let forgiveness and patience be my milk-cows, and let the calf of my mind intuitively drink in this milk.
I beg for the clothes of modesty and the Lord's Praise; Nanak chants the Glorious Praises of the Lord. |4|7|

Prabhaatee, First Mehl:
No one can hold anyone back from coming; how could anyone hold anyone back from going?
He alone thoroughly understands this, from whom all beings come; all are merged and immersed in Him. |1|

Waaho! - You are Great, and Wondrous is Your Will.
Whatever You do, surely comes to pass. Nothing else can happen. |1|Pause|

The buckets on the chain of the Persian wheel rotate; one empties out to fill another.
This is just like the Play of our Lord and Master; such is His Glorious Greatness. |2|

Following the path of intuitive awareness, one turns away from the world, and one's vision is enlightened.
Contemplate this in your mind, and see, O spiritual teacher. Who is the householder, and who is the renunciate? |3|

Hope comes from the Lord; surrendering to Him, we remain in the state of nirvaanaa.

We come from Him; surrendering to Him, O Nanak, one is approved as a householder, and a renunciate. |4|8|

Prabhaatee, First Mehl:
I am a sacrifice to that one who binds in bondage his evil and corrupted gaze.
One who does not know the difference between vice and virtue wanders around uselessly. |1|

Speak the True Name of the Creator Lord.
Then, you shall never again have to come into this world. |1|Pause|

The Creator transforms the high into the low, and makes the lowly into kings.
Those who know the All-knowing Lord are approved and certified as perfect in this world. |2|

If anyone is mistaken and fooled, you should go to instruct him.

Section 34 - Raag Prabhaatee - Part 004

The Creator Himself plays all the games; only a few understand this. |3|

Meditate on the Name, and the Word of the Shabad, in the early hours before dawn; leave your worldly entanglements behind.
Prays Nanak, the slave of God's slaves: the world loses, and he wins. |4|9|

Prabhaatee, First Mehl:
The mind is Maya, the mind is a chaser; the mind is a bird flying across the sky.
The thieves are overpowered by the Shabad, and then the body-village prospers and celebrates.
Lord, when You save someone, he is saved; his capital is safe and sound. |1|

Such is my Treasure, the Jewel of the Naam;
please bless me with the Guru's Teachings, so that I may fall at Your Feet. |1|Pause|

The mind is a Yogi, the mind is a pleasure-seeker; the mind is foolish and ignorant.

The mind is the giver, the mind is the beggar; the mind is the Great Guru, the Creator.

The five thieves are conquered, and peace is attained; such is the contemplative wisdom of God. |2|

The One Lord is said to be in each and every heart, but no one can see Him.

The false are cast upside-down into the womb of reincarnation; without the Name, they lose their honor.

Those whom You unite, remain united, if it is Your Will. |3|

God does not ask about social class or birth; you must find your true home.

That is your social class and that is your status - the karma of what you have done.

The pains of death and rebirth are eradicated; O Nanak, salvation is in the Lord's Name. |4|10|

Prabhaatee, First Mehl:

He is awake, and even happy, but he is being plundered - he is blind!

The noose is around his neck, and yet, his head is busy with worldly affairs.

In hope, he comes and in desire, he leaves.

The strings of his life are all tangled up; he is utterly helpless. |1|

The Lord of Awareness, the Lord of Life is awake and aware.

He is the Ocean of peace, the Treasure of Ambrosial Nectar. |1|Pause|

He does not understand what he is told; he is blind - he does not see, and so he does his evil deeds.

The Transcendent Lord Himself showers His Love and Affection; by His Grace, He bestows glorious greatness. |2|

With the coming of each and every day, his life is wearing away, bit by bit; but still, his heart is attached to Maya.

Without the Guru, he is drowned, and finds no place of rest, as long as he is caught in duality. |3|

Day and night, God watches over and takes care of His living beings; they receive pleasure and pain according to their past actions.

Nanak, the unfortunate one, begs for the charity of Truth; please bless him with this glory. |4|11|

Prabhaatee, First Mehl:
If I remain silent, the world calls me a fool.
If I talk too much, I miss out on Your Love.
My mistakes and faults will be judged in Your Court.
Without the Naam, the Name of the Lord, how can I maintain good conduct? |1|

Such is the falsehood which is plundering the world.
The slanderer slanders me, but even so, I love him. |1|Pause|

He alone knows the way, who has been slandered.
Through the Word of the Guru's Shabad, he is stamped with the Lord's Insignia in His Court.
He realizes the Naam, the Cause of causes, deep within himself.
He alone knows the way, who is blessed by the Lord's Glance of Grace. |2|

I am filthy and polluted; the True Lord is Immaculate and Sublime.
Calling oneself sublime, one does not become exalted.
The self-willed manmukh openly eats the great poison.
But one who becomes Gurmukh is absorbed in the Name. |3|

I am blind, deaf, foolish and ignorant,

Section 34 - Raag Prabhaatee - Part 005

the lowest of the low, the worst of the worst.
I am poor, but I have the Wealth of Your Name, O my Beloved.
This is the most excellent wealth; all else is poison and ashes. |4|

I pay no attention to slander and praise; I contemplate the Word of the Shabad.
I celebrate the One who blesses me with His Bounty.
Whomever You forgive, O Lord, is blessed with status and honor.
Says Nanak, I speak as He causes me to speak. |5|12|

Prabhaatee, First Mehl:

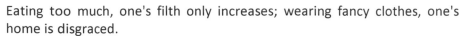

Eating too much, one's filth only increases; wearing fancy clothes, one's home is disgraced.
Talking too much, one only starts arguments. Without the Name, every-thing is poison - know this well. |1|

O Baba, such is the treacherous trap which has caught my mind;
riding out the waves of the storm, it will be enlightened by intuitive wisdom. |1|Pause|

They eat poison, speak poison and do poisonous deeds.
Bound and gagged at Death's door, they are punished; they can be saved only through the True Name. |2|

As they come, they go. Their actions are recorded, and go along with them.
The self-willed manmukh loses his capital, and is punished in the Court of the Lord. |3|

The world is false and polluted; only the True One is Pure. Contemplate Him through the Word of the Guru's Shabad.
Those who have God's spiritual wisdom within, are known to be very rare. |4|

They endure the unendurable, and the Nectar of the Lord, the Embodiment of Bliss, trickles into them continuously.
O Nanak, the fish is in love with the water; if it pleases You, Lord, please enshrine such love within me. |5|13|

Prabhaatee, First Mehl:
Songs, sounds, pleasures and clever tricks;
joy, love and the power to command;
fine clothes and food - these have no place in one's consciousness.
True intuitive peace and poise rest in the Naam. |1|

What do I know about what God does?
Without the Naam, the Name of the Lord, nothing makes my body feel good. |1|Pause|

Yoga, thrills, delicious flavors and ecstasy;
wisdom, truth and love all come from devotion to the Lord of the Universe.
My own occupation is to work to praise the Lord.

Deep within, I dwell on the Lord of the sun and the moon. |2|

I have lovingly enshrined the love of my Beloved within my heart.
My Husband Lord, the Lord of the World, is the Master of the meek and the poor.
Night and day, the Naam is my giving in charity and fasting.
The waves have subsided, contemplating the essence of reality. |3|

What power do I have to speak the Unspoken?
I worship You with devotion; You inspire me to do so.
You dwell deep within; my egotism is dispelled.
So whom should I serve? There is no other than You. |4|

The Word of the Guru's Shabad is utterly sweet and sublime.
Such is the Ambrosial Nectar I see deep within.
Those who taste this, attain the state of perfection.
O Nanak, they are satisfied, and their bodies are at peace. |5|14|

Prabhaatee, First Mehl:
Deep within, I see the Shabad, the Word of God; my mind is pleased and appeased. Nothing else can touch and imbue me.
Day and night, God watches over and cares for His beings and creatures; He is the Ruler of all. |1|

My God is dyed in the most beautiful and glorious color.
Merciful to the meek and the poor, my Beloved is the Enticer of the mind; He is so very sweet, imbued with the deep crimson color of His Love. |1|Pause|

The Well is high up in the Tenth Gate; the Ambrosial Nectar flows, and I drink it in.
The creation is His; He alone knows its ways and means. The Gurmukh contemplates spiritual wisdom. |2|

Section 34 - Raag Prabhaatee - Part 006

The rays of light spread out, and the heart-lotus joyfully blossoms forth; the sun enters into the house of the moon.
I have conquered death; the desires of the mind are destroyed. By Guru's Grace, I have found God. |3|

I am dyed in the deep crimson color of His Love. I am not colored by any other color.

O Nanak, my tongue is saturated with the taste of God, who is permeating and pervading everywhere. |4|15|

Prabhaatee, First Mehl:
The Yogis are divided into twelve schools, the Sannyaasees into ten.
The Yogis and those wearing religious robes, and the Jains with their all hair plucked out - without the Word of the Shabad, the noose is around their necks. |1|

Those who are imbued with the Shabad are the perfectly detached renunciates.
They beg to receive charity in the hands of their hearts, embracing love and affection for the One. |1|Pause|

The Brahmins study and argue about the scriptures; they perform ceremonial rituals, and lead others in these rituals.
Without true understanding, those self-willed manmukhs understand nothing. Separated from God, they suffer in pain. |2|

Those who receive the Shabad are sanctified and pure; they are approved in the True Court.
Night and day, they remain lovingly attuned to the Naam; throughout the ages, they are merged in the True One. |3|

Good deeds, righteousness and Dharmic faith, purification, austere self-discipline, chanting, intense meditation and pilgrimages to sacred shrines - all these abide in the Shabad.
O Nanak, united in union with the True Guru, suffering, sin and death run away. |4|16|

Prabhaatee, First Mehl:
The dust of the feet of the Saints, the Company of the Holy, and the Praises of the Lord carry us across to the other side.
What can the wretched, terrified Messenger of Death do to the Gurmukhs? The Lord abides in their hearts. |1|

Without the Naam, the Name of the Lord, life might just as well be burnt down.
The Gurmukh chants and meditates on the Lord, chanting the chant on the mala; the Flavor of the Lord comes into the mind. |1|Pause|

Those who follow the Guru's Teachings find true peace - how can I even describe the glory of such a person?
The Gurmukh seeks and finds the gems and jewels, diamonds, rubies and treasures. |2|

So center yourself on the treasures of spiritual wisdom and meditation; remain lovingly attuned to the One True Lord, and the Word of His Shabad.
Remain absorbed in the Primal State of the Fearless, Immaculate, Independent, Self-sufficient Lord. |3|

The seven seas are overflowing with the Immaculate Water; the inverted boat floats across.
The mind which wandered in external distractions is restrained and held in check; the Gurmukh is intuitively absorbed in God. |4|

He is a householder, he is a renunciate and God's slave, who, as Gurmukh, realizes his own self.
Says Nanak, his mind is pleased and appeased by the True Word of the Shabad; there is no other at all. |5|17|

Raag Prabhaatee, Third Mehl, Chau-Padas:
One Universal Creator God. By The Grace Of The True Guru:
Those who become Gurmukh and understand are very rare; God is permeating and pervading through the Word of His Shabad.
Those who are imbued with the Naam, the Name of the Lord, find everlasting peace; they remain lovingly attuned to the True One. |1|

Section 34 - Raag Prabhaatee - Part 007

Chant the Name of the Lord, Har, Har, O Siblings of Destiny.
By Guru's Grace, the mind becomes steady and stable; night and day, it remains satisfied with the Sublime Essence of the Lord. |1|Pause|

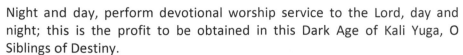
Night and day, perform devotional worship service to the Lord, day and night; this is the profit to be obtained in this Dark Age of Kali Yuga, O Siblings of Destiny.
The humble beings are forever immaculate; no filth ever sticks to them. They focus their consciousness on the True Name. |2|

The True Guru has revealed the ornamentation of peace; the Glorious Greatness of the Naam is Great!
The Inexhaustible Treasures are overflowing; they are never exhausted. So serve the Lord forever, O Siblings of Destiny. |3|

The Creator comes to abide in the minds of those whom He Himself has blessed.
O Nanak, meditate forever on the Naam, which the True Guru has revealed. |4|1|

Prabhaatee, Third Mehl:
I am unworthy; please forgive me and bless me, O my Lord and Master, and unite me with Yourself.
You are Endless; no one can find Your limits. Through the Word of Your Shabad, You bestow understanding. |1|

O Dear Lord, I am a sacrifice to You.
I dedicate my mind and body and place them in offering before You; I shall remain in Your Sanctuary forever. |1|Pause|

Please keep me forever under Your Will, O my Lord and Master; please bless me with the Glorious Greatness of Your Name.
Through the Perfect Guru, God's Will is revealed; night and day, remain absorbed in peace and poise. |2|

Those devotees who accept Your Will are pleasing to You, Lord; You Yourself forgive them, and unite them with Yourself.
Accepting Your Will, I have found everlasting peace; the Guru has extinguished the fire of desire. |3|

Whatever You do comes to pass, O Creator; nothing else can be done.
O Nanak, nothing is as great as the Blessing of the Name; it is obtained through the Perfect Guru. |4|2|

Prabhaatee, Third Mehl:
The Gurmukhs praise the Lord; praising the Lord, they know Him.
Doubt and duality are gone from within; they realize the Word of the Guru's Shabad. |1|

O Dear Lord, You are my One and Only.
I meditate on You and praise You; salvation and wisdom come from You. |1|Pause|

The Gurmukhs praise You; they receive the most excellent and sweet Ambrosial Nectar.
This Nectar is forever sweet; it never loses its taste. Contemplate the Word of the Guru's Shabad. |2|

He makes it seem so sweet to me; I am a sacrifice to Him.
Through the Shabad, I praise the Giver of peace forever. I have eradicated self-conceit from within. |3|

My True Guru is forever the Giver. I receive whatever fruits and rewards I desire.
O Nanak, through the Naam, glorious greatness is obtained; through the Word of the Guru's Shabad, the True One is found. |4|3|

Prabhaatee, Third Mehl:
Those who enter Your Sanctuary, Dear Lord, are saved by Your Protective Power.
I cannot even conceive of any other as Great as You. There never was, and there never shall be. |1|

O Dear Lord, I shall remain in Your Sanctuary forever.
As it pleases You, You save me, O my Lord and Master; this is Your Glorious Greatness. |1|Pause|

O Dear Lord, You cherish and sustain those who seek Your Sanctuary.

Section 34 - Raag Prabhaatee - Part 008

O Dear Lord, the Messenger of Death cannot even touch those whom You, in Your Mercy, protect. |2|

True Is Your Sanctuary, O Dear Lord; it never diminishes or goes away.
Those who abandon the Lord, and become attached to the love of duality, shall continue to die and be reborn. |3|

Those who seek Your Sanctuary, Dear Lord, shall never suffer in pain or hunger for anything.
O Nanak, praise the Naam, the Name of the Lord forever, and merge in the True Word of the Shabad. |4|4|

Prabhaatee, Third Mehl:
As Gurmukh, meditate on the Dear Lord forever, as long as there is the breath of life.
Through the Word of the Guru's Shabad, the mind becomes immaculate, and egotistical pride is expelled from the mind.
Fruitful and prosperous is the life of that mortal being, who is absorbed in the Name of the Lord. |1|

O my mind, listen to the Teachings of the Guru.
The Name of the Lord is the Giver of peace forever. With intuitive ease, drink in the Sublime Essence of the Lord. |1|Pause|

Those who understand their own origin dwell within the home of their inner being, in intuitive peace and poise.
Through the Word of the Guru's Shabad, the heart-lotus blossoms forth, and egotism and evil-mindedness are eradicated.
The One True Lord is pervading amongst all; those who realize this are very rare. |2|

Through the Guru's Teachings, the mind becomes immaculate, speaking the Ambrosial Essence.
The Name of the Lord dwells in the mind forever; within the mind, the mind is pleased and appeased.
I am forever a sacrifice to my Guru, through whom I have realized the Lord, the Supreme Soul. |3|

Those human beings who do not serve the True Guru - their lives are uselessly wasted.
When God bestows His Glance of Grace, then we meet the True Guru, merging in intuitive peace and poise.

O Nanak, by great good fortune, the Naam is bestowed; by perfect destiny, meditate. |4|5|

Prabhaatee, Third Mehl:
God Himself fashioned the many forms and colors; He created the Universe and staged the play.
Creating the creation, He watches over it. He acts, and causes all to act; He gives sustenance to all beings. |1|

In this Dark Age of Kali Yuga, the Lord is All-pervading.
The One God is pervading and permeating each and every heart; the Name of the Lord, Har, Har, is revealed to the Gurmukh. |1|Pause|

The Naam, the Name of the Lord, is hidden, but it is pervasive in the Dark Age. The Lord is totally pervading and permeating each and every heart.
The Jewel of the Naam is revealed within the hearts of those who hurry to the Sanctuary of the Guru. |2|

Whoever overpowers the five sense organs, is blessed with forgiveness, patience and contentment, through the Guru's Teachings.
Blessed, blessed, perfect and great is that humble servant of the Lord, who is inspired by the Fear of God and detached love, to sing the Glorious Praises of the Lord. |3|

If someone turns his face away from the Guru, and does not enshrine the Guru's Words in his consciousness

- he may perform all sorts of rituals and accumulate wealth, but in the end, he will fall into hell. |4|

The One Shabad, the Word of the One God, is prevailing everywhere. All the creation came from the One Lord.
O Nanak, the Gurmukh is united in union. When the Gurmukh goes, he blends into the Lord, Har, Har. |5|6|

Prabhaatee, Third Mehl:
O my mind, praise your Guru.

Section 34 - Raag Prabhaatee - Part 009

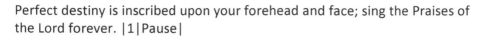

Perfect destiny is inscribed upon your forehead and face; sing the Praises of the Lord forever. |1|Pause|

The Lord bestows the Ambrosial Food of the Naam.
Out of millions, only a rare few receive it
- only those who are blessed by God's Glance of Grace. |1|

Whoever enshrines the Guru's Feet within his mind,
is rid of pain and darkness from within.
The True Lord unites him with Himself. |2|

So embrace love for the Word of the Guru's Bani.
Here and hereafter, this is your only Support.
The Creator Lord Himself bestows it. |3|

One whom the Lord inspires to accept His Will,
is a wise and knowing devotee.
Nanak is forever a sacrifice to him. |4|7|17|7|24|

Prabhaatee, Fourth Mehl, Bibhaas:
One Universal Creator God. By The Grace Of The True Guru:
Through the Guru's Teachings, I sing the Glorious Praises of the Lord with joyous love and delight; I am enraptured, lovingly attuned to the Naam, the Name of the Lord.
Through the Word of the Guru's Shabad, I drink in the Ambrosial Essence; I am a sacrifice to the Naam. |1|

The Lord, the Life of the World, is my Breath of Life.
The Lofty and Exalted Lord became pleasing to my heart and my inner being, when the Guru breathed the Mantra of the Lord into my ears. |1|Pause|

Come, O Saints: let us join together, O Siblings of Destiny; let us meet and chant the Name of the Lord, Har, Har.
How am I to find my God? Please bless me with the Gift of the Lord's Teachings. |2|

The Lord, Har, Har, abides in the Society of the Saints; joining this Sangat, the Lord's Glories are known.

By great good fortune, the Society of the Saints is found. Through the Guru, the True Guru, I receive the Touch of the Lord God. |3|

I sing the Glorious Praises of God, my Inaccessible Lord and Master; singing His Praises, I am enraptured.
The Guru has showered His Mercy on servant Nanak; in an instant, He blessed him with the Gift of the Lord's Name. |4|1|

Prabhaatee, Fourth Mehl:
With the rising of the sun, the Gurmukh speaks of the Lord. All through the night, he dwells upon the Sermon of the Lord.
My God has infused this longing within me; I seek my Lord God. |1|

My mind is the dust of the feet of the Holy.
The Guru has implanted the Sweet Name of the Lord, Har, Har, within me. I dust the Guru's Feet with my hair. |1|Pause|

Dark are the days and nights of the faithless cynics; they are caught in the trap of attachment to Maya.
The Lord God does not dwell in their hearts, even for an instant; every hair of their heads is totally tied up in debts. |2|

Joining the Sat Sangat, the True Congregation, wisdom and understanding are obtained, and one is released from the traps of egotism and possessiveness.
The Lord's Name, and the Lord, seem sweet to me. Through the Word of His Shabad, the Guru has made me happy. |3|

I am just a child; the Guru is the Unfathomable Lord of the World. In His Mercy, He cherishes and sustains me.
I am drowning in the ocean of poison; O God, Guru, Lord of the World, please save Your child, Nanak. |4|2|

Prabhaatee, Fourth Mehl:
The Lord God showered me with His Mercy for an instant; I sing His Glorious Praises with joyous love and delight.

Section 34 - Raag Prabhaatee - Part 010

Both the singer and the listener are liberated, when, as Gurmukh, they drink in the Lord's Name, even for an instant. |1|

The Sublime Essence of the Name of the Lord, Har, Har, is enshrined within my mind.
As Gurmukh, I have obtained the cooling, soothing Water of the Naam. I eagerly drink in the sublime essence of the Name of the Lord, Har, Har. |1|Pause|

Those whose hearts are imbued with the Love of the Lord have the mark of radiant purity upon their foreheads.
The Glory of the Lord's humble servant is manifest throughout the world, like the moon among the stars. |2|

Those whose hearts are not filled with the Lord's Name - all their affairs are worthless and insipid.
They may adorn and decorate their bodies, but without the Naam, they look like their noses have been cut off. |3|

The Sovereign Lord permeates each and every heart; the One Lord is all-pervading everywhere.
The Lord has showered His Mercy upon servant Nanak; through the Word of the Guru's Teachings, I have meditated on the Lord in an instant. |4|3|

Prabhaatee, Fourth Mehl:
God, the Inaccessible and Merciful, has showered me with His Mercy; I chant the Name of the Lord, Har, Har, with my mouth.
I meditate on the Name of the Lord, the Purifier of sinners; I am rid of all my sins and mistakes. |1|

O mind, chant the Name of the All-pervading Lord.
I sing the Praises of the Lord, Merciful to the meek, Destroyer of pain.
Following the Guru's Teachings, I gather in the Wealth of the Naam, the Name of the Lord. |1|Pause|

The Lord abides in the body-village; through the Wisdom of the Guru's Teachings, the Lord, Har, Har, is revealed.
In the lake of the body, the Lord's Name has been revealed. Within my own home and mansion, I have obtained the Lord God. |2|

Those beings who wander in the wilderness of doubt - those faithless cynics are foolish, and are plundered.
They are like the deer: the scent of musk comes from its own navel, but it wanders and roams around, searching for it in the bushes. |3|

You are Great and Unfathomable; Your Wisdom, God, is Profound and Incomprehensible. Please bless me with that wisdom, by which I might attain You, O Lord God.
The Guru has placed His Hand upon servant Nanak; he chants the Name of the Lord. |4|4|

Prabhaatee, Fourth Mehl:
My mind is in love with the Name of the Lord, Har, Har; I meditate on the Great Lord God.
The Word of the True Guru has become pleasing to my heart. The Lord God has showered me with His Grace. |1|

O my mind, vibrate and meditate on the Lord's Name every instant.
The Perfect Guru has blessed me with the gift of the Name of the Lord, Har, Har. The Lord's Name abides in my mind and body. |1|Pause|

The Lord abides in the body-village, in my home and mansion. As Gurmukh, I meditate on His Glory.
Here and hereafter, the Lord's humble servants are embellished and exalted; their faces are radiant; as Gurmukh, they are carried across. |2|

I am lovingly attuned to the Fearless Lord, Har, Har, Har; through the Guru, I have enshrined the Lord within my heart in an instant.
Millions upon millions of the faults and mistakes of the Lord's humble servant are all taken away in an instant. |3|

Your humble servants are known only through You, God; knowing You, they becomes supreme.
The Lord, Har, Har, has enshrined Himself within His humble servant. O Nanak, the Lord God and His servant are one and the same. |4|5|

Section 34 - Raag Prabhaatee - Part 011

Prabhaatee, Fourth Mehl:

The Guru, the True Guru, has implanted the Naam, the Name of the Lord within me. I was dead, but chanting the Name of the Lord, Har, Har, I have been brought back to life.

Blessed, blessed is the Guru, the Guru, the Perfect True Guru; He reached out to me with His Arm, and pulled me up and out of the ocean of poison. |1|

O mind, meditate and worship the Lord's Name.

God is never found, even by making all sorts of new efforts. The Lord God is obtained only through the Perfect Guru. |1|Pause|

The Sublime Essence of the Lord's Name is the source of nectar and bliss; drinking in this Sublime Essence, following the Guru's Teachings, I have become happy.

Even iron slag is transformed into gold, joining the Lord's Congregation. Through the Guru, the Lord's Light is enshrined within the heart. |2|

Those who are continually lured by greed, egotism and corruption, who are lured away by emotional attachment to their children and spouse

- they never serve at the feet of the Saints; those self-willed manmukhs are filled with ashes. |3|

O God, You alone know Your Glorious Virtues; I have grown weary - I seek Your Sanctuary.

As You know best, You preserve and protect me, O my Lord and Master; servant Nanak is Your slave. |4|6|

First Set Of Six|

Prabhaatee, Bibhaas, Partaal, Fourth Mehl:
One Universal Creator God. By The Grace Of The True Guru:
O mind, meditate on the Treasure of the Name of the Lord, Har, Har.
You shall be honored in the Court of the Lord.
Those who chant and meditate shall be carried across to the other shore. |1|Pause|

Listen, O mind: meditate on the Name of the Lord, Har, Har.
Listen, O mind: the Kirtan of the Lord's Praises is equal to bathing at the sixty-eight sacred shrines of pilgrimage.

Listen, O mind: as Gurmukh, you shall be blessed with honor. |1|

O mind, chant and meditate on the Supreme Transcendent Lord God.
Millions of sins shall be destroyed in an instant.
O Nanak, you shall meet with the Lord God. |2|1|7|

Prabhaatee, Fifth Mehl, Bibhaas:
One Universal Creator God. By The Grace Of The True Guru:
The Lord created the mind, and fashioned the entire body.
From the five elements, He formed it, and infused His Light within it.
He made the earth its bed, and water for it to use.
Do not forget Him for an instant; serve the Lord of the World. |1|

O mind, serve the True Guru, and obtain the supreme status.
If you remain unattached and unaffected by sorrow and joy, then you shall find the Lord of Life. |1|Pause|

He makes all the various pleasures, clothes and foods for you to enjoy.
He made your mother, father and all relatives.
He provides sustenance to all, in the water and on the land, O friend.
So serve the Lord, forever and ever. |2|

He shall be your Helper and Support there, where no one else can help you.
He washes away millions of sins in an instant.
He bestows His Gifts, and never regrets them.
He forgives, once and for all, and never asks for one's account again. |3|

Section 34 - Raag Prabhaatee - Part 012

By pre-ordained destiny, I have searched and found God.
In the Saadh Sangat, the Company of the Holy, the Lord of the World abides.
Meeting with the Guru, I have come to Your Door.
O Lord, please bless servant Nanak with the Blessed Vision of Your Darshan. |4|1|

Prabhaatee, Fifth Mehl:
Serving God, His humble servant is glorified.
Unfulfilled sexual desire, unresolved anger and unsatisfied greed are eradicated.

Your Name is the treasure of Your humble servant.
Singing His Praises, I am in love with the Blessed Vision of God's Darshan. |1|

You are known, O God, by Your devotees.
Breaking their bonds, You emancipate them. |1|Pause|

Those humble beings who are imbued with God's Love
find peace in God's Congregation.
They alone understand this, to whom this subtle essence comes.
Beholding it, and gazing upon it, in their minds they are wonderstruck. |2|

They are at peace, the most exalted of all,
within whose hearts God dwells.
They are stable and unchanging; they do not come and go in reincarnation.
Night and day, they sing the Glorious Praises of the Lord God. |3|

All bow down in humble respect to those
whose minds are filled with the Formless Lord.
Show mercy unto me, O my Divine Lord and Master.
May Nanak be saved, by serving these humble beings. |4|2|

Prabhaatee, Fifth Mehl:
Singing His Glorious Praises, the mind is in ecstasy.
Twenty-four hours a day, I meditate in remembrance on God.
Remembering Him in meditation, the sins go away.
I fall at the Feet of that Guru. |1|

O beloved Saints, please bless me with wisdom;
let me meditate on the Naam, the Name of the Lord, and be emancipated. |1|Pause|

The Guru has shown me the straight path;
I have abandoned everything else. I am enraptured with the Name of the Lord.
I am forever a sacrifice to that Guru;
I meditate in remembrance on the Lord, through the Guru. |2|

The Guru carries those mortal beings across, and saves them from drowning.

By His Grace, they are not enticed by Maya;
in this world and the next, they are embellished and exalted by the Guru.
I am forever a sacrifice to that Guru. |3|

From the most ignorant, I have been made spiritually wise,
through the Unspoken Speech of the Perfect Guru.
The Divine Guru, O Nanak, is the Supreme Lord God.
By great good fortune, I serve the Lord. |4|3|

Prabhaatee, Fifth Mehl:
Eradicating all my pains, He has blessed me with peace, and inspired me to
chant His Name.
In His Mercy, He has enjoined me to His service, and has purged me of all
my sins. |1|

I am only a child; I seek the Sanctuary of God the Merciful.
Erasing my demerits and faults, God has made me His Own. My Guru, the
Lord of the World, protects me. |1|Pause|

My sicknesses and sins were erased in an instant, when the Lord of the
World became merciful.
With each and very breath, I worship and adore the Supreme Lord God; I
am a sacrifice to the True Guru. |2|

My Lord and Master is Inaccessible, Unfathomable and Infinite. His limits
cannot be found.
We earn the profit, and become wealthy, meditating on our God. |3|

Section 34 - Raag Prabhaatee - Part 013

Twenty-four hours a day, I meditate on the Supreme Lord God; I sing His
Glorious Praises forever and ever.
Says Nanak, my desires have been fulfilled; I have found my Guru, the
Supreme Lord God. |4|4|

Prabhaatee, Fifth Mehl:
Meditating in rememberance on the Naam, all my sins have been erased.
The Guru has blessed me with the Capital of the True Name.
God's servants are embellished and exalted in His Court;
serving Him, they look beauteous forever. |1|

Chant the Name of the Lord, Har, Har, O my Siblings of Destiny.
All sickness and sin shall be erased; your mind shall be rid of the darkness of ignorance. |1|Pause|

The Guru has saved me from death and rebirth, O friend;
I am in love with the Name of the Lord.
The suffering of millions of incarnations is gone;
whatever pleases Him is good. |2|

I am forever a sacrifice to the Guru;
by His Grace, I meditate on the Lord's Name.
By great good fortune, such a Guru is found;
meeting Him, one is lovingly attuned to the Lord. |3|

Please be merciful, O Supreme Lord God, O Lord and Master,
Inner-knower, Searcher of Hearts.
Twenty-four hours a day, I am lovingly attuned to You.
Servant Nanak has come to the Sanctuary of God. |4|5|

Prabhaatee, Fifth Mehl:
In His Mercy, God has made me His Own.
He has blessed me with the Naam, the Name of the Lord.
Twenty-four hours a day, I sing the Glorious Praises of the Lord of the Universe.
Fear is dispelled, and all anxiety has been alleviated. |1|

I have been saved, touching the Feet of the True Guru.
Whatever the Guru says is good and sweet to me. I have renounced the intellectual wisdom of my mind. |1|Pause|

That Lord God abides within my mind and body.
There are no conflicts, pains or obstacles.
Forever and ever, God is with my soul.
Filth and pollution are washed away by the Love of the Name. |2|

I am in love with the Lotus Feet of the Lord;
I am no longer consumed by sexual desire, anger and egotism.
Now, I know the way to meet God.

Through loving devotional worship, my mind is pleased and appeased with the Lord. |3|

Listen, O friends, Saints, my exalted companions.
The Jewel of the Naam, the Name of the Lord, is unfathomable and immeasurable.
Forever and ever, sing the Glories of God, the Treasure of Virtue.
Says Nanak, by great good fortune, He is found. |4|6|

Prabhaatee, Fifth Mehl:
They are wealthy, and they are the true merchants,
who have the credit of the Naam in the Court of the Lord. |1|

So chant the Name of the Lord, Har, Har, in your mind, my friends.
The Perfect Guru is found by great good fortune, and then one's lifestyle becomes perfect and immaculate. |1|Pause|

They earn the profit, and the congratulations pour in;
by the Grace of the Saints, they sing the Glorious Praises of the Lord. |2|

Their lives are fruitful and prosperous, and their birth is approved;
by Guru's Grace, they enjoy the Love of the Lord. |3|

Sexuality, anger and egotism are wiped away;
O Nanak, as Gurmukh, they are carried across to the other shore. |4|7|

Prabhaatee, Fifth Mehl:
The Guru is Perfect, and Perfect is His Power.

Section 34 - Raag Prabhaatee - Part 014

The Word of the Guru's Shabad is unchanging, forever and ever.
All pains and afflictions run away from those, whose minds are filled with the Word of the Guru's Bani. |1|

Imbued with the Lord's Love, they sing the Glorious Praises of the Lord.
They are liberated, bathing in the dust of the feet of the Holy. |1|Pause|

By Guru's Grace, they are carried across to the other shore;
they are rid of fear, doubt and corruption.

The Guru's Feet abide deep within their minds and bodies.
The Holy are fearless; they take to the Sanctuary of the Lord. |2|

They are blessed with abundant bliss, happiness, pleasure and peace.
Enemies and pains do not even approach them.
The Perfect Guru makes them His Own, and protects them.
Chanting the Lord's Name, they are rid of all their sins. |3|

The Saints, spiritual companions and Sikhs are exalted and uplifted.
The Perfect Guru leads them to meet God.
The painful noose of death and rebirth is snapped.
Says Nanak, the Guru covers their faults. |4|8|

Prabhaatee, Fifth Mehl:
The Perfect True Guru has bestowed the Naam, the Name of the Lord.
I am blessed with bliss and happiness, emancipation and eternal peace. All
my affairs have been resolved. |1|Pause|

The Lotus Feet of the Guru abide within my mind.
I am rid of pain, suffering, doubt and fraud. |1|

Rise early, and sing the Glorious Word of God's Bani.
Twenty-four hours a day, meditate in remembrance on the Lord, O mortal.
|2|

Inwardly and outwardly, God is everywhere.
Wherever I go, He is always with me, my Helper and Support. |3|

With my palms pressed together, I offer this prayer.
O Nanak, I meditate forever on the Lord, the Treasure of Virtue. |4|9|

Prabhaatee, Fifth Mehl:
The Supreme Lord God is All-wise and All-knowing.
The Perfect Guru is found by great good fortune. I am a sacrifice to the
Blessed Vision of His Darshan. |1|Pause|

My sins are cut away, through the Word of the Shabad, and I have found
contentment.
I have become worthy of worshipping the Naam in adoration.
In the Saadh Sangat, the Company of the Holy, I have been enlightened.

The Lord's Lotus Feet abide within my mind. |1|

The One who made us, protects and preserves us.
God is Perfect, the Master of the masterless.
Those, upon whom He showers His Mercy
- they have perfect karma and conduct. |2|

They sing the Glories of God, continually, continuously, forever fresh and new.
They do not wander in the 8.4 million incarnations.
Here and hereafter, they worship the Lord's Feet.
Their faces are radiant, and they are honored in the Court of the Lord. |3|

That person, upon whose forehead the Guru places His Hand
- out of millions, how rare is that slave.
He sees God pervading and permeating the water, the land and the sky.
Nanak is saved by the dust of the feet of such a humble being. |4|10|

Prabhaatee, Fifth Mehl:
I am a sacrifice to my Perfect Guru.
By His Grace, I chant and meditate on the Lord, Har, Har. |1|Pause|

Listening to the Ambrosial Word of His Bani, I am exalted and enraptured.
My corrupt and poisonous entanglements are gone. |1|

I am in love with the True Word of His Shabad.
The Lord God has come into my consciousness. |2|

Chanting the Naam, I am enlightened.

Section 34 - Raag Prabhaatee - Part 015

The Word of the Guru's Shabad has come to dwell within my heart. |3|

The Guru is All-powerful and Merciful forever.
Chanting and meditating on the Lord, Nanak is exalted and enraptured. |4|11|

Prabhaatee, Fifth Mehl:
Chanting Guru, Guru, I have found eternal peace.

God, Merciful to the meek, has become kind and compassionate; He has inspired me to chant His Name. |1|Pause|

Joining the Society of the Saints, I am illumined and enlightened.
Chanting the Name of the Lord, Har, Har, my hopes have been fulfilled. |1|

I am blessed with total salvation, and my mind is filled with peace.
I sing the Glorious Praises of the Lord; O Nanak, the Guru has been gracious to me. |2|12|

Prabhaatee, Fifth Mehl, Second House, Bibhaas:
One Universal Creator God. By The Grace Of The True Guru:
There is no other place of rest,
none at all, without the Lord's Name.
There is total success and salvation,
and all affairs are perfectly resolved. |1|

Constantly chant the Name of the Lord.
Sexuality, anger and egotism are wiped away; let yourself fall in love with the One Lord. |1|Pause|

Attached to the Naam, the Name of the Lord, pain runs away. In His Sanctuary, He cherishes and sustains us.
Whoever has such pre-ordained destiny meets with the True Guru; the Messenger of Death cannot grab him. |2|

Night and day, meditate on the Lord, Har, Har; abandon the doubts of your mind.
One who has perfect karma joins the Saadh Sangat, the Company of the Holy, and meets the Lord. |3|

The sins of countless lifetimes are erased, and one is protected by the Lord Himself.
He is our Mother, Father, Friend and Sibling; O servant Nanak, meditate on the Lord, Har, Har. |4|1|13|

Prabhaatee, Fifth Mehl, Bibhaas, Partaal:
One Universal Creator God. By The Grace Of The True Guru:
Chant the Name of the Lord, Raam, Raam, Raam.

Conflict, suffering, greed and emotional attachment shall be dispelled, and the fever of egotism shall be relieved. |1|Pause|

Renounce your selfishness, and grasp the feet of the Saints; your mind shall be sanctified, and your sins shall be taken away. |1|

Nanak, the child, does not know anything at all. O God, please protect me; You are my Mother and Father. |2|1|14|

Prabhaatee, Fifth Mehl:
I have taken the Shelter and Support of the Lord's Lotus Feet.
You are Lofty and Exalted, Grand and Infinite, O my Lord and Master; You alone are above all. |1|Pause|

He is the Support of the breath of life, the Destroyer of pain, the Giver of discriminating understanding. |1|

So bow down in respect to the Savior Lord; worship and adore the One God.
Bathing in the dust of the feet of the Saints, Nanak is blessed with countless comforts. |2|2|15|

Section 34 - Raag Prabhaatee - Part 016

Prabhaatee, Ashtapadees, First Mehl, Bibhaas:
One Universal Creator God. By The Grace Of The True Guru:
The insanity of duality has driven the mind insane.
In false greed, life is wasting away.
Duality clings to the mind; it cannot be restrained.
The True Guru saves us, implanting the Naam, the Name of the Lord within. |1|

Without subduing the mind, Maya cannot be subdued.
The One who created this, He alone understands. Contemplating the Word of the Shabad, one is carried across the terrifying world-ocean. |1|Pause|

Gathering the wealth of Maya, kings become proud and arrogant.
But this Maya that they love so much shall not go along with them in the end.
There are so many colors and flavors of attachment to Maya.

Except for the Name, no one has any friend or companion. |2|

According to one's own mind, one sees the minds of others.
According to one's desires, one's condition is determined.
According to one's actions, one is focused and tuned in.
Seeking the advice of the True Guru, one finds the home of peace and poise. |3|

In music and song, the mind is caught by the love of duality.
Filled with deception deep within, one suffers in terrible pain.
Meeting with the True Guru, one is blessed with clear understanding,
and remains lovingly attuned to the True Name. |4|

Through the True Word of the Shabad, one practices Truth.
He sings the Glorious Praises of the Lord, through the True Word of His Bani.
He dwells in the home of his own heart deep within, and obtains the immortal status.
Then, he is blessed with honor in the Court of the True Lord. |5|

Without serving the Guru, there is no devotional worship,
even though one may make all sorts of efforts.
If one eradicates egotism and selfishness through the Shabad,
the Immaculate Naam comes to abide in the mind. |6|

In this world, the practice of the Shabad is the most excellent occupation.
Without the Shabad, everything else is the darkness of emotional attachment.
Through the Shabad, the Naam is enshrined within the heart.
Through the Shabad, one obtains clear understanding and the door of salvation. |7|

There is no other Creator except the All-seeing Lord God.
The True Lord Himself is Infinite and Incomparably Beautiful.
Through the Lord's Name, one obtains the most sublime and exalted state.
O Nanak, how rare are those humble beings, who seek and find the Lord. |8|1|

Prabhaatee, First Mehl:
Emotional attachment to Maya is spread out all over the world.

Seeing a beautiful woman, the man is overcome with sexual desire.
His love for his children and gold steadily increases.
He sees everything as his own, but he does not own the One Lord. |1|

I meditate as I chant on such a mala,
that I rise above pleasure and pain; I attain the most wondrous devotional worship of the Lord. |1|Pause|

O Treasure of Virtue, Your limits cannot be found.
Through the True Word of the Shabad, I am absorbed into You.
You Yourself created the comings and goings of reincarnation.
They alone are devotees, who focus their consciousness on You. |2|

Spiritual wisdom and meditation on the Lord, the Lord of Nirvaanaa
- without meeting the True Guru, no one knows this.
The Lord's Light fills the sacred pools of all beings.
I am a sacrifice to the Embodiment of Bliss. |3|

Through the Guru's Teachings, one achieves loving devotional worship.
The Shabad burns away egotism from within.

Section 34 - Raag Prabhaatee - Part 017

The wandering mind is restrained and held in its place.
The True Name is enshrined in the mind. |4|

The exciting and intoxicating worldly plays come to an end,
for those who accept the Guru's Teachings, and become lovingly attuned to the One Lord.
Seeing this, the fire in the water is extinguished.
They alone realize this, who are blessed by great good fortune. |5|

Serving the True Guru, doubt is dispelled.
Those who are lovingly attuned to the True Lord remain awake and aware night and day.
They know the One Lord, and no other.
Serving the Giver of peace, they become immaculate. |6|

Selfless service and intuitive awareness come by reflecting upon the Word of the Shabad.

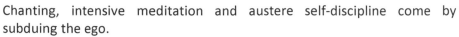

Chanting, intensive meditation and austere self-discipline come by subduing the ego.

One becomes Jivan-mukta - liberated while yet alive, by listening to the Shabad.

Living a truthful way of life, one finds true peace. |7|

The Giver of peace is the Eradicator of pain.

I cannot conceive of serving any other.

I place my body, mind and wealth in offering before Him.

Says Nanak, I have tasted the supreme, sublime Essence of the Lord. |8|2|

Prabhaatee, First Mehl:

You may perform exercises of inner purification, and fire up the furnace of the Kundalini, inhaling and exhaling and holding the breath.

Without the True Guru, you will not understand; deluded by doubt, you shall drown and die.

The spiritually blind are filled with filth and pollution; they may wash, but the filth within shall never depart.

Without the Naam, the Name of the Lord, all their actions are useless, like the magician who deceives through illuions. |1|

The merits of the six religious rituals are obtained through the Immaculate Naam.

You, O Lord, are the Ocean of virtue; I am so unworthy. |1|Pause|

Running around chasing the entanglements of Maya is an evil-minded act of corruption.

The fool makes a show of his self-conceit; he does not know how to behave.

The self-willed manmukh is enticed by his desires for Maya; his words are useless and empty.

The ritual cleansings of the sinner are fradulent; his rituals and decorations are useless and empty. |2|

False is the wisdom of the mind; its actions inspire useless disputes.

The false are filled with egotism; they do not obtain the sublime taste of their Lord and Master.

Without the Name, whatever else they do is tasteless and insipid.

Associating with their enemies, they are plundered and ruined. Their speech is poison, and their lives are useless. |3|

Do not be deluded by doubt; do not invite your own death.
Serve the True Guru, and you shall be at peace forever.
Without the True Guru, no one is liberated.
They come and go in reincarnation; they die, only to be reborn and die again. |4|

This body wanders, caught in the three dispositions.
It is afflicted by sorrow and suffering.
So serve the One who has no mother or father.
Desire and selfishness shall depart from within. |5|

Wherever I look, I see Him.
Without meeting the True Guru, no one is liberated.
Enshrine the True One in your heart; this is the most excellent action.
All other hypocritical actions and devotions bring only ruin. |6|

When one is rid of duality, then he realizes the Word of the Shabad.
Inside and out, he knows the One Lord.
This is the most Excellent Wisdom of the Shabad.
Ashes fall on the heads of those who are in duality. |7|

To praise the Lord through the Guru's Teachings is the most excellent action.
In the Society of the Saints, contemplate the Glories of God and His spiritual wisdom.
Whoever subdues his mind, knows the state of being dead while yet alive.
O Nanak, by His Grace, the Gracious Lord is realized. |8|3|

Section 34 - Raag Prabhaatee - Part 018

Prabhaatee, First Mehl, Dakhnee:
Ahalyaa was the wife of Gautam the seer. Seeing her, Indra was enticed.
When he received a thousand marks of disgrace on his body, then he felt regret in his mind. |1|

O Siblings of Destiny, no one knowingly makes mistakes.
He alone is mistaken, whom the Lord Himself makes so. He alone understands, whom the Lord causes to understand. |1|Pause|

Harichand, the king and ruler of his land, did not appreciate the value of his pre-ordained destiny.
If he had known that it was a mistake, he would not have made such a show of giving in charity, and he would not have been sold in the market. |2|

The Lord took the form of a dwarf, and asked for some land.
If Bal the king has recognized Him, he would not have been deceived, and sent to the underworld. |3|

Vyaas taught and warned the king Janmayjaa not to do three things.
But he performed the sacred feast and killed eighteen Brahmins; the record of one's past deeds cannot be erased. |4|

I do not try to calculate the account; I accept the Hukam of God's Command. I speak with intuitive love and respect.
No matter what happens, I will praise the Lord. It is all Your Glorious Greatness, O Lord. |5|

The Gurmukh remains detached; filth never attaches itself to him. He remains forever in God's Sanctuary.
The foolish self-willed manmukh does not think of the future; he is overtaken by pain, and then he regrets. |6|

The Creator who created this creation acts, and causes all to act.
O Lord, egotistical pride does not depart from the soul. Falling into egotistical pride, one is ruined. |7|

Everyone makes mistakes; only the Creator does not make mistakes.
O Nanak, salvation comes through the True Name. By Guru's Grace, one is released. |8|4|

Prabhaatee, First Mehl:
To chant and listen to the Naam, the Name of the Lord, is my Support.
Worthless entanglements are ended and gone.
The self-willed manmukh, caught in duality, loses his honor.
Except for the Name, I have no other at all. |1|

Listen, O blind, foolish, idiotic mind.

Aren't you ashamed of your comings and goings in reincarnation? Without the Guru, you shall drown, over and over again. |1|Pause|

This mind is ruined by its attachment to Maya.
The Command of the Primal Lord is pre-ordained. Before whom should I cry?
Only a few, as Gurmukh, understand this.
Without the Naam, no one is liberated. |2|

People wander lost, staggering and stumbling through 8.4 million incarnations.
Without knowing the Guru, they cannot escape the noose of Death.
This mind, from one moment to the next, goes from the heavens to the underworld.
The Gurmukh contemplates the Naam, and is released. |3|

When God sends His Summons, there is no time to delay.
When one dies in the Word of the Shabad, he lives in peace.
Without the Guru, no one understands.
The Lord Himself acts, and inspires all to act. |4|

Inner conflict comes to an end, singing the Glorious Praises of the Lord.
Through the Perfect True Guru, one is intuitively absorbed into the Lord.
This wobbling, unsteady mind is stabilized,
and one lives the lifestyle of true actions. |5|

If someone is false within his own self, then how can he be pure?
How rare are those who wash with the Shabad.
How rare are those who, as Gurmukh, live the Truth.
Their comings and goings in reincarnation are over and done. |6|

Section 34 - Raag Prabhaatee - Part 019

Those who eat and drink the Fear of God, find the most excellent peace.
Associating with the humble servants of the Lord, they are carried across.
They speak the Truth, and lovingly inspire others to speak it as well.
The Word of the Guru's Shabad is the most excellent occupation. |7|

Those who take the Lord's Praises as their karma and Dharma, their honor and worship service

- their sexual desire and anger are burnt off in the fire.
They taste the sublime essence of the Lord, and their minds are drenched with it.
Prays Nanak, there is no other at all. |8|5|

Prabhaatee, First Mehl:
Chant the Lord's Name, and worship Him deep within your being.
Contemplate the Word of the Guru's Shabad, and no other. |1|

The One is pervading all places.
I do not see any other; unto whom should I offer worship? |1|Pause|

I place my mind and body in offering before You; I dedicate my soul to You.
As it pleases You, You save me, Lord; this is my prayer. |2|

True is that tongue which is delighted by the sublime essence of the Lord.
Following the Guru's Teachings, one is saved in the Sanctuary of God. |3|

My God created religious rituals.
He placed the glory of the Naam above these rituals. |4|

The four great blessings are under the control of the True Guru.
When the first three are put aside, one is blessed with the fourth. |5|

Those whom the True Guru blesses with liberation and meditation
realize the Lord's State, and become sublime. |6|

Their minds and bodies are cooled and soothed; the Guru imparts this understanding.
Who can estimate the value of those whom God has exalted? |7|

Says Nanak, the Guru has imparted this understanding;
without the Naam, the Name of the Lord, no one is emancipated. |8|6|

Prabhaatee, First Mehl:
Some are forgiven by the Primal Lord God; the Perfect Guru makes the true making.
Those who are attuned to the Love of the Lord are imbued with Truth forever; their pains are dispelled, and they obtain honor. |1|

False are the clever tricks of the evil-minded.
They shall disappear in no time at all. |1|Pause|

Pain and suffering afflict the self-willed manmukh. The pains of the self-willed manmukh shall never depart.
The Gurmukh recognizes the Giver of pleasure and pain. He merges in His Sanctuary. |2|

The self-willed manmukhs do not know loving devotional worship; they are insane, rotting away in their egotism.
This mind flies in an instant from the heavens to the underworld, as long as it does not know the Word of the Shabad. |3|

The world has become hungry and thirsty; without the True Guru, it is not satisfied.
Merging intuitively in the Celestial Lord, peace is obtained, and one goes to the Lord's Court wearing robes of honor. |4|

The Lord in His Court is Himself the Knower and Seer; the Word of the Guru's Bani is Immaculate.
He Himself is the Awareness of Truth; He Himself understands the state of nirvaanaa. |5|

He made the waves of water, the fire and the air, and then joined the three together to form the world.
He blessed these elements with such power, that they remain subject to His Command. |6|

How rare are those humble beings in this world, whom the Lord tests and places in His Treasury.
They rise above social status and color, and rid themselves of possessiveness and greed. |7|

Attuned to the Naam, the Name of the Lord, they are like immaculate sacred shrines; they are rid of the pain and pollution of egotism.
Nanak washes the feet of those who, as Gurmukh, love the True Lord. |8|7|

Section 34 - Raag Prabhaatee - Part 020

Prabhaatee, Third Mehl, Bibhaas:
One Universal Creator God. By The Grace Of The True Guru:
By Guru's Grace, see that the Temple of the Lord is within you.
The Temple of the Lord is found through the Word of the Shabad; contemplate the Lord's Name. |1|

O my mind, be joyfully attuned to the Shabad.
True is devotional worship, and True is the Temple of the Lord; True is His Manifest Glory. |1|Pause|

This body is the Temple of the Lord, in which the jewel of spiritual wisdom is revealed.
The self-willed manmukhs do not know anything at all; they do not believe that the Lord's Temple is within. |2|

The Dear Lord created the Temple of the Lord; He adorns it by His Will.
All act according to their pre-ordained destiny; no one can erase it. |3|

Contemplating the Shabad, peace is obtained, loving the True Name.
The Temple of the Lord is embellished with the Shabad; it is an Infinite Fortress of God. |4|

This world is the Temple of the Lord; without the Guru, there is only pitch darkness.
The blind and foolish self-willed manmukhs worship in the love of duality. |5|

One's body and social status do not go along to that place, where all are called to account.
Those who are attuned to Truth are saved; those in the love of duality are miserable. |6|

The treasure of the Naam is within the Temple of the Lord. The idiotic fools do not realize this.
By Guru's Grace, I have realized this. I keep the Lord enshrined within my heart. |7|

Those who are attuned to the love of the Shabad know the Guru, through the Word of the Guru's Bani.

Sacred, pure and immaculate are those humble beings who are absorbed in the Name of the Lord. |8|

The Temple of the Lord is the Lord's Shop; He embellishes it with the Word of His Shabad.
In that shop is the merchandise of the One Name; the Gurmukhs adorn themselves with it. |9|

The mind is like iron slag, within the Temple of the Lord; it is lured by the love of duality.
Meeting with the Guru, the Philosopher's Stone, the mind is transformed into gold. Its value cannot be described. |10|

The Lord abides within the Temple of the Lord. He is pervading in all.
O Nanak, the Gurmukhs trade in the merchandise of Truth. |11|1|

Prabhaatee, Third Mehl:
Those who remain awake and aware in the Love and Fear of God, rid themselves of the filth and pollution of egotism.
They remain awake and aware forever, and protect their homes, by beating and driving out the five thieves. |1|

O my mind, as Gurmukh, meditate on the Naam, the Name of the Lord.
O mind, do only those deeds which will lead you to the Path of the Lord. |1|Pause|

The celestial melody wells up in the Gurmukh, and the pains of egotism are taken away.
The Name of the Lord abides in the mind, as one intuitively sings the Glorious Praises of the Lord. |2|

Those who follow the Guru's Teachings - their faces are radiant and beautiful. They keep the Lord enshrined in their hearts.
Here and hereafter, they find absolute peace; chanting the Name of the Lord, Har, Har, they are carried across to the other shore. |3|

Section 34 - Raag Prabhaatee - Part 021

In egotism, one cannot remain awake and aware, and one's devotional worship of the Lord is not accepted

The self-willed manmukhs find no place in the Court of the Lord; they do their deeds in the love of duality. |4|

Cursed is the food, and cursed are the clothes, of those who are attached to the love of duality.
They are like maggots in manure, sinking into manure. In death and rebirth, they are wasted away to ruin. |5|

I am a sacrifice to those who meet with the True Guru.
I shall continue to associate with them; devoted to Truth, I am absorbed in Truth. |6|

By perfect destiny, the Guru is found. He cannot be found by any efforts.
Through the True Guru, intuitive wisdom wells up; through the Word of the Shabad, egotism is burnt away. |7|

O my mind, hurry to the Sanctuary of the Lord; He is Potent to do every-thing.
O Nanak, never forget the Naam, the Name of the Lord. Whatever He does, comes to pass. |8|2|7|2|9|

Bibhaas, Prabhaatee, Fifth Mehl, Ashtapadees:
One Universal Creator God. By The Grace Of The True Guru:
Mother, father, siblings, children and spouse
- involved with them, people eat the food of bliss.
The mind is entangled in sweet emotional attachment.
Those who seek God's Glorious Virtues are the support of my breath of life.
|1|

My One Lord is the Inner-Knower, the Searcher of hearts.
He alone is my Support; He is my only Protection. My Great Lord and Master is over and above the heads of kings. |1|Pause|

I have broken my ties to that deceitful serpent.
The Guru has told me that it is false and fraudulent.
Its face is sweet, but it tastes very bitter.
My mind remains satisfied with the Ambrosial Naam, the Name of the Lord.
|2|

I have broken my ties with greed and emotional attachment.

The Merciful Guru has rescued me from them.
These cheating thieves have plundered so many homes.
The Merciful Guru has protected and saved me. |3|

I have no dealings whatsoever with sexual desire and anger.
I listen to the Guru's Teachings.
Wherever I look, I see the most horrible goblins.
My Guru, the Lord of the World, has saved me from them. |4|

I have made widows of the ten sensory organs.
The Guru has told me that these pleasures are the fires of corruption.
Those who associate with them go to hell.
The Guru has saved me; I am lovingly attuned to the Lord. |5|

I have forsaken the advice of my ego.
The Guru has told me that this is foolish stubbornness.
This ego is homeless; it shall never find a home.
The Guru has saved me; I am lovingly attuned to the Lord. |6|

I have become alienated from these people.
We cannot both live together in one home.
Grasping the hem of the Guru's Robe, I have come to God.
Please be fair with me, All-knowing Lord God. |7|

God smiled at me and spoke, passing judgement.
He made all the demons perform service for me.
You are my Lord and Master; all this home belongs to You.
Says Nanak, the Guru has passed judgement. |8|1|

Prabhaatee, Fifth Mehl:

Section 34 - Raag Prabhaatee - Part 022

Within the mind dwell anger and massive ego.
Worship services are performed with great pomp and ceremony.
Ritual cleansing baths are taken, and sacred marks are applied to the body.
But still, the filth and pollution within never depart. |1|

No one has ever found God in this way.

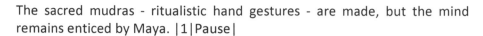

The sacred mudras - ritualistic hand gestures - are made, but the mind remains enticed by Maya. |1|Pause|

They commit sins, under the influence of the five thieves.
They bathe at sacred shrines, and claim that everything has been washed off.
Then they commit them again, without fear of the consequences.
The sinners are bound and gagged, and taken to the City of Death. |2|

The ankle-bells shake and the cymbals vibrate,
but those who have deception within wander lost like demons.
By destroying its hole, the snake is not killed.
God, who created you, knows everything. |3|

You worship fire and wear saffron colored robes.
Stung by your misfortune, you abandon your home.
Leaving your own country, you wander in foreign lands.
But you bring the five rejects with you. |4|

You have split your ears, and now you steal crumbs.
You beg from door to door, but you fail to be satisfied.
You have abandoned your own wife, but now you sneak glances at other women.
God is not found by wearing religious robes; you are utterly miserable! |5|

He does not speak; he is on silence.
But he is filled with desire; he is made to wander in reincarnation.
Abstaining from food, his body suffers in pain.
He does not realize the Hukam of the Lord's Command; he is afflicted by possessiveness. |6|

Without the True Guru, no one has attained the supreme status.
Go ahead and ask all the Vedas and the Simritees.
The self-willed manmukhs do useless deeds.
They are like a house of sand, which cannot stand. |7|

One unto whom the Lord of the Universe becomes Merciful,
sews the Word of the Guru's Shabad into his robes.
Out of millions, it is rare that such a Saint is seen.
O Nanak, with him, we are carried across. |8|

If one has such good destiny, then the Blessed Vision of His Darshan is obtained.

He saves himself, and carries across all his family as well. |1|SECOND PAUSE|2|

Prabhaatee, Fifth Mehl:

Meditating in remembrance on the Naam, all the sins are erased.

The accounts held by the Righteous Judge of Dharma are torn up.

Joining the Saadh Sangat, the Company of the Holy,

I have found the Sublime Essence of the Lord. The Supreme Lord God has melted into my heart. |1|

Dwelling on the Lord, Har, Har, I have found peace.

Your slaves seek the Sanctuary of Your Feet. |1|Pause|

The cycle of reincarnation is ended, and darkness is dispelled.

The Guru has revealed the door of liberation.

My mind and body are forever imbued with loving devotion to the Lord.

Now I know God, because He has made me know Him. |2|

He is contained in each and every heart.

Without Him, there is no one at all.

Hatred, conflict, fear and doubt have been eliminated.

God, the Soul of Pure Goodness, has manifested His Righteousness. |3|

He has rescued me from the most dangerous waves.

Separated from Him for countless lifetimes, I am united with Him once again.

Chanting, intense meditation and strict self-discipline are the contemplation of the Naam.

My Lord and Master has blessed me with His Glance of Grace. |4|

Bliss, peace and salvation are found in that place,

Section 34 - Raag Prabhaatee - Part 023

where the servants of the Lord of the World abide.

God, the Lord of the World, is pleased and satisfied with me.

My disharmony with Him of so many lifetimes is ended. |5|

Burnt offerings, sacred feasts, intense meditations with the body upside-
down, worship services
and taking millions of cleansing baths at sacred shrines of pilgrimage
- the merits of all these are obtained by enshrining the Lord's Lotus Feet
within the heart, even for an instant.
Meditating on the Lord of the Universe, all one's affairs are resolved. |6|

God's Place is the highest of the high.
The Lord's humble servants intuitively focus their meditation on Him.
I long for the dust of the slaves of the Lord's slaves.
My Beloved Lord is overflowing with all powers. |7|

My Beloved Lord, my Mother and Father, is always near.
O my Friend and Companion, You are my Trusted Support.
God takes His slaves by the hand, and makes them His Own.
Nanak lives by meditating on the Lord, the Treasure of Virtue.
|8|3|2|7|12|

Bibhaas, Prabhaatee, The Word Of Devotee Kabeer Jee:
One Universal Creator God. By The Grace Of The True Guru:
My anxious fears of death and rebirth have been taken away.
The Celestial Lord has shown His Love for me. |1|

The Divine Light has dawned, and darkness has been dispelled.
Contemplating the Lord, I have obtained the Jewel of His Name. |1|Pause|

Pain runs far away from that place where there is bliss.
The jewel of the mind is focused and attuned to the essence of reality. |2|

Whatever happens is by the Pleasure of Your Will.
Whoever understands this, is intuitively merged in the Lord. |3|

Says Kabeer, my sins have been obliterated.
My mind has merged into the Lord, the Life of the World. |4|1|

PRABHAATEE:
If the Lord Allah lives only in the mosque, then to whom does the rest of
the world belong?

According to the Hindus, the Lord's Name abides in the idol, but there is no truth in either of these claims. |1|

O Allah, O Raam, I live by Your Name.
Please show mercy to me, O Master. |1|Pause|

The God of the Hindus lives in the southern lands, and the God of the Muslims lives in the west.
So search in your heart - look deep into your heart of hearts; this is the home and the place where God lives. |2|

The Brahmins observe twenty-four fasts during the year, and the Muslims fast during the month of Ramadaan.
The Muslims set aside eleven months, and claim that the treasure is only in the one month. |3|

What is the use of bathing at Orissa? Why do the Muslims bow their heads in the mosque?
If someone has deception in his heart, what good is it for him to utter prayers? And what good is it for him to go on pilgrimage to Mecca? |4|

You fashioned all these men and women, Lord. All these are Your Forms.
Kabeer is the child of God, Allah, Raam. All the Gurus and prophets are mine. |5|

Says Kabeer, listen, O men and women: seek the Sanctuary of the One.
Chant the Naam, the Name of the Lord, O mortals, and you shall surely be carried across. |6|2|

PRABHAATEE:
First, Allah created the Light; then, by His Creative Power, He made all mortal beings.
From the One Light, the entire universe welled up. So who is good, and who is bad? |1|

Section 34 - Raag Prabhaatee - Part 024

O people, O Siblings of Destiny, do not wander deluded by doubt.
The Creation is in the Creator, and the Creator is in the Creation, totally pervading and permeating all places. |1|Pause|

The clay is the same, but the Fashioner has fashioned it in various ways.
There is nothing wrong with the pot of clay - there is nothing wrong with the Potter. |2|

The One True Lord abides in all; by His making, everything is made.
Whoever realizes the Hukam of His Command, knows the One Lord. He alone is said to be the Lord's slave. |3|

The Lord Allah is Unseen; He cannot be seen. The Guru has blessed me with this sweet molasses.
Says Kabeer, my anxiety and fear have been taken away; I see the Immaculate Lord pervading everywhere. |4|3|

PRABHAATEE:
Do not say that the Vedas, the Bible and the Koran are false. Those who do not contemplate them are false.
You say that the One Lord is in all, so why do you kill chickens? |1|

O Mullah, tell me: is this God's Justice?
The doubts of your mind have not been dispelled. |1|Pause|

You seize a living creature, and then bring it home and kill its body; you have killed only the clay.
The light of the soul passes into another form. So tell me, what have you killed? |2|

And what good are your purifications? Why do you bother to wash your face? And why do you bother to bow your head in the mosque?
Your heart is full of hypocrisy; what good are your prayers or your pilgrimage to Mecca? |3|

You are impure; you do not understand the Pure Lord. You do not know His Mystery.
Says Kabeer, you have missed out on paradise; your mind is set on hell. |4|4|

PRABHAATEE:
Hear my prayer, Lord; You are the Divine Light of the Divine, the Primal, All-pervading Master.

The Siddhas in Samaadhi have not found Your limits. They hold tight to the Protection of Your Sanctuary. |1|

Worship and adoration of the Pure, Primal Lord comes by worshipping the True Guru, O Siblings of Destiny.
Standing at His Door, Brahma studies the Vedas, but he cannot see the Unseen Lord. |1|Pause|

With the oil of knowledge about the essence of reality, and the wick of the Naam, the Name of the Lord, this lamp illluminates my body.
I have applied the Light of the Lord of the Universe, and lit this lamp. God the Knower knows. |2|

The Unstruck Melody of the Panch Shabad, the Five Primal Sounds, vibrates and resounds. I dwell with the Lord of the World.
Kabeer, Your slave, performs this Aartee, this lamp-lit worship service for You, O Formless Lord of Nirvaanaa. |3|5|

Prabhaatee, The Word Of Devotee Naam Dayv Jee:
One Universal Creator God. By The Grace Of The True Guru:
The mind alone knows the state of the mind; I tell it to the Knowing Lord.
I chant the Name of the Lord, the Inner-knower, the Searcher of hearts - why should I be afraid? |1|

My mind is pierced through by the love of the Lord of the World.
My God is All-pervading everywhere. |1|Pause|

The mind is the shop, the mind is the town, and the mind is the shopkeeper.
The mind abides in various forms, wandering all across the world. |2|

This mind is imbued with the Word of the Guru's Shabad, and duality is easily overcome.

Section 34 - Raag Prabhaatee - Part 025

He Himself is the Commander; all are under His Command. The Fearless Lord looks on all alike. |3|

That humble being who knows, and meditates on the Supreme Primal Being - his word becomes eternal.
Says Naam Dayv, I have found the Invisible, Wondrous Lord, the Life of the World, within my heart. |4|1|

PRABHAATEE:
He existed in the beginning, in the primeval age, and all throughout the ages; His limits cannot be known.
The Lord is pervading and permeating amongst all; this is how His Form can be described. |1|

The Lord of the Universe appears when the Word of His Shabad is chanted.
My Lord is the Embodiment of Bliss. |1|Pause|

The beautiful fragrance of sandalwood emanates from the sandalwood tree, and attaches to the other trees of the forest.
God, the Primal Source of everything, is like the sandalwood tree; He transforms us woody trees into fragrant sandalwood. |2|

You, O Lord, are the Philosopher's Stone, and I am iron; associating with You, I am transformed into gold.
You are Merciful; You are the gem and the jewel. Naam Dayv is absorbed in the Truth. |3|2|

PRABHAATEE:
The Primal Being has no ancestry; He has staged this play.
God is hidden deep within each and every heart. |1|

No one knows the Light of the soul.
Whatever I do, is known to You, Lord. |1|Pause|

Just as the pitcher is made from clay,
everything is made from the Beloved Divine Creator Himself. |2|

The mortal's actions hold the soul in the bondage of karma.
Whatever he does, he does on his own. |3|

Prays Naam Dayv, whatever this soul wants, it obtains.
Whoever abides in the Lord, becomes immortal. |4|3|

Prabhaatee, The Word Of Devotee Baynee Jee:
One Universal Creator God. By The Grace Of The True Guru:
You rub your body with sandalwood oil, and place basil leaves on your forehead.
But you hold a knife in the hand of your heart.
You look like a thug; pretending to meditate, you pose like a crane.
You try to look like a Vaishnaav, but the breath of life escapes through your mouth. |1|

You pray for hours to God the Beautiful.
But your gaze is evil, and your nights are wasted in conflict. |1|Pause|

You perform daily cleansing rituals,
wear two loin-cloths, perform religious rituals and put only milk in your mouth.
But in your heart, you have drawn out the sword.
You routinely steal the property of others. |2|

You worship the stone idol, and paint ceremonial marks of Ganesha.
You remain awake throughout the night, pretending to worship God.
You dance, but your consciousness is filled with evil.
You are lewd and depraved - this is such an unrighteous dance! |3|

You sit on a deer-skin, and chant on your mala.
You put the sacred mark, the tilak, on your forehead.
You wear the rosary beads of Shiva around your neck, but your heart is filled with falsehood.
You are lewd and depraved - you do not chant God's Name. |4|

Whoever does not realize the essence of the soul
- all his religious actions are hollow and false.
Says Baynee, as Gurmukh, meditate.
Without the True Guru, you shall not find the Way. |5|1|

RAAG JAIJAAVANTEE

Section 35 - Raag Jaijaavantee - Part 001

ONE Universal Creator God. Truth Is The Name. Creative Being Personified. No Fear. No Hatred. Image Of The Undying. Beyond Birth. Self-Existent. By Guru's Grace:

Raag Jaijaavantee, Ninth Mehl:
Meditate in remembrance on the Lord - meditate on the Lord; this alone shall be of use to you.
Abandon your association with Maya, and take shelter in the Sanctuary of God.
Remember that the pleasures of the world are false; this whole show is just an illusion. |1|Pause|

You must understand that this wealth is just a dream. Why are you so proud?
The empires of the earth are like walls of sand. |1|

Servant Nanak speaks the Truth: your body shall perish and pass away.
Moment by moment, yesterday passed. Today is passing as well. |2|1|

Jaijaavantee, Ninth Mehl:
Meditate on the Lord - vibrate on the Lord; your life is slipping away.
Why am I telling you this again and again? You fool - why don't you understand?
Your body is like a hail-stone; it melts away in no time at all. |1|Pause|

So give up all your doubts, and utter the Naam, the Name of the Lord.
At the very last moment, this alone shall go along with you. |1|

Forget the poisonous sins of corruption, and enshrine the Praises of God in your heart.
Servant Nanak proclaims that this opportunity is slipping away. |2|2|

Jaijaavantee, Ninth Mehl:

O mortal, what will your condition be?

In this world, you have not listened to the Lord's Name.

You are totally engrossed in corruption and sin; you have not turned your mind away from them at all. |1|Pause|

You obtained this human life, but you have not remembered the Lord in meditation, even for an instant.

For the sake of pleasure, you have become subservient to your woman, and now your feet are bound. |1|

Servant Nanak proclaims that the vast expanse of this world is just a dream. Why not meditate on the Lord? Even Maya is His slave. |2|3|

Jaijaavantee, Ninth Mehl:

Slipping away - your life is uselessly slipping away.

Night and day, you listen to the Puraanas, but you do not understand them, you ignorant fool!

Death has arrived; now where will you run? |1|Pause|

SHALOK SEHSKRITEE, FIRST MEHL & FIFTH MEHL

Section 36 - Shalok Sehskritee, First Mehl & Fifth Mehl - Part 001

You believed that this body was permanent, but it shall turn to dust.
Why don't you chant the Name of the Lord, you shameless fool? |1|

Let devotional worship of the Lord enter into your heart, and abandon the intellectualism of your mind.
O Servant Nanak, this is the way to live in the world. |2|4|

One Universal Creator God. Truth Is The Name. Creative Being Personified. No Fear. No Hatred. Image Of The Undying. Beyond Birth. Self-Existent. By Guru's Grace:

Shalok Sehskritee, First Mehl:
You study the scriptures, say your prayers and argue;
you worship stones and sit like a crane, pretending to meditate.
You speak lies and well-ornamented falsehood,
and recite your daily prayers three times a day.
The mala is around your neck, and the sacred tilak mark is on your forehead.
You wear two loin cloths, and keep your head covered.
If you know God and the nature of karma,
you know that all these rituals and beliefs are useless.
Says Nanak, meditate on the Lord with faith.
Without the True Guru, no one finds the Way. |1|

The mortal's life is fruitless, as long as he does not know God.
Only a few, by Guru's Grace, cross over the world-ocean.
The Creator, the Cause of causes, is All-powerful. Thus speaks Nanak, after deep deliberation.
The Creation is under the control of the Creator. By His Power, He sustains and supports it. |2|

The Shabad is Yoga, the Shabad is spiritual wisdom; the Shabad is the Vedas for the Brahmin.

The Shabad is heroic bravery for the Khshaatriya; the Shabad is service to others for the Soodra.
The Shabad for all is the Shabad, the Word of the One God, for one who knows this secret.
Nanak is the slave of the Divine, Immaculate Lord. |3|

The One Lord is the Divinity of all divinities. He is the Divinity of the soul.
Nanak is the slave of that one who knows the Secrets of the soul and the Supreme Lord God. He is the Divine Immaculate Lord Himself. |4|

Shalok Sehskritee , Fifth Mehl:
One Universal Creator God. Truth Is The Name. Creative Being Personified. No Fear. No Hatred. Image Of The Undying. Beyond Birth. Self-Existent. By Guru's Grace:

Who is the mother, and who is the father? Who is the son, and what is the pleasure of marriage?
Who is the brother, friend, companion and relative? Who is emotionally attached to the family?
Who is restlessly attached to beauty? It leaves, as soon as we see it.
Only the meditative remembrance of God remains with us. O Nanak, it brings the blessings of the Saints, the sons of the Imperishable Lord. |1|

Section 36 - Shalok Sehskritee, First Mehl & Fifth Mehl - Part 002

Cursed is loving attachment to one's mother and father; cursed is loving attachment to one's siblings and relatives.
Cursed is attachment to the joys of family life with one's spouse and children.
Cursed is attachment to household affairs.
Only loving attachment to the Saadh Sangat, the Company of the Holy, is True. Nanak dwells there in peace. |2|

The body is false; its power is temporary.
It grows old; its love for Maya increases greatly.
The human is only a temporary guest in the home of the body, but he has high hopes.
The Righteous Judge of Dharma is relentless; he counts each and every breath.

The human body, so difficult to obtain, has fallen into the deep dark pit of emotional attachment. O Nanak, its only support is God, the Essence of Reality.

O God, Lord of the World, Lord of the Universe, Master of the Universe, please be kind to me. |3|

This fragile body-fortress is made up of water, plastered with blood and wrapped in skin.

It has nine gates, but no doors; it is supported by pillars of wind, the channels of the breath.

The ignorant person does not meditate in remembrance on the Lord of the Universe; he thinks that this body is permanent.

This precious body is saved and redeemed in the Sanctuary of the Holy, O Nanak,

chanting the Name of the Lord, Har, Har, Har, Har, Har, Haray. |4|

O Glorious, Eternal and Imperishable, Perfect and Abundantly Compassionate,

Profound and Unfathomable, Lofty and Exalted, All-knowing and Infinite Lord God.

O Lover of Your devoted servants, Your Feet are a Sanctuary of Peace.

O Master of the masterless, Helper of the helpless, Nanak seeks Your Sanctuary. |5|

Seeing the deer, the hunter aims his weapons.

But if one is protected by the Lord of the World, O Nanak, not a hair on his head will be touched. |6|

He may be surrounded on all four sides by servants and powerful warriors; he may dwell in a lofty place, difficult to approach, and never even think of death.

But when the Order comes from the Primal Lord God, O Nanak, even an ant can take away his breath of life. |7|

To be imbued and attuned to the Word of the Shabad; to be kind and compassionate; to sing the Kirtan of the Lord's Praises - these are the most worthwhile actions in this Dark Age of Kali Yuga.

In this way, one's inner doubts and emotional attachments are dispelled.

God is pervading and permeating all places.

So obtain the Blessed Vision of His Darshan; He dwells upon the tongues of the Holy.
O Nanak, meditate and chant the Name of the Beloved Lord, Har, Har, Har, Haray. |8|

Beauty fades away, islands fade away, the sun, moon, stars and sky fade away.
The earth, mountains, forests and lands fade away.
One's spouse, children, siblings and loved friends fade away.
Gold and jewels and the incomparable beauty of Maya fade away.
Only the Eternal, Unchanging Lord does not fade away.
O Nanak, only the humble Saints are steady and stable forever. |9|

Do not delay in practicing righteousness; delay in committing sins.
Implant the Naam, the Name of the Lord, within yourself, and abandon greed.
In the Sanctuary of the Saints, the sins are erased. The character of righteousness is received by that person,

O Nanak, with whom the Lord is pleased and satisfied. |10|

The person of shallow understanding is dying in emotional attachment; he is engrossed in pursuits of pleasure with his wife.
With youthful beauty and golden earrings,
wondrous mansions, decorations and clothes - this is how Maya clings to him.
O Eternal, Unchanging, Benevolent Lord God, O Sanctuary of the Saints, Nanak humbly bows to You. |11|

If there is birth, then there is death. If there is pleasure, then there is pain.
If there is enjoyment, then there is disease.
If there is high, then there is low. If there is small, then there is great.

Section 36 - Shalok Sehskritee, First Mehl & Fifth Mehl - Part 003

If there is power, then there is pride. If there is egotistical pride, then there will be a fall.
Engrossed in worldly ways, one is ruined.

Meditating and vibrating on the Lord of the Universe in the Company of the Holy, you shall become steady and stable. Nanak vibrates and meditates on the Lord God. |12|

By the Grace of God, genuine understanding comes to the mind.
The intellect blossoms forth, and one finds a place in the realm of celestial bliss.
The senses are brought under control, and pride is abandoned.
The heart is cooled and soothed, and the wisdom of the Saints is implanted within.
Reincarnation is ended, and the Blessed Vision of the Lord's Darshan is obtained.
O Nanak, the musical instrument of the Word of the Shabad vibrates and resounds within. |13|

The Vedas preach and recount God's Glories; people hear them by various ways and means.
The Merciful Lord, Har, Har, implants spiritual wisdom within.
Nanak begs for the Gift of the Naam, the Name of the Lord. The Guru is the Great Giver, the Lord of the World. |14|

Do not worry so much about your mother, father and siblings. Do not worry so much about other people.
Do not worry about your spouse, children and friends. You are obsessed with your involvements in Maya.
The One Lord God is Kind and Compassionate, O Nanak. He is the Cherisher and Nurturer of all living beings. |15|

Wealth is temporary; conscious existence is temporary; hopes of all sorts are temporary.
The bonds of love, attachment, egotism, doubt, Maya and the pollution of corruption are temporary.
The mortal passes through the fire of the womb of reincarnation countless times. He does not remember the Lord in meditation; his understanding is polluted.
O Lord of the Universe, when You grant Your Grace, even sinners are saved.
Nanak dwells in the Saadh Sangat, the Company of the Holy. |16|

You may drop down from the mountains, and fall into the nether regions of the underworld, or be burnt in the blazing fire, or swept away by the unfathomable waves of water; but the worst pain of all is household anxiety, which is the source of the cycle of death and rebirth.

No matter what you do, you cannot break its bonds, O Nanak. Man's only Support, Anchor and Mainstay is the Word of the Shabad, and the Holy, Friendly Saints. |17|

Excruciating pain, countless killings, reincarnation, poverty and terrible misery

are all destroyed by meditating in remembrance on the Lord's Name, O Nanak, just as fire reduces piles of wood to ashes. |18|

Meditating in remembrance on the Lord, the darkness is illuminated. Dwelling on His Glorious Praises, the ugly sins are destroyed.

Enshrining the Lord deep within the heart, and with the immaculate karma of doing good deeds, one strikes fear into the demons.

The cycle of coming and going in reincarnation is ended, absolute peace is obtained, and the Fruitful Vision of the Lord's Darshan.

He is Potent to give Protection, He is the Lover of His Saints. O Nanak, the Lord God blesses all with bliss. |19|

Those who were left behind - the Lord brings them to the front. He fulfills the hopes of the hopeless.

He makes the poor rich, and cures the illnesses of the ill.

He blesses His devotees with devotion. They sing the Kirtan of the Praises of the Lord's Name.

O Nanak, those who serve the Guru find the Supreme Lord God, the Great Giver|20|

He gives Support to the unsupported. The Name of the Lord is the Wealth of the poor.

The Lord of the Universe is the Master of the masterless; the Beautiful-haired Lord is the Power of the weak.

The Lord is Merciful to all beings, Eternal and Unchanging, the Family of the meek and humble.

The All-knowing, Perfect, Primal Lord God is the Lover of His devotees, the Embodiment of Mercy.

Section 36 - Shalok Sehskritee, First Mehl & Fifth Mehl   Part 004

The Supreme Lord God, the Transcendent, Luminous Lord, dwells in each and every heart.
Nanak begs for this blessing from the Merciful Lord, that he may never forget Him, never forget Him. |21|

I have no power; I do not serve You, and I do not love You, O Supreme Sublime Lord God.
By Your Grace, Nanak meditates on the Naam, the Name of the Merciful Lord, Har, Har. |22|

The Lord feeds and sustains all living beings; He blesses them gifts of restful peace and fine clothes.
He created the jewel of human life, with all its cleverness and intelligence.
By His Grace, mortals abide in peace and bliss.
O Nanak, meditating in remembrance on the Lord, Har, Har, Haray,
the mortal is released from attachment to the world. |23|

The kings of the earth are eating up the blessings of the good karma of their past lives.
Those cruel-minded rulers who oppress the people, O Nanak, shall suffer in pain for a very long time. |24|

Those who meditate in remembrance on the Lord in their hearts, look upon even pain as God's Grace.
The healthy person is very sick, if he does not remember the Lord, the Embodiment of Mercy. |25|

To sing the Kirtan of God's Praises is the righteous duty incurred by taking birth in this human body.
The Naam, the Name of the Lord, is Ambrosial Nectar, O Nanak. The Saints drink it in, and never have enough of it. |26|

The Saints are tolerant and good-natured; friends and enemies are the same to them.
O Nanak, it is all the same to them, whether someone offers them all sorts of foods, or slanders them, or draws weapons to kill them. |27|

They pay no attention to dishonor or disrespect.

They are not bothered by gossip; the miseries of the world do not touch them.

Those who join the Saadh Sangat, the Company of the Holy, and chant the Name of the Lord of the Universe - O Nanak, those mortals abide in peace. |28|

The Holy people are an invincible army of spiritual warriors; their bodies are protected by the armor of humility.

Their weapons are the Glorious Praises of the Lord which they chant; their Shelter and Shield is the Word of the Guru's Shabad.

The horses, chariots and elephants they ride are their way to realize God's Path.

They walk fearlessly through the armies of their enemies; they attack them with the Kirtan of God's Praises.

They conquer the entire world, O Nanak, and overpower the five thieves. |29|

Misled by evil-mindedness, mortals are engrossed in the mirage of the illusory world, like the passing shade of a tree.

Emotional attachment to family is false, so Nanak meditates in remembrance on the Name of the Lord, Raam, Raam. |30|

I do not possess the treasure of the wisdom of the Vedas, nor do I possess the merits of the Praises of the Naam.

I do not have a beautiful voice to sing jewelled melodies; I am not clever, wise or shrewd.

By destiny and hard work, the wealth of Maya is obtained. O Nanak, in the Saadh Sangat, the Company of the Holy, even fools become religious scholars. |31|

The mala around my neck is the chanting of the Lord's Name. The Love of the Lord is my silent chanting.

Chanting this most Sublime Word brings salvation and joy to the eyes. |32|

That mortal who lacks the Guru's Mantra - cursed and contaminated is his life.

That blockhead is just a dog, a pig, a jackass, a crow, a snake. |33|

Whoever contemplates the Lord's Lotus Feet, and enshrines His Name within the heart,

Section 36 - Shalok Sehskritee, First Mehl & Fifth Mehl - Part 005

and sings the Kirtan of His Praises in the Saadh Sangat, O Nanak, shall never see the Messenger of Death. |34|

Wealth and beauty are not so difficult to obtain. Paradise and royal power are not so difficult to obtain.
Foods and delicacies are not so difficult to obtain. Elegant clothes are not so difficuilt to obtain.
Children, friends, siblings and relatives are not so difficult to obtain. The pleasures of woman are not so difficult to obtain.
Knowledge and wisdom are not so difficult to obtain. Cleverness and trickery are not so difficult to obtain.
Only the Naam, the Name of the Lord, is difficult to obtain. O Nanak, it is only obtained by God's Grace, in the Saadh Sangat, the Company of the Holy. |35|

Wherever I look, I see the Lord, whether in this world, in paradise, or the nether regions of the underworld.
The Lord of the Universe is All-pervading everywhere. O Nanak, no blame or stain sticks to Him. |36|

Poison is transformed into nectar, and enemies into friends and companions.
Pain is changed into pleasure, and the fearful become fearless.
Those who have no home or place find their place of rest in the Naam, O Nanak, when the Guru, the Lord, becomes Merciful. |37|

He blesses all with humility; He has blessed me with humility as well. He purifies all, and He has purified me as well.
The Creator of all is the Creator of me as well. O Nanak, no blame or stain sticks to Him. |38|

The moon-god is not cool and calm, nor is the white sandalwood tree.
The winter season is not cool; O Nanak, only the Holy friends, the Saints, are cool and calm. |39|

Through the Mantra of the Name of the Lord, Raam, Raam, one meditates on the All-pervading Lord.

Those who have the wisdom to look alike upon pleasure and pain, live the immaculate lifestyle, free of vengeance.

They are kind to all beings; they have overpowered the five thieves.

They take the Kirtan of the Lord's Praise as their food; they remain untouched by Maya, like the lotus in the water.

They share the Teachings with friend and enemy alike; they love the devotional worship of God.

They do not listen to slander; renouncing self-conceit, they become the dust of all.

Whoever has these six qualities, O Nanak, is called a Holy friend. |40|

The goat enjoys eating fruits and roots, but if it lives near a tiger, it is always anxious.

This is the condition of the world, O Nanak; it is afflicted by pleasure and pain. |41|

Fraud, false accusations, millions of diseases, sins and the filthy residues of evil mistakes;

doubt, emotional attachment, pride, dishonor and intoxication with Maya

- these lead mortals to death and rebirth, wandering lost in hell. In spite of all sorts of efforts, salvation is not found.

Chanting and meditating on the Name of the Lord in the Saadh Sangat, the Company of the Holy, O Nanak, mortals become immaculate and pure.

They continually dwell upon the Glorious Praises of God. |42|

In the Sanctuary of the Kind-hearted Lord, our Transcendent Lord and Master, we are carried across.

God is the Perfect, All-powerful Cause of causes; He is the Giver of gifts.

He gives hope to the hopeless. He is the Source of all riches.

Nanak meditates in remembrance on the Treasure of Virtue; we are all beggars, begging at His Door. |43|

The most difficult place becomes easy, and the worst pain turns into pleasure.

Evil words, differences and doubts are obliterated, and even faithless cynics and malicious gossips become good people.

They become steady and stable, whether happy or sad; their fears are taken away, and they are fearless.

Section 36 - Shalok Sehskritee, First Mehl & Fifth Mehl - Part 00G

The dreadful woods become a well-populated city; such are the merits of the righteous life of Dharma, given by God's Grace.

Chanting the Lord's Name in the Saadh Sangat, the Company of the Holy, O Nanak, the Lotus Feet of the Merciful Lord are found. |44|

O emotional attachment, you are the invincible warrior of the battlefield of life; you totally crush and destroy even the most powerful.

You entice and fascinate even the heavenly heralds, celestial singers, gods, mortals, beasts and birds.

Nanak bows in humble surrender to the Lord; he seeks the Sanctuary of the Lord of the Universe. |45|

O sexual desire, you lead the mortals to hell; you make them wander in reincarnation through countless species.

You cheat the consciousness, and pervade the three worlds. You destroy meditation, penance and virtue.

But you give only shallow pleasure, while you make the mortals weak and unsteady; you pervade the high and the low.

Your fear is dispelled in the Saadh Sangat, the Company of the Holy, O Nanak, through the Protection and Support of the Lord. |46|

O anger, you are the root of conflict; compassion never rises up in you.

You take the corrupt, sinful beings in your power, and make them dance like monkeys.

Associating with you, mortals are debased and punished by the Messenger of Death in so many ways.

O Destroyer of the pains of the poor, O Merciful God, Nanak prays for You to protect all begins from such anger. |47|

O greed, you cling to even the great, assaulting them with countless waves.

You cause them to run around wildly in all directions, wobbling and wavering unsteadily.

You have no respect for friends, ideals, relations, mother or father.

You make them do what they should not do. You make them eat what they should not eat. You make them accomplish what they should not accomplish.

Save me, save me - I have come to Your Sanctuary, O my Lord and Master; Nanak prays to the Lord. |48|

O egotism, you are the root of birth and death and the cycle of reincarnation; you are the very soul of sin.

You forsake friends, and hold tight to enemies. You spread out countless illusions of Maya.

You cause the living beings to come and go until they are exhausted. You lead them to experience pain and pleasure.

You lead them to wander lost in the terrible wilderness of doubt; you lead them to contract the most horrible, incurable diseases.

The only Physician is the Supreme Lord, the Transcendent Lord God. Nanak worships and adores the Lord, Har, Har, Haray. |49|

O Lord of the Universe, Master of the Breath of life, Treasure of Mercy, Guru of the World.

O Destroyer of the fever of the world, Embodiment of Compassion, please take away all my pain.

O Merciful Lord, Potent to give Sanctuary, Master of the meek and humble, please be kind to me.

Whether his body is healthy or sick, let Nanak meditate in remembrance on You, Lord. |50|

I have come to the Sanctuary of the Lord's Lotus Feet, where I sing the Kirtan of His Praises.

In the Saadh Sangat, the Company of the Holy, Nanak is carried across the utterly terrifying, difficult world-ocean. |51|

The Supreme Lord God has procted my head and forehead; the Transcendent Lord has protected my hands and body.

God, my Lord and Master, has saved my soul; the Lord of the Universe has saved my wealth and feet.

The Merciful Guru has protected everything, and destroyed my fear and suffering.

God is the Lover of His devotees, the Master of the masterless. Nanak has entered the Sanctuary of the Imperishable Primal Lord God. |52|

His Power supports the sky, and locks fire within wood.

His Power supports the moon, the sun and the stars, and infuses light and breath into the body.

Section 36 - Shalok Sehskritee, First Mehl & Fifth Mehl - Part 007

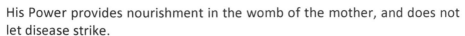

His Power provides nourishment in the womb of the mother, and does not let disease strike.
His Power holds back the ocean, O Nanak, and does not allow the waves of water to destroy the land. |53|

The Lord of the World is Supremely Beautiful; His Meditation is the Life of all.
In the Society of the Saints, O Nanak, He is found on the path of devotional worship of the Lord. |54|

The mosquito pierces the stone, the ant crosses the swamp,
the cripple crosses the ocean, and the blind sees in the darkness,
meditating on the Lord of the Universe in the Saadh Sangat. Nanak seeks the Sanctuary of the Lord, Har, Har, Haray. |55|

Like a Brahmin without a sacred mark on his forehead, or a king without the power of command,
or a warrior without weapons, so is the devotee of God without Dharmic Faith. |56|

God has no conch-shell, no religious mark, no paraphernalia; he does not have blue skin.
His Form is Wondrous and Amazing. He is beyond incarnation.
The Vedas say that He is not this, and not that.
The Lord of the Universe is Lofty and High, Great and Infinite.
The Imperishable Lord abides in the hearts of the Holy. He is understood, O Nanak, by those who are very fortunate. |57|

Living in the world, it is like a wild jungle. One's relatives are like dogs, jackals and donkeys.
In this difficult place, the mind is intoxicated with the wine of emotional attachment; the five unconquered thieves lurk there.
The mortals wander lost in love and emotional attachment, fear and doubt; they are caught in the sharp, strong noose of egotism.
The ocean of fire is terrifying and impassable. The distant shore is so far away; it cannot be reached.
Vibrate and meditate on the Lord of the World, in the Saadh Sangat, the Company of the Holy; O Nanak, by His Grace, we are saved at the Lotus Feet of the Lord. |58|

When the Lord of the Universe grants His Grace, all illnesses are cured.
Nanak chants His Glorious Praises in the Saadh Sangat, in the Sanctuary of the Perfect Transcendent Lord God. |59|

The mortal is beautiful and speaks sweet words, but in the farm of his heart, he harbors cruel vengeance.
He pretends to bow in worship, but he is false. Beware of him, O friendly Saints. |60|

The thoughtless fool does not know that each day, his breaths are being used up.
His most beautiful body is wearing away; old age, the daughter of death, has seized it.
He is engrossed in family play; placing his hopes in transitory things, he indulges in corrupt pleasures.
Wandering lost in countless incarnations, he is exhausted. Nanak seeks the Sanctuary of the Embodiment of Mercy. |61|

O tongue, you love to enjoy the sweet delicacies.
You are dead to the Truth, and involved in great disputes. Instead, repeat the holy words:
Gobind, Daamodar, Maadhav. |62|

Those who are proud, and intoxicated with the pleasures of sex,
and asserting their power over others,
never contemplate the Lord's Lotus Feet. Their lives are cursed, and as worthless as straw.
You are as tiny and insignificant as an ant, but you shall become great, by the Wealth of the Lord's Meditation.
Nanak bows in humble worship, countless times, over and over again. |63|

The blade of grass becomes a mountain, and the barren land becomes green.
The drowning one swims across, and the empty is filled to overflowing.
Millions of suns illuminate the darkness,
prays Nanak, when the Guru, the Lord, becomes Merciful. |64|

FIFTH MEHL, GAAT'HAA

Section 37 - Fifth Mehl, Gaat'haa - Part 001

Associating with the Brahmin, one is saved, if his actions are perfect and God-like.
Those whose souls are imbued with the world - O Nanak, their lives are fruitless. |65|

The mortal steals the wealth of others, and makes all sorts of problems; his preaching is only for his own livelihood.
His desire for this and that is not satisfied; his mind is caught in Maya, and he is acting like a pig. |66|

Those who are intoxicated and absorbed in the Lord's Lotus Feet are saved from the terrifying world-ocean.
Countless sins are destroyed, O Nanak, in the Saadh Sangat, the Company of the Holy; there is no doubt about this. |67|4|

Fifth Mehl, Gaat'haa:
One Universal Creator God. By The Grace Of The True Guru:
Camphor, flowers and perfume become contaminated, by coming into contact with the human body.
O Nanak, the ignorant one is proud of his foul-smelling marrow, blood and bones. |1|

Even if the mortal could reduce himself to the size of an atom, and shoot through the ethers, worlds and realms in the blink of an eye, O Nanak, without the Holy Saint, he shall not be saved. |2|

Know for sure that death will come; whatever is seen is false.
So chant the Kirtan of the Lord's Praises in the Saadh Sangat, the Company of the Holy; this alone shall go along with you in the end. |3|

The consciousness wanders lost in Maya, attached to friends and relatives.
Vibrating and meditating on the Lord of the Universe in the Saadh Sangat, O Nanak, the eternal place of rest is found. |4|

The lowly nim tree, growing near the sandalwood tree, becomes just like the sandalwood tree.
But the bamboo tree, also growing near it, does not pick up its fragrance; it is too tall and proud. |5|

In this Gaat'haa, the Lord's Sermon is woven; listening to it, pride is crushed.
The five enemies are killed, O Nanak, by shooting the Arrow of the Lord. |6|

The Words of the Holy are the path of peace. They are obtained by good karma.
The cycle of birth and death is ended, O Nanak, singing the Kirtan of the Lord's Praises. |7|

When the leaves wither and fall, they cannot be attached to the branch again.
Without the Naam, the Name of the Lord, O Nanak, there is misery and suffering. The mortal wanders in reincarnation day and night. |8|

One is blessed with love for the Saadh Sangat, the Company of the Holy, by great good fortune.
Whoever sings the Glorious Praises of the Lord's Name, O Nanak, is not affected by the world-ocean. |9|

This Gaat'haa is profound and infinite; how rare are those who understand it.
They forsake sexual desire and worldly love, O Nanak, and praise the Lord in the Saadh Sangat. |10|

The Words of the Holy are the most sublime Mantra. They eradicate millions of sinful mistakes.
Meditating on the Lotus Feet of the Lord, O Nanak, all one's generations are saved. |11|

That palace is beautiful, in which the Kirtan of the Lord's Praises are sung.
Those who dwell on the Lord of the Universe are liberated. O Nanak, only the most fortunate are so blessed. |12|

I have found the Lord, my Friend, my very Best Friend.
He shall never break my heart.
His dwelling is eternal; His weight cannot be weighed.
Nanak has made Him the Friend of his soul. |13|

One's bad reputation is erased by a true son,
who meditates in his heart on the Guru's Mantra.

PHUNHAY, FIFTH MEHL

Section 38 - Phunhay, Fifth Mehl - Part 001

The Beloved Eternal Lord God,
O Nanak, carries us across the world-ocean. |14|

It is death to forget the Lord of the Universe.
It is life to meditate on the Name of the Lord.
The Lord is found in the Saadh Sangat, the Company of the Holy,
O Nanak, by pre-ordained destiny. |15|

The snake-charmer, by his spell, neutralizes the poison and leaves the snake without fangs.
Just so, the Saints remove suffering;
O Nanak, they are found by good karma. |16|

The Lord is All-pervading everywhere; He gives Sanctuary to all living beings.
The mind is touched by His Love, O Nanak,
by Guru's Grace, and the Blessed Vision of His Darshan. |17|

My mind is pierced through by the Lord's Lotus Feet.
I am blessed with total happiness.
Holy people have been singing this Gaat'haa, O Nanak, since the very beginning of time. |18|

Chanting and singing the Sublime Word of God in the Saadh Sangat, mortals are saved from the world-ocean. O Nanak, they shall never again be consigned to reincarnation. |19|

People contemplate the Vedas, Puraanas and Shaastras.
But by enshrining in their hearts the Naam, the Name of the One and Only Creator of the Universe,
everyone can be saved.
By great good fortune, O Nanak, a few cross over like this. |20|

Meditating in remembrance on the Naam, the Name of Lord of the Universe, all one's generations are saved.

It is obtained in the Saadh Sangat, the Company of the Holy. O Nanak, by great good fortune, the Blessed Vision of His Darshan is seen. |21|

Abandon all your evil habits, and implant all Dharmic faith within.

The Saadh Sangat, the Company of the Holy, is obtained, O Nanak, by those who have such destiny written upon their foreheads. |22|

God was, is, and shall always be. He sustains and destroys all.

Know that these Holy people are true, O Nanak; they are in love with the Lord. |23|

The mortal is engrossed in sweet words and transitory pleasures which shall soon fade away.

Disease, sorrow and separation afflict him; O Nanak, he never finds peace, even in dreams. |24|

Phunhay, Fifth Mehl:

One Universal Creator God. By The Grace Of The True Guru:

With Pen in Hand, the Unfathomable Lord writes the mortal's destiny upon his forehead.

The Incomparably Beautiful Lord is involved with all.

I cannot utter Your Praises with my mouth.

Nanak is fascinated, gazing upon the Blessed Vision of Your Darshan. I am a sacrifice to You. |1|

Seated in the Society of the Saints, I chant the Lord's Praises.

I dedicate all my adornments to Him, and give all this soul to Him.

With hopeful yearning for Him, I have made the bed for my Husband.

O Lord! If such good destiny is inscribed upon my forehead, then I shall find my Friend. |2|

O my companion, I have prepared everything: make-up, garlands and betel-leaves.

I have embellished myself with the sixteen decorations, and applied the mascara to my eyes.

If my Husband Lord comes to my home, then I obtain everything.

O Lord! Without my Husband, all these adornments are useless. |3|

Very fortunate is she, within whose home the Husband Lord abides.
She is totally adorned and decorated; she is a happy soul-bride.
I sleep in peace, without anxiety; the hopes of my mind have been fulfilled.
O Lord! When my Husband came into the home of my heart, I obtained everything. |4|

Section 38 - Phunhay, Fifth Mehl - Part 002

My hope is so intense, that this hope alone should fulfill my hopes.
When the True Guru becomes merciful, then I attain the Perfect Lord.
My body is filled with so many demerits; I am covered with faults and demerits.
O Lord! When the True Guru becomes Merciful, then the mind is held in place. |5|

Says Nanak, I have meditated on the Lord, Infinite and Endless.
This world-ocean is so difficult to cross; the True Guru has carried me across.
My comings and goings in reincarnation ended, when I met the Perfect Lord.
O Lord! I have obtained the Ambrosial Nectar of the Name of the Lord from the True Guru. |6|

The lotus is in my hand; in the courtyard of my heart I abide in peace.
O my companion, the Jewel is around my neck; beholding it, sorrow is taken away.
I abide with the Lord of the World, the Treasury of Total Peace. O Lord!
All wealth, spiritual perfection and the nine treasures are in His Hand. |7|

Those men who go out to enjoy other men's women shall suffer in shame.
Those who steal the wealth of others - how can their guilt be concealed?
Those who chant the Sacred Praises of the Lord save and redeem all their generations.
O Lord! Those who listen and contemplate the Supreme Lord God become pure and holy. |8|

The sky above looks lovely, and the earth below is beautiful.
Lightning flashes in the ten directions; I behold the Face of my Beloved.
If I go searching in foreign lands, how can I find my Beloved?

O Lord! If such destiny is inscribed upon my forehead, I am absorbed in the Blessed Vision of His Darshan. |9|

I have seen all places, but none can compare to You.
The Primal Lord, the Architect of Destiny, has established You; thus You are adorned and embellished.
Ramdaspur is prosperous and thickly populated, and incomparably beautiful.
O Lord! Bathing in the Sacred Pool of Raam Daas, the sins are washed away, O Nanak. |10|

The rainbird is very smart; in its consciousness, it longs for the friendly rain.
It longs for that, to which its breath of life is attached.
It wanders depressed, from forest to forest, for the sake of a drop of water.
O Lord! In just the same way, the humble servant of the Lord begs for the Naam, the Name of the Lord. Nanak is a sacrifice to him. |11|

The Consciousness of my Friend is incomparably beautiful. Its mystery cannot be known.
One who purchases the priceless virtues realizes the essence of reality.
When the consciousness is absorbed in the supreme consciousness, great joy and bliss are found.
O Lord! When the fickle thieves are overcome, the true wealth is obtained. |12|

In a dream, I was lifted up; why didn't I grasp the hem of His Robe?
Gazing upon the Beautiful Lord relaxing there, my mind was charmed and fascinated.
I am searching for His Feet - tell me, where can I find Him?
O Lord! Tell me how I can find my Beloved, O my companion. |13|

The eyes which do not see the Holy - those eyes are miserable.
The ears which do not hear the Sound-current of the Naad - those ears might just as well be plugged.
The tongue which does not chant the Naam ought to be cut out, bit by bit.
O Lord! When the mortal forgets the Lord of the Universe, the Sovereign Lord King, he grows weaker day by day. |14|

The wings of the bumble bee are caught in the intoxicating fragrant petals of the lotus.

With its limbs entangled in the petals, it loses its senses.

CHAUBOLAS, FIFTH MEHL

Section 39 - Chaubolas, Fifth Mehl - Part 001

Is there any such friend, who can untie this difficult knot?
O Nanak, the One Supreme Lord and Master of the earth reunites the separated ones. |15|

I run around in all directions, searching for the love of God.
The five evil enemies are tormenting me; how can I destroy them?
Shoot them with the sharp arrows of meditation on the Name of God.
O Lord! The way to slaughter these terrible sadistic enemies is obtained from the Perfect Guru. |16|

The True Guru has blessed me with the bounty which shall never be exhausted.
Eating and consuming it, all the Gurmukhs are emancipated.
The Lord, in His Mercy, has blessed me with the treasure of the Ambrosial Naam.
O Nanak, worship and adore the Lord, who never dies. |17|

Wherever the Lord's devotee goes is a blessed, beautiful place.
All comforts are obtained, meditating on the Lord's Name.
People praise and congratulate the devotee of the Lord, while the slanderers rot and die.
Says Nanak, O friend, chant the Naam, and your mind shall be filled with bliss. |18|

The mortal never serves the Immaculate Lord, the Purifier of sinners.
The mortal wastes away in false pleasures. How long can this go on?
Why do you take such pleasure, looking at this mirage?
O Lord! I am a sacrifice to those who are known and approved in the Court of the Lord. |19|

The fool commits countless foolish actions and so many sinful mistakes.
The fool's body smells rotten, and turns to dust.
He wanders lost in the darkness of pride, and never thinks of dying.

O Lord! The mortal gazes upon the mirage; why does he think it is true? |20|

When someone's days are over, who can save him?
How long can the physicians go on, suggesting various therapies?
You fool, remember the One Lord; only He shall be of use to you in the end.
O Lord! Without the Name, the body turns to dust, and everything goes to waste. |21|

Drink in the medicine of the Incomparable, Priceless Name.
Meeting and joining together, the Saints drink it in, and give it to everyone.
He alone is blessed with it, who is destined to receive it.
O Lord! I am a sacrifice to those who enjoy the Love of the Lord. |22|

The physicians meet together in their assembly.
The medicines are effective, when the Lord Himself stands in their midst.
Their good deeds and karma become apparent.
O Lord! Pains, diseases and sins all vanish from their bodies. |23|

Chaubolas, Fifth Mehl:
One Universal Creator God. By The Grace Of The True Guru:
O Samman, if one could buy this love with money,
then consider Raawan the king. He was not poor, but he could not buy it, even though he offered his head to Shiva. |1|

My body is drenched in love and affection for the Lord; there is no distance at all between us.
My mind is pierced through by the Lotus Feet of the Lord. He is realized when one's intuitive consciousness is attuned to Him. |2|

SHALOKS OF DEVOTEE KABEER JEE

Section 40 - Shaloks Of Devotee Kabeer Jee - Part 001

I would cross the oceans, mountains, wilderness, forests and the nine regions of the earth in a single step, O Musan, for the Love of my Beloved. |3|

O Musan, the Light of the Lord's Love has spread across the sky;
I cling to my Lord, like the bumble bee caught in the lotus flower. |4|

Chanting and intense meditation, austere self-discipline, pleasure and peace, honor, greatness and pride
- O Musan, I would dedicate and sacrifice all these for a moment of my Lord's Love. |5|

O Musan, the world does not understand the Mystery of the Lord; it is dying and being plundered.
It is not pierced through by the Love of the Beloved Lord; it is entangled in false pursuits. |6|

When someone's home and property are burnt, because of his attachment to them, he suffers in the sorrow of separation.
O Musan, when mortals forget the Merciful Lord God, then they are truly plundered. |7|

Whoever enjoys the taste of the Lord's Love, remembers His Lotus Feet in his mind.
O Nanak, the lovers of God do not go anywhere else. |8|

Climbing thousands of steep hillsides, the fickle mind becomes miserable.
Look at the humble, lowly mud, O Jamaal: the beautiful lotus grows in it. |9|

My Lord has lotus-eyes; His Face is so beautifully adorned.
O Musan, I am intoxicated with His Mystery. I break the necklace of pride into bits. |10|

I am intoxicated with the Love of my Husband Lord; remembering Him in meditation, I am not conscious of my own body.
He is revealed in all His Glory, all throughout the world. Nanak is a lowly moth at His Flame. |11|

Shaloks Of Devotee Kabeer Jee:
One Universal Creator God. By The Grace Of The True Guru:
Kabeer, my rosary is my tongue, upon which the Lord's Name is strung.
From the very beginning, and throughout the ages, all the devotees abide in tranquil peace. |1|

Kabeer, everyone laughs at my social class.
I am a sacrifice to this social class, in which I chant and meditate on the Creator. |2|

Kabeer, why do you stumble? Why does your soul waver?
He is the Lord of all comforts and peace; drink in the Sublime Essence of the Lord's Name. |3|

Kabeer, earrings made of gold and studded with jewels,
look like burnt twigs, if the Name is not in the mind. |4|

Kabeer, rare is such a person, who remains dead while yet alive.
Singing the Glorious Praises of the Lord, he is fearless. Wherever I look, the Lord is there. |5|

Kabeer, on the day when I die, afterwards there shall be bliss.
I shall meet with my Lord God. Those with me shall meditate and vibrate on the Lord of the Universe. |6|

Kabeer, I am the worst of all. Everyone else is good.
Whoever understands this is a friend of mine. |7|

Kabeer, she came to me in various forms and disguises.
My Guru saved me, and now she bows humbly to me. |8|

Kabeer, kill only that, which, when killed, shall bring peace.
Everyone shall call you good, very good, and no one shall think you are bad. |9|

Kabeer, the night is dark, and men go about doing their dark deeds.

Section 40 - Shaloks Of Devotee Kabeer Jee - Part 002

They take the noose and run around; but rest assured that God shall destroy them. |10|

Kabeer, the sandalwood tree is good, even though it is surrounded by weeds.
Those who dwell near the sandalwood tree, become just like the sandalwood tree. |11|

Kabeer, the bamboo is drowned in its egotistical pride. No one should drown like this.
Bamboo also dwells near the sandalwood tree, but it does not take up its fragrance. |12|

Kabeer, the mortal loses his faith, for the sake of the world, but the world shall not go along with him in the end.
The idiot strikes his own foot with the axe by his own hand. |13|

Kabeer, wherever I go, I see wonders everywhere.
But without the devotees of the One Lord, it is all wilderness to me. |14|

Kabeer, the dwelling of the Saints is good; the dwelling of the unrighteous burns like an oven.
Those mansions in which the Lord's Name is not chanted might just as well burn down. |15|

Kabeer, why cry at the death of a Saint? He is just going back to his home.
Cry for the wretched, faithless cynic, who is sold from store to store. |16|

Kabeer, the faithless cynic is like a piece of garlic.
Even if you eat it sitting in a corner, it becomes obvious to everyone. |17|

Kabeer, Maya is the butter-churn, and the breath is the churning-stick.
The Saints eat the butter, while the world drinks the whey. |18|

Kabeer, Maya is the butter-churn; the breath flows like ice water.

Whoever does the churning eats the butter; the others are just churning-sticks. |19|

Kabeer, Maya is the thief, which breaks in and plunders the store.
Only Kabeer is not plundered; he has cut her into twelve pieces. |20|

Kabeer, peace does not come in this world by making lots of friends.
Those who keep their consciousness focused on the One Lord shall find eternal peace. |21|

Kabeer, the world is afraid of death - that death fills my mind with bliss.
It is only by death that perfect, supreme bliss is obtained. |22|

The Treasure of the Lord is obtained, O Kabeer, but do not undo its knot.
There is no market to sell it, no appraiser, no customer, and no price. |23|

Kabeer, be in love with only that one, whose Master is the Lord.
The Pandits, the religious scholars, kings and landlords - what good is love for them? |24|

Kabeer, when you are in love with the One Lord, duality and alienation depart.
You may have long hair, or you may shave your head bald. |25|

Kabeer, the world is a room filled with black soot; the blind fall into its trap.
I am a sacrifice to those who are thrown in, and still escape. |26|

Kabeer, this body shall perish; save it, if you can.
Even those who have tens of thousands and millions, must depart bare-footed in the end. |27|

Kabeer, this body shall perish; place it on the path.
Either join the Saadh Sangat, the Company of the Holy, or sing the Glorious Praises of the Lord. |28|

Kabeer, dying, dying, the whole world has to die, and yet, none know how to die.

Section 40 - Shaloks Of Devotee Kabeer Jee - Part 003

Let those who die, die such a death, that they shall never have to die again. |29|

Kabeer, it is so difficult to obtain this human body; it does not just come over and over again.
It is like the ripe fruit on the tree; when it falls to the ground, it cannot be re-attached to the branch. |30|

Kabeer, you are Kabeer; your name means great.
O Lord, You are Kabeer. The Jewel of the Lord is obtained, when the mortal first gives up his body. |31|

Kabeer, do not struggle in stubborn pride; nothing happens just because you say so.
No one can erase the actions of the Merciful Lord. |32|

Kabeer, no one who is false can withstand the Touchstone of the Lord.
He alone can pass the test of the Lord's Touchstone, who remains dead while yet alive. |33|

Kabeer, some wear gaudy robes, and chew betel leaves and betel nuts.
Without the Name of the One Lord, they are bound and gagged and taken to the City of Death. |34|

Kabeer, the boat is old, and it has thousands of holes.
Those who are light get across, while those who carry the weight of their sins on their heads are drowned. |35|

Kabeer, the bones burn like wood, and the hair burns like straw.
Seeing the world burning like this, Kabeer has become sad. |36|

Kabeer, do not be so proud of your bones wrapped up in skin.
Those who were on their horses and under their canopies, were eventually buried under the ground. |37|

Kabeer, do not be so proud of your tall mansions.
Today or tomorrow, you shall lie beneath the ground, and the grass shall grow above you. |38|

Kabeer, do not be so proud, and do not laugh at the poor.

Your boat is still out at sea; who knows what will happen? |39|

Kabeer, do not be so proud, looking at your beautiful body.
Today or tomorrow, you will have to leave it behind, like the snake shedding its skin. |40|

Kabeer, if you must rob and plunder, then plunder the plunder of the Lord's Name.
Otherwise, in the world hereafter, you will regret and repent, when the breath of life leaves the body. |41|

Kabeer, there is no one born, who burns his own home,
and burning his five sons, remains lovingly attuned to the Lord. |42|

Kabeer, how rare are those who sell their son and sell their daughter
and, entering into partnership with Kabeer, deal with the Lord. |43|

Kabeer, let me remind you of this. Do not be skeptical or cynical.
Those pleasures which you enjoyed so much in the past - now you must eat their fruits. |44|

Kabeer, at first, I thought learning was good; then I thought Yoga was better.
I shall never abandon devotional worship of the Lord, even though people may slander me. |45|

Kabeer, how can the wretched people slander me? They have no wisdom or intelligence.
Kabeer continues to dwell upon the Lord's Name; I have abandoned all other affairs. |46|

Kabeer, the robe of the stranger-soul has caught fire on all four sides.
The cloth of the body has been burnt and reduced to charcoal, but the fire did not touch the thread of the soul. |47|

Kabeer, the cloth has been burnt and reduced to charcoal, and the begging bowl is shattered into pieces.
The poor Yogi has played out his game; only ashes remain on his seat. |48|

Section 40 - Shaloks Of Devotee Kabeer Jee - Part 004

Kabeer, the fish is in the shallow water; the fisherman has cast his net.
You shall not escape this little pool; think about returning to the ocean.
|49|

Kabeer, do not leave the ocean, even if it is very salty.
If you poke around searching from puddle to puddle, no one will call you smart. |50|

Kabeer, those who have no guru are washed away. No one can help them.
Be meek and humble; whatever happens is what the Creator Lord does. |51|

Kabeer, even the dog of a devotee is good, while the mother of the faithless cynic is bad.
The dog hears the Praises of the Lord's Name, while the other is engaged in sin. |52|

Kabeer, the deer is weak, and the pool is lush with green vegetation.
Thousands of hunters are chasing after the soul; how long can it escape death? |53|

Kabeer, some make their homes on the banks of the Ganges, and drink pure water.
Without devotional worship of the Lord, they are not liberated. Kabeer proclaims this. |54|

Kabeer, my mind has become immaculate, like the waters of the Ganges.
The Lord follows after me, calling, "Kabeer! Kabeer!"|55|

Kabeer, tumeric is yelow, and lime is white.
You shall meet the Beloved Lord, only when both colors are lost. |56|

Kabeer, tumeric has lost its yellow color, and no trace of lime's whiteness remains.
I am a sacrifice to this love, by which social class and status, color and ancestry are taken away. |57|

Kabeer, the door of liberation is very narrow, less than the width of a mustard seed.

Your mind is larger than an elephant; how will it pass through? |58|

Kabeer, if I meet such a True Guru, who mercifully blesses me with the gift, then the door of liberation will open wide for me, and I will easily pass through. |59|

Kabeer, I have no hut or hovel, no house or village.
I hope that the Lord will not ask who I am. I have no social status or name. |60|

Kabeer, I long to die; let me die at the Lord's Door.
I hope that the Lord does not ask, "Who is this, lying at my door?" |61|

Kabeer, I have not done anything; I shall not do anything; my body cannot do anything.
I do not know what the Lord has done, but the call has gone out: "Kabeer, Kabeer." |62|

Kabeer, if someone utters the Name of the Lord even in dreams,
I would make my skin into shoes for his feet. |63|

Kabeer, we are puppets of clay, but we take the name of mankind.
We are guests here for only a few days, but we take up so much space. |64|

Kabeer, I have made myself into henna, and I grind myself into powder.
But You, O my Husband Lord, have not asked about me; You have never applied me to Your Feet. |65|

Kabeer, that door, through which people never stop coming and going
- how can I leave such a door as that? |66|

Kabeer, I was drowning, but the waves of virtue saved me in an instant.

Section 40 - Shaloks Of Devotee Kabeer Jee - Part 005

When I saw that my boat was rotten, then I immediately got out. |67|

Kabeer, the sinner does not like devotion to the Lord; he does not appreciate worship.

The fly abandons the sandalwood tree, and goes after the rotten smell. |68|

Kabeer, the physician is dead, and the patient is dead; the whole world is dead.
Only Kabeer is not dead; there is no one to mourn for him. |69|

Kabeer, I have not meditated on the Lord; such is the bad habit I have developed.
The body is a wooden pot; it cannot be put back on the fire. |70|

Kabeer, it came to pass, that I did whatever I pleased.
Why should I be afraid of death? I have invited death for myself. |71|

Kabeer, the mortals suck at the sugar cane, for the sake of the sweet juice.
They should work just as hard for virtue.
The person who lacks virtue - no one calls him good. |72|

Kabeer, the pitcher is full of water; it will break, today or tomorrow.
Those who do not remember their Guru, shall be plundered on the way. |73|

Kabeer, I am the Lord's dog; Moti is my name.
There is a chain around my neck; wherever I am pulled, I go. |74|

Kabeer, why do you show other people your rosary beads?
You do not remember the Lord in your heart, so what use is this rosary to you? |75|

Kabeer, the snake of separation from the Lord abides within my mind; it does not respond to any mantra.
One who is separated from the Lord does not live; if he does live, he goes insane. |76|

Kabeer, the philosopher's stone and sandalwood oil have the same good quality.
Whatever comes into contact with them is uplifted. Iron is transformed into gold, and ordinary wood becomes fragrant. |77|

Kabeer, Death's club is terrible; it cannot be endured.

I have met with the holy man; he has attached me to the hem of his robe. |78|

Kabeer, the physician says that he alone is good, and all the medicine is under his control.
But these things belong to the Lord; He takes them away whenever He wishes. |79|

Kabeer, take your drum and beat it for ten days.
Life is like people meeting on a boat on a river; they shall not meet again. |80|

Kabeer, if I could change the seven seas into ink and make all the vegetation my pen,
and the earth my paper, even then, I could not write the Praises of the Lord. |81|

Kabeer, what can my lowly status as a weaver do to me? The Lord dwells in my heart.
Kabeer, the Lord hugs me close in His Embrace; I have forsaken all my entanglements. |82|

Kabeer, will anyone set fire to his home
and kill his five sons (the five thieves) to remain lovingly attached to the Lord? |83|

Kabeer, will anyone burn his own body?
The people are blind - they do not know, although Kabeer continues to shout at them. |84|

Kabeer, the widow mounts the funeral pyre and cries out, "Listen, O brother funeral pyre.
All people must depart in the end; it is only you and I." |85|

Section 40 - Shaloks Of Devotee Kabeer Jee - Part 006

Kabeer, the mind has become a bird; it soars and flies in the ten directions.
According to the company it keeps, so are the fruits it eats. |86|

Kabeer, you have found that place which you were seeking.

You have become that which you thought was separate from yourself. |87|

Kabeer, I have been ruined and destroyed by bad company, like the banana plant near the thorn bush.
The thorn bush waves in the wind, and pierces the banana plant; see this, and do not associate with the faithless cynics. |88|

Kabeer, the mortal wants to walk on the path, carrying the load of others' sins on his head.
He is not afraid of his own load of sins; the road ahead shall be difficult and treacherous. |89|

Kabeer, the forest is burning; the tree standing in it is crying out,
"Do not let me fall into the hands of the blacksmith, who would burn me a second time."|90|

Kabeer, when one died, two were dead. When two died, four were dead.
When four died, six were dead, four males and two females. |91|

Kabeer, I have seen and observed, and searched all over the world, but I have found no place of rest anywhere.
Those who do not remember the Lord's Name - why do they delude themselves in other pursuits? |92|

Kabeer, associate with the Holy people, who will take you to Nirvaanaa in the end.
Do not associate with the faithless cynics; they would bring you to ruin. |93|

Kabeer, I contemplate the Lord in the world; I know that He is permeating the world.
Those who do not contemplate the Name of the Lord - their birth into this world is useless. |94|

Kabeer, place your hopes in the Lord; other hopes lead to despair.
Those who dissociate themselves from the Lord's Name - when they fall into hell, then they will appreciate its value. |95|

Kabeer has made many students and disciples, but he has not made God his friend.

He set out on a journey to meet the Lord, but his consciousness failed him half-way. |96|

Kabeer, what can the poor creature do, if the Lord does not give him assistance?
Whatever branch he steps on breaks and collapses. |97|

Kabeer, those who only preach to others - sand falls into their mouths.
They keep their eyes on the property of others, while their own farm is being eaten up. |98|

Kabeer, I will remain in the Saadh Sangat, the Company of the Holy, even if I have only coarse bread to eat.
Whatever will be, will be. I will not associate with the faithless cynics. |99|

Kabeer, in the Saadh Sangat, love for the Lord doubles day by day.
The faithless cynic is like a black blanket, which does not become white by being washed. |100|

Kabeer, you have not shaved your mind, so why do you shave your head?
Whatever is done, is done by the mind; it is useless to shave your head. |101|

Kabeer, do not abandon the Lord; your body and wealth shall go, so let them go.
My consciousness is pierced by the Lord's Lotus Feet; I am absorbed in the Name of the Lord. |102|

Kabeer, all the strings of the instrument I played are broken.
What can the poor instrument do, when the player has departed as well. |103|

Kabeer, shave the mother of that guru, who does not take away one's doubt.

Section 40 - Shaloks Of Devotee Kabeer Jee - Part 007

He himself is drowning in the four Vedas; he drowns his disciples as well. |104|

Kabeer, whatever sins the mortal has committed, he tries to keep hidden under cover.
But in the end, they shall all be revealed, when the Righteous Judge of Dharma investigates. |105|

Kabeer, you have given up meditating on the Lord, and you have raised a large family.
You continue to involve yourself in worldly affairs, but none of your brothers and relatives remain. |106|

Kabeer, those who give up meditation on the Lord, and get up at night to wake the spirits of the dead,
shall be reincarnated as snakes, and eat their own offspring. |107|

Kabeer, the woman who gives up meditation on the Lord, and observes the ritual fast of Ahoi,
shall be reincarnated as a donkey, to carry heavy burdens. |108|

Kabeer, it is the most clever wisdom, to chant and meditate on the Lord in the heart.
It is like playing on a pig; if you fall off, you will find no place of rest. |109|

Kabeer, blessed is that mouth, which utters the Lord's Name.
It purifies the body, and the whole village as well. |110|

Kabeer, that family is good, in which the Lord's slave is born.
But that family in which the Lord's slave is not born is as useless as weeds. |111|

Kabeer, some have lots of horses, elephants and carriages, and thousands of banners waving.
But begging is better than these comforts, if one spends his days meditating in remembrance on the Lord. |112|

Kabeer, I have wandered all over the world, carrying the drum on my shoulder.
No one belongs to anyone else; I have looked and carefully studied it. |113|

The pearls are scattered on the road; the blind man comes along.

Without the Light of the Lord of the Universe, the world just passes them by. |114|

My family is drowned, O Kabeer, since the birth of my son Kamaal.
He has given up meditating on the Lord, in order to bring home wealth. |115|

Kabeer, go out to meet the holy man; do not take anyone else with you.
Do not turn back - keep on going. Whatever will be, will be. |116|

Kabeer, do not bind yourself with that chain, which binds the whole world.
As the salt is lost in the flour, so shall your golden body be lost. |117|

Kabeer, the soul-swan is flying away, and the body is being buried, and still he makes gestures.
Even then, the mortal does not give up the cruel look in his eyes. |118|

Kabeer: with my eyes, I see You, Lord; with my ears, I hear Your Name.
With my tongue I chant Your Name; I enshrine Your Lotus Feet within my heart. |119|

Kabeer, I have been spared from heaven and hell, by the Grace of the True Guru.
From beginning to end, I abide in the joy of the Lord's Lotus Feet. |120|

Kabeer, how can I even describe the extent of the joy of the Lord's Lotus Feet?
I cannot describe its sublime glory; it has to be seen to be appreciated. |121|

Kabeer, how can I describe what I have seen? No one will believe my words.
The Lord is just as He is. I dwell in delight, singing His Glorious Praises. |122|

Section 40 - Shaloks Of Devotee Kabeer Jee - Part 008

Kabeer, the flamingo pecks and feeds, and remembers her chicks. She pecks and pecks and feeds, and remembers them always. Her chicks are

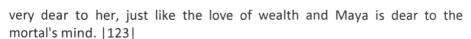

very dear to her, just like the love of wealth and Maya is dear to the mortal's mind. |123|

Kabeer, the sky is overcast and cloudy; the ponds and lakes are overflowing with water.
Like the rainbird, some remain thirsty - what is their condition? |124|

Kabeer, the chakvi duck is separated from her love through the night, but in the morning, she meets him again.
Those who are separated from the Lord do not meet Him in the day, or in the night. |125|

Kabeer: O conch shell, remain in the ocean.
If you are separated from it, you shall scream at sunrise from temple to temple. |126|

Kabeer, what are you doing sleeping? Wake up and cry in fear and pain.
Those who live in the grave - how can they sleep in peace? |127|

Kabeer, what are you doing sleeping? Why not rise up and meditate on the Lord?
One day you shall sleep with your legs outstretched. |128|

Kabeer, what are you doing sleeping? Wake up, and sit up.
Attach yourself to the One, from whom you have been separated. |129|

Kabeer, do not leave the Society of the Saints; walk upon this Path.
See them, and be sanctified; meet them, and chant the Name. |130|

Kabeer, do not associate with the faithless cynics; run far away from them.
If you touch a vessel stained with soot, some of the soot will stick to you. |131|

Kabeer, you have not contemplated the Lord, and now old age has overtaken you.
Now that the door of your mansion is on fire, what can you take out? |132|

Kabeer, the Creator does whatever He pleases.
There is none other than Him; He alone is the Creator of all. |133|

Kabeer, the fruit trees are bearing fruit, and the mangoes are becoming ripe.
They will reach the owner, only if the crows do not eat them first. |134|

Kabeer, some buy idols and worship them; in their stubborn-mindedness, they make pilgrimages to sacred shrines.
They look at one another, and wear religious robes, but they are deluded and lost. |135|

Kabeer, someone sets up a stone idol and all the world worships it as the Lord.
Those who hold to this belief will be drowned in the river of darkness. |136|

Kabeer, the paper is the prison, and the ink of rituals are the bars on the windows.
The stone idols have drowned the world, and the Pandits, the religious scholars, have plundered it on the way. |137|

Kabeer, that which you have to do tomorrow - do it today instead; and that which you have to do now - do it immediately!

Later on, you will not be able to do anything, when death hangs over your head. |138|

Kabeer, I have seen a person, who is as shiny as washed wax.
He seems very clever and very virtuous, but in reality, he is without understanding, and corrupt. |139|

Kabeer, the Messenger of Death shall not compromise my understanding.
I have meditated on the Lord, the Cherisher, who created this Messenger of Death. |140|

Kabeer, the Lord is like musk; all His slaves are like bumble bees.

Section 40 - Shaloks Of Devotee Kabeer Jee - Part 009

The more Kabeer worships Him, the more the Lord abides within his mind. |141|

Kabeer, the mortal has fallen into the grip of family life, and the Lord has been set aside.
The messengers of the Righteous Judge of Dharma descend upon the mortal, in the midst of all his pomp and ceremony. |142|

Kabeer, even a pig is better than the faithless cynic; at least the pig keeps the village clean.
When the wretched, faithless cynic dies, no one even mentions his name. |143|

Kabeer, the mortal gathers wealth, shell by shell, accumulating thousands and millions.
But when the time of his departure comes, he takes nothing at all with him. He is even stripped of his loin-cloth. |144|

Kabeer, what good is it to become a devotee of Vishnu, and wear four malas?
On the outside, he may look like pure gold, but on the inside, he is stuffed with dust. |145|

Kabeer, let yourself be a pebble on the path; abandon your egotistical pride.
Such a humble slave shall meet the Lord God. |146|

Kabeer, what good would it be, to be a pebble? It would only hurt the traveller on the path.
Your slave, O Lord, is like the dust of the earth. |147|

Kabeer, what then, if one could become dust? It is blown up by the wind, and sticks to the body.
The humble servant of the Lord should be like water, which cleans everything. |148|

Kabeer, what then, if one could become water? It becomes cold, then hot.
The humble servant of the Lord should be just like the Lord. |149|

The banners wave above the lofty mansions, filled with gold and beautiful women.
But better than these is dry bread, if one sings the Glorious Praises of the Lord in the Society of the Saints. |150|

Kabeer, the wilderness is better than a city, if the Lord's devotees live there.
Without my Beloved Lord, it is like the City of Death for me. |151|

Kabeer, between the Ganges and Jamunaa Rivers, on the shore of Celestial Silence,
there, Kabeer has made his home. The silent sages and the humble servants of the Lord search for the way to get there. |152|

Kabeer, if the mortal continues to love the Lord in the end, as he pledged in the beginning,
no poor diamond, not even millions of jewels, can equal him. |153|

Kabeer, I saw a strange and wonderful thing. A jewel was being sold in a store.
Because there was no buyer, it was going in exchange for a shell. |154|

Kabeer, where there is spiritual wisdom, there is righteousness and Dharma. Where there is falsehood, there is sin.
Where there is greed, there is death. Where there is forgiveness, there is God Himself. |155|

Kabeer, what good is it to give up Maya, if the mortal does not give up his pride?
Even the silent sages and seers are destroyed by pride; pride eats up everything. |156|

Kabeer, the True Guru has met me; He aimed the Arrow of the Shabad at me.
As soon as it struck me, I fell to the ground with a hole in my heart. |157|

Kabeer, what can the True Guru do, when His Sikhs are at fault?
The blind do not take in any of His Teachings; it is as useless as blowing into bamboo. |158|

Kabeer, the wife of the king has all sorts of horses, elephants and carriages.

Section 40 - Shaloks Of Devotee Kabeer Jee - Part 010

But she is not equal to the water-carrier of the Lord's humble servant. |159|

Kabeer, why do you slander the wife of the king? Why do you honor the slave of the Lord?
Because one combs her hair for corruption, while the other remembers the Name of the Lord. |160|

Kabeer, with the Support of the Lord's Pillar, I have become steady and stable.
The True Guru has given me courage. Kabeer, I have purchased the diamond, on the banks of the Mansarovar Lake. |161|

Kabeer, the Lord is the Diamond, and the Lord's humble servant is the jeweller who has set up his shop.
As soon as an appraiser is found, the price of the jewel is set. |162|

Kabeer, you remember the Lord in meditation, only when the need arises.
You should remember Him all the time.
You shall dwell in the city of immortality, and the Lord shall restore the wealth you lost. |163|

Kabeer, it is good to perform selfless service for two - the Saints and the Lord.
The Lord is the Giver of liberation, and the Saint inspires us to chant the Naam. |164|

Kabeer, the crowds follow the path which the Pandits, the religious scholars, have taken.
There is a difficult and treacherous cliff on that path to the Lord; Kabeer is climbing that cliff. |165|

Kabeer, the mortal dies of his worldly troubles and pain, after worrying about his family.
Whose family is dishonored, when he is placed on the funeral pyre? |166|

Kabeer, you shall drown, you wretched being, from worrying about what other people think.
You know that whatever happens to your neighbors, will also happen to you. |167|

Kabeer, even dry bread, made of various grains, is good.
No one brags about it, throughout the vast country and great empire. |168|

Kabeer, those who brag, shall burn. Those who do not brag remain carefree.
That humble being who does not brag, looks upon the gods and the poor alike. |169|

Kabeer, the pool is filled to overflowing, but no one can drink the water from it.
By great good fortune, you have found it; drink it in handfuls, O Kabeer. |170|

Kabeer, just as the stars disappear at dawn, so shall this body disappear.
Only the letters of God's Name do not disappear; Kabeer holds these tight. |171|

Kabeer, the wooden house is burning on all sides.
The Pandits, the religious scholars, have been burnt to death, while the illiterate ones run to safety. |172|

Kabeer, give up your skepticism; let your papers float away.
Find the essence of the letters of the alphabet, and focus your consciousness on the Lord. |173|

Kabeer, the Saint does not forsake his Saintly nature, even though he meets with millions of evil-doers.
Even when sandalwood is surrounded by snakes, it does not give up its cooling fragrance. |174|

Kabeer, my mind is cooled and soothed; I have become God-conscious.
The fire which has burnt the world is like water to the Lord's humble servant. |175|

Kabeer, no one knows the Play of the Creator Lord.
Only the Lord Himself and the slaves at His Court understand it. |176|

Kabeer, it is good that I feel the Fear of God; I have forgotten everything else.

Section 40 - Shaloks Of Devotee Kabeer Jee - Part 011

The hail-stone has melted into water, and flowed into the ocean. |177|

Kabeer, the body is a pile of dust, collected and packed together.
It is a show which lasts for only a few days, and then dust returns to dust. |178|

Kabeer, bodies are like the rising and setting of the sun and the moon.
Without meeting the Guru, the Lord of the Universe, they are all reduced to dust again. |179|

Where the Fearless Lord is, there is no fear; where there is fear, the Lord is not there.
Kabeer speaks after careful consideration; hear this, O Saints, in your minds. |180|

Kabeer, those who do not know anything, pass their lives in peaceful sleep.
But I have understood the riddle; I am faced with all sorts of troubles. |181|

Kabeer, those who are beaten cry a lot; but the cries of the pain of separation are different.
Struck by the Mystery of God, Kabeer remains silent. |182|

Kabeer, the stroke of a lance is easy to bear; it takes away the breath.
But one who endures the stroke of the Word of the Shabad is the Guru, and I am his slave. |183|

Kabeer: O Mullah, why do you climb to the top of the minaret? The Lord is not hard of hearing.
Look within your own heart for the One, for whose sake you shout your prayers. |184|

Why does the Shaykh bother to go on pilgrimage to Mecca, if he is not content with himself?

Kabeer, one whose heart is not healthy and whole - how can he attain his Lord? |185|

Kabeer, worship the Lord Allah; meditating in remembrance on Him, troubles and pains depart.
The Lord shall be revealed within your own heart, and the burning fire within shall be extinguished by His Name. |186|

Kabeer, to use force is tyranny, even if you call it legal.
When your account is called for in the Court of the Lord, what will your condition be then? |187|

Kabeer, the dinner of beans and rice is excellent, if it is flavored with salt.
Who would cut his throat, to have meat with his bread? |188|

Kabeer, one is known to have been touched by the Guru, only when his emotional attachment and physical illnesses are eradicated.
He is not burned by pleasure or pain, and so he becomes the Lord Himself. |189|

Kabeer, it does make a difference, how you chant the Lord's Name, 'Raam'. This is something to consider.
Everyone uses the same word for the son of Dasrath and the Wondrous Lord. |190|

Kabeer, use the word 'Raam', only to speak of the All-pervading Lord. You must make that distinction.
One 'Raam' is pervading everywhere, while the other is contained only in himself. |191|

Kabeer, those houses in which neither the Holy nor the Lord are served
- those houses are like cremation grounds; demons dwell within them. |192|

Kabeer, I have become mute, insane and deaf.
I am crippled - the True Guru has pierced me with His Arrow. |193|

Kabeer, the True Guru, the Spiritual Warrior, has shot me with His Arrow.
As soon as it struck me, I fell to the ground, with a hole in my heart. |194|

Kabeer, the pure drop of water falls from the sky, onto the dirty ground.

Section 40 - Shaloks Of Devotee Kabeer Jee - Part 012

You must acknowledge this, that without the Sangat, the Holy Congregation, it turns into burnt ashes. |195|

Kabeer, the pure drop of water falls from the sky, and mixes with the dust. Millions of clever people may try, but they will fail - it cannot be made separate again. |196|

Kabeer, I was going on a pilgrimage to Mecca, and God met me on the way. He scolded me and asked, "Who told you that I am only there?" |197|

Kabeer, I went to Mecca - how many times, Kabeer?
O Lord, what is the problem with me? You have not spoken to me with Your Mouth. |198|

Kabeer, they oppress living beings and kill them, and call it proper.
When the Lord calls for their account, what will their condition be? |199|

Kabeer, it is tyranny to use force; the Lord shall call you to account.
When your account is called for, your face and mouth shall be beaten. |200|

Kabeer, it is easy to render your account, if your heart is pure.
In the True Court of the Lord, no one will seize you. |201|

Kabeer: O duality, you are mighty and powerful in the earth and the sky.
The six Shaastras and the eighty-four Siddhas are entrenched in skepticism. |202|

Kabeer, nothing is mine within myself. Whatever there is, is Yours, O Lord.
If I surrender to You what is already Yours, what does it cost me? |203|

Kabeer, repeating, "You, You", I have become like You. Nothing of me remains in myself.
When the difference between myself and others is removed, then wherever I look, I see only You. |204|

Kabeer, those who think of evil and entertain false hopes
- none of their desires shall be fulfilled; they shall depart in despair. |205|

Kabeer, whoever meditates in remembrance on the Lord, he alone is happy in this world.
One who is protected and saved by the Creator Lord, shall never waver, here or hereafter. |206|

Kabeer, I was being crushed like sesame seeds in the oil-press, but the True Guru saved me.
My pre-ordained primal destiny has now been revealed. |207|

Kabeer, my days have passed, and I have postponed my payments; the interest on my account continues to increase.
I have not meditated on the Lord and my account is still pending, and now, the moment of my death has come! |208|

Fifth Mehl:
Kabeer, the mortal is a barking dog, chasing after a carcass.
By the Grace of good karma, I have found the True Guru, who has saved me. |209|

Fifth Mehl:
Kabeer, the earth belongs to the Holy, but it is being occupied by thieves.
They are not a burden to the earth; they receive its blessings. |210|

Fifth Mehl:
Kabeer, the rice is beaten with a mallet to get rid of the husk.
When people sit in evil company, the Righteous Judge of Dharma calls them to account. |211|

Trilochan says, O Naam Dayv, Maya has enticed you, my friend.
Why are you printing designs on these sheets, and not focusing your consciousness on the Lord? |212|

Naam Dayv answers, O Trilochan, chant the Lord's Name with your mouth.

Section 40 - Shaloks Of Devotee Kabeer Jee - Part 013

With your hands and feet, do all your work, but let your consciousness remain with the Immaculate Lord. |213|

Fifth Mehl:
Kabeer, no one belongs to me, and I belong to no one else.
The One who created the creation - into Him I shall be absorbed. |214|

Kabeer, the flour has fallen into the mud; nothing has come into my hands.
That which was eaten while it was being ground - that alone is of any use. |215|

Kabeer, the mortal knows everything, and knowing, he still makes mistakes.
What good is a lamp in one's hand, if he falls into the well? |216|

Kabeer, I am in love with the All-knowing Lord; the ignorant ones try to hold me back.
How could I ever break with the One, who owns our soul and breath of life. |217|

Kabeer, why kill yourself for your love of decorations of your home and mansion?
In the end, only six feet, or a little more, shall be your lot. |218|

Kabeer, whatever I wish for does not happen. What can I accomplish by merely thinking?
The Lord does whatever He wishes; it is not up to me at all. |219|

Third Mehl:
God Himself makes the mortals anxious, and He Himself takes the anxiety away.
O Nanak, praise the One, who takes care of all. |220|

Fifth Mehl:
Kabeer, the mortal does not remember the Lord; he wanders around, engrossed in greed.
Committing sins, he dies, and his life ends in an instant. |221|

Kabeer, the body is like a clay vessel or a brittle metal pot.

If you wish to keep it safe and sound, then vibrate and meditate on the Lord; otherwise, the thing shall break. |222|

Kabeer, chant the Name of the Beautifully-haired Lord; do not sleep unaware.
Chanting His Name night and day, the Lord will eventually hear your call. |223|

Kabeer, the body is a banana forest, and the mind is an intoxicated elephant.
The jewel of spiritual wisdom is the prod, and the rare Saint is the rider. |224|

Kabeer, the Lord's Name is the jewel, and the mouth is the purse; open this purse to the Appraiser.
If a buyer can be found, it will go for a high price. |225|

Kabeer, the mortal does not know the Lord's Name, but he has raised a very large family.
He dies in the midst of his worldly affairs, and then he is not heard in the external world. |226|

Kabeer, in the blink of an eye, moment by moment, life is passing by.
The mortal does not give up his worldly entanglements; the Messenger of Death walks in and beats the drum. |227|

Kabeer, the Lord is the tree, and disillusionment with the world is the fruit.
The Holy man, who has abandoned useless arguments, is the shade of the tree. |228|

Kabeer, plant the seeds of such a plant, which shall bear fruit throughout the twelve months,
with cooling shade and abundant fruit, upon which birds joyously play. |229|

Kabeer, the Great Giver is the tree, which blesses all with the fruit of compassion.
When the birds migrate to other lands, O Tree, you bear the fruits. |230|

Kabeer, the mortal finds the Saadh Sangat, the Company of the Holy, if he has such destiny written upon his forehead.

SHALOKS OF SHAYKH FAREED JEE

Section 41 - Shaloks Of Shaykh Fareed Jee - Part 001

He obtains the treasure of liberation, and the difficult road to the Lord is not blocked. |231|

Kabeer, whether is is for an hour, half an hour, or half of that,
whatever it is, it is worthwhile to speak with the Holy. |232|

Kabeer, those mortals who consume marijuana, fish and wine
- no matter what pilgrimages, fasts and rituals they follow, they will all go to hell. |233|

Kabeer, I keep my eyes lowered, and enshrine my Friend within my heart.
I enjoy all pleasures with my Beloved, but I do not let anyone else know. |234|

Twenty-four hours a day, every hour, my soul continues to look to You, O Lord.
Why should I keep my eyes lowered? I see my Beloved in every heart. |235|

Listen, O my companions: my soul dwells in my Beloved, and my Beloved dwells in my soul.
I realize that there is no difference between my soul and my Beloved; I cannot tell whether my soul or my Beloved dwells in my heart. |236|

Kabeer, the Brahmin may be the guru of the world, but he is not the Guru of the devotees.
He rots and dies in the perplexities of the four Vedas. |237|

The Lord is like sugar, scattered in the sand; the elephant cannot pick it up.
Says Kabeer, the Guru has given me this sublime understanding: become an ant, and feed on it. |238|

Kabeer, if you desire to play the game of love with the Lord, then cut off your head, and make it into a ball.
Lose yourself in the play of it, and then whatever will be, will be. |239|

Kabeer, if you desire to play the game of love with the Lord, play it with someone with committment.
Pressing the unripe mustard seeds produces neither oil nor flour. |240|

Searching, the mortal stumbles like a blind person, and does not recognize the Saint.
Says Naam Dayv, how can one obtain the Lord God, without His devotee? |241|

Forsaking the Diamond of the Lord, the mortals put their hopes in another.
Those people shall go to hell; Ravi Daas speaks the Truth. |242|

Kabeer, if you live the householder's life, then practice righteousness; otherwise, you might as well retire from the world.
If someone renounces the world, and then gets involved in worldly entanglements, he shall suffer terrible misfortune. |243|

Shaloks Of Shaykh Fareed Jee:
One Universal Creator God. By The Grace Of The True Guru:
The day of the bride's wedding is pre-ordained.
On that day, the Messenger of Death, of whom she had only heard, comes and shows its face.
It breaks the bones of the body and pulls the helpless soul out.
That pre-ordained time of marriage cannot be avoided. Explain this to your soul.
The soul is the bride, and death is the groom. He will marry her and take her away.
After the body sends her away with its own hands, whose neck will it embrace?
The bridge to hell is narrower than a hair; haven't you heard of it with your ears?
Fareed, the call has come; be careful now - don't let yourself be robbed. |1|

Fareed, it is so difficult to become a humble Saint at the Lord's Door.

Section 41 - Shaloks Of Shaykh Fareed Jee - Part 002

I am so accustomed to walking in the ways of the world. I have tied and picked up the bundle; where can I go to throw it away? |2|

I know nothing; I understand nothing. The world is a smouldering fire.
My Lord did well to warn me about it; otherwise, I would have been burnt as well. |3|

Fareed, if I had known that I had so few sesame seeds, I would have been more careful with them in my hands.
If I had known that my Husband Lord was so young and innocent, I would not have been so arrogant. |4|

If I had known that my robe would come loose, I would have tied a tighter knot.
I have found none as great as You, Lord; I have looked and searched throughout the world. |5|

Fareed, if you have a keen understanding, then do not write black marks against anyone else.
Look underneath your own collar instead. |6|

Fareed, do not turn around and strike those who strike you with their fists.
Kiss their feet, and return to your own home. |7|

Fareed, when there was time for you to earn good karma, you were in love with the world instead.
Now, death has a strong foothold; when the load is full, it is taken away. |8|

See, Fareed, what has happened: your beard has become grey.
That which is coming is near, and the past is left far behind. |9|

See, Fareed, what has happened: sugar has become poison.
Without my Lord, who can I tell of my sorrow? |10|

Fareed, my eyes have become weak, and my ears have become hard of hearing.
The body's crop has become ripe and turned color. |11|

Fareed, those who did not enjoy their Spouse when their hair was black - hardly any of them enjoy Him when their hair turns grey.
So be in love with the Lord, so that your color may ever be new. |12|

Third Mehl:
Fareed, whether one's hair is black or grey, our Lord and Master is always here if one remembers Him.
This loving devotion to the Lord does not come by one's own efforts, even though all may long for it.
This cup of loving devotion belongs to our Lord and Master; He gives it to whomever He likes. |13|

Fareed, those eyes which have enticed the world - I have seen those eyes.
Once, they could not endure even a bit of mascara; now, the birds hatch their young in them! |14|

Fareed, they shouted and yelled, and constantly gave good advice.
But those whom the devil has spoiled - how can they turn their conscious-ness towards God? |15|

Fareed, become the grass on the path,
if you long for the Lord of all.
One will cut you down, and another will trample you underfoot;
then, you shall enter the Court of the Lord. |16|

Fareed, do not slander the dust; noting is as great as dust.
When we are alive, it is under our feet, and when we are dead, it is above us. |17|

Fareed, when there is greed, what love can there be? When there is greed, love is false.
How long can one remain in a thatched hut which leaks when it rains? |18|

Fareed, why do you wander from jungle to jungle, crashing through the thorny trees?
The Lord abides in the heart; why are you looking for Him in the jungle? |19|

Fareed, with these small legs, I crossed deserts and mountains.

But today, Fareed, my water jug seems hundreds of miles away. |20|

Fareed, the nights are long, and my sides are aching in pain.

Section 41 - Shaloks Of Shaykh Fareed Jee - Part 003

Cursed are the lives of those who place their hopes in others. |21|

Fareed, if I had been there when my friend came, I would have made myself a sacrifice to him.
Now my flesh is burning red on the hot coals. |22|

Fareed, the farmer plants acacia trees, and wishes for grapes.
He is spinning wool, but he wishes to wear silk. |23|

Fareed, the path is muddy, and the house of my Beloved is so far away.
If I go out, my blanket will get soaked, but if I remain at home, then my heart will be broken. |24|

My blanket is soaked, drenched with the downpour of the Lord's Rain.
I am going out to meet my Friend, so that my heart will not be broken. |25|

Fareed, I was worried that my turban might become dirty.
My thoughtless self did not realize that one day, dust will consume my head as well. |26|

Fareed: sugar cane, candy, sugar, molasses, honey and buffalo's milk
- all these things are sweet, but they are not equal to You. |27|

Fareed, my bread is made of wood, and hunger is my appetizer.
Those who eat buttered bread, will suffer in terrible pain. |28|

Eat dry bread, and drink cold water.
Fareed, if you see someone else's buttered bread, do not envy him for it. |29|

This night, I did not sleep with my Husband Lord, and now my body is suffering in pain.
Go and ask the deserted bride, how she passes her night. |30|

She finds no place of rest in her father-in-law's home, and no place in her parents' home either.

Her Husband Lord does not care for her; what sort of a blessed, happy soul-bride is she? |31|

In her father-in-law's home hereafter, and in her parents' home in this world, she belongs to her Husband Lord. Her Husband is Inaccessible and Unfathomable.

O Nanak, she is the happy soul-bride, who is pleasing to her Carefree Lord. |32|

Bathing, washing and decorating herself, she comes and sleeps without anxiety.

Fareed, she still smells like asafoetida; the fragrance of musk is gone. |33|

I am not afraid of losing my youth, as long as I do not lose the Love of my Husband Lord.

Fareed, so many youths, without His Love, have dried up and withered away. |34|

Fareed, anxiety is my bed, pain is my mattress, and the pain of separation is my blanket and quilt.

Behold, this is my life, O my True Lord and Master. |35|

Many talk of the pain and suffering of separation; O pain, you are the ruler of all.

Fareed, that body, within which love of the Lord does not well up - look upon that body as a cremation ground. |36|

Fareed, these are poisonous sprouts coated with sugar.

Some die planting them, and some are ruined, harvesting and enjoying them. |37|

Fareed, the hours of the day are lost wandering around, and the hours of the night are lost in sleep.

God will call for your account, and ask you why you came into this world. |38|

Fareed, you have gone to the Lord's Door. Have you seen the gong there?

This blameless object is being beaten - imagine what is in store for us sinners! |39|

Each and every hour, it is beaten; it is punished every day.
This beautiful body is like the gong; it passes the night in pain. |40|

Section 41 - Shaloks Of Shaykh Fareed Jee - Part 004

Shaykh Fareed has grown old, and his body has begun to tremble.
Even if he could live for hundreds of years, his body will eventually turn to dust. |41|

Fareed begs, O Lord, do not make me sit at another's door.
If this is the way you are going to keep me, then go ahead and take the life out of my body. |42|

With the axe on his shoulder, and a bucket on his head, the blacksmith is ready to cut down the tree.
Fareed, I long for my Lord; you long only for the charcoal. |43|

Fareed, some have lots of flour, while others do not even have salt.
When they go beyond this world, it shall be seen, who will be punished. |44|

Drums were beaten in their honor, there were canopies above their heads, and bugles announced their coming.
They have gone to sleep in the cemetary, buried like poor orphans. |45|

Fareed, those who built houses, mansions and lofty buildings, are also gone.
They made false deals, and were dropped into their graves. |46|

Fareed, there are many seams on the patched coat, but there are no seams on the soul.
The shaykhs and their disciples have all departed, each in his own turn. |47|

Fareed, the two lamps are lit, but death has come anyway.
It has captured the fortress of the body, and plundered the home of the heart; it extinguishes the lamps and departs. |48|

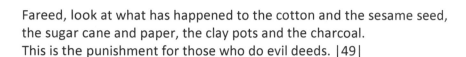

Fareed, look at what has happened to the cotton and the sesame seed, the sugar cane and paper, the clay pots and the charcoal.
This is the punishment for those who do evil deeds. |49|

Fareed, you wear your prayer shawl on your shoulders and the robes of a Sufi; your words are sweet, but there is a dagger in your heart.
Outwardly, you look bright, but your heart is dark as night. |50|

Fareed, not even a drop of blood would issue forth, if someone cut my body.
Those bodies which are imbued with the Lord - those bodies contain no blood. |51|

Third Mehl:
This body is all blood; without blood, this body could not exist.
Those who are imbued with their Lord, do not have the blood of greed in their bodies.
When the Fear of God fills the body, it becomes thin; the blood of greed departs from within.
Just as metal is purified by fire, the Fear of God removes the filthy residues of evil-mindedness.
O Nanak, those humble beings are beautiful, who are imbued with the Lord's Love. |52|

Fareed, seek that sacred pool, in which the genuine article is found.
Why do you bother to search in the pond? Your hand will only sink into the mud. |53|

Fareed, when she is young, she does not enjoy her Husband. When she grows up, she dies.
Lying in the grave, the soul-bride cries, "I did not meet You, my Lord."|54|

Fareed, your hair has turned grey, your beard has turned grey, and your moustache has turned grey.
O my thoughtless and insane mind, why are you indulging in pleasures? |55|

Fareed, how long can you run on the rooftop? You are asleep to your Husband Lord - give it up!

The days which were allotted to you are numbered, and they are passing, passing away. |56|

Fareed, houses, mansions and balconies - do not attach your consciousness to these.
When these collapse into heaps of dust, none of them will be your friend. |57|

Fareed, do not focus on mansions and wealth; center your consciousness on death, your powerful enemy.

Section 41 - Shaloks Of Shaykh Fareed Jee - Part 005

Remember that place where you must go. |58|

Fareed, those deeds which do not bring merit - forget about those deeds.
Otherwise, you shall be put to shame, in the Court of the Lord. |59|

Fareed, work for your Lord and Master; dispel the doubts of your heart.
The dervishes, the humble devotees, have the patient endurance of trees. |60|

Fareed, my clothes are black, and my outfit is black.
I wander around full of sins, and yet people call me a dervish - a holy man. |61|

The crop which is burnt will not bloom, even if it is soaked in water.
Fareed, she who is forsaken by her Husband Lord, grieves and laments. |62|

When she is a virgin, she is full of desire; but when she is married, then her troubles begin.
Fareed, she has this one regret, that she cannot be a virgin again. |63|

The swans have landed in a small pond of salt water.
They dip in their bills, but do not drink; they fly away, still thirsty. |64|

The swans fly away, and land in the fields of grain. The people go to chase them away.

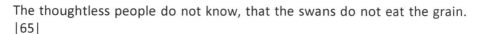

The thoughtless people do not know, that the swans do not eat the grain. |65|

The birds which lived in the pools have flown away and left.
Fareed, the overflowing pool shall also pass away, and only the lotus flowers shall remain. |66|

Fareed, a stone will be your pillow, and the earth will be your bed. The worms shall eat into your flesh.
Countless ages will pass, and you will still be lying on one side. |67|

Fareed, your beautiful body shall break apart, and the subtle thread of the breath shall be snapped.
In which house will the Messenger of Death be a guest today? |68|

Fareed, your beautiful body shall break apart, and the subtle thread of the breath shall be snapped.
Those friends who were a burden on the earth - how can they come today? |69|

Fareed: O faithless dog, this is not a good way of life.
You never come to the mosque for your five daily prayers. |70|

Rise up, Fareed, and cleanse yourself; chant your morning prayer.
The head which does not bow to the Lord - chop off and remove that head. |71|

That head which does not bow to the Lord - what is to be done with that head?
Put it in the fireplace, instead of firewood. |72|

Fareed, where are your mother and father, who gave birth to you?
They have left you, but even so, you are not convinced that you shall also have to go. |73|

Fareed, flatten out your mind; smooth out the hills and valleys.
Hereafter, the fires of hell shall not even approach you. |74|

Fifth Mehl:
Fareed, the Creator is in the Creation, and the Creation abides in God.

Whom can we call bad? There is none without Him. |75|

Fareed, if on that day when my umbilical cord was cut, my throat had been cut instead,
I would not have fallen into so many troubles, or undergone so many hardships. |76|

My teeth, feet, eyes and ears have stopped working.
My body cries out, "Those whom I knew have left me!"|77|

Fareed, answer evil with goodness; do not fill your mind with anger.

Section 41 - Shaloks Of Shaykh Fareed Jee - Part 006

Your body shall not suffer from any disease, and you shall obtain everything. |78|

Fareed, the bird is a guest in this beautiful world-garden.
The morning drums are beating - get ready to leave! |79|

Fareed, musk is released at night. Those who are sleeping do not receive their share.
Those whose eyes are heavy with sleep - how can they receive it? |80|

Fareed, I thought that I was in trouble; the whole world is in trouble!
When I climbed the hill and looked around, I saw this fire in each and every home. |81|

Fifth Mehl:
Fareed, in the midst of this beautiful earth, there is a garden of thorns.
Those humble beings who are blessed by their spiritual teacher, do not suffer even a scratch. |82|

Fifth Mehl:
Fareed, life is blessed and beautiful, along with the beautiful body.
Only a rare few are found, who love their Beloved Lord. |83|

O river, do not destroy your banks; you too will be asked to give your account.
The river flows in whatever direction the Lord orders. |84|

Fareed, the day passes painfully; the night is spent in anguish.
The boatman stands up and shouts, "The boat is caught in the whirl-pool!" |85|

The river flows on and on; it loves to eat into its banks.
What can the whirlpool do to the boat, if the boatman remains alert? |86|

Fareed, there are dozens who say they are friends; I search, but I cannot find even one.
I yearn for my beloved like a smouldering fire. |87|

Fareed, this body is always barking. Who can stand this constant suffering?
I have put plugs in my ears; I don't care how much the wind is blowing. |88|

Fareed, God's dates have ripened, and rivers of honey flow.
With each passing day, your life is being stolen away. |89|

Fareed, my withered body has become a skeleton; the crows are pecking at my palms.
Even now, God has not come to help me; behold, this is the fate of all mortal beings. |90|

The crows have searched my skeleton, and eaten all my flesh.
But please do not touch these eyes; I hope to see my Lord. |91|

O crow, do not peck at my skeleton; if you have landed on it, fly away.
Do not eat the flesh from that skeleton, within which my Husband Lord abides. |92|

Fareed, the poor grave calls out, "O homeless one, come back to your home.
You shall surely have to come to me; do not be afraid of death." |93|

These eyes have seen a great many leave.
Fareed, the people have their fate, and I have mine. |94|

God says, "If you reform yourself, you shall meet me, and meeting me, you shall be at peace.

O Fareed, if you will be mine, the whole world will be yours."|95|

How long can the tree remain implanted on the river-bank?
Fareed, how long can water be kept in a soft clay pot? |96|

Fareed, the mansions are vacant; those who lived in them have gone to live underground.

Section 41 - Shaloks Of Shaykh Fareed Jee - Part 007

They remain there, in those unhonored graves.
O Shaykh, dedicate yourself to God; you will have to depart, today or tomorrow. |97|

Fareed, the shore of death looks like the river-bank, being eroded away.
Beyond is the burning hell, from which cries and shrieks are heard.
Some understand this completely, while others wander around carelessly.
Those actions which are done in this world, shall be examined in the Court of the Lord. |98|

Fareed, the crane perches on the river bank, playing joyfully.
While it is playing, a hawk suddenly pounces on it.
When the Hawk of God attacks, playful sport is forgotten.
God does what is not expected or even considered. |99|

The body is nourished by water and grain.
The mortal comes into the world with high hopes.
But when the Messenger of Death comes, it breaks down all the doors.
It binds and gags the mortal, before the eyes of his beloved brothers.
Behold, the mortal being is going away, carried on the shoulders of four men.
Fareed, only those good deeds done in the world will be of any use in the Court of the Lord. |100|

Fareed, I am a sacrifice to those birds which live in the jungle.
They peck at the roots and live on the ground, but they do not leave the Lord's side. |101|

Fareed, the seasons change, the woods shake and the leaves drop from the trees.

I have searched in the four directions, but I have not found any resting place anywhere. |102|

Fareed, I have torn my clothes to tatters; now I wear only a rough blanket. I wear only those clothes which will lead me to meet my Lord. |103|

Third Mehl:
Why do you tear apart your fine clothes, and take to wearing a rough blanket?
O Nanak, even sitting in your own home, you can meet the Lord, if your mind is in the right place. |104|

Fifth Mehl:
Fareed, those who are very proud of their greatness, wealth and youth,
shall return empty-handed from their Lord, like sandhills after the rain. |105|

Fareed, the faces of those who forget the Lord's Name are dreadful.
They suffer terrible pain here, and hereafter they find no place of rest or refuge. |106|

Fareed, if you do not awaken in the early hours before dawn, you are dead while yet alive.
Although you have forgotten God, God has not forgotten you. |107|

Fifth Mehl:
Fareed, my Husband Lord is full of joy; He is Great and Self-sufficient.
To be imbued with the Lord God - this is the most beautiful decoration. |108|

Fifth Mehl:
Fareed, look upon pleasure and pain as the same; eradicate corruption from your heart.
Whatever pleases the Lord God is good; understand this, and you will reach His Court. |109|

Fifth Mehl:
Fareed, the world dances as it dances, and you dance with it as well.
That soul alone does not dance with it, who is under the care of the Lord God. |110|

Fifth Mehl:
Fareed, the heart is imbued with this world, but the world is of no use to it at all.

Section 41 - Shaloks Of Shaykh Fareed Jee - Part 008

It is so difficult to be like the fakeers - the Holy Saints; it is only achieved by perfect karma. |111|

The first watch of the night brings flowers, and the later watches of the night bring fruit.
Those who remain awake and aware, receive the gifts from the Lord. |112|

The gifts are from our Lord and Master; who can force Him to bestow them?
Some are awake, and do not receive them, while He awakens others from sleep to bless them. |113|

You search for your Husband Lord; you must have some fault in your body.
Those who are known as happy soul-brides, do not look to others. |114|

Within yourself, make patience the bow, and make patience the bowstring.
Make patience the arrow, the Creator will not let you miss the target. |115|

Those who are patient abide in patience; in this way, they burn their bodies.
They are close to the Lord, but they do not reveal their secret to anyone. |116|

Let patience be your purpose in life; implant this within your being.
In this way, you will grow into a great river; you will not break off into a tiny stream. |117|

Fareed, it is difficult to be a dervish - a Holy Saint; it is easier to love bread when it is buttered.
Only a rare few follow the way of the Saints. |118|

My body is cooking like an oven; my bones are burning like firewood.

If my feet become tired, I will walk on my head, if I can meet my Beloved. |119|

Do not heat up your body like an oven, and do not burn your bones like firewood.
What harm have your feet and head done to you? Behold your Beloved within yourself. |120|

I search for my Friend, but my Friend is already with me.
O Nanak, the Unseen Lord cannot be seen; He is revealed only to the Gurmukh. |121|

Seeing the swans swimming, the cranes became excited.
The poor cranes were drowned to death, with their heads below the water and their feet sticking out above. |122|

I knew him as a great swan, so I associated with him.
If I had known that he was a only wretched crane, I would never in my life have crossed paths with him. |123|

Who is a swan, and who is a crane, if God blesses him with His Glance of Grace?
If it pleases Him, O Nanak, He changes a crow into a swan. |124|

There is only one bird in the lake, but there are fifty trappers.
This body is caught in the waves of desire. O my True Lord, You are my only hope! |125|

What is that word, what is that virtue, and what is that magic mantra?
What are those clothes, which I can wear to captivate my Husband Lord? |126|

Humility is the word, forgiveness is the virtue, and sweet speech is the magic mantra.
Wear these three robes, O sister, and you will captivate your Husband Lord. |127|

If you are wise, be simple;
if you are powerful, be weak;
and when there is nothing to share, then share with others.

How rare is one who is known as such a devotee. |128|

Do not utter even a single harsh word; your True Lord and Master abides in all.
Do not break anyone's heart; these are all priceless jewels. |129|

The minds of all are like precious jewels; to harm them is not good at all.
If you desire your Beloved, then do not break anyone's heart. |130|

SWAIYAS FROM THE MOUTH OF THE GREAT FIFTH MEHL

Section 42 - Swaiyas From The Mouth Of The Great Fifth Mehl - Part 001

ONE Universal Creator God. Truth Is The Name. Creative Being Personified. No Fear. No Hatred. Image Of The Undying. Beyond Birth. Self-Existent. By Guru's Grace:

Swaiyas From The Mouth Of The Great Fifth Mehl:
O Primal Lord God, You Yourself are the Creator, the Cause of all causes.
You are All-pervading everywhere, totally filling all hearts.
You are seen pervading the world; who can know Your State? You protect all; You are our Lord and Master.
O my Imperishable and Formless Lord, You formed Yourself.
You are the One and Only; no one else is like You.
O Lord, You have no end or limitation. Who can contemplate You? You are the Father of the world, the Support of all life.
Your devotees are at Your Door, O God - they are just like You. How can servant Nanak describe them with only one tongue?
I am a sacrifice, a sacrifice, a sacrifice, a sacrifice, forever a sacrifice to them. |1|

Streams of Ambrosial Nectar flow; Your Treasures are unweighable and overflowing in abundance. You are the Farthest of the far, Infinite and Incomparably Beautiful.
You do whatever You please; You do not take advice from anyone else. In Your Home, creation and destruction happen in an instant.
No one else is equal to You; Your Light is Immaculate and Pure. Millions of sins are washed away, chanting Your Name, Har, Har.
Your devotees are at Your Door, God - they are just like You. How can servant Nanak describe them with only one tongue?
I am a sacrifice, a sacrifice, a sacrifice, a sacrifice, forever a sacrifice to them. |2|

You established all the worlds from within Yourself, and extended them outward. You are All-pervading amongst all, and yet You Yourself remain detached.

O Lord, there is no end or limit to Your Glorious Virtues; all beings and creatures are Yours. You are the Giver of all, the One Invisible Lord.

Section 42 - Swaiyas From The Mouth Of The Great Fifth Mehl - Part 002

He Himself supports the Universe, revealing His All-powerful Creative Potency. He has no color, form, mouth or beard.

Your devotees are at Your Door, O God - they are just like You. How can servant Nanak describe them with only one tongue?

I am a sacrifice, a sacrifice, a sacrifice, a sacrifice, forever a sacrifice to them. |3|

You are the Treasure of all virtue; who can know the value of Your spiritual wisdom and meditation? O God, Your Place is known as the highest of the high.

Mind, wealth and the breath of life belong to You alone, Lord. The world is strung upon Your Thread. What praises can I give to You? You are the Greatest of the great.

Who can know Your Mystery? O Unfathomable, Infinite, Divine Lord, Your Power is unstoppable. O God, You are the Support of all.

Your devotees are at Your Door, O God - they are just like You. How can servant Nanak describe them with only one tongue?

I am a sacrifice, a sacrifice, a sacrifice, a sacrifice, forever a sacrifice to them. |4|

O Formless, Formed, Undeceivable, Perfect, Imperishable,

Blissful, Unlimited, Beautiful, Immaculate, Blossoming Lord:

Countless are those who sing Your Glorious Praises, but they do not know even a tiny bit of Your extent.

That humble being upon whom You shower Your Mercy meets with You, O God.

Blessed, blessed, blessed are those humble beings, upon whom the Lord, Har, Har, showers His Mercy.

Whoever meets with the Lord through Guru Nanak is rid of both birth and death. |5|

The Lord is said to be True, True, True, True, the Truest of the True.

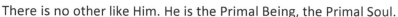

There is no other like Him. He is the Primal Being, the Primal Soul.

Chanting the Ambrosial Name of the Lord, the mortal is blessed with all comforts.

Those who taste it with their tongues, those humble beings are satisfied and fulfilled.

That person who becomes pleasing to his Lord and Master, loves the Sat Sangat, the True Congregation.

Whoever meets with the Lord through Guru Nanak, saves all his generations. |6|

True is His Congregation and His Court. The True Lord has established Truth.

Sitting upon His Throne of Truth, He administers True Justice.

The True Lord Himself fashioned the Universe. He is Infallible, and does not make mistakes.

The Naam, the Name of the Infinite Lord, is the jewel. Its value cannot be appraised - it is priceless.

That person, upon whom the Lord of the Universe showers His Mercy obtains all comforts.

Those who touch the Feet of the Lord through Guru Nanak, do not have to enter the cycle of reincarnation ever again. |7|

What is the Yoga, what is the spiritual wisdom and meditation, and what is the way, to praise the Lord?

The Siddhas and seekers and the three hundred thirty million gods cannot find even a tiny bit of the Lord's Value.

Neither Brahma, nor Sanak, nor the thousand-headed serpent king can find the limits of His Glorious Virtues.

The Inapprehensible Lord cannot be apprehended. He is pervading and permeating amongst all.

Those whom God has mercifully freed from their nooses - those humble beings are attached to His devotional worship.

Those who meet with the Lord through Guru Nanak are liberated forever, here and hereafter. |8|

I am a beggar; I seek the Sanctuary of God, the Giver of givers.

Please bless me with the gift of the dust of the feet of the Saints; grasping them, I cross over the terrifying world-ocean.

Please listen to my prayer, if it pleases You, O my Lord and Master.

Section 42 - Swaiyas From The Mouth Of The Great Fifth Mehl - Part 003

My mind yearns for the Blessed Vision of Your Darshan. This mind abides in devotional worship.

The lamp is lit in the darkness; all are saved in this Dark Age of Kali Yuga, through the One Name and faith in the Dharma.

The Lord is revealed in all the worlds. O servant Nanak, the Guru is the Supreme Lord God. |9|

Swaiyas From The Mouth Of The Great Fifth Mehl:

One Universal Creator God. By The Grace Of The True Guru:

This body is frail and transitory, and bound to emotional attachment. I am foolish, stone-hearted, filthy and unwise.

My mind wanders and wobbles, and will not hold steady. It does not know the state of the Supreme Lord God.

I am intoxicated with the wine of youth, beauty and the riches of Maya. I wander around perplexed, in excessive egotistical pride.

The wealth and women of others, arguments and slander, are sweet and dear to my soul.

I try to hide my deception, but God, the Inner-knower, the Searcher of Hearts, sees and hears all.

I have no humility, faith, compassion or purity, but I seek Your Sanctuary, O Giver of life.

The All-powerful Lord is the Cause of causes. O Lord and Master of Nanak, please save me! |1|

The Praises of the Creator, the Enticer of the mind, are potent to destroy sins.

The All-powerful Lord is the boat, to carry us across; He saves all our generations.

O my unconscious mind, contemplate and remember Him in the Sat Sangat, the True Congregation. Why are you wandering around, enticed by the darkness of doubt?

Remember Him in meditation, for an hour, for a moment, even for an instant. Chant the Name of the Lord with your tongue.

You are bound to worthless deeds and shallow pleasures; why do you spend millions of lifetimes wandering in such pain?

Chant and vibrate the Name of the Lord, O Nanak, through the Teachings of the Saints. Meditate on the Lord with love in your soul. |2|

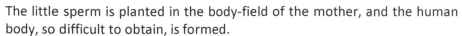

The little sperm is planted in the body-field of the mother, and the human body, so difficult to obtain, is formed.

He eats and drinks, and enjoys pleasures; his pains are taken away, and his suffering is gone.

He is given the understanding to recognize mother, father, siblings and relatives.

He grows day by day, as the horrible specter of old age comes closer and closer.

You worthless, petty worm of Maya - remember your Lord and Master, at least for an instant!

Please take Nanak's hand, O Merciful Ocean of Mercy, and take away this heavy load of doubt. |3|

O mind, you are a mouse, living in the mousehole of the body; you are so proud of yourself, but you act like an absolute fool.

You swing in the swing of wealth, intoxicated with Maya, and you wander around like an owl.

You take pleasure in your children, spouse, friends and relatives; your emotional attachment to them is increasing.

You have planted the seeds of egotism, and the sprout of possessiveness has come up. You pass your life making sinful mistakes.

The cat of death, with his mouth wide-open, is watching you. You eat food, but you are still hungry.

Meditate in remembrance on the Merciful Lord of the World, O Nanak, in the Sat Sangat, the True Congregation. Know that the world is just a dream. |4|

Section 42 - Swaiyas From The Mouth Of The Great Fifth Mehl - Part 004

Neither body, nor house, nor love last forever. You are intoxicated with Maya; how long will you be proud of them?

Neither crown, nor canopy, nor servants last forever. You do not consider in your heart that your life is passing away.

Neither chariots, nor horses, nor elephants or royal thrones shall last forever. In an instant, you will have to leave them, and depart naked.

Neither warrior, nor hero, nor king or ruler last forever; see this with your eyes.

Neither fortress, nor shelter, nor treasure will save you; doing evil deeds, you shall depart empty-handed.

Friends, children, spouses and friends - none of them last forever; they change like the shade of a tree.

God is the Perfect Primal Being, Merciful to the meek; each and every instant, meditate in remembrance on Him, the Inaccessible and Infinite.

O Great Lord and Master, servant Nanak seeks Your Sanctuary; please shower him with Your Mercy, and carry him across. |5|

I have used up my breath of life, sold my self-respect, begged for charity, committed highway robbery, and dedicated my consciousness to the love and pursuit of acquiring wealth.

I have kept it secretly hidden from my friends, relatives, companions, children and siblings.

I ran around practicing falsehood, burning up my body and growing old.

I gave up good deeds, righteousness and Dharma, self-discipline, purity, religious vows and all good ways; I associated with the fickle Maya.

Beasts and birds, trees and mountains - in so many ways, I wandered lost in reincarnation.

I did not remember the Naam, the Name of the Lord, for a moment, or even an instant. He is the Master of the meek, the Lord of all life.

The food and drink, and the sweet and tasty dishes became totally bitter at the last moment.

O Nanak, I was saved in the Society of the Saints, at their feet; the others, intoxicated with Maya, have gone, leaving everything behind. |6|

Brahma, Shiva, the Vedas and the silent sages sing the Glorious Praises of their Lord and Master with love and delight.

Indra, Vishnu and Gorakh, who come to earth and then go to heaven again, seek the Lord.

The Siddhas, human beings, gods and demons cannot find even a tiny bit of His Mystery.

The Lord's humble servants are imbued with love and affection for God their Beloved; in the delight of devotional worship, they are absorbed in the Blessed Vision of His Darshan.

But those who forsake Him, and beg from another, shall see their mouths, teeth and tongues wear away.

O my foolish mind, meditate in remembrance on the Lord, the Giver of peace. Slave Nanak imparts these teachings. |7|

The pleasures of Maya shall fade away. In doubt, the mortal falls into the deep dark pit of emotional attachment.

He is so proud, even the sky cannot contain him. His belly is filled with manure, bones and worms.

He runs around in the ten directions, for the sake of the great poison of corruption. He steals the wealth of others, and in the end, he is destroyed by his own ignorance.

His youth passes away, the illnesses of old age seize him, and the Messenger of Death punishes him; such is the death he dies.

He suffers the agony of hell in countless incarnations; he rots away in the pit of pain and condemnation.

O Nanak, those whom the Saint mercifully takes as his own, are carried across by their loving devotional worship. |8|

All virtues are obtained, all fruits and rewards, and the desires of the mind; my hopes have been totally fulfilled.

The Medicine, the Mantra, the Magic Charm, will cure all illnesses and totally take away all pain.

Section 42 - Swaiyas From The Mouth Of The Great Fifth Mehl - Part 005

Lust, anger, egotism, jealousy and desire are eliminated by chanting the Name of the Lord.

The merits of cleansing baths, charity, penance, purity and good deeds, are obtained by enshrining the Lotus Feet of God within the heart.

The Lord is my Friend, my Very Best Friend, Companion and Relative. God is the Sustenance of the soul, the Support of the breath of life.

I have grasped the Shelter and Support of my All-powerful Lord and Master; slave Nanak is forever a sacrifice to Him. |9|

Weapons cannot cut that person who delights in the love of the Lord's Lotus Feet.

Ropes cannot bind that person whose mind is pierced through by the Vision of the Lord's Way.

Fire cannot burn that person who is attached to the dust of the feet of the Lord's humble servant.

Water cannot drown that person whose feet walk on the Lord's Path.

O Nanak, diseases, faults, sinful mistakes and emotional attachment are pierced by the Arrow of the Name. |1|10|

People are engaged in making all sorts of efforts; they contemplate the various aspects of the six Shaastras.

Rubbing ashes all over their bodies, they wander around at the various sacred shrines of pilgrimage; they fast until their bodies are emaciated, and braid their hair into tangled messes.

Without devotional worship of the Lord, they all suffer in pain, caught in the tangled web of their love.

They perform worship ceremonies, draw ritual marks on their bodies, cook their own food fanatically, and make pompous shows of themselves in all sorts of ways. |2|11|20|

Swaiyas In Praise Of The First Mehl:

One Universal Creator God. By The Grace Of The True Guru:

Meditate single-mindedly on the Primal Lord God, the Bestower of blessings.

He is the Helper and Support of the Saints, manifest forever.

Grasp His Feet and enshrine them in your heart.

Then, let us sing the Glorious Praises of the most exalted Guru Nanak. |1|

I sing the Glorious Praises of the most exalted Guru Nanak, the Ocean of peace, the Eradicator of sins, the sacred pool of the Shabad, the Word of God.

The beings of deep and profound understanding, oceans of wisdom, sing of Him; the Yogis and wandering hermits meditate on Him.

Indra and devotees like Prahlaad, who know the joy of the soul, sing of Him.

KAL the poet sings the Sublime Praises of Guru Nanak, who enjoys mastery of Raja Yoga, the Yoga of meditation and success. |2|

King Janak and the great Yogic heroes of the Lord's Way, sing the Praises of the All-powerful Primal Being, filled with the sublime essence of the Lord.

Sanak and Brahma's sons, the Saadhus and Siddhas, the silent sages and humble servants of the Lord sing the Praises of Guru Nanak, who cannot be deceived by the great deceiver.

Dhoma the seer and Dhroo, whose realm is unmoving, sing the Glorious Praises of Guru Nanak, who knows the ecstasy of loving devotional worship.

KAL the poet sings the Sublime Praises of Guru Nanak, who enjoys mastery of Raja Yoga. |3|

Kapila and the other Yogis sing of Guru Nanak. He is the Avataar, the Incarnation of the Infinite Lord.

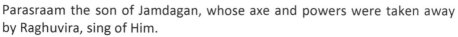
Parasraam the son of Jamdagan, whose axe and powers were taken away by Raghuvira, sing of Him.

Udho, Akrur and Bidur sing the Glorious Praises of Guru Nanak, who knows the Lord, the Soul of All.

KAL the poet sings the Sublime Praises of Guru Nanak, who enjoys mastery of Raja Yoga. |4|

Section 42 - Swaiyas From The Mouth Of The Great Fifth Mehl - Part 006

The four castes and the six Shaastras sing His Glorious Praises; Brahma and the others contemplate His Virtues.

The thousand-tongued serpent king sings His Praises with delight, remaining lovingly attached to Him.

Shiva, detached and beyond desire, sings the Glorious Praises of Guru Nanak, who knows the Lord's endless meditation.

KAL the poet sings the Sublime Praises of Guru Nanak, who enjoys mastery of Raja Yoga. |5|

He mastered Raja Yoga, and enjoys sovereignty over both worlds; the Lord, beyond hate and revenge, is enshrined within His Heart.

The whole world is saved, and carried across, chanting the Naam, the Name of the Lord.

Sanak and Janak and the others sing His Praises, age after age.

Blessed, blessed, blessed and fruitful is the sublime birth of the Guru into the world.

Even in the nether regions, His Victory is celebrated; so says KAL the poet.

You are blessed with the Nectar of the Lord's Name, O Guru Nanak; You have mastered Raja Yoga, and enjoy sovereignty over both worlds. |6|

In the Golden Age of Sat Yuga, You were pleased to deceive Baal the king, in the form of a dwarf.

In the Silver Age of Traytaa Yuga, You were called Raam of the Raghu dynasty.

In the Brass Age of Dwaapur Yuga, You were Krishna; You killed Mur the demon and saved Kans.

You blessed Ugrasain with a kingdom, and You blessed Your humble devotees with fearlessness.

In the Iron Age, the Dark Age of Kali Yuga, You are known and accepted as Guru Nanak, Guru Angad and Guru Amar Das.

The sovereign rule of the Great Guru is unchanging and permanent, according the Command of the Primal Lord God. |7|

His Glorious Praises are sung by the devotees Ravi Daas, Jai Dayv and Trilochan.
The devotees Naam Dayv and Kabeer praise Him continually, knowing Him to be even-eyed.
The devotee Baynee sings His Praises; He intuitively enjoys the ecstasy of the soul.
He is the Master of Yoga and meditation, and the spiritual wisdom of the Guru; He knows none other except God.
Sukh Dayv and Preekhyat sing His Praises, and Gautam the rishi sings His Praise.
Says KAL the poet, the ever-fresh praises of Guru Nanak are spread throughout the world. |8|

In the nether worlds, His Praises are sung by the devotees like Shaysh-naag in serpent form.
Shiva, the Yogis and the wandering hermits sing His Praises forever.
Vyaas the silent sage, who studied the Vedas and its grammar, sings His Praise.
His Praises are sung by Brahma, who created the entire universe by God's Command.
God fills the galaxies and realms of the universe; He is known to be the same, manifest and unmanifest.
KAL chants the Sublime Praises of Guru Nanak, who enjoys mastery of Yoga. |9|

The nine masters of Yoga sing His Praises; blessed is the Guru, who is merged into the True Lord.
Maandhaataa, who called himself ruler of all the world, sings His Praises.
Bal the king, dwelling in the seventh underworld, sings His Praises.
Bhart'har, abiding forever with Gorakh, his guru, sings His Praises.
Doorbaasaa, King Puro and Angra sing the Praises of Guru Nanak.
Says KAL the poet, the Sublime Praises of Guru Nanak intuitively permeate each and every heart. |10|

Section 42 - Swaiyas From The Mouth Of The Great Fifth Mehl - Part 007

Swaiyas In Praise Of The Second Mehl:

One Universal Creator God. By The Grace Of The True Guru:

Blessed is the Primal Lord God, the Creator, the All-powerful Cause of causes.

Blessed is the True Guru Nanak, who placed His hand upon Your forehead.

When He placed His hand upon Your forehead, then the celestial nectar began to rain down in torrents; the gods and human beings, heavenly heralds and sages were drenched in its fragrance.

You challenged and subdued the cruel demon of death; You restrained Your wandering mind; You overpowered the five demons and You keep them in one home.

Through the Guru's Door, the Gurdwara, You have conquered the world; You play the game even-handedly. You keep the flow of your love steady for the Formless Lord.

O KAL SAHAAR, chant the Praises of Lehnaa throughout the seven continents; He met with the Lord, and became Guru of the World. |1|

The Stream of Ambrosial Nectar from His eyes washes away the slime and filth of sins; the sight of His door dispels the darkness of ignorance.

Whoever accomplishes this most difficult task of contemplating the most sublime Word of the Shabad - those people cross over the terrifying world-ocean, and cast off their loads of sin.

The Sat Sangat, the True Congregation, is celestial and sublime; whoever remains awake and aware, contemplating the Guru, embodies humility, and is imbued forever with the Supreme Love of the Lord.

O KAL SAHAAR, chant the Praises of Lehnaa throughout the seven continents; He met with the Lord, and became Guru of the World. |2|

You hold tight to the Naam, the Name of the Infinite Lord; Your expanse is immaculate. You are the Support of the Siddhas and seekers, and the good and humble beings.

You are the incarnation of King Janak; the contemplation of Your Shabad is sublime throughout the universe. You abide in the world like the lotus on the water.

Like the Elyisan Tree, You cure all illnesses and take away the sufferings of the world. The three-phased soul is lovingly attuned to You alone.

O KAL SAHAAR, chant the Praises of Lehnaa throughout the seven continents; He met with the Lord, and became Guru of the World. |3|

You were blessed with glory by the Prophet; You serve the Guru, certified by the Lord, who has subdued the snake of the mind, and who abides in the state of sublime bliss.

Your Vision is like that of the Lord, Your soul is a fount of spiritual wisdom; You know the unfathomable state of the certified Guru.

Your Gaze is focused upon the unmoving, unchanging place. Your Intellect is immaculate; it is focused upon the most sublime place. Wearing the armor of humility, you have overcome Maya.

O KAL SAKAAR, chant the Praises of Lehnaa throughout the seven continents; He met with the Lord, and became Guru of the World. |4|

Casting Your Glance of Grace, you dispel the darkness, burn away evil, and destroy sin.

You are the Heroic Warrior of the Shabad, the Word of God. Your Power destroys sexual desire and anger.

You have overpowered greed and emotional attachment; You nurture and cherish those who seek Your Sanctuary.

You gather in the joyful love of the soul; Your Words have the Potency to bring forth Ambrosial Nectar.

You are appointed the True Guru, the True Guru in this Dark Age of Kali Yuga; whoever is truly attached to You is carried across.

The lion, the son of Pheru, is Guru Angad, the Guru of the World; Lehnaa practices Raja Yoga, the Yoga of meditation and success. |5|

Section 42 - Swaiyas From The Mouth Of The Great Fifth Mehl - Part 008

Your mind remains lovingly attuned to the Lord forever; You do whatever you desire.

Like the tree heavy with fruit, You bow in humility, and endure the pain of it; You are pure of thought.

You realize this reality, that the Lord is All-pervading, Unseen and Amazing.

With intuitive ease, You send forth the rays of the Ambrosial Word of power.

You have risen to the state of the certified Guru; you grasp truth and contentment.

KAL proclaims, that whoever attains the Blessed Vision of the Darshan of Lehnaa, meets with the Lord. |6|

My mind has faith, that the Prophet has given You access to the Profound Lord.

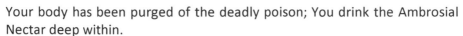

Your body has been purged of the deadly poison; You drink the Ambrosial Nectar deep within.

Your Heart has blossomed forth in awareness of the Unseen Lord, who has infused His Power throughout the ages.

O True Guru, You are intuitively absorbed in Samaadhi, with continuity and equality.

You are open-minded and large-hearted, the Destroyer of poverty; seeing You, sins are afraid.

Says KAL, I lovingly, continually, intuitively chant the Praises of Lehnaa with my tongue. |7|

The Naam, the Name of the Lord, is our medicine; the Naam is our support; the Naam is the peace of Samaadhi. The Naam is the insignia which embellishes us forever.

KAL is imbued with the Love of the Naam, the Naam which is the fragrance of gods and human beings.

Whoever obtains the Naam, the Philosopher's Stone, becomes the embodiment of Truth, manifest and radiant throughout the world.

Gazing upon the Blessed Vision of the Guru's Darshan, it is as if one has bathed at the sixty-eight sacred shrines of pilgrimage. |8|

The True Name is the sacred shrine, the True Name is the cleansing bath of purification and food. The True Name is eternal love; chant the True Name, and be embellished.

The True Name is obtained through the Word of the Guru's Shabad; the Sangat, the Holy Congregation, is fragrant with the True Name.

KAL the poet utters the Praises of the one whose self-discipline is the True Name, and whose fast is the True Name.

Gazing upon the Blessed Vision of the Guru's Darshan, one's life is approved and certified in the True Name. |9|

When You bestow Your Ambrosial Glance of Grace, You eradicate all wickedness, sin and filth.

Sexual desire, anger, greed and emotional attachment - You have over-come all these powerful passions.

Your mind is filled with peace forever; You banish the sufferings of the world.

The Guru is the river of the nine treasures, washing off the dirt of our lives.

So speaks TAL the poet: serve the Guru, day and night, with intuitive love and affection.

Gazing upon the Blessed Vision of the Guru, the pains of death and rebirth are taken away. |10|

Swaiyas In Praise Of The Third Mehl:
One Universal Creator God. By The Grace Of The True Guru:
Dwell upon that Primal Being, the True Lord God; in this world, His One Name is Undeceivable.
He carries His devotees across the terrifying world-ocean; meditate in remembrance on His Naam, Supreme and Sublime.
Nanak delighted in the Naam; He established Lehnaa as Guru, who was imbued with all supernatural spiritual powers.
So speaks KALL the poet: the glory of the wise, sublime and humble Amar Daas is spread throughout the world.
His Praises radiate throughout the world, like the rays of the sun, and the branches of the maulsar (fragrant) tree.
In the north, south, east and west, people proclaim Your Victory.

Section 42 - Swaiyas From The Mouth Of The Great Fifth Mehl - Part 009

The Guru spoke the Lord's Name with His mouth and broadcast it through-out the world, to turn the tide of the hearts of men.
That Undeceivable Naam, which carries the devotees across the world-ocean, came into Guru Amar Daas. |1|

The gods and heavenly heralds, the Siddhas and seekers and Shiva in Samaadhi meditate in remembrance on the Naam, the Name of the Lord.
The stars and the realms of Dhroo, and devotees like Naaraad and Prahlaad meditate on the Naam.
The moon and the sun long for the Naam; it has saved even mountain ranges.
That Undeceivable Naam, which carries the devotees across the world-ocean, came into Guru Amar Daas. |2|

Dwelling upon that Immaculate Naam, the nine Yogic masters, Shiva and Sanak and many others have been emancipated.
The eighty-four Siddhas, the beings of supernatural spiritual powers, and the Buddhas are imbued with the Naam; it carried Ambreek across the terrifying world-ocean.
It has erased the sins of Oodho, Akroor, Trilochan, Naam Dayv and Kabeer, in this Dark Age of Kali Yuga.

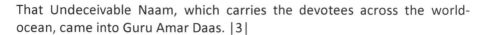

That Undeceivable Naam, which carries the devotees across the world-ocean, came into Guru Amar Daas. |3|

The three hundred thirty million angels meditate, attached to the Naam; it is enshrined within the minds of the celibates and ascetics.
Bhisham Pitama, the son of the Ganges, meditated on that Naam; his consciousness delighted in the Ambrosial Nectar of the Lord's Feet.
The great and profound Guru has brought forth the Naam; accepting the teachings as true, the Holy Congregation has been saved.
That Undeceivable Naam, which carries the devotees across the world-ocean, came into Guru Amar Daas. |4|

The Glory of the Naam shines forth, like the rays of the sun, and the branches of the Elysian Tree.
In the countries of the north, south, east and west, the Praises of the Naam are chanted.
Life is fruitful, when the Name of the Lord abides in the heart.
The angelic beings, heavenly heralds, celestial singers and the six Shaastras yearn for the Naam.
The son of Tayj Bhaan of the Bhalla dynasty is noble and famous; with his palms pressed together, KALL meditates on Him.
The Naam takes away the fears of the devotees about the word-ocean; Guru Amar Daas has obtained it. |5|

The thirty-one million gods meditate on the Naam, along with the Siddhas and seekers; the Naam supports solar systems and galaxies.
One who meditates on the Naam in Samaadhi, endures sorrow and joy as one and the same.
The Naam is the most sublime of all; the devotees remain lovingly attuned to it.
Guru Amar Daas was blessed with the treasure of the Naam, by the Creator Lord, in His Pleasure. |6|

He is the Warrior Hero of Truth, humility is His Power. His Loving Nature inspires the Congregation with deep and profound understanding; He is absorbed in the Lord, free of hate and vengeance.
Patience has been His white banner since the beginning of time, planted on the bridge to heaven.
The Saints meet their Beloved Guru, who is united with the Creator Lord.

Serving the True Guru, they find peace; Guru Amar Daas has given them this ability. |7|

The Naam is His cleansing bath; the Naam is the food He eats; the Naam is the taste He enjoys. With deep yearning, He chants the Sweet Bani of the Guru's Word forever.
Blessed is service to the True Guru; by His Grace, the State of the Unfathomable Lord is known.
All Your generations are totally saved; You dwell in the Naam, the Name of the Lord.

Section 42 - Swaiyas From The Mouth Of The Great Fifth Mehl - Part 010

So speaks KALL: fruitful is the life of one who meets with Guru Amar Daas, radiant with the Light of God. |8|

On His right hand is the sign of the lotus; the Siddhis, the supernatural spiritual powers, await His Command.
On His left are worldly powers, which fascinate the three worlds.
The Inexpressible Lord abides in His Heart; He alone knows this joy.
Guru Amar Daas utters the words of devotion, imbued with the Love of the Lord.
On His forehead is the true insignia of the Lord's Mercy; with his palms pressed together, KALL meditates on Him.
Whoever meets with the Guru, the certified True Guru, has all his desires fulfilled. |9|

Supremely fruitful are the feet which walk upon the path of Guru Amar Daas.
Supremely fruitful are the hands which touch the feet of Guru Amar Daas.
Supremely fruitful is the tongue which utters the praises of Guru Amar Daas.
Supremely fruitful are the eyes which behold Guru Amar Daas.
Supremely fruitful are the ears which hear the Praises of Guru Amar Daas.
Fruitful is the heart in which Guru Amar Daas, the Father of the world, Himself abides.
Fruitful is the head, says JAALAP, which bows forever before Guru Amar Daas. |1|10|

They do not suffer pain or hunger, and they cannot be called poor.

They do not grieve, and their limits cannot be found.

They do not serve anyone else, but they give gifts to hundreds and thousands.

They sit on beautiful carpets; they establish and disestablish at will.

They find peace in this world, and live fearlessly amidst their enemies.

They are fruitful and prosperous, says JAALAP. Guru Amar Daas is pleased with them. |2|11|

You read about the One Lord, and enshrine Him in Your mind; You realize the One and Only Lord.

With Your eyes and the words You speak, You dwell upon the One Lord; You do not know any other place of rest.

You know the One Lord while dreaming, and the One Lord while awake. You are absorbed in the One.

At the age of seventy-one, You began to march towards the Indestructible Lord.

The One Lord, who takes hundreds of thousands of forms, cannot be seen. He can only be described as One.

So speaks JAALAP: O Guru Amar Daas, You long for the One Lord, and believe in the One Lord alone. |3|12|

The understanding which Jai Dayv grasped, the understanding which permeated Naam Dayv,

the understanding which was in the consciousness of Trilochan and known by the devotee Kabeer,

by which Rukmaangad constantly meditated on the Lord, O Siblings of Destiny,

which brought Ambreek and Prahlaad to seek the Sanctuary of the Lord of the Universe, and which brought them to salvation

-says JALL that sublime understanding has brought You to renounce greed, anger and desire, and to know the way.

Guru Amar Daas is the Lord's own devotee; gazing upon the Blessed Vision of His Darshan, one is liberated. |4|13|

Meeting with Guru Amar Daas, the earth is purged of its sin.

The Siddhas and seekers long to meet with Guru Amar Daas.

Meeting with Guru Amar Daas, the mortal meditates on the Lord, and his journey comes to its end.

Meeting with Guru Amar Daas, the Fearless Lord is obtained, and the cycle of reincarnation is brought to an end.

Section 42 - Swaiyas From The Mouth Of The Great Fifth Mehl - Part 011

Realizing the One Lord, love of duality ceases, and one comes to accept the Sublime Mantra of the Guru.
So speaks JAALAP: countless treasures are obtained, by the sight of Guru Amar Daas. |5|14|

Guru Nanak gathered up the True Name of the Creator Lord, and implanted it within.
Through Him, Lehnaa became manifest in the form of Guru Angad, who remained lovingly attuned to His Feet.
Guru Amar Daas of that dynasty is the home of hope. How can I express His Glorious Virtues?
His Virtues are unknowable and unfathomable. I do not know the limits of His Virtues.
The Creator, the Architect of Destiny, has made Him a boat to carry all His generations across, along with the Sangat, the Holy Congregation.
So speaks KEERAT: O Guru Amar Daas, please protect me and save me; I seek the Sanctuary of Your Feet. |1|15|

The Lord Himself wielded His Power and entered the world.
The Formless Lord took form, and with His Light He illuminated the realms of the world.
He is All-pervading everywhere; the Lamp of the Shabad, the Word, has been lit.
Whoever gathers in the essence of the teachings shall be absorbed in the Feet of the Lord.
Lehnaa, who became Guru Angad, and Guru Amar Daas, have been reincarnated into the pure house of Guru Nanak.
Guru Amar Daas is our Saving Grace, who carries us across; in lifetime after lifetime, I seek the Sanctuary of Your Feet. |2|16|

Gazing upon the Blessed Vision of His Darshan, the Gursikh is blessed with chanting and deep meditation, truth and contentment.
Whoever seeks His Sanctuary is saved; his account is cleared in the City of Death.

His heart is totally filled with loving devotion; he chants to the Creator Lord.

The Guru is the river of pearls; in an instant, he carries the drowning ones across.

He was reincarnated into the House of Guru Nanak; He chants the Glorious Praises of the Creator Lord.

Those who serve Guru Amar Daas - their pains and poverty are taken away, far away. |3|17|

I consciously pray within my consciousness, but I cannot express it in words.

I place all my worries and anxieties before You; I look to the Saadh Sangat, the Company of the Holy, for help.

By the Hukam of Your Command, I am blessed with Your Insignia; I serve my Lord and Master.

When You, O Guru, gaze at me with Your Glance of Grace, the fruit of the Naam, the Name of the Creator, is placed within my mouth.

The Unfathomable and Unseen Primal Lord God, the Cause of causes - as He orders, so do I speak.

O Guru Amar Daas, Doer of deeds, Cause of causes, as You keep me, I remain; as You protect me, I survive. |4|18|

OF BHIKHAA:
In deep meditation, and the spiritual wisdom of the Guru, one's essence merges with the essence of reality.

In truth, the True Lord is recognized and realized, when one is lovingly attuned to Him, with one-pointed consciousness.

Lust and anger are brought under control, when the breath does not fly around, wandering restlessly.

Dwelling in the land of the Formless Lord, realizing the Hukam of His Command, His contemplative wisdom is attained.

In this Dark Age of Kali Yuga, the Guru is the Form of the Creator, the Primal Lord God; he alone knows, who has tried it.

So speaks BHIKHAA: I have met the Guru. With love and intuitive affection, He has bestowed the Blessed Vision of His Darshan. |1|19|

I have been searching for the Saints; I have seen so many Holy and spiritual people.

The hermits, Sannyaasees, ascetics, penitents, fanatics and Pandits all speak sweetly.

I wandered around lost for a year, but no one touched my soul.

Section 42 - Swaiyas From The Mouth Of The Great Fifth Mehl - Part 012

I listened to preachers and teachers, but I could not be happy with their lifestyles.
Those who have abandoned the Lord's Name, and become attached to duality - why should I speak in praise of them?
So speaks BHIKHAA: the Lord has led me to meet the Guru. As You keep me, I remain; as You protect me, I survive. |2|20|

Wearing the armor of Samaadhi, the Guru has mounted the saddled horse of spiritual wisdom.
Holding the bow of Dharma in His Hands, He has shot the arrows of devotion and humility.
He is fearless in the Fear of the Eternal Lord God; He has thrust the spear of the Word of the Guru's Shabad into the mind.
He has cut down the five demons of unfulfilled sexual desire, unresolved anger, unsatisfied greed, emotional attachment and self-conceit.
Guru Amar Daas, the son of Tayj Bhaan, of the noble Bhalla dynasty, blessed by Guru Nanak, is the Master of kings.
SALL speaks the truth; O Guru Amar Daas, you have conquered the army of evil, fighting the battle this way. |1|21|

The raindrops of the clouds, the plants of the earth, and the flowers of the spring cannot be counted.
Who can know the limits of the rays of the sun and the moon, the waves of the ocean and the Ganges?
With Shiva's meditation and the spiritual wisdom of the True Guru, says BHALL the poet, these may be counted.
O Guru Amar Daas, Your Glorious Virtues are so sublime; Your Praises belong only to You. |1|22|

Swaiyas In Praise Of The Fourth Mehl:
One Universal Creator God. By The Grace Of The True Guru:
Meditate single-mindedly on the Immaculate Primal Lord God.
By Guru's Grace, sing the Glorious Praises of the Lord forever.
Singing His Praises, the mind blossoms forth in ecstasy.
The True Guru fulfills the hopes of His humble servant.
Serving the True Guru, the supreme status is obtained.

Meditate on the Imperishable, Formless Lord God.

Meeting with Him, one escapes poverty.

KAL SAHAAR chants His Glorious Praises.

I chant the pure praises of that humble being who has been blessed with the Ambrosial Nectar of the Naam, the Name of the Lord.

He served the True Guru and was blessed with the sublime essence of the Shabad, the Word of God. The Immaculate Naam has been enshrined in his heart.

He enjoys and savors the Lord's Name, and purchases the Glorious Virtues of the Lord of the Universe. He seeks the essence of reality; he is the Fountain of even-handed justice.

So speaks KALL the poet: Guru Raam Daas, the son of Har Daas, fills the empty pools to overflowing. |1|

The stream of ambrosial nectar flows and the immortal status is obtained; the pool is forever overflowing with Ambrosial Nectar.

Those Saints who have served the Lord in the past drink in this Nectar, and bathe their minds in it.

God takes their fears away, and blesses them with the state of fearless dignity. Through the Word of His Shabad, He has saved them.

So speaks KALL the poet: Guru Raam Daas, the son of Har Daas, fills the empty pools to overflowing. |2|

The True Guru's understanding is deep and profound. The Sat Sangat is His Pure Congregation. His Soul is drenched in the deep crimson color of the Lord's Love.

The Lotus of His mind remains awake and aware, illuminated with intuitive wisdom. In His own home, He has obtained the Fearless, Immaculate Lord.

Section 42 - Swaiyas From The Mouth Of The Great Fifth Mehl - Part 013

The Merciful True Guru has implanted the Lord's Name within me, and by His Grace, I have overpowered the five thieves.

So speaks KALL the poet: Guru Raam Daas, the son of Har Daas, fills the empty pools to overflowing. |3|

With intuitive detachment, He is lovingly attuned to the Fearless, Unmanif-est Lord; He met with Guru Amar Daas, the Philosopher's Stone, within his own home.

By the Grace of the True Guru, He attained the supreme status; He is overflowing with the treasures of loving devotion.

He was released from reincarnation, and the fear of death was taken away.

His consciousness is attached to the Lord, the Ocean of contentment.

So speaks KALL the poet: Guru Raam Daas, the son of Har Daas, fills the empty pools to overflowing. |4|

He fills the empty to overflowing; He has enshrined the Infinite within His heart.

Within His mind, He contemplates the essence of reality, the Destroyer of pain, the Enlightener of the soul.

He yearns for the Lord's Love forever; He Himself knows the sublime essence of this Love.

By the Grace of the True Guru, He intuitively enjoys this Love.

By the Grace of Guru Nanak, and the sublime teachings of Guru Angad, Guru Amar Daas broadcast the Lord's Command.

So speaks KALL: O Guru Raam Daas, You have attained the status of eternal and imperishable dignity. |5|

You abide in the pool of contentment; Your tongue reveals the Ambrosial Essence.

Meeting with You, a tranquil peace wells up, and sins run far away.

You have attained the Ocean of peace, and You never grow tired on the Lord's path.

The armor of self-restraint, truth, contentment and humility can never be pierced.

The Creator Lord certified the True Guru, and now the world blows the trumpet of His Praises.

So speaks KALL: O Guru Raam Daas, You have attained the state of fearless immortality. |6|

O certified True Guru, You have conquered the world; You meditate single-mindedly on the One Lord.

Blessed, blessed is Guru Amar Daas, the True Guru, who implanted the Naam, the Name of the Lord, deep within.

The Naam is the wealth of the nine treasures; prosperity and supernatural spiritual powers are His slaves.

He is blessed with the ocean of intuitive wisdom; He has met with the Imperishable Lord God.

The Guru has implanted the Naam deep within; attached to the Naam, the devotees have been carried across since ancient times.

So speaks KALL: O Guru Raam Daas, You have obtained the wealth of the Lord's Love. |7|

The flow of loving devotion and primal love does not stop.

The True Guru drinks in the stream of nectar, the sublime essence of the Shabad, the Infinite Word of God.

Wisdom is His mother, and contentment is His father; He is absorbed in the ocean of intuitive peace and poise.

The Guru is the Embodiment of the Unborn, Self-illumined Lord; by the Word of His Teachings, the Guru carries the world across.

Within His mind, the Guru has enshrined the Shabad, the Word of the Unseen, Unfathomable, Infinite Lord.

So speaks KALL: O Guru Raam Daas, You have attained the Lord, the Saving Grace of the world. |8|

The Saving Grace of the world, the nine treasures, carries the devotees across the world-ocean.

The Drop of Ambrosial Nectar, the Lord's Name, is the antidote to the poison of sin.

The tree of intuitive peace and poise blossoms and bears the ambrosial fruit of spiritual wisdom.

Blessed are those fortunate people who receive it, by Guru's Grace.

They are liberated through the Shabad, the Word of the True Guru; their minds are filled with the Guru's Wisdom.

So speaks KALL: O Guru Raam Daas, You beat the drum of the Shabad. |9|

Section 42 - Swaiyas From The Mouth Of The Great Fifth Mehl - Part 014

On the bed of faith, with the blankets of intuitive peace and poise and the canopy of contentment, You are embellished forever with the armor of humility.

Through the Word of the Guru's Shabad, you practice the Naam; You lean on its Support, and give Your Fragrance to Your companions.

You abide with the Unborn Lord, the Good and Pure True Guru.

So speaks KALL: O Guru Raam Daas, You abide in the sacred pool of intuitive peace and poise. |10|

The Lord's Name abides in the hearts of those who are pleasing to the Guru.

Sins run far away from those who are pleasing to the Guru.

Those who are pleasing to the Guru eradicate pride and egotism from within.

Those who are pleasing to the Guru are attached to the Shadad, the Word of God; they are carried across the terrifying world-ocean.

Those who are blessed with the wisdom of the certified Guru - blessed and fruitful is their birth into the world.

KALL the poet runs to the Sanctuary of the Great Guru; attached to the Guru, they are blessed with worldly enjoyments, liberation and everything. |11|

The Guru has pitched the tent; under it, all the ages are gathered.

He carries the spear of intuition, and takes the Support of Naam, the Name of the Lord, through which the devotees are fulfilled.

Guru Nanak, Guru Angad and Guru Amar Daas, through devotional worship, have merged into the Lord.

O Guru Raam Daas, You alone know the taste of this Raja Yoga. |12|

He alone is enlightened like Janaka, who links the chariot of his mind to the state of ecstatic realization.

He gathers in truth and contentment, and fills up the empty pool within.

He speaks the Unspoken Speech of the eternal city. He alone obtains it, unto whom God gives it.

O Guru Raam Daas, Your sovereign rule, like that of Janak, is Yours alone. |13|

Tell me, how can sin and suffering cling to that humble being who chants the Naam, given by the Guru, with single-minded love and firm faith?

When the Lord, the Boat to carry us across, bestows His Glance of Grace, even for an instant, the mortal contemplates the Shabad within his heart; unfulfilled sexual desire and unresolved anger are eradicated.

The Guru is the Giver to all beings; He speaks the spiritual wisdom of the Unfathomable Lord, and meditates on Him day and night. He never sleeps, even for an instant.

Seeing Him, poverty vanishes, and one is blessed with the treasure of the Naam, the Name of the Lord. The spiritual wisdom of the Guru's Word washes away the filth of evil-mindedness.

Tell me, how can sin and suffering cling to that humble being who chants the Naam, given by the Guru, with single-minded love and firm faith? |1|

Dharmic faith and the karma of good deeds are obtained from the Perfect True Guru.

The Siddhas and Holy Saadhus, the silent sages and angelic beings, yearn to serve Him; through the most excellent Word of the Shabad, they are lovingly attuned to the One Lord.

Who can know Your limits? You are the Embodiment of the Fearless, Formless Lord. You are the Speaker of the Unspoken Speech; You alone understand this.

O foolish worldly mortal, you are deluded by doubt; give up birth and death, and you shall not be punished by the Messenger of Death. Meditate on the Guru's Teachings.

You foolish mortal being, reflect on this in your mind; chant and meditate day and night. Dharmic faith and the karma of good deeds are obtained from the Perfect True Guru. |2|

I am a sacrifice, a sacrifice, to the True Name, O my True Guru.

What Praises can I offer to You? What service can I do for You? I have only one mouth and tongue; with my palms pressed together, I chant to You with joy and delight.

In thought, word and deed, I know the Lord; I do not worship any other. The Guru has enshrined the most excellent Name of the Infinite Lord within my heart.

Section 42 - Swaiyas From The Mouth Of The Great Fifth Mehl - Part 015

So speaks NALL the poet: touching the Philosopher's Stone, glass is transformed into gold, and the sandalwood tree imparts its fragrance to other trees; meditating in remembrance on the Lord, I am transformed.

Seeing His Door, I am rid of sexual desire and anger. I am a sacrifice, a sacrifice, to the True Name, O my True Guru. |3|

Guru Raam Daas was blessed with the Throne of Raja Yoga.

First, Guru Nanak illuminated the world, like the full moon, and filled it with bliss. To carry humanity across, He bestowed His Radiance.

He blessed Guru Angad with the treasure of spiritual wisdom, and the Unspoken Speech; He overcame the five demons and the fear of the Messenger of Death.

The Great and True Guru, Guru Amar Daas, has preserved honor in this Dark Age of Kali Yuga. Seeing His Lotus Feet, sin and evil are destroyed.

When His mind was totally satisfied in every way, when He was totally pleased, He bestowed upon Guru Raam Daas the Throne of Raja Yoga. |4|

RADD:
He established the earth, the sky and the air, the water of the oceans, fire and food.

He created the moon, the starts and the sun, night and day and mountains; he blessed the trees with flowers and fruits.

He created the gods, human beings and the seven seas; He established the three worlds.

Guru Amar Daas was blessed with the Light of the One Name, the True Name of the Lord. |1|5|

Glass is transformed into gold, listening to the Word of the Guru's Shabad.

Poison is transformed into ambrosial nectar, speaking the Name of the True Guru.

Iron is transformed into jewels, when the True Guru bestows His Glance of Grace.

Stones are transformed into emeralds, when the mortal chants and contemplates the spiritual wisdom of the Guru.

The True Guru transforms ordinary wood into sandalwood, eradicating the pains of poverty.

Whoever touches the Feet of the True Guru, is transformed from a beast and a ghost into an angelic being. |2|6|

One who has the Guru on his side - how could he be proud of his wealth?

One who has the Guru on his side - what would hundreds of thousands of supporters do for him?

One who has the Guru on his side, does not depend on anyone else for spiritual wisdom and meditation.

One who has the Guru on his side contemplates the Shabad and the Teachings, and abides in the Home of Truth.

The Lord's humble slave and poet utters this prayer: whoever chants to the Guru night and day,

whoever enshrines the Name of the Guru within his heart, is rid of both birth and death. |3|7|

Without the Guru, there is utter darkness; without the Guru, understanding does not come.

Without the Guru, there is no intuitive awareness or success; without the Guru, there is no liberation.

So make Him your Guru, and contemplate the Truth; make Him your Guru, O my mind.

Make Him your Guru, who is embellished and exalted in the Word of the Shabad; all your sins shall be washed away.

So speaks NALL the poet: with your eyes, make Him your Guru; with the words you speak, make Him your Guru, your True Guru.

Those who have not seen the Guru, who have not made Him their Guru, are useless in this world. |4|8|

Dwell upon the Guru, the Guru, the Guru, O my mind.

Section 42 - Swaiyas From The Mouth Of The Great Fifth Mehl - Part 016

The All-powerful Guru is the Boat to carry us across in this Dark Age of Kali Yuga. Hearing the Word of His Shabad, we are transported into Samaadhi.

He is the Spiritual Hero who destroys pain and brings peace. Whoever meditates on Him, dwells near Him.

He is the Perfect Primal Being, who meditates in remembrance on the Lord within his heart; seeing His Face, sins run away.

If you long for wisdom, wealth, spiritual perfection and properity, O my mind, dwell upon the Guru, the Guru, the Guru. |5|9|

Gazing upon the Face of the Guru, I find peace.

I was thirsty, yearning to drink in the Nectar; to fulfill that wish, the Guru laid out the way.

My mind has become perfect; it dwells in the Lord's Place; it had been wandering in all directions, in its desire for tastes and pleasures.

Goindwal is the City of God, built on the bank of the Beas River.

The pains of so many years have been taken away; gazing upon the Face of the Guru, I find peace. |6|10|

The All-powerful Guru placed His hand upon my head.

The Guru was kind, and blessed me with the Lord's Name. Gazing upon His Feet, my sins were dispelled.

Night and day, the Guru meditates on the One Lord; hearing His Name, the Messenger of Death is scared away.

So speaks the Lord's slave: Guru Raam Daas placed His Faith in Guru Amar Daas, the Guru of the World; touching the Philosopher's Stone, He was transformed into the Philosopher's Stone.

Guru Raam Daas recognized the Lord as True; the All-powerful Guru placed His hand upon His head. |7|11|

Now, please preserve the honor of Your humble slave.

God saved the honor of the devotee Prahlaad, when Harnaakhash tore him apart with his claws.

And the Dear Lord God saved the honor of Dropadi; when her clothes were stripped from her, she was blessed with even more.

Sudaamaa was saved from misfortune; and Ganikaa the prostitute - when she chanted Your Name, her affairs were perfectly resolved.

O Great True Guru, if it pleases You, please save the honor of Your slave in this Dark Age of kali Yuga. |8|12|

JHOLNAA:

Chant Guru, Guru, Guru, Guru, Guru, O mortal beings.

Chant the Shabad, the Word of the Lord, Har, Har; the Naam, the Name of the Lord, brings the nine treasures. With your tongue, taste it, day and night, and know it as true.

Then, you shall obtain His Love and Affection; become Gurmukh, and meditate on Him. Give up all other ways; vibrate and meditate on Him, O spiritual people.

Enshrine the Word of the Guru's Teachings within your heart, and overpower the five passions. Your life, and your generations, shall be saved, and you shall be honored at the Lord's Door.

If you desire all the peace and comforts of this world and the next, then chant Guru, Guru, Guru, Guru, Guru, O mortal beings. |1|13|

Chant Guru, Guru, Guru, Guru, Guru, and know Him as true.

Know that the Lord is the Treasure of Excellence. Enshrine Him in your mind, and meditate on Him. Enshrine the Word of the Guru's Teachings within your heart.

Then, cleanse yourself in the Immaculate and Unfathomable Water of the Guru; O Gursikhs and Saints, cross over the Ocean of Love of the True Name.

Meditate lovingly forever on the Lord, free of hate and vengeance, Formless and Fearless; lovingly savor the Word of the Guru's Shabad, and implant devotional worship of the Lord deep within.

O foolish mind, give up your doubts; as Gurmukh, vibrate and meditate on the Naam. Chant Guru, Guru, Guru, Guru, Guru, and know Him as true. |2|14|

Section 42 - Swaiyas From The Mouth Of The Great Fifth Mehl - Part 017

Chant Guru, Guru, Guru; through the Guru, the Lord is obtained.
The Guru is an Ocean, deep and profound, infinite and unfathomable.
Lovingly attuned to the Lord's Name, you shall be blessed with jewels, diamonds and emeralds.
And, the Guru makes us fragrant and fruitful, and His Touch transforms us into gold. The filth of evil-mindedness is washed away, meditating on the Word of the Guru's Shabad.
The Stream of Ambrosial Nectar flows constantly from His Door. The Saints and Sikhs bathe in the immaculate pool of the Guru's spiritual wisdom.
Enshrine the Naam, the Name of the Lord, within your heart, and dwell in Nirvaanaa. Chant Guru, Guru, Guru; through the Guru, the Lord is obtained. |3|15|

Chant Guru, Guru, Guru, Guru, Guru, O my mind.
Serving Him, Shiva and the Siddhas, the angels and demons and servants of the gods, and the thrity-three million gods cross over, listening to the Word of the Guru's Teachings.
And, the Saints and loving devotees are carried across, chanting Guru, Guru. Prahlaad and the silent sages met the Guru, and were carried across.
Naarad and Sanak and those men of God who became Gurmukh were carried across; attached to the One Name, they abandoned other tastes and pleasures, and were carried across.
This is the prayer of the Lord's humble slave: the Gurmukh obtains the Naam, the Name of the Lord, chanting Guru, Guru, Guru, Guru, Guru, O my mind. |4|16|29|

The Great, Supreme Guru showered His Mercy upon all;
in the Golden Age of Sat Yuga, He blessed Dhroo.
He saved the devotee Prahlaad,
placing the Lotus of His Hand upon his forehead.
The Unseen Form of the Lord cannot be seen.
The Siddhas and seekers all seek His Sanctuary.
True are the Words of the Guru's teachings. Enshrine them in your soul.
Emancipate your body, and redeem this human incarnation.

The Guru is the Boat, and the Guru is the Boatman. Without the Guru, no one can cross over.

By Guru's Grace, God is obtained. Without the Guru, no one is liberated.

Guru Nanak dwells near the Creator Lord.

He established Lehnaa as Guru, and enshrined His Light in the world.

Lehnaa established the path of righteousness and Dharma,

which He passed on to Guru Amar Daas, of the Bhalla dynasty.

Then, He firmly established the Great Raam Daas of the Sodhi dynasty.

He was blessed with the inexhaustible treasure of the Lord's Name.

He was blessed with the treasure of the Lord's Name; throughout the four ages, it is inexhaustible. Serving the Guru, He received His reward.

Those who bow at His Feet and seek His Sanctuary, are blessed with peace; those Gurmukhs are blessed with supreme bliss.

The Guru's Body is the Embodiment of the Supreme Lord God, our Lord and Master, the Form of the Primal Being, who nourishes and cherishes all.

So serve the Guru, the True Guru; His ways and means are inscrutable. The Great Guru Raam Daas is the Boat to carry us across. |1|

The Holy people chant the Ambrosial Words of His Bani with delight in their minds.

The Blessed Vision of the Guru's Darshan is fruitful and rewarding in this world; it brings lasting bliss and joy.

The Guru's Darshan is fruitful and rewarding in this world, like the Ganges. Meeting Him, the supreme sacred status is obtained.

Even sinful people conquer the realm of Death, if they become the Lord's humble servants, and are imbued with the Guru's spiritual wisdom.

He is certified, like the handsome Ram Chander in the house of Dasrath of the Raghwa dynasty. Even the silent sages seek His Sanctuary.

Section 42 - Swaiyas From The Mouth Of The Great Fifth Mehl - Part 018

So serve the Guru, the True Guru; His ways and means are inscrutable. The Great Guru Raam Daas is the Boat to carry us across. |2|

The Name of the Lord, from the Mouth of the Guru, is the Raft to cross over the unfathomable world-ocean.

The cycle of birth and death in this world is ended for those who have this faith in their hearts.

Those humble beings who have this faith in their hearts, are awarded the highest status.

They forsake Maya, emotional attachment and greed; they are rid of the frustrations of possessiveness, sexual desire and anger.

They are blessed with the Inner Vision to see God, the Cause of causes, and all their doubts are dispelled.

So serve the Guru, the True Guru; His ways and means are inscrutable. The Great Guru Raam Daas is the Boat to carry us across. |3|

The Glorious Greatness of the Guru is manifest forever in each and every heart. His humble servants sing His Praises.

Some read and listen and sing of Him, taking their cleansing bath in the early hours of the morning before the dawn.

After their cleansing bath in the hours before the dawn, they worship the Guru with their minds pure and clear.

Touching the Philosopher's Stone, their bodies are transformed into gold. They focus their meditation on the Embodiment of Divine Light.

The Master of the Universe, the very Life of the World pervades the sea and the land, manifesting Himself in myriads of ways.

So serve the Guru, the True Guru; His ways and means are inscrutable. The Great Guru Raam Daas is the Boat to carry us across. |4|

Those who realize the Eternal, Unchanging Word of God, like Dhroo, are immune to death.

They cross over the terrifying world-ocean in an instant; the Lord created the world like a bubble of water.

The Kundalini rises in the Sat Sangat, the True Congregation; through the Word of the Guru, they enjoy the Lord of Supreme Bliss.

The Supreme Guru is the Lord and Master over all; so serve the True Guru, in thought, word and deed. |5|

Waahay Guru, Waahay Guru, Waahay Guru, Waahay Jee-o.

You are lotus-eyed, with sweet speech, exalted and embellished with millions of companions. Mother Yashoda invited You as Krishna to eat the sweet rice.

Gazing upon Your supremely beautiful form, and hearing the musical sounds of Your silver bells tinkling, she was intoxicated with delight.

Death's pen and command are in Your hands. Tell me, who can erase it? Shiva and Brahma yearn to enshrine Your spiritual wisdom in their hearts.

You are forever True, the Home of Excellence, the Primal Supreme Being.

Waahay Guru, Waahay Guru, Waahay Guru, Waahay Jee-o. |1|6|

You are blessed with the Lord's Name, the supreme mansion, and clear understanding. You are the Formless, Infinite Lord; who can compare to You?

For the sake of the pure-hearted devotee Prahlaad, You took the form of the man-lion, to tear apart and destroy Harnaakhash with your claws.

You are the Infinite Supreme Lord God; with your symbols of power, You deceived Baliraja; who can know You?

You are forever True, the Home of Excellence, the Primal Supreme Being. Waahay Guru, Waahay Guru, Waahay Guru, Waahay Jee-o. |2|7|

As Krishna, You wear yellow robes, with teeth like jasmine flowers; You dwell with Your lovers, with Your mala around Your neck, and You joyfully adorn Your head with the crow of peacock feathers.

Section 42 - Swaiyas From The Mouth Of The Great Fifth Mehl - Part 019

You have no advisors, You are so very patient; You are the Upholder of the Dharma, unseen and unfathomable. You have staged the play of the Universe with joy and delight.

No one can speak Your Unspoken Speech. You are pervading the three worlds. You assume the form of spiritual perfection, O King of kings.

You are forever True, the Home of Excellence, the Primal Supreme Being. Waahay Guru, Waahay Guru, Waahay Guru, Waahay Jee-o. |3|8|

The True Guru, the True Guru, the True Guru is the Lord of the Universe Himself.

Enticer of Baliraja, who smothers the mighty, and fulfills the devotees; the Prince Krishna, and Kalki; the thunder of His army and the beat of His drum echoes across the Universe.

The Lord of contemplation, Destroyer of sin, who brings pleasure to the beings of all realms, He Himself is the God of gods, Divinity of the divine, the thousand-headed king cobra.

He took birth in the Incarnations of the Fish, Tortoise and Wild Boar, and played His part. He played games on the banks of the Jamunaa River.

Enshrine this most excellent Name within your heart, and renounce the wickedness of the mind, O GAYAND the True Guru, the True Guru, the True Guru is the Lord of the Universe Himself. |4|9|

The Supreme Guru, the Supreme Guru, the Supreme Guru, the True, Dear Lord.

Respect and obey the Guru's Word; this is your own personal treasure - know this mantra as true. Night and day, you shall be saved, and blessed with the supreme status.

Renounce sexual desire, anger, greed and attachment; give up your games of deception. Snap the noose of egotism, and let yourself be at home in the Saadh Sangat, the Company of the Holy.

Free your consciousness of attachment to your body, your home, your spouse, and the pleasures of this world. Serve forever at His Lotus Feet, and firmly implant these teachings within.

Enshrine this most excellent Name within your heart, and renounce the wickedness of the mind, O GAYAND. the Supreme Guru, the Supreme Guru, the Supreme Guru, the True, Dear Lord. |5|10|

Your servants are totally fulfilled, throughout the ages; O Waahay Guru, it is all You, forever.

O Formless Lord God, You are eternally intact; no one can say how You came into being.

You created countless Brahmas and Vishnus; their minds were intoxicated with emotional attachment.

You created the 8.4 million species of beings, and provide for their sustanance.

Your servants are totally fulfilled, throughout the ages; O Waahay Guru, it is all You, forever. |1|11|

Waaho! Waaho! Great! Great is the Play of God!

He Himself laughs, and He Himself thinks; He Himself illumines the sun and the moon.

He Himself is the water, He Himself is the earth and its support. He Himself abides in each and every heart.

He Himself is male, and He Himself is female; He Himself is the chessman, and He Himself is the board.

As Gurmukh, join the Sangat, and consider all this: Waaho! Waaho! Great! Great is the Play of God! |2|12|

You have formed and created this play, this great game. O Waahay Guru, this is all You, forever.

You are pervading and permeating the water, land, skies and nether regions; Your Words are sweeter than Ambrosial Nectar.

Brahmas and Shivas respect and obey You. O Death of death, Formless Lord, I beg of You.

Section 42 - Swaiyas From The Mouth Of The Great Fifth Mehl - Part 020

By Guru's Grace, the greatest thing is obtained, and the mind is involved with the Sat Sangat, the True Congregation.

You have formed and created this play, this great game. O Waahay Guru, this is all Your making. |3|13|42|

The Lord is Inaccessible, Infinite, Eternal and Primordial; no one knows His beginning.

Shiva and Brahma meditate on Him; the Vedas describe Him again and again.

The Lord is Formless, beyond hate and vengeance; there is no one else like Him.

He creates and destroys - He is All-powerful; God is the Boat to carry all across.

He created the world in its various aspects; His humble servant MAT'HURAA delights in His Praises.

Sat Naam, the Great and Supreme True Name of God, the Personification of Creativity, dwells in the Consciousness of Guru Raam Daas. |1|

I have grasped hold of the All-powerful Guru; He has made my mind steady and stable, and embellished me with clear consciousness.

And, His Banner of Righteousness waves proudly forever, to defend against the waves of sin.

His humble servant MAT'HRAA knows this as true, and speaks it from his soul; there is nothing else to consider.

In this Dark Age of Kali Yuga, the Lord's Name is the Great Ship, to carry us all across the terrifying world-ocean, safely to the other side. |2|

The Saints dwell in the Saadh Sangat, the Company of the Holy; imbued with pure celestial love, they sing the Lord's Praises.

The Support of the Earth has established this Path of Dharma; He Himself remains lovingly attuned to the Lord, and does not wander in distraction.

So speaks MAT'HURAA: those blessed with good fortune receive the fruits of their minds' desires.

Those who focus their consciousness on the Guru's Feet, they do not fear the judgement of Dharamraj. |3|

The Immaculate, Sacred Pool of the Guru is overflowing with the waves of the Shabad, radiantly revealed in the early hours before the dawn.

He is Deep and Profound, Unfathomable and utterly Great, eternally overflowing with all sorts of jewels.

The Saint-swans celebrate; their fear of death is erased, along with the accounts of their pain.

In this Dark Age of Kali Yuga, the sins are taken away; the Blessed Vision of the Guru's Darshan is the Ocean of all peace and comfort. |4|

For His Sake, the silent sages meditated and focused their consciousness, wandering all the ages through; rarely, if ever, their souls were enlightened.

In the Hymns of the Vedas, Brahma sang His Praises; for His Sake, Shiva the silent sage held his place on the Kailaash Mountain.

For His Sake, the Yogis, celibates, Siddhas and seekers, the countless sects of fanatics with matted hair wear religious robes, wandering as detached renunciates.

That True Guru, by the Pleasure of His Will, showered His Mercy upon all beings, and blessed Guru Raam Daas with the Glorious Greatness of the Naam. |5|

He focuses His Meditation deep within; the Embodiment of Light, He illuminates the three worlds.

Gazing upon the Blessed Vision of His Darshan, doubt runs away, pain is eradicated, and celestial peace spontaneously wells up.

The selfless servants and Sikhs are always totally captivated by it, like bumble bees lured by the fragrance of the flower.

The Guru Himself established the Eternal Throne of Truth, in Guru Raam Daas. |6|

Section 42 - Swaiyas From The Mouth Of The Great Fifth Mehl - Part 021

The Universe is intoxicated with the wine of Maya, but it has been saved; the All-powerful Guru has blessed it with the Ambrosial Nectar of the Naam.

And, the Praiseworthy Guru is blessed with eternal peace, wealth and prosperity; the supernatural spiritual powers of the Siddhis never leave him.

His Gifts are vast and great; His awesome Power is supreme. Your humble servant and slave speaks this truth.

One, upon whose head the Guru has placed His Hand - with whom should he be concerned? |7|49|

He is totally pervading and permeating the three realms;
in all the world, He has not created another like Himself.
He Himself created Himself.
The angels, human beings and demons have not found His limits.
The angels, demons and human beings have not found His limits; the heavenly heralds and celestial singers wander around, searching for Him.
The Eternal, Imperishable, Unmoving and Unchanging, Unborn, Self-Existent, Primal Being of the Soul, the Infinity of the Infinite,

the Eternal All-powerful Cause of causes - all beings meditate on Him in their minds.
O Great and Supreme Guru Raam Daas, Your Victory resounds across the universe. You have attained the supreme status of the Lord. |1|

Nanak, the True Guru, worships God single-mindedly; He surrenders His body, mind and wealth to the Lord of the Universe.
The Infinite Lord enshrined His Own Image in Guru Angad. In His heart, He delights in the spiritual wisdom of the Unfathomable Lord.
Guru Amar Daas brought the Creator Lord under His control. Waaho! Waaho! Meditate on Him!
O Great and Supreme Guru Raam Daas, Your Victory resounds across the universe. You have attained the supreme status of the Lord. |2|

Naarad, Dhroo, Prahlaad and Sudaamaa are accounted among the Lord's devotees of the past.
Ambreek, Jai Dayv, Trilochan, Naam Dayv and Kabeer are also remembered.
They were incarnated in this Dark Age of Kali Yuga; their praises have spread over all the world.
O Great and Supreme Guru Raam Daas, Your Victory resounds across the universe. You have attained the supreme status of the Lord. |3|

Those who meditate in remembrance on You within their minds - their sexual desire and anger are taken away.
Those who remember You in meditation with their words, are rid of their poverty and pain in an instant.

Those who obtain the Blessed Vision of Your Darshan, by the karma of their good deeds, touch the Philosopher's Stone, and like BALL the poet, sing Your Praises.

O Great and Supreme Guru Raam Daas, Your Victory resounds across the universe. You have attained the supreme status of the Lord. |4|

Those who meditate in remembrance on the True Guru - the darkness of their eyes is removed in an instant.

Those who meditate in remembrance on the True Guru within their hearts, are blessed with the Lord's Name, day by day.

Those who meditate in remembrance on the True Guru within their souls - the fire of desire is extinguished for them.

Those who meditate in remembrance on the True Guru, are blessed with wealth and prosperity, supernatural spiritual powers and the nine treasures.

So speaks BALL the poet: Blessed is Guru Raam Daas; joining the Sangat, the Congregation, call Him blessed and great.

Meditate on the True Guru, O men, through Whom the Lord is obtained. |5|54|

Living the Word of the Shabad, He attained the supreme status; while performing selfless service, He did not leave the side of Guru Amar Daas.

From that service, the light from the jewel of spiritual wisdom shines forth, radiant and bright; it has destroyed pain, poverty and darkness.

Section 42 - Swaiyas From The Mouth Of The Great Fifth Mehl - Part 022

So speaks KEERAT the poet: those who grasp hold of the feet of the Saints, are not afraid of death, sexual desire or anger.

Just as Guru Nanak was part and parcel, life and limb with Guru Angad, so is Guru Amar Daas one with Guru Raam Daas. |1|

Whoever serves the True Guru obtains the treasure; night and day, he dwells at the Lord's Feet.

And so, the entire Sangat loves, fears and respects You. You are the sandalwood tree; Your fragrance spreads gloriously far and wide.

Dhroo, Prahlaad, Kabeer and Trilochan chanted the Naam, the Name of the Lord, and His Illumination radiantly shines forth.

Seeing Him, the mind is totally delighted; Guru Raam Daas is the Helper and Support of the Saints. |2|

Guru Nanak realized the Immaculate Naam, the Name of the Lord. He was lovingly attuned to loving devotional worship of the Lord.

Gur Angad was with Him, life and limb, like the ocean; He showered His consciousness with the Word of the Shabad.

The Unspoken Speech of Guru Amar Daas cannot be expressed with only one tongue.

Guru Raam Daas of the Sodhi dynasty has now been blessed with Glorious Greatness, to carry the whole world across. |3|

I am overflowing with sins and demerits; I have no merits or virtues at all. I abandoned the Ambrosial Nectar, and I drank poison instead.

I am attached to Maya, and deluded by doubt; I have fallen in love with my children and spouse.

I have heard that the most exalted Path of all is the Sangat, the Guru's Congregation. Joining it, the fear of death is taken away.

KEERAT the poet offers this one prayer: O Guru Raam Daas, save me! Take me into Your Sanctuary! |4|58|

He has crushed and overpowered emotional attachment. He seized sexual desire by the hair, and threw it down.

With His Power, He cut anger into pieces, and sent greed away in disgrace.

Life and death, with palms pressed together, respect and obey the Hukam of His Command.

He brought the terrifying world-ocean under His Control; by His Pleasure, He carried His Sikhs across.

He is seated upon the Throne of Truth, with the canopy above His Head; He is embellished with the powers of Yoga and the enjoyment of pleasures.

So speaks SALL the poet: O Guru Raam Daas, Your sovereign power is eternal and unbreakable; Your army is invincible. |1|

You are the True Guru, throughout the four ages; You Yourself are the Transcendent Lord.

The angelic beings, seekers, Siddhas and Sikhs have served You, since the very beginning of time.

You are the Primal Lord God, from the very beginning, and throughout the ages; Your Power supports the three worlds.

You are Inaccessible; You are the Saving Grace of the Vedas. You have conquered old age and death.

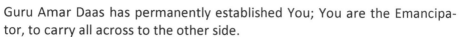

Guru Amar Daas has permanently established You; You are the Emancipa-
tor, to carry all across to the other side.
So speaks SALL the poet: O Guru Raam Daas, You are the Destroyer of sins;
I seek Your Sanctuary. |2|60|

Swaiyas In Praise Of The Fifth Mehl:
One Universal Creator God. By The Grace Of The True Guru:
Meditate in remembrance on the Primal Lord God, Eternal and Imperisha-
ble.
Remembering Him in meditation, the filth of evil-mindedness is eradicated.
I enshrine the Lotus Feet of the True Guru within my heart.

Section 42 - Swaiyas From The Mouth Of The Great Fifth Mehl - Part 023

With intuitive peace and poise, I contemplate the Glorious Virtues of Guru
Arjun.
He was revealed in the House of Guru Raam Daas,
and all hopes and desires were fulfilled.
From birth, He realized God through the Guru's Teachings.
With palms pressed together, KALL the poet speaks His praises.
The Lord brought Him into the world, to practice the Yoga of devotional
worship.
The Word of the Guru's Shabad has been revealed, and the Lord dwells on
His tongue.
Attached to Guru Nanak, Guru Angad and Guru Amar Daas, He attained the
supreme status.
In the House of Guru Raam Daas, the devotee of the Lord, Guru Arjun was
born. |1|

By great good fortune, the mind is uplifted and exalted, and the Word of
the Shabad dwells in the heart.
The jewel of the mind is contented; the Guru has implanted the Naam, the
Name of the Lord, within.
The Inaccessible and Unfathomable, Supreme Lord God is revealed through
the True Guru.
In the House of Guru Raam Daas, Guru Arjun has appeared as the Embodi-
ment of the Fearless Lord. |2|

The benign rule of Raja Janak has been established, and the Golden Age of
Sat Yuga has begun.

Through the Word of the Guru's Shabad, the mind is pleased and appeased; the unsatisfied mind is satisfied.

Guru Nanak laid the foundation of Truth; He is blended with the True Guru.

In the House of Guru Raam Daas, Guru Arjun has appeared as the Embodiment of the Infinite Lord. |3|

The Sovereign Lord King has staged this wondrous play; contentment was gathered together, and pure understanding was infused in the True Guru.

KALL the poet utters the Praises of the Unborn, Self-existent Lord.

Guru Nanak blessed Guru Angad, and Guru Angad blessed Guru Amar Daas with the treasure.

Guru Raam Daas blessed Guru Arjun, who touched the Philosopher's Stone, and was certified. |4|

O Guru Arjun, You are Eternal, Invaluable, Unborn, Self-existent,

the Destroyer of fear, the Dispeller of pain, Infinite and Fearless.

You have grasped the Ungraspable, and burnt away doubt and skepticism. You bestow cooling and soothing peace.

The Self-existent, Perfect Primal Lord God Creator has taken birth.

First, Guru Nanak, then Guru Angad and Guru Amar Daas, the True Guru, have been absorbed into the Word of the Shabad.

Blessed, blessed is Guru Raam Daas, the Philosopher's Stone, who transformed Guru Arjun unto Himself. |5|

His victory is proclaimed all over the world; His Home is blessed with good fortune; He remains united with the Lord.

By great good fortune, He has found the Perfect Guru; He remains lovingly attuned to Him, and endures the load of the earth.

He is the Destroyer of fear, the Eradicator of the pains of others. KALL SAHAAR the poet utters Your Praise, O Guru.

In the Sodhi family, is born Arjun, the son of Guru Raam Daas, the holder of the banner of Dharma and the devotee of God. |6|

The Support of the Dharma, immersed in the deep and profound Teachings of the Guru, the Remover of the pains of others.

The Shabad is excellent and sublime, kind and generous like the Lord, the Destroyer of egotism.

The Great Giver, the spiritual wisdom of the True Guru, His mind does not grow weary of its yearning for the Lord.

The Embodiment of Truth, the Mantra of the Lord's Name, the nine treasures are never exhausted.

O Son of Guru Raam Daas, You are contained amidst all; the canopy of intuitive wisdom is spread above You.

So speaks KALL the poet: O Guru Arjun, You know the sublime essence of Raja Yoga, the Yoga of meditation and success. |7|

Section 42 - Swaiyas From The Mouth Of The Great Fifth Mehl - Part 024

In the Fear of God, You enjoy the Fearless Lord; among the thousands of beings, You see the Unseen Lord.

Through the True Guru, You have realized the state of the Inaccessible, Unfathomable, Profound Lord.

Meeting with the Guru, You are certified and approved; You practice Yoga in the midst of wealth and power.

Blessed, blessed, blessed is the Guru, who has filled to overflowing the pools which were empty.

Reaching up to the certified Guru, You endure the unendurable; You are immersed in the pool of contentment.

So speaks KALL: O Guru Arjun, You have intuitively attained the state of Yoga within Yourself. |8|

Nectar drips from Your tongue, and Your mouth gives Blessings, O Incomprehensible and Infinite Spiritual Hero. O Guru, the Word of Your Shabad eradicates egotism.

You have overpowered the five enticers, and established with intuitive ease the Absolute Lord within Your own being.

Attached to the Lord's Name, the world is saved; enshrine the True Guru within your heart.

So speaks KALL: O Guru Arjun, You have illiminated the highest pinnacle of wisdom. |9|

SORAT'H
: Guru Arjun is the certified Primal Person; like Arjuna, He never leaves the field of battle.

The Naam, the Name of the Lord, is His spear and insignia. He is embellished with the Shabad, the Word of the True Guru. |1|

The Lord's Name is the Boat, the Bridge to cross over the terrifying world-ocean.

You are in love with the True Guru; attached to the Naam, You have saved the world. |2|

The Naam is the Saving Grace of the world; by the Pleasure of the True Guru, it is obtained.
Now, I am not concerned with anything else; at Your Door, I am fulfilled. |3|12|

The Embodiment of Light, the Lord Himself is called Guru Nanak.
From Him, came Guru Angad; His essence was absorbed into the essence.
Guru Angad showed His Mercy, and established Amar Daas as the True Guru.
Guru Amar Daas blessed Guru Raam Daas with the umbrella of immortality.
So speaks MAT'HURAA: gazing upon the Blessed Vision, the Darshan of Guru Raam Daas, His speech became as sweet as nectar.
With your eyes, see the certified Primal Person, Guru Arjun, the Fifth Manifestation of the Guru. |1|

He is the Embodiment of Truth; He has enshrined the True Name, Sat Naam, Truth and contentment within His heart.
From the very beginning, the Primal Being has written this destiny upon His forehead.
His Divine Light shines forth, dazzling and radiant; His Glorious Grandeur pervades the realms of the world.
Meeting the Guru, touching the Philosopher's Stone, He was acclaimed as Guru.
So speaks MAT'HURAA: I constantly focus my consciousness on Him; as sunmukh, I look to Him.
In this Dark Age of Kali Yuga, Guru Arjun is the Boat; attached to him, the entire universe is safely carried across. |2|

I beg from that humble being who is known all over the world, who lives in, and loves the Name, night and day.
He is supremely unattached, and imbued with the Love of the Transcendent Lord; he is free of desire, but he lives as a family man.
He is dedicated to the Love of the Infinite, Limitless Primal Lord God; he has no concerns for any other pleasure, except for the Lord God.
Guru Arjun is the All-pervading Lord God of MAT'HURAA. Devoted to His Worship, he remains attached to the Lord's Feet. |3|

Section 42 - Swaiyas From The Mouth Of The Great Fifth Mehl - Part 025

All the gods, silent sages, Indra, Shiva and Yogis have not found the Lord's limits
- not even Brahma who contemplates the Vedas. I shall not give up meditating on the Lord, even for an instant.
The God of MAT'HURAA is Merciful to the meek; He blesses and uplifts the Sangats throughout the Universe.
Guru Raam Daas, to save the world, enshrined the Guru's Light into Guru Arjun. |4|

In the great darkness of this world, the Lord revealed Himself, incarnated as Guru Arjun.
Millions of pains are taken away, from those who drink in the Ambrosial Nectar of the Naam, says MAT'HURAA.
O mortal being, do not leave this path; do not think that there is any difference between God and Guru.
The Perfect Lord God has manifested Himself; He dwells in the heart of Guru Arjun. |5|

As long as the destiny written upon my forehead was not activated, I wandered around lost, running in all directions.
I was drowning in the horrible world-ocean of this Dark Age of Kali Yuga, and my remorse would never have ended.
O MAT'HURAA, consider this essential truth: to save the world, the Lord incarnated Himself.
Whoever meditates on Guru Arjun Dayv, shall not have to pass through the painful womb of reincarnation ever again. |6|

In the ocean of this Dark Age of Kali Yuga, the Lord's Name has been revealed in the Form of Guru Arjun, to save the world.
Pain and poverty are taken away from that person, within whose heart the Saint abides.
He is the Pure, Immaculate Form of the Infinite Lord; except for Him, there is no other at all.
Whoever knows Him in thought, word and deed, becomes just like Him.
He is totally pervading the earth, the sky and the nine regions of the planet. He is the Embodiment of the Light of God.
So speaks MAT'HURAA: there is no difference between God and Guru; Guru Arjun is the Personification of the Lord Himself. |7|19|

The stream of the Lord's Name flows like the Ganges, invincible and unstoppable. The Sikhs of the Sangat all bathe in it.

It appears as if the holy texts like the Puraanaas are being recited there and Brahma himself sings the Vedas.

The invincible chauri, the fly-brush, waves over His head; with His mouth, He drinks in the Ambrosial Nectar of the Naam.

The Transcendent Lord Himself has placed the royal canopy over the head of Guru Arjun.

Guru Nanak, Guru Angad, Guru Amar Daas and Guru Raam Daas met together before the Lord.

So speaks HARBANS: Their Praises echo and resound all over the world; who can possibly say that the Great Gurus are dead? |1|

When it was the Will of the Transcendent Lord Himself, Guru Raam Daas went to the City of God.

The Lord offered Him His Royal Throne, and seated the Guru upon it.

The angels and gods were delighted; they proclaimed and celebrated Your victory, O Guru.

The demons ran away; their sins made them shake and tremble inside.

Those people who found Guru Raam Daas were rid of their sins.

He gave the Royal Canopy and Throne to Guru Arjun, and came home. |2|21|9|11|10|10|22|60|143|

SHALOKS IN ADDITION TO THE VAARS

Section 43 - Shaloks In Addition To The Vaars - Part 001

ONE Universal Creator God. Truth Is The Name. Creative Being Personified. No Fear. No Hatred. Image Of The Undying. Beyond Birth. Self-Existent. By Guru's Grace:

Shaloks In Addition To The Vaars.
First Mehl:
O you with swollen breasts, let your consciousness become deep and profound.
O mother-in-law, how can I bow? Because of my stiff nipples, I cannot bow.
O sister, those mansions built as high as mountains
- I have seen them come crumbling down. O bride, do not be so proud of your nipples. |1|

O bride with deer-like eyes, listen to the words of deep and infinite wisdom.
First, examine the merchandise, and then, make the deal.
Proclaim that you will not associate with evil people; celebrate victory with your friends.
This proclamation, to meet with your friends, O bride - give it some thought.
Surrender mind and body to the Lord your Friend; this is the most excellent pleasure.
Do not fall in love with one who is destined to leave.
O Nanak, I am a sacrifice to those who understand this. |2|

If you wish to swim across the water, then consult those who know how to swim.
Those who have survived these treacherous waves are very wise. |3|

The storm rages and the rain floods the land; thousands of waves rise and surge.
If you cry out for help from the True Guru, you have nothing to fear - your boat will not sink. |4|

O Nanak, what has happened to the world?
There is no guide or friend.
There is no love, even among brothers and relatives.
For the sake of the world, people have lost their faith. |5|

They cry and weep and wail.
They slap their faces and pull their hair out.
But if they chant the Naam, the Name of the Lord, they shall be absorbed into it.
O Nanak, I am a sacrifice to them. |6|

O my mind, do not waver or walk on the crooked path; take the straight and true path.
The terrible tiger is behind you, and the pool of fire is ahead.
My soul is skeptical and doubtful, but I cannot see any other way to go.
O Nanak, as Gurmukh, dwell with your Beloved Lord, and you shall be saved. |7|

The tiger is killed, and the mind is killed, through the Teachings of the True Guru.
One who understands himself, meets with the Lord, and never dies again.

Section 43 - Shaloks In Addition To The Vaars - Part 002

One who sees the One and Only Lord with his eyes - his hands shall not get muddy and dirty.
O Nanak, the Gurmukhs are saved; the Guru has surrounded the ocean with the embankment of Truth. |8|

If you wish to put out the fire, then look for water; without the Guru, the ocean of water is not found.
You shall continue to wander lost in reincarnation through birth and death, even if you do thousands of other deeds.
But you shall not be taxed by the Messenger of Death, if you walk in harmony with the Will of the True Guru.
O Nanak, the immaculate, immortal status is obtained, and the Guru will unite you in the Lord's Union. |9|

The crow rubs and washes itself in the mud puddle.

Its mind and body are polluted with its own mistakes and demerits, and its beak is filled with dirt.
The swan in the pool associated with the crow, not knowing that it was evil.
Such is the love of the faithless cynic; understand this, O spiritually wise ones, through love and devotion.
So proclaim the victory of the Society of the Saints, and act as Gurmukh.
Immaculate and pure is that cleansing bath, O Nanak, at the sacred shrine of the Guru's river. |10|

What should I account as the rewards of this human life, if one does not feel love and devotion to the Lord?
Wearing clothes and eating food is useless, if the mind is filled with the love of duality.
Seeing and hearing is false, if one speaks lies.
O Nanak, praise the Naam, the Name of the Lord; everything else is coming and going in egotism. |11|

The Saints are few and far between; everything else in the world is just a pompous show. |12|

O Nanak, one who is struck by the Lord dies instantaneously; the power to live is lost.
If someone dies by such a stroke, then he is accepted.
He alone is struck, who is struck by the Lord; after such a stroke, he is approved.
The arrow of love, shot by the All-knowing Lord, cannot be pulled out. |13|

Who can wash the unbaked clay pot?
Joining the five elements together, the Lord made a false cover.
When it pleases Him, He makes it right.
The supreme light shines forth, and the celestial song vibrates and resounds. |14|

Those who are totally blind in their minds, do not have the integrity to keep their word.
With their blind minds, and their upside-down heart-lotus, they look totally ugly.
Some know how to speak and understand what they are told. Those people are wise and good-looking.

Some do not know the Sound-current of the Naad, spiritual wisdom or the joy of song. They do not even understand good and bad.

Some have no idea of perfection, wisdom or understanding; they know nothing about the mystery of the Word.

O Nanak, those people are really donkeys; they have no virtue or merit, but still, they are very proud. |15|

He alone is a Brahmin, who knows God.

He chants and meditates, and practices austerity and good deeds.

He keeps to the Dharma, with faith, humility and contentment.

Breaking his bonds, he is liberated.

Such a Brahmin is worthy of being worshipped. |16|

He alone is a Kh'shaatriyaa, who is a hero in good deeds.

He uses his body to give in charity;

he understands his farm, and plants the seeds of generosity.

Such a Kh'shaatriyaa is accepted in the Court of the Lord.

Whoever practices greed, possessiveness and falsehood,

shall receive the fruits of his own labors. |17|

Do not heat your body like a furnace, or burn your bones like firewood.

What have your head and feet done wrong? See your Husband Lord within yourself. |18|

Section 43 - Shaloks In Addition To The Vaars - Part 003

God the Cosmic Husband dwells within all hearts; without Him, there is no heart at all.

O Nanak, the Gurmukhs are the happy, virtuous soul-brides; the Lord is revealed to them. |19|

If you desire to play this game of love with Me,

then step onto My Path with your head in hand.

When you place your feet on this Path,

give Me your head, and do not pay any attention to public opinion. |20|

False is friendship with the false and greedy. False is its foundation.

O Moollah, no one knows where death shall strike. |21|

Without spiritual wisdom, the people worship ignorance.

They grope in the darkness, in the love of duality. |22|

Without the Guru, there is no spiritual wisdom; without Dharma, there is no meditation.
Without Truth, there is no credit; without capital, there is no balance. |23|

The mortals are sent into the world; then, they arise and depart.
There is no joy in this. |24|

Raam Chand, sad at heart, assembled his army and forces.
The army of monkeys was at his service; his mind and body became eager for war.
Raawan captured his wife Sita, and Lachhman was cursed to die.
O Nanak, the Creator Lord is the Doer of all; He watches over all, and destroys what He has created. |25|

In his mind, Raam Chand mourned for Sita and Lachhman.
Then, he remembered Hanuman the monkey-god, who came to him.
The misguided demon did not understand that God is the Doer of deeds.
O Nanak, the actions of the Self-existent Lord cannot be erased. |26|

The city of Lahore suffered terrible destruction for four hours. |27|

Third Mehl:
The city of Lahore is a pool of ambrosial nectar, the home of praise. |28|

First Mehl:
What are the signs of a prosperous person? His stores of food never run out.
Prosperity dwells in his home, with the sounds of girls and women.
All the women of his home shout and cry over useless things.
Whatever he takes, he does not give back. Seeking to earn more and more, he is troubled and uneasy. |29|

O lotus, your leaves were green, and your blossoms were gold.
What pain has burnt you, and made your body black? O Nanak, my body is battered.
I have not received that water which I love.
Seeing it, my body blossomed forth, and I was blessed with a deep and beautiful color. |30|

No one lives long enough to accomplish all he wishes.

Only the spiritually wise live forever; they are honored for their intuitive awareness.

Bit by bit, life passes away, even though the mortal tries to hold it back.

O Nanak, unto whom should we complain? Death takes one's life away without anyone's consent. |31|

Do not blame the Sovereign Lord; when someone grows old, his intellect leaves him.

The blind man talks and babbles, and then falls into the ditch. |32|

All that the Perfect Lord does is perfect; there is not too little, or too much.

O Nanak, knowing this as Gurmukh, the mortal merges into the Perfect Lord God. |33|

Section 43 - Shaloks In Addition To The Vaars - Part 004

Shalok, Third Mehl:

One Universal Creator God. By The Grace Of The True Guru:

Do not call the wandering beggars holy men, if their minds are filled with doubt.

Whoever gives to them, O Nanak, earns the same sort of merit. |1|

One who begs for the supreme status of the Fearless and Immaculate Lord

- how rare are those who have the opportunity, O Nanak, to give food to such a person. |2|

If I were a religious scholar, an astrologer, or one who could recite the four Vedas,

I could be famous throughout the nine regions of the earth, for my wisdom and thoughtful contemplation. |3|

If a Brahmin kills a cow or a female infant, and accepts the offerings of an evil person,

he is cursed with the leprosy of curses and criticism; he is forever and ever filled with egotistical pride.

One who forgets the Naam, O Nanak, is covered by countless sins.

Let all wisdom be burnt away, except for the essence of spiritual wisdom. |4|

No one can erase that primal destiny written upon one's forehead.
O Nanak, whatever is written there, comes to pass. He alone understands, who is blessed by God's Grace. |5|

Those who forget the Naam, the Name of the Lord, and become attached to greed and fraud,
are engrossed in the entanglements of Maya the enticer, with the fire of desire within them.
Those who, like the pumpkin vine, are too stubborn climb the trellis, are cheated by Maya the cheater.
The self-willed manmukhs are bound and gagged and led away; the dogs do not join the herd of cows.
The Lord Himself misleads the misguided ones, and He Himself unites them in His Union.
O Nanak, the Gurmukhs are saved; they walk in harmony with the Will of the True Guru. |6|

I praise the Praiseworthy Lord, and sing the Praises of the True Lord.
O Nanak, the One Lord alone is True; stay away from all other doors. |7|

O Nanak, wherever I go, I find the True Lord.
Wherever I look, I see the One Lord. He reveals Himself to the Gurmukh. |8|

The Word of the Shabad is the Dispeller of sorrow, if one enshrines it in the mind.
By Guru's Grace, it dwells in the mind; by God's Mercy, it is obtained. |9|

O Nanak, acting in egotism, countless thousands have wasted away to death.
Those who meet with the True Guru are saved, through the Shabad, the True Word of the Inscrutable Lord. |10|

Those who serve the True Guru single-mindedly - I fall at the feet of those humble beings.
Through the Word of the Guru's Shabad, the Lord abides in the mind, and the hunger for Maya departs.
Immaculate and pure are those humble beings, who, as Gurmukh, merge in the Naam.

O Nanak, other empires are false; they alone are true emperors, who are imbued with the Naam. |11|

The devoted wife in her husband's home has a great longing to perform loving devotional service to him;
she prepares and offers to him all sorts of sweet delicacies and dishes of all flavors.
In the same way, the devotees praise the Word of the Guru's Bani, and focus their consciousness on the Lord's Name.
They place mind, body and wealth in offering before the Guru, and sell their heads to Him.
In the Fear of God, His devotees yearn for His devotional worship; God fulfills their desires, and merges them with Himself.

Section 43 - Shaloks In Addition To The Vaars - Part 005

My Lord God is Self-existent and Independent. What does He need to eat to be satisfied?
Whoever walks in harmony with the Will of the True Guru, and sings the Glorious Praises of the Lord, is pleasing to Him.
Blessed, blessed are they, in this Dark Age of Kali Yuga, O Nanak, who walk in harmony with the Will of the True Guru. |12|

Those who do not serve the True Guru, and do not keep the Shabad enshrined in their hearts
- cursed are their lives. Why did they even come into the world?
If one follows the Guru's Teachings, and keeps the Fear of God in his mind, then he is lovingly attuned to the sublime essence of the Lord.
By his primal destiny, he obtains the Name; O Nanak, he is carried across. |13|

The world wanders lost in emotional attachment to Maya; it does not realize that its own home is being plundered.
The self-willed manmukh is blind in the world; his mind is lured away by sexual desire and anger.
With the sword of spiritual wisdom, kill the five demons. Remain awake and aware to the Guru's Teachings.
The Jewel of the Naam is revealed, and the mind and body are purified.
Those who lack the Naam wander around lost, with their noses cut off; without the Name, they sit and cry.

O Nanak, no one can erase that which is pre-ordained by the Creator Lord. |14|

The Gurmukhs earn the wealth of the Lord, contemplating the Word of the Guru's Shabad.
They receive the wealth of the Naam; their treasures are overflowing.
Through the Word of the Guru's Bani, they utter the Glorious Praises of the Lord, whose end and limitations cannot be found.
O Nanak, the Creator is the Doer of all; the Creator Lord beholds all. |15|

Within the Gurmukh is intuitive peace and poise; his mind ascends to the Tenth Plane of the Akaashic Ethers.
No one is sleepy or hungry there; they dwell in the peace of the Ambrosial Name of the Lord.
O Nanak, pain and pleasure do not afflict anyone, where the Light of the Lord, the Supreme Soul, illuminates. |16|

All have come, wearing the robes of sexual desire and anger.
Some are born, and some pass away. They come and go according to the Hukam of the Lord's Command.
Their comings and goings in reincarnation do not end; they are imbued with the love of duality.
Bound in bondage, they are made to wander, and they cannot do anything about it. |17|

Those, upon whom the Lord showers His Mercy, come and meet the True Guru.
Meeting with the True Guru, they turn away from the world; they remain dead while still alive, with intuitive peace and poise.
O Nanak, the devotees are imbued with the Lord; they are absorbed in the Name of the Lord. |18|

The intellect of the self-willed manmukh is fickle; he is very tricky and clever within.
Whatever he has done, and all that he does, is useless. Not even an iota of it is acceptable.
The charity and generosity he pretends to give will be judged by the Righteous Judge of Dharma.
Without the True Guru, the Messenger of Death does not leave the mortal alone; he is ruined by the love of duality.

Youth slips away imperceptibly, old age comes, and then he dies.

The mortal is caught in love and emotional attachment to children and spouse, but none of them will be his helper and support in the end.

Whoever serves the True Guru finds peace; the Name comes to abide in the mind.

O Nanak, great and very fortunate are those who, as Gurmukh, are absorbed in the Naam. |19|

The self-willed manmukhs do not even think of the Name; without the Name, they cry in pain.

Section 43 - Shaloks In Addition To The Vaars - Part 006

They do not worship the Lord, the Supreme Soul; how can they find peace in duality?

They are filled with the filth of egotism; they do not wash it away with the Word of the Shabad.

O Nanak, without the Name, they die in their filth; they waste the priceless opportunity of this human life. |20|

The self-willed manmukhs are deaf and blind; they are filled with the fire of desire.

They have no intuitive understanding of the Guru's Bani; they are not illumined with the Shabad.

They do not know their own inner being, and they have no faith in the Guru's Word.

The Word of the Guru's Shabad is within the being of the spiritually wise ones. They always blossom in His love.

The Lord saves the honor of the spiritually wise ones.I am forever a sacrifice to them.

Servant Nanak is the slave of those Gurmukhs who serve the Lord. |21|

The poisonous snake, the serpent of Maya, has surrounded the world with its coils, O mother!

The antidote to this poisonous venom is the Name of the Lord; the Guru places the magic spell of the Shabad into the mouth.

Those who are blessed with such pre-ordained destiny come and meet the True Guru.

Meeting with the True Guru, they become immaculate, and the poison of egotism is eradicated.

Radiant and bright are the faces of the Gurmukhs; they are honored in the Court of the Lord.

Servant Nanak is forever a sacrifice to those who walk in harmony with the Will of the True Guru. |22|

The True Guru, the Primal Being, has no hatred or vengeance. His heart is constantly attuned to the Lord.

Whoever directs hatred against the Guru, who has no hatred at all, only sets his own home on fire.

Anger and egotism are within him night and day; he burns, and suffers constant pain.

They babble and tell lies, and keep on barking, eating the poison of the love of duality.

For the sake of the poison of Maya, they wander from house to house, and lose their honor.

They are like the son of a prostitute, who does not know the name of his father.

They do not remember the Name of the Lord, Har, Har; the Creator Himself brings them to ruin.

The Lord showers His Mercy upon the Gurmukhs, and reunites the separated ones with Himself.

Servant Nanak is a sacrifice to those who fall at the Feet of the True Guru. |23|

Those who are attached to the Naam, the Name of the Lord, are saved; without the Name, they must go to the City of Death.

O Nanak, without the Name, they find no peace; they come and go in reincarnation with regrets. |24|

When anxiety and wanderings come to an end, the mind becomes happy.

By Guru's Grace, the soul-bride understands, and then she sleeps without worry.

Those who have such pre-ordained destiny meet with the Guru, the Lord of the Universe.

O Nanak, they merge intuitively into the Lord, the Embodiment of Supreme Bliss. |25|

Those who serve their True Guru, who contemplate the Word of the Guru's Shabad, who honor and obey the Will of the True Guru, who keep the Lord's Name enshrined within their hearts,

are honored, here and hereafter; they are dedicated to the business of the Lord's Name.

Through the Word of the Shabad, the Gurmukhs gain recognition in that Court of the True Lord.

The True Name is their merchandise, the True Name is their expenditure; the Love of their Beloved fills their inner beings.

The Messenger of Death does not even approach them; the Creator Lord Himself forgives them.

Section 43 - Shaloks In Addition To The Vaars - Part 007

O Nanak, they alone are wealthy, who are imbued with the Naam; the rest of the world is poor. |26|

The Lord's Name is the Support of the Lord's humble servants. Without the Lord's Name, the there is no other place, no place of rest.

Following the Guru's Teachings, the Name abides in the mind, and one is intuitively, automatically absorbed in the Lord.

Those with great good fortune meditate on the Naam; night and day, they embrace love for the Name.

Servant Nanak begs for the dust of their feet; I am forever a sacrifice to them. |27|

The 8.4 million species of beings burn in desire and cry in pain.

All this show of emotional attachment to Maya shall not go with you at that very last instant.

Without the Lord, peace and tranquility do not come; unto whom should we go and complain?

By great good fortune, one meets the True Guru, and comes to understand the contemplation of God.

The fire of desire is totally extinguished, O servant Nanak, enshrining the Lord within the heart. |28|

I make so many mistakes, there is no end or limit to them.

O Lord, please be merciful and forgive me; I am a sinner, a great offender.

O Dear Lord, if You made an account of my mistakes, my turn to be forgiven would not even come. Please forgive me, and unite me with Yourself.

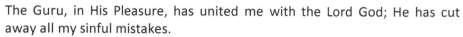

The Guru, in His Pleasure, has united me with the Lord God; He has cut away all my sinful mistakes.

Servant Nanak celebrates the victory of those who meditate on the Name of the Lord, Har, Har. |29|

Those who have been separated and alienated from the Lord are united with Him again, through the Fear and the Love of the True Guru.

They escape the cycle of birth and death, and, as Gurmukh, they meditate on the Naam, the Name of the Lord.

Joining the Saadh Sangat, the Guru's Congregation, the diamonds and jewels are obtained.

O Nanak, the jewel is priceless; the Gurmukhs seek and find it. |30|

The self-willed manmukhs do not even think of the Naam. Cursed are their lives, and cursed are their homes.

That Lord who gives them so much to eat and wear - they do not enshrine that Lord, the Treasure of Virtue, in their minds.

This mind is not pierced by the Word of the Shabad; how can it come to dwell in its true home?

The self-willed manmukhs are like discarded brides, ruined by coming and going in the cycle of reincarnation.

The Gurmukhs are embellished and exalted by the Naam, the Name of the Lord; the jewel of destiny is engraved upon their foreheads.

They enshrine the Name of the Lord, Har, Har, within their hearts; the Lord illumines their heart-lotus.

I am forever a sacrifice to those who serve their True Guru.

O Nanak, radiant and bright are the faces of those whose inner beings are illuminated with the Light of the Naam. |31|

Those who die in the Word of the Shabad are saved. Without the Shabad, no one is liberated.

They wear religious robes and perform all sorts of rituals, but they are ruined; in the love of duality, their world is ruined.

O Nanak, without the True Guru, the Name is not obtained, even though one may long for it hundreds of times. |32|

The Name of the Lord is utterly great, lofty and high, the highest of the high.

No one can climb up to it, even though one may long for it, hundreds of times.

Speaking about self-discipline, no one become pure; everyone walks around wearing religious robes.

Those blessed by the karma of good deeds go and climb the ladder of the Guru.

The Lord comes and dwells within that one who contemplates the Word of the Guru's Shabad.

Section 43 - Shaloks In Addition To The Vaars - Part 008

O Nanak, when someone dies in the Word of the Shabad, the mind is pleased and appeased. True is the reputation of those who are true. |33|

Emotional attachment to Maya is a treacherous ocean of pain and poison, which cannot be crossed.

Screaming, "Mine, mine!", they rot and die; they pass their lives in egotism.

The self-willed manmukhs are in limbo, neither on this side, nor the other; they are stuck in the middle.

They act as they are pre-destined; they cannot do anything else.

Following the Guru's Teachings, the jewel of spiritual wisdom abides in the mind, and then God is easily seen in all.

O Nanak, the very fortunate ones embark on the Boat of the True Guru; they are carried across the terrifying world-ocean. |34|

Without the True Guru, there is no giver who can bestow the Support of the Lord's Name.

By Guru's Grace, the Name comes to dwell in the mind; keep it enshrined in your heart.

The fire of desire is extinguished, and one finds satisfaction, through the Love of the Name of the Lord.

O Nanak, the Gurmukh finds the Lord, when He showers His Mercy. |35|

Without the Shabad, the world is so insane, that it cannot even be described.

Those who are protected by the Lord are saved; they remain lovingly attuned to the Word of the Shabad.

O Nanak, the Creator who made this making knows everything. |36|

The Pandits, the religious scholars, have grown weary of making fire-offerings and sacrifices, making pilgrimages to all the sacred shrines, and reading the Puraanas.

But they cannot get rid of the poison of emotional attachment to Maya; they continue to come and go in egotism.

Meeting with the True Guru, one's filth is washed off, meditating on the Lord, the Primal Being, the All-knowing One.

Servant Nanak is forever a sacrifice to those who serve their Lord God. |37|

Mortals give great thought to Maya and emotional attachment; they harbor great hopes, in greed and corruption.

The self-willed manmukhs do not become steady and stable; they die and are gone in an instant.

Only those who are blessed with great good fortune meet the True Guru, and leave behind their egotism and corruption.

Chanting the Name of the Lord, they find peace; servant Nanak contemplates the Word of the Shabad. |38|

Without the True Guru, there is no devotional worship, and no love of the Naam, the Name of the Lord.

Servant Nanak worships and adores the Naam, with love and affection for the Guru. |39|

Do not trust greedy people, if you can avoid doing so.

At the very last moment, they will deceive you there, where no one will be able to lend a helping hand.

Whoever associates with the self-willed manmukhs, will have his face blackened and dirtied.

Black are the faces of those greedy people; they lose their lives, and leave in disgrace.

O Lord, let me join the Sat Sangat, the True Congregation; may the Name of the Lord God abide in my mind.

The filth and pollution of birth and death is washed away, O servant Nanak, singing the Glorious Praises of the Lord. |40|

Whatever is pre-destined by the Lord God Creator, cannot be erased.

Body and soul are all His. The Sovereign Lord King cherishes all.

The gossipers and slanderers shall remain hungry and die, rolling in the dust; their hands cannot reach anywhere.

Outwardly, they do all the proper deeds, but they are hypocrites; in their minds and hearts, they practice deception and fraud.

Whatever is planted in the farm of the body, shall come and stand before them in the end.

Section 43 - Shaloks In Addition To The Vaars - Part 009

Nanak offers this prayer: O Lord God, please forgive me, and unite me with Yourself. |41|

The mortal being does not understand the comings and goings of reincarnation; he does not see the Court of the Lord.
He is wrapped up in emotional attachment and Maya, and within his being is the darkness of ignorance.
The sleeping person wakes, only when he is hit on the head by a heavy club.
The Gurmukhs dwell upon the Lord; they find the door of salvation.
O Nanak, they themselves are saved, and all their relatives are carried across as well. |42|

Whoever dies in the Word of the Shabad, is known to be truly dead.
By Guru's Grace, the mortal is satisfied by the sublime essence of the Lord.
Through the Word of the Guru's Shabad, he is recognized in the Court of the Lord.
Without the Shabad, everyone is dead.
The self-willed manmukh dies; his life is wasted.
Those who do not remember the Name of the Lord, shall cry in pain in the end.
O Nanak, whatever the Creator Lord does, comes to pass. |43|

The Gurmukhs never grow old; within them is intuitive understanding and spiritual wisdom.
They chant the Praises of the Lord, forever and ever; deep within, they intuitively meditate on the Lord.
They dwell forever in blissful knowledge of the Lord; they look upon pain and pleasure as one and the same.
They see the One Lord in all, and realize the Lord, the Supreme Soul of all. |44|

The self-willed manmukhs are like stupid children; they do not keep the Lord in their thoughts.
They do all their deeds in egotism, and they must answer to the Righteous Judge of Dharma.

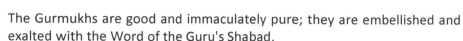

The Gurmukhs are good and immaculately pure; they are embellished and exalted with the Word of the Guru's Shabad.

Not even a tiny bit of filth sticks to them; they walk in harmony with the Will of the True Guru.

The filth of the manmukhs is not washed away, even if they wash hundreds of times.

O Nanak, the Gurmukhs are united with the Lord; they merge into the Guru's Being. |45|

How can someone do bad things, and still live with himself?

By his own anger, he only burns himself.

The self-willed manmukh drives himself crazy with worries and stubborn struggles.

But those who become Gurmukh understand everything.

O Nanak, the Gurmukh struggles with his own mind. |46|

Those who do not serve the True Guru, the Primal Being, and do not reflect upon the Word of the Shabad

- do not call them human beings; they are just animals and stupid beasts.

They have no spiritual wisdom or meditation within their beings; they are not in love with the Lord.

The self-willed manmukhs die in evil and corruption; they die and are reborn, again and again.

They alone live, who join with the living; enshrine the Lord, the Lord of Life, within your heart.

O Nanak, the Gurmukhs look beautiful in that Court of the True Lord. |47|

The Lord built the Harimandir, the Temple of the Lord; the Lord dwells within it.

Following the Guru's Teachings, I have found the Lord; my emotional attachment to Maya has been burnt away.

Countless things are in the Harimandir, the Temple of the Lord; contemplate the Naam, and the nine treasures will be yours.

Blessed is that happy soul-bride, O Nanak, who, as Gurmukh, seeks and finds the Lord.

By great good fortune, one searches the temple of the body-fortress, and finds the Lord within the heart. |48|

The self-willed manmukhs wander lost in the ten directions, led by intense desire, greed and corruption.

Section 43 - Shaloks In Addition To The Vaars - Part 010

Their attachment to Maya does not cease; they die, only to be reborn, over and over again.
Serving the True Guru, peace is found; intense desire and corruption are discarded.
The pains of death and birth are taken away; servant Nanak reflects upon the Word of the Shabad. |49|

Meditate on the Name of the Lord, Har, Har, O mortal being, and you shall be honored in the Court of the Lord.
All your sins and terrible mistakes shall be taken away, and you shall be rid of your pride and egotism.
The heart-lotus of the Gurmukh blossoms forth, realizing God, the Soul of all.
O Lord God, please shower Your Mercy upon servant Nanak, that he may chant the Name of the Lord. |50|

In Dhanaasaree, the soul-bride is known to be wealthy, O Siblings of Destiny, when she works for the True Guru.
She surrenders her body, mind and soul, O Siblings of Destiny, and lives according to the Hukam of His Command.
I sit where He wishes me to sit, O Siblings of Destiny; wherever He sends me, I go.
There is no other wealth as great, O Siblings of Destiny; such is the greatness of the True Name.
I sing forever the Glorious Praises of the True Lord; I shall remain with the True One forever.
So wear the clothes of His Glorious Virtues and goodness, O Siblings of Destiny; eat and enjoy the flavor of your own honor.
How can I praise Him, O Siblings of Destiny? I am a sacrifice to the Blessed Vision of His Darshan.
Great is the Glorious Greatness of the True Guru, O Siblings of Destiny; if one is blessed with good karma, He is found.
Some do not know how to submit to the Hukam of His Command, O Siblings of Destiny; they wander around lost in the love of duality.

They find no place of rest in the Sangat, O Siblings of Destiny; they find no place to sit.

Nanak: they alone submit to His Command, O Siblings of Destiny, who are pre-destined to live the Name.

I am a sacrifice to them, O Siblings of Destiny, I am forever a sacrifice to them. |51|

Those beards are true, which brush the feet of the True Guru.

Those who serve their Guru night and day, live in bliss, night and day.

O Nanak, their faces appear beautiful in the Court of the True Lord. |52|

True are the faces and true are the beards, of those who speak the Truth and live the Truth.

The True Word of the Shabad abides in their minds; they are absorbed in the True Guru.

True is their capital, and true is their wealth; they are blessed with the ultimate status.

They hear the Truth, they believe in the Truth; they act and work in the Truth.

They are given a place in the Court of the True Lord; they are absorbed in the True Lord.

O Nanak, without the True Guru, the True Lord is not found. The self-willed manmukhs leave, wandering around lost. |53|

The rainbird cries, "Pri-o! Pri-o! Beloved! Beloved!" She is in love with the treasure, the water.

Meeting with the Guru, the cooling, soothing water is obtained, and all pain is taken away.

My thirst has been quenched, and intuitive peace and poise have welled up; my cries and screams of anguish are past.

O Nanak, the Gurmukhs are peaceful and tranquil; they enshrine the Naam, the Name of the Lord, within their hearts. |54|

O rainbird, chirp the True Name, and let yourself be attuned to the True Lord.

Your word shall be accepted and approved, if you speak as Gurmukh.

Remember the Shabad, and your thirst shall be relieved; surrender to the Will of the Lord.

Section 43 - Shaloks In Addition To The Vaars - Part 011

The clouds are heavy, hanging low, and the rain is pouring down on all sides; the rain-drop is received, with natural ease.

From water, everything is produced; without water, thirst is not quenched.

O Nanak, whoever drinks in the Water of the Lord, shall never feel hunger again. |55|

O rainbird, speak the Shabad, the True Word of God, with natural peace and poise.

Everything is with you; the True Guru will show you this.

So understand your own self, and meet your Beloved; His Grace shall rain down in torrents.

Drop by drop, the Ambrosial Nectar rains down softly and gently; thirst and hunger are completely gone.

Your cries and screams of anguish have ceased; your light shall merge into the Light.

O Nanak, the happy soul-brides sleep in peace; they are absorbed in the True Name. |56|

The Primal Lord and Master has sent out the True Hukam of His Command.

Indra mercifully sends forth the rain, which falls in torrents.

The body and mind of the rainbird are happy. only when the rain-drop falls into its mouth.

The corn grows high, wealth increases, and the earth is embellished with beauty.

Night and day, people worship the Lord with devotion, and are absorbed in the Word of the Guru's Shabad.

The True Lord Himself forgives them, and showering them with His Mercy, He leads them to walk in His Will.

O brides, sing the Glorious Praises of the Lord, and be absorbed in the True Word of His Shabad.

Let the Fear of God be your decoration, and remain lovingly attuned to the True Lord.

O Nanak, the Naam abides in the mind, and the mortal is saved in the Court of the Lord. |57|

The rainbird wanders all over the earth, soaring high through the skies.

But it obtains the drop of water, only when it meets the True Guru, and then, its hunger and thirst are relieved.

Soul and body and all belong to Him; everything is His.

He knows everything, without being told; unto whom should we offer our prayers?

O Nanak, the One Lord is prevading and permeating each and every heart; the Word of the Shabad brings illumination. |58|

O Nanak, the season of spring comes to one who serves the True Guru.

The Lord rains His Mercy down upon him, and his mind and body totally blossom forth; the entire world becomes green and rejuvenated. |59|

The Word of the Shabad brings eternal spring; it rejuvenates the mind and body.

O Nanak, do not forget the Naam, the Name of the Lord, which has created everyone. |60|

O Nanak, it is the spring season, for those Gurmukhs, within whose minds the Lord abides.

When the Lord showers His Mercy, the mind and body blossom forth, and all the world turns green and lush. |61|

In the early hours of the morning, whose name should we chant?

Chant the Name of the Transcendent Lord, who is All-powerful to create and destroy. |62|

The Persian wheel also cries out, "Too! Too! You! You!", with sweet and sublime sounds.

Our Lord and Master is always present; why do you cry out to Him in such a loud voice?

I am a sacrifice to that Lord who created the world, and who loves it.

Give up your selfishness, and then you shall meet your Husband Lord. Consider this Truth.

Speaking in shallow egotism, no one understands the Ways of God.

The forests and fields, and all the three worlds meditate on You, O Lord; this is the way they pass their days and nights forever.

Without the True Guru, no one finds the Lord. People have grown weary of thinking about it.

Section 43 - Shaloks In Addition To The Vaars - Part 012

But if the Lord casts His Glance of Grace, then He Himself embellishes us.

O Nanak, the Gurmukhs meditate on the Lord; blessed and approved is their coming into the world. |63|

Yoga is not obtained by wearing saffron robes; Yoga is not obtained by wearing dirty robes.
O Nanak, Yoga is obtained even while sitting in your own home, by following the Teachings of the True Guru. |64|

You may wander in all four directions, and read the Vedas throughout the four ages.
O Nanak, if you meet with the True Guru, the Lord shall come to dwell within your mind, and you shall find the door of salvation. |65|

O Nanak, the Hukam, the Command of your Lord and Master, is prevailing. The intellectually confused person wanders around lost, misled by his fickle consciousness.
If you make friends with the self-willed manmukhs, O friend, who can you ask for peace?
Make friends with the Gurmukhs, and focus your consciousness on the True Guru.
The root of birth and death will be cut away, and then, you shall find peace, O friend. |66|

The Lord Himself instructs those who are misguided, when He casts His Glance of Grace.
O Nanak, those who are not blessed by His Glance of Grace, cry and weep and wail. |67|

Shalok, Fourth Mehl:
One Universal Creator God. By The Grace Of The True Guru:
Blessed and very fortunate are those happy soul-brides who, as Gurmukh, meet their Sovereign Lord King.
The Light of God shines within them; O Nanak, they are absorbed in the Naam, the Name of the Lord. |1|

Waaho! Waaho! Blessed and Great is the True Guru, the Primal Being, who has realized the True Lord.
Meeting Him, thirst is quenched, and the body and mind are cooled and soothed.

Waaho! Waaho! Blessed and Great is the True Guru, the True Primal Being, who looks upon all alike.

Waaho! Waaho! Blessed and Great is the True Guru, who has no hatred; slander and praise are all the same to Him.

Waaho! Waaho! Blessed and Great is the All-knowing True Guru, who has realized God within.

Waaho! Waaho! Blessed and Great is the Formless True Guru, who has no end or limitation.

Waaho! Waaho! Blessed and Great is the True Guru, who implants the Truth within.

O Nanak, Blessed and Great is the True Guru, through whom the Naam, the Name of the Lord, is received. |2|

For the Gurmukh, the true Song of Praise is to chant the Name of the Lord God.

Chanting the Praises of the Lord, their minds are in ecstasy.

By great good fortune, they find the Lord, the Embodiment of perfect, supreme bliss.

Servant Nanak praises the Naam, the Name of the Lord; no obstacle will block his mind or body. |3|

I am in love with my Beloved; how can I meet my Dear Friend?

I seek that friend, who is embellished with Truth.

The True Guru is my Friend; if I meet Him, I will offer this mind as a sacrifice to Him.

He has shown me my Beloved Lord, my Friend, the Creator.

O Nanak, I was searching for my Beloved; the True Guru has shown me that He has been with me all the time. |4|

I stand by the side of the road, waiting for You; O my Friend, I hope that You will come.

If only someone would come today and unite me in Union with my Beloved.

Section 43 - Shaloks In Addition To The Vaars - Part 013

I would cut my living body into four pieces for anyone who shows me my Beloved.

O Nanak, when the Lord becomes merciful, then He leads us to meet the Perfect Guru. |5|

The power of egotism prevails within, and the body is controlled by Maya; the false ones come and go in reincarnation.

If someone does not obey the Command of the True Guru, he cannot cross over the treacherous world-ocean.

Whoever is blessed with the Lord's Glance of Grace, walks in harmony with the Will of the True Guru.

The Blessed Vision of the True Guru's Darshan is fruitful; through it, one obtains the fruits of his desires.

I touch the feet of those who believe in and obey the True Guru.

Nanak is the slave of those who, night and day, remain lovingly attuned to the Lord. |6|

Those who are in love with their Beloved - how can they find satisfaction without His Darshan?

O Nanak, the Gurmukhs meet Him with ease, and this mind blossoms forth in joy. |7|

Those who are in love with their Beloved - how can they live without Him?

When they see their Husband Lord, O Nanak, they are rejuvenated. |8|

Those Gurmukhs who are filled with love for You, my True Beloved,

O Nanak, remain immersed in the Lord's Love, night and day. |9|

The love of the Gurmukh is true; through it, the True Beloved is attained.

Night and day, remain in bliss, O Nanak, immersed in intuitive peace and poise. |10|

True love and affection are obtained from the Perfect Guru.

They never break, O Nanak, if one sings the Glorious Praises of the Lord. |11|

How can those who have true love within them live without their Husband Lord?

The Lord unites the Gurmukhs with Himself, O Nanak; they were separated from Him for such a long time. |12|

You grant Your Grace to those whom You Yourself bless with love and affection.

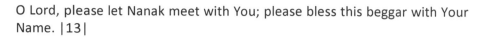

O Lord, please let Nanak meet with You; please bless this beggar with Your Name. |13|

The Gurmukh laughs, and the Gurmukh cries.
Whatever the Gurmukh does, is devotional worship.
Whoever becomes Gurmukh contemplates the Lord.
The Gurmukh, O Nanak, crosses over to the other shore. |14|

Those who have the Naam within, contemplate the Word of the Guru's Bani.
Their faces are always radiant in the Court of the True Lord.
Sitting down and standing up, they never forget the Creator, who forgives them.
O Nanak, the Gurmukhs are united with the Lord. Those united by the Creator Lord, shall never be separated again. |15|

To work for the Guru, or a spiritual teacher, is terribly difficult, but it brings the most excellent peace.
The Lord casts His Glance of Grace, and inspires love and affection.
Joined to the service of the True Guru, the mortal being crosses over the terrifying world-ocean.
The fruits of the mind's desires are obtained, with clear contemplation and discriminating understanding within.
O Nanak, meeting the True Guru, God is found; He is the Eradicator of all sorrow. |16|

The self-willed manmukh may perform service, but his consciousness is attached to the love of duality.
Through Maya, his emotional attachment to children, spouse and relatives increases.
He shall be called to account in the Court of the Lord, and in the end, no one will be able to save him.

Section 43 - Shaloks In Addition To The Vaars - Part 014

Without the Lord's Name, all is pain. Attachment to Maya is agonizingly painful.
O Nanak, the Gurmukh comes to see, that attachment to Maya separates all from the Lord. |17|

The Gurmukh obeys the Order of her Husband Lord God; through the Hukam of His Command, she finds peace.

In His Will, she serves; in His Will, she worship and adores Him.

In His Will, she merges in absorption. His Will is her fast, vow, purity and self-discipline; through it, she obtains the fruits of her mind's desires.

She is always and forever the happy, pure soul-bride, who realizes His Will; she serves the True Guru, inspired by loving absorption.

O Nanak, those upon whom the Lord showers His Mercy, are merged and immersed in His Will. |18|

The wretched, self-willed manmukhs do not realize His Will; they continually act in ego.

By ritualistic fasts, vows, purities, self-disciplines and worship ceremonies, they still cannot get rid of their hypocrisy and doubt.

Inwardly, they are impure, pierced through by attachment to Maya; they are like elephants, who throw dirt all over themselves right after their bath.

They do not even think of the One who created them. Without thinking of Him, they cannot find peace.

O Nanak, the Primal Creator has made the drama of the Universe; all act as they are pre-ordained. |19|

The Gurmukh has faith; his mind is contented and satisfied. Night and day, he serves the Lord, absorbed in Him.

The Guru, the True Guru, is within; all worship and adore Him. Everyone comes to see the Blessed Vision of His Darshan.

So believe in the True Guru, the supreme sublime Contemplator. Meeting with Him, hunger and thirst are completely relieved.

I am forever a sacrifice to my Guru, who leads me to meet the True Lord God.

O Nanak, those who come and fall at the Feet of the Guru are blessed with the karma of Truth. |20|

That Beloved, with whom I am in love, that Friend of mine is with me.

I wander around inside and outside, but I always keep Him enshrined within my heart. |21|

Those who meditate on the Lord single-mindedly, with one-pointed concentration, link their consciousness to the True Guru.

They are rid of pain, hunger, and the great illness of egotism; lovingly attuned to the Lord, they become free of pain.

They sing His Praises, and chant His Praises; in His Glorious Praises, they sleep in absorption.

O Nanak, through the Perfect Guru, they come to meet God with intuitive peace and poise. |22|

The self-willed manmukhs are emotionally attached to Maya; they are not in love with the Naam.

They practice falsehood, gather falsehood, and eat the food of falsehood.

Gathering the poisonous wealth and property of Maya, they die; in the end, they are all reduced to ashes.

They perform religious rituals of purity and self-discipline, but they are filled with greed, evil and corruption.

O Nanak, the actions of the self-willed manmukhs are not accepted; in the Court of the Lord, they are miserable. |23|

Among all Ragas, that one is sublime, O Siblings of Destiny, by which the Lord comes to abide in the mind.

Those Ragas which are in the Sound-current of the Naad are totally true; their value cannot be expressed.

Those Ragas which are not in the Sound-current of the Naad - by these, the Lord's Will cannot be understood.

O Nanak, they alone are right, who understand the Will of the True Guru.

Everything happens as He wills. |24|

Section 43 - Shaloks In Addition To The Vaars - Part 015

The Ambrosial Nectar of the Naam, the Name of the Lord, is within the True Guru.

Following the Guru's Teachings, one meditates on the Immaculate Naam, the Pure and Holy Naam.

The Ambrosial Word of His Bani is the true essence. It comes to abide in the mind of the Gurmukh.

The heart-lotus blossoms forth, and one's light merges in the Light.

O Nanak, they alone meet with the True Guru, who have such pre-ordained destiny inscribed upon their foreheads. |25|

Within the self-willed manmukhs is the fire of desire; their hunger does not depart.

Emotional attachments to relatives are totally false; they remain engrossed in falsehood.

Night and day, they are troubled by anxiety; bound to anxiety, they depart.
Their comings and goings in reincarnation never end; they do their deeds in egotism.
But in the Guru's Sanctuary, they are saved, O Nanak, and set free. |26|

The True Guru meditates on the Lord, the Primal Being. The Sat Sangat, the True Congregation, loves the True Guru.
Those who join the Sat Sangat, and serve the True Guru - the Guru unites them in the Lord's Union.
This world, this universe, is a terrifying ocean. On the Boat of the Naam, the Name of the Lord, the Guru carries us across.
The Sikhs of the Guru accept and obey the Lord's Will; the Perfect Guru carries them across.
O Lord, please bless me with the dust of the feet of the Guru's Sikhs. I am a sinner - please save me.
Those who have such pre-ordained destiny written upon their foreheads by the Lord God, come to meet Guru Nanak.
The Messenger of Death is beaten and driven away; we are saved in the Court of the Lord.
Blessed and celebrated are the Sikhs of the Guru; in His Pleasure, the Lord unites them in His Union. |27|

The Perfect Guru has implanted the Lord's Name within me; it has dispelled my doubts from within.
Singing the Kirtan of the Praises of the Lord's Name, the Lord's path is illuminated and shown to His Sikhs.
Conquering my egotism, I remain lovingly attuned to the One Lord; the Naam, the Name of the Lord, dwells within me.
I follow the Guru's Teachings, and so the Messenger of Death cannot even see me; I am immersed in the True Name.
The Creator Himself is All-pervading; as He pleases, He links us to His Name.
Servant Nanak lives, chanting the Name. Without the Name, he dies in an instant. |28|

Within the minds of the faithless cynics is the disease of egotism; these evil people wander around lost, deluded by doubt.
O Nanak, this disease is eradicated only by meeting with the True Guru, the Holy Friend. |29|

Following the Guru's Teachings, chant the Name of the Lord, Har, Har.

Attracted by the Lord's Love, day and night, the body-robe is imbued with the Lord's Love.

I have not found any being like the Lord, although I have searched and looked all over the world.

The Guru, the True Guru, has implanted the Naam within; now, my mind does not waver or wander anywhere else.

Servant Nanak is the slave of the Lord, the slave of the slaves of the Guru, the True Guru. |30|

Section 43 - Shaloks In Addition To The Vaars - Part 016

Shalok, Fifth Mehl:

One Universal Creator God. By The Grace Of The True Guru:

They alone are imbued with the Lord, who do not turn their faces away from Him - they realize Him.

The false, immature lovers do not know the way of love, and so they fall. |1|

Without my Master, I will burn my silk and satin clothes in the fire.

Even rolling in the dust, I look beautiful, O Nanak, if my Husband Lord is with me. |2|

Through the Word of the Guru's Shabad, I worship and adore the Naam, with love and balanced detachment.

When the five enemies are overcome, O Nanak, this musical measure of Raga MAAROO becomes frtuiful. |3|

When I have the One Lord, I have tens of thousands. Otherwise, people like me beg from door to door.

O Brahmin, your life has passed away uselessly; you have forgotten the One who created you. |4|

In Raga Sorat'h, drink in this sublime essence, which never loses its taste.

O Nanak, singing the Glorious Praises of the Lord's Name, one's reputation is immaculate in the Court of the Lord. |5|

No one can kill those whom God Himself protects.

The treasure of the Naam, the Name of the Lord, is within them. They cherish His Glorious Virtues forever.

They take the Support of the One, the Inaccessible Lord; they enshrine God in their mind and body.

They are imbued with the Love of the Infinite Lord, and no one can wipe it away.

The Gurmukhs sing the Glorious Praises of the Lord; they obtain the most excellent celestial peace and poise.

O Nanak, they enshrine the treasure of the Naam in their hearts. |6|

Whatever God does, accept that as good; leave behind all other judgements.

He shall cast His Glance of Grace, and attach you to Himself.

Instruct yourself with the Teachings, and doubt will depart from within.

Everyone does that which is pre-ordained by destiny.

Everything is under His control; there is no other place at all.

Nanak is in peace and bliss, accepting the Will of God. |7|

Those who meditate in remembrance on the Perfect Guru, are exalted and uplifted.

O Nanak, dwelling on the Naam, the Name of the Lord, all affairs are resolved. |8|

The sinners act, and generate bad karma, and then they weep and wail.

O Nanak, just as the churning stick churns the butter, so does the Righteous Judge of Dharma churn them. |9|

Meditating on the Naam, O friend, the treasure of life is won.

O Nanak, speaking in Righteousness, one's world becomes sanctified. |10|

I am stuck in an evil place, trusting the sweet words of an evil advisor.

O Nanak, they alone are saved, who have such good destiny inscribed upon their foreheads. |11|

They alone sleep and dream in peace, who are imbued with the Love of their Husband Lord.

Those who have been separated from the Love of their Master, scream and cry twenty-four hours a day. |12|

Millions are asleep, in the false illusion of Maya.

O Nanak, they alone are awake and aware, who chant the Naam with their tongues. |13|

Seeing the mirage, the optical illusion, the people are confused and deluded.

Those who worship and adore the True Lord, O Nanak, their minds and bodies are beautiful. |14|

The All-powerful Supreme Lord God, the Infinite Primal Being, is the Saving Grace of sinners.

SHALOK, NINTH MEHL

Section 44 - Shalok, Ninth Mehl - Part 001

Those whom He saves, meditate in remembrance on the Creator Lord. |15|

Forsake duality and the ways of evil; focus your consciousness on the One Lord.
In the love of duality, O Nanak, the mortals are being washed downstream. |16|

In the markets and bazaars of the three qualities, the merchants make their deals.
Those who load the true merchandise are the true traders. |17|

Those who do not know the way of love are foolish; they wander lost and confused.
O Nanak, forgetting the Lord, they fall into the deep, dark pit of hell. |18|

In his mind, the mortal does not forget Maya; he begs for more and more wealth.
That God does not even come into his consciousness; O Nanak, it is not in his karma. |19|

The mortal does not run out of capital, as long as the Lord Himself is merciful.
The Word of the Shabad is Guru Nanak's inexhaustible treasure; this wealth and capital never runs out, no matter how much it is spent and consumed. |20|

If I could find wings for sale, I would buy them with an equal weight of my flesh.
I would attach them to my body, and seek out and find my Friend. |21|

My Friend is the True Supreme King, the King over the heads of kings.

Sitting by His side, we are exalted and beautified; He is the Support of all. |22|

One Universal Creator God. By The Grace Of The True Guru:
Shalok, Ninth Mehl:
If you do not sing the Praises of the Lord, your life is rendered useless.
Says Nanak, meditate, vibrate upon the Lord; immerse your mind in Him, like the fish in the water. |1|

Why are you engrossed in sin and corruption? You are not detached, even for a moment!
Says Nanak, meditate, vibrate upon the Lord, and you shall not be caught in the noose of death. |2|

Your youth has passed away like this, and old age has overtaken your body.
Says Nanak, meditate, vibrate upon the Lord; your life is fleeting away! |3|

You have become old, and you do not understand that death is overtaking you.
Says Nanak, you are insane! Why do you not remember and meditate on God? |4|

Your wealth, spouse, and all the possessions which you claim as your own - none of these shall go along with you in the end. O Nanak, know this as true. |5|

He is the Saving Grace of sinners, the Destroyer of fear, the Master of the masterless.
Says Nanak, realize and know Him, who is always with you. |6|

He has given you your body and wealth, but you are not in love with Him.
Says Nanak, you are insane! Why do you now shake and tremble so helplessly? |7|

He has given you your body, wealth, property, peace and beautiful mansions.
Says Nanak, listen, mind: why don't you remember the Lord in meditation? |8|

The Lord is the Giver of all peace and comfort. There is no other at all.

Says Nanak, listen, mind: meditating in remembrance on Him, salvation is attained. |9|

Section 44 - Shalok, Ninth Mehl - Part 002

Remembering Him in meditation, salvation is attained; vibrate and meditate on Him, O my friend.
Says Nanak, listen, mind: your life is passing away! |10|

Your body is made up of the five elements; you are clever and wise - know this well.
Believe it - you shall merge once again into the One, O Nanak, from whom you originated. |11|

The Dear Lord abides in each and every heart; the Saints proclaim this as true.
Says Nanak, meditate and vibrate upon Him, and you shall cross over the terrifying world-ocean. |12|

One who is not touched by pleasure or pain, greed, emotional attachment and egotistical pride
- says Nanak, listen, mind: he is the very image of God. |13|

One who is beyond praise and slander, who looks upon gold and iron alike
- says Nanak, listen, mind: know that such a person is liberated. |14|

One who is not affected by pleasure or pain, who looks upon friend and enemy alike
- says Nanak, listen, mind: know that such a person is liberated. |15|

One who does not frighten anyone, and who is not afraid of anyone else
- says Nanak, listen, mind: call him spiritually wise. |16|

One who has forsaken all sin and corruption, who wears the robes of neutral detachment
- says Nanak, listen, mind: good destiny is written on his forehead. |17|

One who renounces Maya and possessiveness and is detached from everything
- says Nanak, listen, mind: God abides in his heart. |18|

That mortal, who forsakes egotism, and realizes the Creator Lord
- says Nanak, that person is liberated; O mind, know this as true. |19|

In this Dark Age of Kali Yuga, the Name of the Lord is the Destroyer of fear, the Eradicator of evil-mindedness.
Night and day, O Nanak, whoever vibrates and meditates on the Lord's Name, sees all of his works brought to fruition. |20|

Vibrate with your tongue the Glorious Praises of the Lord of the Universe; with your ears, hear the Lord's Name.
Says Nanak, listen, man: you shall not have to go to the house of Death. |21|

That mortal who renounces possessiveness, greed, emotional attachment and egotism
- says Nanak, he himself is saved, and he saves many others as well. |22|

Like a dream and a show, so is this world, you must know.
None of this is true, O Nanak, without God. |23|

Night and day, for the sake of Maya, the mortal wanders constantly.
Among millions, O Nanak, there is scarcely anyone, who keeps the Lord in his consciousness. |24|

As the bubbles in the water well up and disappear again,
so is the universe created; says Nanak, listen, O my friend! |25|

The mortal does not remember the Lord, even for a moment; he is blinded by the wine of Maya.
Says Nanak, without meditating on the Lord, he is caught by the noose of Death. |26|

If you yearn for eternal peace, then seek the Sanctuary of the Lord.
Says Nanak, listen, mind: this human body is difficult to obtain. |27|

For the sake of Maya, the fools and ignorant people run all around.
Says Nanak, without meditating on the Lord, life passes away uselessly. |28|

That mortal who meditates and vibrates upon the Lord night and day - know him to be the embodiment of the Lord.

Section 44 - Shalok, Ninth Mehl - Part 003

There is no difference between the Lord and the humble servant of the Lord; O Nanak, know this as true. |29|

The mortal is entangled in Maya; he has forgotten the Name of the Lord of the Universe.
Says Nanak, without meditating on the Lord, what is the use of this human life? |30|

The mortal does not think of the Lord; he is blinded by the wine of Maya.
Says Nanak, without meditating on the Lord, he is caught in the noose of Death. |31|

In good times, there are many companions around, but in bad times, there is no one at all.
Says Nanak, vibrate, and meditate on the Lord; He shall be your only Help and Support in the end. |32|

Mortals wander lost and confused through countless lifetimes; their fear of death is never removed.
Says Nanak, vibrate and meditate on the Lord, and you shall dwell in the Fearless Lord. |33|

I have tried so many things, but the pride of my mind has not been dispelled.
I am engrossed in evil-mindedness, Nanak. O God, please save me! |34|

Childhood, youth and old age - know these as the three stages of life.
Says Nanak, without meditating on the Lord, everything is useless; you must appreciate this. |35|

You have not done what you should have done; you are entangled in the web of greed.
Nanak, your time is past and gone; why are you crying now, you blind fool? |36|

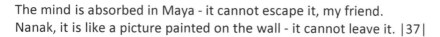

The mind is absorbed in Maya - it cannot escape it, my friend.
Nanak, it is like a picture painted on the wall - it cannot leave it. |37|

The man wishes for something, but something different happens.
He plots to deceive others, O Nanak, but he places the noose around his own neck instead. |38|

People make all sorts of efforts to find peace and pleasure, but no one tries to earn pain.
Says Nanak, listen, mind: whatever pleases God comes to pass. |39|

The world wanders around begging, but the Lord is the Giver of all.
Says Nanak, meditate in remembrance on Him, and all your works will be successful. |40|

Why do you take such false pride in yourself? You must know that the world is just a dream.
None of this is yours; Nanak proclaims this truth. |41|

You are so proud of your body; it shall perish in an instant, my friend.
That mortal who chants the Praises of the Lord, O Nanak, conquers the world. |42|

That person, who meditates in remembrance on the Lord in his heart, is liberated - know this well.
There is no difference between that person and the Lord: O Nanak, accept this as the Truth. |43|

That person, who does not feel devotion to God in his mind
- O Nanak, know that his body is like that of a pig, or a dog. |44|

A dog never abandons the home of his master.
O Nanak, in just the same way, vibrate, and meditate on the Lord, single-mindedly, with one-pointed consciousness. |45|

Those who make pilgrimages to sacred shrines, observe ritualistic fasts and make donations to charity while still taking pride in their minds

- O Nanak, their actions are useless, like the elephant, who takes a bath, and then rolls in the dust. |46|

The head shakes, the feet stagger, and the eyes become dull and weak. Says Nanak, this is your condition. And even now, you have not savored the sublime essence of the Lord. |47|

MUNDAAVANEE, FIFTH MEHL & RAAG MAALAA

Section 45 - Mundaavanee, Fifth Mehl & Raag Maalaa - Part 001

I had looked upon the world as my own, but no one belongs to anyone else.
O Nanak, only devotional worship of the Lord is permanent; enshrine this in your mind. |48|

The world and its affairs are totally false; know this well, my friend.
Says Nanak, it is like a wall of sand; it shall not endure. |49|

Raam Chand passed away, as did Raawan, even though he had lots of relatives.
Says Nanak, nothing lasts forever; the world is like a dream. |50|

People become anxious, when something unexpected happens.
This is the way of the world, O Nanak; nothing is stable or permanent. |51|

Whatever has been created shall be destroyed; everyone shall perish, today or tomorrow.
O Nanak, sing the Glorious Praises of the Lord, and give up all other entanglements. |52|

DOHRAA:
My strength is exhausted, and I am in bondage; I cannot do anything at all.
Says Nanak, now, the Lord is my Support; He will help me, as He did the elephant. |53|

My strength has been restored, and my bonds have been broken; now, I can do everything.
Nanak: everything is in Your hands, Lord; You are my Helper and Support. |54|

My associates and companions have all deserted me; no one remains with me.
Says Nanak, in this tragedy, the Lord alone is my Support. |55|

The Naam remains; the Holy Saints remain; the Guru, the Lord of the Universe, remains.

Says Nanak, how rare are those who chant the Guru's Mantra in this world. |56|

I have enshrined the Lord's Name within my heart; there is nothing equal to it.

Meditating in remembrance on it, my troubles are taken away; I have received the Blessed Vision of Your Darshan. |57|1|

Mundaavanee, Fifth Mehl:

Upon this Plate, three things have been placed: Truth, Contentment and Contemplation.

The Ambrosial Nectar of the Naam, the Name of our Lord and Master, has been placed upon it as well; it is the Support of all.

One who eats it and enjoys it shall be saved.

This thing can never be forsaken; keep this always and forever in your mind.

The dark world-ocean is crossed over, by grasping the Feet of the Lord; O Nanak, it is all the extension of God. |1|

Shalok, Fifth Mehl:

I have not appreciated what You have done for me, Lord; only You can make me worthy.

I am unworthy - I have no worth or virtues at all. You have taken pity on me.

You took pity on me, and blessed me with Your Mercy, and I have met the True Guru, my Friend.

O Nanak, if I am blessed with the Naam, I live, and my body and mind blossom forth. |1|

One Universal Creator God. By The Grace Of The True Guru:

Raag Maalaa:

Each Raga has five wives,

and eight sons, who emit distinctive notes.

In the first place is Raag Bhairao.

Section 45 - Mundaavanee, Fifth Mehl & Raag Maalaa - Part 002

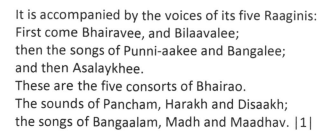

It is accompanied by the voices of its five Raaginis:
First come Bhairavee, and Bilaavalee;
then the songs of Punni-aakee and Bangalee;
and then Asalaykhee.
These are the five consorts of Bhairao.
The sounds of Pancham, Harakh and Disaakh;
the songs of Bangaalam, Madh and Maadhav. |1|

Lalat and Bilaaval - each gives out its own melody.
when these eight sons of Bhairao are sung by accomplished musicians. |1|

In the second family is Maalakausak,
who brings his five Raaginis:
Gondakaree and Dayv Gandhaaree,
the voices of Gandhaaree and Seehutee,
and the fifth song of Dhanaasaree.
This chain of Maalakausak brings along :
Maaroo, Masta-ang and Mayvaaraa,
Prabal, Chandakausak,
Khau, Khat and Bauraanad singing.
These are the eight sons of Maalakausak. |1|

Then comes Hindol with his five wives and eight sons;
it rises in waves when the sweet-voiced chorus sings. |1|

There come Taylangee and Darvakaree;
Basantee and Sandoor follow;
then Aheeree, the finest of women.
These five wives come together.
The sons: Surmaanand and Bhaaskar come,
Chandrabinb and Mangalan follow.
Sarasbaan and Binodaa then come,
and the thrilling songs of Basant and Kamodaa.
These are the eight sons I have listed.
Then comes the turn of Deepak. |1|

Kachhaylee, Patamanjaree and Todee are sung;
Kaamodee and Goojaree accompany Deepak. |1|

Kaalankaa, Kuntal and Raamaa,

Kamalakusam and Champak are their names;
Gauraa, Kaanaraa and Kaylaanaa;
these are the eight sons of Deepak. |1|

All join together and sing Siree Raag,
which is accompanied by its five wives.:
Bairaaree and Karnaatee,
the songs of Gawree and Aasaavaree;
then follows Sindhavee.
These are the five wives of Siree Raag. |1|

Saaloo, Saarang, Saagaraa, Gond and Gambheer
- the eight sons of Siree Raag include Gund, Kumb and Hameer. |1|

In the sixth place, Maygh Raag is sung,
with its five wives in accompaniment:
Sorat'h, Gond, and the melody of Malaaree;
then the harmonies of Aasaa are sung.
And finally comes the high tone Soohau.
These are the five with Maygh Raag. |1|

Bairaadhar, Gajadhar, Kaydaaraa,
Jabaleedhar, Nat and Jaladhaaraa.
Then come the songs of Shankar and Shi-aamaa.
These are the names of the sons of Maygh Raag. |1|

So all together, they sing the six Raagas and the thirty Raaginis,
and all the forty-eight sons of the Raagas. |1|1|